HBJ TREASURY OF LITERATURE

ENDLESS WORLDS

ANNOTATED TEACHER'S EDITION · VOLUME TWO

SENIOR AUTHORS
ROGER C. FARR
DOROTHY S. STRICKLAND

AUTHORS
RICHARD F. ABRAHAMSON
ELLEN BOOTH CHURCH
BARBARA BOWEN COULTER
MARGARET A. GALLEGO
JUDITH L. IRVIN
KAREN KUTIPER
JUNKO YOKOTA LEWIS
DONNA M. OGLE
TIMOTHY SHANAHAN
PATRICIA SMITH

SENIOR CONSULTANTS
BERNICE E. CULLINAN
W. DORSEY HAMMOND
ASA G. HILLIARD III

CONSULTANTS
ALONZO A. CRIM
ROLANDO R. HINOJOSA-SMITH
LEE BENNETT HOPKINS
ROBERT J. STERNBERG

 HARCOURT BRACE JOVANOVICH, INC.

Orlando   Austin   San Diego   Chicago   Dallas   New York

Acknowledgments appear on pg R114.

Printed in the United States of America

ISBN 0-15-300453-3

1 2 3 4 5 6 7 8 9 10   048   96 95 94 93 92

DEAR EDUCATOR,

HBJ TREASURY OF LITERATURE, an integrated reading and language arts program, offers a wealth of literature to touch the hearts and minds of its readers. Readers grow in confidence with the turn of every page because the program is built on the following principles.

Reading is an interactive process of constructing meaning. Good readers are strategic readers. They learn, practice, and apply strategies as part of this dynamic process. Authentic literature provides a richness of opportunities for children to interact with concepts and ideas, setting the foundation for a lifelong love of reading.

Effective instruction is meaning-based and integrates listening, speaking, reading, writing, spelling, and thinking. Integrating language arts instruction across the curriculum enables students to make critical connections to all subject areas.

Meeting individual needs in a classroom means access to a wide variety of instructional activities that provide for different learning modalities, varying language proficiencies, and individual learning styles.

Multicultural literature and activities, infused throughout the curriculum, enable children to appreciate cultural diversity, to grasp the concept that all groups have contributed to society, and to take pride in cultural heritage.

Assessment is an ongoing, natural part of the reading and language process. Whether formal or informal, it should help teachers determine, in a meaningful context, what students know and what they need to learn.

HBJ TREASURY OF LITERATURE offers your students a collection of trade books under one cover and sets the foundation for a lifelong love of reading.

SINCERELY,
THE AUTHORS

UNIT ONE / CONTENTS
• • • • • • • • • • • • • • • •
D I S C O V E R I E S

UNIT TWO/CONTENTS
T A L E S

UNIT THREE/CONTENTS
BONANZAS

UNIT FOUR/CONTENTS
••••••••••••••••
CHALLENGES

UNIT FIVE/CONTENTS
• • • • • • • • • • • • • • • •
OBSERVATIONS

UNIT SIX / CONTENTS
•••••••••••••
S O L U T I O N S

HBJ TREASURY OF LITERATURE

A variety of components designed to nurture a lifelong love of reading

Literature Components

Student Anthologies (1-8)
A collection of trade books under one cover, featuring authentic children's literature and stunning illustrations that help students become successful, enthusiastic readers.

Big Books (1-3)
Authentic children's literature on large, easy-to-see pages.

Literature Cassettes (1-8)
Delightful recordings of literature selections to model good reading.

Libraries (1-8)
Classroom collections of children's trade books that connect with Student Anthology themes and authors, plus teacher's guides with suggestions, activities, and projects.

Teacher Materials

Teacher's Editions (1-8)
Integrated lesson plans that provide teaching strategies, activities, and practical suggestions for all types of learners and needs.

Teacher's ResourceBank™ (1-8)
A wealth of classroom tools for reading success, including teacher's resources for skills instruction, practice, enrichment, and assessment.

Picture Cards (1)
Colorful pictures that help build visual literacy.

Word Cards (1)
Vocabulary and letter cards that help introduce new words and enable students to build sentences, match words, and play vocabulary games.

Instructional Charts (1-3) and Transparencies (1-8)
Eye-catching wall charts and transparencies for building story background and developing vocabulary.

HBJ Staff Development Series
Innovative videotapes of professional workshops which explore a variety of current reading issues.

Student Support

Writer's Journal (1-8)
A colorful, consumable write-in book that encourages students to record their personal reactions to literature. (Teacher's Edition available separately.)

Practice Book (1-8)
An appealing write-in book filled with activities that strengthen and enhance skills. (Teacher's Edition available separately.)

Integrated Spelling (1-8)
Suggestions, activities, and assessment for integrated spelling instruction. (Teacher's Edition available separately.)

Project Cards (1-8)
Independent projects—for individuals and small groups—that include integrated language arts, integrated curriculum, multicultural, challenge, and reader response activities.

Family Activities

Take-Home Books (1)
Special books which children make to read with their families, reinforcing vocabulary development.

Family Involvement Activities (1-6)
Copying-master activities for extending each theme, including a Read-at-Home Story to share.

Continued on back page

Components

Assessment Choices

Unit Skills Assessment and Teacher's Edition (1-8)
Tests to evaluate mastery of strategies and skills taught in Learning Through Literature.

Unit Holistic Assessment and Teacher's Edition (1-8)
Options for evaluating students' ability to read and understand excerpts from literature.

Unit Integrated Performance Assessment and Teacher's Edition (1-8)
Strategies for assessing students' use of reading and writing strategies modeled and practiced in the classroom.

Portfolio Assessment Teacher's Guide (K-8)
A convenient booklet and copying masters that provide suggestions and checklists for effective portfolio assessment.

Individual Inventory for Reading and Writing (1-8)
An effective tool for evaluating an individual student's reading and writing abilities.

Group Placement Tests, Teacher's Edition with Copying Masters (1-8)
Primary, intermediate, and advanced tests that suggest appropriate placement.

Computer Management System (1-8)
A microcomputer management system and teacher's guide for scoring tests, writing curriculum objectives, and creating tailor-made reports of student, group, or class progress (available for Apple and IBM computers).

Learning Technology

Laserdisc (1-8)
Dynamic full-motion videos and inviting still images that build concepts, illustrate key vocabulary, and stimulate critical thinking—all accessed easily by bar codes.

Reading Software (3-8)
A reading skills practice program with activities that reinforce vocabulary, comprehension, thinking, study, and language skills (available for Apple IIe, IIc, and IIGS computers).

Second Language Support

Second-Language Support Manual (1-8)
Designed for *HBJ Treasury of Literature* users, a valuable teaching resource guide with lesson-by-lesson strategies for helping second-language students build English language and reading skills.

Transition for ESL Students, Teacher's Manual (1-6)
Useful suggestions and strategies for helping ESL students make a comfortable transition to *HBJ Treasury of Literature*.

English as a Second Language (1-5)
Colorful classroom posters and a helpful teacher's manual for developing English language skills.

Harcourt Brace Jovanovich

For more information call:
1-800-CALL-HBJ (1-800-225-5425)

CONTENTS
REFERENCE FILE

INTEGRATED INSTRUCTION / R21

CLASSROOM MANAGEMENT / R29

RETEACH LESSONS / R35

Endless Worlds

Reflecting on the Literature

Invite students to think about what they have read.

Ask students to look at the Contents for Units 1–3 on pages 4–9. Use questions such as the following to help them reflect on what they have read so far in *Endless Worlds*.

- Which theme has been your favorite so far? Why?
- Which story has been your favorite so far? Why?
- Which author has been your favorite so far? What makes his or her writing so special?
- Which was your favorite library or Bookshelf book?

Help students preview the rest of the book.

Ask students to preview the Contents for Units 4–6 (pages 10–15). Have them examine the illustrations and read the theme and selection titles. Encourage them to use this information to make predictions about the remaining literature in the Student Anthology. Remind students that the Handbook for Readers and Writers, the Glossary, and the Index of Titles and Authors appear at the back of the book, and ask volunteers to tell how they can use each resource.

Thinking About Classroom Management

Consider management options.

At this point, you may find it useful to ask yourself the following questions, and use the answers as you think about classroom management options for the last three units of *Endless Worlds*.

- What kinds of stories and which authors did my students find the most enjoyable? How can I use this information to further "hook" my students on reading? (Additional Reading in the lesson plans and Bookshelf in the Student Anthology will help you gather a list of titles to use with students.)
- What kinds of activities worked well with my students? How can I use this information to help me plan classroom management for the rest of the year? (Managing the Literature–Based Classroom, Options for Reading, and cooperative reading suggestions offer a variety of alternatives from which to choose.)

HBJ TREASURY OF LITERATURE

ENDLESS WORLDS

SENIOR AUTHORS
ROGER C. FARR
DOROTHY S. STRICKLAND

AUTHORS
RICHARD F. ABRAHAMSON
ELLEN BOOTH CHURCH
BARBARA BOWEN COULTER
MARGARET A. GALLEGO
JUDITH L. IRVIN
KAREN KUTIPER
JUNKO YOKOTA LEWIS
DONNA M. OGLE
TIMOTHY SHANAHAN
PATRICIA SMITH

SENIOR CONSULTANTS
BERNICE E. CULLINAN
W. DORSEY HAMMOND
ASA G. HILLIARD III

CONSULTANTS
ALONZO A. CRIM
ROLANDO R. HINOJOSA-SMITH
LEE BENNETT HOPKINS
ROBERT J. STERNBERG

HBJ HARCOURT BRACE JOVANOVICH, INC.
Orlando   Austin   San Diego   Chicago   Dallas   New York

Copyright © 1993 by Harcourt Brace Jovanovich, Inc.

All rights reserved. No part of this publication may be reproduced or transmitted in any form or by any means, electronic or mechanical, including photocopy, recording, or any information storage and retrieval system, without permission in writing from the publisher.

Requests for permission to make copies of any part of the work should be mailed to: Permissions Department, Harcourt Brace Jovanovich, Publishers, 8th Floor, Orlando, Florida 32887

Printed in the United States of America

ISBN 0-15-300427-4

1 2 3 4 5 6 7 8 9 10   048   96 95 94 93 92
Acknowledgments continue on pages 623–624, which constitute an extension of this copyright page.

Acknowledgments
For permission to reprint copyrighted material, grateful acknowledgment is made to the following sources:

Isaac Asimov: From "The Story Machine" by Isaac Asimov in *Plays* Magazine, May 1977.

Atheneum Publishers, an imprint of Macmillan Publishing Company: Cover illustration by Judith Gwyn Brown from *I Am the Universe* by Barbara Corcoran. Illustration copyright © 1986 by Judith Gwyn Brown. "The First" from *Something New Begins* by Lilian Moore. Text copyright © 1980, 1982 by Lilian Moore.

Avon Books: Cover illustration from *Bearstone* by Will Hobbs. Copyright © 1989 by Will Hobbs.

Bantam Books, a division of Bantam Doubleday Dell Publishing Group, Inc.: Cover illustration by Vladimir Kordic from *Where the Red Fern Grows* by Wilson Rawls. Copyright © 1961 by Wilson Rawls; copyright © 1961 by The Curtis Publishing Company.

William Bentzen, on behalf of the heirs of Knud Rasmussen: "And I think over again . . ." (Retitled: "Song") from *Intellectual Culture of the Copper Eskimos,* translated by Knud Rasmussen.

Bradbury Press, an Affiliate of Macmillan, Inc.: "Gnats, Mammoths, and Saber-toothed Tigers" and "Layers of Fossils" from *Dinosaurs Walked Here and Other Stories Fossils Tell* by Patricia Lauber. Text copyright © 1987 by Patricia Lauber.

Curtis Brown, Ltd.: "The Microscope" by Maxine Kumin. Text copyright © 1963 by Maxine Kumin. Originally published in *The Atlantic Monthly.*

Clarion Books, a Houghton Mifflin Company imprint: From "Discovering Gold" in *Klondike Fever: The Famous Gold Rush of 1898* by Michael Cooper. Text copyright © 1989 by Michael Cooper.

Cobblehill Books, an affiliate of Dutton Children's Books, a division of Penguin Books USA Inc.: From "Helping Hands" in *People Who Make a Difference* by Brent Ashabranner. Text copyright © 1989 by Brent Ashabranner.

Coward-McCann, Inc.: "Peki, The Musician" from *The Crest and the Hide* by Harold Courlander. Text copyright © 1982 by Harold Courlander.

Crown Publishers, Inc.: From *Nadja on My Way* (Retitled: "A Life in Music") by Nadja Salerno-Sonnenberg, cover photographs by Janette Beckman. Text copyright © 1989 by Nadja Salerno-Sonnenberg; cover photographs copyright © 1989 by Janette Beckman.

Dell Books, a division of Bantam Doubleday Dell Publishing Group, Inc.: From pp. 15-26 in *The Outside Shot* (Retitled: "A Nice Touch") by Walter Dean Myers. Text copyright © 1984 by John Ballard. "Playing God" (Retitled: "The Second Highest Point") by Ouida Sebestyen from *Visions,* edited by Donald R. Gallo. Text copyright © 1987 by Ouida Sebestyen.

Doubleday, a division of Bantam Doubleday Dell Publishing Group, Inc.: Text from pp. 669-681 and cover illustration from *Roots* (Retitled: "Mister Kintel") by Alex Haley. Text and cover illustration copyright © 1976 by Alex Haley.

E. P. Dutton, a division of Penguin Books USA, Inc.: Cover illustration from *The El Dorado Adventure* by Lloyd Alexander. Copyright © 1987 by Lloyd Alexander. Text and cover illustration from *The Astronaut Training Book for Kids* by Kim Long. Copyright © 1990 by Kim Long. Cover illustration from *Rascal* by Sterling North. Illustration copyright © 1963 by E. P. Dutton, a division of Penguin Books USA Inc.

Farrar, Straus and Giroux, Inc.: Cover photo by Rob McEwan from *Anne of Green Gables* by L. M. Montgomery. Adapted from "Naftali the Storyteller and His Horse, Sus" in *Stories for Children* by Isaac Bashevis Singer. Text copyright © 1973, 1976, 1984 by Isaac Bashevis Singer. Cover illustration by Leslie W. Bowman from *El Guero* by Elizabeth Borton de Treviño. Illustration copyright © 1989 by Leslie W. Bowman. Adapted from *Here Is Mexico* (Retitled: "Mexico: A Wealth of Beauty") by Elizabeth Borton de Treviño. Text copyright © 1970 by Elizabeth Borton de Treviño.

Michael Garland: Cover illustration by Michael Garland from *My Side of the Mountain* by Jean Craighead George. Illustration copyright © 1989 by Michael Garland.

Grosset & Dunlap, a division of G. P. Putnam's Sons: Cover illustration by Kyuzo Tsugami from *The Call of the Wild and Other Stories* by Jack London. Illustration copyright © 1965 by Grosset & Dunlap, Inc.

Harcourt Brace Jovanovich, Inc.: "One" from *When I Dance* by James Berry. Text copyright © 1991, 1988 by James Berry. Originally published by Hamish Hamilton Children's Books, 1988. Cover illustration by Fritz Eichenberg from *Rainbows Are Made: Poems* by Carl Sandburg, selected by Lee Bennett Hopkins. Illustration copyright © 1982 by Fritz Eichenberg. "The No-Guitar Blues" from *Baseball in April* by Gary Soto. Text copyright © 1990 by Gary Soto. From *Be An Inventor* by Barbara Taylor. Text copyright © 1987 by Field Publications. Pronunciation Key from *HBJ School Dictionary,* Third Edition. Text copyright © 1990 by Harcourt Brace Jovanovich, Inc.

HarperCollins Publishers: Cover illustration by John Schoenherr from *Julie of the Wolves* by Jean Craighead George. Illustration copyright © 1972 by John Schoenherr. "Little Green Men" by Barry B. Longyear. Text © 1987 by Barry B. Longyear. Cover illustration by Colin Thiele. Illustration copyright © 1988 by HarperCollins Publishers. From pp. 63-86 in *Sea Glass* (Retitled: "At the Cove") by Laurence Yep. Text copyright © 1979 by Laurence Yep.

Harrap Publishing Group, Ltd.: From "Mayans, Toltecs and Aztecs" in *Let's Visit Mexico* by John C. Caldwell. Text © by John C. Caldwell.

continued on pages 623 and 624

2

HBJ TREASURY OF LITERATURE

Dear Reader,

"If a thing doesn't happen today, it might easily happen tomorrow. If not in one country, then in another. There are ENDLESS WORLDS. . . ." So says Isaac Bashevis Singer, who wrote one of the selections you will read this year. These selections will tell you about fascinating worlds, worlds in which people lead their daily lives in a variety of ways and enjoy exciting events.

You will read about Peki, a young musician in Africa who faces a big challenge, and Fausto, a Mexican American student who's eager to learn to play the guitar. You will read about the hardships faced by people who discovered gold in Canada and about the challenges faced by archaeologists uncovering ancient treasures in Mexico. You will learn how astronauts have increased our knowledge of Earth, and you will also discover how fossils of saber-toothed tigers and even gnats can tell us about the past.

During the year you will also learn about spirit—the spirit of discovery and the spirit of freedom. You will read about the spirit of discovery Alex Haley feels when he learns about his heritage during a visit to Africa. You will come to understand the spirit of freedom, the freedom poet Paul Laurence Dunbar expresses in the line "I know why the caged bird sings."

We hope that you will enjoy discovering the many worlds collected here.

Sincerely,
The Authors

ENDLESS WORLDS

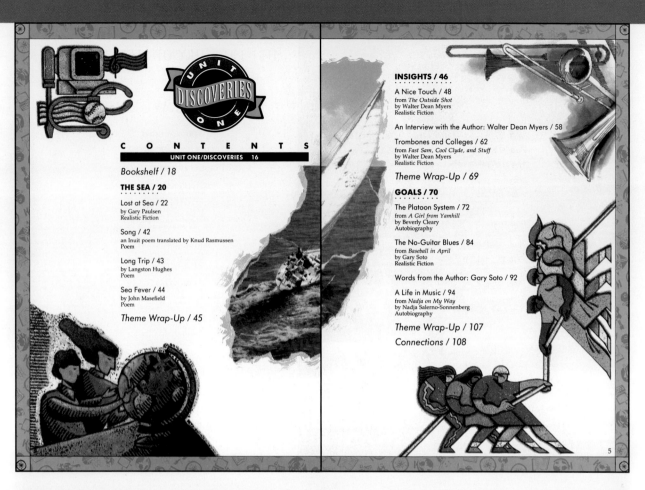

UNIT ONE DISCOVERIES

C O N T E N T S

5

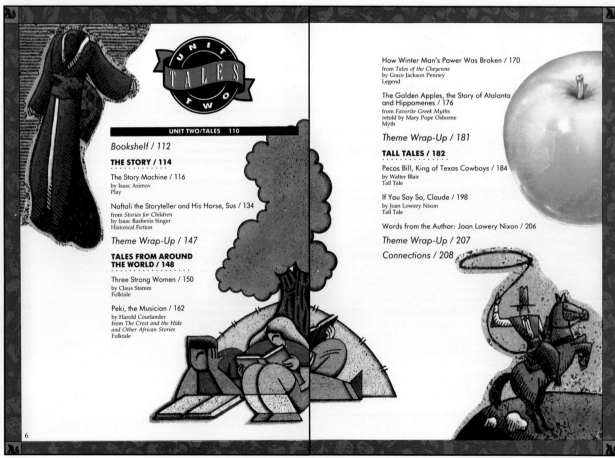

UNIT TWO TALES

6

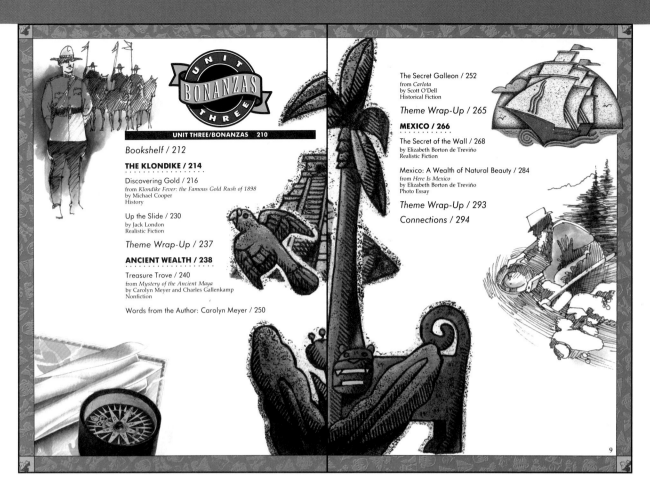

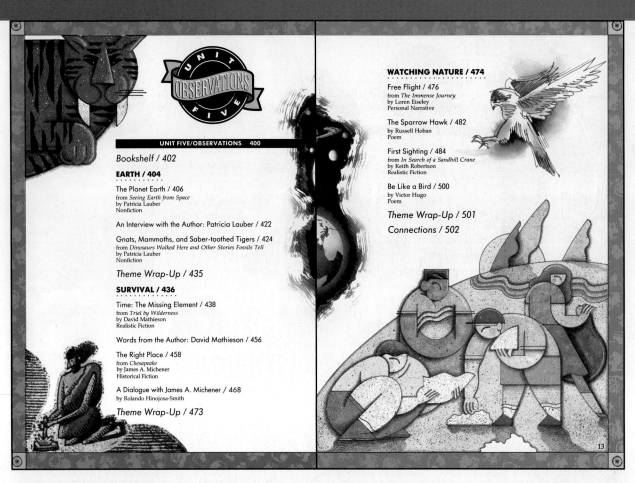

13

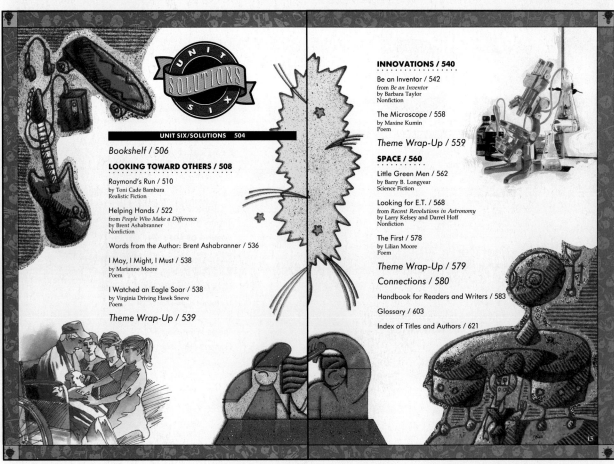

15

UNIT CHALLENGES FOUR

Planning Center

What's Ahead in "Challenges"?

FORTITUDE: PAGES 300–331B   What would demand all of a person's effort and skill? Your students will find out when you introduce them to Ralph Helfer and Susan Butcher, two special people who face extraordinary challenges with incredible "Fortitude."

SEARCHING: PAGES 332–359B   Searching for one's identity is an ongoing process. Invite your students to read the autobiographical excerpt about one man's search for his roots and eight poems about the freedom to be who you are.

COMING OF AGE: PAGES 360–397B   "Coming of Age" is a challenging experience. Your students may discover that their own feelings and experiences are very similar to those of the characters in the selections.

Pacing

This unit is designed to take approximately five or six weeks, depending on your students' needs.

Assessment and Evaluation

ASSESSMENT OPTIONS		
Title	**Description**	**When and How It's Used**
INFORMAL ASSESSMENT OPTIONS (Ongoing)		
Reading/Writing Portfolio	Contains samples of students' literacy development.	Collect samples of personal journals and writing throughout the unit. Hold periodic Portfolio Conferences.
Informal Assessment Notes	Appear throughout the *Teacher's Edition*.	Observe students' reading, writing, listening, and speaking behaviors. Complete checklists on an ongoing basis.
Student Self-Assessment Notes	Appear throughout the *Teacher's Edition*.	Students monitor their use of reading and writing strategies.
Running Records	Ongoing assessment of students' reading skills and strategies as they read both fiction and nonfiction.	Record periodically to track students' progress.
FORMAL ASSESSMENT OPTIONS (End of Unit)		
Skills Assessment	Assesses mastery of strategies and skills taught in Learning Through Literature.	Administer at end of the unit.
Holistic Assessment	Evaluates students' ability to read and understand excerpts from literature.	Administer at end of the unit.
Integrated Performance Assessment	Assesses use of reading and writing strategies modeled and practiced in the classroom.	Administer at end of the unit.

HBJ Literature Cassette 2

Recordings of the following selections in "Challenges" may be used for instruction or for students' listening enjoyment:

- "Sympathy"
- "One"
- "The Road Not Taken"
- "Advice to Travelers"
- "I Saw a Man"
- "The Forecast"
- "I'm Nobody!"
- "To Make a Prairie"
- "The Second Highest Point"

Audiovisual Materials and Software

After the Rain by Norma F. Mazer. American School Publishers, 1990. Rachel's grandfather is dying of cancer, and he becomes the most important thing in her life. AUDIOCASSETTE OR VIDEO

Meet the Newbery Author: Laurence Yep. Random House, 1981. Summaries of Yep's novels are combined with background information about the author. FILMSTRIP

Mending Wall by Robert Frost. Aims Media. With a background of fitting visual effects, Leonard Nimoy reads Frost's poem. FILM OR VIDEO

Poetry Express. Learning Well. Students learn about style, theme, and mood in a wide variety of poetry examples. COMPUTER SOFTWARE

World Cultures and Youth: Richard's Totem Pole. Coronet/MTI. A Gitskan Indian in British Columbia takes an interest in his heritage. INTERACTIVE VIDEODISC

"Rubbing my eyes, I looked to the hillside above our home. There it stood in all its wild beauty, a waving red banner in a carpet of green. It seemed to be saying 'Good-bye, and don't worry, for I'll be here always.' "

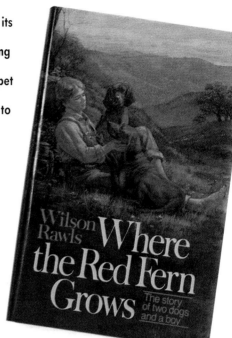

HBJ Treasury of Literature Library

Here are some of the options you will find in the *HBJ Treasury of Literature Library Guide* for *Where the Red Fern Grows*:

- **Reading Cooperatively** in response groups
- **Reading Independently** during sustained silent reading periods
- **Directing the Reading** through questioning strategies
- **Reading Aloud** to encourage literature appreciation

Bulletin Board Idea

Begin a bulletin board display labeled "Challenges" with a newspaper photograph that depicts a challenge—for example, an Olympic athlete taking part in an event. Either include the caption from the newspaper, or write one that ties the photograph to the theme, "Challenges." Invite students to add other theme-related pictures they find in newspapers or magazines and have them write a caption that explains what each picture shows and how it depicts a challenge. Encourage students to include as many different kinds of challenges as they can. Students also can add their own drawings to the display.

Challenges

Ask students to suggest different kinds of challenges that people face in life. Encourage a variety of responses, such as ''conquering nature'' and ''finding oneself.'' Ask students to read the unit introduction and to preview the theme and selection titles to help them set a purpose for reading the unit. Have them speculate about possible connections among the themes of ''Challenges'': ''Fortitude,'' ''Searching,'' and ''Coming of Age.'' CULTURAL AWARENESS

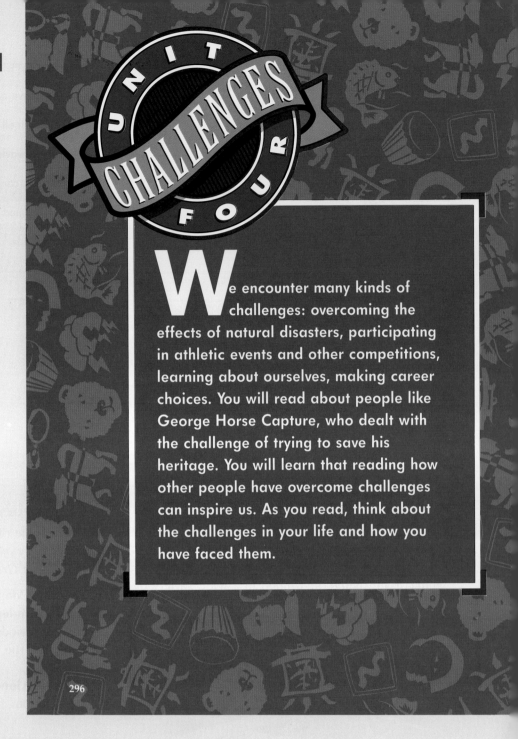

We encounter many kinds of challenges: overcoming the effects of natural disasters, participating in athletic events and other competitions, learning about ourselves, making career choices. You will read about people like George Horse Capture, who dealt with the challenge of trying to save his heritage. You will learn that reading how other people have overcome challenges can inspire us. As you read, think about the challenges in your life and how you have faced them.

THEMES

FORTITUDE
. . . .
300

SEARCHING
. . . .
332

COMING OF AGE
. . . .
360

297

Focus on Literary Genre

If you wish to have students focus on literary genre, or form, as they read the selections in "Challenges," refer to the Literary Genre list. (A complete Table of Contents classified by literary genre appears on pages R98–R101.) The labels on the numbered annotations beside the reduced student pages will help you guide students to note and analyze the literary elements and characteristics of each genre.

BOOKSHELF

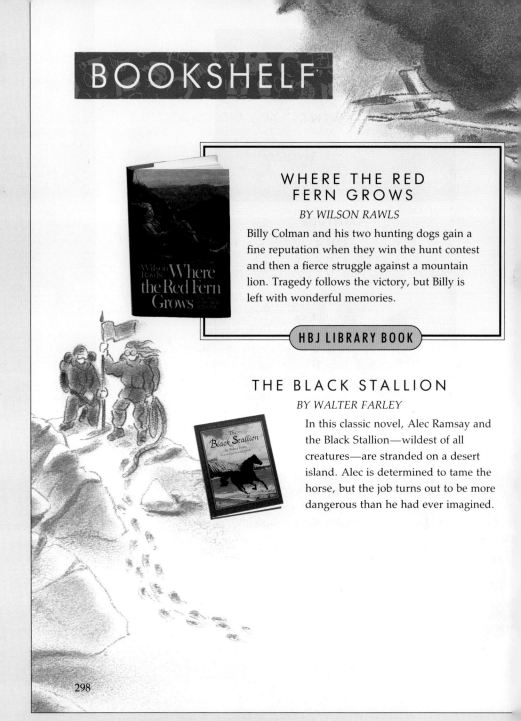

WHERE THE RED FERN GROWS

BY WILSON RAWLS

Billy Colman and his two hunting dogs gain a fine reputation when they win the hunt contest and then a fierce struggle against a mountain lion. Tragedy follows the victory, but Billy is left with wonderful memories.

HBJ LIBRARY BOOK

THE BLACK STALLION

BY WALTER FARLEY

In this classic novel, Alec Ramsay and the Black Stallion—wildest of all creatures—are stranded on a desert island. Alec is determined to tame the horse, but the job turns out to be more dangerous than he had ever imagined.

298

HBJ Library Book

Have students read the information about *Where the Red Fern Grows* and look at the cover illustration. Have them discuss what they know about the book so far. Page 295F provides a preview of the lesson plans that can be found in the *HBJ Treasury of Literature Library Guide*.

RAINBOWS ARE MADE

BY CARL SANDBURG
COLLECTED BY LEE BENNETT HOPKINS

These poems by one of America's greatest writers are
enhanced by stunning woodcut engravings. ALA
NOTABLE BOOK

ANTHONY BURNS:
THE DEFEAT AND TRIUMPH
OF A FUGITIVE SLAVE

BY VIRGINIA HAMILTON

In this true story, Anthony Burns, born a slave,
becomes the center of attention after he escapes
to Boston. When he is arrested under the Fugitive
Slave Act, Anthony becomes a symbol of freedom
in peril. ALA NOTABLE BOOK, SCHOOL LIBRARY
JOURNAL BEST BOOK

JODIE'S JOURNEY

BY COLIN THIELE

After winning a jumping championship riding her
beloved horse, Monarch, Jodie faces far more challenging
hurdles. She learns that she has a crippling disease and
will never ride Monarch again.

299

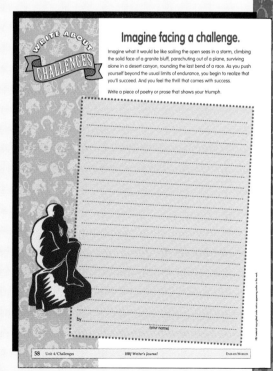

WRITER'S JOURNAL pages 56–58:

Reading and writing about "Challenges"

Imagine facing a challenge.

Imagine what it would be like sailing the open seas in a storm, climbing
the solid face of a granite bluff, parachuting out of a plane, surviving
alone in a desert canyon, rounding the last bend of a race. As you push
yourself beyond the usual limits of endurance, you begin to realize that
you'll succeed. And you feel the thrill that comes with success.

Write a piece of poetry or prose that shows your triumph.

by _____
[your name]

Writer's Journal

Read aloud to students.

The Fastest Woman in the World

by Tom Biracree

When she was only four years old, Wilma Rudolph was stricken by polio. For several years, she couldn't walk without a leg brace. Remarkably, she set herself to meet this challenge and became a world-famous track star. At the 1960 Olympics, she faced her greatest track challenge—the 400-meter relay.

The crowd of 80,000 spectators in the Stadio Olympico was more than double the population of Wilma Rudolph's hometown of Clarksville, Tennessee. She knew that, in addition, more than 100 million people were watching her on television as she went through her final warm-up exercises. Yet, like Jesse Owens before her, Rudolph had a reserve of quiet strength that enabled her to maintain a firm resolve, even under the most intense pressures.

Her opponents were not the only runners affecting Rudolph's chances of winning her third gold medal. The performance of her teammates was vitally important. A relay race is a symphony of intricate movements, each of which must fall into place like notes in a musical score. Just as one wrong note can ruin a piece of music, any one of an infinite number of small mishaps can turn a winning relay ream into losers.

The coordination required between teammates must be so precise that relay runners routinely endure endless practice sessions. Rudolph and her three teammates—Martha Hudson, Barbara Jones, and Lucinda Williams—had one major advantage: They were already finely attuned partners.

But the four women had never performed under the pressure of the Olympic Games—pressure that was compounded by the excitement of the crowd cheering the other events conducted simultaneously in the stadium's infield. Then, too, in the preliminary heats (qualifying races) of the men's and women's relays, seven highly trained teams had already been disqualified. One lapse in concentration by Rudolph and her partners could make their team the eighth.

And a week before this climactic race, Rudolph had twisted her ankle. Somehow, she had still managed to best her opponents in the 100-meter

SELECTION SUMMARY The pressure is intense as American runner Wilma Rudolph awaits the start of the 400-meter relay race at the 1960 Olympics. Although the U.S. team is not favored to win, Rudolph is eager to try for a third gold medal. The U.S. team falls behind, but somehow Rudolph finds the power to close the gap and to finish first. The team sets a new record and Rudolph becomes the most celebrated female athlete in the world.

ABOUT THE AUTHOR Tom Biracree is the author of over thirty-five books. He was a high school coach and sportswriter before beginning his writing career.

Strategies for Listening

LISTENING/THINKING STRATEGY—IDENTIFYING MOOD USING DETAILS Tell students that a biographer not only tries to re-create the time, place, and events in a person's life, but the mood or atmosphere as well. Explain to students that listening for details about the mood or atmosphere will help them to better understand the actions and feelings of the characters.

SET A PURPOSE FOR LISTENING Explain that this excerpt is about an actual relay race that took place at the 1960 Rome Olympics. Students should pay attention to details to understand what the main character is experiencing.

dash the next day, and the 200-meter contest the day after. But those races had been run on straight tracks, whereas the relay was run on a challenging, curved course that put a punishing strain on a runner's ankles. Occasional twinges of pain reminded Rudolph that one slightly misplaced step could send her crashing to the cinders.

The starter called the runners to the starting blocks. Rudolph took her place near the 300-meter mark of the 400-meter track. She always ran "anchor" (the final leg of the race), partly because she was the team's fastest runner and partly because her one shortcoming as a racer was her inability to make a perfect start from the blocks. That weakness had bothered her a great deal until she learned that Jesse Owens had also been a poor starter who relied on later bursts of speed for his triumphs.

Rudolph knelt to check her track shoes one more time. Suddenly, the crowd grew silent, and without looking she knew the race was about to begin. The crack of the starter's pistol was followed instantaneously by the roar of the spectators.

The runners, sprinting like thoroughbreds, completed the first 100 meters in a little more than 11 seconds without a clear leader emerging. But by the time the second American runner, Barbara Jones, passed the baton to Lucinda Williams, it was clear that the experts had been wrong: The U.S. team had a good chance of capturing the race.

As Williams hurtled toward her, Wilma Rudolph studied the competition. The West German anchor, Jutta Heine, had easily outstripped her opponents in a preliminary race, and Rudolph knew that Heine would be gunning for a victory today. She also knew that Irina Press, a powerfully built

sprinter from the Soviet Union, would also be a formidable competitor. When Rudolph saw that Lucinda Williams had come abreast of the West German and Russian racers, she felt a small surge of relief. It looked as if she would not have to chase Heine and Press.

But disaster struck during the hand-off, when Rudolph fumbled and nearly dropped the baton. She regained control scarcely a foot before reaching the point where the American team would have been disqualified. Rudolph was still in the race, but the U.S. team had fallen behind.

For Rudolph, the final 90 meters of the race seemed to be run in slow motion. Every fiber of strength she had built up in seven years of intensive training was put to the test. She fixed her gaze fiercely on the backs of the other runners as she closed the gap inch by inch.

Coming into the final stretch, she was still two meters behind Irina Press, who had taken the lead. But Rudolph dug down for extra reserves of power. Pushing for the tape that stretched across the finish line, she made a final, desperate lunge. The Soviet runner dropped from sight as Rudolph burst through the tape and collapsed to the ground.

An instant later she was joined by her teammates. They hugged her, sobbing, as they waited for the judges to examine photographs of the finish. The agitated crowd hushed as the announcement blared over the loud-speaker—the U.S. team had won! They had triumphed by inches, to set a new record time of 44.5 seconds.

Wilma Rudolph, a shy black woman from a small town in Tennessee, had become the most celebrated female athlete in the world.

Responding to Literature

1. **How would you describe Rudolph's state of mind as she waits for the starting gun to be fired? Explain.** (Accept reasonable responses: She feels confident, but she is challenged by the excitement and the crowds.)
DETERMINING CHARACTERS' EMOTIONS

2. **How do you think you would feel if your team lost because one of your teammates dropped the baton? Explain.** (Accept reasonable responses: furious with the person who dropped the baton; happy that you at least got to the Olympics.) CRITICAL: EXPRESSING PERSONAL OPINIONS

SPEAKING Invite students to take the part of a sports announcer describing to a radio audience in America the details of Wilma Rudolph's Olympic race. Remind students that they must re-create all of the details of the race because their radio audience can't see the actual race. CREATIVE: VISUALIZING

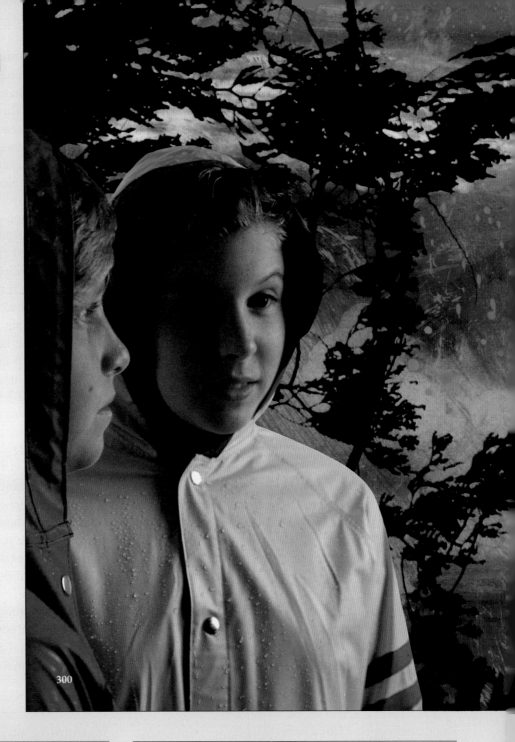

Fortitude

Ask students what they understand by the word *fortitude*. Point out that the root of the word means "strong," and elicit synonyms such as *strength of character* or *courage*. Have students look at the illustration on Student Anthology page 301. Ask students for what types of situations a person might have to master a degree of fortitude. Then have students read the selection titles on that page. Discuss what is happening in the picture and what kind of fortitude the characters in the selections might possess.

PACING   Although you may need to adapt to the individual needs within your classroom, this theme has been designed to take about two weeks to complete.

300

Management Options

THE LITERATURE-BASED CLASSROOM   Providing a literature-rich curriculum creates unique classroom management challenges. Some management options for the selections in this theme follow.

COMMUNICATE WITH THE SCHOOL LIBRARIAN
Students will be required to do research to complete the Writer's Workshop activity on Student Anthology page 331. Inform the school librarian of the assignment ahead of time. Some students may require assistance locating and using library resources. Be sure to inform the librarian of the unit theme and the titles in the Bookshelf features as well.

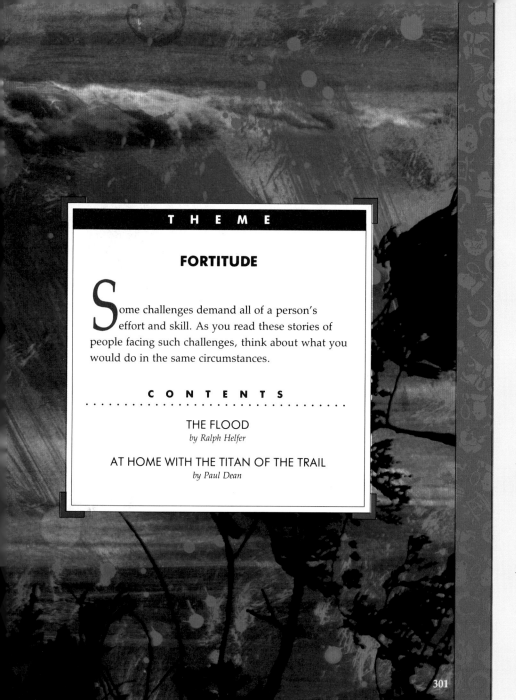

THEME

FORTITUDE

Some challenges demand all of a person's effort and skill. As you read these stories of people facing such challenges, think about what you would do in the same circumstances.

CONTENTS

THE FLOOD
by Ralph Helfer

AT HOME WITH THE TITAN OF THE TRAIL
by Paul Dean

301

EXCHANGING RESEARCH REPORTS When students are working independently on research reports, you may want to set up a system by which they can read and comment on each other's work in an objective way. You might assign each student an identification number. Both the writer and the reviewer should use their identification numbers rather than their names on the report and on the comment sheet drawn up by the reviewer.

READING/WRITING PORTFOLIO Instruct students to keep in their portfolios their writing responses to the theme selections. Remind them also to add to their personal journals notes on their independent reading.

THE FLOOD

by Ralph Helfer

RALPH HELFER, renowned animal trainer and founder of Africa U.S.A., has devoted his life to training wild animals to appear on television and in the movies. In his book, Helfer tells how he trained Clyde, Clint Eastwood's orangutan, and many other famous animals to work safely on the set with both stars and extras. The book strongly advocates Helfer's system of affection training, a method of domesticating wild animals that relies on love, patience, and understanding.

OTHER BOOKS ABOUT FORTITUDE
Moxie by Phyllis Rossiter. Macmillan, 1990. AVERAGE
Sniper by Theodore Taylor. Harcourt Brace Jovanovich, 1989. AVERAGE
The Wounded Wolf by Jean Craighead George. HarperCollins, 1978. EASY

SELECTION SUMMARY
In this excerpt from his nonfiction book, *The Beauty of the Beasts*, Ralph Helfer explains that he uses affection training to train animals for movies and television. He has 1,500 wild animals on his California ranch when a flood hits. Helfer, his wife, and his staff struggle heroically to save the animals. Some animals are swept away, but affection training has conditioned them to cooperate with human rescuers, so most survive. The flood destroys the ranch, but Helfer resolves to start over.

LESSON PLANNER	Materials	Integrated Curriculum	Meeting Individual Needs
1 READING LITERATURE pp. 301B–321	Student Anthology pp. 302–321 Transparency 17 Second-Language Support Manual Practice Book p. 92 Integrated Spelling p. 45 Integrated Spelling T.E. pp. 64–65	Spelling Spelling Pretest Spelling-Vocabulary Connection (science words)	Second-Language Support Vocabulary 301C Strategic Reading 301D, 304, 314 Cooperative Reading 302, 320
2 RESPONDING TO LITERATURE pp. 321A–321D	Writer's Journal p. 59 Practice Book pp. 93–94 Integrated Spelling p. 46 Integrated Spelling T.E. pp. 64–65	Vocabulary Workshop Reviewing Key Words Extending Vocabulary Writing About the Literature Speaking/Listening Spelling Review	Cooperative Learning 321B, 321C, 321D
3 LEARNING THROUGH LITERATURE pp. 321E–321J	Second-Language Support Manual Writer's Journal pp. 60–61 Practice Book pp. 95–96	Math Science Social Studies/Health Multicultural	Reteach 321F, 321H Challenge 321F, 321H Second-Language Support 321F, 321H Cooperative Learning 321H, 321I

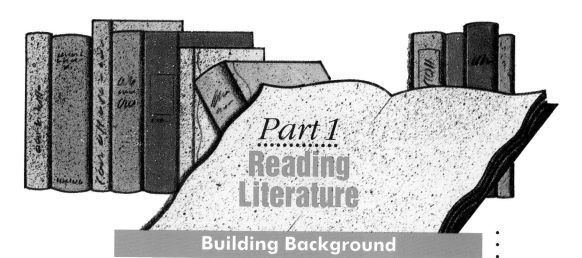

Part 1
Reading Literature

Building Background

Access prior knowledge and develop vocabulary concepts.

Tell students they will be reading a nonfiction narrative, a true story called "The Flood." Explain that the author keeps hundreds of wild animals on his California ranch and trains them for roles in movies and television. Write the following headings on the board and invite students to add specific details about what it might be like to experience a flood.

FLOOD

Description	Events	Feelings
rising water roads flooded	people swept downstream heroic rescues	terror suspense relief

Have students quickwrite sentences.

Ask students to imagine they are caught in a flood or other disaster. Have them write a few sentences about what they would do and share them with a friend.

Vocabulary Strategies

Introduce Key Words and strategies.

Tell students that they may find some unfamiliar words in "The Flood." Display Transparency 17, or write the paragraph on the board. Have students read the paragraph silently and use context clues, phonics, and structural analysis to figure out the meanings of the underlined words.

Transparency 17   Key Words

The storm struck at dawn. By noon the earth was saturated and could hold no more water. We had believed that the cabins inside the walled compound were safe from flooding, but we could see the rising river causing erosion along the wall. We finally succumbed to our fears and fled to the haven of high ground. We had been indoctrinated by the camp counselors to follow safety procedures, so we all made it. But it was heartrending to see our cabin destroyed by the river's turbulence.

KEY WORDS DEFINED

saturated   soaked

compound   buildings in an enclosed yard

erosion   a wearing away

succumbed   gave in

haven   safe place

indoctrinated   thoroughly taught

heartrending   heartbreaking

turbulence   agitation, swirling

Ask a volunteer to read the paragraph aloud. Provide help with pronunciation if necessary.

**Check students'
understanding.**
Write the synonyms in the right-hand column on the board. Then read aloud the Key Words and have students identify the synonym for each Key Word. STRATEGY: SYNONYMS

1. heartrending (g)
2. erosion (f)
3. succumbed (a)
4. haven (h)
5. saturated (b)
6. turbulence (d)
7. indoctrinated (c)
8. compound (e)

a. *gave in*
b. *soaked*
c. *instructed*
d. *disturbance*
e. *fenced-in buildings*
f. *a wearing away*
g. *distressing*
h. *shelter*

After discussing the Key Words with students, encourage them to add some of the words to the chart they completed in Building Background. For example, they might place *turbulence* under *Description* and *erosion* under *Events*.

**Encourage use of
the Glossary.**
GLOSSARY Point out that this narrative may contain other unfamiliar words, such as *chaos* and *leverage*, that students can look up in the Glossary or in a dictionary. Remind students that they can also use the Glossary to confirm or clarify their understanding of Key Words.

**Integrate spelling
with vocabulary.**
SPELLING-VOCABULARY CONNECTION *Integrated Spelling* page 45 reinforces spellings of science words, including the Key Words *erosion, saturated,* and *turbulence.*

**SECOND-LANGUAGE
SUPPORT** Have students work with a peer tutor to look up the Key Words in a dictionary and match them to their meanings. They may demonstrate their mastery by using the new words in oral sentences. (See *Second-Language Support Manual.*)

**PRACTICE BOOK
page 92:** Reinforcing Key Words

**INTEGRATED SPELLING
page 45:** Writing and spelling science words

NOTE: These pages may be completed now or after students have read the narrative.

Practice Book

• • • THE FLOOD • • •

Name _____

Read the following paragraphs. Use clues in the story to determine the meaning of each underlined word. Then write the word on the line next to its meaning.

I've heard that my grandfather's college years were filled with turbulence. He began his studies intending to do medical research. But there was a gradual erosion of his interest in medicine. His father, a doctor, complained that he was being indoctrinated by his roommate, who was an early believer in protecting animals and their habitats. My grandmother remembers hours of debate about the subject and heartrending pictures of hungry animals. Eventually, my grandfather succumbed to his roommate's arguments and changed his field of study.

Finally, after years of study, and with degrees in zoology and botany, my grandfather felt saturated with book knowledge and was ready to begin his career.

He began his work in a small compound at the edge of the rain forest in Brazil. By the time he retired, my grandfather had helped to preserve 450,000 acres of rain forest as a haven for endangered animals.

1. taught certain principles or beliefs ___indoctrinated___
2. a gradual wearing away or something gradually worn away
   ___erosion___
3. an enclosed yard with buildings in it ___compound___
4. gave in, yielded ___succumbed___
5. disorder, violent agitation ___turbulence___
6. causing much grief, heartbreaking ___heartrending___
7. unable to hold any more water, knowledge, and so on
   ___saturated___
8. a safe place, refuge ___haven___

92 Vocabulary

Practice Book • ENDLESS WORLDS

Integrated Spelling

INTEGRATED SPELLING
Science Words

Name _____

Read the Spelling Words. Write them on a separate sheet of paper. Check your spelling.

SPELLING STRATEGY

Spelling science words is easier if you connect them with words you know. For example, **earthen** means "made of **earth**."

Often, science words come from foreign languages, such as Greek or Latin. For example, **debris** comes from the French word **debriser**, which meant "to break into pieces." In French, the final s is not usually pronounced, so **debris** has a silent s.

When you are not sure how to spell a science word, think about what the word means. Are there other related words that you know? Do you recognize the base word or a prefix or suffix from another language?

Write the related Spelling Word for each word below.

danger ___endanger___ earth ___earthen___
erode ___erosion___ generate ___generator___ survive ___survival___

Write each Spelling Word next to its origin.

Greek: *a* ("without") + *byssos* ("depth") = ___abyss___
French: *debriser* ("break into pieces") = ___debris___
Latin: *instinctus* ("impulse") = ___instinct___
Latin: *saturatus* ("full") = ___saturate___
Latin: *turba* ("confusion") = ___turbulence___

SPELLING WORDS
abyss
debris
earthen
endanger
erosion
generator
instinct
saturate
survival
turbulence

MEMORY JOGGER

End anger in the wild—don't **endanger** the animals!

Here's a Memory Jogger to help you spell **endanger**.

ENDLESS WORLDS • "The Flood"   45

Practice Book   **Integrated Spelling**

Preview and Predict

Discuss the value of previewing and predicting.

Remind students that making predictions about what they are reading can help them understand it better. Point out that while this selection is nonfiction, it is narrative—it tells a story. Have a volunteer suggest ways of previewing narrative nonfiction in order to make predictions. (reading the title and the first paragraph; looking at the pictures; reading about the author) Then have students preview.

Introduce the sequence diagram.

Point out that a nonfiction narrative, like a fictional story, moves from one event to the next. Use a sequence diagram to help students predict what will happen in "The Flood."

SEQUENCE DIAGRAM

First: *Rains cause flood.*	Next: *Helfner uses affection training to save animals.*	Next:
Next:	Next:	Finally:

PERSONAL JOURNAL Have students copy the sequence diagram into their personal journals, or have them use *Practice Book* page 93. (See page 321B in this Teacher's Edition.) Have them complete the diagram as they read "The Flood" or afterward. (Students will return to the diagram after reading, in Summarizing the Literature.)

Setting a Purpose

Have students set purposes.

Have students use the predictions they have made to write questions that they would like answered by the end of the selection. Invite volunteers to share their questions.

Model purpose-setting, if necessary.

If students have difficulty setting a purpose for reading, model the thinking process:

> **I know from previewing that Helfer uses something called affection training. I also predict that there will be a flood. Therefore, I'll read to find out whether affection training will help Helfer save the animals from the flood.**

SECOND-LANGUAGE SUPPORT Students may benefit from the Guided Reading activities and the additional guidance under the Student Anthology pages. (See *Second-Language Support Manual.*)

OPTIONS FOR READING

Independent Reading
Have students read the selection silently with their purpose for reading in mind.

Guided Reading
Follow the Guided Reading suggestions that appear on pages 302, 312, and 320. These suggestions model strategic reading.

Cooperative Reading
Suggestions for Cooperative Reading appear on pages 302 and 319.

Numbered Annotations
Use the numbered annotations beside the Student Anthology pages to heighten students' appreciation of the selection.

302

Guided Reading

SET PURPOSE/PREDICT: PAGES 302–312 Have students read to the end of the last complete paragraph on page 312 to find out how Helfer and his crew respond to the flood. As students read, suggest that they think about how the events fit in their sequence diagrams.

Cooperative Reading

Have group members read the selection silently and agree on which events to record on their sequence diagrams.

THE FLOOD

from
THE BEAUTY OF THE BEASTS
▼▼▼▼▼▼▼▼▼▼▼▼▼▼▼▼▼▼▼▼▼▼

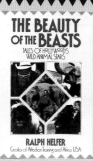

by Ralph Helfer

Ralph Helfer, one of the world's foremost animal trainers, is determined to stop the use of methods of animal training that use fear and violence to influence an animal's behavior. Using affection training, which is based on love, patience, understanding, and respect, Helfer has schooled animal performers for more than 5,000 movies and television programs. He has received recognition from the American Humane Society, and he and his animal friends have won many awards for the best animal performances on the screen.

◀ *In the history of the motion picture and TV industries, no child had ever worked in complete safety with an African lion until Pamela Franklin teamed up with Zamba for* The Lion. *Their affection for each other continued long after filming was finished.*

303

BACKGROUND INFORMATION
The events in this true story take place in California in the mid-1960s, on Ralph Helfer's ranch in Soledad Canyon, thirty miles north of Los Angeles. Ralph Helfer is an animal trainer. At the time of the narrative, he has recently completed outfitting his new ranch, called Africa U.S.A., to accommodate 1,500 wild animals and their trainers and keepers.

From whose point of view is the account being told? *(Ralph Helfer's)*
INFERENTIAL: DRAWING CONCLUSIONS

How do you know that Helfer is the narrator? *(He is the author of this nonfiction selection, and he is using I and my.)*
METACOGNITIVE: NOTING IMPORTANT DETAILS

2 AUTHOR'S PURPOSE
Why does Helfer tell his readers that he built a channel that should handle the worst possible flooding? *(Accept reasonable responses: to let readers know he cares about the safety of the animals and staff; to show his thoroughness; to indicate the immensity of the flood to come; to show that even the well prepared are vulnerable.)*
CRITICAL: MAKING JUDGMENTS

Amanda Blake and Mickey Rooney were cohosts of the PATSY ceremonies when I received an award from the American Humane Society for outstanding achievement in motion pictures.

It was raining that morning, as usual. For weeks it had been coming down—sometimes heavily, with thunder and lightning, and sometimes with just a mist of light rain. But it was always there, and by now the blankets, the beds, and the whole house were constantly damp.

My career was at a peak. I'd spent twelve years struggling to get to the top, and I had finally made it. My life was pretty good. I had just completed the back-to-back shooting of *Daktari* and *Gentle Ben*, and I was living at our new ranch, Africa U.S.A., with 1,500 wild animals and a crew of dedicated keepers and trainers.

The ranch was beautiful. Nestled at the bottom of Soledad Canyon, about thirty miles north of Los Angeles, the property snaked for a mile down the canyon beside the banks of the Santa Clarita stream. The highway wound above it on one side, the railroad track on the other.

We'd had heavy rains before, and even a few floods, but nothing we couldn't handle. There was a flood-control dam above us, fifteen miles up the canyon, and we weren't too worried about the stream's overflowing. But just to make sure, we had asked the city's flood-control office to advise us. They checked their records for the biggest flood in the office's hundred-year history, and calculated that to handle one that size we would need a channel 100 feet wide, 12 feet deep, and 1 mile long. It cost us $100,000 and three months of hard work, but we built it. It was worth it to feel safe.

Toni and I had grabbed a few hours' sleep before leaving the house, which was located off the ranch up on a hill, and heading out

304

Second-Language Support
Make sure students understand that in paragraph 2 *shooting* refers to making a movie, that *back-to-back* means "one right after the other," and that *Daktari* and *Gentle Ben* are movie titles. Also, since this selection contains many idioms, you may want to assign peer tutors to help students with idiomatic expressions as necessary.

into the rain again early this morning to make sure our animals were dry and safe.

On arriving at the compound, Toni went over to check on the "wild string," a group of lions, tigers, bears, and leopards that had been donated to us by people who never should have had them in the first place. Hopeless animal lovers that we were, we had taken them in, even though we knew that very few spoiled mature animals could ever be indoctrinated with affection training.

I checked at the office for messages, then headed for "Beverly Hills," our nickname for the area where our movie-star animals lived—Gentle Ben, Clarence the cross-eyed lion, Judy the chimp, Bullfrog the "talking" buffalo, Modoc the elephant, and many others. The rain had become a steady downpour by the time I arrived there. Everything seemed to be in order, so I went on to the rhinos. No problems there, either.

As I left the rhinos, I noticed that I could no longer jump over the stream that ran beside their barn. I was starting to get a little concerned. The sky was now opening up with a vengeance. I wrapped my poncho around me and continued my tour of inspection.

I was wondering how Toni was making out with the wild string when Miguel, a Mexican keeper who had been with us for six years, arrived to care for the animals in the Beverly Hills section. He smiled his broad, gold-capped grin, then disappeared around a bend of the stream.

Then my head trainer, Frank Lamping, arrived. He told me that the earthen dam above us was about to go. To prevent the dam from bursting, the flood-control people were opening the floodgates to release the pressure. We were to watch out for some heavy water coming downstream.

The crew had all been working continuously from morning until night since the rains had begun, to make sure that the ranch was safe. Now we had to redouble our efforts.

I told Frank to check the stock area. A trainer yelled from the roadway above that he had the nursery section under control.

I found some pretty badly undermined cages in my area and set to work with a shovel to fill the erosion. I was looking down at my shovel, working hard, when I heard a noise. It was a low roar, and

3 AUTHOR'S VIEWPOINT
Ralph Helfer says that the animals in the "wild string" came from "people who never should have had them in the first place." What is he expressing, a fact or an opinion? *(an opinion)*
CRITICAL: MAKING JUDGMENTS

How do you know this is an opinion? *(He says people* should not *have had the animals. The word* should *is a clue that he is expressing an opinion.)*
METACOGNITIVE: MAKING JUDGMENTS

4 NARRATION: ACTIONS/EVENTS
What do Helfer and the others expect to happen when they open the floodgates? *(They expect a lot of water to come down, but not as much as would come if the dam broke.)*
LITERAL: NOTING IMPORTANT DETAILS

Vocabulary Strategy Point out the word *undermined* (line 1 of the last paragraph), and have students break it into its component parts to determine its meaning. (*under-*, meaning "beneath," and *mine*, "to dig"; thus *undermined*, meaning "dug out beneath," "weakened") Ask students for other examples of words with the word part *under-*.
STRATEGY: STRUCTURAL ANALYSIS

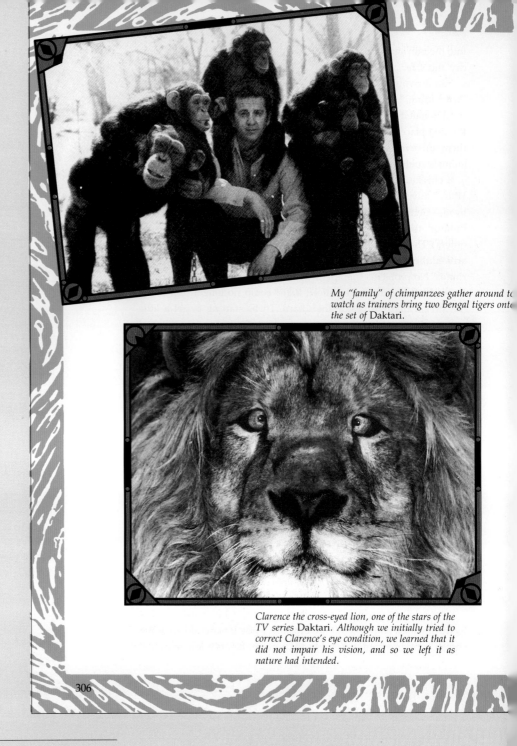

My "family" of chimpanzees gather around to watch as trainers bring two Bengal tigers onto the set of Daktari.

Clarence the cross-eyed lion, one of the stars of the TV series Daktari. Although we initially tried to correct Clarence's eye condition, we learned that it did not impair his vision, and so we left it as nature had intended.

306

Informal Assessment You can informally assess students' abilities to summarize by occasionally presenting the following scenario:

> Pretend that this narrative is something you are watching on television. There is a commercial break right now, and someone comes into the room and asks you what has happened so far. What can you explain while the commercial is still on?

By encouraging students to talk freely about their own thinking, you will get important diagnostic insights into how well they are reading.

it was quickly becoming louder and closer. I remember just looking over my shoulder, and suddenly there it was—a wall of water carrying with it full-sized oak trees, sheds, branches. Down it came, crashing and exploding against the compound, uprooting cages, overturning buildings, trucks—anything in its way.

Instantly, everything was in chaos. Sheer panic broke out among the animals in the Beverly Hills section. Lions were roaring and hitting against the sides of their cages; bears were lunging against the bars; chimps were screaming. The water was starting to rock the cages. Some were already floating and were about to be swept downstream.

I didn't know what to do first! I raced for the cages, but was thrown down by the weight of the water. Miguel came running over, yelling half in English and half in Spanish. I told him to grab a large coil of rope that was hanging in a tree nearby. I fastened it around me and, with Miguel holding the other end, I started out into the water. If I could just get to the cages, I could unlock them and set the animals free. At least then they could fend for themselves. It was their only chance. Otherwise, they would all drown in their cages.

The water was rushing past me furiously. I struggled through it to Gentle Ben's cage, fumbling for the key. "Don't *drop* it!" I mumbled to myself. The key turned, I threw open the door, and the great old bear landed right on top of me in his panic for freedom.

I grabbed Ben's heavy coat and hung on as his massive body carried me to a group of cages holding more than twenty animals. The water was now five or six feet deep. Cages were starting to come loose from their foundations; the animals were swimming inside them, fighting for breath. I let go of Ben and grabbed onto the steel bars of one of the cages. My heart sank as I saw Ben dog-paddling, trying to reach the embankment. He never did. I could just barely make out his form as he was carried through some rough white water and around a bend before he was lost from view.

One by one I released the animals—leopards, tigers, bears— talking as calmly as I could, even managing an occasional pat or kiss of farewell. I watched as they were carried away, swept along with the torrent of water. Some would come together for a moment and would then be whisked away, as though a giant hand had come up

5 AUTHOR'S CRAFT
Suspense builds when the reader feels concerned or worried about what will happen next and when the author withholds the final outcome. How does this author build suspense as he tells about trying to set the bear free? *(He uses words like* furiously, rushing, *and* struggled; *and he brings up the worst things that could happen—the animals' drowning in their cages, his dropping the key.)*
CRITICAL: SYNTHESIZING

6 AUTHOR'S VIEWPOINT
How does the author feel about what happens to Ben? *(He is terribly distressed.)*
INFERENTIAL: DRAWING CONCLUSIONS

How do you know how he feels? *(He is obviously very attached to the bear; he says his "heart sank" as he watched him being carried away.)*
METACOGNITIVE: NOTING IMPORTANT DETAILS

7 NARRATION: CONFLICT
What are the two factors that Helfer is now struggling against? *(the flood and time)*
INFERENTIAL: DETERMINING MAIN IDEA

8 AUTHOR'S CRAFT
Adventure writing contains action and suspense. Do you think Helfer's narrative qualifies as adventure writing? Why or why not? *(Accept reasonable responses: Yes; there is a lot of fast-paced action, with the animals being swept away and the water rushing. There is also a lot of suspense, because the author suggests that animals are drowning and the reader does not know which—if any—will survive.)*
INFERENTIAL: CLASSIFYING

9 NARRATION: ACTIONS/EVENTS
What causes the flood? *(The ground is too wet to absorb any of the water from the dam, and more rain keeps falling.)*
LITERAL: RECOGNIZING CAUSE-EFFECT

and shoved them. Some went under. I strained to see whether any of these came up again, but I couldn't tell.

My wonderful, beloved animals were all fighting for their lives. I felt sick and helpless.

To my right, about thirty feet out in the water and half submerged, was a large, heavy steel cage on wheels with a row of four compartments in it. I managed to get to it just as the force of the current started to move it. I began to open the compartments, one by one, but now the cage was moving faster downstream, carrying me with it. I looked back to the shore, at Miguel. He saw the problem, and with his end of the rope he threw a dally around a large tree branch. We were running out of time. If the rope came to the end of its slack before I could get it off me and onto the cage, we would lose the cage. It was picking up speed, and the animals inside were roaring and barking in terror.

I decided to hold the cage myself, with the rope tied around my waist. There were two beautiful wolves in the last cage, Sheba and Rona. Toni and I had raised them since they were pups. I was at their door, fumbling with the lock, when the rope went taut. I thought it would cut me in half. I grabbed the steel bars with both hands, leaving the key in the lock, praying it wouldn't drop out. When I reached down once more to open the lock, the key fell into the water! I was stunned, frozen. I knew I had just signed those animals' death warrants. The water behind the cage was building up a wall of force. I held on as tightly as I could, but finally the cage was ripped out of my hands.

I fell backward into the churning water; when I surfaced, I could see the cage out in the mainstream, racing with the trees, bushes, and sides of buildings, heading on down the raging river. I looked for the last time at Sheba and Rona. They were looking at us quietly as if they knew, but their eyes begged for help. My tears joined the flood as my beloved friends were washed away.

By this time it had become clear to me what had happened. The floodgates on the dam had been opened, all right, but because the ground was already saturated with the thirty inches of rain that had fallen in the last few weeks, it wouldn't absorb any more. At the same time, the new storm had hit, pouring down another fourteen inches in just twenty-four

Teaching Tip You may want to explain that *throw a dally* (line 7 of the second complete paragraph) is a ranching term that means to twist a rope around something solid, like a saddle horn or tree branch, to keep the rope from slipping out of one's grasp.

hours. Together, these conditions had caused the flood.

It was a larger flood than any that had been recorded in the area in the last hundred years, and it was made worse because the water had been held up occasionally on its fifteen-mile journey down the canyon by debris in its path. When suddenly released, the water that had built up behind the naturally formed logjams doubled in force. By the time it reached us, huge waves had been built up: the water and debris came crashing down on us like a wall, then subsided, only to come crashing down again. We were to struggle through two days and nights of unbelievable havoc and terror, trying desperately to salvage what we could of the ranch.

Gentle Ben relaxes his 600 pounds on my shoulder during a morning workout on the set of his popular TV series.

309

Vocabulary Strategy Help students with the pronunciation of *debris* [də·brē′] on line 15, if necessary. Have them use context to figure out its meaning. Suggest that they look back at page 307 for the description of what is in the water when the flood first hits. (trees, sheds, branches, things swept along by the flood) STRATEGY: CONTEXT CLUES

10 FIGURATIVE LANGUAGE

What comparisons does the author use to describe the flood? How do they help explain what it was like?
(He describes the river as moving "with the speed and force of an express train," picking up a large building "like a matchbox" and tumbling it over "like a toy." These images suggest the tremendous force and violence of the water and the helplessness of the people.)
INFERENTIAL: MAKING COMPARISONS

11 DESCRIPTION

Imagine the sights, sounds, and feelings of a horrible rainstorm. Then imagine a wildly rushing river and a zoo full of terrified animals. Describe how the animal compound must have looked and sounded as the flood continued.
(Accept reasonable responses: There must have been great confusion, with many people and animals swimming and wading, and a great deal of noise from the rushing water, shouts, and the cries of animals.)
CREATIVE: VISUALIZING

The storm grew worse. Heavy sheets of rain filled and overflowed our flood channel, undermining its sides until they caved in. By mid-morning the Santa Clarita had become a raging, murderous torrent, 150 feet wide and 15 feet deep, moving through Africa U.S.A. with the speed and force of an express train. In its fury it wiped out a two-lane highway, full-grown oak trees, generator buildings—everything. Our soundstage was in a full-sized building, 100 feet long by 50 feet wide, but the water just picked it up like a matchbox and carried it away downstream, end over end, rolling it like a toy and depositing it on a sand embankment a mile away. Electric wires flared brightly as the water hit them. We rushed for the main switch to the soundstage, shutting everything down for fear of someone being electrocuted. Everywhere, animals and people were in the water, swimming for safety.

We'd be half drowned, and then we'd make our way to the shore, cough and sputter, and go back into the water. You don't think at a time like that—you *do*. My people risked their lives over and over again for the animals.

The waves next hit the elephant pens, hard. We moved the elephants out as the building collapsed and was carried downstream. Then the waves caught the camels' cage, pulling it into the water. One huge camel was turning over and over as he was swept along. (I thought at the time that somewhere, someday, if that animal drowned, some archeologist would dig up its bones and say, "There must have been camels in Los Angeles!")

We worked frenziedly. Bears, lions, and tigers were jumping out of their cages and immediately being swept downstream. Others were hanging onto our legs and pulling us under, or we were hanging onto them and swimming for shore. I unlocked the cheetah's cage and he sprang out over my head, right into the water, and was gone. Animals were everywhere.

I remember grabbing hold of a mature tiger as he came out of his cage. He carried me on his back to temporary security on the opposite bank as smoothly as if we'd rehearsed it.

Another time I found myself being carried downstream with Zamba, Jr., who was caught in the same whirlpool that I was. I grabbed his mane, and together we swam for the safety of the shore. After resting a bit, I managed to get back to the main area,

310

Oral Rereading Invite students to read aloud either the four paragraphs on page 310 beginning with *The storm grew worse* (paragraph 1) or some other episode within the narrative that expresses action and suspense. Encourage students to work in pairs to master reading the passage fluently and with expression. After students have practiced, ask volunteers to read portions aloud.

Sultan, a cross-breed of Siberian and Bengal species, poses with me for a portrait. Although I generally disapprove of interbreeding tigers, some have come to me with various subspecies already bred into them. Sultan exhibited the best qualities of the two species: the larger size of the Siberian and the more pliant intelligence of the Bengal.

311

12 NARRATION: ACTIONS/EVENTS

How does the behavior of the animals support the author's belief in affection training? *(The animals show no fear of the people and let themselves be helped; they cooperate, and they even help each other.)*
INFERENTIAL: DRAWING CONCLUSIONS

13 AUTHOR'S CRAFT

Why does the author tell about grabbing the pipe and, later, about the rope tangled around Frank's foot? *(Accept reasonable responses: He wants to show that the rescuers are all risking their lives and, indeed, more than once come close to death.)*
CRITICAL: MAKING JUDGMENTS

---

leaving the lion in as good a spot as any. At least for the moment he was safe.

12 As the storm rode on, the river was full of animals and people swimming together; there was no "kill" instinct in operation, only that of survival. Men were grabbing fistfuls of fur, clinging for life. A monkey grabbed a lion's tail, which allowed him to make it to safety.

Clarence the cross-eyed lion was in a state of panic. The river had surrounded him and was now flooding his cage. His trainer, Bob, waded across the water, put a chain on Clarence, took him out of his cage, and attempted to jump across the raging stream with him. But the lion wouldn't jump. The water was rising rapidly. Bob threw part of the chain to me. To gain some leverage, I grabbed a pipe that was running alongside a building. As we both pulled, Clarence finally jumped, and just then the pipe I was holding onto came loose. It turned out to be a "hot" electric conduit, for when Clarence leaped and the pipe came loose, we all got a tremendous electric shock! Fortunately, the pipe also pulled the wires loose, so the shock only lasted for an instant. Had it continued, it would certainly have killed us, as we were standing knee-deep in water.

13 We noticed a group of monkeys trapped in a small outcropping of dirt and debris in the middle of the river. Frank almost died trying to save them: he tied a rope around his waist and started across, but about halfway over he slipped and went under. We didn't know whether to pull on the rope or not. We finally saw him in midstream, trying to stay afloat. Whenever we pulled on the rope, he would go under. (We found out later that the rope had become tangled around his foot, and every time we yanked it we were pulling him under!) But he made it, and he was able to swim the animals to safety.

We were racing against time. The river was still rising, piling up roots and buildings and pushing them along in front, forming a wall of destruction. The shouts of half-drowned men and the screams of drowning animals filled the air, along with thunder and lightning and the ever-increasing downpour of rain.

Throughout the turmoil and strife one thing was crystal clear to me, and that is that without affection training, all would have been lost. It was extraordinary. As dangerous and frightening as the

---

Guided Reading

MONITOR COMPREHENSION: PAGES 302–312
How do Ralph Helfer and his crew respond to the flood? (Their first thought is to save the animals. They risk their lives to free the animals.) STRATEGIC READING: RETURNING TO PURPOSE

What problems does the flood cause for Helfer and his crew? (The animals are in cages. If the flood reaches them, many animals will drown. The workers do not have time to release the animals from their cages before the flood hits.) STRATEGIC READING: SUMMARIZING

SET PURPOSE/PREDICT: PAGES 312–321 Ask students to predict whether Helfer will succeed in saving his animals and what the animals will do if they are freed. Remind students to continue noting the sequence of events as they read. Then invite them to read the rest of the narrative.

emergency was, these animals remained calm enough to let themselves be led to safety when it was possible for us to do so.

Imagine yourself in a raging storm, with buildings crashing alongside of you. You make your way to a cage that houses a lion or a tiger, and the animal immediately understands why you're there and is happy to see you. You open the door, put a leash on the animal, and you both jump out into the freezing, swirling water. Together, you're swept down the stream, hitting logs, rolling over and over, as you try to keep your arms around the animal. Together, you get up onto the safety of dry land. You dry off, give your animal a big hug, and then go back in for another one.

There was one big cage left in the back section containing a lion. This lion was a killer who had been fear trained rather than affection trained. We went out to him. The other lions were being saved because we could swim with them, but this fellow was too rough. I got to the cage and opened the door. A couple of my men threw ropes on the lion and pulled, **14** trying to get him out of his potential grave—but he wouldn't come out. He was petrified! We pulled and struggled and fought to get him out of the cage, but we couldn't do it, and we finally had to let him go.

Then the "wild string" panicked, and in their hysteria they attacked their rescuers as if they were enemies. In the end, we had to resort to tranquilizer guns. We fired darts into each fear-trained animal, and as they succumbed to the medication,

Many nights I would find this duckling curled up in one of C. J.'s massive hairy arms. The powerful orangutan would gently stroke the duckling's head with one of his large fingers—a rare and touching sight to behold.

313

14 AUTHOR'S VIEWPOINT
What contrast does the author make between affection-trained and fear-trained animals? *(The affection-trained animals trust the people who are trying to rescue them, so they work with their rescuers. The fear-trained lion dies because he does not cooperate with his rescuers.)*
INFERENTIAL: COMPARING AND CONTRASTING

Do you think the author's belief in affection training is fair and unbiased? How do you know? *(Accept reasonable responses: No; he gives only positive examples of affection training and only negative ones of what he calls fear training. The name* fear training *suggests that he is biased against that method.)*
METACOGNITIVE: MAKING JUDGMENTS

15 CHARACTER'S EMOTIONS
What feelings does Ralph Helfer experience when he notices that Bullfrog is gone? How do you know? *(Accept reasonable responses: Helfer seems discouraged and overwhelmed by a sense of loss and devastation. He fears that the buffalo has not survived; he wonders whether the nightmare will ever end.)*
METACOGNITIVE: DRAWING CONCLUSIONS

we held their bodies up above the water and carried them to safety. Tragically, there was not enough time to drag all of them to safety; several drowned in their drugged sleep before we could reach them.

The storm continued on into the night, and with the darkness came a nightmare of confusion. We worked on without sleep, sustained by coffee and desperation.

During that first night, it became clear that ancient Modoc, the elephant, the one-eyed wonder of the big top, had by no means outlived her capacity for calmness and courage in the face of disaster. Modoc took over, understanding fully what was at stake and what was required of her. Animal after animal was saved as she labored at the water's edge, hauling their cages to safety on higher ground. When the current tore a cage free and washed it downstream, Modoc got a firmer grip on the rope with her trunk and, with the power of several bulldozers, steadily dragged the cage back to safety. Then a trainer would attach the rope to another endangered pen, and Modoc would resume her labors.

We eventually became stranded with some of the animals on an island—this was all that was left of Africa U.S.A., plus the area alongside the railroad track. When the dam had burst upstream, the wall of water that hit the ranch divided into two fast-moving rivers. As time passed, the rivers widened and deepened until they were impossible to cross. As dusk fell on the second day, we realized that we were cut off from the mainland. Since it was the highest ground on the ranch, the island in the center had become the haven for all the survivors. The office building, the vehicles, and about twenty cages were all well above the flooded zone and so were safe for the time being. The giraffes, some monkeys, and one lion were all housed in makeshift cages on the island. We all hoped the water would not rise any further.

Behind the office building ran a railroad track. By following the tracks for three miles, it would be possible to reach the highway. The problem would then be in crossing the torrent of water to get to the road.

15 I noticed that Bullfrog, our thousand-pound Indian buffalo, was gone. Buffalos are known to be excellent swimmers. Surely *he* could survive! I asked around to see whether anyone had seen him. No one had. Bullfrog's cage had been at the entrance to the ranch,

314

Second-Language Support
Explain, or have a peer tutor explain, that the reference to *the big top* (circus tent) in line 2 of the second paragraph means that the elephant was once in a circus. Encourage students to describe what they know about circus elephants—for example, students might know that they are trained to work as well as perform.

MEETING INDIVIDUAL NEEDS

because he always greeted visitors with a most unusual bellow that sounded exactly like the word "Hi." Now he was gone, too. Would it ever end? I felt weak. The temperature had dropped, and the wind had come up. The windchill factor was now thirty degrees below zero.

There's something horrible about tragedy that occurs in the dark. I could hear the water running behind me, and every once in a while I'd hear a big timber go, or an animal cry, or a person shouting. It all seemed very unreal.

Throughout the night and all the next day the rain continued, and we worked on. Luckily, help came from everywhere. The highway, which we could no longer get to but which we could see, was lined with cars. Some people had successfully rigged up a bos'n chair 50 feet in the air and were sending hot food and drink over to us, a distance of some 200 yards. Other people were walking three miles over the hills to bring supplies. Radio communication was set up by a citizens-band club. Gardner McKay, the actor and a true friend, put his Mercedes on the track, deflated the tires, and slowly drove down to help us. One elderly woman prepared ham and coffee and brought it in at two o'clock in the morning, only to find on her return that her car had been broken into and robbed!

Then a train engine came down the track to help (just an engine—no cars). Three girls from the affection-training school volunteered to rescue the snakes. The girls climbed onto the cowcatcher on the front of the engine. We then wrapped about thirty feet of pythons and boa constrictors around their shoulders and told them where to take the snakes once they were on the other side. (There was, of course, no more electricity in the reptile and nursery area, and unless we could get the reptiles to some heat, they would surely die.) Goats, aoudads, and llamas all rode in the coal bin behind the engine. I'll never forget the look on one girl's face as the engine pulled out and a python crawled through her hair.

By four the next morning, some twenty people had, by one method or another, made it over to our island to help. Some chose a dangerous way, tying ropes around their middles and entering the water slowly, with those on the island holding the other ends of the ropes. Then, with the current carrying them quickly downstream, they would look for a logjam or boulder to stop them so they could

315

Teaching Tip You may want to explain that a *bos'n chair* (lines 4–5 of the second paragraph) is a sling on an arrangement of ropes and pulleys. It is usually used to move people or materials from one ship to another or from ship to shore. A *bos'n* (boatswain) is a ship's officer in charge of maintaining the hull (the frame or body of the ship).

You may also want to explain that *citizens band* (line 8 of the same paragraph), or CB, is a radio frequency reserved for private citizens to use.

Vocabulary Strategy Remind students that sometimes they do not need to know the precise meaning of a word. For example, near the end of the third paragraph, they will find the word *aoudads* [ä′o͞o·dadz]. The context will tell them that an aoudad is a type of animal, perhaps like a goat or a llama, but the precise type of animal is not important. (For the simply curious, an aoudad is a bearded sheep native to North Africa.) STRATEGY: CONTEXT CLUES

What do the clues the author gives suggest is happening to Bullfrog? How do these clues help build suspense? *(Accept reasonable responses: The clues suggest that Bullfrog is being swept away to his death. They build suspense because the reader does not know whether Bullfrog will live or die.)*
METACOGNITIVE: DRAWING CONCLUSIONS

What is the situation at the ranch when the rain finally stops? *(Most of the property is underwater. Buildings and cages have been destroyed. Most of the animals have disappeared or drowned.)*
INFERENTIAL: SUMMARIZING

make their way to where we were.

I was having some coffee in the watchmen's trailer when the scream of an animal shattered the night. I dashed out to find a small group of people huddled together, trying to shine their flashlights on the animal who was out there in the dark, desperately struggling in the raging water. It had succeeded in swimming out of the turbulence in the middle of the stream, but the sides of the river were too slippery for it to get a foothold and climb to safety. In the dark, I couldn't make out which animal it was. Then I heard it: "Hi! Hi!" It was a call of desperation from Bullfrog, the buffalo, as he fought for his life. There was nothing we could do to help him, and his "Hi's" trailed down the dark, black abyss, fading as he was carried away around the bend.

Then Toni screamed at me in the dark, "Ralph, over here!" I fought my way through a maze of debris and water and burst into a clearing. There was Toni, holding a flashlight on—lo and behold—a big steel cage from Beverly Hills! It had been washed downstream and was lodged in the trunk of a toppled tree. It was still upright, but its back was facing us, and we couldn't see inside. We waded out to the cage. Toni kept calling, "Sheba, Rona, are you there? Please answer!" Our hearts were beating fast, and Toni was crying.

Hoping against hope that the wolves were still alive, we rounded the corner, half swimming, half falling. Then we eased up to the front of the cage and looked straight into two sets of the most beautiful eyes I'd ever seen. Rona and Sheba had survived! They practically jumped out of their skins when they saw us, as though to say, "Is it really *you?*" Toni had her key, and we unlocked the door. Both wolves fell all over us, knocking us into the water. They couldn't seem to stop licking our faces and whimpering. At least *they* were safe!

The rain finally let up on the morning of the third day. The sun came out, and at last we had time to stop, look around, and assess the damage. It was devastating, and heartrending.

Most of the animals had been let out of their cages and had totally disappeared, including Judy, Clarence, Pajama Tops, the zebra, and Raunchy, our star jaguar. We knew a few others had definitely drowned. Both rhinos were missing, and so were the hippos. Our beloved Gentle Ben had been washed away, along with hundreds of other animals.

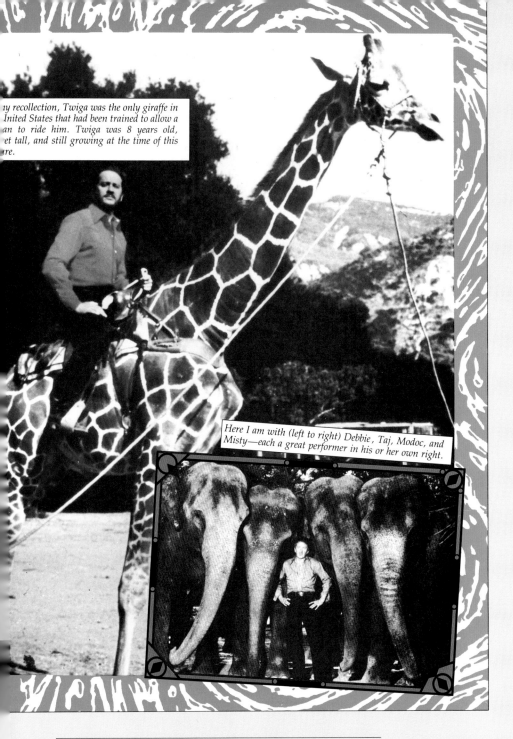

...y recollection, Twiga was the only giraffe in ...United States that had been trained to allow a ...an to ride him. Twiga was 8 years old, ...et tall, and still growing at the time of this ...re.

Here I am with (left to right) Debbie, Taj, Modoc, and Misty—each a great performer in his or her own right.

Teaching Tip Remind students that pictures and captions can help them understand and appreciate a selection. **How do the photos and captions tell you more about the author and his work with animals?** (Accept reasonable responses: They inform the reader of the author's success in working with all kinds of animals.) **What kind of feeling do the photos and captions give the selection?** (Accept reasonable responses: an informal, homey feeling as from a family photo album.)

18 NARRATION: CHARACTERIZATION
What kind of person is Toni? How do you know? *(Accept reasonable responses: She seems very caring, supportive, and unselfish. She takes an active role in saving the animals and thinks of her husband's needs. The baby animals seem to love her, so she must be kind to them. Her husband exclaims, ''What a woman!'')*
METACOGNITIVE: DRAWING CONCLUSIONS

18 I was sitting there looking at the wreckage when somebody put a cup of hot chocolate in my hand. It was Toni. She stood before me, as exhausted as I was, clothes torn and wet, hair astray, cold and shivering. What a woman! Earlier, she had managed to make her way to the Africa U.S.A. nursery, where all of the baby animals were quartered. Without exception, the babies had all followed her to safety. Not one baby animal had been lost.

The hot liquid felt good going down. I stood up and hugged and kissed Toni, and arm in arm we walked. The sun was just topping the cottonwoods. The river had subsided. All was quiet, except for an occasional animal noise: a yelp, a growl, a snort. All of the animals were happy to see the sun, to feel its warmth.

Toni and I felt only the heavy, leaden feeling of loss. Ten years were, literally, down the drain. We had just signed a contract with Universal Studios to open our beautiful ranch to their tours: this would now be impossible. A million dollars was gone, maybe more. But what was far worse was the loss of some of our beloved animals.

We hiked to a ridge above the railroad track. Something caught my eye, and as we came near an outcrop of trees where we could have a better view, we looked over. There, on top of a nearby hill, we saw an incredible sight. Lying under the tree was Zamba, and at his feet, resting, were a multitude of animals. Deer, bears,

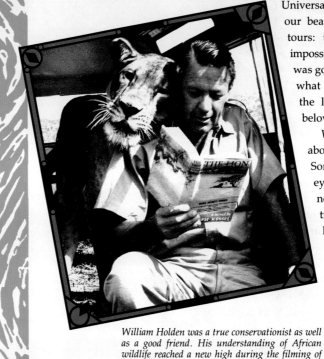

William Holden was a true conservationist as well as a good friend. His understanding of African wildlife reached a new high during the filming of The Lion. *Here he takes a break while Tammy asks for attention.*

318

tigers, llamas, all lying together peacefully. The animals must have fought their way clear of the treacherous waters and, together, climbed the hill, slept, and then dried off in the morning sun. They hadn't run away. In fact, they seemed to be waiting for our next move. It was as though God had caused the flood to make me realize how powerful affection training is, how deep it had gone. The lamb could truly lie down with the lion, without fear, and could do it by choice!

We called Zam over to us and smothered him with hugs and kisses. As we climbed down to the ranch, the other animals joined us. Camels, giraffes, eland—all came along as we wound our way down.

So many people were there at the ranch! We were once again connected with the rest of the world. Exhausted, wet, wonderful people—true animal lovers. They had come from everywhere. Some were employees, some friends, some strangers. All greeted us as we came down the hill. Their faces expressed hope and love. They cared . . . and it showed.

We took the animals one by one and fed, cleaned, and housed them as best we could.

"Ralph, come quickly!" screamed a voice. "He made it, he made it! *He's alive!*"

"Who, who?" I screamed, and was met by a resounding "Hi, Hi!" From around the corner came Bullfrog—disheveled and muddy, but alive!

"Hi, hi!"

Yes, *hi*, you big, lovable . . . hi! hi!

We began searching for the animals that were still lost. The ranch was a network of people and animals working together on the massive cleanup effort. Animals were straining to pull big trucks out of the water and muck. Bakery trucks were coming by with stale bread for the elephants. Farmers loaned us their skip loaders to round up the hippos and rhinos. (One hippo fell in love with the skip-loader bucket and coyly followed it home!) Charley and Madeline Franks, two loyal helpers, kept hot chili coming and must have dished out hundreds of meals. People from the Humane Society, Fish and Game, Animal Regulation, and the SPCA[1] all helped to comfort and tend the animals.

---

[1] SPCA: Society for the Prevention of Cruelty to Animals

319

21 NARRATION: ACTIONS/EVENTS
What is unusual about the behavior of the animals after the flood? *(They cause no trouble. They do not become wild but remain tame and friendly.)*
INFERENTIAL: DRAWING CONCLUSIONS

22 AUTHOR'S PURPOSE
Why does the author mention that five of the animals that drowned had not been affection trained? *(Accept reasonable responses: He uses this statistic to support his viewpoint that affection training is a better method than fear training.)*
INFERENTIAL: DETERMINING CAUSE-EFFECT

Everyone was busy constructing makeshift cages. The medical-lab trailer was pulled out of the mud. The nursery building and all of its kitchen storage area had been completely submerged, and some of it had been washed away. However, what could be salvaged was taken up to the island for immediate use.

21 Outside the ranch, the animals began turning up everywhere. Elephants showed up in people's backyards. Eagles sat in the limbs of trees. Llamas and guanacos cruised the local restaurants and were seen in parking lots. There was no difficulty between animals and people.

We had had dozens of alligators, some weighing two hundred to three hundred pounds. The whole pen had been hit by the water; we lost most of them because the water was ice-cold, and it battered and beat them. For seven months afterward we'd read in the paper that the bodies of alligators were being found everywhere, up to forty-five miles away. There were helicopter and airplane photos of alligators that had been killed, their bodies lying in the sand as the water subsided.

22 Of 1,500 other animals, only 9 had drowned. Five of these were animals that had not been affection trained.

Only one animal remained lost and unaccounted for, and that was old Gentle Ben. I had last seen him being swept sideways down the river. We didn't have much hope for him.

I was starting to feel the full shock of everything that had happened. True, by some miracle most of the animals were safe, but other losses had been enormous. As the emergency lessened and mopping-up operations took over, I felt worse and worse. The shakes set in, and then I developed a high fever. The doctors said it was a walking pneumonia, and that rest, good food, and warmth were in order. But there were still too many things to do—now was not the time to stop. I did, however, need to find a place to sit down and relax for a while.

As I sat on a log, my body trembled with shock as well as illness. In looking over the debris, it seemed to me that everything I had worked for was gone. The emotional pain, the sheer physical exhaustion, and the pneumonia had overloaded me. I just couldn't handle any more. I had no more tears, no pain of any kind. I was numb. I sat in the middle of the chaos with an old blanket wrapped

320

Guided Reading

MONITOR COMPREHENSION: PAGES 312–321
How does Helfer succeed in saving his animals— and what do the animals do once they are free?
(He and his helpers are able to let them out of their cages and help them swim to safety. The animals wait peacefully together until he rounds them up, or they come home by themselves. STRATEGIC READING: RETURNING TO PURPOSE

What theory, or belief, does Helfer use the flood and the behavior of the animals to illustrate?
(affection training) CRITICAL: MAKING JUDGMENTS

What kinds of emotions does the author experience? Give examples that explain the cause of each emotion. (Accept reasonable responses: He feels frustration as he watches many animals drift out of sight. He feels cared for when many community members come out to help him and his animals. He feels joy when some of the animals he thought drowned are brought back to him. He feels pride when he realizes his affection-trained animals have shown a higher survival rate.) STRATEGIC READING: SUMMARIZING

around me, unmoving, unable to give any more orders.

I had closed my eyes and was drifting off to sleep when something warm and wet on my face woke me up. I opened my eyes and saw Ben. *Gentle Ben had come home!!* I hugged him and cried **23** like a big kid. I turned to get up to tell everyone, but I didn't have to. They were all there. Toni, joined by the rest, had brought him to me. He'd been found two miles down the canyon, mud-covered and a few pounds lighter, but safe! Tears were in everybody's eyes—and if you looked closely, it seemed that even old Ben had a few.

A beautiful rainbow arched its brilliant colors across the ravaged countryside, then was gone.

*****

There was a time in my life when I felt I had reached the end of the rainbow. I had touched it, had dug my hand deep into its treasures of happiness and prosperity.

Suddenly, everything had changed. All that I had created was gone. I hadn't realized how vulnerable the world is, how delicate the balance of forces that sustain our existence.

I stood up and dusted off my jeans. In the distance I could see the sky clearing, and I knew that some day there would be another rainbow, its treasure awaiting. Until then, we had a job to do. We would need to start all over again.

THINK IT OVER

1. Ralph Helfer said, "without affection training, all would have been lost." Explain how affection training made a difference during the disaster.
2. In what ways were volunteers from the surrounding area helpful to the animals and the workers at Africa U.S.A.?
3. How was Modoc especially helpful in rescuing the animals?
4. Ralph Helfer said he "hadn't realized how vulnerable the world is, how delicate the balance of forces that sustain our existence." Explain how this remark is true of many disasters like the one in this selection.

24

WRITE

Write several paragraphs in which you explain the advantages affection training has over fear training.

25

321

---

23 NARRATION: RESOLUTION
How does Gentle Ben's return make the story of the flood complete? *(Accept reasonable responses: The bear's return answers one unanswered question and ends the narrative on a happy note.)*
CRITICAL: MAKING JUDGMENTS

---

24 THINK IT OVER
1. *Affection training made it possible for the people to save the animals, because the animals loved and trusted them.*
INFERENTIAL: DETERMINING CAUSE-EFFECT
2. *They brought food, helped set up makeshift cages, and helped round up the animals.*
LITERAL: NOTING IMPORTANT DETAILS
3. *She helped pull caged animals out of the water.*
LITERAL: NOTING IMPORTANT DETAILS
4. *Accept reasonable responses: A natural or human-caused disaster can wipe out a life—or a lifetime of work—in a few minutes.*
CRITICAL: MAKING JUDGMENTS

---

25 WRITE
You may want to help students get started with a prewriting graphic such as the following:

Affection Training vs. Fear Training

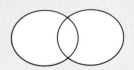

Accept reasonable responses: Affection training seems to produce better and more permanent results, with happier animals. Students should support their assertions with evidence from the selection.
CRITICAL: CLASSIFYING/SUMMARIZING

NOTE **Additional writing activities appear on page 321D.**

Returning to the Predictions Invite students to recall the predictions that they made before reading and that they may have written in their personal journals. Encourage students to talk about how their predictions changed as they read and why.

Returning to the Purpose for Reading Have students tell whether affection training helped Helfer save his animals. (Accept reasonable responses: Yes; affection training, many people working together, strength and courage, and being somewhat prepared all helped.)

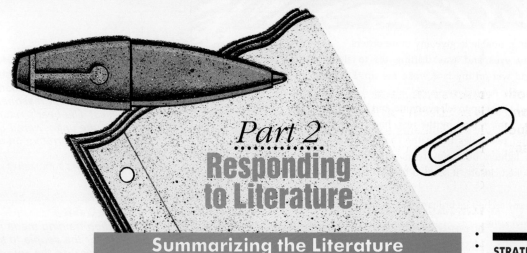

Part 2
Responding to Literature

Summarizing the Literature

Have students retell the selection and write a summary.

Invite students to summarize the story, using the sequence diagram. If they have not yet completed the diagram, have them do so now. (See *Practice Book* page 93, on 321B.) Students may use their completed diagrams to retell the selection and write a brief summary statement.

SEQUENCE DIAGRAM

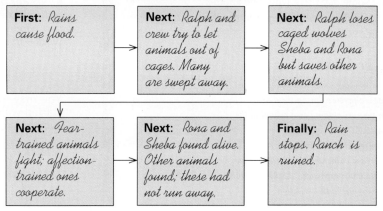

First: Rains cause flood.	**Next:** Ralph and crew try to let animals out of cages. Many are swept away.	**Next:** Ralph loses caged wolves Sheba and Rona but saves other animals.
Next: Fear-trained animals fight; affection-trained ones cooperate.	**Next:** Rona and Sheba found alive. Other animals found; these had not run away.	**Finally:** Rain stops. Ranch is ruined.

Appreciating Literature

Have students share personal responses.

Divide students into groups to discuss the excerpt. Provide questions such as the following to help them get started:

• **What kind of person is the author? Do you agree with his ideas? What makes you feel this way?**

You may want to circulate among the groups, encouraging participation in the discussions.

PERSONAL JOURNAL Have students use their personal journals to write about ideas and feelings that are expressed in the groups.

STRATEGY CONFERENCE

Discuss the sequence diagram, asking students whether it helped them understand, remember, and appreciate the narrative. Invite students to share other strategies they may have used—such as summarizing—to understand and enjoy the narrative.

INFORMAL ASSESSMENT

Having students order the details of a selection in this way will help you informally assess how well they understood **key relationships**. Ask yourself: Did students grasp **time relationships**? Did students recognize the **causes** of **effects** and the effects of causes? Can students tell which details are more important than others?

Critical Thinking Activities

Encourage both cooperative and individual responses.

DISCUSS AN ISSUE Do you think that affection training is as effective as Ralph Helfer claims? Why or why not? Invite students to form discussion groups to talk about this issue, using evidence from the selection and using their own experience in training pets to support their viewpoints. CRITICAL: MAKING JUDGMENTS

WRITE A JOURNAL ENTRY How might this story have been different if the animals had been fear trained? Have students write journal entries that describe imaginary similar disasters in which animals' training affects their own fates or the fate of one or more human beings. CREATIVE: SPECULATING

EXPRESS PERSONAL OPINIONS Some animal lovers feel that wild animals should never be taken out of their natural habitats and taught to perform just for human entertainment. Do you agree? What do you think Ralph Helfer would say to these people? Have students work individually to express a point of view. Remind them to support their opinions with evidence. CRITICAL: MAKING JUDGMENTS

Writer's Journal

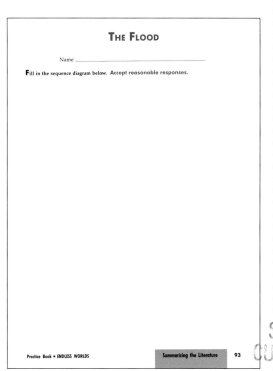

Practice Book

WRITER'S JOURNAL
page 59: Writing a creative response

PRACTICE BOOK
page 93: Summarizing the selection

VO·CAB·U·LAR·Y Workshop

Reviewing Key Words

To review how the new vocabulary is used in this selection, display the Key Words. Read and discuss the analogies below, and ask students to supply a Key Word to complete each one.

1. *calm : stillness :: churning :* (turbulence)
2. *happy : sad :: heartwarming :* (heartrending)
3. *damp : moist :: soaked :* (saturated)
4. *keep : lose :: resisted :* (succumbed)
5. *stores : mall :: buildings :* (compound)
6. *danger : peril :: shelter :* (haven)
7. *dozed : slept :: instructed :* (indoctrinated)
8. *gain : loss :: buildup :* (erosion)

Extending Vocabulary

EMOTIONAL LANGUAGE Ask students how the word *heartrending* makes them feel. Explain that *heartrending* has an emotional impact because it describes something painful. If an author uses a number of words that describe strong feelings, readers will react emotionally to the language. Ralph Helfer uses a great many "emotional" words in his narrative. For example, *affection* and *fear* are both emotionally charged words.

COOPERATIVE LEARNING Ask students to work in pairs to skim the selection for emotional words the author uses about his animals (*wonderful, beloved, beautiful*); the flood (*raging, murderous, torrent, fury, havoc, terror*); and the fear-trained animals (*killer, petrified, panicked, hysteria, tragically*). Invite students to identify feelings that these words arouse and to discuss how Helfer uses them to reach readers' emotions.

PRACTICE BOOK

page 94: Understanding and interpreting emotional language

Beloved

RAGING

HYSTERIA

· · · THE FLOOD · · ·

Name _____

A. Writers often use emotional words to sway readers to their point of view. Read each sentence. Then rewrite each one to remove the emotionally charged language. **Responses will vary.**

1. The golden lion tamarins at the zoo are adorable because their darling faces are surrounded by a sunburst of red fur. The faces of the golden lion tamarins are surrounded by a red ruff.

2. My friend and I can hardly stop giggling when we look at the funny red crested macaques. My friend and I find the red crested macaques amusing.

3. The gorillas are nothing short of majestic. The gorillas are large.

4. They seem such ancient presences, as they take stock of us, scrutinizing our every move. As they look at us, I am reminded of how long they've been on the earth.

B. Rewrite each sentence. Use emotional language to express your point of view. **Accept reasonable responses.**

1. Sometimes I watch the snakes curl around the limbs of a tree. _____

2. My friend and I watch the lions pacing in their dens. _____

3. My younger brother always wants to feed the animals in the petting zoo. _____

94 Slanted Language   Practice Book ■ ENDLESS WORLDS

Practice Book

Teacher Choices

Language Arts

WRITING

Writing About the Literature

AVAILABLE ON PROJECT CARD

CREATIVE: ADVENTURE NARRATIVE Ask students to imagine that they are scriptwriters for a television program called "Suspense." As a prewriting activity, suggest that they use a diagram like the one below. Groups of students should then develop a plot outline. LISTENING/SPEAKING/WRITING

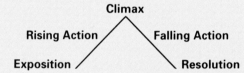

Climax

Rising Action   Falling Action

Exposition   Resolution

CRITICAL: PERSUASIVE ESSAY Point out that Helfer used the story of the flood to persuade readers that affection training was superior to other methods. Have students think of something *they* feel should be done differently and write an essay in which they use an anecdote or example to support an opinion. WRITING

NOTE: An additional writing activity appears on page 321.

SPEAKING/LISTENING

Speaking to Entertain

Have students prepare short narrative speeches about an animal they have experience with or have read about. Have them make an outline with a beginning, middle, and ending. Before they deliver their speeches, have them practice with a partner. LISTENING/SPEAKING/WRITING

SPELLING

Spelling Review

SPELLING WORDS: *abyss, debris, earthen, endanger, erosion, generator, instinct, saturate, survival, turbulence*

Display the words. Have students read each word aloud in unison, listening to the sounds of each syllable. Then have students copy the words on a sheet of paper and arrange them in webs around general science topics. For example, the words *earthen, debris,* and *erosion* might be placed around the topic *Soil.* Display students' work. LISTENING/READING/WRITING/SPELLING

INTEGRATED SPELLING

page 46: Writing science words

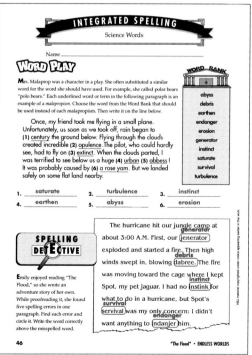

Integrated Spelling

**COMPREHENSION
INTRODUCE**

Author's Purpose and Viewpoint

OBJECTIVE: *To infer meaning by identifying the author's purpose and viewpoint in a selection*

1 Focus

Explain the value of recognizing an author's purpose and viewpoint.

Explain that Ralph Helfer in "The Flood" may have had more than one purpose for writing. He may have wanted to persuade, as well as entertain and inform. Ask students why it is useful to know when someone is trying to influence them. (Accept reasonable responses: so that they can evaluate the information and make their own decisions.)

2 Teach/Model

Model the thinking.

Explain that authors often weave persuasion into their writing if they have a strong viewpoint or opinion. For example, they may choose to use only examples that support their opinion. Model how to detect the author's viewpoint:

> **I see that "The Flood" has action and suspense and tells a story. Therefore, I feel that one of the author's purposes is to entertain. I also notice that the author says only good things about affection training, while he says only bad things about fear training. I think he is trying to influence me to believe in affection training as he does.**

Have students look for clues to the author's viewpoint.

Ask students to reread the second complete paragraph on page 313 and determine the author's viewpoint. (He tells how a fear-trained animal resisted people and died. The author is definitely against fear training.)

3 | **Practice/Apply**

Have students identify opinions.

Have students identify in the narrative other places in which the author reveals an opinion.

4 | **Summarize**

Informally assess the learning.

Ask volunteers to give examples from the narrative that imply a particular viewpoint. Check understanding by having students summarize what they learned. (An author may have more than one purpose for writing. He or she may have a strong viewpoint. Readers can look for clues as to whether the selection is slanted.)

READER ↔ WRITER CONNECTION

Author's Purpose and Viewpoint

▶ **Writers** always begin with a purpose. Their viewpoint may be objective, or it may be biased if their purpose is to persuade.

▶ **Readers** identify an author's purpose and viewpoint to decide if the author's ideas are biased or unbiased, so they can more clearly judge the writing.

WRITE AN ESSAY Have students imagine that they work for a zoo. They want to organize the animals into groups by habitat rather than by type. Have them write an essay to persuade, entertain, or inform others with their idea.

RETEACH Follow the visual, auditory, and kinesthetic/motor models on page R47.

CHALLENGE Have a small group of students analyze newspaper editorials and letters to the editor for bias, fairness, and emotional language.

SECOND-LANGUAGE SUPPORT Have students work with a peer tutor to classify words in the selection as positive, negative, or neutral. (See *Second-Language Support Manual*.)

WRITER'S JOURNAL page 60: Writing an essay

PRACTICE BOOK page 95: Determining an author's purpose and viewpoint

---

WHAT IS YOUR PURPOSE?

A zoo is changing its method of organizing animals into groups. Instead of grouping them by type (for example, all primates together, all hoofed animals together), the zoo keepers will group them by habitat. Rattlesnakes, raccoons, mice, coyotes, bobcats, and rabbits will be in one compound, animals from the African plains will inhabit another compound, and so on.

Use this as a topic for an essay. Before you begin writing, decide what your purpose will be: to persuade, to entertain, or to inform.

_____

by _____ (your name)

60 "The Flood"   HBJ Writer's Journal   ENDLESS WORLDS   Author's Purpose and Viewpoint

Writer's Journal

• • • THE FLOOD • • •

Name _____

Read the passage. Then answer the questions.

The Monterey Bay Aquarium in California is quite amazing. If nothing else, it is a truly phenomenal feat of engineering! Imagine the water pressure on the glass walls of those enormous tanks. It is great fun to be able to watch the darling sea otters playing at close range.

Nevertheless, if I had but one day to spend in Monterey, I would spend it strolling the peaceful trails of Point Lobos. Point Lobos is a protected reserve where animals frolic happily in their own habitat. There, you can hike through tranquil forests or amble along breathtaking shore trails. You may encounter sea otters; you may not. Part of the joy of Point Lobos is the unexpected. One day you may see a baby sea otter snuggled on its mother's furry chest; at another time you may gaze in astonishment as migrating gray whales spout and dive offshore.

1. What emotionally charged words do you recognize in the passage?
   Accept reasonable responses. Students may include *amazing, phenomenal, feat, enormous, fun, darling, strolling, peaceful, frolic, tranquil, amble, breathtaking, joy, snuggled, furry, gaze, astonishment.*

2. The author mentioned several interesting sights along Point Lobos. Write two examples that support the author's viewpoint. **The author mentions a baby sea otter and migrating whales.**

3. Which sentence states an opinion as fact? **The best answer is** *Point Lobos is a protected reserve where animals frolic happily in their own habitat.*

4. Why do you think the author chose the phrase *baby sea otter* instead of *juvenile sea otter?* **Accept reasonable responses. It carries more emotional charge.**

5. What is the author's main purpose in writing this passage? Support your answer. **to persuade the reader to visit Point Lobos**

SUMMARIZING the LEARNING Writers always write with a **purpose** in mind. Readers should be aware that the writer's **viewpoint** may be either objective or biased.

Practice Book ■ ENDLESS WORLDS   Author's Purpose-Viewpoint   95

Practice Book

Making Generalizations

OBJECTIVE: *To recognize and to make valid generalizations*

1	Focus

Demonstrate the usefulness of generalizing.

Ask students to suggest an easier and shorter way to say "I like cats, dogs, horses, snakes, alligators, birds, and so on." ("I like animals.") Then ask them to suggest a shorter way to say "I like cats, dogs, and horses, but I don't like snakes and alligators." ("I like most [or some] animals.") Tell students that the shorter statements are called generalizations, because they use several specific details to make a broad, or general, statement.

2	Teach/Model

Model the thinking.

Explain that a generalization is a judgment or conclusion drawn from information that may include many details. Point out that a generalization that is too broad may not be useful. Explain that a good, or valid, generalization, which may contain such words as *some, many,* or *often,* can have many applications.

Explain that people make generalizations by identifying a main idea and details, drawing a conclusion about them, and seeing how this might apply in a different context. Model making and limiting a generalization:

> **Helfer tells about all the people who risked their lives to help the animals. I generalize by saying, "A disaster brings out the best in people." Then I remember that the car of one of the helpers was broken into, so I realize my generalization is not valid. I modify it: "A disaster brings out the best in most people."**

Have students discuss generalizations.

Copy this diagram on the board. Have a volunteer explain it. Then have students use the diagram to make a generalization. Remind them that their generalization should not be too broad.

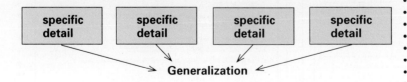

3	Practice/Apply

Have students apply the learning.

COOPERATIVE LEARNING   Have students work in groups to make generalizations about information in "The Flood."

4	Summarize

Informally assess the learning.

Ask volunteers to state a generalization they made from Helfer's account and to diagram support for it on the board. Tell them to add one piece of support from their own experience. Check understanding by having students summarize what they learned. (Generalizations are broad conclusions, drawn from facts, that can be applied to situations beyond a particular set of circumstances. Limiting words can make generalizations valid.)

READER ⬌ WRITER CONNECTION

Making Generalizations

▶ **Writers** often generalize to help their readers see how details are related to broader ideas.
▶ **Readers** make generalizations to extend ideas and apply information beyond the selection.

WRITE A DESCRIPTION   Have students imagine they are writing a description of a favorite place—their hometown, their neighborhood, a national park—for a travel book. Have them include both details and generalizations for travelers.

RETEACH   Follow the visual, auditory, and kinesthetic/motor models on page R48.

CHALLENGE   Have a small group of students identify overly broad generalizations in letters to the editor, advertisements, and editorials. Tell them to suggest ways to make these generalizations valid.

SECOND-LANGUAGE SUPPORT   Students can demonstrate their understanding by describing orally the information they would include in the generalization diagram. (See Second-Language Support Manual.)

WRITER'S JOURNAL
page 61:   Writing a description

PRACTICE BOOK
page 96:   Making generalizations

Writer's Journal

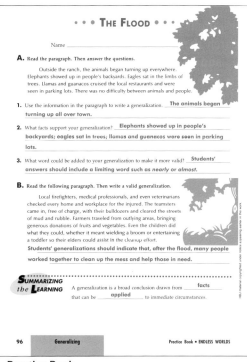

Practice Book

Integrated Curriculum

MATH

Figuring on the Flood

COOPERATIVE LEARNING Remind students that the flood-control office had advised Ralph Helfer to build a channel 12 feet deep, 100 feet wide, and 1 mile long, at a cost of $100,000. The actual flood waters were 15 feet deep and 150 feet wide. Ask students to calculate how much deeper and wider a new channel of the same length should have been to contain the flood. (3 feet deeper, 50 feet wider) Challenge students to work in small groups to write word problems using these figures, for example: How many cubic feet of water would the original channel hold? How many cubic feet would the new channel have to hold? How much did the old channel cost per cubic foot? How much would the new channel cost? LISTENING/SPEAKING/WRITING

SCIENCE

From Alligator to Zebra

Have students each choose an animal from those on Ralph Helfer's ranch and research the animal's natural habitat, its appearance, and its behavior. Tell students to prepare oral reports on their animals to present to their classmates. LISTENING/SPEAKING/READING/WRITING

SOCIAL STUDIES/HEALTH

Stormy Weather

Remind students that "The Flood" is about a natural disaster. Ask students to find out more about natural disasters in the United States, such as hurricanes, tornadoes, blizzards, earthquakes, volcanic eruptions, and floods. Have students choose one kind of natural disaster and write a brief composition describing causes and effects of such a disaster and steps that people can take to minimize damage in the event of one of these natural disasters. READING/WRITING

SCIENCE

News from Zoos

AVAILABLE ON PROJECT CARD

COOPERATIVE LEARNING Point out that zoos used to be places where animals were kept in cages. People are now aware that animals in captivity have special needs, and zoos are changing in response. Ask a group of students to research how modern zoos work. Suggest that the group prepare a list of questions about modern zoos. Each group member can find out the answer to one question. Then the group members can combine their findings into an oral report to present to their classmates. LISTENING/SPEAKING/ READING/WRITING

Saving the Animals

READ ALOUD TO STUDENTS:

PEOPLE AROUND THE WORLD ARE WORKING TO PROTECT ANIMALS.

In 1989, President Daniel arap Moi of Kenya set fire to a 20-foot-high mound of elephant tusks worth $3 million. He burned the tusks from 2,500 elephants as part of a campaign to stop the world trade in ivory. Kenya was willing to give up the ivory in order to gain support and protection for the elephants.

The California condor, an ancient bird species that lived almost a million years ago, in the time of mammoths and mastodons, is almost extinct. Condors have been killed by hunters and have died from eating lead bullets in animal carcasses. In 1987 the California Condor Recovery Team, led by Lloyd Kiff, rounded up the last living birds and have been breeding them in zoos. Following a process Colombian scientists used with the Andean condor, the Recovery Team is beginning to return condor chicks to the wild. The scientists hope to establish new wild condor populations in California wildlife preserves.

Sometimes the demands of new industries and old ways of life are difficult to reconcile. The oil industry is damaging the traditional way of life of Indians and Inuit, or Eskimos, in western Canada and Alaska. Indians and Eskimos have long depended on whales and caribou for their survival. Now the

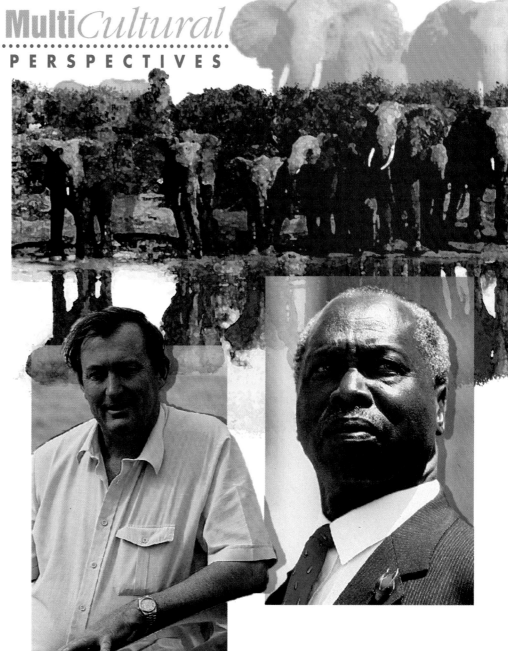

President Moi (right) and Dr. Leakey, Kenya's Director of Wildlife Conservation, work to keep Kenyan elephants alive.

oil wells and pipelines have scared away the animals. Whales stay farther offshore, and caribou have changed their travel routes, making hunting difficult. Although the native people benefit from the oil industry through cash subsidies, some question whether the money is worth the loss of the old way of life. ■

ACTIVITY CORNER

■ Ask students to identify cultures that have special relationships with animals, such as the Plains Indians had with the buffalo. Have them write brief, illustrated feature articles on the people and animals.

■ Have students use clippings from magazines, newspapers, and mail solicitations to make a "Worldwatch" bulletin board of efforts people are making to save endangered animals around the world.

AT HOME WITH THE TITAN OF THE TRAIL

by Paul Dean

PAUL DEAN (1941–) was born in Pittsburgh, Pennsylvania, and attended school at the State University of Pennsylvania, where he studied engineering. His interests in science and language led him to forge a career as an editor of motorcycle magazines, first *Cycle Guide* and then *Cycle* and *Cycle World*. He has served as a trustee for the American Motorcycle Association and has arranged competitions for them. His fascination with racing inspired this newspaper feature article on Susan Butcher, champion dog sled racer.

OTHER BOOKS ABOUT DETERMINATION

Bicycle Rider by Mary Scioscia. HarperCollins, 1983. EASY

Black Star, Bright Dawn by Scott O'Dell. Houghton Mifflin, 1988. AVERAGE

Jackie Robinson by Richard Scott. Chelsea House, 1989. CHALLENGING

Zan Hagen's Marathon by R.R. Knudson. Farrar, Straus and Giroux, 1984. AVERAGE

- **SELECTION SUMMARY**
- This article describes
- the life of a singular
- woman. Susan
- Butcher raises
- huskies in Eureka,
- Alaska. Butcher loves
- the ruggedness, the
- solitude, and the
- huskies. The dogs are
- bred for sled racing,
- and one race in
- particular: the
- Iditarod. She has
- won the Iditarod four
- times, and her
- champion dog,
- Granite, has won it
- three times. Susan
- Butcher lives an
- unusual life, with the
- risks and the cold,
- but her courage and
- fierce commitment
- have made her one
- of the best dog sled
- racers in the world.

LESSON PLANNER			
	Materials	**Integrated Curriculum**	**Meeting Individual Needs**

1 READING LITERATURE pp. 321L–330	Student Anthology pp. 322–330
	 Transparency 18
	 Second-Language Support Manual
	 Practice Book p. 97
	 Integrated Spelling p. 47
	 Integrated Spelling T.E. pp. 66–67
	 Response Card 5: Author's Viewpoint
		Spelling
		   Spelling Pretest
		   Spelling-Vocabulary Connection
		   (prefixes *in-, re-, un-*)
			Second-Language Support
			   Vocabulary 321M
			   Strategic Reading 321N, 324
			 Cooperative Reading 322, 324, 329

2 RESPONDING TO LITERATURE pp. 330A–330E	Writer's Journal p. 62
	 Practice Book pp. 98–99
	 Integrated Spelling p. 48
	 Integrated Spelling T.E. pp. 66–67
		Vocabulary Workshop
		   Reviewing Key Words
		   Extending Vocabulary
		 Writing About the Literature
		 Speaking/Listening
		 Spelling Review
			Cooperative Learning 330B, 330D

3 LEARNING THROUGH LITERATURE pp. 330F–330L	Second-Language Support Manual Writer's Journal p. 63 Practice Book pp. 100–101	Science Social Studies/Math Health Multicultural	Challenge 330G, 330H, 330I Second-Language Support 330G Cooperative Learning 330G

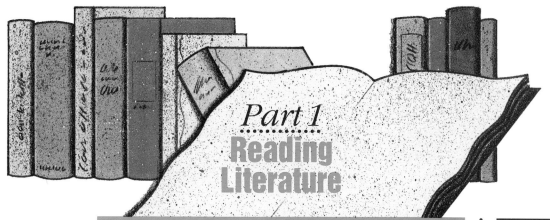

Part 1
Reading Literature

CULTURAL AWARENESS

To help students appreciate the cultural background and setting of "At Home with the Titan of the Trail," share with them the information under Cultural Background/Setting on page 322.

Access prior knowledge and develop vocabulary concepts.

Tell students they will be reading an article about a woman who races huskies in Alaska. Encourage students to recall what they already know about the Far North from "Discovering Gold" or other sources. You may wish to draw a web on the board and have students complete it.

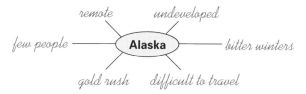

remote   undeveloped

few people ——— **Alaska** ——— bitter winters

gold rush   difficult to travel

Have students quickwrite questions.

Have students write down one or two questions they would ask someone who lives there about life in a cold, remote region of Alaska. Call on volunteers to share their questions.

Vocabulary Strategies

KEY WORDS DEFINED

muskeg soft, swampy ground

inadequacies failings

masochism enjoyment of suffering

intrusion unwelcome entry, invasion

privation lack of necessities

hutches pens, enclosures

rejuvenated renewed

rapport friendship, relationship of mutual trust

stoicism indifference to pain or pleasure

stamina endurance

Introduce Key Words and strategies.

Tell students they will meet some unfamiliar words in the article. Display Transparency 18, or write the paragraph on the board.

Transparency 18 Key Words

Kim, the guide, lived in a cabin surrounded by marshy <u>muskeg</u>. The cabin's <u>inadequacies</u>—no electricity or running water—appealed to Kim. There was no <u>masochism</u>, or enjoyment of suffering, in him, but he saw modern conveniences as an <u>intrusion</u> and preferred the <u>privation</u> of the frozen waste. His dog inhabited one of the wooden <u>hutches</u> nearby. If boredom ever set in, Kim and the dog went on difficult hikes and returned happy and lively, <u>rejuvenated</u> by the adventure. Kim and his dog shared a special feeling, or <u>rapport</u>. Kim saw his own <u>stoicism</u>, or indifference to pain and pleasure, in his pet's strength and <u>stamina</u>.

Have students read silently, and then encourage them to use phonics and context clues to determine the meanings of the underlined words. Ask a volunteer to read the paragraph aloud. Help with pronunciation, if necessary.

Check students' understanding.

Have students demonstrate their understanding by matching the Key Words to their definitions.

1. **muskeg** (f)
2. **hutches** (c)
3. **masochism** (h)
4. **privation** (i)
5. **intrusion** (b)
6. **stamina** (e)
7. **rejuvenated** (j)
8. **stoicism** (a)
9. **inadequacies** (g)
10. **rapport** (d)

a. indifference to pain
b. unwelcome entry
c. pens, enclosures
d. mutual trust
e. endurance
f. soft, swampy ground
g. lacks, failings
h. taste for suffering
i. lack of necessities
j. renewed

Integrate spelling with vocabulary.

SPELLING-VOCABULARY CONNECTION *Integrated Spelling* page 47 reinforces spellings of words containing prefixes *in-, re-,* and *un-,* including the following Key Words: *inadequacies, intrusion, rejuvenated.* The spelling of the Key Word *rapport* is also included.

SECOND-LANGUAGE SUPPORT Have students use Key Words in sentences with the help of a peer tutor. (See *Second-Language Support Manual.*)

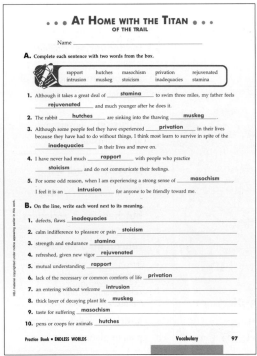

Practice Book

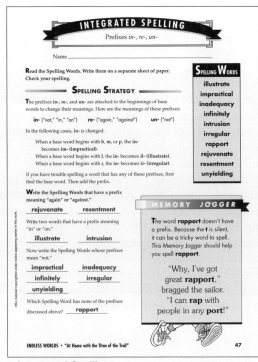

Integrated Spelling

PRACTICE BOOK
page 97: Reinforcing Key Words

INTEGRATED SPELLING
page 47: Writing and spelling words with prefixes: *in-, re-, un-*

NOTE: These pages may be completed now or after students have read the article.

Using the K-W-L Strategy

Have students use prior knowledge.

Explain that this feature article originally appeared in a newspaper. A feature article is a special, in-depth treatment of persons or events that are of high interest to readers. Then write *K-W-L* on the board. Call on a volunteer to explain how the K-W-L strategy works. (You begin by reviewing what you *know* about a topic; you develop questions about what you *want* to find out; as you read or afterward, you write down what you have *learned* and see if you answered your questions.)

Have students preview the selection.

Have students use the title, photographs, and captions to preview the article. Explain that the Titans were giants who, according to Greek mythology, ruled the earth.

Introduce the K-W-L chart.

Write the following headings on the board:

K-W-L CHART

What I Know	What I Want to Know	What I Learned

PERSONAL JOURNAL   Instruct students to write the headings in their personal journals, or have them use *Practice Book* page 98. (See page 330B in this Teacher's Edition.) Then have them brainstorm what they know about sled dogs in the Arctic. Help students fill in the first column with this information. Then have them fill in the second column with questions they would like answered as they read the article.

Setting a Purpose

Have students set purposes.

Have students use their questions from the second column of the chart to set a purpose for reading. Suggest that, as they read, they take notes on the answers and add more questions to the chart.

Model purpose-setting, if necessary.

If students have difficulty setting a purpose for reading, model the thinking process:

> **I already know that Susan Butcher has won the Iditarod four times. After looking at the photographs and reading the title and caption, my purpose for reading will be to find out more about Butcher, her dog Granite, and the way she trains her dog team to win the race.**

Alaska has been and still is home to many people of Aleut and Inuit (Eskimo) descent. Inuit people used dogs and sleds for transportation long before other people knew Alaska existed. The favored type of sled among Inuits in this area was the frame sled, which has a basketlike frame built on runners. The same basic construction devised and used by the ancient Inuit is used today in dog sled races like the Iditarod.

1 DESCRIPTION

What contrast does the author draw between the general setting and the atmosphere of the kennel? *(He contrasts the "chilly, unyielding land" with the warmth Susan Butcher shows her dogs.)*
INFERENTIAL: COMPARING AND CONTRASTING

2 CHARACTERIZATION

What verbs does the author use to describe Susan Butcher's movements? (crouched, wrapped [arms], flopped, wrinkled [her nose])
LITERAL: NOTING IMPORTANT DETAILS

What do these verbs suggest about her? *(She feels great affection for her dogs and becomes one with them. Some of her movements are like those of her huskies.)*
INFERENTIAL: MAKING COMPARISONS

1 EUREKA, Alaska—It was a moment of warmth in a chilly, unyielding land. Twelve dozen Alaskan huskies yelped, growled, yipped and howled from their hutches on thawing muskeg and stretched wet paws toward Susan Butcher.

Butcher returned the adoration. She chanted.

"Bugga, bugga, buggabeen . . . the fastest dog there's ever been." Her song was for Sluggo, a honey-beige husky with a sore paw. It was raw from ice balls that formed between his toes last month when he was leading Butcher's team to victory in an 11-day streak of masochism known as the Iditarod Sled Dog Race. It was Sluggo's first win. It was Susan Butcher's fourth.

"Dugadee. Dugadoo. Dugadog." That was for Granite. He has won three Iditarods and, says Butcher, is the finest sled dog of this decade. If Granite were a horse he'd be Secretariat.

2 Then this iron woman crouched deep among her dogs and the spring-softened snow and wrapped arms around Elan's shaggy neck; flopped on her belly on a plywood doghouse to say boo to Tolstoy; and wrinkled her nose against the wet black plug of Heifer's nose.

And Susan Butcher—emotionally stale from airlines and motels and real clothes, mentally exhausted by 10 days of victory greetings, public speaking and a meeting with President Bush—finally was home.

Susan Butcher with sled dogs Tolstoy, Granite, and Mattie

AT HOM
Titan o

Guided Reading

SET PURPOSE/PREDICT: PAGES 322–325 Have students read through the first complete paragraph on page 325 to find out the answers to some of their questions. Ask students which questions they might expect to have answered in the first section. (What is a dog sled race like? What makes it challenging or dangerous?)

Cooperative Reading

READER RESPONSE STRATEGY: PAGES 322–325 Form groups of students, and have each group select a leader. Ask group members to read pages 322–325 silently, and then have the leader use dialogue questions such as those below to encourage discussion. (Response Card 5: Author's Viewpoint, on page R66, offers a variety of dialogue questions.)

- What is the author trying to tell you? How do you know?
- Can you tell what kinds of people the author admires?

VITH THE
he Trail

by Paul Dean
Los Angeles Times

Informal Assessment You can informally assess whether students understand an author's viewpoint. On occasion, ask students these questions:

- Why did the author write this article? What does he think about the topic?
- What about the article makes you think this is the author's viewpoint?

By encouraging students to talk freely about their own thinking, you will get important diagnostic insights into how well they are reading.

Teaching Tip Explain to students that Secretariat (page 322, third paragraph) was one of the few racehorses ever to win the Triple Crown of horse racing, which includes the Kentucky Derby, the Preakness, and the Belmont Stakes horse races. Some regard him as the greatest racehorse of modern times.

324

3 CHARACTERIZATION

What does the description of Susan Butcher's home tell the reader about her? *(She loves her rugged and remote life-style and dislikes the modern conveniences most of us could not live without.)*
INFERENTIAL: DRAWING CONCLUSIONS

4 TEXT STRUCTURE

In this paragraph, the author uses *only* **to introduce three sentences in a row. Why do you think he does that?** *(Accept reasonable responses: He recognizes there is something different about Susan Butcher's unusual need for solitude, and he wants to explain or defend it. The repetition adds impact.)*
CRITICAL: MAKING JUDGMENTS

5 EXPOSITORY TEXT: MAIN IDEA

What are Susan Butcher's credentials as the best dog sled racer in the world? *(She has won the Iditarod four times and has set speed records in it. She has also won many less-demanding races.)*
LITERAL: NOTING IMPORTANT DETAILS

3

Home. That's Trail Breaker Kennel, five acres of bush surrounding an 80-year-old log cabin that once belonged to a Gold Rush blacksmith. It is most of Eureka (Elev. 270, Pop. 6). Just a scatter of mining shacks among stands of silver birch at the end of 140 miles of dirt road not far beneath the Arctic Circle.

Hers is life without television, running water, flush toilets or a bathtub. There's a single telephone hooked by satellite to a Seattle area code, but that's for husband Dave Monson to use because Butcher regards a ringing phone as the ultimate intrusion and refuses to answer it. A run to the grocery store is a four-hour rattle by truck to Fairbanks.

4

Only in isolation approaching privation, Butcher says, can she maintain an uninterrupted focus on breeding and training sled dogs. Only away from the noise, stink and structures of man can she intensify an unusual personal bonding with her dogs. Only from here can she concentrate on winning next **5** year's Iditarod.

For a decade, she explains, she has concentrated on a companionship that starts with a puppy's first breath and produces dogs ready to drop for her—huskies that have made her not just the *best woman* dog sled racer in the world, but the *best* dog sled racer in the world.

In any endurance athlete's life the Iditarod stands as a death wish—a lopsided gamble against survival across 1,130 frost-bitten miles, mountain ranges, blizzards, and frozen seas between Anchorage and Nome. Only two persons have won the Iditarod four times—Rick Swenson, 38, of Two Rivers, Alaska, and Susan Butcher, 35.

The race record is 11 days, 1 hour and 53 minutes. It belongs to Butcher. Her fifth Iditarod championship, said Joe Redding-ton Jr., a racer and son of the 1972 founder of the Iditarod, may be considered an inevitability. If anyone breaks the 10-day barrier, believe other experts, it will be Susan Butcher.

In the past winter's schedule of sled dog races —marked by such contests as the John Beargrease Marathon and the Coldfoot Classic—Butcher entered six events. She won four and was second in the others.

"What was the total frustration for the mushers is that Susan took three totally separate teams [to the races]," Butcher said. In conversation she often inserts herself in the narrative. "Both Susan's A and B dogs blew away the other teams and took 10 hours off the record in the Beargrease.

"The C team finished just seven minutes behind the winner in another event and would have won it if Susan hadn't been sicker [with flu] than a dog."

There are few places in Alaska where this happy woman with a smile stretching from here to the Aleutians can move unrecognized. She has visited two Presidents, been commended by legislatures, won the medals and awards of world organizations and visited the Soviet Union to counsel *perestroik*

Second-Language Support

Make sure students understand that a musher (column 3, first complete paragraph) is a driver of a husky team. The root of the word is *mush*, a command that means "run" to a dog team.

MEETING INDIVIDUAL NEEDS

Cooperative Reading

READER RESPONSE STRATEGY: PAGES 325–330
Groups should continue reading silently, pausing occasionally to discuss how their predictions and conclusions change as they learn more about Susan Butcher.

mushers and set trails for next year's Alaska-Siberia race.

Butcher has run her dogs in Switzerland and is a friend of Gen. Colin Powell, chairman of the Joint Chiefs of Staff, because each has been elected to membership in the American Academy of Achievement. Her racing has produced a major cottage industry in her home state; the smug legend of a million T-shirts sold says: "Alaska—Where Men are Men and Women Win the Iditarod."

Rarely is Butcher an also-ran, except to a media darling like Granite. On this month's victory tour, the 9-year-old husky, now retired, was given his own room at the Ritz-Carlton in St. Louis and the Four Seasons in Washington, D.C.

Letters from hotel managers were addressed to "Mr. Granite" and propped against baskets of Evian water from the French Alps and silver platters of ground round.

"There were times," Monson joked, "when we felt the introduction would be: Here's Granite who won the Iditarod three times with . . . er . . . um,

Susan Butcher cooks at Iditarod checkpoint

the couple that owns him."

Yet such world attention has cost.

Resentment has been raised against Butcher by veterans who raced in obscurity for years be-cause nobody cared much about the Iditarod—until a woman won. Then came reporters from *Sports Illustrated* and ABC's "Wide World of Sports" and Australia and Japan.

Said former champion Swenson: "She's a good competitor, but that's all I can say." Then he said more. "You could ask yourself what have they [Butcher and Monson] done for anyone else in the sport? They just take, take, take."

Butcher, a woman of uncluttered beliefs, sees another root of the resentment.

"I have become a symbol to women across the country—and internationally, in fact—and I'm not going to say that there wasn't a lot of strength gained by that thought and by the support [from women] that I got," she said.

Most competitors also don't recognize the spiritual link Butcher says she has with her huskies.

325

6 TONE

Why do you think the author now introduces criticism that has been leveled at the racer? *(Accept reasonable responses: He wants to paint a rounded portrait or present both sides of an issue.)*
INFERENTIAL: DRAWING CONCLUSIONS

Do you think the author gives Butcher's critics a fair hearing? Explain. *(Accept reasonable responses: probably not. For one thing, he suggests the critics are motivated by jealousy. For another, he quotes a charge that he neither explains nor refutes: "They [Susan Butcher and her husband] just take, take, take.")*
CRITICAL: DETECTING BIAS

Guided Reading

MONITOR COMPREHENSION: PAGES 322–325
What is a dog sled race like? What makes it challenging or dangerous? (A dog sled race involves a several-day-long run over difficult terrain. The race tests the courage and endurance of both the dogs and the driver.) STRATEGIC READING: RETURNING TO PURPOSE

What have you learned about Susan Butcher so far? (She leads a life free from modern-day conveniences; she loves her dogs and spends many hours caring for and training them; she has been honored for her achievements by governments and dignitaries all over the world.) STRATEGIC READING: SUMMARIZING

SET PURPOSE/PREDICT: PAGES 325–330 Ask students to predict what questions they will find the answers to in the remainder of the article. ("How does Susan Butcher raise her huskies? What sort of person is she?") Have students read the remainder of "At Home with the Titan of the Trail" to answer their questions.

What do you learn about Susan Butcher's training methods? *(She takes care of each dog personally from the moment it is born. She forms a close bond with each husky.)*
INFERENTIAL: DETERMINING MAIN IDEA

To what does the author compare Butcher and the dogs? *(to a parent and children; to a family)*
INFERENTIAL: MAKING COMPARISONS

"I was born with a particular ability with animals and a particular love for them," she said. "I think that what you get from animals, and what I got from my first dog, one of my first close friends, is the security of constant love.

"An animal loves you and you love them and that is just constant. I needed that as a child. I have some compositions here, some of those one-liners you write in the first grade. Mine said: 'I hate the city, I love the country and I love animals.'"

All animals, she added. A pet iguana. A crow on a fence post. Even a hundred cows in a field "send me into a total thrill."

So in spring when husky pups are born to her 150-dog kennel, she holds each blind thing in her hands and breathes into its nose. That way, she says, the dog will associate her smell with comfort and encouragement. The rapport begins.

She feeds the dogs. *She* exercises and trains them. *She* massages them after

runs. On a rotation basis, each dog sleeps in the cabin. The family forms.

Once, when a young Granite suffered renal failure from driving himself to dehydration, Butcher sat up for five nights with the dog's head in her lap. Granite survived and remained a champion.

"But I don't say I *need* to bond with these puppies early," Butcher explains. "I

want to bond with them.

"I'm not saying that if I don't bond with this puppy I might not win the Iditarod, so therefore I *have* to go out and bond with this puppy. I'm going out because I'm absolutely drawn to that."

She also will not ask more of her dogs than they can deliver, she says. The huskies know that. So, they often give more than they

Iditarod Champion Susan Butcher at the finish line for the 1987 race

326

Oral Rereading   Invite a pair of students to orally reread part of the article as an interview between Paul Dean and Susan Butcher. Have students write questions that Dean might have asked to get the answers Butcher gives. For example, on the third paragraph of this page, the student playing Dean's role might ask, "Do you love all animals?" Allow students to choose the section they would like to perform. Have them practice before presenting their interview.

thought they had. And she is infinitely patient with the dogs.

"I want every one of these dogs to make my Iditarod team," Butcher continued. "So I give everybody their sixth, seventh, and eighth or ninth chance. Whereas my competitors—and I think this is one of the biggest differences—often don't give them a second or third chance."

Granite was a loser. She once offered him for sale for $250. "He didn't come around at least until his 10th chance. Sluggo was probably on his 20th chance before he came around.

"So you've got two superstars there who would not have even made it in someone else's team." And further, "every dog I run was raised in my own kennel by me and through my scheme . . . whereas often less than half of somebody else's team is raised in their own kennel, and they buy the others."

They buy from Butcher, paying from $1,000 to $10,000 for a trained dog. But even at that price, Butcher says, the animal is still one of her discards.

Her childhood was filled with daring. During summers spent in Maine she raced 13-foot sailing dinghies when gales sent others heading for the dock. Her description of childhood is that she was "an individualist . . . hard core, big time tomboy . . . a real gambler who took dangers fairly lightly . . . and very lopsided academically, because I was a dyslexic who excelled at math."

Her first dog, at 15, was Manganak, named for Zachary Manganak, a Canadian Eskimo in one of her children's books. Then she bought a second husky. Her mother said two dogs in one house was too much.

"So I left the house rather than not get the dog," Butcher remembered. "But happily so, and we maintained a wonderful relationship."

She was 16 then. Butcher went to Nova Scotia and learned to farm and train horses and picked up enough carpentry to build a boathouse. She went to join her father in Boulder, Colo., where her step-mother bought her a dog sled.

"We went to pick it up from a woman who had 50 huskies," Butcher said. "Ten minutes later I had moved in. I lived with her for a couple of years, worked as a veterinary technician and mushed and was frustrated by every minute of it."

Butcher wanted the life of yesteryear. There must be a place, she reasoned, where human survival depended on instincts and dogs were not domestic pets but working animals "needed for transportation, to haul your water, to haul your wood."

She eyed Western Canada. On her way, she paused in Fairbanks. "I felt at home the second I got there."

Butcher worked at a musk ox farm, found a companion and headed for her first winter in the lonely Wrangell Mountains before she had learned her partner's last name.

"It was one of the purest places left in Alaska," she recalled. "The closest road was 50 miles away. In

327

8 EXPOSITORY TEXT: CAUSE-EFFECT
What qualities did Susan Butcher have as a youth that pointed toward her future career? *(She was independent and prone to risk-taking, and she adored animals.)*
INFERENTIAL: DETERMINING CAUSE-EFFECT

9 AUTHOR'S PURPOSE
At this point the author is inserting events that concern Butcher's past. What do you think is the author's purpose in writing of events that occurred many years earlier? *(Accept reasonable responses: to explain what led this extraordinary woman to live in remote Alaska and become a champion racer.)*
INFERENTIAL: DRAWING CONCLUSIONS

10 EXPOSITORY TEXT: DETAILS
What evidence is there in the article that Susan Butcher is probably more sensitive to animals than she is to people? *(Accept reasonable responses: She left home at sixteen and describes the parting with her mother as "happy." She headed for the Wrangell Mountains with a partner before she learned her partner's last name. She can tolerate civilization for only a month or two at a time. She treats her dogs like "family.")*
INFERENTIAL: SUMMARIZING

11 EXPOSITORY TEXT: DETAILS
What evidence does the author provide that the dogs return Susan Butcher's devotion? *(Granite and others have performed heroic feats to save her life.)*
INFERENTIAL: DRAWING CONCLUSIONS

Does this prove the dogs' devotion, or can their acts be interpreted in some other way? *(The dogs may have been trying to save themselves.)*
CRITICAL: DISTINGUISHING FACT FROM OPINION

Canada. We took in a sack of flour and a slab of bacon and a jar of peanut butter and lived off moose and caribou and ptarmigan and whatever we could hunt.

"I was a vegetarian when I went out there. I wasn't a vegetarian when I came back."

Butcher found "Utopia." She also discovered life in its basic form. "If you were going to eat meat, you shot it. You saw its death. You caused its death and you ate it and you survived because of its death.

"And you hauled all your own water and everything was dependent on you and the reward was living in the most gorgeous spot on Earth.

10 "I found out after that second winter that I was totally rejuvenated," she said. "I knew that if I could spend the majority of a year away from people, then I could actually adore human beings for about two months . . . even strangers."

But only for a short while. "Then I'd fall off and it would be big time bad news. Get me out into the bush again. Susan is

328

ready to flip out."

In 1977, she moved to Eureka with two objectives: To form a kennel of at least 100 dogs and build a team to run the Iditarod.

They were long, lonely years. She lived alone or with handlers when she could afford them. Debts grew. Equipment broke. One winter she survived by eating meat bought for the dogs.

But Butcher had goals, a stiff spine, a stubborn mind-set and an eye for any opportunity to focus attention on her and the dogs.

So in 1979, with Iditarod founder Joe Reddington, she took a dog team to the 20,320-foot summit of Mt. McKinley. It took 44 days. **11** It also brought public interest to the earnest young woman with the braided hair.

She trains her pups in harness at $4\frac{1}{2}$ months. Each one has been bred for essentials. Stamina. Resistance to injury. A sense of teamwork. Courage. Stoicism and flexibility of limbs.

Her aim is always to run behind the best dog team anyone ever hitched to a

sled. Each dog must also have total communication with Butcher.

She deepens the telepathy by singing to the dogs when they are racing, old folk songs by Bob Dylan and Joan Baez and maybe some Irish lullabies.

And in the worst moments of several Iditarods—when there were hallucinations from sleep deprivation—the dogs have saved her life.

In 1984, jockeying for the lead with two other teams, Butcher was told by race supervisors there was no overland trail between Unalakleet and Shaktoolik on Norton Sound, which pokes toward the Bering Sea. Crossing sea ice on a moonless night was the only choice.

"I noticed the ice was almost billowing," she recalled. "Just as I saw that, I told Granite [in lead] to go to the left. Which he did. He was terrified because the whole thing [ice] was going like this [rocking] . . . when the sled fell through and the whole team and I went in about 30 feet of water."

Vocabulary Strategy   Ask students how context clues can help them determine the meaning of *Utopia* (column 1, second complete paragraph). (Accept reasonable responses: The reader is told that the Wrangell Mountains are "one of the purest places left in Alaska" and that one lives close to nature there. Students may be able to figure out that *Utopia* means "an ideal place.") STRATEGY: CONTEXT CLUES

But then "Granite hit hard ice and he got up on top of it. Him and Maddie. Then, two [dogs] by two, they pulled us out. I thought we were goners."

A moose once attacked the team and that cost Butcher the 1985 race, seven years of preparation, two dogs killed and 13 injured.

Butcher has crossed Norton Sound in a blizzard when she couldn't see the lead dog. Navigation was by a small compass. For five blind hours she traveled the ice, wondering how close she was to the spot where a friend drowned earlier in the year.

"But there's a fun thing about it," she said. She mentioned a quirk known to all adventurers. "It's thrilling, isn't it? Especially when you conquer it."

2 There are activists who see sled dog racing as cruelty to animals.

Butcher snorts at the thought. It is an expression, she says, of uninformed city dwellers who know only pampered pets.

Pulling sleds "is what they live for . . . it is instinc-

Susan Butcher with her dog team

tive for them to want to pull.

"From the time they see the harness come out or see the sled, they are absolutely going crazy, jumping around, wanting to go and then literally jumping into harness."

There also are times when the adrenaline pumps and 12 dogs are galloping as one. Then, Butcher says, they don't want to stop. There was the

time a tired Butcher was racing in the Brooks Range and thought her weariness would be contagious.

"I felt these dogs would be fried or at least pick up on my feelings of being fried," she said. "But I could not stop them. It was a total thrill. I hooked a five-inch diameter tree with my snow hook and they pulled the tree over. I tried stopping them for five or six miles and then gave up.

329

13 FIGURATIVE LANGUAGE
What does the author mean when he asks, "Is there still a call of the wild for Susan Butcher?" *(Accept reasonable responses: Is she drawn to even fiercer confrontations with nature?)*
INFERENTIAL: DRAWING CONCLUSIONS

14 THINK IT OVER
1. *Susan Butcher trains her dogs by giving them constant attention and affection. She differs from other trainers in that she herself breeds, trains, and cares for each dog, and she rarely gives up on a loser.*
INFERENTIAL: COMPARING AND CONTRASTING
2. *Granite has won the Iditarod three times.*
LITERAL: NOTING IMPORTANT DETAILS
3. *The Iditarod is a dog sled race run over 1,130 miles of mountains and frozen seas. Both the length of the race and the hazardous conditions make it a challenge.*
INFERENTIAL: SUMMARIZING
4. *She was elected to the Academy because of her impressive record of victories.*
INFERENTIAL: DETERMINING CAUSE-EFFECT
5. *Accept reasonable responses: Her being a woman has won her some support and attention, but it has also caused some resentment among veteran male racers who are envious of all the attention she has received.*
INFERENTIAL: DETERMINING CAUSE-EFFECT

15 WRITE
Suggest that students outline their introduction with a graphic such as this:

What I Should Say

why speaker is important — *why she would interest teenagers*

Responses will vary.
CREATIVE: SYNTHESIZING

NOTE Additional writing activities appear on pages 330D and 330E.

"So they went 35 miles into the next village."

Such moments, she says, make Susan complete.

The childhood inadequacies have gone. She no longer hunts for role models—because she has become the very person she was always searching for.

Yet is there still a call of the wild for Susan Butcher?

She thought long about that.

Outside the log cabin, Sluggo and Tolstoy and Co-Star and Hermit lie flat, with furry bellies toasting in the warm Arctic sun. Monson was playing a tape and porch speakers carried the Modern Mandolin Quartet over snow to thicket and silent hill. A gray jay snoozed in a tree.

"Oh, no," Butcher whispered. "It's still calling."

THINK IT OVER

1. *What method does Susan Butcher use to train her dogs? How is her method different from that of other trainers?*
2. *Why is Granite so famous?*
3. *Describe the Iditarod race, and explain what makes this race such a great challenge.*
4. *Why do you think Butcher was elected as a member of the American Academy of Achievement?*
5. *How has being a woman been both an advantage and a disadvantage to Butcher in her career?*

WRITE

15 *Suppose Susan Butcher were speaking at an assembly program at your school. Write a short introduction you could present before her speech.*

330

Returning to the Purpose for Reading Invite students to review the questions that they asked before reading and that they may have written in their personal journals. Ask students whether they found answers to the questions. Call on volunteers to share other questions they added to their K-W-L charts while they were reading.

Part 2
Responding to Literature

Summarizing the Literature

Have students retell the selection and write a summary.

Have students summarize "At Home with the Titan of the Trail," using the chart they completed as they read. If they did not complete the chart, have them do so now. (See *Practice Book* page 98, on 330B.) Students may use their completed charts to retell the selection and write a brief summary statement.

K-W-L CHART

What I Know	What I Want to Know	What I Learned
Huskies are strong, long-haired dogs, native to the Arctic.	What is a dog sled race like?	Dogs in harness, with one dog leading the team, race for days over difficult terrain.
Husky-pulled sleds are a common means of transportation in the North.	What makes the race challenging or dangerous?	Racers must cross ice that may not hold and travel in blizzards over mountains.

Appreciating Literature

Have students share personal responses.

Divide students into small groups to discuss the article. Provide an open-ended question such as the following to help students get started:

- **What character trait, if any, does Susan Butcher possess that you admire? Explain your answer.**

PERSONAL JOURNAL   Have students use their personal journals to write about ideas and feelings that are expressed in the groups. You may also wish to refer students to their personal journals after they complete the Critical Thinking Activities.

STRATEGY CONFERENCE

Ask students how completing their K–W–L charts helped them understand and appreciate the article. Then invite volunteers to discuss questions on their K–W–L charts that were not answered by the article.

STUDENT SELF-ASSESSMENT

To help students self-assess their listening skills, write the following questions on the board:

- Would I be able to paraphrase the speakers' ideas about this article?
- Were any of the ideas discussed similar to what I was thinking? Did I offer support for those ideas?

Encourage both cooperative and individual responses.

DISCUSS ROLE MODELS **Would you choose Susan Butcher as a role model or recommend her as one? Why or why not?** Encourage students to examine both the positive and negative aspects of the racer's career and life before they formulate their answers. Also ask them to consider what qualities a role model should have. Call on volunteers to argue the pros and cons of considering Butcher a role model. CRITICAL: MAKING JUDGMENTS

ROLE-PLAY AN INTERVIEW **Suppose the author were to interview Susan Butcher's mother or husband for additional segments of the article. What questions might he ask, and how might each party respond?** Have small groups of students prepare questions and then role-play the discussions that might take place. CREATIVE: INVENTING NEW SCENES

WRITE AN ESSAY **Susan Butcher risks her life and those of her dogs for the sake of pitting herself against nature. In general, do you think this is an acceptable thing to do?** Ask students to write brief essays in answer to this question. Suggest that they back up their arguments with reasons and with analogies to other dangerous ventures, such as mountain climbing or sailing across the ocean in a small boat. CRITICAL: MAKING JUDGMENTS

Writer's Journal

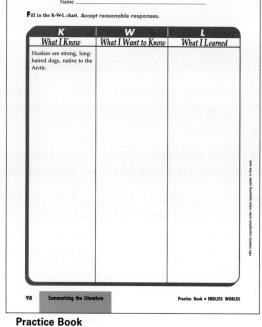

Practice Book

WRITER'S JOURNAL
page 62: Writing a creative response

PRACTICE BOOK
page 98: Summarizing the selection

VO·CAB·U·LAR·Y Workshop

Reviewing Key Words

To review how the new vocabulary was used in this selection, display the Key Words. Read each activity below aloud, and ask students to indicate the appropriate Key Word.

A. Match the Key Word to its definition.

1. masochism   endurance (3)
2. stoicism   a taste for suffering (1)
3. stamina   indifference to pleasure and pain (2)

B. Add the Key Word to its synonyms.

4. pens, coops, cages, *(hutches)*
5. swamp, bog, marsh, *(muskeg)*
6. harmony, accord, friendship, *(rapport)*

C. Add the related Key Word.

7. juvenile
   rejuvenate
   rejuvenation
   (rejuvenated)

8. deprive
   deprived
   deprivation
   (privation)

9. intrude
   intruded
   intrusive
   intrusively
   intrusiveness
   (intrusion)

10. adequate
    adequacy
    adequately
    inadequately
    (inadequacies)

Extending Vocabulary

CHARGED LANGUAGE   Explain to students that the purpose of a headline in a newspaper or magazine is to attract readers and to make them want to read the article. That is why headlines often contain very dramatic language. Ask students to discuss the differences between the following two headlines:

HEROIC HOUND RESCUES
MUCH–LOVED MASTER

DOG SAVES WOMAN

Then ask students to create dramatic headlines about Susan Butcher, dog sled racing, and the huskies. You might start students off by suggesting that they rewrite headlines like the following:

Woman Wins Iditarod   Team Victory

PRACTICE BOOK

page 99: Interpreting charged language

> ··· AT HOME WITH THE TITAN ···
> OF THE TRAIL
>
> Name _____
>
> **A.** Rewrite the headlines below. Use exciting words to attract your readers' attention. You may use the charged words at the right or think of some of your own. **Accept reasonable responses.**
>
> 1. Weather Turns Cold
>   cold snap / blast / mercury
>   plunge / icy / wintry
>   chills / frigid / bitter
>
> 2. People Look for Boy Lost in Snow
>   blizzard / wind / scour
>   blinding / rescue team / piercing
>   fierce / search / worried
>
> 3. Anchorage Welcomes Racers
>   receives / entertains / sledders
>   mushers / greets / hosts
>   accepts / competitors / enthusiastic
>
> 4. Alaskan Dogsled Race Begins
>   wilderness / endurance / tundra
>   survival / pit / marathon
>   huskies / cross-country / dash
>
> **B.** Think of an event that recently took place in your school or community. Write three headlines to describe the event. **Responses will vary.**
>
> Practice Book ▪ ENDLESS WORLDS   Charged Language   99

Practice Book

Integrated **Language Arts**

<table>
<tr><td></td></tr>
</table>

WRITING

Writing About the Literature

CREATIVE: PERSONAL NARRATIVE Point out to students that they face challenges every day in sports, academics, and their personal lives. Ask students to write about a challenge they or someone else faced. They should describe both the challenge and the response to it. Tell students that they may write their narratives in the third person. WRITING

CRITICAL: PERSUASIVE ESSAY Explain to students that many sports are criticized for their danger or violence. Ask students how they react when they hear football criticized as violent. Ask them to write persuasive essays arguing that football or another sport is or is not too violent. Suggest that as they write, they try to respond to the arguments of those who hold the opposite view. Remind students to include in their essays an opening statement, supportive reasons, and a conclusion. You may wish to have students use a schedule like the one below to plan their work. LISTENING/ SPEAKING/WRITING

Monday	Tuesday	Wednesday	Thursday	Friday
Paper assigned. Due Friday.	Trip to library. Began research.	Read books. Wrote outline. First draft.	Revision, second draft.	Turned in paper.

NOTE: An additional writing activity appears on page 330.

SPEAKING/LISTENING

Conquering the Cold

AVAILABLE ON PROJECT CARD

COOPERATIVE LEARNING The frozen parts of the world have long drawn the adventurous, bent on conquest or discovery. Have groups of students research such heroic expeditions as Henson and Peary's journey to the North Pole or the climbing of Mt. Everest by Sir Edmund Hillary and Tenzing Norgay. Have each group reenact the most exciting parts of one expedition. After several reenactments have been given, discuss with students the lure of these perilous places and why people will risk their lives to explore them. You may wish to point out that when Hillary was asked why he climbed Everest, he answered, "Because it was there." Ask students what they think he meant by that. LISTENING/SPEAKING/READING

WRITING

I Nominate You

AVAILABLE ON PROJECT CARD

Susan Butcher was elected to membership in the American Academy of Achievement. Have students write a nomination speech for someone they think should be recognized for demonstrating outstanding achievement. Explain that the person they nominate can be a famous person whose achievements they admire or someone they know who, similarly, they think deserves recognition for a special talent or accomplishment. Point out that they should give reasons for their nominations in their writing. After writing their speeches, students should present them to classmates. LISTENING/SPEAKING/WRITING

SPEAKING/LISTENING

What a Thrill!

In describing her love for sled racing, Susan Butcher said "It's thrilling, isn't it? Especially when you conquer it." Have students think about some activity they have done that was thrilling and gave them a feeling of exhilaration, such as skiing down a slope or running a race. Have students interview each other about their experiences and then report on the interview. Before beginning, partners will want to tell each other what their experience was so that the interviewer can have time to write some probing questions. One question you might suggest each student ask is "If you had to use four adjectives to describe your sport or activity, what words would you choose?" Follow up by having the interviewers summarize the interview, including whether they would enjoy such an experience. LISTENING/SPEAKING/WRITING

SPELLING

Spelling Review

SPELLING WORDS: *illustrate, impractical, inadequacy, infinitely, intrusion, irregular, rapport, rejuvenate, resentment, unyielding*

Have students look up the prefixes *in-, re-,* and *un-* in a dictionary. Tell them to write these prefixes, and their meanings, at the top of a sheet of paper. Then ask the students to look up each Spelling Word. For each word, have the students write the etymology. (If students are unfamiliar with looking up a word's etymology, direct them to the appropriate explanatory notes contained in the dictionary.) Then ask volunteers to explain the etymology and meaning of each Spelling Word, including the meaning of any prefix. SPEAKING/READING/WRITING/SPELLING

INTEGRATED SPELLING

page 48: Writing words

with prefixes: *in-, re-, un-*

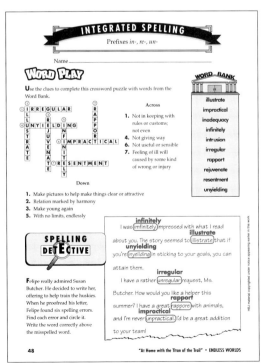

Integrated Spelling

Learning Through Literature

LITERARY APPRECIATION
REVIEW

Literary Forms

OBJECTIVE: *To understand the purpose of a newspaper feature article*

Review

Discuss feature articles.

Remind students that "At Home with the Titan of the Trail" originally appeared in a newspaper. Explain that the article is a newspaper feature article and that such articles present people and events that are of special interest to readers.

Model the thinking.

Explain that a feature article offers in-depth coverage of its subject and that the author's purpose is generally to entertain as well as to inform. Because a feature article may contain opinions, the author's name is given in a byline. A "hard news" article, in contrast, simply presents the facts in their order of importance. The writer's name is not usually given. Model how you would recognize a feature story:

> **As I begin to read "At Home with the Titan of the Trail," I notice that the author catches my interest by telling a story about Susan Butcher's homecoming. I do not find out why she is in the paper until the end of the third paragraph. This use of suspense to catch the reader's interest is typical of a newspaper feature article.**

330F / *ENDLESS WORLDS,* UNIT 4

Practice/Apply

Have students apply the learning.

COOPERATIVE LEARNING   Ask students to list the *5W* facts (who, what, where, when, and why) about Susan Butcher that they can glean from the selection. Then ask them to describe what information the feature article provides in addition to these facts.

Summarize

Informally assess the learning.

Check students' understanding by asking them to summarize what they have learned. (Feature articles offer in-depth coverage of newsworthy people and events. They may entertain as well as inform.)

READER ↔ WRITER CONNECTION

Feature Articles

▶ **Writers** write newspaper features to provide in-depth coverage on a topic of interest.
▶ **Readers** learn more about a topic by reading a feature article.

WRITE A NEWSPAPER FEATURE ARTICLE   Ask students to write a feature article about what students at your school are doing to protect the environment. Have students make their articles realistic by writing about projects actually being done at your school.

CHALLENGE   Challenge a group of students to prepare a class newspaper with feature articles, news articles, and catchy headlines.

SECOND-LANGUAGE SUPPORT   Students may demonstrate their understanding by pointing out feature articles in a newspaper. (See *Second-Language Support Manual.*)

WRITER'S JOURNAL
page 63:   Writing a feature article

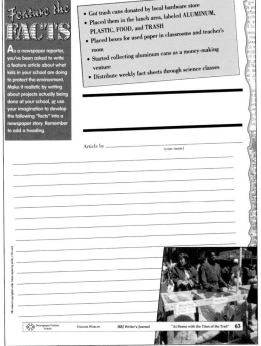

Writer's Journal

Reference Sources

OBJECTIVE: *To use a dictionary to find word meanings*

Review

Review the use of a dictionary.

Have students turn to page 327, and model how to find the meaning of the word *dyslexic* in the dictionary.

I can't figure out *dyslexic* from context clues, so I look in a dictionary. I see it means "one who has a reading problem." The phonetic respelling tells me how to pronounce it.

Practice/Apply

Have students apply the learning.

Have students use a dictionary to look up the meanings of *renal, veterinary,* and *ptarmigan.*

Summarize

Informally assess the learning.

Ask students to summarize what they learned. (If using context clues and other strategies doesn't work, look up a new word in a dictionary.)

CHALLENGE Have students look in the back of the dictionary to see what additional kinds of information are offered. Ask them to share what they find by writing and displaying a table of contents for the dictionary.

PRACTICE BOOK

page 100: Using reference sources

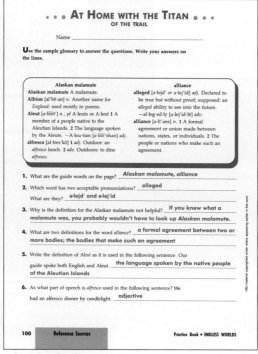

Practice Book

Fact-Opinion/Viewpoint

OBJECTIVE: *To separate fact from opinion as a strategy for determining author's purpose and viewpoint*

Review

Review how fact and opinion can indicate purpose and viewpoint.

Ask students how distinguishing fact from opinion can help them determine an author's purpose and viewpoint. (The opinions an author expresses show his or her attitude about a subject. An author's purpose may be to express an opinion.)

Practice/Apply

Have students apply the learning.

Have students find opinions in the article about Susan Butcher and infer the author's attitude.

Summarize

Informally assess the learning.

Have students summarize what they learned. (Distinguishing fact from opinion can help determine an author's purpose and viewpoint.)

CHALLENGE Have students write a letter to the editor on a community issue, in which they incorporate both facts and opinions. For their first drafts, ask them to put an *F* in the margin next to facts, and an *0* next to sentences expressing an opinion.

PRACTICE BOOK

page 101: Determining author's purpose and viewpoint by distinguishing fact from opinion

---

···· AT HOME WITH THE TITAN ····
OF THE TRAIL

Name _____

Read the paragraph and answer the questions.

On May 1, 1986, an adventurous team of five men, one woman, and twenty dogs stood at the top of the world. It had taken them fifty-six days to get here. However, they were the first team in more than seventy-seven years to reach the North Pole by dogsled without any resupply or electronic navigation. It was an exhausting experience. One team member compared it to pushing a truck out of a snowdrift for twelve hours straight each day. But what a challenge! "This journey stands for hope," said Ann Bancroft at the Pole, "hope that other seemingly impossible goals can be met."

1. List three facts from the passage. __Accept reasonable responses. Arrived May 1, 1986; group included five men, one woman, and twenty dogs; made it to the North Pole; made it in fifty-six days; were first team in more than seventy-seven years to reach it by dogsled without any resupply or electronic navigation.

2. What makes you think these are facts? __Accept reasonable responses. The writer uses specific dates and figures that could be verified.

3. Which sentences or phrases give the author's opinions? __It was an exhausting experience. But what a challenge!

4. What opinions does the author quote? __One participant compared the experience to pushing a truck out of a snowdrift for twelve hours straight each day. "This journey stands for hope, hope that other seemingly impossible goals can be met."

5. What do you think the author's purpose was in writing the piece? __Accept reasonable responses. Students may note that the passage is uplifting and may encourage others to meet their challenges with hope.

Practice Book ● ENDLESS WORLDS

Fact-Opinion/Author's Purpose-Viewpoint

101

Practice Book

Integrated Curriculum

SCIENCE

The Land of the Midnight Sun
AVAILABLE ON PROJECT CARD

Invite students to find out about seasonal patterns of sunlight in the Arctic regions. Ask students to explain why lands near the North Pole are dark all day much of the winter but enjoy a "midnight sun" at the height of summer. Students might draw diagrams showing the angle of the sun's rays striking the earth, to clarify the phenomenon. Encourage students to investigate reference sources on their own in the astronomy section of the school or local library. LISTENING/SPEAKING/READING

SOCIAL STUDIES/MATH

The Last Frontier
AVAILABLE ON PROJECT CARD

USE A MAP Ask interested students to bring a detailed map of Alaska to class and locate the major places mentioned in the article. Suggest that students also find out some important facts about Alaska, such as the size and population, and present these in an attention-getting manner. They might want to include the ratio of population to area compared to other states. (The state is several times larger than most but inhabited by far fewer people.) Some students might research the state's natural resources and the role that oil has played in its economy. LISTENING/SPEAKING/READING/WRITING

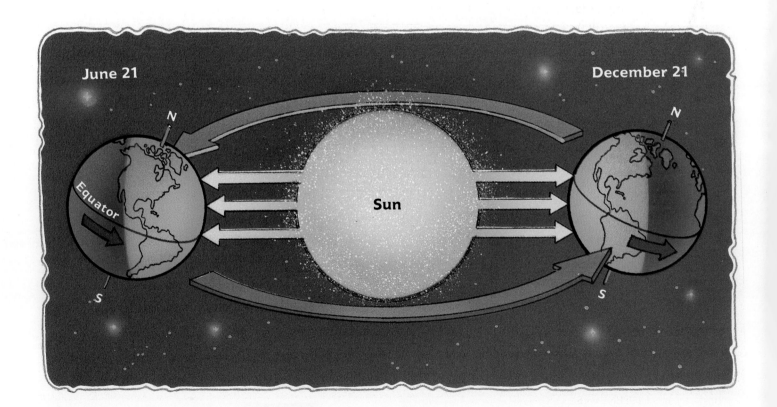

June 21 December 21 Sun N S Equator

SOCIAL STUDIES

The Igloo Builders

CULTURAL AWARENESS Susan Butcher sought out the cold and isolation of Alaska, but many Inuit (Eskimos) are born to it. Have a group of students look into the culture of this Far Northern people. A short presentation might cover the distinctive diet and housing that enabled the Inuit to survive in this harsh climate. The presentation should take into account both traditional and present-day Inuit culture. LISTENING/SPEAKING/READING/WRITING

HEALTH

Living on Next to Nothing

Ask students to suppose they were going to pass the winter in a cabin in a remote region of Alaska. They would need to take food and other supplies with them. Have students prepare a list of food items they would take in order to stay healthy throughout the winter. Suggest they consult a nutrition text for foods that meet minimum daily requirements. Encourage students to take along those foods that best resist spoilage. READING/WRITING

SOCIAL STUDIES

She's a Winner

Susan Butcher's victory in the Iditarod brought her national attention. She was the first woman who had ever won this challenging race. Have students research other women who have excelled in sports or other challenging activities. Some students might want to collaborate as a group and work on a particular sport, such as tennis or track, in which there are many outstanding women athletes. Encourage students to spend time in choosing the person they will research. For example, by scanning books of sports history, students might discover someone, like Susan Butcher, who is at the top of her field, though not well known to the general public. Have students present their research in an oral report. LISTENING/SPEAKING/READING/WRITING

SCIENCE

Hello from Eureka

Susan Butcher and her husband live without electricity, but they have a telephone because of a satellite linked to a Seattle area code. Have students find out about communications satellites. They might investigate how satellites work as well as some of the various ways they are used. Encourage students to draw a labeled diagram showing how satellites are linked worldwide and how a transmission via a satellite from Eureka, Alaska, is received in Seattle, Washington. Ask volunteers to explain their diagrams.
LISTENING/SPEAKING/READING/WRITING

MultiCultural
PERSPECTIVES

Peoples of the North

READ ALOUD TO STUDENTS:

THE PEOPLES OF THE FAR NORTH HAVE DEVELOPED RICH AND SATISFYING WAYS OF LIFE IN SPITE OF THE HARSH CLIMATE.

The dogsled described in "At Home with the Titan of the Trail" is just one invention for coping with the snow and ice of Alaskan winters.

Traveling in weather that is forty degrees or more below zero, in blinding snowstorms, people without snowmobiles in the Far North depend on their dogs for their lives. Therefore, they protect their dogs' paws with shoes made of caribou hide. These shoes prevent ice and crusted snow from crippling the dogs, which are needed to pull the sleds.

Glazing the runners of a sled with ice is another trick used to overcome the difficulty of travel in the Far North. When it is very cold, the snow is sometimes grainy, and the runners stick as though sliding over sand. Ice would help the runners move smoothly, but ice does not adhere to wood, bone, or metal. Therefore, the musher, or driver, plasters the sled runners with a paste made of earth, reindeer moss, and water. Once the paste freezes, the musher spreads melted snow over the coated runner, creating a smooth, icy glaze. ■

ACTIVITY CORNER

■ The people who live in the Far North of North America are closely related to the Northern peoples of Asia and Europe. Have students research the various groups who live in and near the Arctic. Students can present their findings in oral reports, using maps or a globe to show each group's area.

■ Northern life has changed drastically with the introduction of new tools and technology. Today, Far Northern peoples use snowmobiles more often than dogsleds. They fly planes, operate earth-moving equipment, and use computers and other sophisticated electronic equipment. Have students present a TV newscast expressing the concerns of modern-day Northern peoples. They may read newspapers and magazines to find out about Northern people's reactions to the loss of the traditional ways of life.

For many Eskimos, the traditional way of life has been replaced by new technology.

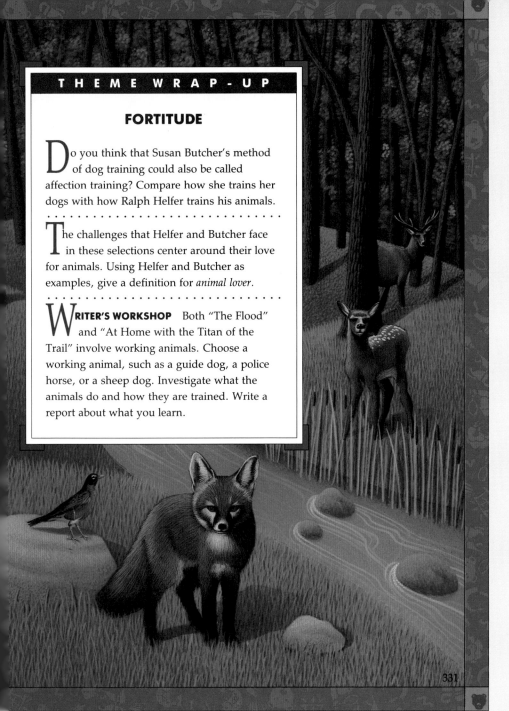

THEME WRAP-UP

FORTITUDE

Do you think that Susan Butcher's method of dog training could also be called affection training? Compare how she trains her dogs with how Ralph Helfer trains his animals.

· ·

The challenges that Helfer and Butcher face in these selections center around their love for animals. Using Helfer and Butcher as examples, give a definition for *animal lover*.

· ·

WRITER'S WORKSHOP Both "The Flood" and "At Home with the Titan of the Trail" involve working animals. Choose a working animal, such as a guide dog, a police horse, or a sheep dog. Investigate what the animals do and how they are trained. Write a report about what you learn.

331

Remind students that in "Challenges," they have read about two animal trainers. Discuss the challenges each trainer faced and how he or she responded to them. Ask why each selection is included in the theme "Fortitude." Explain that the Theme Wrap-Up questions and activity on page 331 will inspire students to define the qualities needed by animal lovers and trainers.

Note that pages 331A–331B provide support for applying the writing process to the last question.

1 Have students first think about each trainer's method separately and then identify common elements. *(Accept reasonable responses: Both Susan Butcher and Ralph Helfer form bonds of trust with the animals they raise.)*
INFERENTIAL: MAKING COMPARISONS

2 Ask students to provide a general definition of the term *animal lover,* using the trainers as a starting point. *(Accept reasonable responses: An animal lover is someone who cares deeply about animals and treats them with respect and kindness.)*
INFERENTIAL: MAKING GENERALIZATIONS

Writer's Workshop

See pages 331A–331B for suggestions for applying the writing process. Responses will require research. You may prefer to allow students to respond to the theme in their own way. WRITING PROCESS: A RESEARCH REPORT

Writer's Workshop

Discuss research reports. Remind students that a research report provides information to answer a question. Point out that it has an introduction, a body, and a conclusion and that in a research report, writers use transitional expressions to explain or link a chain of events. Suggest that students refer to the Handbook in the *Writer's Journal* as they write, revise, and proofread their research reports.

Prewriting

Before students write, have them discuss possible reference sources: an encyclopedia, a card catalog, the *Readers' Guide to Periodical Literature.* Remind them to look in indexes under related topics—for example, under *blindness* for information about guide dogs. Encourage them to interview animal trainers, if possible. Then have students

- undertake their research.
- organize their data in outline form, using main ideas and details. For guide dogs, the outline might start like this:

Guide Dog
I. Breed: Often a German shepherd 　　A. Intelligent 　　B. Responsive 　　C. Obedient **II.** Training methods

Have students complete the outline with three or four main ideas before they start drafting.

Drafting

Have students write a draft of the research report. Remind them to

- begin with an introductory paragraph and end with a conclusion.
- write a topic sentence for every paragraph, referring to the main ideas in their outlines.
- expand each topic sentence with appropriate detail.
- use language and a tone suited to research reports—that is, formal but not pretentious language and tone.
- write without worrying about spelling, punctuation, or grammar for the present.

COMPUTER CONNECTION　Students may want to use a computer during the drafting and revising stages of the writing process so they can easily add, delete, or rearrange details.

Responding and Revising

Have students work with partners to review their drafts for language and organization. Offer the following evaluation and revision tips. Then have students revise their work.

- Is the connection clear between the animal's eventual use and its training? If not, the writer should make clear the link between them.
- Is the report unified and coherent? If not, the writer should improve the outline's organization and should supply appropriate transitions. (See the Language/Literature Link below.)

STUDENT SELF-ASSESSMENT OPTION   Students may use the Writing Self-Assessment Checklist in the *Portfolio Teacher's Guide.* Suggest that as they use the checklist, they focus on the organization of the research report and on their transitional expressions.

Proofreading

Offer these tips to help students proofread their draft and make changes:

- If you quote an authority in your report, put the expert's words in quotation marks.
- Check to see whether you have used the correct style in listing your sources.

Publishing

Discuss publishing options with students. Some students may wish to submit their reports to the local ASPCA or a similar organization and then save their reports in their reading/writing portfolios.

LANGUAGE/LITERATURE LINK

Checking for Unity and Coherence

Explain that in a unified work, the details support the main idea, and the transitions are smooth. For an example of unified writing, turn to page 324 of "At Home with the Titan of the Trail." Have students read the first three paragraphs and discuss how the writer uses facts, figures, and description to create a single image—that of a bare and isolated place with few creature comforts. Suggest that students check their own paragraphs to make sure the details build to a central idea.

Speaking Option

TV BROADCAST   You may want to adapt the *Writer's Workshop* so that students can present their research report as a TV broadcast. Have students follow the guidelines offered for Prewriting, Drafting, and Responding and Revising. Suggest that students pretend to be newscasters, filming a segment of a TV show on the training of working animals. Give students the following speaking tips to help them with their broadcasts:

- Look at the camera, not down at your notes.
- Make your important points within the time constraints.
- Keep your facial expressions and your gestures natural.
- Speak with confidence.

Have students hold a "mock" microphone as they broadcast their report.

Searching

Have students read the introduction and the selection titles on Student Anthology page 333. Then ask students how the illustration relates to the theme "Searching." You might ask, for example, "What might someone search for in his or her reflection?" Ask students if they have ever heard of *Roots* and its author, Alex Haley. Encourage speculation on the subject of the search in "Mister Kinte!" Ask why the poems about freedom of choice might entail a similar search.

PACING Although you may need to adapt to the individual needs of the students in your classes, this theme has been designed to take about two weeks to complete.

332

Management Options

THE LITERATURE-BASED CLASSROOM Providing a literature-rich curriculum creates unique classroom management challenges. Some management options for the selections in this theme follow.

PULL-OUT SKILLS GROUPS Many of your students may not need the Learning Through Literature review lessons on figurative language and on using facts and opinions to identify the author's purpose and viewpoint. You may wish to have these students begin an Integrated Curriculum activity while you work with small groups on the review lessons.

THEME

SEARCHING

Some challenges require only physical strength. Others require emotional stability and determination as well. Searching for one's identity is one challenge that may require all three.

C O N T E N T S

MISTER KINTE!
by Alex Haley

WORDS FROM THE AUTHOR:
ALEX HALEY

FREEDOM OF CHOICE: EIGHT POEMS

STUDENTS AT RISK
Have students work in small groups to preview the selection and formulate questions about what they hope to learn when they read "Mister Kinte!" Then have the group cooperatively read and discuss the selection.

GIFTED AND TALENTED
Suggest that students choose fine arts illustrations for favorite poems or for poems they have written. Provide a place for students to display the poems and illustrations. Also see the *Challenge Cards.*

SPECIAL EDUCATION STUDENTS
Pre-record selection passages. Invite students with low vision to listen to the passages and take notes. This will provide students with additional practice following the Learning Through Literature lesson on taking notes as well as strengthen their listening skills.

LIMITED ENGLISH PROFICIENT STUDENTS
Some students may have difficulty understanding the poems in this theme. Pair students with English-fluent students and have them read the poems cooperatively, helping each other with any words and phrases they find difficult.

ENCOURAGING PEER BOOK CHATS   You may want to help students schedule times when they can meet in small groups for informal discussions of books they have read or are currently reading. Groups of four or five students may be able to meet in corners of the room while you are working on skills with others. Book chat discussions should be interactive and spontaneous, but students might also take time beforehand to think about specific ideas they would like to share.

READING/WRITING PORTFOLIO   Instruct students to keep in their portfolios their writing responses to the theme selections. Remind them also to add to their personal journals notes on their independent reading.

MISTER KINTE!

by Alex Haley

ALEX HALEY (1921–1992) first heard the story of his family's history at his grandparents' home in Henning, Tennessee. At seventeen, he joined the U.S. Coast Guard; after finishing all available reading material on the ship, he began writing stories. He explains, "The idea that one could roll a blank sheet of paper into a typewriter and write something on it that other people would care to read challenged, intrigued, exhilarated me—and does to this day." *Roots: The Saga of an American Family,* published in 1976, made Alex Haley famous.

OTHER BOOKS ABOUT CONNECTIONS

Going Home by Nicholas Mohr. Dial, 1986.
EASY

Her Own Song by Ellen Howard. Atheneum, 1988.
AVERAGE

My Name Is Not Angelica by Scott O'Dell. Houghton Mifflin, 1989. AVERAGE

The Return by Sonia Levitin. Atheneum, 1986.
AVERAGE

"The idea that one could . . . write something . . . that other people would care to read . . . exhilarated me."

SELECTION SUMMARY
Alex Haley recounts how he set out to research family stories about an African ancestor named "Kin-tay." A few fragments of African words led Haley to a language, Mandinka, and then to the part of Africa where it is spoken. There he met a *griot,* a man who memorizes and recites the history of a clan, and was astonished to hear him tell the same story Haley's American relatives had told. Haley was then warmly welcomed as a member of the Kinte clan.

LESSON PLANNER			
	Materials	**Integrated Curriculum**	**Meeting Individual Needs**
1 READING LITERATURE pp. 333B–347	Student Anthology pp. 334–347 Transparency 19 Second-Language Support Manual Practice Book p. 102 Integrated Spelling p. 49 Integrated Spelling T.E. pp. 68–69 Response Card 7: Free Response	Spelling Spelling Pretest Spelling-Vocabulary Connection (the sounds /k/ and /kw/)	Second-Language Support Vocabulary 333C Strategic Reading 333D, 339 Cooperative Reading 334, 346
2 RESPONDING TO LITERATURE pp. 347A–347D	Writer's Journal p. 64 Practice Book p. 103 Integrated Spelling p. 50 Integrated Spelling T.E. pp. 68–69	Vocabulary Workshop Reviewing Key Words Extending Vocabulary Writing About the Literature Speaking/Listening Spelling Review	Cooperative Learning 347B, 347C, 347D
3 LEARNING THROUGH LITERATURE pp. 347E–347L	Second-Language Support Manual Practice Book pp. 104–107	Math/Social Studies Art Social Studies Science Multicultural	Challenge 347F, 347H, 347I, 347J Second-Language Support 347F, 347H Cooperative Learning 347H, 347I, 347J, 347K

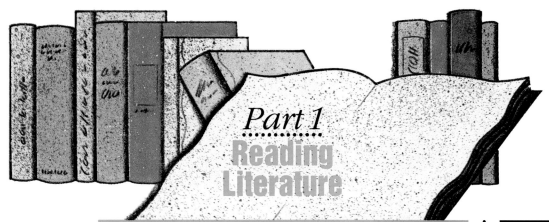

Part 1
Reading Literature

Building Background

Access prior knowledge and develop vocabulary concepts.

Tell students that they will be reading about a man who researches his family tree. Remind students that most families in America came originally from somewhere else. Begin the following web on the board. Invite students to suggest ways people can find out about their own roots.

family stories — relatives

older people — **Searching for Roots** — family albums

libraries — public records

Have students quickwrite sentences.

Ask students to choose something of interest from their own or someone else's family history and write a few sentences about it. Students may volunteer to share their anecdotes.

Vocabulary Strategies

Introduce Key Words and strategies.

Tell students that "Mister Kinte!" may contain unfamiliar words. Display Transparency 19, or write the paragraph on the board. Have students read the paragraph silently and use vocabulary strategies to figure out the meanings of the underlined words. Ask a volunteer to read the paragraph aloud. Provide help with pronunciation if necessary.

Transparency 19   Key Words

Lee tried to ignore the cacophony of scraping and banging that came intermittently from outside, each period of silence a relief from the noise. She was entranced by the wall hieroglyphics. Until now, this picture writing had been undeciphered, its message unknown. Now Lee had a thesis. She believed the marks told the chronicles of a lost tribe, its entire history, and showed the lineage from which its rulers came. Her idea had many ramifications. For one thing, it might lead to a generic way of reading all such writing.

CULTURAL AWARENESS

To help students appreciate the cultural background and setting of "Mister Kinte!" share with them the information under Cultural Background/Setting on page 335.

KEY WORDS DEFINED

cacophony harsh sound

intermittently periodically

entranced fascinated

hieroglyphics picture writing

undeciphered not decoded or understood

thesis unproved idea

chronicles historical accounts

lineage ancestry

ramifications implications

generic general

Check students' understanding.

Have students demonstrate their understanding of the Key Words by selecting the Key Word that fits each category of words. STRATEGY: SYNONYMS

1. accounts, histories, _____ (*chronicles*)
2. symbols, signs, _____ (*hieroglyphics*)
3. charmed, fascinated, _____ (*entranced*)
4. occasionally, periodically, _____ (*intermittently*)
5. ancestry, descent, _____ (*lineage*)
6. typical, general, _____ (*generic*)
7. implications, extensions, _____ (*ramifications*)
8. noise, discord, _____ (*cacophony*)
9. proposal, unproved idea, _____ (*thesis*)
10. unknown, undecoded, _____ (*undeciphered*)

After discussing the Key Words with students, encourage them to add Key Words such as *chronicles* and *lineage* to the web they completed in Building Background.

Integrate spelling with vocabulary.

SPELLING-VOCABULARY CONNECTION *Integrated Spelling* page 49 reinforces **spellings of words with the /k/ and /kw/ sounds,** including the Key Words *cacophony, chronicles, generic,* and *ramification.*

SECOND-LANGUAGE SUPPORT Encourage students to use structural analysis to decode those Key Words that have prefixes, suffixes, or inflectional endings. Have them work with a peer tutor to identify affixes and examine how those word parts affect meaning. (See *Second-Language Support Manual.*)

PRACTICE BOOK page 102: Reinforcing Key Words

INTEGRATED SPELLING page 49: Writing and spelling words with the /k/ and /kw/ sounds

NOTE: These pages may be completed now or after students have read the selection.

• • • MISTER KINTE! • • •

Name _____

A. Read the paragraphs. Use the context clues to fill in the missing words. Choose from the words in the box, and write them on the lines.

| cacophony | lineage | generic | undeciphered | ramifications |
| entranced | hieroglyphics | thesis | chronicles | intermittently |

My mother has always been interested in history. In fact, she is positively ___entranced___ by the subject. It all began when her father brought home a game from the Metropolitan Museum of Art that taught children to write ___hieroglyphics___. The results, or ___ramifications___, of the gift were startling. As a young child, my mother began to study the ___chronicles___, or records, of ancient civilizations. She became interested in tracing the ___lineage___ of kings and queens, noting which families produced the best leaders.

Later, her interests expanded to include a study of ancient languages. Over the years, when her schedule permitted, my mother ___intermittently___ left school and took part in archaeological digs. She planned to write her ___thesis___ on ancient languages and needed to narrow her field of study to one particular ___undeciphered___ language that had not been translated. My mother told me that at the dig sites she heard a ___cacophony___ of languages because the workers came from many countries. Finally, she noticed a sound that is ___generic___ to many languages, ancient and modern. Many scholars think she may have found an important key to the history of language.

B. Match each word with its definition. Write the letter for the definition on the line.

1. __e__ cacophony   a. not translated into plain language
2. __d__ lineage   b. records of historical events
3. __c__ generic   c. characteristic of a whole group
4. __a__ undeciphered   d. line of descent, ancestry
5. __b__ chronicles   e. an unpleasant mixture of sounds

102 **Vocabulary**   Practice Book • ENDLESS WORLDS

Practice Book

INTEGRATED SPELLING
The Sounds /k/ and /kw/

Name _____

Read the Spelling Words. Write them on a separate sheet of paper. Check your spelling.

SPELLING STRATEGY

Here are five ways to spell the sound /k/: **c** as in **can**, **k** as in **peak**, **cc** as in **occupy**, **ck** as in **flock**, and **ch** as in **character**. The sound /kw/ is usually spelled with **qu**, as in **banquet**.

To spell a word that has the /k/ or /kw/ sound, first think of the possible spellings for that sound. Then try to picture the word in your mind. Also try writing the word with the various spellings of the /k/ or /kw/ sound. Which spelling *looks* correct? If these strategies don't work, look up the word in a dictionary.

Which Spelling Word uses both a *c* and a *qu* to spell /kw/?
___acquainted___

Which word uses only a *qu* to spell /kw/?
___quest___

Which word has *two* /k/ sounds, both spelled with *c*?
___cacophony___

Which other three words use *c* to spell the /k/ sound?
___colleague___
___generic___
___ramification___

Which word spells /k/ with *cc*?
___unaccustomed___

Which word uses *ch* to spell /k/?
___chronicle___

Which word spells /k/ with a *ck*?
___thickening___

| **SPELLING WORDS** |
| acquainted |
| cacophony |
| chronicle |
| colleague |
| generic |
| lineage |
| quest |
| ramification |
| thickening |
| unaccustomed |

MEMORY JOGGER

The word **lineage** gives many spellers trouble because both vowels in the middle are pronounced. This Memory Jogger may help you remember how to spell **lineage**.

Your **lineage** is your family **line**, traced through the **ages**.

ENDLESS WORLDS • "Mister Kinte!"   49

Integrated Spelling

Using the K-W-L Strategy

Have students preview the literature.

Remind students that an autobiography is a person's story of his or her own life. Have a volunteer explain how to preview an autobiography. (by reading the title, author's name, and introduction, if any; by looking at the illustrations; and by reading the captions) Have students follow the previewing suggestions.

Introduce the K-W-L chart.

Write the following headings on the board: *What I Know, What I Want to Know, What I Learned.*

PERSONAL JOURNAL   Have students copy the headings in their personal journals, or have them use *Practice Book* page 103. (See page 347B in this Teacher's Edition.) Tell students to use the ideas they generated in Building Background to help them fill in column one. Tell students to use the second column to write questions for which they want to find answers. (Students will return to the chart after reading, in Summarizing the Literature.) Students' charts may resemble the following:

K-W-L CHART

What I Know	What I Want to Know	What I Learned
People find out about their ancestors by doing research. African people were kidnapped and brought to America as slaves.	What made the author try to find out about his ancestor?	

Setting a Purpose

Have students set purposes.

Have students use the questions in the second column of the chart to set a purpose for reading the excerpt. Invite them to share their purposes with classmates.

Model purpose-setting, if necessary.

If students have difficulty setting a purpose for reading, model the thinking process:

> **My purpose for reading will be to find out what discoveries Haley made about his ancestry and how they affected him. I will also look for answers to the questions on my K-W-L chart.**

OPTIONS FOR READING

Independent Reading
Have students read the selection silently with their purpose for reading in mind. Suggest that after reading each section, they add notes to the third column of their charts.

Guided Reading
Follow the Guided Reading suggestions that appear on pages 334, 341 and 346. These suggestions model strategic reading.

Cooperative Reading
Suggestions for Cooperative Reading appear on pages 334 and 346.

Numbered Annotations
Use the numbered annotations beside the Student Anthology pages to heighten students' appreciation of the narrative.

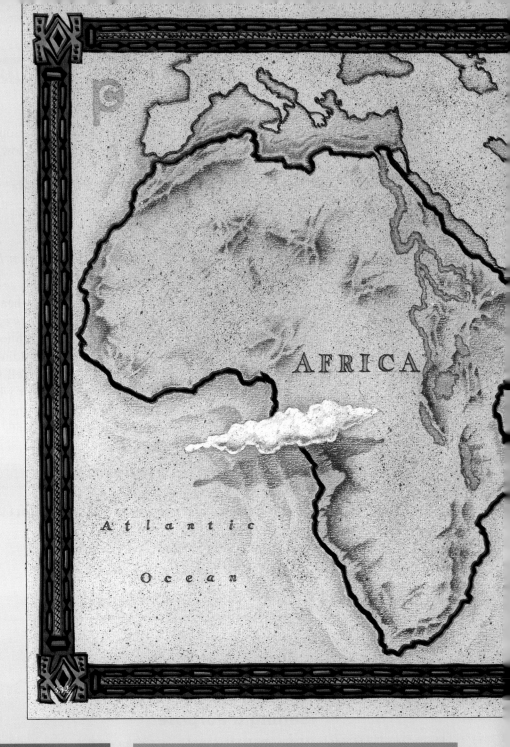

Guided Reading

SET PURPOSE/PREDICT: PAGES 334–341 Have
students read to the break on page 341 to find out
what Alex Haley discovered about his ancestry.
Have students read silently, pausing from time to
time to note new questions and to state a new
purpose for reading. As students read, you may wish
to have them make notes and add questions to their
K-W-L charts.

Cooperative Reading

READER RESPONSE STRATEGY: PAGES 334–347
Have students work in pairs. Ask each pair to decide
whether they will read silently or aloud and how
frequently they will stop. At designated stopping
points, each member of the pair should respond
freely to what he or she has read so far. Have pairs
continue the procedure until they reach the end of
the selection. (Response Card 7: Free Response, on
page R68, gives complete directions for using the
strategy.)

MISTER KINTE!

from *Roots*
by Alex Haley

AWARD-WINNING
AUTHOR

*When he was a boy in Tennessee, Alex Haley's
grandmother and other relatives used to tell him stories
about their ancestors through the generations all the
way back to a man they called* the African. *The
following excerpt describes journalist Haley's attempts
to find out more about his ancestors and tells how his
discoveries led him to write* Roots, *which became a
best-selling book and popular TV series.*

illustrations by Clarence Porter

CULTURAL BACKGROUND/SETTING

When Alex Haley set out on his
search for his ancestral background,
he did not know if there was any
way to find out whether the family
stories he had heard were true. He
had assumed that because his
African ancestor had come to this
country as a slave and left no
written records, his family history
could never be traced. The setting
in this story changes continually as
the author's research takes him
around the world. An important part
of his search takes place in the
small country of The Gambia (also
known as simply "Gambia") in
West Africa, from which Haley's
ancestor "Kin-tay" came.

The Gambia is one of the smallest
independent nations in Africa. It lies
on the western coast, between 13°
and 14° north latitude, and is
surrounded by the larger country of
Senegal. This area belonged to the
powerful Mali Empire during the
thirteenth, fourteenth, and fifteenth
centuries. During the sixteenth
century the coast of The Gambia
became a center of the English and
Portuguese slave trades.

1 DESCRIPTION
Explain how Champollion was able to figure out the meaning of the hieroglyphics on the Rosetta Stone. *(He matched unknown characters and symbols with the known Greek letters and explained that the three inscriptions said the same thing.)*
INFERENTIAL: SUMMARIZING

2 EXPOSITORY TEXT: MAIN IDEA
What analogy, or comparison, does Alex Haley make? *(He compares the snatches of an unidentified language in his family's history with the once-unknown languages written on the Rosetta Stone.)*
INFERENTIAL: MAKING COMPARISONS

How was Alex Haley's family history like the Rosetta Stone? *(Both contained unknown languages. Both could be figured out by matching them with known information.)*
INFERENTIAL: MAKING COMPARISONS

ROOTS
The Saga of an American Family
ALEX HALEY

Soon, a magazine sent me on an assignment to London. Between appointments, utterly fascinated with a wealth of history everywhere, I missed scarcely a guided tour anywhere within London's area during the next several days. Poking about one day in the British Museum, I found myself looking at something I'd heard of vaguely: The Rosetta Stone. I don't know why, it just about entranced me. I got a book there in the museum library to learn more about it.

Discovered in the Nile delta, I learned, the stone's face had chiseled into it three separate texts: one in known Greek characters, the second in a then-unknown set of characters, the third in the ancient hieroglyphics, which it had been assumed no one ever would be able to translate. But a French scholar, Jean Champollion, successively matched, character for character, both the unknown text and the hieroglyphics with the known Greek text, and he offered a thesis that the texts read the same. Essentially, he had cracked the mystery of the previously undeciphered hieroglyphics in which much of mankind's earliest history was recorded.

The key that had unlocked a door into the past fascinated me. I seemed to feel it had some special personal significance, but I couldn't imagine what. I was on a plane returning to the United States when an idea hit me. Using language chiseled into stone, the French scholar had deciphered a historic unknown by matching it with that which was known. That presented me a rough analogy: In the oral history that Grandma, Aunt Liz, Aunt Plus, Cousin Georgia, and the others had always told on the boyhood Henning front

porch, I had an unknown quotient in those strange words or sounds passed on by the African. I got to thinking about them: "Kin-tay," he had said, was his name. "*Ko*" he had called a guitar. "Kamby Bolongo" he had called a river in Virginia. They were mostly sharp, angular sounds, with *k* predominating. These sounds probably had undergone some changes across the generations of being passed down, yet unquestionably they represented phonetic snatches of whatever was the specific tongue spoken by my African ancestor who was a family legend. My plane from London was circling to land at New York with me wondering: What specific African tongue was it? Was there any way in the world that maybe I could find out?

Now the thing was where, what, how could I pursue those strange phonetic sounds that it was always said our African ancestor had spoken. It seemed obvious that I had to reach as wide a range of actual Africans as I possibly could, simply because so many different tribal tongues are spoken in Africa. There in New York City, I began doing what seemed logical: I began arriving at the United Nations around quitting time; the elevators were spilling out people who were thronging through the lobby on their way home. It wasn't hard to spot the Africans, and every one I was able to stop, I'd tell my sounds to. Within a couple of weeks, I guess I had stopped about two dozen Africans, each of whom had given me a quick look, a quick listen, and then took off. I can't say I blame them—me trying to communicate some African sounds in a Tennessee accent.

Increasingly frustrated, I had a long talk with George Sims, with whom I'd grown up in Henning, and who is a master researcher. After a few days, George brought me a list of about a dozen people academically renowned for their knowledge of African linguistics. One whose background intrigued me quickly was a Belgian, Dr. Jan Vansina. After study at the University of London's School of African and Oriental Studies, he had done his early work living in African villages and written a book called *La Tradition Orale*. I telephoned Dr. Vansina where he now taught at the University of Wisconsin, and he gave me an appointment to see him. It was a Wednesday morning that I flew to Madison, Wisconsin, motivated by my intense curiosity about some strange phonetic sounds . . . and with no dream in this world of what was about to start happening. . . .

3 EXPOSITORY TEXT: SEQUENCE
What language problem did Alex Haley have to solve first? *(He had to identify a specific African language.)*
INFERENTIAL: DETERMINING MAIN IDEA

Why might this have been a difficult problem to solve? *(Accept reasonable responses: There are many African languages; most people in America are not familiar with African languages; even those who are probably know only one or two.)*
INFERENTIAL: SPECULATING

4 AUTHOR'S CRAFT
How do the author's words foreshadow, or give a hint of, what is to come? *(He says he had "no dream in this world" of what would start happening. This suggests that he is going to tell us about something important that took place.)*
INFERENTIAL: MAKING PREDICTIONS

Vocabulary Strategy Draw students' attention to the use of the word *tongue* in line 8 and again in the first complete paragraph on this page. Ask them to use context clues to figure out its meaning. (language) Point out that even a familiar word may have more than one meaning, so it is always essential to note the context in which a word is used. STRATEGY: MULTIPLE-MEANING WORDS

Cultural Awareness Explain that *La Tradition Orale* (last paragraph) is French (a language spoken in Belgium) for *The Oral Tradition*. Make certain all students understand that *oral tradition*, or *oral history*, refers to information passed down by word of mouth rather than in writing. You may wish to point out that Africa has a particularly strong oral tradition.

5 EXPOSITORY TEXT: MAIN IDEA AND DETAILS
Summarize Dr. Vansina's explanation for sounds Haley remembered. *(The words come from a language called Mandinka, in which* ko *could mean "a stringed instrument," and* Kamby Bolongo *could mean the "Gambia River.")*
INFERENTIAL: SUMMARIZING

6 FORESHADOWING
How does the author build suspense by suggesting that the next thing to happen will be important and unusual? *(He says he had the feeling of being watched by his ancestors.)*
INFERENTIAL: DRAWING CONCLUSIONS

That evening in the Vansinas' living room, I told him every syllable I could remember of the family narrative heard since little boyhood—recently buttressed by Cousin Georgia in Kansas City. Dr. Vansina, after listening intently throughout, then began asking me questions. Being an oral historian, he was particularly interested in the physical transmission of the narrative down across generations.

We talked so late that he invited me to spend the night, and the next morning Dr. Vansina, with a very serious expression on his face, said, "I wanted to sleep on it. The ramifications of phonetic sounds preserved down across your family's generations can be immense." He said that he had been on the phone with a colleague Africanist, Dr. Philip Curtin; they both felt certain that the sounds I'd conveyed to him were from the "Mandinka" tongue. I'd never heard that word; he told me that it was the language spoken by the Mandingo people. Then he guess-translated certain of the sounds. One of them probably meant cow or cattle; another probably meant the baobab tree, generic in West Africa. The word *ko*, he said, could refer to the *kora*, one of the Mandingo people's oldest stringed instruments, made of a halved large dried gourd covered with

5 goatskin, with a long neck, and twenty-one strings with a bridge. An enslaved Mandingo might relate the *kora* visually to some among the types of stringed instruments that U.S. slaves had.

The most involved sound I had heard and brought was Kamby Bolongo, my ancestor's sound to his daughter Kizzy as he had pointed to the Mattaponi River in Spotsylvania County, Virginia. Dr. Vansina said that without question, bolongo meant, in the Mandinka tongue, a moving water, as a river; preceded by *Kamby*, it could indicate the Gambia River.

I'd never heard of it.

An incident happened that would build my feelings—especially

6 as more uncanny things occurred—that, yes, they were up there watching. . . .

I was asked to speak at a seminar held at Utica College, Utica, New York. Walking down a hallway with the professor who had invited me, I said I'd just flown in from Washington and why I'd been there. "The Gambia? If I'm not mistaken, someone mentioned recently that an outstanding student from that country is over at Hamilton."

The old, distinguished Hamilton College was maybe a half hour's drive away, in Clinton, New York. Before I could finish asking, a Professor Charles Todd said, "You're talking about Ebou Manga." Consulting a course roster, he told me where I could find him in an agricultural economics class. Ebou Manga was small of build, with careful eyes, a reserved manner, and black as soot. He tentatively confirmed my sounds, clearly startled to have heard me uttering them. Was Mandinka his home tongue? "No, although I am familiar with it." He was a Wolof, he said. In his dormitory room, I told him about my quest. We left for The Gambia at the end of the following week.

Arriving in Dakar, Senegal, the next morning, we caught a light plane to small Yundum Airport in The Gambia. In a passenger van, we rode into the capital city of Banjul (then Bathurst). Ebou and his father, Alhaji Manga—Gambians are mostly Moslem—assembled a small group of men knowledgeable in their small country's history, who met with me in the lounge of the Atlantic Hotel. As I had told Dr. Vansina in Wisconsin, I told these men the family narrative that had come down across the generations.

When I had finished, they said almost with wry amusement, "Well, of course 'Kamby Bolongo' would mean Gambia River; anyone would know that." I told them hotly that no, a great many people *wouldn't* know it! Then they showed a much greater interest that my 1760s ancestor had insisted his name was "Kin-tay." "Our country's oldest villages tend to be named for the families that settled those villages centuries ago," they said. Sending for a map, pointing, they said, "Look, here is the village of Kinte-Kundah. And not too far from it, the village of Kinte-Kundah Janneh-Ya."

Then they told me something of which I'd never have dreamed: of very old men, called *griots,* still to be found in the older back-country villages, men who were in effect living, walking archives of oral history. A senior *griot* would be a man usually in his late sixties or early seventies; below him would be progressively younger *griots*—and apprenticing boys, so a boy would be exposed to those *griots'* particular line of narrative for forty or fifty years before he could qualify as a senior *griot,* who told on special occasions the centuries-old histories of villages, of clans, of families, of great heroes. Throughout the whole of black Africa such oral chronicles had been handed down

7

7 NARRATION: EVENTS
What can you predict from what Alex Haley tells you about *griots*? What clues lead you to your prediction? *(Accept reasonable responses: A* griot *might provide details of Haley's African history dating back to his ancestor in the 1760s. Clues include the fact a* griot *can tell centuries-old family histories.)*
METACOGNITIVE: MAKING PREDICTIONS

Second-Language Support
Make sure that students understand what a *griot* is and what one does (paragraph 4). You may want to have a peer tutor work with nonnative speakers to look up and discuss the meaning in context of such words as *archives, apprenticing, forefathers,* and *facets.*

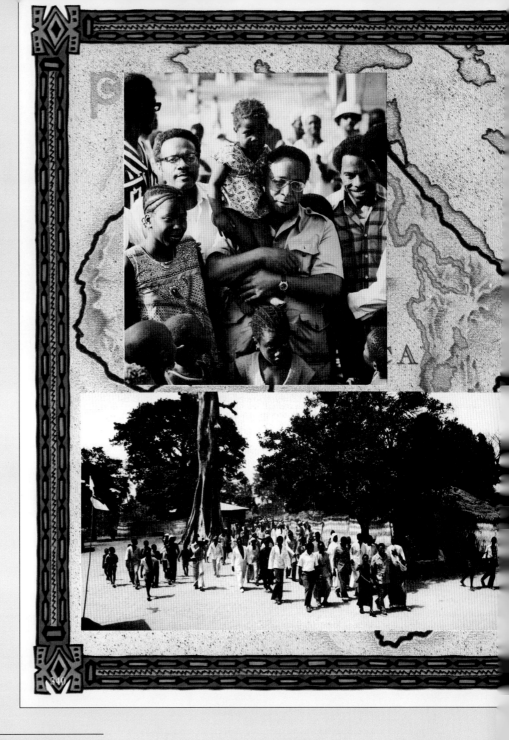

Informal Assessment   Informally assessing
whether students are fulfilling the established
purpose for reading involves asking questions like
the following:

- Has this selection told you what you need to
  know to fulfill your purpose for reading it?
- If so, what ideas and details were the most
  important in helping you do that?
- If not, what did the selection fail to tell you?

This assessment will indicate how well students are
focusing as they read, and it will encourage them to
watch for details that fulfill their purpose.

since the time of the ancient forefathers, I was informed, and there were certain legendary *griots* who could narrate facets of African history literally for as long as three days without ever repeating themselves.

Seeing how astounded I was, these Gambian men reminded me that every living person ancestrally goes back to some time and some place where no writing existed; and then human memories and mouths and ears were the only ways those human beings could store and relay information. They said that we who live in the Western culture are so conditioned to the "crutch of print" that few among us comprehend what a trained memory is capable of.

Since my forefather had said his name was "Kin-tay"—properly spelled "Kinte," they said—and since the Kinte clan was old and well known in The Gambia, they promised to do what they could to find a *griot* who might be able to assist my search.

Back in the United States, I began devouring books on African history. It grew quickly into some kind of obsession to correct my ignorance concerning the earth's second-largest continent. It embarrasses me to this day that up to then my images about Africa had been largely derived or inferred from Tarzan movies and my very little authentic knowledge had come from only occasional leafings through the *National Geographic*. All of a sudden now, after reading all day, I'd sit on the edge of my bed at night studying a map of Africa, memorizing the different countries' relative positions and the principal waters where slave ships had operated.

After some weeks, a registered letter came from The Gambia; it suggested that when possible, I should come back.

I again visited Cousin Georgia in Kansas City—something had urged me to do so, and I found her quite ill. But she was thrilled to hear both what I had learned and what I hoped to learn. She wished me Godspeed, and I flew then to Africa.

The same men with whom I had previously talked told me now in a rather matter-of-fact manner that they had caused word to be put out in the back country, and that a *griot* very knowledgeable of the Kinte clan had indeed been found—his name, they said, was

◀ Author Alex Haley returned to the village of Joffure after the publication of *Roots*.

8 FIGURATIVE LANGUAGE
What does the phrase *crutch of print* mean? What attitude on the part of the Gambians does the phrase reveal? *(The Gambians are saying that people in the West depend on the printed word, rather than on their minds or memories. This metaphoric use of the word* crutch *connotes leaning on something when such support is not really needed; the Gambians are suggesting that their way is better.)*
INFERENTIAL: MAKING COMPARISONS

9 LITERARY FORMS: AUTOBIOGRAPHY
What is influencing Alex Haley's actions at this point? *(Haley's first trip to Africa has created a thirst for knowledge about his ancestral home.)* Point out that an autobiography often discusses important events or influences in a person's life.
INFERENTIAL: DETERMINING CAUSE-EFFECT

Guided Reading

MONITOR COMPREHENSION: PAGES 334–341 **What did Alex Haley discover as he researched his ancestry?** (He learned that the bits of African speech that had been passed down in his family are from a language called Mandinka; that the name *Kinte* is from a large and important African clan; and, most amazingly, that there are men called *griots* who can recite hundreds of years of clan history from memory.) STRATEGIC READING: RETURNING TO PURPOSE

What steps did Alex Haley take in researching his ancestry? (First, he identified the sounds he knew. Then he met someone who directed him to a student from Africa. He traveled to The Gambia with the student and talked to other men from that country. They told him that he needed to find a *griot*, or oral historian, from his clan.) STRATEGIC READING: SUMMARIZING

SET PURPOSE/PREDICT: PAGES 341–347 Have students read the rest of the selection to determine what additional information Haley learned about his ancestry.

10 FORESHADOWING
How does Alex Haley let you know
that the climax, or high point, of
his narrative is approaching? *(He*
says that he had "the peak
experience" of his life in the back
country of West Africa.)
INFERENTIAL: DRAWING CONCLUSIONS

11 DESCRIPTION
How did Alex Haley recognize the
***griot*?** *(Haley saw that he had an*
aura of "somebodiness.")
LITERAL: NOTING IMPORTANT DETAILS

What do you think Haley means by
this description? *(Accept*
reasonable responses: The griot
probably had an air of importance
and dignity and commanded
respect from the villagers.)
INFERENTIAL: DRAWING CONCLUSIONS

"Kebba Kanji Fofana." I was ready to have a fit. "Where *is* he?" They looked at me oddly: "He's in his village."

I discovered that if I intended to see this *griot*, I was going to have to do something I'd never have dreamed I'd ever be doing—organizing what seemed, at least to me then, a kind of mini-safari! It took me three days of negotiating through unaccustomed endless African palaver finally to hire a launch to get upriver; to rent a lorry and a vehicle to take supplies by a roundabout land route; to hire finally a total of fourteen people, including three interpreters and four musicians, who had told me that the old *griots* in the back country wouldn't talk without music in the background.

10 There is an expression called "the peak experience"—that which, emotionally, nothing in your life ever transcends. I've had mine, that first day in the back country of black West Africa.

When we got within sight of Juffure, the children who were playing outside gave the alert, and the people came flocking from their huts. It's a village of only about seventy people. Like most back-country villages, it was still very much as it was two hundred years ago, with its circular mud houses and their conical thatched roofs. Among the people as they gathered was a small man wearing **11** an off-white robe, a pillbox hat over an aquiline-featured black face, and about him was an aura of "somebodiness" until I knew he was the man we had come to see and hear.

As the three interpreters left our party to converge upon him, the seventy-odd other villagers gathered closely around me, in a kind of horseshoe pattern, three or four deep all around; had I stuck out my arms, my fingers would have touched the nearest ones on either side. They were all staring at me. The eyes just raked me. Their foreheads were furrowed with their very intensity of staring. A kind of visceral surging or a churning sensation started up deep inside me; bewildered, I was wondering what on earth was this . . . then in a little while it was rather as if some full-gale force of realization rolled in on me: Many times in my life I had been among crowds of people, but never where *every one was jet black!*

Rocked emotionally, my eyes dropped downward as we tend to do when we're uncertain, insecure, and my glance fell upon my own hands' brown complexion. This time more quickly than before, and

even harder, another gale-force emotion hit me: I felt myself some variety of a hybrid . . . I felt somehow impure among the pure; it was a terribly shaming feeling. About then, abruptly the old man left the interpreters. The people immediately also left me now to go crowding about him. **12**

One of my interpreters came up quickly and whispered in my ear, "They stare at you so much because they have never here seen a black American." When I grasped the significance, I believe that hit me harder than what had already happened. They hadn't been looking at me as an individual, but I represented in their eyes a symbol of the twenty-five millions of us black people whom they had never seen, who lived beyond an ocean.

The people were clustered thickly about the old man, all of them intermittently flicking glances toward me as they talked animatedly in their Mandinka tongue. After a while, the old man turned, walked briskly through the people, past my three interpreters, and right up to me. His eyes piercing into mine, seeming to feel I should understand his Mandinka, he expressed what they had all decided they *felt* concerning those unseen millions of us who lived in those places that had been slave ships' destinations—and the translation came: "We have been told by the forefathers that there are many of us from this place who are in exile in that place called America—and in other places."

The old man sat down, facing me, as the people hurriedly gathered behind him. Then he began to recite for me the ancestral history of the Kinte clan, as it had been passed along orally down across centuries from the forefathers' time. It was not merely conversational, but more as if a scroll were being read; for the still, silent villagers, it was clearly a formal occasion. The *griot* would speak, bending forward from the waist, his body rigid, his neck cords standing out, his words seeming almost physical objects. After a sentence or two, seeming to go limp, he would lean back, listening to an interpreter's translation. Spilling from the *griot's* head came an incredibly complex Kinte clan lineage that reached back across many generations: who married whom; who had what children; what children then married whom; then their offspring. It was all just unbelievable. I was struck not only by the profusion of details, but

12 NARRATION: CHARACTERIZATION
How did Alex Haley feel as he met the villagers? What caused his emotional response? (*Accept reasonable responses: He was almost overcome by his feelings, especially the feeling of being different. The villagers were staring at him, and suddenly he was sharply aware that he is only part African.*)
LITERAL: RECOGNIZING MAIN IDEA

How does the superimposition of the photographs onto the map of Africa, which also appears on the first page of the selection, underscore Haley's purpose?
(Accept reasonable responses: (Haley is visually associated with Africa, his ancestral home.)
INFERENTIAL: DRAWING CONCLUSIONS

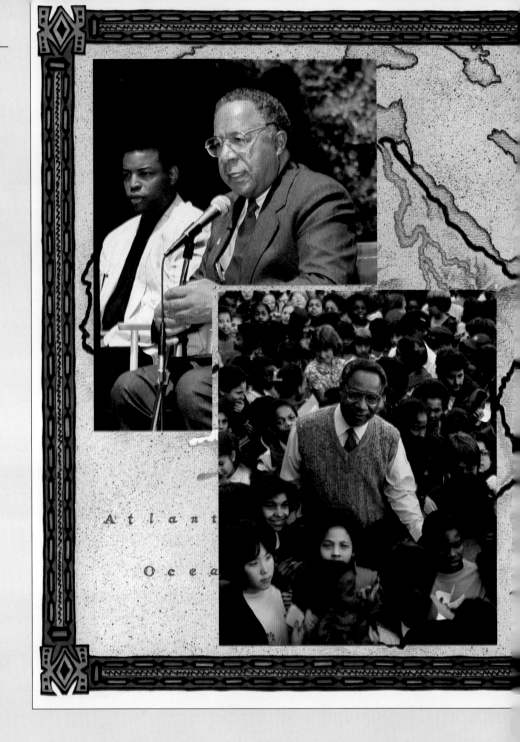

also by the narrative's biblical style, something like: "—and so-and-so took as a wife so-and-so, and begat . . . and begat . . . and begat . . ." He would next name each begat's eventual spouse, or spouses, and their averagely numerous offspring, and so on. To date things the *griot* linked them to events, such as "—in the year of the big water" —a flood—"he slew a water buffalo." To determine the calendar date, you'd have to find out when that particular flood occurred.

The old *griot* had talked for nearly two hours up to then, and perhaps fifty times the narrative had included some detail about someone whom he had named. Now after he had just named those four sons, again he appended a detail, and the interpreter translated—

"About the time the King's soldiers came"—another of the *griot's* time-fixing references—"the eldest of these four sons, Kunta, went away from his village to chop wood . . . and he was never seen again . . ." And the *griot* went on with his narrative.

I sat as if I were carved of stone. My blood seemed to have congealed. This man whose lifetime had been in this back-country African village had no way in the world to know that he had just echoed what I had heard all through my boyhood years on my grandma's front porch in Henning, Tennessee . . . of an African who always had insisted that his name was "Kin-tay"; who had called a guitar a "*ko*," and a river within the state of Virginia, "Kamby Bolongo"; and who had been kidnapped into slavery while not far from his village, chopping wood to make himself a drum.

I managed to fumble from my dufflebag my basic notebook, whose first pages containing grandma's story I showed to an interpreter. After briefly reading, clearly astounded, he spoke rapidly while showing it to the old *griot*, who became agitated; he got up, exclaiming to the people, gesturing at my notebook in the interpreter's hands, and *they* all got agitated.

I don't remember hearing anyone giving an order, I only recall becoming aware that those seventy-odd people had formed a wide human ring around me, moving counterclockwise, chanting softly, loudly, softly; their bodies close together, they were lifting their knees high, stamping up reddish puffs of the dust. . . .

◀ Alex Haley with La Var Burton, star of the television series *Roots*. Alex Haley greets students.

---

13 EXPOSITORY TEXT: MAIN IDEA
Explain how, in this culture where written records are not kept, people have knowledge of who their ancestors are and when they lived. *(An oral historian, called a* griot, *in West Africa learns and recites the clan's lineage. People's lives are dated by being linked to events.)*
LITERAL: RECOGNIZING SEQUENCE

---

14 NARRATION: ACTIONS/EVENTS
Why was Alex Haley so struck by the *griot's* words about Kunta? What did they mean to him? *(He recognized the same story he had heard from his relatives. He realized that the story told in his family about his ancestor must be correct.)*
INFERENTIAL: DETERMINING MAIN IDEA

---

15 AUTHOR'S CRAFT
What sensory language does Alex Haley use to describe this event? What does his description help you do? *(Accept reasonable responses:* wide human ring; moving counterclockwise; chanting softly, loudly, softly; reddish puffs of dust; *the language helps the reader visualize the scene.)*
METACOGNITIVE: VISUALIZING

Oral Rereading   Invite students to read aloud the three paragraphs beginning with *I managed to fumble* . . . on page 345 and ending with . . . *and you are us* on page 346. This describes the villagers' ceremony showing their union with Haley. Encourage students to pay particular attention to the rich descriptive language and to try to visualize the scene as they read. Have students work in pairs to practice reading the passage. After they have practiced, ask volunteers to read their passages aloud. You may wish instead to have students choose other passages for rereading that had special meaning or value to them.

16 NARRATION: CLIMAX
What was the people's reason for shouting "Meester Kinte!" to Alex Haley? *(They, too, were excited by the news that a lost member of the clan had found them. Haley is a member of the Kinte clan, and they were acknowledging kinship.)*
METACOGNITIVE: DRAWING CONCLUSIONS

The woman who broke from the moving circle was one of about a dozen whose infant children were within cloth slings across their backs. Her jet-black face deeply contorting, the woman came charging toward me, her bare feet slapping the earth, and snatching her baby free, she thrust it at me almost roughly, the gesture saying "Take it!" . . . and I did, clasping the baby to me. Then she snatched away her baby; and another woman was thrusting her baby, then another, and another . . . until I had embraced probably a dozen babies. I wouldn't learn until maybe a year later, from a Harvard University professor, Dr. Jerome Bruner, a scholar of such matters, "You didn't know you were participating in one of the oldest ceremonies of humankind, called 'The laying on of hands'! In their way, they were telling you 'Through this flesh, which is us, we are you, and you are us!'"

Since we had come by the river, I wanted to return by land. As I sat beside the wiry young Mandingo driver who was leaving dust pluming behind us on the hot, rough, pitted, back-country road toward Banjul, there came from somewhere into my head a staggering awareness . . . that *if* any black American could be so blessed as I had been to know only a few ancestral clues—could he or she know *who* was either the paternal or maternal African ancestor or ancestors, and about *where* that ancestor lived when taken, and finally about *when* the ancestor was taken—then only those few clues might well see that black American able to locate some wizened old black *griot* whose narrative could reveal the black American's ancestral clan, perhaps even the very village.

My mind reeled with it all as we approached another, much larger village. Staring ahead, I realized that word of what had happened in Juffure must have left there well before I did. The driver slowing down, I could see this village's people thronging the road ahead; they were waving, amid their cacophony of crying out something; I stood up in the Land-Rover, waving back as they seemed grudging to open a path for the Land-Rover.

I guess we had moved a third of the way through the village when it suddenly registered in my brain what they were all crying out . . . the wizened, robed elders and younger men, the mothers and the naked tar-black children, they were all waving up to me;

Guided Reading

MONITOR COMPREHENSION: PAGES 341–347 **What discovery did Alex Haley make about his ancestry?** (He found that the family story was true and that his ancestor came from the village of Juffure.) STRATEGIC READING: RETURNING TO PURPOSE

What did Alex Haley learn about himself and his family? (He discovered that he has roots stretching back to a proud tradition in Africa.) STRATEGIC READING: SUMMARIZING

Cooperative Reading

READER RESPONSE STRATEGY: PAGES 334–347 After students finish the selection, have each student respond freely to the selection as a whole. Remind students to draw from their discussions during reading as they participate in the Responding to Literature activities on pages 347A–347B.

their expressions buoyant, beaming, all were crying out together, *"Meester Kinte! Meester Kinte!"*

Let me tell you something: I am a man. A sob hit me somewhere around my ankles; it came surging upward, and flinging my hands over my face, I was just bawling, as I hadn't since I was a baby. *"Meester Kinte!"* I just felt like I was weeping for all of history's incredible atrocities against fellow men, which seems to be mankind's greatest flaw. . . .

Flying homeward from Dakar, I decided to write a book. My own ancestors would automatically also be a symbolic saga of all African-descent people—who are without exception the seeds of someone like Kunta who was born and grew up in some black African village, someone who was captured and chained down in one of those slave ships that sailed them across the same ocean, into some succession of plantations, and since then a struggle for freedom.

17

THINK IT OVER

1. Explain how the Rosetta Stone played a big part in Alex Haley's decision to write Roots.
2. What is the "laying on of hands" ceremony? What is its significance?
3. What effect does the "crutch of print" have on memory in Western civilization?
4. Who are griots, and what is their role as historians? Explain why Alex Haley's visit to a griot was so complicated.
5. Consider the steps Haley took before he decided to write a book. How did each new discovery lead to the next?

18

WRITE

List several impressions that the African people may have had of Alex Haley.

19

Returning to the Purpose for Reading Have students summarize the discoveries Alex Haley made in his search for his roots. (Accept reasonable responses: He discovered a great deal about African cultures. He discovered the way history is passed down by *griots*. He also discovered the village from which his ancestor had come.)

17 NARRATION: RESOLUTION
Do you think Haley's decision to write about his experiences was a good one? *(Accept reasonable responses: Yes; his experience could encourage others to search for their roots.)*
CRITICAL: MAKING JUDGMENTS

18 THINK IT OVER
1. *Alex Haley thought that if the Rosetta Stone could be deciphered, the unknown sounds from his family's past might also.*
INFERENTIAL: MAKING COMPARISONS
2. *The Kinte women handed Haley their babies to show that he and they are all one family.*
LITERAL: NOTING IMPORTANT DETAILS
3. *According to the Africans that Haley met, it keeps people from developing their memories.*
INFERENTIAL: DRAWING CONCLUSIONS
4. Griots *are men trained to commit clan history to memory. To meet one, Haley had to arrange a difficult trip, requiring vehicles, supplies, interpreters, and musicians.*
INFERENTIAL: SUMMARIZING
5. *The Rosetta Stone led him to research the family words. He consulted a researcher, who put him in touch with a language expert. Chance led him to someone from The Gambia; that meeting led him to Africa, where a* griot *was found to help him. Finally, Haley decided to write his book.*
INFERENTIAL: DETERMINING SEQUENCE

19 WRITE
You may want to help students get started by having them note on a prewriting graphic ways in which Haley says he is different from the Africans he met.

Alex Haley	African People
trained to rely on print	*trained to rely on memory*

Accept reasonable responses. Students should use selection details to compare and contrast Haley and his African relatives.
INFERENTIAL: COMPARING AND CONTRASTING

NOTE Additional writing activities appear on page 347D.

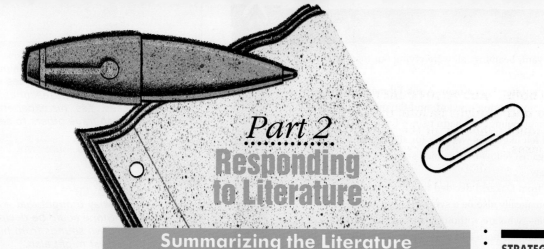

Part 2
Responding to Literature

Summarizing the Literature

Have students retell the selection and write a summary.

Invite students to summarize "Mister Kinte!" using their K-W-L charts. If they did not complete the chart, have them do so now. (See *Practice Book* page 103, on 347B.) Students may use their completed charts to retell the selection and write a brief summary statement.

K-W-L CHART

What I Know	What I Want to Know	What I Learned
People find out about their ancestors by doing research.	What made the author try to find out about his ancestor?	He got the idea from looking at the Rosetta Stone.
African people were kidnapped and brought to America as slaves.		

Appreciating Literature

Have students share personal responses.

Divide the class into small groups to discuss "Mister Kinte!" Provide general questions such as the following to help the groups get started:

- **Imagine that Alex Haley had not written *Roots* but that another author had written about Haley's search for his origins. How would the account be different? What would be lost and what could be gained?**

PERSONAL JOURNAL Encourage students to use their personal journals to write about ideas and feelings that are expressed in the groups. You may also wish to refer students to their personal journals after they complete the Critical Thinking Activities.

STRATEGY CONFERENCE

Discuss the K-W-L chart, asking students whether it helped them understand, remember, and appreciate the excerpt. Invite students to share other reading strategies, such as taking notes, that helped them understand and enjoy "Mister Kinte!"

INFORMAL ASSESSMENT

Having students discuss the **details** they thought were most and least informative will encourage them to **organize** and **evaluate** the content of the selection while summarizing it. Doing this will enable you to see whether key details of the selection have been noted and appreciated and whether students can focus on and select details that serve purposes for reading.

Encourage both cooperative and individual responses.

ADD TO AN ORAL HISTORY *How do you think the* griot *might include the story of Alex Haley's visit in the oral history of the Kinte clan?* Have pairs of students work together to write the *griot's* reference to Haley. Remind them to include a time reference so that the timing of the visit can be easily remembered in the clan's oral history. CREATIVE: INVENTING NEW SCENES

PREPARE A SPEECH *Do you think that books like Alex Haley's* Roots *have a purpose beyond entertaining their readers? If so, what might their authors' intentions be?* Invite students to prepare short speeches in which they respond to this question. Remind them to support their arguments with reasons and examples. CRITICAL: SPECULATING

WRITE INSTRUCTIONS *Review the steps that Alex Haley took to track down his family history. Then write steps that other people could use to discover their ancestry.* Have students work in small groups to review Haley's quest and then write a series of steps on how to search for one's roots. Point out that the steps should appear in a progressive order, with such words as *first, then,* and *next* to signal sequence. CRITICAL: WRITING INSTRUCTIONS/ DETERMINING SEQUENCE

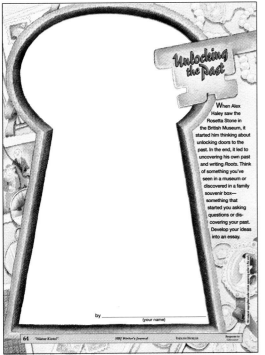

Writer's Journal

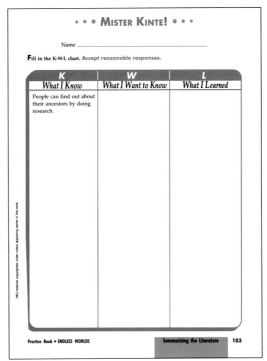

Practice Book

WRITER'S JOURNAL

page 64: Writing a creative response

PRACTICE BOOK

page 103: Summarizing the selection

VO·CAB·U·LAR·Y Workshop

Reviewing Key Words

To review how the new vocabulary was used in this selection, display the Key Words. Read each answer below and ask students to supply a question using a Key Word. (Possible questions are shown.)

1. *Answer:* **ancient writing systems**
   Question: What are hieroglyphics?
2. *Answer:* **a loud, harsh noise**
   Question: What is cacophony?
3. *Answer:* **implications**
   Question: What are ramifications?
4. *Answer:* **a statement yet to be proved**
   Question: What is a thesis?
5. *Answer:* **not read or figured out**
   Question: What does *undeciphered* mean?
6. *Answer:* **annals of history; accounts**
   Question: What are chronicles?
7. *Answer:* **occasionally**
   Question: What does *intermittently* mean?
8. *Answer:* **a line of descent; ancestry**
   Question: What is lineage?
9. *Answer:* **enraptured**
   Question: What is another word for *entranced*?
10. *Answer:* **general**
    Question: What is the meaning of *generic*?

Extending Vocabulary

LANGUAGE HISTORY   Explain that a word may have a family tree. The word *lineage* comes from the Middle English *linage,* which in turn comes from the Old French *lignage.* That word came from the Latin *linea,* meaning a "linen or flaxen line." Explain that, like these three languages, most languages that originated in Europe belong to the Indo-European group. Linguists think there must have been a common language from which other languages developed, even though no one knows who spoke it or what it sounded like. Some of the languages that can be traced to Indo-European origins include Greek, Latin, French, Spanish, Italian, Portuguese, Russian, Czech, Polish, German, Dutch, English, and several languages of India.

COOPERATIVE LEARNING   Have students research how languages develop. They might be interested to learn about languages *not* in the Indo-European family, such as Asian, Native American, Turkish, and African tongues. Ask volunteers to suggest good sources for this information. (encyclopedia; nonfiction books about language) Students may work in pairs or small groups. They should present their findings in oral reports. Suggest that they hold the attention of their audience by using visual aids, such as charts showing words in English that have come from the language they studied.

Language Arts

WRITING

Writing About the Literature

AVAILABLE ON PROJECT CARD

CREATIVE: DESCRIPTIVE NARRATIVE Ask students to write a narrative from Kunta Kinte's point of view in which they describe what happened to him and what he thought and felt. Suggest that students begin with a web:

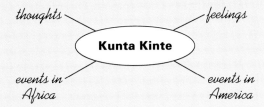

READING/WRITING

CRITICAL: EXPOSITORY ESSAY Point out that Alex Haley "wept for all of history's incredible atrocities." Ask students to write an essay about how such atrocities might be prevented. Remind them to provide an opening statement, supporting evidence, and a concluding statement in their work. WRITING

NOTE: An additional writing activity appears on page 347.

SPEAKING/LISTENING

Creative Dramatics

COOPERATIVE LEARNING Suggest that students form small groups to dramatize parts of Alex Haley's story as a radio play. After they have written and practiced their play, they may enjoy tape-recording and playing it for their classmates. LISTENING/SPEAKING/READING/WRITING

SPELLING

Spelling Review

SPELLING WORDS: *acquainted, cacophony, chronicle, colleague, generic, lineage, quest, ramification, thickening, unaccustomed*

Have students write each Spelling Word at the top of a column. Then have them make word families for each Spelling Word. In the column beneath each word, students should list the word's base word or root and any other words they can think of that share that base or root. In addition, for words with the /k/ or /kw/ sound, have students circle the letter or letters that stand for the sound. READING/WRITING/SPELLING

INTEGRATED SPELLING

page 50: Writing words with the /k/ or /kw/ sound

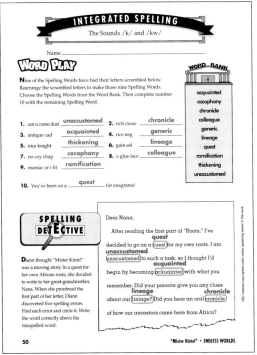

Integrated Spelling

STUDY SKILLS
INTRODUCE

Note-Taking Strategies

OBJECTIVE: *To develop note-taking strategies*

1	Focus

Discuss the value of taking notes effectively.

Discuss with students how taking notes can help them. For example, having notes to look at eliminates the need to read material twice, and the notes act as a memory refresher. Point out that knowing some note-taking strategies will help students take more effective notes.

2	Teach/Model

Model the thinking.

Explain that good note-takers do not write down every word. They look for words that will help them remember important ideas. Model how to take good notes:

> **When I take notes, I look for key ideas—that is, main ideas and really important details. I jot down just the important words or phrases. I abbreviate words and names. Sometimes I use symbols like arrows or plus signs, or I draw a little sketch. The most important ideas I star or underline as I write.**

Have students discuss note-taking.

Direct students to look at the first three paragraphs of "Mister Kinte!" (pages 336–337). Discuss what main facts they would write down if they were taking notes. (Accept reasonable responses: Alex Haley/London/saw Rosetta Stone used to decipher hieroglyph. Gave idea to trace Afr. lang. sounds from family. Problem: How?)

3   Practice/Apply

Have students recall from notes.

Have students take notes on the next five paragraphs of the selection. Then have them form small groups and use their notes for help in recalling main ideas and details from what they have just read. Suggest that students compare notes to see which ideas they thought were most important and to identify helpful abbreviations and symbols they used in taking notes.

4   Summarize

Informally assess the learning.

Ask students to suggest notes for the introductory paragraph of the selection. Write the notes on the board. Have other students use the notes to summarize that part of the narrative. Check understanding by having students summarize what they learned. (Note-taking strategies such as looking for main ideas and important details, using symbols, and using abbreviations can make note taking easier and more helpful.)

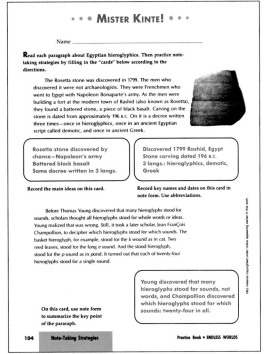

Practice Book

CHALLENGE Encourage students to select a topic that interests them and to use their note-taking skills to research the topic for an informative speech.

SECOND-LANGUAGE SUPPORT Reassure students that since their notes are for themselves alone, it is acceptable for them to take notes in their first language occasionally. Encourage them to concentrate on finding main ideas and important details. (See *Second-Language Support Manual*.)

PRACTICE BOOK
page 104: Using note-taking strategies

Book Parts

OBJECTIVE: *To use the parts of a book for information*

1   Focus

Explain the value of knowing the parts of a book.

Remind students that books have features that make it easier to extract information from them. Knowing how to use these book parts will help students find and evaluate the information they need.

2   Teach/Model

Model the thinking.

Model how information can be obtained from different parts of a book:

> **When I first look at a book, I turn to the front matter: the title page, the copyright page, and the table of contents. These pages tell me the title and author of the book and the place and date of publication. I also see how the book is divided and on what pages I can locate specific sections. Next, I turn to the back and look at the back matter: the index, glossary, and bibliography. Here are listed the book's topics with their page numbers, potentially unfamiliar words with definitions, and the sources the author used to write the book.**

You may wish to point out that the front matter of a book may not have page numbers or may be numbered with small roman numerals or in another way to distinguish it from the main text. The back matter may be numbered as a continuation of the main text, as a continuation of the front matter, or in another fashion.

Have students examine the parts of a book.

Ask students to find the following parts in their textbooks: title page, copyright page with publication date, acknowledgments, table of contents, index, and glossary. Discuss how each part might be helpful to a reader or researcher.

3   Practice/Apply

Have students ask questions about book parts.

COOPERATIVE LEARNING Have students work in pairs to make up ten short questions about information that may be found in the front and back matter of a book. (Sample question: "On what page can you find the author's name?") Have students take turns posing their questions to other pairs until all questions have been answered correctly.

4   Summarize

Informally assess the learning.

Ask students to use their Student Anthology texts to find information such as the following and then explain how they found it:

- the date of publication
- the author of "First Sighting"

Check understanding by having students summarize what they learned. (Knowing what type of information is in each book part helps readers find it quickly and easily.)

CHALLENGE Have students work in small groups to make up a question-and-answer game using information that can be found in the front and back matter of a book.

SECOND-LANGUAGE SUPPORT Encourage students to bring in books written in their first language and to use them to demonstrate to the class where the information contained in the front and back matter may be found. (See *Second-Language Support Manual.*)

PRACTICE BOOK page 105: Using book parts

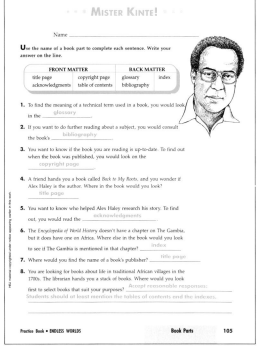

Practice Book

Figurative Language

OBJECTIVE: *To appreciate figurative language*

Review

Review figures of speech.

Review the idea that metaphors and similes compare two unlike things. Personification gives human qualities to things. Model how to recognize figurative language:

> **When Haley writes about "the key that had unlocked a door into the past," he is not being literal. He is comparing the way the deciphering of hieroglyphics led to a knowledge of the past with the way a key opens a door.**

Practice/Apply

Have students identify figurative language.

COOPERATIVE LEARNING Invite groups to find figurative language in the selection and to analyze and share what the expressions mean.

Summarize

Informally assess the learning.

Ask students to summarize what they learned. (Figurative language uses words to mean something different from their literal meanings.)

CHALLENGE Have small groups of students use what they have learned about figurative language to write metaphors and similes of their own. If they like, they may work individually to develop a metaphor or simile into a poem.

PRACTICE BOOK
page 106: Understanding figurative language

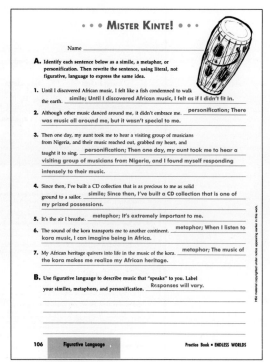

Practice Book

Fact-Opinion/Viewpoint

OBJECTIVE: *To identify facts and opinions in order to distinguish an author's viewpoint and purpose*

Review

Review how the skills are related.

Review that noticing facts and opinions can help students identify an author's viewpoint and purpose. Model how:

> **When Haley tells about meeting the villagers, he does not present any negative facts. He states his opinion that this has been "the peak experience" of his life. I see that his viewpoint is positive and his purpose is to inspire others.**

Practice/Apply

Have students apply the learning.

COOPERATIVE LEARNING Have small groups of students identify facts and opinions on pages 339–341 and then use them to discuss the author's viewpoint and purpose.

Summarize

Informally assess the learning.

Check understanding by having students summarize what they reviewed. (An author's presentation of facts and opinions can reveal the author's viewpoint and purpose.)

CHALLENGE Ask students to bring in editorials clipped from a local newspaper and to explain how the editor uses facts and opinions to support his or her viewpoint. Discuss whether the facts cited, as well as the opinions expressed, would have been different if the editor had had a different viewpoint.

PRACTICE BOOK page 107: Using fact and opinion to determine author's purpose and viewpoint

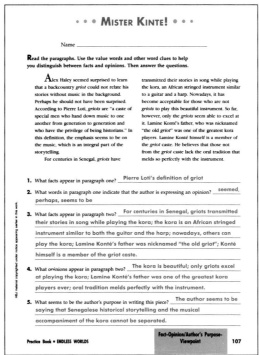

Practice Book

Integrated **Curriculum**

MATH/SOCIAL STUDIES

Planes, Trucks, and Automobiles

USE MAPS Remind students of all the places to which Alex Haley's work and research took him. Have students locate on maps the places mentioned in the selection and use the information to create a map that delineates Haley's route. Finally, have them calculate how many miles Haley traveled in search of his roots. READING/WRITING

ART

Master Mask Makers

Explain that African art—including fine weavings, wood carvings, and metalwork—is prized by collectors from all over the world for its beauty, strong design, and high quality and that masks are probably the African art objects we see most often. Many of these masks have special meaning or significance. Invite students to research African art and to create an African-style mask, using homemade papier-mâché or a light wood. When the masks are finished, students may display them while giving oral reports on African masks and the way they are made and used, and any special significance of the masks they have designed and made. LISTENING/SPEAKING/READING

SOCIAL STUDIES

African Awareness
AVAILABLE ON PROJECT CARD

COOPERATIVE LEARNING Remind students that Alex Haley became fascinated with Africa. Invite students to form groups to research the world's second-largest continent. Divide the continent into North, West, South, East, and Central Africa, and assign each group a different section. Have each group concentrate on what is special about that section. They may look at food, customs, art, history, resources, and political organization. Then hold an African Awareness Day, in which each group shares information with the others. LISTENING/SPEAKING/READING/WRITING

SCIENCE

Good Gnus, Bad Gnus

Point out that parts of Africa are known for their wildlife, including elephants, lions, gorillas, antelope, gnus, hyenas, and many species of birds. Invite students interested in natural history to choose an African animal and research its habits and habitat, along with any threats to its survival. Have students write reports on their animals and make the reports available to classmates. READING/WRITING

Going Back in Time

WRITERS OFTEN SEARCH OUT STORIES FROM THEIR FAMILY HISTORIES.

Amy Tan, for example, is the author of two best-selling books based on her mother's childhood experiences in China. Tan's novels are rich with details from another time and culture. Her stories transport readers to a time in China when enemy soldiers were invading people's homes, and refugees were forced to abandon their precious belongings. Her mother's memories of these chilling events have helped to establish Tan as an important novelist.

Another writer who traveled back in time to discover lost or hidden stories is Rayford Logan, an eminent black historian. A distinguished professor of history, Logan was associated with Howard University from 1938 to 1982. He used his position there to enlighten the world about the contributions of African Americans to American culture. His goal was to foster a sense of identity and pride among blacks by revealing the truth about their ancestors. In 1980 Logan received the Spingarn Medal, the NAACP's highest achievement award, for his efforts. ■

ACTIVITY CORNER
■ Ask students to interview older relatives to find out about their family's origins. Have students record these interviews and share them with the group if they wish.
■ Encourage students to draw simple family trees, with dates and place names, to see how much they know about their families. Discuss what more they might like to know and how they might discover this information.

ANCESTORS & DESCENDANTS OF Chapter Number **SIMON AND ELIZABETH (WHITE) MASON** in Parentheses

People researching their family histories often record information on genealogy charts such as this one.

Amy Tan wove stories her mother told her into best-selling books.

Dr. Rayford Logan's work has inspired many African Americans with a vision of their heritage.

Words About the Author: Alex Haley

Words about the Author:

Alex Haley

Alex Haley illustration by Scott Scheidly

Childhood stories about a puzzling but fascinating ancestor spurred Alex Haley's search for the truth and in time produced a phenomenal historical novel—one that has inspired readers to discover more about themselves and their roots.

As a young boy, Haley sat on his grandmother's porch in Henning, Tennessee, and listened as his grandmother and other older relatives told stories about his ancestors. They were all fascinating stories, yes, but none more so than the stories about "the African."

Born in Ithaca, New York, in 1921 to Simon Alexander Haley, a professor, and Bertha Palmer Haley, a teacher, Alex Palmer Haley spent most of his youth in Henning. The oral tradition was strong in Haley's family, and from an early age he understood the power of words—spoken or written.

As he grew to manhood, his fascination with "the African" increased accordingly, stirring in him a desire to investigate further and to discover more about his roots. And so Alex Haley began the long journey that 1 led him to The Gambia, West Africa—home of "the African"—and later led him to the publication of *Roots: The Saga of an American Family.*

His understanding of the power of words helped prepare him for his career in journalism, which he began when he joined the United States Coast Guard in 1939. When he retired from the Coast Guard as chief journalist in 1959, Haley said he was "prepared to starve" in his determination to pursue a full-time writing career. And in those early years, starvation was always close by.

348

Reading the Author Feature

Invite students to share what they know about Alex Haley. Discuss where they have heard his name and in what connection. Then ask students to draw on their reading of Haley's "Mister Kinte!" (from *Roots*) to predict what the author might be like, what inspired him to write the book, and what other information they might learn in a biographical sketch about him.

Teaching Tip Remind students that Alex Haley spent twenty years of his life serving in the United States Coast Guard. Point out that the Coast Guard is a branch of the armed services and has been active since 1790. It protects property and life at sea and enforces federal laws and treaties on the high seas.

2 SYMBOLISM
How do the two cans of sardines and the eighteen cents stand for, or symbolize, Haley's "determination to be independent"? *(Haley didn't give up his pursuit of a writing career and get a more secure job, even in the face of severe financial difficulties.)*
INFERENTIAL: DRAWING CONCLUSIONS

3 NARRATION: EVENTS
Why did it take Alex Haley twelve years to gather the material for *Roots*? Why is such painstaking research necessary for writing historical fiction? *(Accept reasonable responses: He had to travel to many places, including Africa, to look for clues about his ancestor who was kidnapped and sold as a slave; the background information must be based on historical events.)*
CRITICAL: MAKING JUDGMENTS

At one point he was down to eighteen cents and two cans of sardines. Then, finally, he received a check, payment for an article he had written. Receiving the check gave him the incentive to continue as a writer. The framed eighteen cents and the cans of sardines—symbols of his "determination to be independent"—now hang in the library at his home.

When *Roots* was published in 1976, critics called it "a phenomenon," not only because it told the story of the journey of all African Americans from slavery to freedom, but also because it changed the way people viewed themselves, their families, and their ancestry. The book sparked many readers' search for knowledge about their lineage. Aware of the excitement he had created, Haley provided more information about genealogical research in *My Search for Roots*. That book contains an account of the twelve years of intense research Haley undertook in the United States and Africa to gather material for *Roots*.

Haley served as script consultant for three televised miniseries: *Roots*; *Roots: The Next Generation*; and *Palmerstown, U. S. A.*

Among the awards he received for *Roots* are special citations in 1977 from the National Book Award committee and from the Pulitzer Prize committee.

349

Second-Language Support
Students may need help understanding the expression *prepared to starve* on page 348. Explain that its literal meaning is "ready to suffer extreme hunger." The expression describes a person's determination and willingness to make great personal sacrifices in order to achieve a certain goal. Remind students that in Alex Haley's case, he was once almost out of food and money early in his writing career.

MEETING INDIVIDUAL NEEDS

Responding to the Author Feature
Discuss with students whether they think they would be "prepared to starve" as Alex Haley was willing to do. Invite volunteers to suggest goals or ideals for which they would be willing to make great sacrifices.

FREEDOM OF CHOICE

From ancient times poetry has been memorized and passed on from generation to generation. But what is poetry? It sometimes has rhyme, but this is not essential for a poem. What *is* essential is for a poem to stir our emotions through our imagination. The poet uses the powerful magic of words to move us. The other essential is rhythm, achieved through the use of accented and unaccented syllables and the sounds of words.

Carl Sandburg may have defined poetry best when he said, "Poetry is a language that tells us, through a more or less emotional reaction, something that cannot be said."

"**P**oetry . . . tells us . . . something that cannot be said."

COLLECTIONS OF POETRY

Poems for Youth by Emily Dickinson. Little, Brown, 1934.

The Poetry of Robert Frost, edited by Edward Connery Lathem. Holt, Rinehart and Winston, 1970.

Something New Begins: New and Selected Poems by Lilian Moore. Atheneum, 1982. AVERAGE

The Whispering Wind: Poetry by Young American Indians, edited by Terry Allen. Doubleday, 1972.

• SELECTION SUMMARY
• The common theme
• of these eight poems
• is freedom of choice.
• "Sympathy" laments
• lack of freedom,
• while "One"
• addresses our
• uniqueness. "The
• Road Not Taken"
• recalls a moment of
• choice. "Advice to
• Travelers" counsels
• us to express
• ourselves, and "I Saw
• a Man" sketches an
• encounter with
• someone who insists
• upon pursuing
• dreams. "The
• Forecast" concerns
• our flight from
• freedom, but "I'm
• Nobody!" extols the
• freedom to choose
• privacy, and "To
• Make a Prairie"
• celebrates the
• importance of the
• individual.

LESSON PLANNER

	Materials	Integrated Curriculum	Meeting Individual Needs

1 READING LITERATURE pp. 349B–358	Student Anthology pp. 350–358
	Transparency 20
	Second-Language Support Manual
	Practice Book p. 108
	Integrated Spelling p. 51
	Integrated Spelling T.E. pp. 70–71
		Spelling
		  Spelling Pretest
		  Spelling-Vocabulary Connection
		  (words with shifting accents)
			Second-Language Support
			  Vocabulary 349C
			  Strategic Reading 349D

2 RESPONDING TO LITERATURE pp. 358A–358E	Writer's Journal p. 65
	Practice Book p. 109
	Integrated Spelling p. 52
	Integrated Spelling T.E. pp. 70–71
		Vocabulary Workshop
		  Reviewing Key Words
		  Extending Vocabulary
		Writing About the Literature
		Speaking/Listening
		Spelling Review
			Cooperative Learning 358B, 358C

3 LEARNING THROUGH LITERATURE pp. 358F–358N	Second-Language Support Manual Writer's Journal p. 66 Practice Book pp. 110–111	Science Social Studies Art Multicultural	Cooperative Learning 358I Challenge 358G, 358I, 358K Second-Language Support 358G, 358I

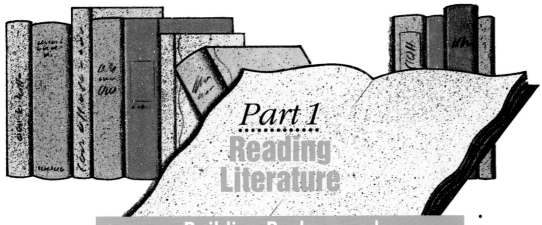

Part 1
Reading Literature

Building Background

Access prior knowledge and develop vocabulary concepts.

Have students name some poems or lyrics they have memorized. Point out that students are often asked to memorize poems but rarely prose. Write *Why poetry is easier to memorize than prose* on the board at the center of a web, and ask students to suggest reasons why this is so.

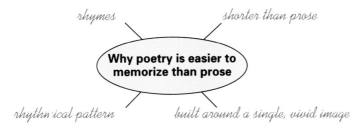

rhymes   shorter than prose

Why poetry is easier to memorize than prose

rhythmical pattern   built around a single, vivid image

Have students quickwrite a list.

Ask students to list one or two reasons why people might want to memorize poetry. Call on volunteers to share their ideas with the group.

Vocabulary Strategies

Introduce Key Words and strategies.

Tell students that they may encounter some unfamiliar words in the poems. Display Transparency 20, or write the paragraph on the board.

Transparency 20   Key Words

Lost in <u>revery</u>, the distracted mouse did not notice that she had run over a lion's tail. The lion <u>accosted</u> the mouse and threatened her. Though she believed her pleas were <u>futile</u>, the mouse begged the lion to let her go and promised to help him sometime. The lion laughed but let the mouse go. The mouse rushed away. Though their paths <u>diverged</u>, she was sure that she and the lion would meet again.

KEY WORDS DEFINED

revery   daydream

accosted   stopped and spoke to

futile   pointless, useless

diverged   branched off, went in different directions

After students have read the paragraph silently, encourage them to use context clues, phonics, and structural analysis to figure out the meanings of the underlined words. Help with pronunciation as a volunteer reads the paragraph aloud.

Check students' understanding.

Have students answer the following questions, either orally or in writing, to show their understanding of the Key Words.

1. *futile*   **If a bucket has a hole in the bottom, why would carrying water in it be a futile action?** (because the water would leak through the hole)   STRATEGY: EXPLANATION
2. *revery*   **What is a word that means the same as revery?** (Accept reasonable responses: *daydream, daze.*)   STRATEGY: SYNONYMS
3. *diverged*   **What kinds of things might diverge?** (Accept reasonable responses: streets, paths, two people's lives.)   STRATEGY: EXAMPLES
4. *accosted*   **If you are accosted by someone whom you want to avoid, what might you say?** (Responses will vary.)   STRATEGY: EXPLANATION

Integrate spelling with vocabulary.

SPELLING-VOCABULARY CONNECTION *Integrated Spelling* page 51 reinforces spellings of **words with shifting accents,** including the Key Word *futile*.

SECOND-LANGUAGE SUPPORT   Ask students to work with peer tutors to role-play or draw pictures illustrating the meanings of the Key Words. (See *Second-Language Support Manual.*)

PRACTICE BOOK
• **page 108:** *Reinforcing Key Words*

INTEGRATED SPELLING
• **page 51:** Writing and spelling words with shifting accents

• **NOTE:** These pages may be completed now or after students have read the poetry.

Practice Book

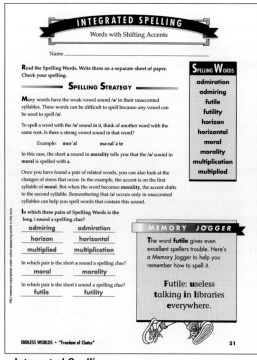

Integrated Spelling

Strategic Reading: Poetry

Preview and Predict

Discuss ways of previewing poetry.

Explain that as with prose, readers can preview a poem by reading and thinking about the title and scanning the illustrations. Tell students that many poems have no plot, so readers cannot predict what will happen, but they can make predictions about what the theme or the subject will be.

Have students preview and predict.

To establish a pattern for students to follow with the other poems, read aloud the first stanza of "Sympathy." Ask students what the poet feels deprived of. (Accept reasonable responses: He feels a lack of freedom.)

Introduce the poetry theme chart.

Display the poetry theme chart to encourage students to think about what the poems say about freedom.

POETRY THEME CHART

Title	Subject	Theme

PERSONAL JOURNAL   Have students copy the poetry theme chart in their personal journals, or have them use *Practice Book* page 109. (See page 358B in this Teacher's Edition.) Suggest that when students preview a poem, they write their predictions about the subject in the second column. Explain that they will want to read and study a poem before they write its theme. (Students will return to the chart after reading, in Summarizing the Literature.)

Setting a Purpose

Have students set purposes.

Have students use the predictions they make to develop questions they would like answered through their reading of the poems.

Model purpose-setting, if necessary.

If students have difficulty setting a purpose for reading, model the thinking process:

> **After previewing the first poem, I get a sense that the poet is talking about being an individual who is free to make choices. My purpose for reading will be to find out what each of these poems has to say about a person's freedom to choose.**

SECOND-LANGUAGE SUPPORT   Students may benefit from participating in the Guided Reading activities and the additional guidance under the Student Anthology pages. (See *Second-Language Support Manual*.)

OPTIONS FOR READING

Independent Reading
Have students read the poems silently with their purpose for reading in mind.

Guided Reading
Follow the Guided Reading suggestions that appear on pages 350 and 358. These suggestions model strategic reading.

Numbered Annotations
Use the numbered annotations beside the Student Anthology pages to heighten students' appreciation of the poetry.

ARTIST'S CRAFT
The fine-art reproductions that accompany these poems are intended to complement, rather than illustrate. After discussing the poems, you may want to encourage students to express their ideas and feelings about the artwork. **How does this art, taken by itself, make you feel? How does it relate to the theme or mood of the poem?** *(Responses will vary.)*
CRITICAL: SYNTHESIZING

FREEDOM OF CHOICE:
Eight Poems

Mirage, 1985, Pat Steir, Installation Promenades, Parc Lullin, Geneva, Switzerland

350

Guided Reading

SET PURPOSE/PREDICT: PAGES 350–358   Share with students the information about the poets, and have them read each poem. Ask them, as they read, to think about what kinds of feelings each poet expresses.

Informal Assessment   You can informally assess whether your students use vocabulary strategies as they read, which ones they tend to use, and how effectively they use them. To do this, ask the following questions on occasion:

- Are there any words in this poem that are new to you? Point out one.
- How did you figure out what this word meant? If that hadn't worked, what could you have done?

Sympathy

by Paul Laurence Dunbar

I know what the caged bird feels, alas!
When the sun is bright on the upland slopes;
When the wind stirs soft through the springing grass
And the river flows like a stream of glass;
When the first bird sings and the first bud opes,
And the faint perfume from its chalice steals—
I know what the caged bird feels!

I know why the caged bird beats his wing
Till its blood is red on the cruel bars;
For he must fly back to his perch and cling
When he fain would be on the bough a-swing;
And a pain still throbs in the old, old scars
And they pulse again with a keener sting—   **1**
I know why he beats his wing!

I know why the caged bird sings, ah me,
When his wing is bruised and his bosom sore,
When he beats his bars and would be free;
It is not a carol of joy or glee,
But a prayer that he sends from his heart's deep core,
But a plea, that upward to Heaven he flings—
I know why the caged bird sings!

351

PAUL LAURENCE DUNBAR
(1872–1906), whose father was enslaved for some of his life, earned renown as the nation's first established and well-known African American poet.

1 DESCRIPTION
What does the poet mean by "the old, old scars"? Why do they pulse "with a keener sting"? *(Accept reasonable responses: They may be physical scars from beatings that slaves endured, or they may be psychological scars inflicted by prejudiced people. A "keener sting" might be felt by people who are not slaves but still are not truly free.)*
INFERENTIAL: DETERMINING MAIN IDEA

Vocabulary Strategy Point out *fain*, in the fourth line of the second stanza, as archaic, or old-fashioned, language. Ask whether students can figure out its meaning. (*Fain* means "rather"; context clues come from the bird's preferring to be on the open bough.) Ask students to find other examples of archaic language. (*alas, opes, chalice, a-swing*) STRATEGY: CONTEXT CLUES

JAMES BERRY
(1924–   ) was born and raised in
Jamaica and lives in England. He
received the Order of the British
Empire in 1990 in recognition of his
poetry and short stories. He has
done much work in the field of
multicultural education.

2 DESCRIPTION
What is unique about the speaker?
*(his fingerprints, tears, laughter, and
sense of expectancy)*
LITERAL: NOTING IMPORTANT DETAILS

3 THEME
**Why can't anyone exactly copy the
speaker?** *(The qualities that make
him unique are internal, involving
feelings and his personal
perceptions. Only the externals can
be copied.)*
INFERENTIAL: DETERMINING MAIN IDEA

One

by James Berry

Only one of me
and nobody can get a second one
from a photocopy machine.

2 Nobody has the fingerprints I have.
Nobody can cry my tears, or laugh my laugh
or have my expectancy when I wait.

But anybody can mimic my dance with my dog.
Anybody can howl how I sing out of tune.
And mirrors can show me multiplied
many times, say, dressed up in red
or dressed up in grey.

3 Nobody can get into my clothes for me
or feel my fall for me, or do my running.
Nobody hears my music for me, either.

I am just this one.
Nobody else makes the words
I shape with sound, when I talk.

But anybody can act how I stutter in a rage.
Anybody can copy echoes I make.
And mirrors can show me multiplied
many times, say, dressed up in green
or dressed up in blue.

The Musician, 1917-1918, Georges
Braque, Collection of Basel Museum

352

The Road Not Taken ⁴

by Robert Frost

AWARD-WINNING
AUTHOR

Two roads <u>diverged</u> in a yellow wood,
And sorry I could not travel both
And be one traveler, long I stood
And looked down one as far as I could
To where it bent in the undergrowth;

Then took the other, as just as fair,
And having perhaps the better claim,
Because it was grassy and wanted wear;
Though as for that, the passing there
Had worn them really about the same,

And both that morning equally lay
In leaves no step had trodden black.
Oh, I kept the first for another day!
Yet knowing how way leads on to way,
I doubted if I should ever come back.

I shall be telling this with a sigh
Somewhere ages and ages hence:
Two roads diverged in a wood, and I—
I took the one less traveled by,
And that has made all the difference.

353

ROBERT FROST
(1874–1963) wrote about New
England and spoke with its native
voice. Writing verse in general
delighted him, and he spoke with
relish of "the surprise of
remembering something I didn't
know I knew."

4 THEME
**How does the fact that the poem is
titled "The Road Not Taken," rather
than "The Road Taken," suggest
the theme?** *(The title suggests the
author's emphasis on wondering
how his life might have been
different. The speaker knows the
road taken and the results of that
decision, but he will never know
what would have happened had he
chosen the other, more commonly
traveled route.)*
INFERENTIAL: DETERMINING MAIN IDEA

WALKER GIBSON

(1919–   ) has taught English at the college level. In the 1960s, he appeared on television teaching "Sunrise Semester." He has written a handbook on English and such works as *Poems in the Making.*

5 MOOD
What clues are there that the mood of the poem is meant to be humorous? *(the phrase* like to died *and the image of a burro eating up his identity)*
METACOGNITIVE: NOTING IMPORTANT DETAILS

STEPHEN CRANE

(1871–1900) went to college in his early teens and thought of becoming a baseball player. Instead, he tried journalism. Soon after publishing his classic novel about the Civil War, *The Red Badge of Courage,* he died of tuberculosis. Until shortly before his death, he continued writing stories to pay his bills.

6 CONFLICT
What opposing views of dreams are presented in this poem? *(One person is committed to their pursuit. The other believes it is useless.)*
INFERENTIAL: DETERMINING MAIN IDEA

Advice to Travelers

by Walker Gibson

A burro once, sent by express,
His shipping ticket on his bridle,
Ate up his name and his address,
And in some warehouse, standing idle,
5 He waited till he like to died.
The moral hardly needs the showing:
Don't keep things locked up deep inside—
Say who you are and where you're going.

I Saw a Man

by Stephen Crane

I saw a man pursuing the horizon;
Round and round they sped.
I was disturbed at this;
I accosted the man.
6 "It is futile," I said,
"You can never—"

"You lie," he cried,
And ran on.

Mist in Kanab Canyon, Utah, Thomas Moran, 1892, oil on canvas, 44 ³/₈" X 38 ³/₈". National Museum of American Art, Smithsonian Institution, Bequest of Bessie B. Croffut.

354

355

Informal Assessment You can informally assess whether your students understand a poet's viewpoint and can identify the poet's purpose for writing a poem. On occasion, ask questions like these:

- Why did the poet write this poem? What does he or she think about this topic?
- What in the poem makes you think this was the poet's purpose?
- How well does the poet succeed in fulfilling this purpose? Is there anything else the poet should have done or said?

DAN JAFFE
(1933–) has taught English at several colleges and has written essays, poems, reviews, and a libretto for a jazz opera. He has also served as editor-in-chief of BookMark Press.

7 AUTHOR'S CRAFT
What does the poem predict will happen to people and the way they look at the world? *(They will become dependent on television and removed from nature; they will not see things directly but rather through words and images on television.)*
INFERENTIAL: DETERMINING MAIN IDEA

Why do you think the poet calls this poem "The Forecast"? *(Accept reasonable responses: The forecast is what "the weather man will tell us" and it is also the prediction the poet is making; the title connects the two ideas.)*
INFERENTIAL: SYNTHESIZING

The Forecast

by Dan Jaffe

Perhaps our age has driven us indoors.
We sprawl in the semi-darkness, dreaming sometimes
Of a vague world spinning in the wind.
But we have snapped our locks, pulled down our shades,
Taken all precautions. We shall not be disturbed.
If the earth shakes, it will be on a screen;
7 And if the prairie wind spills down our streets
And covers us with leaves, the weatherman will tell us.

Untitled, Helen Pashgian, epoxy on canvas 60" X 90". Collection of the Security Pacific Corporation, Los Angeles, California.

356

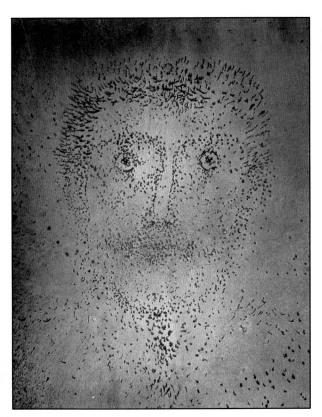

Portrait of Mr. A.L.,
Paul Klee, 1924,
Zurich, Germany

EMILY DICKINSON
(1830–1886) spent her life as
something of a hermit, publishing
only three of her many poems. "I
do not go from home," she wrote in
a letter, but instead explored the
vast inner world of her imagination.

8 FIGURATIVE LANGUAGE
**In what way do "somebodies"
resemble frogs?** *(They swell up with
pride and croak about themselves.)*
INFERENTIAL: MAKING COMPARISONS

I'm Nobody!

by Emily Dickinson

I'm nobody! Who are you?
Are you nobody, too?
Then there's a pair of us—don't tell!
They'd banish us, you know.

How dreary—to be—somebody!
How public, like a frog
To tell your name the livelong day **8**
To an admiring bog!

357

Oral Rereading Have students read through the
poems silently. Then call on volunteers to read one
of the poems orally. Point out that although it may
seem easy to read poetry aloud, the trick is to make
it sound easy. Instruct students to pay attention to
punctuation and line breaks for pauses when
reading. Give students time to rehearse quietly with
a partner. Then ask them to read their poems aloud
to the group. Encourage a variety of interpretations.

9 AUTHOR'S PURPOSE
Why do you think the poet wants to tell the reader how "To Make a Prairie"? (*Accept reasonable responses: She wants to explain how wonderful the imagination is.*)
INFERENTIAL: DETERMINING MAIN IDEA

10 FIGURATIVE LANGUAGE
How can revery alone create a prairie? (*The individual can dream up a prairie through the imagination.*)
INFERENTIAL: MAKING COMPARISONS

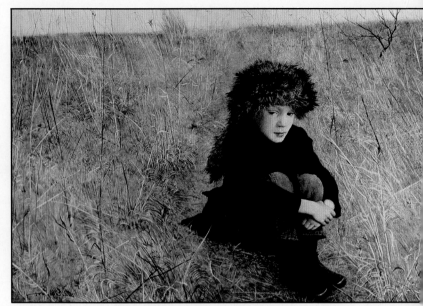

Faraway, 1952, Andrew Wyeth, drybrush watercolor on paper, 13 ¾"
X 21 ½". Collection of Jamie Wyeth, Brandywine River Museum

To Make a Prairie

by Emily Dickinson

To make a prairie it takes a clover and one bee,
9 One clover, and a bee,
And revery.
The revery alone will do,
10 If bees are few.

358

Guided Reading

MONITOR COMPREHENSION: PAGES 350–358
What feelings do the poets express? (Some of the poems express a sense of captivity ["Sympathy," "The Forecast"], while others rejoice in freedom and individuality ["One," "I'm Nobody!" "To Make a Prairie"]. Some seem to express ambiguous or unresolved feelings about freedom of choice ["The Road Not Taken," "I Saw a Man"]. "Advice to Travelers" expresses a belief in decisiveness.)
STRATEGIC READING: SUMMARIZING/RETURNING TO PURPOSE

Returning to the Predictions Invite students to discuss the predictions that they made before reading and that they may have written in their personal journals. Encourage students to talk about how those predictions changed as they read the poems.

Returning to the Purpose for Reading
Discuss the overall impression students gained about freedom of choice and its importance to the poets.
(Accept reasonable responses: The poets rebel against restriction and assert their value as individuals.)

Part 2
Responding to Literature

Summarizing the Literature

Return to the poetry theme chart.

Invite students to complete their poetry theme charts now, if they have not already done so. (See *Practice Book* page 109, on 358B.) Students may use their completed charts to write a brief statement about how the poems are related.

POETRY THEME CHART

Title	Subject	Theme
"Sympathy"	Lack of freedom; oppression	The oppressed pray for freedom.
"One"	Individuality; uniqueness	Everyone is unique.
"The Road Not Taken"	Decisions, choices	Decisions affect people forever.
"Advice to Travelers"	Being yourself	Do not hide who you are.
"I Saw a Man"	Pursuing dreams	Dreamers are incurable.
"The Forecast"	Living life	People do not live life, but watch it.
"I'm Nobody!"	Private life	A private life is fulfilling.
"To Make a Prairie"	Importance of imagination	Imagination is a great gift.

Appreciating Literature

Have students share personal responses.

Divide students into small groups to discuss the poetry. Provide a general question to get the groups started:

• **Which poem did you find the most moving? Why?**

PERSONAL JOURNAL Encourage students to use their personal journals to write about ideas and feelings that are expressed in the groups. You may also wish to refer students to their personal journals after they complete the Critical Thinking Activities.

STRATEGY CONFERENCE

Discuss the poetry theme chart, asking students how it helped them understand and appreciate the selected poems. Invite volunteers to share other strategies they used, such as reading aloud.

INFORMAL ASSESSMENT

Having students summarize in this way will help you informally assess how well they comprehended the **theme** or message of each poem. It also will help you see how well they recognized the importance of specific **language** and **images** in contributing to this theme.

Encourage both cooperative and individual responses.

RESPOND TO ART   Turn to page 358, and study the painting, titled *Faraway*. **If you asked this boy what he is doing, how would he respond?** Invite students to write the boy's answer. Have volunteers share their ideas. CREATIVE: SPECULATING

ROLE-PLAY POETS' RESPONSES   **Suppose that Paul Laurence Dunbar, Dan Jaffe, and Stephen Crane were guests on a panel and were asked, "What does this country need more of?" How do you think each might have answered?** Invite students to role-play the responses. CREATIVE: INVENTING NEW SCENES

WRITE A POEM   **Do you believe that Emily Dickinson would have had a different attitude toward a private life if she had lived today?** Ask students to write a poem about solitude in today's society. Encourage a variety of responses. CRITICAL: SPECULATING

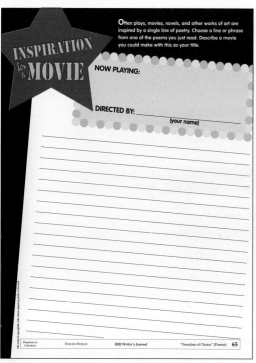

Writer's Journal

Practice Book

WRITER'S JOURNAL
page 65: Writing a creative response

PRACTICE BOOK
page 109: Summarizing the selection

VO·CAB·U·LAR·Y Workshop

Reviewing Key Words

To review how the new vocabulary was used in these poems, display the Key Words. Have students select the Key Word that belongs with each group of synonyms.

1. **dream, trance,** _____ *(revery)*
2. **vain, useless,** _____ *(futile)*
3. **met, stopped,** _____ *(accosted)*
4. **parted, separated,** _____ *(diverged)*

Extending Vocabulary

VISUALIZING THROUGH WORDS   Point out to students that poets use vivid language to describe people, places, things, and ideas so that a mental picture is formed in the reader's mind. Explain that through their use of language, poets often appeal to the senses.

Ask students to reread "Sympathy" and to discuss how the poet appeals to the senses of sight, hearing, touch, and smell in the first stanza. Have them point out specific words and phrases that help them visualize what the poet is writing about.

COOPERATIVE LEARNING   Encourage students to write descriptive phrases about a particular food (without naming it), using words that enable the reader to "see," "touch," "taste," and "smell" that food. Suggest that they use a thesaurus to find the most vivid, exact words. Have partners exchange papers to see whether each can correctly guess the food the other describes. Ask the partners to identify the words or phrases that were the best clues for them.

Integrated Language Arts

WRITING

Writing About the Literature

CRITICAL: EXPOSITORY LETTER Remind students that we all face choices. Invite students to name some choices for which they might seek the advice of someone they trust, such as whether or not to pursue a college-bound track in high school. Ask students to write a letter to an imagined advisor, setting forth both sides of the issue. Suggest they begin by listing as many reasons as they can think of for and against their choice.

Reasons For	Reasons Against

Once students have set down reasons, ask them to rearrange them in order of importance and use the most important ones for writing.
WRITING

AVAILABLE ON PROJECT CARD

CREATIVE: SONG LYRICS Point out that song lyrics often rhyme and are often written in a regular meter. Ask students to decide whether or not that makes the song lyrics poetry. Then invite students to write new lyrics to a familiar tune. They may want to use "freedom of choice" as their theme. Have volunteers sing or display their lyrics.
LISTENING/SPEAKING/WRITING

SPEAKING/LISTENING

A Symbol of Freedom
AVAILABLE ON PROJECT CARD

Elicit from students some of the different symbols that the poets used to stand for individual freedom or the lack of it. Then ask students to work with a partner to choose one of these symbols that is meaningful to them. Partners should prepare a presentation of their symbol. Invite students to be original and creative by thinking of options, including writing about the symbol, making it, being it, role-playing a scene that demonstrates it, or choosing their own form of presentation.
LISTENING/SPEAKING/READING/WRITING

SPEAKING/LISTENING

Emote! (a Little)

Ask students to find a poem they like, not included in the Student Anthology, and to memorize it for recitation. Suggest that they rehearse the poem as they would for Readers Theatre, thinking first about the speaker's mood, tone, and so on. Call on volunteers to recite their poems, and ask the rest of the group to comment. LISTENING/SPEAKING/READING

E. PASSARELLI

SPELLING

Spelling Review

SPELLING WORDS: *admiring, admiration, futile, futility, horizon, horizontal, moral, morality, multiplied, multiplication*

Ask the students to look up each Spelling Word in a dictionary. Have them write the word, its pronunciation (including all stress and other diacritical marks), and its meaning. Then tell the students to write five different sentences. In each one, they must use two different words that come from the same word families as the Spelling Words. These words may be the Spelling Words, the base words used to make the Spelling Words, roots, or new words formed by adding prefixes, suffixes, or inflectional endings. When students are finished, ask them to share their sentences orally. LISTENING/SPEAKING/READING/WRITING/SPELLING

INTEGRATED SPELLING

page 52: Writing words with shifting accents

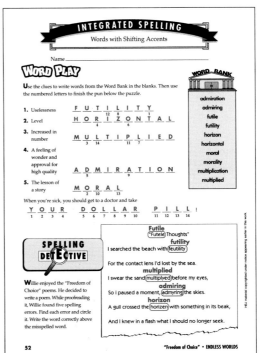

Integrated Spelling

LITERARY APPRECIATION
INTRODUCE

Poetry

OBJECTIVE: *To identify the elements that distinguish poetry from prose*

1	Focus

Explain what makes poetry different from prose.

Remind students that early in "Freedom of Choice" they named some reasons why poetry is easier to memorize than prose. Ask them to review those reasons. (Students may suggest rhyme, meter, imagery, length, sounds.) Point out that because these same elements make poetry different from prose, we read poetry differently. We read it slowly to savor the imagery, and we listen for the sound as much as for the meaning of the words.

2	Teach/Model

Discuss how a theme might be handled in poetry and in prose.

Have students reread "I'm Nobody!" on page 357. Discuss how Emily Dickinson might have expressed in an essay her thoughts about the virtues of a private life. She might have told us at length that Americans admire famous people but that they are wrong to do so because famous people tend to be pompous. Point out that she gets the same message or theme across more vividly in an eight-line poem.

Model the thinking.

Model how to identify the elements of figurative and vivid language that make a poem different from prose:

> **Unlike the imagined essay, the poem draws you in right away when the first line asks, "Who are you?" The word "banish" conveys society's attitude toward unknown people, and the image of the frog makes you see with few words how famous people puff themselves up with pride.**

Explain that because they use condensed language, poems pack a lot of meaning into a little space. Tell students that not all poems have rhyme or meter, but most use striking images and condensed language.

| 3 | Practice/Apply |

Have students apply the learning.

On the board, write *figurative language, tone, word play, rhyme*. Ask students to discuss how each of these poetic elements makes "Advice to Travelers" different from an essay on the importance of being oneself.

| 4 | Summarize |

Informally assess the learning.

Ask students to discuss the elements that make "The Road Not Taken" a poem. Check students' understanding by having them summarize what they learned. (Unlike prose, poems convey meaning through imagery, tone, sounds, and sometimes rhyme and meter. Poems also make use of condensed language.)

CHALLENGE Ask students to find examples of haiku in the school or local library. Have them read the haiku and any accompanying introduction to find out what distinguishes haiku from other forms of poetry. Then ask them to try writing some haiku. Have students bind their haiku in a poetry collection to share with classmates.

SECOND-LANGUAGE SUPPORT Students may demonstrate their understanding of the literary form by writing poems in their first language. Suggest that after writing, students trade poems and critique each other's work. (See *Second-Language Support Manual*.)

Paraphrasing

OBJECTIVE: *To paraphrase poetic statements in order to understand their meaning*

| 1 | Focus |

Explain the value of paraphrasing poetry.

Have students cite poetry lines they had trouble understanding in "Freedom of Choice." Write their responses on the board. Then ask what is troublesome about these particular lines. (Accept reasonable responses: They are in a special kind of language.) Explain that when we are puzzled by poetic statements, it is helpful to *paraphrase* them, or restate them in everyday English.

| 2 | Teach/Model |

Model the thinking.

Choose one of the examples that students cited, or use lines 5–6 of "Sympathy." Point out that these lines are difficult because they contain both archaic and figurative language.

> **My first step is to change "opes" to "opens" and "chalice" to "cup." But when I read the lines with these changes, I am still puzzled. Why does a cup have perfume? To what does *its* refer? Then I realize that *its* refers to the opened bud and that a flower—the opening bud—is cup-shaped, so perfume must refer to the scent of the flower. In everyday English, the line would read: "When the first flower opens and releases its scent."**

Draw a translation chart on the board to help students visualize what to do.

Poetic Language		Everyday Language
The first perfume from its chalice steals	=	When the first flower opens and releases its scent

3 Practice/Apply

Have students apply the learning.

COOPERATIVE LEARNING Invite students in groups to paraphrase other lines that were cited as troublesome, using similar translation charts. Have the groups share the results of their work.

4 Summarize

Informally assess the learning.

Have students summarize what they learned. (Paraphrasing poetic passages helps readers understand what the passages mean.)

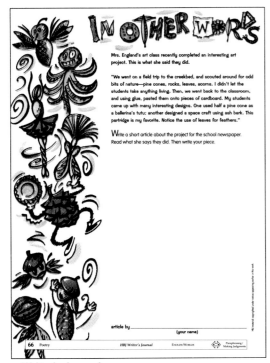

Writer's Journal

Practice Book

Figurative Language

OBJECTIVE: *To appreciate simile and metaphor*

Review

Review the importance of figurative language.

Remind students that both poets and writers of prose use vivid and unexpected comparisons, or figurative language, to help readers imagine things more clearly or share an emotion more deeply. Have students reread "Sympathy" by Paul Dunbar on page 351 and discuss the main comparison of the poem. (The speaker indirectly compares himself, a person who does not feel free, to a caged bird.)

Review types of figurative language.

Remind students that two types of figurative language are similes, which compare two unlike things using the word *like* or *as,* and metaphors, which make an implied comparison.

Have students reread the first stanza of "Sympathy." Model how to distinguish between similes and metaphors:

The line "The river flows like a stream of glass" compares the water to glass, using the word *like*. It is a simile. The poet's comparison of a flower to a chalice is an implied comparison. It does not say directly that a flower is like a chalice. It is a metaphor.

Then have students identify which type of figurative language is used in the main comparison of the poem, that of the speaker to a caged bird. (metaphor)

Draw on the board a chart to record and identify similes and metaphors:

Simile	Comparison	Metaphor	Comparison
"like a stream of glass"	river to glass	"first bud opens . . . perfume from its chalice"	a flower compared to a chalice, or cup

Practice/Apply

Have students identify similes and metaphors.

Call on volunteers to find examples of similes and metaphors in other poems or prose selections and list them on the chart.

Summarize

Informally assess the learning.

Check students' understanding by having them summarize what they reviewed. (Two kinds of figurative language are metaphors and similes. A metaphor implies a comparison between two unlike things. A simile compares things by using *like* or *as*.)

CHALLENGE Invite students to read works by modern poets and to bring in examples of similes and metaphors they like. Encourage them to explain the figurative language they found.

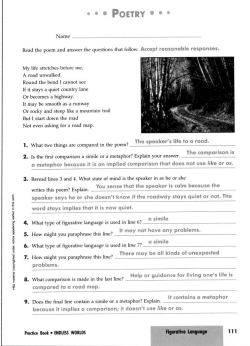

• • • POETRY • • •

Name _____

Read the poem and answer the questions that follow. *Accept reasonable responses.*

My life stretches before me,
A road unwalked.
Round the bend I cannot see
If it stays a quiet country lane
Or becomes a highway.
It may be smooth as a runway
Or rocky and steep like a mountain trail
But I start down the road
Not even asking for a road map.

1. What two things are compared in the poem? ___ *The speaker's life to a road.*

2. Is the first comparison a simile or a metaphor? Explain your answer. ___ *The comparison is a metaphor because it is an implied comparison that does not use like or as.*

3. Reread lines 3 and 4. What state of mind is the speaker in as he or she writes this poem? Explain. ___ *You sense that the speaker is calm because the speaker says he or she doesn't know if the roadway stays quiet or not. The word stays implies that it is now quiet.*

4. What type of figurative language is used in line 6? ___ *a simile*

5. How might you paraphrase this line? ___ *It may not have any problems.*

6. What type of figurative language is used in line 7? ___ *a simile*

7. How might you paraphrase this line? ___ *There may be all kinds of unexpected problems.*

8. What comparison is made in the last line? ___ *Help or guidance for living one's life is compared to a road map.*

9. Does the final line contain a simile or a metaphor? Explain. ___ *It contains a metaphor because it implies a comparison; it doesn't use like or as.*

Practice Book ▪ ENDLESS WORLDS   Figurative Language   111

Practice Book

PRACTICE BOOK
page 111: Identifying figures of speech

Integrated **Curriculum**

SCIENCE
Poetry in Nature

Tell students that Robert Frost often wrote about nature in his native New England. As in "The Road Not Taken," he would take a scene before him and make it stand for a human thought or feeling. In that poem, for example, a forest crossroads stands for choice. Ask students to study some natural spot in their neighborhood, see what plants grow there, and what animals inhabit it. Invite them to speculate on how Frost might have turned the spot into a subject for a poem. Then ask them to write the title of such a poem and to show in the title how something specific in nature suggests a human thought or feeling. WRITING

SOCIAL STUDIES
The Sound of Silence

CULTURAL AWARENESS Ask a group of students to research and report on major events that occurred in America during Emily Dickinson's lifetime (1830–1886). The group might divide the task by decades or by interests, with some doing research on political and military events, others on women's roles, and still others covering literary movements such as Transcendentalism. After the group has made its report, point out that not a hint of these events found its way into Emily Dickinson's poetry. Discuss with students what that suggests about the poet's life and work.
LISTENING/SPEAKING/READING/WRITING

ART
Picture Perfect

Ask students to pretend they have been hired to illustrate a volume of poetry by one of the poets in this selection. Ask them to think about the following questions: What kind of visuals would they choose—photographs, ink drawings, watercolors? Would they use color or only black and white? Would the illustrations be serious or funny? Then have students write a proposal one or two paragraphs long suggesting illustrations and explaining why the style of art fits the poetry. Artistically inclined students may wish to illustrate one of the poems. WRITING

ART
Commentaries in Art
AVAILABLE ON PROJECT CARD

CULTURAL AWARENESS In Paul Dunbar's poem "Sympathy," he speaks about the impact of social oppression. Although his message is relevant now, it applied particularly at the time he was writing. Art in different forms makes social statements about particular times in history. Invite students to choose one period of time in America's history, such as the Revolutionary War or Civil War period, or another period they are currently studying. Suggest that students hunt for paintings, music, poetry, or other artistic forms from the period that indicate what the times were like. Have students share what they learned and if possible show or read some of the work they were particularly inspired by. LISTENING/SPEAKING/READING/WRITING

SOCIAL STUDIES
Freedom to Choose
AVAILABLE ON PROJECT CARD

Discuss with students that throughout history there have been people who have publicly demonstrated their belief in individuality and freedom of choice. Ask them to choose people from history, research their lives, and reveal in a brief essay how their lives are testaments to these beliefs. To help students get started, you might suggest the names of several individuals, such as Socrates, Amelia Earhart, and Martin Luther King, Jr.
READING/WRITING

Multi*Cultural*
P E R S P E C T I V E S

Many Paths

READ ALOUD TO STUDENTS:

AS STEPHEN CRANE SUGGESTS IN "I SAW A MAN," SOME PEOPLE FLATLY REJECT THE NOTION OF "YOU CAN NEVER—."

In New Mexico during the 1940s and 1950s, Al Momaday, a young Kiowa artist, began involving community members in school art programs, building on his Native American artistic and cultural traditions. Momaday's programs won international recognition and inspired many students, including his son, the author N. Scott Momaday.

In Vietnam in 1965, African American army medic Lawrence Joel spent 24 hours under continuous fire, aiding the injured during a surprise attack. "I was afraid," Joel said, "but I knew that was my job." Shot twice, he left his own wounds untended in order to care for others. Joel won the Congressional Medal of Honor.

In Texas during the 1960s, Anita Martinez struggled to get roads paved and lighting improved in her community of West Dallas. Later, as the first Hispanic American to serve on the Dallas City Council, she established a youth recreation center and began a ballet folklórico company to promote cultural pride.

These three people doggedly pursued their own dream—and reached it. ■

ACTIVITY CORNER
AVAILABLE ON PROJECT CARD

■ Have students interview adults they know, asking about accomplishments, large or small, that the adults are proud of. Encourage students to interview people from a variety of ethnic groups. Guide them in creating oral histories based on the interviews. As a group, discuss how each adult used individual strengths, skills, and interests.

■ The *Foxfire* books record individuals' accounts of experiences and daily tasks that were commonplace in rural America a few decades ago. Have students locate these books and present oral reports on some of the individuals whose skills and accomplishments are recorded.

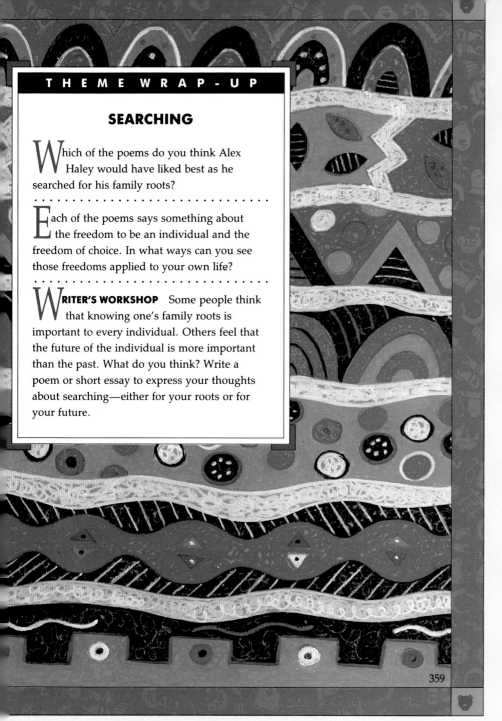

THEME WRAP-UP

SEARCHING

Which of the poems do you think Alex Haley would have liked best as he searched for his family roots?

· ·

Each of the poems says something about the freedom to be an individual and the freedom of choice. In what ways can you see those freedoms applied to your own life?

· ·

WRITER'S WORKSHOP   Some people think that knowing one's family roots is important to every individual. Others feel that the future of the individual is more important than the past. What do you think? Write a poem or short essay to express your thoughts about searching—either for your roots or for your future.

359

Discuss with students the ways in which the poems and "Mister Kinte!" reflect the theme of searching for one's identity. Ask how the problems confronted by Alex Haley and the various poets are alike or different. Explain that the Theme Wrap-Up questions and activity on page 359 will help students think further about roots, individuality, and freedom of choice.

Note that pages 359A–359B provide support for applying the writing process to the last question.

1 Suggest that students first review the eight poems they have read and then decide which one's message might appeal to Alex Haley. *(Accept reasonable responses: Like the speaker in Frost's poem, Haley might feel that he has taken "the road less traveled by, / And that has made all the difference.")*
INFERENTIAL: SYNTHESIZING/SPECULATING

2 As they formulate their answers, encourage students to think about the freedoms they value most. *(Responses will vary.)*
CRITICAL: EXPRESSING PERSONAL OPINIONS

Writer's Workshop

See pages 359A–359B for suggestions for applying the writing process. Responses should express a personal viewpoint and therefore need not draw on the reading. You may prefer to allow students to respond to the theme in their own way. WRITING PROCESS: A POEM OR AN ESSAY

Writer's Workshop

A POEM OR AN ESSAY

For those students who wish to write poems, review the elements of poetry. You might want to use familiar poems and have students recognize imagery, rhythm, and rhyme. Then have students brainstorm a list of images they would use in writing poems about searching for their roots or their future. Suggest that students refer to the Handbook in the *Writer's Journal* as they write, revise, and proofread their poems or essays.

Prewriting

Before students write, have them

- decide whether they will write about searching for their roots or their future.
- select the writing form with which they can best convey their thoughts and feelings.
- use a word web to brainstorm incidents, people, objects, and feelings associated with the subject. The web might look like this:

Drafting

Ask students to write a draft of the poem or essay. Encourage them to

- express feelings, as well as thoughts and perceptions.
- use language and images that evoke a response in the reader.
- write from a consistent, first-person point of view.
- avoid worrying about spelling, punctuation, and grammar for the present.

COMPUTER CONNECTION Students may want to use a computer during the drafting and revising stages so that they can easily experiment with combining sentences by using appositives.

Responding and Revising

Suggest that students trade drafts with a partner working in the same form. Offer the following tips for evaluating and revising:

- Are the images fresh and appropriate? If not, the writer needs to revise them to make sure they convey the sort of feeling he or she intends.
- Has the writer avoided wordy constructions by combining sentences with appositives? (See the Language/Literature Link below.)

STUDENT SELF-ASSESSMENT OPTION Students may use the Writing Self-Assessment Checklist in the *Portfolio Teacher's Guide.* Suggest that as they use the checklist, they focus on the effective use of images and details so that the poem or the essay appeals to both emotions and reason.

Proofreading

Offer these proofreading tips:

- Capitalize the names of countries and continents and adjectives formed from them, such as *Africa, African.*
- Capitalize words that define family relationships only when they are part of a name—for example, *Uncle Ben* (but *my favorite uncle, Ben*).

Publishing

Discuss with students options for publishing their poems and essays. Some students may wish to share their work with a member of their immediate family. Suggest that students also save their work in their reading/writing portfolios.

LANGUAGE/LITERATURE LINK

Combining Sentences

Remind students that an appositive is a noun that defines or explains another noun. Point out that appositives add extra details to writing. To illustrate, have students turn to paragraph two on page 339 of "Mister Kinte!" and read this sentence: "Ebou and his father, Alhaji Manga, assembled." The appositive phrase *Alhaji Manga* adds the Moslem name of Ebou's father—an extra detail that may be interesting to the reader. Have students review their work, looking for opportunities to combine sentences by using appositives.

Speaking Option

ORAL INTERPRETATION You may want to adapt the *Writer's Workshop* to allow students to present an oral presentation of their poem or essay. Have students follow the guidelines for Prewriting, Drafting, and Responding and Revising. Offer these tips to help students present their poem or essay orally:

- Practice reading your poem or essay before a partner or into a tape recorder.
- Make sure you pronounce words correctly and articulate them clearly.
- Try out and choose appropriate tones of voice and facial expressions.

Have each student read aloud his or her poem or essay in front of a small group of classmates.

Coming of Age

Discuss with students the meaning of *coming of age*. Ask to what the phrase might apply besides reaching age twenty-one. Have students read the introduction and the selection titles on Student Anthology page 361. Point out that both titles refer to a place or locality, and ask why this might be so. Then ask students to look at the boys in the illustration and to speculate about how they might mature.

PACING   Although you may need to adapt to the individual needs within your classroom, this theme has been designed to take about two weeks to complete.

360

Management Options

THE LITERATURE-BASED CLASSROOM   Providing a literature-rich curriculum creates unique classroom management challenges. Some management options for the selections in this theme follow.

PREVIEWING A SELECTION   You might occasionally want to ask a small group of students to preview a selection for the whole class. After reading the selection, either independently or cooperatively, students in the preview group should meet to decide what to include in their presentation. Their goal should be to spark interest and motivate other students to read the selection. At some point, you might want to sit in briefly with the preview group to observe their progress and answer any questions they might have.

THEME

COMING OF AGE

Growing up is a challenging experience. As the characters in these selections face new problems and find solutions, think about how you meet your own new experiences.

C O N T E N T S

AT THE COVE
by Laurence Yep

WORDS FROM THE AUTHOR:
LAURENCE YEP

THE SECOND HIGHEST POINT
by Ouida Sebestyen

361

STUDENTS AT RISK
Encourage students to talk with a partner about their own "Coming of Age" experiences before they begin to read the selections. Then have the partners read the selections cooperatively.

GIFTED AND TALENTED
As an extension or alternative to the Writer's Workshop activity, have students work in a group to come up with possible solutions to specific problems their classmates may be experiencing. Invite students to write their concerns anonymously on index cards and place them in a box. The group can discuss possible solutions and record them on another card. Also see the *Challenge Cards.*

SPECIAL EDUCATION STUDENTS
Students may have difficulty focusing on the lines of print and keeping them separate. Suggest that they use a strip of oaktag to help keep their eyes on the line.

LIMITED ENGLISH PROFICIENT STUDENTS
As students read "The Second Highest Point," have them note any of the slang expressions they do not understand and discuss them with an English-fluent student.

GROUPING   You may find that when students are permitted to form their own groups, the same students work together each time. To ensure more variation in groupings, consider assigning each student a number or letter. Students with like numbers or letters can then form groups. Change the students' numbers or letters frequently.

READING/WRITING PORTFOLIO   Instruct students to keep in their portfolios their writing responses to the theme selections. Remind them also to add to their personal journals notes on their independent reading.

AT THE COVE

by Laurence Yep

LAURENCE YEP (1948–) was born in San Francisco, California. As a child, he was the only Chinese boy growing up in his neighborhood. "Probably the reason that much of my writing has found its way to a teenage audience is that I'm always pursuing the theme of being an outsider—an alien— and many teenagers feel they're aliens," he has said. Yep's books have received many awards, including the Newbery Medal, the Children's Choice award, the American Library Association's Notable Book awards, and the Boston Globe–Horn Book Award. Critics have praised Yep's works for their memorable characters and their portraits of relationships.

MORE BOOKS BY LAURENCE YEP
Dragonwings. HarperCollins, 1976. AVERAGE
The Lost Garden. Silver Burdett, 1991. AVERAGE
The Serpent's Children. HarperCollins, 1984. AVERAGE

OTHER BOOKS ABOUT COMING OF AGE
Dicey's Song by Cynthia Voigt. Macmillan, 1982.
    CHALLENGING
The Secret of Gumbo Grove by Eleanora E. Tate.
    Franklin Watts, 1987. AVERAGE

> "**I**'m always pursuing the theme of being an outsider— an alien."

SELECTION SUMMARY
This excerpt from the novel *Sea Glass* concerns a boy who feels like an outsider. Mr. Chin is outstanding at sports. His son Craig seems to lack this talent. Craig visits Uncle Quail, an elderly friend, and the two explore the wonders of Uncle Quail's reef "garden." From Uncle Quail, Craig learns that, as a boy, his father had a strong interest in plants but his grandfather kept his father from pursuing that interest. Uncle Quail points out that Craig needs to accept himself as he is. Craig begins to gain a new perspective on both himself and his father.

LESSON PLANNER			
	Materials	**Integrated Curriculum**	**Meeting Individual Needs**
1 READING LITERATURE pp. 361B–381	Student Anthology pp. 362–381 Transparency 21 Second-Language Support Manual Practice Book p. 112 Integrated Spelling p. 53 Integrated Spelling T.E. pp. 72–73	Spelling Spelling Pretest Spelling-Vocabulary Connection (long *e* sound)	Second-Language Support Vocabulary 361C Strategic Reading 361D, 376
2 RESPONDING TO LITERATURE pp. 381A–381D	Writer's Journal p. 67 Practice Book p. 113 Integrated Spelling p. 54 Integrated Spelling T.E. pp. 72–73	Vocabulary Workshop Reviewing Key Words Extending Vocabulary Writing About the Literature Speaking/Listening Spelling Review	Cooperative Learning 381B, 381C
3 LEARNING THROUGH LITERATURE pp. 381E–381J	Second-Language Support Manual Writer's Journal p. 68 Practice Book pp. 114–115	Science Social Studies/Art Social Studies Art/Science Multicultural	Challenge 381F, 381H Second-Language Support 381F, 381H

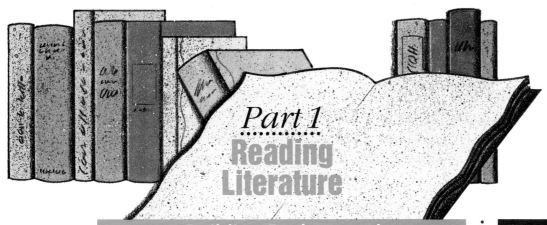

Part 1
Reading Literature

Building Background

Access prior knowledge and develop vocabulary concepts.

Tell students they will be reading a story about a teenage boy and an elderly man who takes a grandfatherly interest in him. Ask students to complete a chart like the one below, contrasting a boy's relationship with an elderly friend and his relationship with his father.

Boy and Father	Boy and Elderly Friend
see each other every day	see each other only on special occasions
have to deal with issues of discipline and responsibility	may make fewer demands on each other

Have students quickwrite a list.

Have students list three activities they could do with an elderly friend. Have volunteers share their writing.

Vocabulary Strategies

Introduce Key Words and strategies.

Tell students that "At the Cove" may contain unfamiliar words. Display Transparency 21, or write the paragraph on the board. Have students read silently and use context, phonics, and structural analysis to figure out the meanings of the underlined words. Invite a volunteer to read the paragraph aloud. Provide help with pronunciation.

Transparency 21 Key Words

Inching along the reef, the little girl lost her balance on the rocky ridge. She flailed about, her arms waving wildly. Quickly, her father's strong, sinewy arms caught her before she fell into the water.

"It was hard for me to balance, too," he remembered, reminiscing about his younger days. Absorbed by his story, the little girl devoured every word. She coaxed him for more in a wheedling, persuasive voice. Smiling indulgently, he gave in to her wish.

CULTURAL AWARENESS

To help students appreciate the cultural background and setting of "At the Cove," share with them the information under Cultural Background/Setting on page 363.

KEY WORDS DEFINED

reef   ridge of sand, coral, or rocks lying near the water's surface

flailed   waved, thrashed

sinewy   strong, firm

reminiscing   remembering, telling about the past

devoured   absorbed, took in eagerly

wheedling   coaxing

indulgently   agreeably, generously

Check students' understanding.

Have students demonstrate their understanding of the Key Words by completing webs like the following. STRATEGY: CATEGORIZING

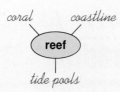

(Accept reasonable responses: *devoured*—swallowed, took in greedily; *indulgently*—mildly, kindly; *wheedling*—flattering, pleading; *sinewy*—strong and thin, muscled; *flailed*—thrashed, waved arms; *reminiscing*—remembering fondly, looking back.)

After discussing the Key Words with students, encourage them to add some of the new words to the chart they completed in Building Background. For example, the boy might listen to the elderly friend *reminiscing*.

Integrate spelling with vocabulary.

SPELLING-VOCABULARY CONNECTION *Integrated Spelling* page 53 reinforces spellings of the **long** *e* sound in the following Key Words: *reef, sinewy, wheedling*.

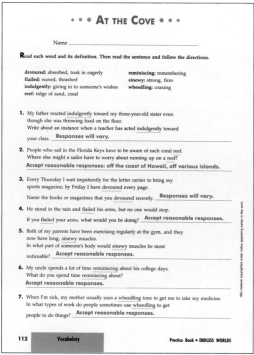

Practice Book

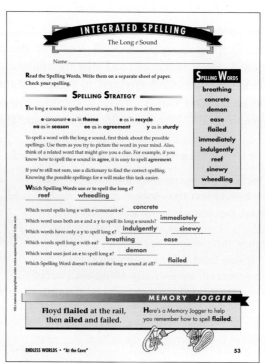

Integrated Spelling

PRACTICE BOOK
page 112: Reinforcing Key Words

INTEGRATED SPELLING
page 53: Writing and spelling words with the long *e* sound

NOTE: These pages may be completed now or after students have read the selection.

Preview and Predict

Have students preview the literature.

Remind students that realistic fiction reflects what happens in real life. Tell them to think about what they already know about relationships as they preview "At the Cove." In addition to having them preview by reading the title and looking at the illustrations, have students read the introduction to the excerpt.

Help students make predictions.

Remind students that in most fiction the main characters have problems, or conflicts, that they are trying to solve. Ask students what the introduction tells them about Craig's problems. Have them predict how his afternoon with an elderly friend might help him solve them.

Introduce the problem-solution chart.

Use the problem-solution chart to encourage students to predict how Craig might solve his problems.

PROBLEM-SOLUTION CHART

Character	Problem	Solution
Craig	can't make friends doesn't agree with father	

PERSONAL JOURNAL Have students copy the headings in their personal journals, or have them use *Practice Book* page 113. (See page 381B in this Teacher's Edition.) Have them begin the first two columns and make predictions for the third column. Students can complete the chart as they read the story or afterward. (Students will return to the chart after reading, in Summarizing the Literature.)

Setting a Purpose

Have students set purposes.

Have students think about the predictions they have just made to develop a question or two that they would like answered by the story's end. Invite volunteers to share one question with the others.

Model purpose-setting, if necessary.

If students have difficulty setting a purpose for reading, model the thinking process:

> **From previewing, I know that Craig has some problems. He's the "new kid on the block" and finds it hard to make friends. He and his father don't agree on the importance of sports. My purpose for reading is to find out whether Uncle Quail will be able to help Craig resolve his disagreement with his father.**

SECOND-LANGUAGE SUPPORT Students may benefit from the Guided Reading activities and the additional guidance under the Student Anthology pages. (See *Second-Language Support Manual.*)

OPTIONS FOR READING

Independent Reading

Have students read the story silently with their purpose for reading in mind.

Guided Reading

Follow the Guided Reading suggestions that appear on pages 362, 370–371, and 380. These suggestions model strategic reading.

Numbered Annotations

Use the numbered annotations beside the Student Anthology pages to heighten students' appreciation of the story.

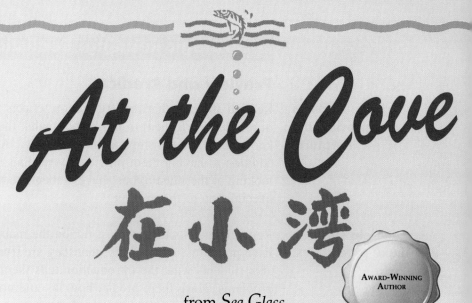

At the Cove

在小湾

AWARD-WINNING
AUTHOR

from *Sea Glass*
by Laurence Yep

Craig Chin, the narrator in Sea Glass, *has grown up in Chinatown in San Francisco. When his family moves to Concepcion, California, he finds it difficult to make "Westerner" friends. He continues to rebel against his father's wishes that he excel in sports. On Saturdays, Craig delivers groceries from his father's store. One of the customers, an elderly man known as Uncle Quail, lives "on a small cove about fifty feet across formed by cliffs and a headland." Craig tells about one Saturday when Uncle Quail invites him back to the cove to swim.*

illustrations by Leslie Wu
Chinese calligraphy by Muns Quan

362

SET PURPOSE/PREDICT: PAGES 362–371 Have students read through the second to the last paragraph on page 371 to find out what kind of people Craig and Uncle Quail are and what additional problems Craig encounters. As students read, suggest they add appropriate material to their charts.

363

CULTURAL BACKGROUND/SETTING

The story takes place on the coast of California, a state with many Chinese Americans. Many Chinese immigrants came to the United States in the 1860s to build the Central Pacific Railroad, part of the first transcontinental railroad in the United States.

Like other immigrants to the United States, Chinese people in the late 1860s and 1870s first settled in their own communities. Today, some Chinese Americans prefer to live within these communities; however, many others have moved into the community at large.

生長
Growth

That Saturday Uncle was already down at the beach. He looked thin and bony and sinewy as he sat with his jacket draped around his shoulders. I turned the wagon around and pushed it before me through the gate. Then I leaned back on my heels and gently lowered it down the path, trying not to look to my right where the edge of the path was. Uncle didn't look up even though the old wagon rattled noisily down the rocky path.

I lifted the carton of groceries out of the wagon onto the porch, sliding it over toward the door. Then I put the old carton with the garbage into the wagon and parked it against the porch so it wouldn't roll down. One lonely sea gull wheeled about, crying over the calm waters of the cove. "Afternoon," I called down to him. My voice echoed on the rocks but Uncle didn't turn around. He just waved his hand vaguely in the air.

I picked up my towel, which was rolled into a cylinder, and with that tucked under my arm I went down to the beach. The tide was really low today. The beach was a lot bigger and I could see a lot of the reef. At the foot of the path, I began to slog across the sand toward where Uncle sat. "I didn't squeeze the bread this time."

"I wait and see." Uncle had a small crowbar in his hand. It was tied to his wrist by a thong. I watched as Uncle slipped the end of the crowbar between the shell and the tan flesh of an abalone.

"You went diving for abalone without me." I stared at him accusingly.

When Uncle had the crowbar positioned just the way he wanted, he shoved it in hard. I suppose he must have broken the abalone's hold on its shell, because he pried it out easily, dropping it into a basket. "I walk through my gardens and I find this one."

I looked around the cove, but it looked especially empty and lifeless now. Even the gull was off to some other place. There were barnacles on the cliffsides, but they were above the water so they were shut up tight and I didn't think they counted. To me, anyway, it looked like the only living things there were me and Uncle.

"What gardens?" I asked skeptically.

Uncle smiled as if it were his secret. "I thought you were one smart boy. Can't you see them?" He slipped the thong of the crowbar from his wrist and dropped it into the basket.

"No, I can't." Sullenly I folded my arms across my chest.

"You think maybe you see, but you don't. Not really." He pointed at my eyes. "Your eyes, they tell your mind a lot of stuff. But your mind, he's one busy fellow. He say, 'I don't have time to listen. Fill out these forms.' So the eyes, they fill out the forms, but there's no place on the forms for everything they see. Just a lot of boxes they are supposed to mark or not. So your mind, he misses a lot." Uncle

364

nodded his head firmly. "You gotta look at the world. Really look."

"Like you?" I was beginning to feel impatient with Uncle.

"No. I only do it in a small, small way. But if you can make your mind listen to your eyes, really listen, what wonders you see." Uncle looked out at his cove wistfully. "You know *the Dragon Mother*?"

4 "No," I said reluctantly.

"Now there was some person who saw the world. *The Dragon Mother* was a human once, but her mind listen to her eyes. She go for a walk, like you and me, we do sometimes. But this woman, she see a dragon's egg." Uncle pretended to look down sharply at the wet sand and hunch his shoulders and hold out his hands from his sides as if he had just seen something.

I looked at the same spot on the beach. "Dragon's egg?"

"You know that the dragons are kings of the sea." Uncle tapped my arm with the back of his hand.

I drew away slightly. "Sure, I know something about that stuff. They live in the sea and in the rivers and they bring rain."

Uncle motioned to the spot on the beach where he had pretended to find the object. "Well, this woman, she find this rock." Uncle pantomimed picking something up from the sand. "She go home and show it to her friends. Everyone tell her, 'You're stupid. This is only a rock.' But she say, 'Mind your own business. This is one special thing.' So she dig a little pool by her home." Uncle scooped some sand from the beach with his hand and set down the imaginary object in his hand. "And she put in seawater over the thing. And she change the water every day for a year. And everyone laugh at her. But she keep doing it because she knows it's special even if they don't. And then, one day, one day . . . the thing hatches." Uncle stretched his fingers wide above the hole he had just dug. "But the baby, it's no sea turtle, no other animal. It's a dragon." Slowly Uncle lifted his arms and spread them as if the dragon were growing in front of us. "She raise this little dragon like

365

4 CONNOTATION
What word tells you that Craig is not eager to hear the story of the Dragon Mother? (reluctantly)
LITERAL: NOTING IMPORTANT DETAILS

Why do you think he reacts the way he does? *(Accept reasonable responses: He may think that old Chinese stories are boring; he knows Uncle Quail is trying to teach him a lesson.)*
INFERENTIAL: SPECULATING

Cultural Awareness At the bottom of the first column, Uncle Quail mentions the Dragon-Kings. You may want to point out to students that in Chinese mythology four Dragon-Kings, all brothers, rule the oceans and other bodies of water. According to myth, the Dragon-Kings control the rain and have the power to cause or relieve droughts and floods.

5 FORESHADOWING
What clue does the author give that something special may happen to Craig in this setting? *(Uncle Quail says that the cove is a special place where magic can happen.)*
METACOGNITIVE: NOTING IMPORTANT DETAILS

6 PLOT: ACTIONS/EVENTS
How do Craig and Uncle Quail differ in their reactions to the water? *(Uncle Quail is physically in good shape, seems not to be bothered by the cold water, and swims well. Craig is somewhat overweight, is intensely aware of the cold water, and does not swim well.)*
INFERENTIAL: COMPARING AND CONTRASTING

7 PLOT: CONFLICT
What problem does Craig encounter as he begins to swim? *(A sudden current knocks him off balance.)*
LITERAL: NOTING IMPORTANT DETAILS

How does his mental attitude contribute to his problem? *(He panics and has to be rescued by Uncle Quail.)*
INFERENTIAL: DETERMINING CAUSE-EFFECT

it maybe her own son. And this dragon, he turn out to be a very important dragon and so humans and dragons, they name her *the Dragon Mother*. She became one important person. And only because this woman, she can see." Uncle dropped his hands back down over his knees with loud slapping noises.

"Oh," I said.

5 "This is one special place here. This is the edge of the world. This is where the magic can happen too." Uncle searched my face, looking for some sign of comprehension, but I could only look at him in confusion. Uncle smiled to himself sadly. He pretended to become stern. "Well, you want to swim, or talk, boy?"

"Let's swim." I started to undress self-consciously on the beach. I was already wearing my swimming trunks underneath my pants, so it didn't take me long. In the meantime, Uncle had shrugged off his jacket and waded into the water to begin swimming. I stared at him in surprise.

He moved almost as quickly and easily through the water as the otter we had seen. There was nothing wasted about his motions when he swam. It was pure, simple, graceful.

"Come on." Uncle turned to me from the water. "You just remember one thing. The currents in my cove, they aren't very strong, but even so, don't fight them."

I adjusted the waistband of my trunks over my stomach, knowing that the waistband would slide back under my belly before long.

366

Uncle hadn't shivered or said anything when he walked into the water. You'd have thought it was warm bathwater to **6** him. But I gave a yelp the moment I waded into the water. The water felt so cold that it felt like someone had been chilling it in the refrigerator. I could feel the goose bumps popping out all over my skin, and I began to shake and to huddle up and hold myself.

Uncle waved one hand from where he was floating. "Come on. You get used to it."

I nodded nervously and kept on walking. I felt the beach slope downward sharply, and I immediately found myself in the water up to my chest. The sea wasn't very pleasant to move around in, but it was better than that first moment of shock. Then a wave broke against the reef and spray went flying and the sea surged through the narrow opening The pull of the sudden current wasn't all that strong, but it caught me by surprise so I got knocked off my feet.

I couldn't see. There was only the clouded, stinging salt water all around me. I flailed with my arms, trying to get **7** my feet on something solid, but I couldn't find anything. And then I felt the current begin to draw me away from the beach as it began to flow out toward the sea. I really panicked then, forgetting everything I'd ever been taught. I wanted air. My lungs tried to drag it in, but all they got was salt water. I began to choke.

Then strong hands appeared magically, gripping me on either side. I tried to grab

hold of Uncle. Something. Anything, as long as I could hold on to it. Somehow, though, Uncle managed to avoid me. My head broke above the surface. I could see the light for a moment before the salt water, running down my face, made my eyes close. I gasped, coughed, and gasped again, trying to get the film of seawater out of my lungs.

Uncle's strong hands pulled steadily in toward the beach. Then I could feel firm sand under me. I stumbled. Uncle's hands held me until I got my balance. I started to stagger toward the beach with Uncle supporting me. Gratefully I felt the air around my shoulders and then my chest and then my stomach. I stretched my arms out like a blind man and stumbled out of the surf to fall onto the beach. I lay on my **8** stomach for a moment, coughing and spitting. I could still feel the sea pulling at my ankles, so I crawled another yard farther up the beach. The sea swept higher. I could feel it tugging at my ankles again, as if it were alive and trying to drag me back in.

Then I felt Uncle's shadow as he sat down heavily beside me. "You sure you can swim, boy?"

I sat up, beginning to shiver. Uncle covered my shoulders with my towel. With one corner of the towel I wiped at my face. "I could have told you. I'm just too fat and clumsy. Sorry."

Uncle put on his ragged jacket and sat down. "You feel too sorry for yourself. And that's not good."

"Are you crazy?" I started to shiver, so I pulled the towel tighter around my neck.

"You're the crazy one." Uncle flung sand over his legs. "You want to stay on the beach when you can be out in the water."

"Drowning isn't my idea of fun." I wiped some of the water from my face.

Uncle put his hands behind him and leaned back. "Well, maybe if you're scared . . . "

With a corner of my towel I finished drying my face. "Who said I was scared?"

"Me," Uncle said. "I say you're scared."

"Nothing scares me," I insisted.

Tunelessly Uncle hummed to himself and tapped his fingers against the sand.

"Well, even if I am," I mumbled, "it's stupid to do something just to prove I'm not scared." **9**

"Yes, no, maybe so. Something good shouldn't scare you." Uncle began to rub his palms together so that the sand sprinkled down. "Maybe I ask you to put your head on a railroad track, and you say no, well, that's different."

"I'm still not going in." I shook my head for emphasis.

Uncle worried at the nail of one finger. Some sand got on his lips. "You can walk on the water then?" Uncle smiled, amused.

I liked Uncle when he said that. I mean, Dad would have gone on shouting or wheedling or both, but instead Uncle **10** turned the whole thing into a joke. He seemed to relax then. "You want to go for a walk instead?" He nodded at the beach. "I mean on solid ground?"

367

8 IMAGERY
What vivid verbs and figurative language help the reader visualize Craig after his rescue and imagine how he feels? *(the words* stumbled, stagger, like a blind man, coughing and spitting, pulling, crawled, tugging, as if it were alive, *and* trying to draw me back in)
CREATIVE: VISUALIZING

9 PLOT: CONFLICT
Who do you think is correct in the conflict between Uncle Quail and Craig about doing things to prove one's courage? *(Responses will vary.)*
CRITICAL: EXPRESSING PERSONAL OPINIONS

10 CHARACTERIZATION
What does Craig's comparison of Uncle Quail to his father reveal about his feelings for his father? *(Craig resents his father's manner of getting him to do something; Craig feels his father harasses him continually.)*
INFERENTIAL: DRAWING CONCLUSIONS

家庭
Family

368

Informal Assessment You can informally assess students' comprehension strategies as they are reading silently. On occasion, ask students these questions:

- Is this what you expected to happen next?
- If so, what did you read earlier that helped you predict this? Which details helped you make your prediction?
- If not, what did you predict would happen? What did you read earlier that led you to believe that?

By encouraging students to talk freely about their own thinking, you will get important diagnostic insights into how well they are reading.

How does the mood of the story change once Uncle Quail convinces Craig to take a walk? *(Accept reasonable responses: The mood is less tense as Craig forgets about himself and begins exploring the environment.)*
INFERENTIAL: MAKING COMPARISONS

"Sure," I said, even though the cove wasn't more than twenty yards wide at any point.

Uncle rose and started across the wet sand toward the cliffs on one side of the cove, and I followed him. When he was by the cliffs, Uncle pointed to the walls above the water at the foot-wide bands of chalky little white bumps. "These are mussels, and those"— he gestured at a blackish band about a foot wide below them —"are barnacles." The bands looked like they were painted on both sides of the cove where the tide would reach it about a yard above its present level. "The water's out or they'd all be open to eat the little things in the water.

"And you see the starfish?" Uncle pointed at the water where there was a bright orange spot just below the surface. "He's waiting now. When the water get higher, he climb back up to the barnacles and mussels." We waded cautiously into the surf; and, as the water **11** sucked at my ankles, he took my wrist and guided it under the water. I felt the rough surface of the starfish. Uncle let go of my

wrist and I traced the shape of the starfish and felt the five legs, one of them curled up slightly. My fingers closed round the body of the starfish and I gave a tug; but it felt as if it were part of the cliff wall.

Uncle laughed in delight, like a kid sharing a new toy with someone else. "You want a starfish, you need a crowbar. Once a starfish sits, nobody can pull it up."

I let go of the starfish. "Is this your garden then?" I looked around the cove, feeling disappointed. The bands of mussels and barnacles and the starfish didn't make up a sea garden in my mind.

"I bet you think this is one real crazy old man, right?" Uncle asked. He bent over so that his hands were near the waterline and ran his hands lightly over the face of the barnacles that were clustered so tightly together. He did it lightly, or the rough faces of the barnacles might have cut up his hands. Suddenly he gave a yelp. He lifted out his hand, and I saw clinging to it a long, greenish-brown worm with lots of legs. And then it let go and dropped with a plunk back into the sea.

370

Vocabulary Strategy Elicit from students that the word *plunk* (at the bottom of the second column) is derived from the sound something makes as it sinks heavily. Ask whether they know any other onomatopoetic words, or words derived from the sounds things make. *(bang, pop, boom, crash)*
STRATEGY: WORD ORIGINS

MONITOR COMPREHENSION: PAGES 362–371
What kind of person is Craig? What kind of person is Uncle Quail? (Craig is self-conscious, lacks confidence, and feels impatient with his own shortcomings; Uncle Quail is a patient, good-natured man, interested in the world.) STRATEGIC READING: RETURNING TO PURPOSE

"Did it hurt?" I asked.

"No, see, not even the skin's broken." He showed me the finger. "That's the hunter that stalks and kills, and this whole place is his jungle." He indicated the bands of mussels and barnacles. "And this is just the start of my garden." Uncle smiled, both proud and pleased—like someone who knows a secret that you do not. "Too bad you don't want to see more of it."

I looked uncertainly at the cove. "You **12** mean I have to swim?"

"Out there." He pointed to the reef that was exposed at low tide.

He was one shameless old man to tempt me that way and he knew it. I almost refused again, but I have to admit I was curious about that garden of his.

"Okay. I'll try just once more," I grumbled.

"We'll stay in the shallow end. Then, if you feel good, we can go out." Uncle walked farther into the water and half turned around as he took off his jacket. I whipped the towel off my shoulders and threw it high up on the beach. Uncle threw his jacket beside it. I waded into the sea until I was waist deep. I kept waiting for Uncle to shout instructions at me the way Dad would have, but he didn't.

I took a deep breath. Then another **13** good one. Holding my arms ahead of me, I bent forward and kicked off from the sand. There was that shock for a moment of letting go of the land, and then I was floating. The cold water didn't feel so

bad this time. I twisted my head to the side and breathed in the air and then slid over, floating on my back, letting the sun warm my face and skin.

Uncle began swimming in the water toward me. The spray from his splashing sent a drizzle over me, and then his body was floating alongside of me. He didn't shout anything at me or tell me how to do things better; he just warned me, "Careful. Don't go out too far."

So we stayed floating on our backs for a few minutes.

"Do you want to swim out to the reef?" I asked Uncle finally.

"Oh-kay." Uncle grinned. He started to move his arms, raising a glittering shower

I LOOKED UNCERTAINLY AT THE COVE. "YOU MEAN I HAVE TO SWIM?" "OUT THERE." HE POINTED TO THE REEF THAT WAS EXPOSED AT LOW TIDE.

誠實
Truth

371

12 PLOT: CONFLICT
What struggle is going on in Craig's mind in this scene? *(He's torn between wanting to see Uncle Quail's special place and being afraid to swim out to the reef.)*
INFERENTIAL: SYNTHESIZING

13 CHARACTER'S EMOTIONS
Do you think Uncle Quail's manner affects Craig's swimming? If so, how? *(Accept reasonable responses: Uncle Quail's easygoing manner helps Craig relax and concentrate on his swimming instead of worrying that somebody is going to yell at him.)*
INFERENTIAL: DETERMINING CAUSE-EFFECT

What problem arises for Craig in this part of the story? How do Craig's feelings about himself affect the problem's outcome? (Craig is knocked off balance by an ocean current; his poor self-image causes him to panic and nearly drown.) STRATEGIC READING: SUMMARIZING

How does Uncle Quail help Craig? (He saves him from drowning, and he attempts to get Craig's mind off himself and to boost Craig's confidence.) INFERENTIAL: DRAWING CONCLUSIONS

SET PURPOSE/PREDICT: PAGES 371–381 Ask students to predict what Uncle Quail might do to help Craig stop worrying about himself and think differently about his father. Remind students to enter their predictions on their problem-solution charts. Then invite students to read the rest of the story for confirmation.

How does the author's use of language make the sea and the reef seem like living creatures? *(He uses words that usually refer to living things: trying, patient, breath, beating of the reef's heart.)*
INFERENTIAL: DETERMINING CAUSE-EFFECT

How does the language help suggest a change in Craig? *(Accept reasonable responses: Since it is Craig who notices these things, the language suggests that he is feeling more at home in the sea and is focusing less on himself and more on the world around him.)*
INFERENTIAL: DRAWING CONCLUSIONS

15 CHARACTERIZATION

How can you tell that Uncle Quail shares Craig's new feeling about the reef? *(He pats a rock "affectionately," as if it were a person.)*
METACOGNITIVE: DRAWING CONCLUSIONS

around his head as he swam out toward the rock reef. I followed him much more slowly and clumsily. Once Uncle was at the reef, he stretched out his arms and clung to a large boulder, hoisting himself up. He perched on the boulder with all the ease of a sea gull, as if he had done this thousands of times. I suppose he had if you thought about all the years he had spent in the cove.

Aware of Uncle watching me, I kept on churning toward the reef. I thought he might have some instructions for improvement by now, but still he didn't say anything.

Instead, he only reached out one hand. I clasped it and Uncle almost pulled me up out of the water to sit beside him—I mean, as if he were as rooted as a starfish to that boulder.

"What—?" I began.

"Shhh. Listen." Uncle swept his hand along, palm downward and parallel to the sea, in a short, sharp gesture for quiet.

At first, though, my main concern was getting a better grip on that big rock, but then as I sat there, I could feel the rhythm of the sea surging against the rocky reef that protected the cove, trying to make the opening in the reef bigger. The sea wasn't pounding so much as steadily pushing, as if it knew it had all the time in the world and could be patient. But after sitting there for a while, I almost felt like the reef was living and I could feel its heart beating.

Even now at low tide, I could feel the fine mist in the air—I suppose it was spray

372

from the waves moving against the reef. But it felt almost like the breath of the rocks around me, breathing slowly and quietly along with the beating of the reef's heart.

"We'll start up there, boy." Uncle pointed toward the top of the reef.

"What about the big waves?" I was too interested to pay attention to the cold air.

Uncle shook his head. "I don't think there will be any more. And if there are, the reef will protect us." He patted a rock affectionately. Then he turned and began climbing. I followed him more cautiously the three feet or so to the top of the reef. I took one look at that big empty sea beyond the reef, and then I turned my head back in toward the cove.

Uncle waved his hand to indicate both sides of the reef. "When the sea goes out, all around here—maybe in little cracks, maybe on ledges—there are pools left. And the rocks, maybe they protect the pools so the big strong waves"—Uncle pantomimed a crashing wave stopped short—"the waves can't reach the pools. Then all kinds of things can grow." He spoke slowly and proudly, as if he were just about to pry up the lid to a treasure chest.

At that moment to my right—from a crevice I thought would be too small for anything to live in—a bright blue-and-purple crab scuttled out. It was only a few inches across. It paused when it saw us, and lifted its claws, ready to defend itself. Tiny bubbles frothed at its mouth.

Uncle reached across my lap to wiggle a finger above its head just out of the reach of its claws. The crab scuttled back into its crevice. "The brave, bold hero," Uncle said with a laugh. "Maybe when he goes home, he tells a lot of tales about fighting us." Carefully Uncle stood up then. He held out his hand, and I took it for support as I got slowly to my feet.

"Now do what I do." Confidently, Uncle turned his back to the sea and began to edge side-ways along the top of the reef.

Uncle made it look real easy, but I found myself spreading my arms for better balance and I began to wish the rocks wouldn't vibrate. It was like walking on the back of some sleeping snake that might wake up and shake me off at any moment.

Uncle stopped where two rectangular slabs of rock leaned their tips against one another. One rock faced toward the sea, the other faced toward the cove. He waited shyly for me. I looked down between the rocks. There was a shallow depression on the giant boulder on which the two slabs rested. I caught my breath. The stone looked gray-black when it was wet, and the seawater was almost clear here; and in the daylight, the colors seemed even brighter. There were anemones of all colors—animals shaped like flowers, whose thin petals moved with a life of their own in the still water. Uncle leaned forward, supporting himself against the slabs. His hand barely stirred the surface of the pool **16** as his finger brushed the petals of a red anemone. In the wink of an eye, the anemone had closed up, looking like a fat, bumpy doughnut. The other anemones closed up too. Uncle removed his hand from the pool. We waited for a little while until one by one they opened once again. They were all kinds of bright colors—orange, red, yellow, solid colors that would make any artist ache inside to be able to use.

Uncle paused where a flat slab of rock leaned against the top of the reef. He pointed inside. "Can you see it?"

I looked in at the shadows. It looked like a big ball of spines within the water under the slab. "What is it?"

"A sea urchin," Uncle explained. "It

373

16 DESCRIPTION
How does the description of the anemones support Uncle Quail's earlier statement that the sea is a magical place? *(They are described as strange animals that look like flowers; they change appearances dramatically, "in the wink of an eye.")*
INFERENTIAL: SYNTHESIZING

17 CHARACTER'S TRAITS
How is Uncle Quail like the Dragon Mother in this scene? *(His patient, careful attention allows him and Craig to witness something "magical.")*
INFERENTIAL: MAKING COMPARISONS

18 CHARACTERIZATION
In what way does Craig see the tide pools even more clearly than Uncle Quail does in this scene? *(Although Uncle Quail says the pools are totally separate, Craig, by paying attention, notices that there is a connection between them.)*
LITERAL: NOTING IMPORTANT DETAILS

Why do you think the author included this scene? *(Accept reasonable responses: to show that Craig could now make his own observations, independent of Uncle Quail; to stress the connections between things and between people.)*
CRITICAL: MAKING JUDGMENTS

come up into the high tide pools."

Even as we watched, the sea urchin retreated farther into the shadows by moving its needlelike spines.

From there we climbed lower on the reef to the top of a small boulder which had crumbled. Uncle squatted down. I did the same.

17 Uncle waited, hands clasped, arms resting on top of his thighs. He looked like he could stay in that position forever. "There." Uncle pointed carefully to the shadow of a rock, at a sluglike thing with little stubby tubes at one end and the rest of its back covered with bright orange-red spots. It crept upside down across the pool as if the surface was a floor to it. Behind it, it left a little silver thread.

"He leaves a trail behind him. You know, like a land slug, that's his cousin. See that silver line? That's it. Watch what happens when I break it." Uncle reached down and touched the silvery thread behind the slug. The slug fell slowly through the water as if whatever invisible wires held it up had suddenly broken. When it landed gently on its back on the bottom of the pool, it slowly twisted about in the water, righting itself, and began crawling up the side again. "He keeps on trying, so I know he's gonna get cross."

Uncle stood up, wiping his hands on

成熟
Maturity

374

the side of his swimming trunks. "You know all the pools around here. Well, some of them are big. Some of them are small. And every pool is cut off from the other. Maybe the pools are this far apart." Uncle held his hands an inch from each other. "But the pools, they might as well be miles and miles apart because the animal in one pool won't know about an animal in another pool. You take any animal around here and it would probably think its own pool is the whole world, and it doesn't know there are pools and pools all around it." Uncle sounded awed by the magic and vastness of what he owned.

18 The sea must have been rising higher because the waves were beginning to splash over the top of the reef. I hadn't noticed the narrow little channel before—it was really more like a scratch along the surface of the rocks. But the anemones' pool at the top of the reef must have begun to fill up, because a little trickle of water began to snake its way down into the pool of the sea urchin and then slipped down the channel again, rounded a corner, and slid in a curve down the surface of a rock, into the pool of the slug and on. So Uncle wasn't exactly right. There was a little thread of water connecting the tide pools sometimes before the sea did come in.

"I never dreamed there was so much to see," I said.

Uncle leaned forward and pretended to peer at something for emphasis. "You have to learn how to pay attention to things." He added, "But first you have to

Oral Rereading Divide students into groups of three to reread the dialogue between Craig and Uncle Quail (pages 374–375), beginning *I never dreamed there was so much to see* (column 2, paragraph 2). Students can choose to be Craig, Uncle Quail, or a narrator who reads the passages that are not dialogue. Tell students to read their parts silently before reading them aloud. Each group can practice together before reading for an audience. You may wish to allow students to choose a different passage to read aloud.

like yourself." He gave a tug to his trunks and sat down. "People who don't like themselves, they spend all their time looking at their faults. They don't have time to look at the world."

"What's there to like about myself?" I sat down and bent my knees so I could wrap my arms around my legs and lean my chest against my thighs. "I'm lousy at swimming. I'm lousy at all the *Westerners'* games. I'm lousy at making friends. I'm even lousy at being Chinese. I'm not like anything Dad wants."

Uncle raised one eyebrow. "Is that all you think your father wants? Play games all the time?"

I hugged my legs tighter against my chest. "That's all we ever do."

"Your father, he want other things too." Uncle ran a finger lightly over a scab on his thumb. "At least he used to. I remember when he was a small boy —smaller than you, maybe only ten or eleven. It was only talk from a small boy, but it was GOOD talk. He tell me, 'Uncle, I'm going to know everything about plants. You want to know something about them, you come to me.'" Uncle cocked his head to one side. "Your father always have some book about plants. Always so he can read from it when he have nothing else to do."

It was funny hearing about Dad when he was a small boy; but what Uncle told me helped explain why Dad had been so hot to start a garden on our very first day here. "I guess he still likes plants," I said.

Uncle, though, was too busy remi-niscing to hear me. "And your father, when he wasn't reading or talking about plants, he was drawing them."

"That's a little hard to swallow," I said. I couldn't associate anything artistic with my dad—not even something like drawing wavy lines on a notepad while he was talking on the phone.

Uncle stiffened and he thrust out his chin. "I'm no liar. I got eyes. I saw them. Maybe the pictures aren't so good, but he say drawing the pictures teach him more than just reading about the plants."

"It's just that I never heard Dad say anything about drawing." I set my chin on top of my knees.

"Your father, he want to grow all kinds of plants and flowers." Uncle pounded his fist against the rock he was sitting on. His fist made a flat, slapping sound. "But your grandfather, he say no. He say it's a waste of money to buy flower seeds. Waste of time to grow them. Your grandfather only let your father grow some vegetables. And your grandfather, he get mad when he find all the drawings. Your grandfather say not to waste good paper that cost so much."

Uncle put his hands down on either side of him and leaned back. "And I watch what happen. Your father was a good boy. It was just like he close a door inside himself. No more books about plants. No more drawing. And," Uncle added sadly, "no more talk about knowing everything about plants. He even tell me he not care about that stuff. But I got eyes. I saw."

375

---

19 THEME
What connection does Uncle Quail make between how people feel about themselves and how they feel about the world? *(People who don't like themselves are so absorbed in their own faults that they don't have time to appreciate the world around them.)*
LITERAL: NOTING IMPORTANT DETAILS

Do you think he is right? Explain. *(Responses will vary.)*
CRITICAL: EXPRESSING PERSONAL OPINIONS

---

20 CHARACTERS' TRAITS
How is Craig's relationship with his father like his father's relationship with Craig's grandfather? *(Both fathers have tried to choose their sons' interests and activities.)*
INFERENTIAL: MAKING COMPARISONS

美麗
Beauty

I bit my lip for a moment and stared at the sea. It was a sad-enough sounding story—whether it was true or not. I guess I could believe some of what Uncle had said—at least the part about Dad's once wanting to grow some flowers, because it would help explain why he had already been planning a garden on our very first day at the store. **21**

It also helped explain his determination to try after the cats had ruined his first plantings. He said he was going to show those cats just who actually ran that backyard. As soon as we could qualify, Dad had taken me to the library to get a card—or so he said—but he'd gotten a card for himself as well. The cards were only temporary cards at first, so we could take out only two books each. Even so, Dad had headed straight for the gardening books like he had memorized their location, and he had taken out two gardening books and talked me into taking out two more. And when we had finally gotten our real cards and could take out six books on each card, Dad had taken out more gardening books.

Finally last month, in March, when Dad had devoured all the gardening books on the library shelves, he had gone to the gardening store and come back with little boxes of flowers to be transplanted. The flowers, Dad informed us, were already large enough to survive the cats and hardy enough to like shady places the best.

Dad had felt so triumphant when he could show us the first flower bud. It was no bigger than my fingernail, and colored

377

21 PLOT: CLIMAX
Why do you think Craig at first doubts the story about his father's boyhood interest? *(Accept reasonable responses: The person Uncle Quail describes doesn't sound like the father Craig knows; Craig is fighting his own sympathy for his father, so he doesn't want to admit that the sad story could be true.)*
INFERENTIAL: DRAWING CONCLUSIONS

Why does Craig start to accept the story and change his view of his father? *(He starts remembering evidence of his father's love for plants, which he had never thought about before.)*
INFERENTIAL: DETERMINING CAUSE-EFFECT

22 CHARACTER'S MOTIVATIONS
How has Craig misjudged until now his father's reasons for being excited about the garden? *(Craig thought his father saw the garden as a competition between himself and the cats who tried to take over the yard.)*
LITERAL: RECOGNIZING CAUSE-EFFECT

23 CHARACTER'S EMOTIONS
Why does Craig start to feel sorry for his father? *(He suddenly realizes that, as a boy, his father had been prevented from doing the one thing that he loved doing most.)*
INFERENTIAL: SYNTHESIZING

lavender. Mom was pleased because Dad was happy, and I said something about how pretty it looked, but in that gray, gloomy backyard the flower bud—I forget the name of the flower—seemed small and insignificant, and even the color didn't seem very bright.

But that didn't seem to stop Dad's enthusiasm as each new bud appeared until there were a lot of them; and that was nothing compared to the time when the first bud began to flower. It was really only half open, with the petals still partly upright, but Dad had pantomimed the opening of the flower with his fingers like he could already see it. I thought Dad had been so happy because he had managed to beat the cats at their own game. Now I could see that the flowers meant more to him.

I looked at Uncle. "Why was Grandfather so mean?"

"All the money have to go home to China. To the wife and the rest of the family there." Uncle shrugged like it was an old story.

"Not even a little something for Dad?"

I wondered. There was a little part inside me that began to feel sorry for Dad.

"The family," Uncle explained simply, "always comes first." He said it as if that should be explanation enough—as if I should already have known that. But Uncle might as well have been talking about the families of people on Jupiter, because it sounded so strange to me.

"That's when your father find other things." Uncle leaned over toward me. "He get real good then at demon[1] games. See, not all the old-timers think demon games are waste of time. Some of the clubs in different Chinatowns, they have teams. Your grandfather, he grumble a little, but he like the respect he get because of your father." Uncle slapped my leg with the back of his hand. "The other Chinese tell your grandfather he must be one strong, quick man if he have a son that strong and that quick. So as long as your father get good grades in school and work hard in the store, he can play the different games. But you

[1]*demon*: Chinese term used for a Westerner

remember that the *demon* games"—Uncle tilted his head up—"they were always your father's second choice."

"I still wish," I said, "that I could be as good as my dad."

Uncle sighed and shook his head. "You try too hard to be Calvin's son." He seemed dissatisfied with what he had said—as if he didn't have enough English to explain all his thoughts to me and he knew I didn't know enough Chinese if we used that language. Uncle folded his legs into a lotus position as if he wanted to become more comfortable before he stretched his arm out toward me. "It's not good if you do everything just like your father. Everyone is different. That's what makes them special." Uncle waved his hand grandly to include the entire reef. "You think it good if all the animals look the same, hah?"

"I have to keep on trying." I shrugged my shoulders, annoyed with Uncle for being so insistent.

There was a long silence while we both listened to the ocean beating against his reef. Finally, I said, "Dad has flower boxes." I thought Uncle might like to know. "He works there every day."

Uncle smiled slowly and nodded his head in approval. "Good. I'm glad Calvin finally got his flowers."

He glanced up at the top of the reef. We could see the spray rising in the air. The drizzle in the air was changing to more like a shower. "Maybe we should go back now," Uncle said. "This reef's not a good place when the tide rises." **24**

"Can't we stay a little while longer?"

"Oh-kay. Oh-kay. A little while then," Uncle said indulgently. I leaned back to look up at the broad sweep of sky overhead. Somehow, sitting on the reef, I felt like the world was a much bigger place than it seemed when I was standing on solid ground. And so much of what I knew when I was on the land didn't seem as certain anymore. I couldn't help hunching my shoulders a little.

Uncle must have been observing me. "Back to the beach, boy. Look at you. You're shivering."

"Not at the cold. It's—"

"No arguments. Come on." Uncle slipped off the rocks into the water.

When we were back on the beach again, I began to shiver for real. A strong wind had begun to sweep in from the sea, so that it was a lot colder than when we had first swum out to the reef. I got my towel from where I had thrown it on the beach and came back toward Uncle, rubbing at my arms and back vigorously.

Uncle did not bother to towel himself. He had rolled around in the sand until he had a thin film covering him. Then he had put on his jacket and sprawled out on the beach to soak up what sun there was.

"Where did you learn how to swim so good?" I sat down beside him.

Uncle turned his head to look at me. "Don't you think we got water in China?"

"You know what I mean." I shrugged my arms through the sleeves of my shirt.

Uncle smiled. "I come from China when I was small. Very small. And I was

379

24 CHARACTER'S MOTIVATIONS
Why do you think Craig wants to stay on the reef a little longer?
(Accept reasonable responses: He now recognizes it as a special place; since he came out there he's begun to understand himself and his father better; the openness of the space seems to help him think more clearly.)
INFERENTIAL: SYNTHESIZING

25 CHARACTER'S EMOTIONS
What problem does Uncle Quail have? *(He's lonely and angry that young people whom he has cared about have forgotten him.)*
INFERENTIAL: DRAWING CONCLUSIONS

Does the fact that Uncle Quail has his own problem make his and Craig's relationship any different? Explain. *(Accept reasonable responses: Yes; now Craig can return Uncle Quail's kindness by giving Uncle Quail some of the company he needs.)*
CRITICAL: MAKING JUDGMENTS

26 PLOT: RESOLUTION
What new discovery does Craig make about something he and his father have in common? *(His father, too, had a relationship with Uncle Quail and went abalone diving with him, just as Craig wants to do.)* **How does this discovery affect Craig?** *(Accept reasonable responses: It makes him even more eager to start diving, perhaps so that he and his father will have something in common.)*
INFERENTIAL: DETERMINING CAUSE-EFFECT

---

raised here. Over in the China Camp near Monterey. There used to be a whole bunch of us catching fish there. My father, he was smart. So the others had him speak to *the white demons.* He learned their language pretty good and he taught me. That's how come I speak American so good." Uncle swept his arms out from his sides and then back down, so that he began to dig shallow depressions in the sand that looked like wings. "You know, a long, long time ago, *the T'ang people,* they call San Francisco the Big City. Sacramento is the Little City. And you know all the tide pools on the reef? Well, I bet there were just as many Chinatowns in this state."

"What happened to them all?" I began to towel off my legs.

Uncle lifted his head and cleared his throat. "One day the sea go out and it never come back, and the pools, they all dry up. And my father and me and some others, we come here."

I spread my towel over my legs like a blanket. "What do you mean?"

"Never mind, boy." He laid his head back down on the sand and stared up at the sky. "Young people, what do they care what happened a long time ago?"

I looked at Uncle. He'd set his jaw firmly like there wasn't any room for argument. "Does anyone visit you?"

"Oh, the older ones in my family, they used to visit." Uncle grasped a handful of sand. "But maybe they're too old now. Maybe they don't like to drive the long way from the City. And the younger ones, they don't remember. They forget about the fun they have swimming here. Even some I teach how to swim." He flung the sand into the air and watched the wind scatter it along the beach. He said as if it were the deadliest insult, "They prefer the tame water in those concrete ponds in their own backyards. They turn their faces from the sea and the things I show them." He added, "Even your father."

I tucked the towel around my legs. "Did you take my father diving for abalone as well?"

"Sure," Uncle said.

"When can I go?" I asked him.

Uncle scratched his cheek for a moment as if he were feeling uncomfortable. "I got to give you real special training to go diving. Not everyone can dive."

"Then when can we start?" I asked impatiently.

"You don't even swim so good. You swim better. Then we can begin your training." Uncle slapped his hands at an imaginary surface. "You still fight the water too much. You must use the sea and you must let it use you."

"But how can I learn to swim better so I can be trained?" I rubbed the back of my neck in annoyance. "You never tell me what to do."

Uncle blinked his eyes, puzzled. "You learn from inside you." He tapped at his heart. "Not from outside. And not from some old man's big mouth."

I'd take Uncle's method of teaching me any day over Dad's way. "So when do you think I'll be ready?"

380

Guided Reading

MONITOR COMPREHENSION: PAGES 371–381
What does Uncle Quail do to help Craig stop worrying about himself so much? (He gets Craig to look at the wonders of the world around him.)
What does Uncle Quail do to help Craig think differently about his father? (He tells Craig about his father's interest in plants as a boy; he tells Craig that being different from his father makes him special.) STRATEGIC READING: RETURNING TO PURPOSE

By the end of the story, how have Craig's feelings changed toward his father? How have his feelings changed toward himself? (Craig has begun to understand his father and feel compassion for him. He has also begun to like himself more and not worry so much about his own shortcomings.)
STRATEGIC READING: SUMMARIZING

Uncle folded his arms across his chest and leaned forward so that his forearms rested on top of his drawn-up knees. "You gotta be comfortable in the water. I can't say."

So maybe his cove wasn't a perfect place. It was still special. For all of his quirks, Uncle still managed to make me feel like a real person. **27**

快樂

Happiness

THINK IT OVER

1. *Do you think Craig makes more discoveries about the cove or about himself in this selection? Explain your answer.*
2. *What does Uncle mean when he says, "But if you can make your mind listen to your eyes, really listen, what wonders you see"?*
3. *What does Craig learn about his father from Uncle? Why is this information so surprising to Craig?*
4. *Explain what Uncle means when he tells Craig, "People who don't like themselves, they spend all their time looking at their faults. They don't have time to look at the world."*
5. *Uncle says, "You gotta look at the world. Really look." Compare how Craig looks at the world at the beginning of the selection with how he looks at the world by the end of the selection. Does he listen to Uncle's advice?*

28

WRITE

Imagine that Craig is telling his father about his trip to the cove. Write a short conversation between them about Craig's experience.

29

381

Returning to the Predictions Invite students to review the predictions that they made before reading and that they may have written in their personal journals. Encourage students to talk about how those predictions changed as they read the story.

Returning to the Purpose for Reading Have students tell whether or not Craig's visit with Uncle Quail resolved his disagreement with his father. (Accept reasonable responses: Yes, because Craig began to change his attitudes; no, because Craig had to work out his problem with his father personally.)

27 CHARACTER'S TRAITS
How does Uncle Quail remind you here of the Dragon Mother? *(By paying attention to Craig, Uncle Quail has helped him start to feel like a special person, just as the Dragon Mother recognized the special nature of the "rock" she found and then helped it hatch.)*
INFERENTIAL: MAKING COMPARISONS

28 THINK IT OVER
1. Accept reasonable responses: He discovers more about himself. He sees himself and his relationship with his father differently.
CRITICAL: MAKING JUDGMENTS
2. Uncle means that Craig has to focus his mind on what his eyes are looking at, instead of thinking about himself so much.
INFERENTIAL: PARAPHRASING
3. Craig learns that his father loves plants but was not allowed to learn about them as a child. Craig has not thought of his father as a person with dreams of his own. He has always thought of his father in terms of their battle over sports.
INFERENTIAL: DETERMINING MAIN IDEA
4. Uncle is telling Craig that the boy is missing the wonders around him because he spends his time thinking about himself.
INFERENTIAL: DETERMINING MAIN IDEA
5. Yes; at the beginning of the story, Craig looks at everything in relation to how it affects him. By the end of the story, Craig is beginning to look at things—and people—for themselves.
INFERENTIAL: COMPARING AND CONTRASTING

29 WRITE
To help students get started, suggest a prewriting graphic such as the following:

(**At the Cove**)

What I Saw   *What I Learned*

Responses will vary. Craig may tell his father only about the sea life, or he may try to tell his father what he learned.
CREATIVE: INVENTING NEW SCENES

NOTE Additional writing activities appear on page 381D.

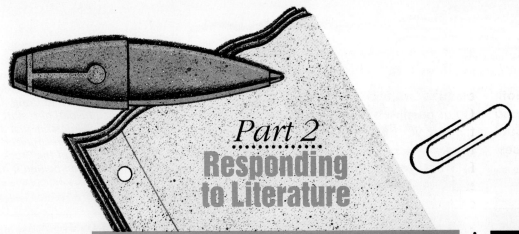

Part 2
Responding to Literature

Summarizing the Literature

Have students retell the selection and write a summary.

Invite students to summarize the selection, using the problem-solution chart. If they have not yet completed the chart, have them do so now. (See *Practice Book* page 113, on 381B.) Students may use their completed charts to retell the selection and write a brief summary statement.

PROBLEM-SOLUTION CHART

Character	Problem	Solution
Craig	can't make friends; doesn't agree with father	begins to understand better
	doesn't like himself	starts thinking about other things
	wants to go abalone diving	must learn to swim better
Mr. Chin	father wouldn't let him learn about plants	took up sports; learned about plants as an adult
Uncle Quail	is lonely	makes friends with Craig

Appreciating Literature

Have students share personal responses.

Divide students into small groups to discuss the selection. Provide general questions to help the groups get started:

- **Often an excerpt, because it is a part of a novel, will leave you with the feeling that something more will happen. Did this excerpt do this? What do you think might happen?**

PERSONAL JOURNAL Encourage students to use their personal journals to write about ideas and feelings that are expressed in the groups. You may also wish to refer students to their personal journals after they complete the Critical Thinking Activities.

Encourage both cooperative and individual responses.

DISCUSS CHARACTER'S MOTIVES **Do you think Uncle Quail purposely invited Craig to visit in order to help the boy with his personal problems? Explain why you think as you do.** Invite students to discuss this issue. Encourage them to find and present supporting evidence for each side. When the evidence is in, students can arrive at a consensus on Uncle Quail's motives. CRITICAL: SPECULATING

ROLE-PLAY NEW DIALOGUE **How might Craig tell or show his father that he knows and understands why Mr. Chin took up athletics?** Assign small groups of students to work together to create and then role-play a dialogue between Mr. Chin and Craig that demonstrates Craig's new understanding of his father. CREATIVE: INVENTING NEW SCENES

WRITE AN ESSAY **Uncle Quail thinks that Craig will begin to feel better about himself if he stops spending so much time thinking about himself. Do you agree or disagree?** Encourage interested students to write short essays stating their opinions. Remind them to support their opinion with reasons. CRITICAL: EXPRESSING PERSONAL OPINIONS

Writer's Journal

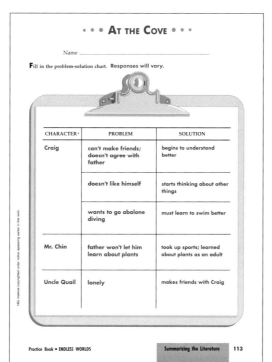

Practice Book

WRITER'S JOURNAL
page 67: Writing a creative response

PRACTICE BOOK
page 113: Summarizing the selection

Reviewing Key Words

To review how the new vocabulary is used in this selection, display the Key Words. Read each analogy below, and have students tell which Key Word completes the analogy correctly.

1. *Wood* is to *table* as *rock* is to _____. *(reef)*
2. *Steel* is to *rigid* as *muscle* is to _____. *(sinewy)*
3. *Said* is to *shouted* as *consumed* is to _____. *(devoured)*
4. *Asked* is to *requested* as *coaxed* is to _____. *(wheedled)*
5. *Legs* is to *kicked* as *arms* is to _____. *(flailed)*
6. *Daydreams* is to *imagining* as *memories* is to _____. *(reminiscing)*
7. *Cruelly* is to *kindly* as *sternly* is to _____. *(indulgently)*

Extending Vocabulary

DESCRIPTIVE LANGUAGE: VIVID VERBS   Point out that the vocabulary word *flailed* is a descriptive verb that vividly describes someone who is struggling in the water. Tell students that Laurence Yep uses many vivid verbs to help readers picture the actions of the story characters and the creatures they observe.

COOPERATIVE LEARNING   Assign students to groups, and have them reread parts of the story to find vivid verbs that describe how someone or something moves. Ask volunteers from each group to pantomime one of their verbs, and let the others guess the verb. Write all of the guesses on the board, and discuss which incorrect guesses might nonetheless be vivid synonyms for the verb in question.

Integrated
Language Arts

Writing About the Literature

CREATIVE: DESCRIPTIVE ESSAY Uncle Quail compares Craig's mind to a busy person who keeps asking his eyes to fill out forms. Ask students to compare their mind to something else. Have them write a descriptive essay using figurative language such as similes, metaphors, and personification. WRITING

AVAILABLE ON PROJECT CARD

CRITICAL: CHARACTER SKETCH Encourage students to write clear, concise character sketches of both Craig and Uncle Quail. As a prewriting activity, they can complete a chart for each character, listing important things that each character says or does and what character trait each behavior reveals. READING/WRITING

What Character Says and Does	→	What His Words and Actions Show

NOTE: An additional writing activity appears on page 381.

SPEAKING/LISTENING

Seaside Serenades

On their own, students can research articles, poems, and short stories that feature the sea. Suggest that they find examples from several genres that further explain or describe the experiences Craig has as he sits on the reef. Encourage volunteers to read aloud from their favorite descriptions.
LISTENING/SPEAKING/READING

SPELLING

Spelling Review

SPELLING WORDS: *breathing, concrete, demon, ease, flailed, immediately, indulgently, reef, sinewy, wheedling*

Tell students to write these column heads on a sheet of paper: *e–consonant–e, e, ea, ee,* and *y.* Then dictate the Spelling Words, and have students list the long *e* words in the correct columns and the word *flailed* separately. Give students five minutes to add at least one more example in each column and one word under *flailed* that has the long *a* sound spelled *ai.* Have volunteers share their examples with their classmates.
LISTENING/SPEAKING/WRITING/SPELLING

INTEGRATED SPELLING

page 54: Writing words with the long e sound

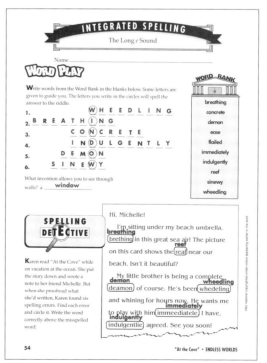

Integrated Spelling

LITERARY APPRECIATION
INTRODUCE

External/Internal Conflict

OBJECTIVE: *To distinguish between external and internal conflicts in a literature selection*

1	Focus

Introduce the concepts of external and internal conflict.

Remind students that fiction such as "At the Cove" revolves around a problem, or conflict. Explain that conflict can be external, such as conflict between a character and other people or between a character and nature. Conflict can also be internal, involving a struggle within a character's mind. Ask students to cite examples of external and internal conflicts.

2	Teach/Model

Model the thinking.

Model how to identify one of the conflicts that Craig experiences in the story:

> **There is a struggle within Craig over his father's demand that he excel at sports. One part of him wants to be as good an athlete as his father, but another part of him says he's too uncoordinated to be any good. Because both sides of the struggle are in Craig's mind, his conflict is internal.**

Have students discuss external and internal conflict.

Have volunteers explain in their own words the difference between internal and external conflict. Then have them recall another internal conflict Craig faces in the story and an external conflict he has with nature.

3 Practice/Apply

Have students identify external and internal conflicts.

Have students use the problem-solution chart that they completed as they read the story. Ask them to tell whether each problem represents an internal or an external conflict and to explain why they think the way they do.

4 Summarize

Informally assess the learning.

Have students summarize what they learned. (External conflict takes place between a character and other people or between a character and nature. Internal conflicts involve problems or struggles in a character's mind.)

READER ↔ WRITER CONNECTION

External and Internal Conflict

▸ **Writers** provide external and/or internal conflicts to make their stories interesting and exciting.
▸ **Readers** identify instances of external and/or internal conflict to understand characters and plots.

WRITE ABOUT CONFLICT Ask students to choose a setting that lends itself to an external conflict. Then ask them to write a scene in which the main character deals with external and internal conflicts at the same time.

CHALLENGE Ask students to use what they have learned about external and internal conflict to create a story plot that has only one kind of conflict. Later, ask students to discuss the problems they had in creating a plot with only one kind of conflict.

SECOND-LANGUAGE SUPPORT Ask students to describe, in their first language and then in English, the conflicts in books they have read or movies they have seen. (See *Second-Language Support Manual.*)

WRITER'S JOURNAL page 68: Writing about external and internal conflicts

Writer's Journal

Narrative Elements

OBJECTIVE: *To interpret mood, or the overall emotional feeling of a literary work, and tone, or the writer's attitude*

Review

Review the concepts of mood and tone.

Tell students that "At the Cove," like other fiction, has mood and tone. Explain that mood is the atmosphere or feeling of a passage or selection and that tone is the attitude a writer takes toward his or her subject and characters. Readers can figure out both by noticing the kinds of words a writer chooses. Ask students to suggest words that a writer might use to create moods of sadness, anticipation, and joy.

Teach/Model

Model identifying mood and tone.

Have students read pages 372–374 aloud, noticing the feeling the author creates. Model how you recognize mood and tone:

> **I notice that in the scenes on the reef, Yep uses words and phrases such as *breathing slowly and quietly, affectionately, proudly, treasure chest,* and *animals shaped like flowers*. By using language with pleasing sounds and connotations, Yep creates a mood of wonder and delight.**
>
> **Yep's tone, or attitude toward his characters, is respectful and affectionate. He uses positive words to describe Uncle Quail and creates sympathy for Craig by allowing him to tell his own story in the first person.**

Have students discuss mood and tone.

Encourage volunteers to explain the meanings of *mood* and *tone,* as well as the difference between the two. Have them describe the mood and tone of a scene in a favorite book, movie, or TV program.

Have students identify mood and tone.

Have students identify the mood and tone of favorite scenes in the selection. Suggest that they find scenes with contrasting moods, such as the scene in which Craig almost drowns and the scene in which he swims to the reef. Encourage them to point to specific words and phrases that indicate mood or tone.

Summarize

Informally assess the learning.

Check students' understanding by having them summarize what they learned. (Mood is the atmosphere or feeling of a selection; tone is the writer's attitude toward the characters and the subject.)

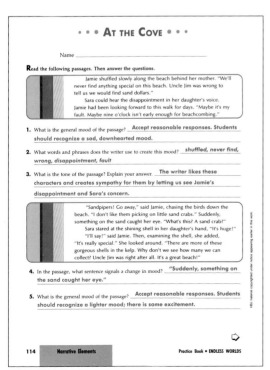

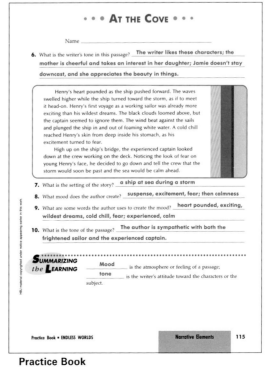

Practice Book

Practice Book

MEETING INDIVIDUAL NEEDS

CHALLENGE Have students read passages or selections from science magazines such as *National Geographic* or *National Wildlife*. Have students work together in small groups to read favorite passages aloud and then discuss the mood and tone of the writing.

SECOND-LANGUAGE SUPPORT Students may need to hear story passages read aloud by a proficient reader before they can identify mood and tone. (See *Second-Language Support Manual.*)

PRACTICE BOOK pages 114–115: Recognizing mood and tone

Integrated
Curriculum

Who's Who in Tidal Pools

Have students choose one form of sea life mentioned as part of Uncle Quail's reef "garden" and research it thoroughly. Interested students can give oral reports on the creatures and decide on the accuracy of the story's description of the sea animal. Ask students to cite evidence as to whether, in the selection, the author changed or exaggerated any of the creature's qualities for dramatic effect.
LISTENING/SPEAKING/READING

Dragon Tales

CULTURAL AWARENESS Encourage students to find out the importance of the dragon and what it symbolizes in Chinese mythology. They can find the information in an encyclopedia or in books on world cultures. Suggest that they also read various descriptions of Chinese dragons, as well as several folktales involving dragons. When they have completed their research, students can create their own dragons in their favorite art medium and have the dragon "tell" its story to an audience.
LISTENING/SPEAKING/READING

Troubled Times

CULTURAL AWARENESS Point out to students that in the 1870s, Chinese workers made up about 20 percent of California's labor force. When the country entered a depression in 1873, recent Chinese immigrants became the targets of hostility and violence. Invite a group of students to research the history of those times. Group members should divide the task among themselves and then present their findings to their classmates, using whatever visual aids are available.
LISTENING/SPEAKING/READING/WRITING

Beauty in Nature
AVAILABLE ON PROJECT CARD

Encourage students to work in groups or alone to observe several flowers, insects, or other living things and create detailed sketches or take photographs of them. They can present their sketches or photo series in an exhibit entitled "Learning to See the Natural World." Tell them to try to experiment with different points of view or camera angles to create interesting effects. Ask students to include a brief caption or description with each sketch or photo in the series. WRITING

Challenge of the Deep

READ ALOUD TO STUDENTS:

MORE THAN 71 PERCENT OF THE EARTH IS COVERED BY WATER.

The vast oceans conceal unexplored new worlds of plants and animals. The era of modern marine biology began with the oceanographic voyage of the British ship *Challenger*, from 1872 to 1876. However, studying sea animals in their natural habitat was difficult until certain inventions made diving to great depths possible. Jacques Cousteau, a French scientist, perfected the aqualung in 1943. With it, a trained diver can reach a depth of 270 feet (75 meters). In 1948 Cousteau helped test a bathyscaphe, or deep-diving vessel, developed by the Swiss physicist Auguste Piccard. Cousteau continued to explore the sea and made underwater films that have fascinated people all over the world.

A more recent development in the technology of deep-sea research is the small, relatively inexpensive submersible. In 1977 the research submersible *Alvin* made the oceanographic discovery of the century off the Galapagos Islands. It found life forms that do not depend in any way on energy from sunlight. Giant clams and tube worms exist without oxygen at incredibly high temperatures in cracks in the ocean floor.

Another marine scientist, Japanese American Eugenie Clark, has won numerous awards and research grants for her studies of sharks. In recent years she has found new species of sea animals and observed them in their natural surroundings for the first time. Using small submersible vehicles and underwater robot cameras, Clark has dived off the Cayman Islands in the Caribbean, in Surguga Bay off the Japanese coast, and in the Red Sea, taking videos of creatures never seen before by humans. ■

ACTIVITY CORNER

■ Have students find Clark's books, *Lady with a Spear, The Lady and the Sharks,* and *Desert Beneath the Sea.* Have them present short reports on Clark's achievements, including their personal comments on her work.
■ Create a classroom bulletin board representing a cross section of the Atlantic or Pacific oceans. Divide the class into five groups. One group will be responsible for laying out and labeling the various levels of the ocean on the bulletin board background paper. The other four groups should bring in pictures and brief descriptions of sea creatures from four levels: 0–200 feet, 200–600 feet, 600–1,000 feet, and below 1,000 feet.

*J*apanese-American Eugenie Clark and the jaws of a shark (top)

*J*acques Cousteau made scuba diving possible and fascinated the world with photos from the ocean depths.

Words from the Author: Laurence Yep

ABOUT THE AUTHOR FEATURE

Laurence Yep shares highlights of his life. He also discusses the book *Sea Glass,* whose main character, he says, is much like himself.

1 NARRATION: EVENTS

How do you think Laurence Yep felt after selling his first story at the age of eighteen? Why? *(Accept reasonable responses: He probably felt inspired and much better about what he was capable of doing, especially since he was so inept at sports.)*
INFERENTIAL: DRAWING CONCLUSIONS

AWARD-WINNING AUTHOR

Laurence YEP

382

Words from the Author:

The character in *Sea Glass*, Craig, is very much like me. I came from a family in which I was the only nonathlete in the bunch. There's a scene in the book in which the father is trying to teach basketball to a hopeless Craig—that was my life during most of the fall and spring. I was inept. I would drop any ball that was thrown to me, and for most of my teenage years, I didn't feel that I fit into my family at all.

I went to a high school that had some wonderful teachers; I had a chemistry teacher who taught us things we wanted to know. I also had an English teacher who said if we wanted to get an A, we had to have a piece accepted by a national **1** publication. Even after he retracted that requirement, I kept sending in things to magazines. I sold my first story when I was eighteen.

I definitely write for the outsider, but there's an age around junior high when almost everyone feels like an outsider and becomes acutely aware of any differences

---

Reading the Author Feature

Invite students to share what they know about Laurence Yep. Discuss where they have heard his name and in what connection. Then ask students to predict, based on their reading of the excerpt "At the Cove" from the novel *Sea Glass,* what the author might be like, what inspired him to write the book, and what kinds of things Yep might choose to share in a short autobiographical sketch.

between themselves and their peers. I felt this especially because I grew up in a black neighborhood. I went to a school in Chinatown, and I was an outsider there, too, because neither I nor my parents spoke Chinese. When I went to the library and librarians tried to get me interested in books like *Homer Price and His Donut Machine*, I couldn't get past the first chapter. Homer had a bicycle, but no one I knew owned one. What I read was science

fiction and fantasy in which kids are taken from our everyday world to some other place where they have to learn new languages and customs. Science fiction and fantasy talked about adjusting, which was something I did every time I got on and off the bus.

2

There was no place I really felt at home, and while I was teaching creative writing at Berkeley, I saw the same thing in the Asian American students there. One has to turn that borderland existence into a source of strength. Because you don't belong to the majority culture, you have a certain flexibility and tolerance others may not have. You become a good listener because you listen to many sides.

When I hear from readers about *Sea Glass*, it's usually because they identify with Craig. There is a lot of pressure at that age to be good at sports. The story shows you that people grow at their own pace, in their own season. I wasn't good at sports, but I was good at writing. There are all sorts of drummers to follow, all sorts of dreams.

3

383

2 ANALOGY
How are Yep's experiences similar to those of science fiction characters? *(Accept reasonable responses: Just as Yep had to adjust to the majority culture, science fiction characters have to adjust to a new, unknown world.)*
INFERENTIAL: MAKING COMPARISONS

3 AUTHOR'S COMMENTARY
What might Laurence Yep say to a teenager who isn't good at sports? *(Accept reasonable responses: Find something you like to do, and do your personal best at your own pace.)*
INFERENTIAL: SPECULATING

Teaching Tip You may wish to point out that Chinatown in San Francisco is the largest Chinese community in the world outside Asia.

Responding to the Author Feature

Invite students to discuss whether or not they agree with the following statement by Laurence Yep: ". . . there's an age around junior high when almost everyone feels like an outsider and becomes acutely aware of any differences between themselves and their peers." Encourage students to give reasons why they agree or disagree with Yep's view.

LAURENCE YEP / **383**

THE SECOND HIGHEST POINT

by Ouida Sebestyen

OUIDA SEBESTYEN (1924–) grew up in a small Texas town and discovered a wider world through library books and movies. Her first novel, *Words by Heart,* was selected as a Best Book by *School Library Journal* and *The New York Times*. Her three subsequent books have also been award-winners. Sebestyen's favorite themes are the worth of the individual, the value of families and relationships, and her belief in the power of good. She seasons her books with vivid dialogue and humor. "I write for readers of all ages," she says, "because I want to nourish the child's idealism and delight in life that we all have in us."

MORE BOOKS BY OUIDA SEBESTYEN
IOU's. Little, Brown, 1986. AVERAGE
Words by Heart. Little, Brown, 1979. AVERAGE

OTHER BOOKS ABOUT RESPONSIBILITY
After the Rain by Norma Fox Mazer. Morrow, 1987. AVERAGE
Big Red by Jim Kjelgaard. Bantam, 1982. AVERAGE
Danza! by Lynn Hall. Macmillan, 1981. AVERAGE

"**I** write for readers of all ages because I want to nourish the . . . delight in life that we all have in us."

SELECTION SUMMARY
Upset by his parents' demands on him, Josh has decided to run away. He is stopped first by his friend Laurel, and then by finding a box of abandoned puppies. Reluctantly accepting responsibility for the pups, Josh attempts to find homes for them. During the afternoon, Josh meets a tramp and a writer who change his mind about running away. When he returns home, the puppy he keeps provides a starting point for communication between Josh and his dad.

LESSON PLANNER		Materials	Integrated Curriculum	Meeting Individual Needs
1	**READING LITERATURE** pp. 383B–396	Student Anthology pp. 384–396 Transparency 22 Second-Language Support Manual Practice Book p. 116 Integrated Spelling p. 55 Integrated Spelling T. E. pp. 74–75 Response Card 4: Theme/Mood	Spelling Spelling Pretest Spelling-Vocabulary Connection (adjective suffixes -able, -ible, -ous)	Second-Language Support Vocabulary 383C Strategic Reading 383D, 388, 389 Cooperative Reading 384, 393, 395
2	**RESPONDING TO LITERATURE** pp. 396A–396E	Writer's Journal p. 69 Practice Book pp. 117–118 Integrated Spelling p. 56 Integrated Spelling T. E. pp. 74–75 Audiocassette 0	Vocabulary Workshop Reviewing Key Words Extending Vocabulary Writing About the Literature Speaking/Listening Spelling Review	Cooperative Learning 396B, 396C
3	**LEARNING THROUGH LITERATURE** pp. 396F–396L	Second-Language Support Manual Practice Book pp. 119–120	Math Physical Education Social Studies Art Multicultural	Challenge 396G, 396H, 396I Second-Language Support 396G Cooperative Learning 396G, 396H, 396I

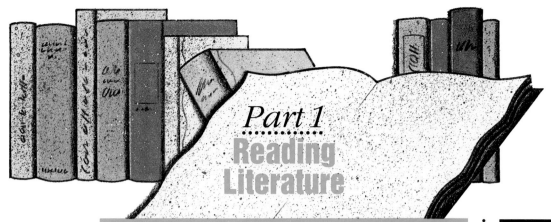

Part 1
Reading Literature

Building Background

Access prior knowledge and develop vocabulary concepts.

Tell students that they will be reading a short story titled "The Second Highest Point." Write the story title on the board, drawing students' attention to the words *Second Highest*. Ask students whether they can think of other expressions using the word *second*, and write their ideas on the board in a web.

second-best

second-rate

The Second Highest Point

second-string

second fiddle

Have students quickwrite sentences.

Ask students to quickly write a few sentences about the feelings people seem to associate with being second rather than first. Invite volunteers to share their writing.

Vocabulary Strategies

Introduce Key Words and strategies.

Tell students that "The Second Highest Point" contains words that may be unfamiliar to them. Display Transparency 22, or write the paragraph on the board. Have students read the paragraph silently. Then encourage students to use context clues and structural analysis to figure out the meanings of the underlined words. As a volunteer reads the paragraph aloud, help with pronunciation.

Transparency 22   Key Words

The seventh graders captured the scary <u>eeriness</u> of the original story in their *Frankenstein* production. They had read the entire <u>unexpurgated</u> story of the lonely monster who wanted love. Their "creature" shuffled <u>warily</u> onto the stage—cautious, watchful. <u>Unobtrusively</u>, the lights dimmed, their fading hardly noticeable. The creature twisted its face. Its mouth <u>warped</u> out of shape and sent out soft moans that were almost <u>inaudible</u>.

CULTURAL AWARENESS

To help students appreciate the cultural background and setting of "The Second Highest Point," share with them the information under Cultural Background/Setting on page 384.

KEY WORDS DEFINED

eeriness strangeness

unexpurgated complete, having no objectionable parts removed

warily cautiously, watchfully

unobtrusively in a way that is not noticeable

warped twisted out of shape

inaudible incapable of being heard

**Check students'
understanding.**

Have students demonstrate their understanding of the Key Words by using some of them to fill in the following chart.
STRATEGY: CONTEXT CLUES

SHY ANIMALS

How They Might Move	How Their Voices Might Sound
warily *unobtrusively*	*inaudible*

Then have students demonstrate their understanding of all the Key Words by matching each with its definition.
STRATEGY: DEFINITION

1. **strangeness; oddness** *(eeriness)*
2. **uncut; complete** *(unexpurgated)*
3. **too soft to be heard** *(inaudible)*
4. **bent out of shape** *(warped)*
5. **cautiously** *(warily)*
6. **without drawing attention to oneself** *(unobtrusively)*

**Integrate spelling
with vocabulary.**

SPELLING-VOCABULARY CONNECTION *Integrated Spelling* page 55 reinforces spellings of words with the **adjective suffixes *-able*, *-ible*, and *-ous*,** including the Key Word *inaudible*. The spelling of the key Word *warped* is also included.

SECOND-LANGUAGE SUPPORT Encourage students to note any slang expressions they do not understand and to discuss the expressions with a peer tutor. (See *Second-Language Support Manual*.)

PRACTICE BOOK
page 116: Reinforcing Key Words

INTEGRATED SPELLING
page 55: Writing and spelling words with the adjective suffixes *-able*, *-ible*, *-ous*

NOTE: These pages may be completed now or after students have read the story.

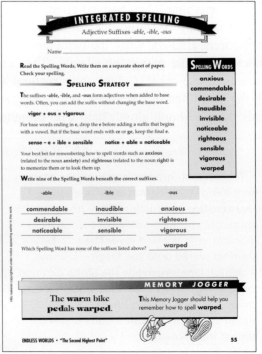

Practice Book

- - - **THE SECOND HIGHEST POINT** - - -

Name _____

A. Read the sentences. Decide on the correct meaning of each underlined word. Circle the letter in front of the correct answer.

1. There was an eeriness about the old library, a musty smell, an odd way the shadows played on the floor.
   a. ugliness   (b.) weirdness
   c. calmness   d. freshness

2. Kate crept warily between the stacks of books on either side of her.
   a. boldly   b. quickly
   c. hungrily   (d.) cautiously

3. She walked quietly throughout the library as she searched unobtrusively for the book.
   a. visibly   (b.) without being seen
   c. quietly   d. without regard for safety

4. The book—the complete, unexpurgated poetry of Percy Bysshe Shelley—was supposed to contain a secret treasure map.
   a. not translated   b. having no rhyme or meter
   c. not published   (d.) uncensored

5. Kate searched the shelves for something that would make the book stand out—a torn book jacket, a warped cover, perhaps.
   (a.) bent out of shape   b. missing
   c. disgusting   d. torn

6. Suddenly an almost inaudible exclamation escaped her lips, and silently, gingerly she took the book from the shelf.
   a. not able to be suppressed   b. not capable of being understood
   (c.) not capable of being heard   d. not capable of being spoken

B. Use *unobtrusively, warily,* and *inaudible* in sentences of your own.

1. Responses will vary.
2. _____
3. _____

116   Vocabulary   Practice Book • ENDLESS WORLDS

Integrated Spelling

INTEGRATED SPELLING
Adjective Suffixes *-able, -ible, -ous*

Name _____

Read the Spelling Words. Write them on a separate sheet of paper. Check your spelling.

SPELLING STRATEGY

The suffixes *-able, -ible,* and *-ous* form adjectives when added to base words. Often, you can add the suffix without changing the base word.

vigor + ous = vigorous

For base words ending in **e**, drop the **e** before adding a suffix that begins with a vowel. But if the base word ends with **ce** or **ge**, keep the final **e**.

sense – e + ible = sensible   notice + able = noticeable

Your best bet for remembering how to spell words such as **anxious** (related to the noun **anxiety**) and **righteous** (related to the noun **right**) is to memorize them or to look them up.

Write nine of the Spelling Words beneath the correct suffixes.

-able	-ible	-ous
commendable	inaudible	anxious
desirable	invisible	righteous
noticeable	sensible	vigorous

Which Spelling Word has none of the suffixes listed above? __warped__

SPELLING WORDS
anxious
commendable
desirable
inaudible
invisible
noticeable
righteous
sensible
vigorous
warped

MEMORY JOGGER

The **war**m bike pedals **warped**.   This Memory Jogger should help you remember how to spell **warped**.

ENDLESS WORLDS • "The Second Highest Point"   55

Strategic Reading: Short Story

Preview and Predict

Have students use prior knowledge.

Remind students to use what they already know about previewing a short story to predict what will happen in "The Second Highest Point." Guide students to recall that story events influence a character's emotions and that these changed emotions can then influence later story events.

Have students preview and predict.

Have students read the first eight paragraphs of the story. Then ask questions such as the following to help students make predictions:

- **What event has influenced Josh's emotions?**
- **What emotions is he feeling, and how will they affect his behavior?**

Introduce the story influences chart.

Use the story influences chart to encourage students to predict how Josh's emotions might change during or after his conversation with Laurel, as well as how his emotional change might affect what he does.

STORY INFLUENCES CHART

Story Event	Influence on Josh's Emotions	Influence on Josh's Behavior

PERSONAL JOURNAL Have students copy the story influences chart in their personal journals, or have them use *Practice Book* page 117. (See page 396B in this Teacher's Edition.) Have them complete it as they read the story or afterward. (Students will return to the chart after reading, in Summarizing the Literature.)

Setting a Purpose

Have students set purposes.

Each student should use the story influences chart to set an individual purpose for reading. Invite volunteers to share with classmates their purpose for reading.

Model purpose-setting, if necessary.

If students have difficulty setting a purpose for reading, model the thinking process:

> **From previewing, I know that Josh is angry and rebellious. These strong feelings have pushed him into a decision to run away. My purpose for reading will be to find out whether Josh runs away or whether something happens that changes his mind.**

SECOND-LANGUAGE SUPPORT Students may benefit from the Guided Reading activities and the additional guidance under the Student Anthology pages. (See *Second-Language Support Manual*.)

OPTIONS FOR READING

Independent Reading Have students read the story silently with their purpose for reading in mind.

Guided Reading Follow the Guided Reading suggestions that appear on pages 384, 392 and 395. These suggestions model strategic reading.

Cooperative Reading Reader response strategies appear on pages 384, 393, and 395.

Numbered Annotations Use the numbered annotations beside the Student Anthology pages to heighten students' appreciation of the story.

CULTURAL BACKGROUND/SETTING
This short story is set in an unnamed American town in the present. By focusing on character rather than setting, the author emphasizes the universal emotional conflicts of adolescence. Students may find the biographical information about Ouida Sebestyen of help before they begin to read. Knowing the characteristics of her stories may help them focus more clearly on the relationships of the characters.

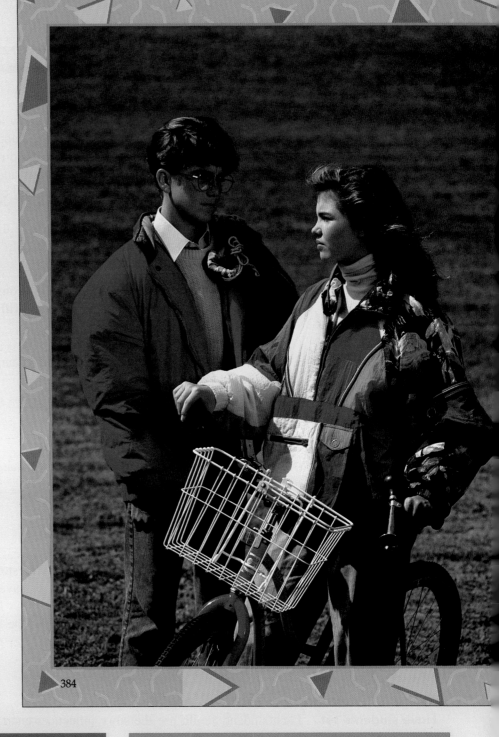
384

Guided Reading

SET PURPOSE/PREDICT: PAGES 384–392 Have students read through the seventh complete paragraph on page 392 to learn more about Josh's feelings and how they influence his behavior. You may wish to suggest that students keep adding details to their story influences charts as they read.

Cooperative Reading

READER RESPONSE STRATEGY: PAGES 384–392
Form groups of three to five students, and have each group select a leader. Ask group members to read pages 384–392 silently, and then encourage the leader to use dialogue questions such as those below to ensure that all members participate in the discussion. (Response Card 4: Theme/Mood on page R65, offers a wide variety of dialogue questions.)

- What do you think the theme is? Explain why.
- What is the mood of the story so far?

The Second Highest Point

by
Ouida Sebestyen

He was almost to the river, walking fast, when he saw Laurel on her bicycle, racing to catch him. In a space between the gusts of raw March wind she yelled, "Josh, wait up, or I'll break your legs."

So he wasn't going to get away without saying good-bye after all.

Laurel came puffing up, fierce and wind-whipped. He braced himself as she stared at the duffel bag he'd taken from his folks' closet and stuffed with all the clothes and things he thought he'd need.

"You're doing it," she said. The pain that came into her eyes hurt him, too. "Why? Without telling me? I thought we were friends! If I hadn't seen you sneaking through the alley—"

• • • • • • • • • • • • • •

385

Informal Assessment Assessing whether students are fulfilling the established purpose for reading involves asking questions like the following:

- Is this what you expected to happen next?
- If so, what did you read earlier that helped you predict this?
- If not, what did you predict would happen? What did you read earlier that led you to believe that?

This assessment will also encourage students to watch for and select details that fulfill their purpose for reading.

1 EXPOSITION
What important information do you learn during the conversation between Josh and Laurel? *(Josh is running away; he's having trouble in school; he's in conflict with his parents; his father has been laid off from work.)*
LITERAL: NOTING IMPORTANT DETAILS

2 CHARACTERIZATION
Josh says that he and Laurel are friends, yet Laurel tells Josh that his running away is dumb and that he's feeling sorry for himself. Do you find this a strange way for a friend to talk? Explain. *(Accept reasonable responses: No, because she's trying to help him; yes, because a real friend would find a less hurtful way to talk.)*
CRITICAL: MAKING JUDGMENTS

3 PLOT: CONFLICT
How do you know that Josh is unsure about running away? *(He turns around to walk backward so that he can talk to Laurel; he asks Laurel to walk to the bridge with him; he has to force himself to stay angry in order to keep going.)*
METACOGNITIVE: DRAWING CONCLUSIONS

We *are* friends, he wanted to assure her. Best friends. The best. But he said, walking on, "So? One more thing I didn't do right today." Suddenly it came pouring out. "At breakfast they jumped down my throat about my grades. Then they got started on why can't I grow up and shape up and do my part now with him out of work. Boy. I didn't get him laid off."

"But it's a hard time for them, Josh."

"Not for her. She's tickled pink. All this schooling's going to get her back into that *career* she gave up when I came along." It seemed vital to stay cold and angry. Even with Laurel. Especially with Laurel, because she knew what he really was. "So I figured I've been enough trouble—I might as well get on out there and do something with my life." He stared at the distant river waiting to be crossed.

"It's dumb," Laurel said, with the directness they had never been afraid to use with each other. "They'll just haul you back. Parents aren't perfect. You're feeling sorry for yourself." She stopped in the road, trying to make him turn around, rethink. But he kept walking. "Please, Josh," she said behind him. "Don't do it."

"*You're* leaving," he said.

"But not until school's out. And I wouldn't be, if we didn't have to move out to the Coast."

"But you are," he said. It wasn't her fault, he knew. She couldn't make her own choices. But he could. "Maybe I'll see you in sunny Cal."

"How'll you live, without money?" she asked into the wind. "Josh? How'll you eat? It scares me."

He turned around. She was outlined against the far-off knob of land called Throne of Kings, where they had sat one day in dusty autumn grass, growing quieter and quieter until their faces turned and their mouths touched in a kiss as intent and sunstruck as the silent hawks gliding over them.

His feet kept moving him backward. "Hey, just don't worry about me," he called. "Nobody else does. Okay?" She didn't answer, but her eyelids blinked fast. He relented. "Would you come as far as the bridge with me?"

She shook her head. "I have to get back to the library. I'm supposed to be helping with the party right now."

Hearing her say she should be getting punch and cookies ready for some stumpy old lady who wrote bad poetry, at the moment he was running away, gave him the new rush of anger he needed to turn around and march out of her life.

The river sprawled ahead of him, more sand than water. There was an eeriness in what he was doing: leaving someone he cared so much about without ending it right. He wished she'd run after him. But what could she say?

When he got to the bridge he looked back, expecting to see her pedaling away, but she stood in the road, her hair blowing across her funny freckled face.

The long bridge turned his footsteps hollow as he started across. He had planned to wait for the bus at the crossroad a mile or so farther on. Between wind gusts he found himself straining to hear the hum of traffic. But the only sound

was closer, a small lonesome squeak like a bird he didn't recognize, or something grating under the bridge.

When would they notice he'd left home? he wondered. Maybe they wouldn't even miss him.

Near the end of the bridge the sound got louder. He scanned the sky and the flat brown horizon. Then he leaned over the bridge rail and looked down into a cardboard box on the sand at the water's edge. A jumble of yips and squeals came from something dark, squirming inside it.

He felt his muscles clamp into knots. He had to catch a bus. He was this far. He had to straighten up and walk on past whatever was down there crying for help. But he couldn't.

He glanced at Laurel. She hadn't moved. He went to the far end of the bridge and climbed down through the weeds. The box twitched as he bent warily and looked in.

Puppies. Five of them, no bigger than fuzzy mittens, crawling in their prison.

Josh drew a weary sigh and squatted to touch them. They went silent, rooting hungrily against his hands. He lifted up a soft black puppy with eyes that melted a hole in his heart, and dropped it back into the pile. "No," he warned them. "I can't do anything, you guys. No."

Their little claws grated on the high sides of the box as they struggled to reach him. He saw Laurel hanging over the bridge rail. "What's down there, Josh?" she called.

"Five puppies," he called back.

She came scrambling down. Her eyes were blazing. "What kind of gutless wonder would throw them into the river! Oh, look at them." She gathered two against her cheeks.

"Maybe somebody couldn't take care of them," he said, trying to be fair. But it wasn't fair. He flicked his hands angrily, staying aloof. "Didn't want to be bothered. So, plop, off the bridge."

"But it's cruel," she said. "It's sad. Like back in early times, in the book Miss Rainey gave you, remember? When people left the defective babies on a mountain so if the gods wanted them saved they could do a miracle." Suddenly she handed him a puppy. "And guess what—along came good old Josh."

"No," he said. "Dang—I've got a bus to catch!" He dropped the puppy into the heap, as trapped as it was. "Why me? What'll I do with the dumb things?"

"You said you've always wanted a dog. You just got five of your wishes." She looked at his eyes and stopped trying to make him smile. "Take them back into town and find them homes. There'll be another bus. If you still . . ."

He followed her gaze down the road he should be striding along, and turned helplessly to the box. "Want a nice puppy?"

387

4 PLOT: RISING ACTION
What complication occurs to interfere with Josh's plans to run away? *(He hears something crying for help.)*
LITERAL: RECOGNIZING CAUSE-EFFECT

5 FIGURATIVE LANGUAGE
How does comparing the puppies to "fuzzy mittens" and their box to a "prison" help suggest Josh's feelings about the puppies? *(Comparing them to fuzzy mittens suggests that Josh finds them warm and appealing; comparing the box to a prison suggests his urge to rescue them.)*
INFERENTIAL: MAKING COMPARISONS

Despite his warning to the puppies, how can you tell that Josh is going to help them? *(because of the image created by* melted a hole through his heart*)*
METACOGNITIVE: MAKING PREDICTIONS

Why does Josh feel defeated?
(because he knows he must take care of the puppies and postpone running away)
INFERENTIAL: DETERMINING CAUSE-EFFECT

Are you surprised at his change of heart? *(Responses will vary.)*
CRITICAL: EXPRESSING PERSONAL OPINIONS

7 PLOT: CONFLICT
What struggle goes on in Josh's mind as he begins to try to give away the puppies? *(He's made his decision because he feels sorry for the puppies, but at the same time he feels angry and resentful that the puppies have changed his plans.)*
INFERENTIAL: SUMMARIZING

"Oh, I do. But my mom's deathly allergic. And when we move I couldn't take it—we'll be renting till we find a house." She nudged him up onto the bridge. "Stand in front of the supermarket, Josh. Won't you? Somebody'll take them. Look, I've got to get back, or I'll get canned."

She went to her bike, but her worried eyes kept studying him. He could feel the box pressing against the folded lump of bus-ticket money in his pocket. What did she want? Why should he be the one to care, when nobody else did?

"Do you think they'd fall out of my basket if I tried to carry them?" she asked.

6 "You just worry about getting on back," he said. Her face fell. It touched him to see how hard she was trying to keep this from being good-bye. He shrugged, defeated. "They're not all that heavy. But you could carry the duffel."

Most of the shoppers glanced into his box and went on past to buy their groceries. A few paused. The children stopped and stayed, cuddling puppies until they were dragged away by their parents.

7 He felt stupid. He resented what those helpless crawling blobs in the box had done to his plans, and was still angry at the person who had left them by the edge of the river. And at himself because he hadn't.

Several times, during the hour he stood in front of the store, he saw a shadowy movement at one of the high library windows down the block. Laurel. Checking to see what luck he was having. Or if he had left.

388

He felt exposed, there in full view of everyone on the street. He knew that his mother was thirty miles away, in one of those nifty workshops that was going to expand her options. But his dad might drive past any minute, checking out a job prospect, and see him and the duffel. He couldn't take a public quarrel, not after leaving that morning feeling so righteous and ready.

A little girl forced her mother to stop at the box.

"Could I have one?" she begged, entranced.

"They'd make great pets. Or watchdogs, or whatever," Josh said quickly, trying to cover every possibility.

The woman smiled. "How much?"

"Oh, free," Josh exclaimed. "Free. And they don't eat much at all."

The woman squeezed the little girl, almost laughing. "Which one do you like?"

The little girl picked up each puppy in turn, studying it nose to nose. The last one stretched to give her a lick. "This one," she breathed, dazzled. "He likes me already!" She turned suddenly to Josh. "We'll love it good."

"We will," the woman agreed. "Thank you."

He felt an unexpected emptiness as they walked away huddled over their treasure. He guessed it was for the puppy leaving the warmth of its brothers and sisters forever, with its little head jiggling trustfully. Or maybe it was because the woman hugged the little girl the way his father hugged him in his fantasies.

Second-Language Support

Help students unfamiliar with the slang term *canned* (paragraph 1, line 8) by asking what might happen to a person who took too long a break on his or her job. (He or she might get fired.)

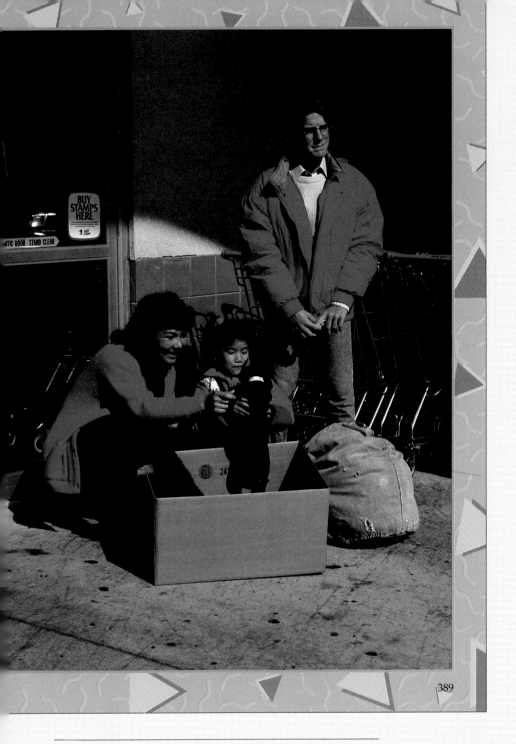
389

Second-Language Support

Remind students that illustrations can help readers understand what the characters are doing and how they feel. Elicit that Josh appears somewhat nervous or confused and that the woman and child seem thrilled with the puppies. Point out that students can use these clues to help them draw conclusions and predict outcomes. For example, students might conclude from the text and photographs together that the woman and child are adopting one of the puppies.

What does the metaphor *a tiny round powder keg of a lady* suggest about Grace Whipple Cox's appearance and personality? *(She is short and probably plump; she might be full of energy and have an "explosive" personality, too.)*
INFERENTIAL: MAKING COMPARISONS

A man came out of the store. Proud of his change of luck, Josh had opened his mouth to say, "How about a beautiful puppy?" when he noticed that the tag on the man's jacket said MANAGER.

He gathered up his duffel and his dogs, and mushed.

As he passed the library, Laurel leaped out onto the top step and beckoned. "Josh! I saved some cookies for you."

He climbed up, weary. "A lady took a puppy."

Her glad smile faded. "You've only given away *one*?"

"Miss Rainey won't like me bringing them into the library, either," he said. "Have you started the party for old lady Snap Crackle Pop?"

Laurel nodded. "Grace Whipple Cox," she corrected him. "She's sitting there, waiting to autograph a stack of books taller than she is, that nobody wants to buy."

8 He went in, trying to be invisible behind Laurel. A tiny, round powder keg of a lady in a velvet hat sat talking to a few matronly types holding punch cups and paper napkins. He could see now why Laurel called her the Gnome de Plume, although at first she'd had to explain the pun to him. He was curious about anybody who could write poetry. He'd tried it himself. Nobody knew, except Laurel, unless Miss Rainey had guessed.

Laurel led him to a little room full of magazines and gave him four pink cookies. "What'll you do now?" she asked. "Oh, Josh, they're hungry. When they're this young they need food every

390

few hours. Could I give them some coffee-creamer stuff, do you think?"

"I don't know. Maybe not." Yips began to come from the box. He put his jacket over it. "I've got to give them *away*. This is crazy."

"Let's try Miss Rainey," Laurel said. "I know she has cats, but maybe—" She winced as the yapping rose in a needle-sharp chorus.

He started through the door with his box and almost bulldozed Miss Rainey off her feet as she started in.

"What on earth!" She flipped through her memory card index for his name. "Josh. What have you got?" She looked in. Her face softened. "Well bless their little deafening hearts."

"Somebody left them under the bridge," Laurel said.

Miss Rainey breathed an angry sigh.

"I found a home for one already." Josh tilted the box so Miss Rainey would see yearning eyes and smell warm puppy. "Laurel thought maybe you'd like one."

"Oh, listen, Josh, they're already trying to zone my house as a zoo. I just couldn't. I'm gone all day. Cats and chameleons and macaws can manage. But a puppy—nope." She turned away. Then she gestured him close again, and muttered, "Try the literary ladies. It's a long shot, but try."

She was leading them out through rows of shelves, when she stopped abruptly. Every face they saw was staring at a long table of refreshments. Another of Miss Rainey's assistants, a little older than

Teaching Tip Explain that the nickname *Gnome de Plume* (paragraph 8, line 6) is a play on the French expression *nom de plume*, which means "pen name," or the name under which an author may write.

Laurel, sat at a punch bowl with her mouth ajar. Her startled eyes were riveted on a scruffy man with no socks who was helping himself to punch and cookies. His hand, the size of a baseball mitt, was already stacked with sand tarts and brownies and macaroons and six of those pink cartwheels Josh had wolfed down in the little room. The man drained his paper cup, smiled at the hypnotized girl, and refilled it. He studied his hand, and added another brownie.

Miss Rainey came alive. "Good lord—he's cleaning us out! Where did he come from?" She headed toward the man so vigorously that Josh thought she was going to grab his cookies. But she drew herself tall and said, "Sir, have you met our distinguished guest, or read her previous books of poetry?"

The scraggy man froze in his tracks. "I can't say I have," he admitted, still chewing. "But I did literally cut my teeth on poetry, ma'am. The complete unexpurgated works of Rudyard Kipling, if I remember rightly." He gave her a big shameless smile, then studied the puppies in Josh's box. "Part shepherd, wouldn't you say—the ears and head shape?"

He left Miss Rainey speechless and walked into the reference section to finish his meal in peace. The girl at the punch bowl exclaimed in a whisper, "I didn't know what to *do*, Miss Rainey! When he

started loading up—"

Miss Rainey patted her shoulder mechanically. "It's all right." Her face had softened as it had when she saw the puppies. "He's hungry."

Laurel elbowed Josh toward the autographing table. A boy from high school was interviewing the Gnome de Plume, scribbling frantically at half the speed of her rushing words. Josh stopped at a distance, not wanting to interrupt but eager to get the women's attention when he could. Somebody had to take another puppy.

"Could you explain why you entitled your newest book *The Second Highest Point in Beymer County*?" the boy asked.

"To make a statement," the Gnome de Plume snapped, from behind the stack of unsold books. "Everybody knows that Crown Hill is the highest point—it's on the maps, it's written about. We act as if second-best is second-rate. I wanted to say that there can be only one topmost *anything*—all the rest of this glorious fascinating world is second. Or third, or tenth. Empty words. Hogwash. Everything has worth, for its own reasons." She knocked the mountain of books askew. "I'm not even a tenth-rate poet, although you don't have to quote me on that. I'm just a funny old lady. But why shouldn't I write a *ton* of poetry if I want to? God doesn't label blades of grass Grade A and Grade B. He creates. For the fun of it!

391

How does Throne of Kings fit Grace Whipple Cox's belief that something doesn't have to be "first" or highest to be important? *(Even though Throne of Kings is only the second highest place in the county, it is a special place for Josh and Laurel.)* INFERENTIAL: DRAWING CONCLUSIONS

Because He's a creator!"

The boy had lost her, back at Crown Hill. Josh watched him write down GRADE A and take a bite of his pencil.

Two of the literary ladies, equally startled, peeped into Josh's box. Miss Rainey said, "Listen, we need homes for these abandoned little things. Someone dropped them in the river without having the decency, or the heart, to finish the job."

The ladies shook their heads sadly. One said, "A ten-to-fifteen-year commitment is too much for me. Besides, they need children to play with. A farm or something." They turned away from the box, unobtrusively putting distance also between themselves and the old lady glaring around her mountain of books.

10 "What's the second highest point in Beymer County?" Josh whispered.

A pink flush crossed Laurel's face. "Throne of Kings," she whispered back.

He felt his own cheeks go warm. There would never be a spot on earth higher than the Throne of Kings on an autumn day, enchanted by hawks. *Why do you have to leave me?* he wanted to beg her through the ache in his throat.

But he was leaving first. You do it to them before they do it to you. You don't just stand there on the reject pile, smiling like it doesn't hurt.

The grungy guy tapped him on the shoulder. "You say you're giving pups away?" His cookies were gone, except for the frosting on his beard.

Josh nodded, surprised.

"I'll take one," the man said.

392

Everyone looked at Josh. The man put his paper cup on the stack of books. It looked like a lighthouse.

"Oh," Miss Rainey said. "I don't think—" She stopped, flustered.

"I don't know," Josh said carefully. "I mean—I don't know you." He hadn't known the woman with the little girl, either, he remembered. "Aren't you just—on the road? I mean, if you don't have a job or anything, how could you feed it, and all?"

"I live here," the man said. "Hey, I wouldn't take it if I couldn't come up with the goods. I take care of *me*, don't I? What's your name? I look like I can manage to take care of a pup, don't I?"

"Josh," he told him, nodding in spite of his doubts.

"Joshua fit the battle of Jericho," the man said, as if he had the habit of telling himself things. "Well, Josh, you trust me or you don't. It's a risk."

"I don't know," Josh said in desperation. How could he tell? What kind of life would a puppy have with a man like that?

But what did it take to beat dying in a box by the river?

Suddenly the man grubbed in the pocket of his ragged pea jacket and brought out a pencil in a handful of lint and crumbs. "I'll tell you what, Josh, my friend, I'll give you my address. You come check on me. Check on your pup—see if I don't do a commendable job on it." He handed Josh a napkin with a street number on it. There were no houses there, Josh knew from his paper route days.

Guided Reading

MONITOR COMPREHENSION: PAGES 384–392
How does Josh feel at the beginning of the story? (unloved, misunderstood, and angry) **Why?** (He believes his parents are taking out their problems on him.) **How have these feelings influenced his behavior?** (He has decided to run away.)
STRATEGIC READING: RETURNING TO PURPOSE

What problem arises that delays Josh's running away? (Josh finds five abandoned puppies and takes on the responsibility of finding homes for them.)
STRATEGIC READING: SUMMARIZING

How do Josh's feelings for the puppies influence his actions? (For the time being, his sympathy and concern for the puppies cause him to change his plans for running away.) INFERENTIAL: DETERMINING CAUSE-EFFECT

SET PURPOSE/PREDICT: PAGES 392–396 Ask students to predict whether Josh's feelings of anger will return and cause him to continue with his original plans. Then invite students to read the rest of the story for confirmation.

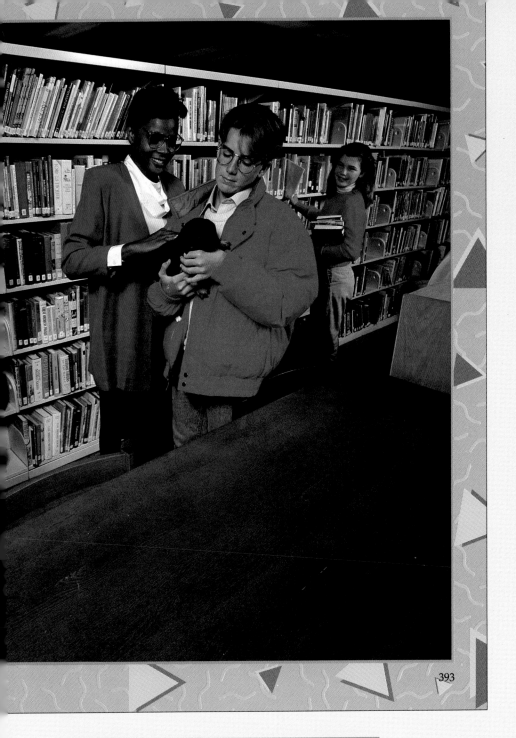

Cooperative Reading

READER RESPONSE STRATEGY: PAGES 392–396

Groups should continue reading silently, pausing periodically to discuss how their predictions and conclusions change as the theme develops and becomes clearer.

11 FORESHADOWING

How does the statement *It's rough by yourself* apply to Josh as well as to the man? (*Accept reasonable responses: Recognizing the man's desperate loneliness may have increased Josh's doubts about running away and trying to survive on his own.*)

INFERENTIAL: MAKING COMPARISONS

12 CHARACTER'S EMOTIONS

How can you tell that in his heart Josh has already decided not to run away, even though he may not realize it? (*He's feeling happier and thinking about how he'll spend his time in his hometown during the next few months, including saying good-bye to Laurel.*)

METACOGNITIVE: DRAWING CONCLUSIONS

13 FIGURATIVE LANGUAGE

What does the comparison *like some kind of neglected machine grinding itself to pieces* tell you about Josh? (*that his negative feelings have been taking control of him and destroying him*)

INFERENTIAL: MAKING COMPARISONS

---

11 A warehouse. So? Guard dogs stayed in warehouses okay. The man gave him a half glance with wary watery eyes. He's begging, Josh thought. It's rough by yourself.

He held out the box. "Which one do you want?"

The man said softly, "The runt." He lifted out the smallest puppy, smoothing its fuzzy head with his thumb. He said, "You keep that address. You come out and check."

"I will," Josh warned him. "You better be telling me the truth."

The man tucked the puppy inside his jacket. "I'll be gentle with it, Josh, my friend. I had a belt taken to me too many times to ever lift my hand to another creature."

He bowed to the ladies, smiling, and went out.

The Gnome de Plume thrust a book into Laurel's hand. "Run catch him," she ordered. Her squinty old eyes glinted with what looked to Josh like pleasure.

12 Laurel darted out. Josh felt a spurt of happiness. Two pups down—three to go. The rest of March, April, May before Laurel left. They'd go to the Throne of Kings again, and this time he would be able to say, *I'm glad we knew each other and liked and loved each other. Even if it can't be the way I wanted it to be.*

The Gnome de Plume brought a box from under the table and began to fill it with her books. The ladies gathered to help.

Josh was folding the napkin into his pocket when his hand froze. What was he

394

doing? He wasn't going to be here to check on anybody's address. He was going to be out there on a bus. Finding his own warehouse to sleep in. There wouldn't be another day on the Throne of Kings. Never another day. He slung his head, blinking as if he'd run into a door in the dark.

He went out blindly and stood on the sidewalk, breathing hard. The box of puppies, lighter now, bulged and bumped in his hands. Laurel came back and stood beside him. They watched the cars go by in the long afternoon shadows.

"Were you just saying that?" she asked, with a pinched, anxious smile. "When you told him you'd check on the puppy?"

A car like his dad's came toward them. He went tight. It passed, driven by a boy in a baseball cap. Josh let out his breath. His voice, sounding far away, said, "Just once, if my folks would just look up and notice I was there. That's all it would take."

13 Laurel nodded. She always nodded, understanding, and he always went on explaining and defending himself, like some kind of neglected machine grinding itself to pieces.

"I mean, they talk to me—sure—but they're doing other things while they're yelling at me. Like I was some emergency they wished they weren't having."

Grace Whipple Cox came out the door with a load of books. Miss Rainey followed with another box and the last of the cookies under plastic on a wobbly paper plate.

Oral Rereading Choose four volunteers to read aloud the passage beginning with the last paragraph on page 394 and continuing through the fifth paragraph in column 2 of page 395 (or some other passage containing dialogue). Assign three volunteers to read the lines spoken by Josh, Laurel, and Grace Whipple Cox, and the fourth to read the narrative paragraphs. Allow students to read through the passage silently before reading aloud, and, if necessary, help them decide on an appropriate tone. Reading the dialogue aloud will enhance students' understanding of the characters' personalities and emotions.

"Let me carry that," Laurel said, taking the Gnome's load. Josh set the puppies down and took the books and plate from Miss Rainey. They followed the Gnome down the chilly street to her beat-up car and put the boxes in the back.

"Not much of an afternoon, dollar-wise," she said. He didn't understand why she followed them back to the library. She looked down at the puppies. "I wish I was sure I *had* ten-to-fifteen years to commit," she said, and laughed. "But so what? We can't wait for life to be perfect, can we?" She lifted up two puppies.

He heard Laurel draw a soft breath.

The Gnome de Plume said, "I can't take all three—I'm tempting fate as it is. But fate has sent them a guardian angel once already." She smiled at Josh. "Fate can do it again, if I don't last long enough. And they'll have each other." She bent closer. "Would you like one of my books?"

He gulped. "Yes," he told her, taking it. "I would."

The Gnome smiled at Laurel and handed her the puppies. "Come, young lady. I'll drive you home."

Laurel turned to Josh. Her anxious eyes tried to read his. "Your duffel is in the little room."

"I know," he said. He didn't move.

Slowly she started after the Gnome. "Josh?" she entreated, looking back.

"It won't work," he said. "I go home—they're madder than ever—we start yelling—"

"Part of that's up to you, isn't it?" she asked.

Her soft words let him down with a thump. Dang—*help* me, he wanted to yell. Don't just pile it back on me.

"Josh, can't you try? We have to get through things the best we can." Her voice was shaking. "I'll listen and listen, if it'll help, but it's up to you finally."

He turned away. Inside the library he stared through the window as the Gnome's car, and then others, and then others, passed in the dusk.

His dad was watching the news. He asked, "Where've you been?" without turning from the TV.

Josh felt the eeriness start again, matching the jumpy light of the screen that lit the room. He took the puppy out of his jacket. It seemed like fate, really, because the one that had been left was the one whose tender eyes had grabbed his heart beside the river.

"What's that?" his dad said, when he noticed. "You can't keep a dog. Your mother's got too much to do already."

15 "She won't have to take care of it," Josh said, keeping his voice even and slow. "I will. Feeding and housebreaking and shots and tags and spaying and everything."

395

14 THEME
How does Miss Cox's saying *We can't wait for life to be perfect, can we?* apply to Josh? *(Up until now, Josh has thought that relationships and events in life should turn out in the way that would be best or happiest for him, but he is starting to accept the imperfections of life and to make the best of them.)*
CRITICAL: MAKING GENERALIZATIONS

15 PLOT: RESOLUTION
How does Josh's answer to his father show that he is changing? *(He answers his father in a calm, mature manner, rather than defensively or angrily.)*
CRITICAL: MAKING JUDGMENTS

Cooperative Reading

READER RESPONSE STRATEGY: PAGES 392–396 After group members have finished reading the story, the group leader may use dialogue questions such as the following to help members discuss the text. (Response Card 4: Theme/Mood, on page R65, offers a wide variety of dialogue questions.)

- What is the theme?
- What is the mood of the story at the end? If it changes, describe where.

Guided Reading

MONITOR COMPREHENSION: PAGES 392–396
Do Josh's feelings of anger return? Does he continue with his original plans? (Josh's anger does return, but comments from both Laurel and Miss Cox cause him to rethink his plans.)
STRATEGIC READING: RETURNING TO PURPOSE

By the end of the story, how have Josh's feelings changed? (He is no longer so angry that he wants to run away. He has come to realize that his anger has often interfered in his relationship with his parents.)
STRATEGIC READING: SUMMARIZING

16 PLOT: RESOLUTION
How does his father's story about his dog give Josh some reassurance that there's a chance for a better relationship? *(It is a sad story that reveals some sympathy and understanding.)*
INFERENTIAL: DRAWING CONCLUSIONS

17 THINK IT OVER
1. *He gives them the kind of care and attention he wants from his own family; he makes sure they end up in good homes.*
INFERENTIAL: DRAWING CONCLUSIONS

2. *Laurel's mother is allergic to dogs; when Laurel moves, her family will be living for a while in a rented place that doesn't allow pets.*
LITERAL: RECOGNIZING CAUSE-EFFECT

3. *Josh sees the display of affection between the mother and her little girl, and it reminds him that he and his parents do not have that sort of relationship.*
INFERENTIAL: DRAWING CONCLUSIONS

4. *At first he is annoyed because they are interfering with his plans. As the afternoon progresses, he is glad that he has rescued them.*
INFERENTIAL: SUMMARIZING

5. *Accept reasonable responses: Simply by being themselves, each character is "worth" something to Josh in helping him mature.*
CRITICAL: MAKING JUDGMENTS

18 WRITE
You may want to help students get started with a prewriting graphic such as the following:

Changes in Next Six Months	
Josh's Feelings	Josh's Actions

Accept reasonable responses. Students should support their judgments with examples from the story.
CREATIVE: SPECULATING

NOTE Additional writing activities appear on page 396D.

His dad looked at him a long time. "Talk is cheap," he said.

"I guess you're going to have to risk it," Josh said, braced against the gaze.

His dad turned back to the news. "She can't do everything. The house, her schooling. She's got big dreams for herself. Give her a chance."

The puppy tried to crawl inside Josh's collar. He had to feed it. He had to buy a bag of something. "I live here too," he said. He felt for his ticket money. Maybe if he called Laurel she'd walk to the store with him and carry the pup while he lugged home a bag of dog chow. And they could talk. "Give me a chance too. Okay?"

His dad switched channels uneasily, testing, rejecting. He doesn't know how to answer me, Josh thought. He doesn't know what to say to any of this—to not having a job, or to her getting ahead of him, or to being my father.

16 A commercial came on. His dad said, watching it, "When I went into the army my folks kept my dog for me. They said he got lost. Ran away. But I was never sure." His face slowly <u>warped</u> in the shifting light. "Maybe he tried to find me. Or maybe he got killed and they hated to tell me. So I never could be sure, you know? For a long time I used to listen to the dogs barking, off in town. For years, I guess. Hoping I'd hear him."

Josh stopped halfway to the door. Hesitantly he came back, and sat on the arm of the couch, stroking the hungry puppy with his thumb. He stared at the television like his dad, not seeing it. Even with the sound turned high, he caught himself trying to hear other things. The far-off whine of buses. The almost <u>inaudible</u> cries and urgings and answers coming from everywhere.

THINK IT OVER

17
1. In what way does Josh give the puppies the chance he is looking for?
2. Why can't Laurel keep one of the puppies?
3. Why does Josh feel an "unexpected emptiness" after he gives away the first puppy?
4. How does Josh feel when he first finds the puppies? How do his feelings change as the afternoon progresses?
5. Grace Whipple Cox says, "Everything has worth, for its own reasons." How does this statement apply to the characters in the story?

WRITE

18 Think about how Josh's life could change during the six months following the end of the story. Write a letter from Josh to Laurel telling about his life at that time.

Returning to the Predictions Invite students to review the predictions that they made before reading and that they may have written in their personal journals. Encourage students to talk about how their predictions changed while reading.

Returning to the Purpose for Reading Have students tell whether Josh ran away or whether something happened to change his mind. (Josh didn't run away, because his taking responsibility for the abandoned puppies led to encounters with people who gave him a new understanding of life.)

Part 2
Responding to Literature

Summarizing the Literature

Have students retell the story and write a summary.

Invite students to summarize the story using the story influences chart. If they have not yet completed the chart, have them do so now. (See *Practice Book* page 117, on 396B.) Students may use their completed charts to retell the story and write a brief summary statement.

STORY INFLUENCES CHART

Story Event	Influence on Josh's Emotions	Influence on Josh's Behavior
finds puppies	wants to save them, but resents change in plans	stays in town to find homes for puppies
hears Grace Whipple Cox's ideas on second highest point	remembers Throne of Kings and regrets that Laurel is moving	decides again to run away
Scruffy man offers to take puppy.	doesn't trust man; wants perfect homes for puppies	decides to trust the man and gives him a puppy

Appreciating Literature

Have students share personal responses.

Have students form small groups to discuss the story. Ask a question such as this to help the groups get started:

- **Did you find the ending satisfactory and appropriate? Why or why not?**

PERSONAL JOURNAL Encourage students to use their personal journals to write about ideas and feelings that are expressed in the groups. You may also wish to refer students to their personal journals after they complete the Critical Thinking Activities.

STRATEGY CONFERENCE

Discuss the story influences chart, asking students how it helped make the story's events clearer. Invite students to share other strategies they used, such as paying special attention to the changes of emotions.

INFORMAL ASSESSMENT

Having students order the details of a selection in this way will help you informally assess how well they understood key relationships. Ask yourself: Did students recognize the **cause-and-effect relationships**? Can students tell which details are more important than others?

Critical Thinking Activities

ROLE-PLAY A SCENE   Do you think Laurel acted wisely in the way she confronted Josh in the story's opening scene? How would you have tried to get Josh to change his mind? Ask small groups of students to role-play the scene they might have had with Josh. When the groups are finished, discuss which suggestions might be the most helpful. CREATIVE: INVENTING NEW SCENES

DISCUSS PROBLEM-SOLVING   How do you think Josh compared in his method of handling his problems with the other characters in the story? Who was the best problem solver? Encourage interested students to reexamine the characters, identify each one's problem and method of solution, and then rank them in order from "best handler of problems" to "poorest handler of problems." Encourage students to debate and support their rankings. CRITICAL: MAKING COMPARISONS/MAKING JUDGMENTS

INVENT NEW PLOT DEVICES   Imagine what might have happened to Josh if he had not found the puppies. Would he have found another good reason not to run away? Give reasons for your opinion. Encourage students to imagine other factors that might have caused Josh to stay. CREATIVE: SPECULATING

Encourage both cooperative and individual responses.

INFORMAL ASSESSMENT

Critical thinking activities provide ample opportunities to note and assess important reading behaviors. Almost all judgments, opinions, and conclusions involve using story details to draw high-level inferences. In addition, the details that a student selects in thinking critically about a reading selection are a clear indication of whether the importance of particular details to the main ideas and themes has been well understood.

Writer's Journal

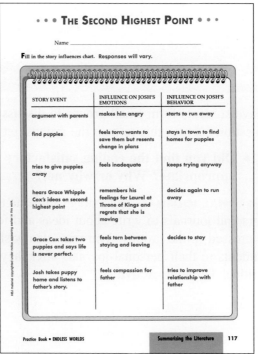

Practice Book

WRITER'S JOURNAL
page 69: Writing a creative response

PRACTICE BOOK
page 117: Summarizing the selection

VO·CAB·U·LAR·Y Workshop

Reviewing Key Words

To review how the new vocabulary was used in this selection, display the Key Words. Read each word and definition below, and ask students to identify the Key Word that is the antonym of each word.

1. *loud* **having the quality of high volume and intensity of sound** *(inaudible)*
2. *normality* **a typical, everyday atmosphere** *(eeriness)*
3. *ostentatiously* **with a great deal of boastful showiness** *(unobtrusively)*
4. *abridged* **shortened, having parts removed** *(unexpurgated)*
5. *undistorted* **not twisted out of shape** *(warped)*
6. *recklessly* **in a careless, incautious manner** *(warily)*

PRACTICE BOOK

page 118: Using formal and informal language

Extending Vocabulary

FORMAL/INFORMAL LANGUAGE Tell students that formal language is the kind used in important documents and on important occasions. Informal language is the kind we use in casual everyday conversation. The vocabulary words *unexpurgated* and *unobtrusively* are examples of formal language, while the slang expressions used by story characters are informal. List the following slang terms from the story: *canned, gutless, grungy, hogwash, jumped down my throat.*

COOPERATIVE LEARNING Divide students into small groups. Have students use dictionaries and thesauruses to find more formal synonyms or near-synonyms for the informal words from the story. Then have them rank the synonyms from most informal to most formal, using a diagram like the one below. Finally, have them write a section of informal dialogue in formal language.

Least Formal		**Most Formal**
canned ⟶	fired ⟶	dismissed
jumped down ⟶	yelled ⟶	reprimanded me
my throat	at me	

THE SECOND HIGHEST POINT

Name _____

A. Fill in the chart by ranking each set of words and expressions from most formal to most informal.

	1	2	3	4
	rough	hush up	frightened	contemplating
	arduous	keep silent	got the creeps	toying with
	tough	be quiet	disquieted	tossing around
	difficult	button your lip	scared out of one's wits	thinking

Most Formal   Most Informal

1. arduous   difficult   rough   tough
2. keep silent   be quiet   hush up   button your lip
3. disquieted   frightened   scared out of one's wits   got the creeps
4. contemplating   thinking   toying with   tossing around

B. Choose one formal and one informal word from each group above. Write a sentence using each word.

1. Pair 1: Accept reasonable responses. Students should write sentences that suit the formality or informality of the words they select.
2. Pair 2: _____
3. Pair 3: _____
4. Pair 4: _____

118   **Formal/Informal Language**   Practice Book ▪ ENDLESS WORLDS

Practice Book

Integrated Language Arts

Teacher Choices

WRITING

Writing About the Literature

AVAILABLE ON PROJECT CARD

CREATIVE: NEWS ARTICLE Ask students to imagine they are the young reporter interviewing Grace Whipple Cox about her book of poetry. As a prewriting activity, suggest they list questions that they would ask in the interview. Remind students to ask questions about *who, what, where, when, why,* and *how.* Suggest that they use a chart to help them.

Interview Questions
Who?
What?
Where?
When?
Why?
How?

Students can then write their interviews, imagining that their work is to be published in a specific newspaper or magazine. WRITING

CRITICAL: PERSUASIVE ESSAY Have students summarize Grace Whipple Cox's opinion on being second-best and write a persuasive essay in which they argue for or against her position. Remind them to use facts, reasons, and examples to support their opinions. WRITING

NOTE: An additional writing activity appears on page 396.

SPEAKING/LISTENING

A Poetry Reading

One way poets gain exposure is by signing autographed copies of their books, as the poet did in the story. Another way is by participating in poetry readings, during which poets read their poems aloud to an audience. Have students conduct a class poetry reading. Students may choose to read one or two of their own poems, saying a few words about each poem and how they came to write it. As an alternative, students may choose a poet and one poem by that person. Students should also find out something about the poet. Students can then discuss the poet briefly before reading the poem. Students may also comment about their reasons for choosing a particular poem.

LISTENING/SPEAKING/READING/WRITING

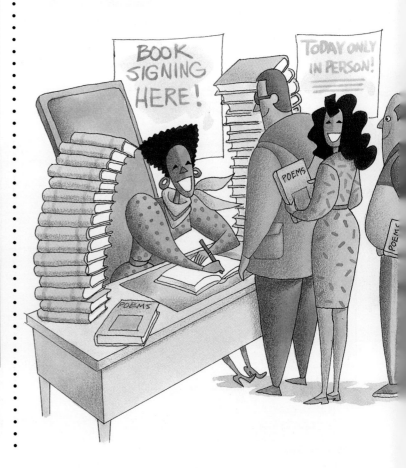

Pet Peeves

AVAILABLE ON PROJECT CARD

Have students prepare a speech on the responsibilities of pet ownership for an audience of children, teenagers, or adults. Students who own pets should use examples from their own experience to support their points. Students can practice by giving their speeches to classmates, while keeping in mind the intended audience. Listening students should help the speakers revise their speeches to be appropriate to their intended audiences. Interested students may then want to present their final speeches to groups of younger students. LISTENING/SPEAKING/READING/WRITING

Spelling Review

SPELLING WORDS: *anxious, commendable, desirable, inaudible, invisible, noticeable, righteous, sensible, vigorous, warped*

Dictate the Spelling Words to students, and have them check their spelling against the list of Spelling Words. Next, give the students five minutes to write a short scene, using as many Spelling Words as possible. Tell them they will receive one point for each Spelling Word they use. At the end of the time, have volunteers read their scenes aloud.
LISTENING/SPEAKING/WRITING/SPELLING

INTEGRATED SPELLING

page 56: Writing words with adjective suffixes *-able*, *-ible*, *-ous*

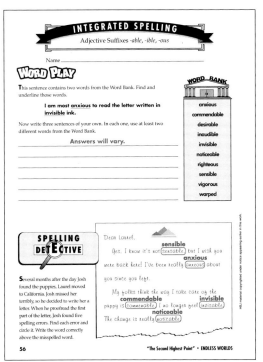

Integrated Spelling

COMPREHENSION
INTRODUCE

Referents

OBJECTIVE: *To identify a word or idea as the referent of a pronoun or other substitute*

1	Focus

Introduce the concept of referents.

Tell students that "The Second Highest Point" contains many referents. Explain that referents are words, often nouns, that are referred to or replaced by other words. The other words that replace nouns are usually pronouns. Remind students that the selection begins with the word *he*, and that *he* refers to the referent *Josh*.

2	Teach/Model

Model the thinking.

Explain that readers identify referents by using the context of the selection. Have students turn to page 387 and read the two paragraphs that begin *Puppies* and *Josh drew a weary sigh*.

Model how you would identify referents:

I notice that the narrator refers to the puppies several times in these sentences, but she uses the word *puppies* only once. After that she refers to the puppies with pronoun substitutes such as *their*, *them*, and *they*. If she had repeated the word *puppies* each time, the paragraphs would have sounded repetitious.

Have students discuss referents.

Encourage volunteers to explain what both a referent and a word substitute are. Have them brainstorm words and phrases that serve as word substitutes. Encourage students to go beyond pronouns to discuss phrases that refer to ideas and reasons; for example: *this (is why), due to these circumstances,* and *thus*.

3 Practice/Apply

Have students identify referents.

COOPERATIVE LEARNING Invite students to work in small groups to identify other referents and their substitute words from the story. Encourage them to keep track of the words by making two lists:

Word Substitutes	Referents

4 Summarize

Informally assess the learning.

Have students share some of the referents and word substitutes they identified from the story. Then have students summarize what they learned. (Pronouns and other word substitutes stand for longer words and phrases, which are their referents.)

CHALLENGE Have students write a paragraph using one of the following: *because of this, in this way, therefore,* or *for these reasons.* Then have students exchange papers and identify the referent of each word or phrase. Ask them to discuss whether the referents are clear.

SECOND-LANGUAGE SUPPORT Students can work with partners who share their first language to compare and contrast the use of referents and word substitutes, if any, in that language and in English. (See *Second-Language Support Manual.*)

PRACTICE BOOK page 119: Understanding referents

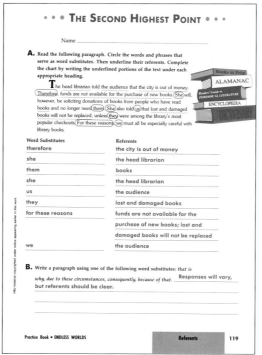

Practice Book

Making Generalizations

OBJECTIVE: *To make generalizations from specific facts and examples*

Review

Review the concept of making generalizations.

Point out that a generalization, or a broad statement, can show how an idea applies to other situations. Model how to generalize from the theme of "The Second Highest Point":

> **Josh decides that running away is not the way to solve his problems. I can generalize by saying that, in general, people should not try to run away from their problems.**

Practice/Apply

Have students apply the learning.

COOPERATIVE LEARNING Have students work in pairs to make generalizations based on the themes of other stories they have read.

Summarize

Informally assess the learning.

Have students summarize what they learned. (A generalization is a broad statement. It can be based on a story theme.)

CHALLENGE Have students use what they have learned about making generalizations to read and generalize from news articles in a local newspaper or a national news magazine.

PRACTICE BOOK
page 120: Making generalizations

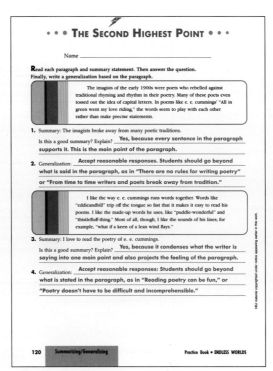

Practice Book

Figurative Language

OBJECTIVE: *To appreciate figurative language and its importance in literature*

Review

Review the concept of figurative language.

Point out to students that many of the slang expressions in "The Second Highest Point" are figurative language. For example, *jumped down my throat* and *tickled pink* are not meant literally. Remind students that *similes*, *metaphors*, and *personification* are other kinds of figurative language:

Model how to identify figurative language:

On page 388 is the sentence *Her face fell*. I know Laurel's face did not *literally* fall. This means that her expression changed from hope to dejection.

Practice/Apply

Have students identify figurative language.

COOPERATIVE LEARNING   Have students work in small groups to identify examples of figurative language in "The Second Highest Point." Encourage them to determine the meaning of each phrase.

Summarize

Informally assess the learning.

Have students summarize what they learned. (Figurative language refers to expressions that have meanings different from the exact or literal meanings of the words.)

CHALLENGE   In a few minutes, have students list as many common expressions that use figurative language as they can. Encourage them to think of their own favorite expressions, those of their family members or friends, and so on. Suggest they choose one or two and draw accompanying cartoons showing the expression's literal meaning.

Integrated Curriculum

How Much Is That Puppy in the Window?

Josh tells his father that he will take full responsibility for the dog, paying for all its expenses. Ask students to list the pet supplies Josh mentions and then brainstorm others. When their list is complete, have them determine the cost of giving a puppy a good start on the road to a healthy, happy life. Suggest they call a veterinarian or humane society for prices of shots, tags, and neutering. Students may visit pet stores or read newspaper advertisements to determine the cost of the supplies a new pup might need. Students should report to classmates on what they learned. They may add interest to their reports by displaying the information on colorful charts. LISTENING/SPEAKING/READING/ WRITING

"In Second Place . . ."

AVAILABLE ON PROJECT CARD

USE *READERS' GUIDE* Challenge students to find out about "second-placers" in any sport of their choosing. Students may want to begin by asking the librarian to help them find rankings in their favorite sport. Suggest that they then check encyclopedias or biographies for information about past champions and the *Readers' Guide to Periodical Literature* for information about contemporary athletes. Challenge students not only to discover pertinent biographical data, but also to find any quotes that tell how these second-placers feel about being second. READING

Going to the Dogs

Invite students to research "man's best friend" and to decide whether the phrase is truly deserved. Challenge them to research the many areas in which dogs work, play, and perform for and with their owners. Suggest that they compile their findings into two lists, *Work* and *Play*. Interested students might also go further and research certain breeds of dogs to learn why they were chosen for the tasks they perform. Students can present their finds at a classroom "Dog Show."
LISTENING/SPEAKING/READING/WRITING

SOCIAL STUDIES

Battles over Public Spaces

USE *READERS' GUIDE* Remind students of how graciously the librarian treated the scruffy man in the library. Then invite them to research the debate over homeless people's right to access to public spaces such as libraries and parks. Suggest they research the issue in the *Readers' Guide to Periodical Literature* and present both sides in a debate. LISTENING/SPEAKING/READING

ART

Caring for Critters

Invite students to create a poster that the Society for the Prevention of Cruelty to Animals might use in promoting awareness of mistreatment or abandonment of animals. Before beginning, students might find out information and statistics useful for their poster. Suggest they contact organizations and agencies such as the Society for the Prevention of Cruelty to Animals, the Audubon Society, the U.S. Fish and Wildlife Service, or state or local groups. LISTENING/SPEAKING/READING/WRITING

SOCIAL STUDIES

Too Much Television!

AVAILABLE ON PROJECT CARD

In the story, Josh's father stared blankly at the television instead of facing Josh to talk to him. Have students look into the effects of television on people. Beyond library research, encourage them to do their own investigations by preparing a questionnaire and having fellow students answer it. They might also want to give the questionnaire to adults and compare the adults' answers with students' answers. Suggest a group brainstorming session to help students generate the questions for their questionnaires. Students might use charts or graphs to tally statistics they gather and to present their findings. LISTENING/SPEAKING/READING/WRITING

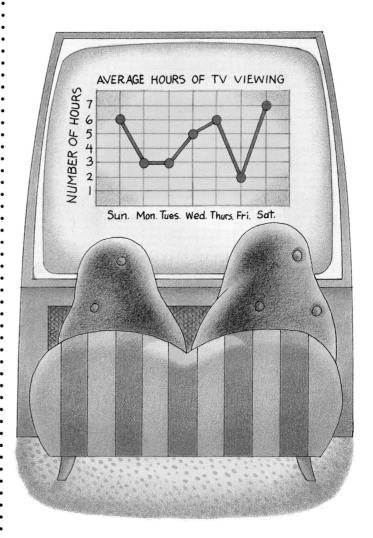

MultiCultural
PERSPECTIVES

Creating Solutions

READ ALOUD TO STUDENTS:

INDIVIDUALS CAN MAKE IMPORTANT CONTRIBUTIONS THROUGH COMMUNITY SERVICE.

Catherine Ferguson, born into slavery in 1779, had two children who died in infancy. This experience inspired her to launch a lifelong career of service to New York's homeless children. During the next four decades, Ferguson raised almost fifty foster children, both black and white.

Annie Dodge Wauneka was born in 1910 on a Navajo reservation in Arizona, where little health care was available and tuberculosis took a high toll each year. In 1951, as the Navajo Tribal Council's first woman member, Annie Dodge Wauneka began a long fight to eradicate tuberculosis. She improved health care and devised health education programs compatible with Navajo culture. In 1963 Wauneka was awarded the Presidential Medal of Freedom. ◼

Annie Dodge Wauneka helped eradicate tuberculosis among the Navajo.

ACTIVITY CORNER
◼ Guide students in creating a community resource handbook for teens. Encourage them to assess teenagers' particular needs, and help them to identify community agencies that can offer appropriate services.
◼ In "The Second Highest Point," Josh and Laura get together at the library. Assign students to interview a librarian to learn of the variety of services, beyond the lending of books, that the library offers. Have them present oral or written reports of their findings.

AVAILABLE ON PROJECT CARD
◼ Identify the health care facilities in your community, and have students list ways that teenagers can help, either by volunteering with the sick or by raising money to combat a particular health problem.

COMING OF AGE

By the end of "At the Cove," Craig has learned about his father's gardening. At the end of "The Second Highest Point," Joshua learns about his father's lost dog. How do you think these stories affect Craig's and Joshua's attitudes about their fathers?

. . . .

Like Craig, Joshua doesn't feel good about himself. Do you think Uncle would give Joshua the same advice he gives Craig? Explain why or why not.

. . . .

WRITER'S WORKSHOP Would Craig and Joshua be able to solve their problems if they could communicate better with their families? Make a list of things that parents and children can do to communicate better with one another. Use your list to write an advice column that you would give to Craig or Josh on better communication.

397

Coming of Age

Remind students that they have read about two boys who are in the process of growing up. Review the reasons why the two characters, Craig and Joshua, don't feel good about themselves. Ask students whether they think these feelings are an inevitable part of growing up and if so, why this might be. Then discuss in what way each boy "comes of age" in the story. Explain that the Theme Wrap-Up questions and activity on page 397 will help them think in more depth about ideas from these selections.

Note that pages 397A–397B provide support for applying the writing process to the last question.

---

1 Tell students first to consider how each boy is affected by the story about his father and then to compare the boys' changing attitudes. *(Accept reasonable responses: Both boys come to see their fathers as human beings who have known loss or disappointment.)*
INFERENTIAL: SYNTHESIZING

---

2 Have students first analyze the gist of Uncle's advice to Craig and then see whether that same advice might apply in Joshua's case. *(Accept reasonable responses: Uncle tells Craig to open his mind to the world and to stop focusing on himself; he might tell Joshua much the same thing with regard to the puppies and Laurel.)*
INFERENTIAL: MAKING JUDGMENTS

Writer's Workshop
See pages 397A–397B for suggestions for applying the writing process. Responses should draw on students' own experience, as well as on one of the selections. You may prefer to allow students to respond to the theme in their own way. WRITING PROCESS: AN ESSAY OF ADVICE

Writer's Workshop

AN ESSAY GIVING ADVICE

Point out to students that in their essays they want to convince their audience to do or to believe in something. Have students brainstorm various thesis statements that they could use to begin their essays. For each statement, have them state one supporting fact. Suggest that students refer to the Handbook in the *Writer's Journal* as they write, revise, and proofread their essays.

Prewriting

Before students write, have them

- choose their intended audience: Craig or Joshua.
- brainstorm with classmates better methods of parent-teenager communication.
- use a list to arrange their thoughts, clarifying each point with an example that relates specifically to Craig's or Joshua's situation. The list might look something like this:

How to Communicate Better with Your Parents

1. Consider their point of view.
   For example: Your father or mother may have lost his or her job and be worried about money. This is not a good time to ask for a raise in your allowance.
2. Think about what you do that causes your parents to become upset.
   For example: Sometimes you may do dangerous things, like not telling them where you are going. If you act sensibly in the future, your parents may also act differently.

Suggest that students list five or six items before they begin drafting.

Drafting

Ask students to write a draft of the advice essay. Remind them to

- identify at the beginning the topic of the essay.
- give advice that is realistic and workable.
- use language appropriate to their audience.
- write freely, without worrying about mechanics for now.

COMPUTER CONNECTION Students may wish to use a computer during the drafting and revising stages so that they can easily tighten or rewrite rambling sentences.

Responding and Revising

Ask students to share their drafts with a small group of classmates and to review one another's drafts for overall effectiveness. Offer the following tips for evaluation and revision.

- Is the language stiff or formal? If so, the writer should try to make it warmer, or more friendly.
- Is there too much about any one point? If so, the writer needs to make his or her prose concise and avoid rambling sentences. (See the Language/ Literature Link below.)

STUDENT SELF-ASSESSMENT OPTION   Students may use the Writing Self-Assessment Checklist in the *Portfolio Teacher's Guide.* Suggest that as they use the checklist, they focus on advice that is realistic and try to avoid rambling sentences.

Proofreading

Offer these tips to help students to proofread their work:

- Indent each new paragraph.
- Check for errors in capitalization and punctuation.

Publishing

Some students may wish to read the advice essay aloud to a partner who is playing the role of Joshua. Other students may wish to submit their work to the school newspaper or a magazine. Suggest that students also save their essays in their reading/writing portfolios.

LANGUAGE/LITERATURE LINK

Avoid Rambling Sentences

Remind students that often when we have a great deal to say, we pack it all into one long sentence. Explain that skillful writers try to cut their sentences down to a readable length. Illustrate the point by turning to page 392 of "The Second Highest Point." Have students read paragraphs five through seven. Then analyze the way the writer conveys the teenagers' thoughts in sentences that are brief and to the point. Tell students to check their own work for rambling sentences and to cut back or rewrite any they find.

Speaking Option

GIVING ADVICE   You may want to adapt the *Writer's Workshop* to allow students to present an oral how-to speech. Have students follow the guidelines for Prewriting, Drafting, and Responding and Revising. Discuss how giving advice on personal matters might differ from making a more formal how-to speech. Offer these speaking tips to help students give advice orally:

- Adapt your language and manner to your audience.
- Deliver your advice in a tone of voice that reflects your empathy and understanding.
- Speak extemporaneously, drawing on your own experience whenever appropriate.

Have each student deliver her or his advice essay to a small group of classmates.

Connections

The Connections activities on Student Anthology pages 398–399 guide students to synthesize multicultural and content-area information with the unit theme. Before students begin, ask them to review quickly the purpose-setting paragraph on page 296.

Then ask students to name the selections they liked best and the characters they found most appealing. As students mention characters, discuss the challenge each character faces and the insight each gains from that challenge.

To prepare students for the Multicultural Connection, share the following information with them. Remind students that the word *Plains* refers to the Great Plains, the vast sweep of grassland in the western United States and Canada, where the buffalo once roamed. Explain that the Plains Indians followed the buffalo, which provided them with food, shelter, clothing, and other necessities of life.

Tell students that great nations of people wandered the Plains. Among them was the Arapaho nation, from which the Gros Ventre nation split off. In winter, the Gros Ventre tribes camped on their own in the woodlands, but in summer, they joined the Arapaho for the great buffalo hunt. Summer was also the time for ritual ceremonies, such as the Sun Dance.

CONNECTIONS

MULTICULTURAL CONNECTION

GEORGE HORSE CAPTURE

George Horse Capture, a member of the Gros Ventre nation, spent a large part of his life helping to preserve the history and culture of the Plains Indians. As curator of the Plains Indian Museum in Cody, Wyoming, he collected and displayed artifacts that tell the story of the great buffalo-hunting nations.

As part of the Buffalo Bill Historical Center, the Plains Indian Museum has many varieties of clothing and other artifacts such as shields, painted buffalo skulls, blankets, and necklaces made of grizzly bear claws.

After helping to design the museum, which faces east just as the Indians' lodges faced east, George Horse Capture worked to make it a place where people can learn about the culture of the Plains Indians past and present.

■ *Imagine that you have been given the job of curator of a museum created to preserve the history and outstanding features of life in your school. Make a list of artifacts and other materials you would display in the museum. Compare your list with those of your classmates.*

398

Multicultural Connection

GEORGE HORSE CAPTURE As students read this feature, remind them to look at the artifacts and to think of the stories these objects tell about the Plains Indians' way of life. When students list school "artifacts," suggest they think of them, too, as silent storytellers. Ask students what facets of school life *they* would choose to record for posterity.

CLIMATIC INFLUENCES

Research two Native American nations from different climatic environments. Concentrate your research on how the climates affected the way the people lived.

Make a chart that illustrates how the climatic conditions caused differences in the ways the groups of Native Americans lived.

	Native American Nations	
Location		
Climate		
Terrain		
Housing		
Clothing		
Food		

EARLY ENVIRONMENTALISTS

Most Native Americans understood the concept of "Waste not, want not." Write an essay describing ways in which these Americans protected their environments in the past and suggesting ways in which all Americans could do so today.

399

Social Studies Connection

CLIMATIC INFLUENCE   You may wish to have students work in pairs for this activity. To help them get started, provide the names of desert nations, such as the Navajo and the Hopi, and the names of northern forest-dwellers, such as the Algonquian and the Ojibwa. When students have completed their work, have them use their charts to give brief oral reports to classmates.

Language Arts Connection

EARLY ENVIRONMENTALISTS   Encourage students to use a graphic organizer to list "then" and "now" practices. Tell them to use the research they did for "Climatic Influences." You may wish to have students illustrate their essays and create a bulletin board display.

Integrated Language Arts

Reviewing Vocabulary—Clues and Double Clues

1. Write six Key Words or other words from Unit 4 on the board.

Key Words
futile	turbulence
revery	stamina
haven	reef

2. Orally provide clues to a cloze activity by giving students a sentence with a missing word for each vocabulary word.

3. Call on volunteers to supply the missing word and to point out the clues to it. You can make the game more challenging by providing two blanks in each sentence.

4. Have students work in groups to make up Clues and Double Clues for other Key Words. You may wish to give points for solving Clues and Double Clues. Groups can exchange clues and compete.

Reviewing Spelling Words

Integrated Spelling page 57 provides a review of the Spelling Words from Unit 4. *Integrated Spelling* page 58 provides practice with homophones.

Writing About "Challenges"

You may wish to have students respond to the unit focus by having them write an advice column that can be either serious or humorous. Encourage students to first write a letter from an imaginary reader asking for advice. Then the student can provide the advice in whatever fashion he or she chooses. You may wish to have students design and create a political advertisement for an imaginary candidate. Provide examples of such advertisements that illustrate the persuasive messages that political ads strive to convey. Either or both of these assignments can be added to the magazine in the *Writer's Journal*. (See *Writer's Journal* pages 70–71.)

INTEGRATED SPELLING
pages 57–58: Reviewing unit words and homophones

WRITER'S JOURNAL
pages 70–71: Making Your Own Magazine

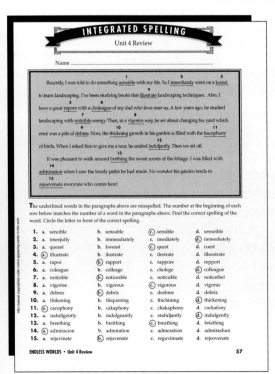

Assessment Options

Informal Assessment

See the suggestions below to informally assess students' progress in Unit 4.

INFORMAL ASSESSMENT NOTES AND CHECKLISTS

If you used the informal assessment notes in the lesson plans to evaluate students' reading and writing behaviors, you may now want to update your Running Records. You may wish to have students complete the Self-Assessment Checklist in the *Portfolio Teacher's Guide*.

PORTFOLIO CONFERENCE

The Portfolio Conference provides you with an opportunity to learn about each student's

- preference for reading fiction or real-life accounts.
- general writing development.
- understanding of figurative language.

Discuss the reading selections in Unit 4, eliciting each student's preferences. Ask about similar works the student has read.

Ask the student to select from his or her reading/portfolio a piece of writing that he or she would like to talk about. Perhaps Joshua's letter to Laurel from "The Second Highest Point" or the Africans' impressions of Alex Haley from "Mister Kinte!" might be shared. Invite the student to comment on what he or she enjoyed most when writing the piece. Compliment the student on some positive aspect of his or her writing.

Formal Assessment

The formal assessment tools described below may be found in the *Teacher's Resource Bank*.

SKILLS ASSESSMENT

The *Skills Assessment* for Unit 4 provides you with feedback about students' mastery of the specific skills and strategies taught in Learning Through Literature. Skills tested in this unit are Figurative Language, Reference Sources (Dictionary), Fact-Opinion/Author's Purpose-Viewpoint. If students had difficulty, refer to pages R35–R52 for visual, auditory, and kinesthetic/motor models that may be used to reteach skills tested in this unit.

HOLISTIC ASSESSMENT

The *Holistic Assessment* for Unit 4 may be used to assess a student's ability to understand passages written at the same level as the selections in the Student Anthology. If students have difficulty, refer them to the appropriate lessons in the Handbook for Readers and Writers: Active Reading Strategies, Reading Nonfiction, and Vocabulary Strategies.

INTEGRATED PERFORMANCE ASSESSMENT

The *Integrated Performance Assessment* for Unit 4 provides you with a profile of how well each student uses reading, writing, listening, and speaking strategies while reading and responding to a piece of literature. Assessment results reflect how well students employ the strategies modeled and practiced in the classroom.

Break Time

A Few Steps to Higher Self-esteem

Self-esteem, that inner sense of worthiness, may be the most important gift you can give yourself. In your challenging world, however, other obligations often compete for the time it takes to reflect on your own accomplishments.

Developing true self-esteem is a lifelong task. Here are some positive steps you can take right now:

1. Accept who you are. Start developing a healthy appreciation for yourself as a unique individual.
2. Give yourself credit. Take a moment at the end of the school day to reflect on things you have done well.
3. Ask someone you respect professionally to come into your room and to observe your teaching. Explain that you are looking for some positive feedback. Then do the same for a colleague.
4. Don't be afraid to take risks. Ask yourself what you've been putting off trying. Then set a goal, and work toward accomplishing it.
5. Go back to school. Accept the challenge of a difficult course.
6. Attend a professional conference or visit another school.
7. Create a support group away from school. Plan dinner with colleagues on a regular basis.
8. Avoid being judgmental. The criticism you send out is seldom returned with positive feelings.

Mastering Classroom Discipline

For novice and veteran alike, the challenge of maintaining an appropriate learning environment often depends on classroom discipline. While no single strategy can be expected to work in all situations, the following suggestions may prove effective in your classroom:

■ Make your discipline policy known to students, parents, and colleagues. Then consistently follow through.

■ Use surprise reinforcers. Make students aware that rewards are a result of their positive behavior.

■ Vary your lessons. Disruptions may be reactions to a curriculum that has become overly routine.

■ Build a caring relationship with your students. People don't risk losing important relationships.

■ Model the behavior you would like to see in your students.

PEANUTS cartoons by Charles M. Schulz. Reprinted by permission of UFS, Inc.

The New Kid in School

Child psychologists say that relocating, even within the same general area, can leave children anxious, angry, depressed, or simply disoriented. Here are a few ideas that might help the new student meet the challenge of adjusting to a new school:

■ Help the student learn about his or her new surroundings within the school and the larger community.

■ Experts say it takes families approximately six months to settle into a new home. Adjust your expectations of the student during this period.

■ One study suggests it takes a new middle-school student an average of twenty-three days to make friends. Scheduling collaborative grouping or paired learning may speed up the process.

UNIT FIVE

OBSERVATIONS

Planning Center

What's Ahead in "Observations"?

EARTH: PAGES 404–435B   Blast off with your students to observe "Earth" from a different perspective—outer space. Then return and go back in time to discover creatures that once roamed the earth and are now extinct.

SURVIVAL: PAGES 436–473B   Meet teenager Elena Bradbury, lone survivor of a plane crash; and Pentaquod, a Native American who lived along the Susquehanna River in the late 1500s. Their survival depends on their courage and ingenuity and their knowledge of nature. As your students read the fictional excerpts, encourage them to think about their own survival skills.

WATCHING NATURE: PAGES 474–501B   Your students will discover the thrill of "Watching Nature" as they read excerpts from a nonfiction book and a novel, and two poems.

Pacing

This unit is designed to take approximately five or six weeks, depending on your students' needs.

Assessment and Evaluation

ASSESSMENT OPTIONS		
Title	**Description**	**When and How It's Used**
INFORMAL ASSESSMENT OPTIONS (Ongoing)		
Reading/Writing Portfolio	Contains samples of students' literacy development.	Collect samples of personal journals and writing throughout the unit. Hold periodic Portfolio Conferences.
Informal Assessment Notes	Appear throughout the *Teacher's Edition.*	Observe students' reading, writing, listening, and speaking behaviors. Complete checklists on an ongoing basis.
Student Self-Assessment Notes	Appear throughout the *Teacher's Edition.*	Students monitor their use of reading and writing strategies.
Running Records	Ongoing assessment of students' reading skills and strategies as they read both fiction and nonfiction.	Record periodically to track students' progress.
FORMAL ASSESSMENT OPTIONS (End of Unit)		
Skills Assessment	Assesses mastery of strategies and skills taught in Learning Through Literature.	Administer at end of the unit.
Holistic Assessment	Evaluates students' ability to read and understand excerpts from literature.	Administer at end of the unit.
Integrated Performance Assessment	Assesses use of reading and writing strategies modeled and practiced in the classroom.	Administer at end of the unit.

HBJ Literature Cassette 2

Recordings of the following selections in "Observations" may be used for instruction or for students' listening enjoyment:

- "The Right Place"
- "The Sparrow Hawk"
- "Be Like the Bird"
- "I May, I Might, I Must"
- "I Watched an Eagle Soar"

Audiovisual Materials and Software

Cougar. Aims, 1990. A brother and sister swept away by a flash flood face survival issues. VIDEO

The Great Dinosaur Hunt. Vestron Video, 1990. This program looks at the mysteries that surround dinosaurs. VIDEO

Michener at Work: The Writing of *Caribbean*. Films for the Humanities, 1991. Viewers travel with the author to the Caribbean as he reveals creative secrets and ideas. VIDEO

Nature's Symphony. Lumivision. Nature's most stunning images are further enhanced by the music of great composers. INTERACTIVE VIDEODISC

One Earth: An Environmental Overview. National Geographic, 1991. This highlights vital environmental issues throughout the world. FILMSTRIP

River Notes: The Dance of the Herons by Barry Lopez. American Audio Prose Library. The author's reading is accompanied by bells and cello. AUDIOCASSETTE

"Five notches into June, my house was done. I could stand in it, lie down in it, and there was room left over for a stump to sit on. On warm evenings I would lie on my stomach and look out the door, listen to the frogs and nighthawks, and hope it would storm so that I could crawl into my tree and be dry."

HBJ Treasury of Literature Library

Here are some of the options you will find in the *HBJ Treasury of Literature Library Guide* for *My Side of the Mountain:*

- **Reading Cooperatively** in response groups
- **Reading Independently** during sustained silent reading periods
- **Directing the Reading** through questioning strategies
- **Reading Aloud** to encourage literature appreciation

Bulletin Board Idea

Start a bulletin board display labeled "What Is It?" with photographs of people or objects taken from odd angles or postcard reproductions of paintings that represent fresh ways of looking at things. Some of these might be Seurat's dotted figures or a Cubist rendition of a violin. Ask students to add to the display. Encourage them to find examples in magazines or advertisements that make the viewer stop and think, "What is it?"

Observations

Ask students what the word *observations* means to them. Have them name real-life situations in which observation skills might be important. Invite them to read the unit introduction and the theme titles in Unit 5. Discuss why the themes "Earth," "Survival," and "Watching Nature" might all appear in a unit called "Observations."

Ask students to discuss what they know about observations that have been important to people in different parts of the world. CULTURAL AWARENESS

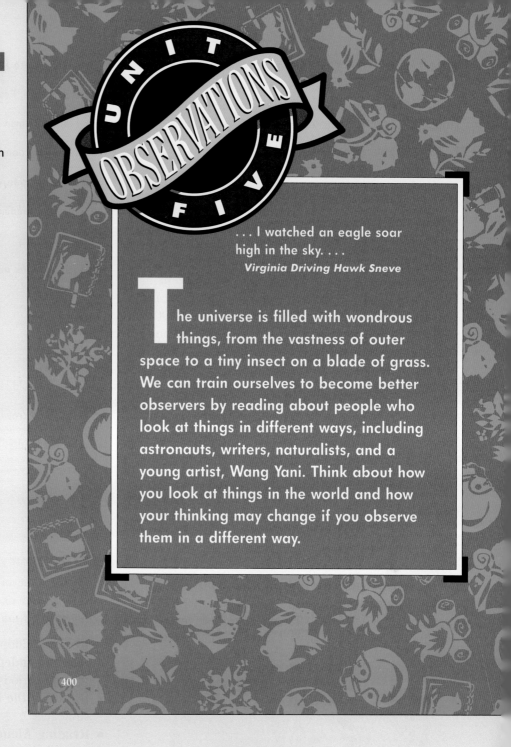

UNIT FIVE

OBSERVATIONS

... I watched an eagle soar high in the sky. ...
Virginia Driving Hawk Sneve

The universe is filled with wondrous things, from the vastness of outer space to a tiny insect on a blade of grass. We can train ourselves to become better observers by reading about people who look at things in different ways, including astronauts, writers, naturalists, and a young artist, Wang Yani. Think about how you look at things in the world and how your thinking may change if you observe them in a different way.

400

THEMES

EARTH
. . . .
404

SURVIVAL
. . . .
436

WATCHING NATURE
. . . .
474

401

Focus on Literary Genre

If you wish to have students focus on literary genre, or form, as they read the selections in "Observations," refer to the Literary Genre list. (A complete Table of Contents classified by literary genre appears on pages R98–R101.) The labels on the numbered annotations beside the reduced student pages will help you guide students to note and analyze the literary elements and characteristics of each genre.

BOOKSHELF

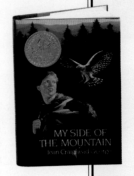

MY SIDE OF THE MOUNTAIN

BY JEAN CRAIGHEAD GEORGE

Sam Gribley goes to the woods and lives off the land. With a tree as his home and a falcon as his companion, Sam relies on his own ingenuity to survive. NEWBERY HONOR BOOK, ALA NOTABLE BOOK, HANS CHRISTIAN ANDERSEN AWARD HONOR BOOK

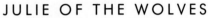

HBJ LIBRARY BOOK

JULIE OF THE WOLVES

BY JEAN CRAIGHEAD GEORGE

Lost in the Alaskan wilderness, a young Eskimo girl is accepted by a pack of Arctic wolves and comes to care for them as though they were her family. NEWBERY MEDAL

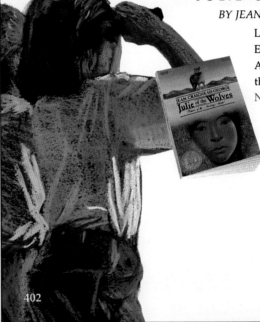

402

HBJ Library Book

Have students read the information about *My Side of the Mountain* and look at the cover illustration. Have them discuss what they know about the book so far. Page 399F provides a preview of the lesson plans that can be found in the *HBJ Treasury of Literature Library Guide*.

THE ASTRONAUT TRAINING BOOK FOR KIDS

BY KIM LONG

This book will tell you all you need to know about preparing for an exciting career. Discover what space will be like when you get there.

SUPERNOVA

BY CHRISTOPHER LAMPTON

In 1987, one of the most exciting astronomical events in modern history took place. It will be years before we learn everything we can from this exploding star.

ANIMALS AT PLAY

BY LAURENCE PRINGLE

Is animal play just for fun? Does play somehow aid the survival of a species? This noted science writer describes and explains many types of animal behavior.

AWARD-WINNING AUTHOR

403

WRITER'S JOURNAL pages 72–74:

Reading and writing about "Observations"

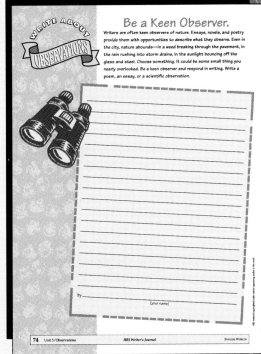

Write About Observations

Be a Keen Observer.

Writers are often keen observers of nature. Essays, novels, and poetry provide them with opportunities to describe what they observe. Even in the city, nature abounds—in a weed breaking through the pavement, in the rain rushing into storm drains, in the sunlight bouncing off the glass and steel. Choose something. It could be some small thing you nearly overlooked. Be a keen observer and respond in writing. Write a poem, an essay, or a scientific observation.

by _____
(your name)

74 Unit 5/Observations   HBJ Writer's Journal   ENDLESS WORLDS

Writer's Journal

**Read aloud
to students.**

Julie of the Wolves

by Jean Craighead George

Miyax pushed back the hood of her sealskin parka and looked at the Arctic sun. It was a yellow disc in a lime-green sky, the colors of six o'clock in the evening and the time when the wolves awoke. Quietly she put down her cooking pot and crept to the top of a dome-shaped frost heave, one of the many earth buckles that rise and fall in the crackling cold of the Arctic winter. Lying on her stomach, she looked across a vast lawn of grass and moss and focused her attention on the wolves she had come upon two sleeps ago. They were wagging their tails as they awoke and saw each other.

Her hands trembled and her heartbeat quickened, for she was frightened, not so much of the wolves, who were shy and many harpoon-shots away, but because of her desperate predicament. Miyax was lost. She had been lost without food for many sleeps on the North Slope of Alaska.

Miyax stared hard at the regal black wolf, hoping to catch his eye. She must somehow tell him that she was starving and ask him for food. This could be done she knew, for her father, an Eskimo hunter, had done so. One year he had camped near a wolf den while on a hunt. When a month had passed and her father had seen no game, he told the leader of the wolves that he was hungry and needed food. The next night the wolf called him from far away and her father went to him and found a freshly killed caribou. Unfortunately, Miyax's father never

explained to her how he had told the wolf of his needs. And not long afterward he paddled his kayak into the Bering Sea to hunt for seal, and he never returned.

She had been watching the wolves for two days, trying to discern which of their sounds and movements expressed goodwill and friendship. Most animals had such signals. The little Arctic ground squirrels flicked their tails sideways to notify others of their kind that they were friendly. By imitating this signal with her forefinger, Miyax had lured many a squirrel to her hand. If she could discover such a gesture for the wolves she would be able to make friends with them and share their food, like a bird or a fox.

Propped on her elbows with her chin in her fists, she stared at the black wolf, trying to catch his eye. She had chosen him because he was much larger than the others, and because he walked like her father, Kapugen, with his head high and his chest out. The black wolf also possessed wisdom, she had observed. The pack looked to him when the wind carried strange scents or the birds cried nervously. If he was alarmed, they were alarmed. If he was calm, they were calm.

Long minutes passed, and the black wolf did not look at her. He had ignored her since she first came upon them, two sleeps ago. True, she moved slowly and quietly, so as not to alarm him; yet she

---

SELECTION SUMMARY Alone and lost on a stretch of Alaskan tundra, thirteen-year-old Miyax struggles to conquer her fear and find a way to survive. Her life depends upon the wolves she has come upon, but she is not sure they will help her. Cautiously, Miyax tries to get the attention of a royal black wolf, the leader, to let him know that she is in desperate need of food.

ABOUT THE AUTHOR Jean Craighead George grew up in a family that was devoted to animals and nature. She continues to explore nature and to express her concern and love for the environment in her work. Ms. George won the 1973 Newbery Medal for her novel *Julie of the Wolves*.

Strategies for Listening

LISTENING/THINKING STRATEGY—NOTING DETAILS
ABOUT THE SETTING Tell students that the setting of a story often influences the plot and characters. Explain that listening for details about the setting will help them to better understand the events and the actions and feelings of the main character.

SET A PURPOSE FOR LISTENING Encourage students to listen for details about the setting and think about how they affect the story and the main character, Miyax (whose American name is Julie).

did wish he would see the kindness in her eyes. Many animals could tell the difference between hostile hunters and friendly people by merely looking at them. But the big black wolf would not even glance her way.

A bird stretched in the grass. The wolf looked at it. A flower twisted in the wind. He glanced at that. Then the breeze rippled the wolverine ruff on Miyax's parka and it glistened in the light. He did not look at that. She waited. Patience with the ways of nature had been instilled in her by her father. And so she knew better than to move or shout. Yet she must get food or die. Her hands shook slightly and she swallowed hard to keep calm.

Miyax was a classic Eskimo beauty, small of bone and delicately wired with strong muscles. Her face was pearl-round and her nose was flat. Her black eyes, which slanted gracefully, were moist and sparkling. Like the beautifully formed polar bears and foxes of the north, she was slightly short-limbed. The frigid environment of the Arctic has sculptured life into compact shapes. Unlike the long-limbed, long-bodied animals of the south that are cooled by dispensing heat on extended surfaces, all live things in the Arctic tend toward compactness, to conserve heat.

The length of her limbs and the beauty of her face were of no use to Miyax as she lay on the lichen-speckled frost heave in the midst of the bleak tundra. Her stomach ached and the royal black wolf was carefully ignoring her.

"*Amaroq, ilaya,* wolf, my friend," she finally called. "Look at me. Look at me."

She spoke half in Eskimo and half in English, as if the instincts of her father and the science of the *gussaks,* the white-faced, might evoke some magical combination that would help her get her message through to the wolf.

Amaroq glanced at his paw and slowly turned his head her way without lifting his eyes. He licked his shoulder. A few matted hairs sprang apart and twinkled individually. Then his eyes sped to each of the three adult wolves that made up his pack and finally to the five pups who were sleeping in a fuzzy mass near the den entrance. The great wolf's eyes softened at the sight of the little wolves, then quickly hardened into brittle yellow jewels as he scanned the flat tundra.

Not a tree grew anywhere to break the monotony of the gold-green plain, for the soils of the tundra are permanently frozen. Only moss, grass, lichens, and a few hardy flowers take root in the thin upper layer that thaws briefly in summer. Nor do many species of animals live in this rigorous land, but those creatures that do dwell here exist in bountiful numbers. Amaroq watched a large cloud of Lapland longspurs wheel up into the sky, then alight in the grasses. Swarms of crane flies, one of the few insects that can survive the cold, darkened the tips of the mosses. Birds wheeled, turned, and called. Thousands sprang up from the ground like leaves in a wind.

The wolf's ears cupped forward and turned in on some distant message from the tundra. Miyax tensed and listened, too. Did he hear some brewing storm, some approaching enemy? Apparently not. His ears relaxed and he rolled to his side. She sighed, glanced at the vaulting sky, and was painfully aware of her predicament.

Responding to Literature

1. **How would you describe Miyax's predicament and her chances of survival? Explain.** (Accept reasonable responses: Miyax is lost in the tundra, has little or no food left, minimal shelter, and no source of food other than to hunt for it herself; Miyax has a good chance to survive because she has determination, patience, and the knowledge that wolves once helped her own father to survive.) INFERENTIAL: SUMMARIZING/DRAWING CONCLUSIONS

2. **How might the wolves help Miyax survive?** (Accept reasonable responses: As animals of prey, they might possibly share the meat from their kills with Miyax, thus providing her with some food and a chance to survive. INFERENTIAL: SPECULATING

SPEAKING   Invite students to form groups to orally compose an adventure that Miyax has with the wolf pack. Encourage groups to tell their adventures to other groups of classmates. CREATIVE: INVENTING NEW SCENES

Earth

Have students look at the photograph and read the information on page 405 of the Student Anthology. Ask them who or what might have taken the photograph of Earth and where the camera was positioned to shoot it. Next, point out that the introduction invites them to "go back in time." Ask students if they were able to do so, what they might learn about the animals such as gnats, mammoths, and saber-toothed tigers mentioned in the selection title.

PACING   This theme has been designed to take about two weeks to complete, depending on your students' needs.

404

Management Options

THE LITERATURE-BASED CLASSROOM   Providing a literature-rich curriculum creates unique classroom management challenges. Some management options for the selections in this theme follow.

"EARTH: PAST, PRESENT, FUTURE" CENTER   To encourage students to read independently and to extend their knowledge of the theme, set aside an area in the classroom where they can refer to books, magazines, newspaper articles, and other resource materials related to "Earth." You may wish to ask the science teacher and the media specialist to suggest filmstrips and videos.

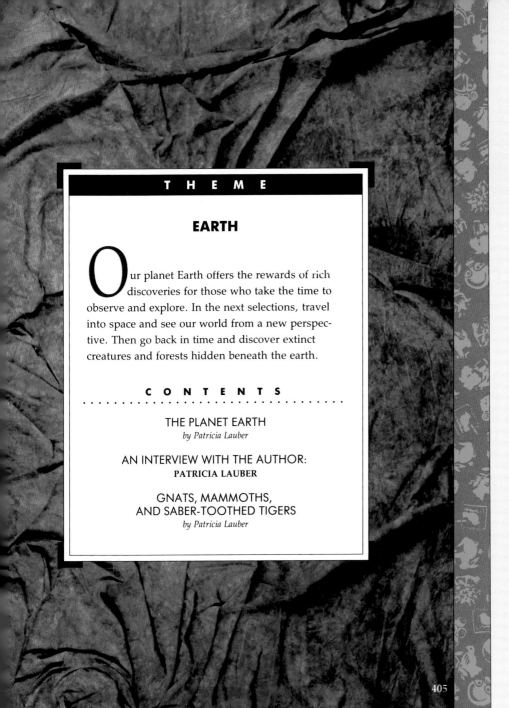

THEME

EARTH

Our planet Earth offers the rewards of rich discoveries for those who take the time to observe and explore. In the next selections, travel into space and see our world from a new perspective. Then go back in time and discover extinct creatures and forests hidden beneath the earth.

CONTENTS

405

STUDENTS AT RISK

To motivate students and better prepare them for the first selection in this theme, you may wish to show filmstrips or videos of pictures that were taken of Earth during space flights.

GIFTED AND TALENTED

As students complete Write activities following the selections and the Writer's Workshop activity on Student Anthology page 435, encourage them to explore a variety of options for publishing their writing. Also see the *Challenge Cards.*

SPECIAL EDUCATION STUDENTS

When students with dyslexia read aloud, suggest that they mark with self-stick notes the parts they will read.

LIMITED ENGLISH PROFICIENT STUDENTS

Some students may have difficulty recalling the rules of punctuation and capitalization when writing in English. Have students make individual punctuation and capitalization reference charts on file folders or large index cards. Suggest that they keep their charts handy whenever they write.

VOCABULARY BUILDUP Begin a cumulative word montage of Key Words and other "problem" words. Write the words on strips of paper and display them randomly on the bulletin board. Then have students try some of these activities to reinforce meaning:

- Identify the verbs (adjectives, adverbs, nouns).
- Choose any two adjectives (verbs, nouns) and use them in a sentence.
- Find as many synonyms as possible for a word.

READING/WRITING PORTFOLIO Instruct students to keep in their portfolios their writing responses to the theme selections. Remind them also to add to their personal journals notes on their independent reading.

THE PLANET EARTH

by Patricia Lauber

PATRICIA LAUBER (1924–) was born in New York City and attended Wellesley College, from which she graduated in 1945. She launched her writing career at Scholastic Magazines, writing classroom magazines for young people, and later became the editor of *Science World*. In 1954 she turned to children's books with *Magic Up Your Sleeve*. Since then, she has produced over forty volumes on a broad range of subjects. She has written about earthquakes and forests, the stars and the sea, and penguins and kangaroos. However, she says, "I won't write about things that don't interest me."

> "**I** won't write about things that don't interest me."

MORE BOOKS BY PATRICIA LAUBER
Journey to the Planets. Crown, 1982. AVERAGE
Voyagers from Space: Meteors and Meteorites. Thomas Y. Crowell, 1989. AVERAGE

OTHER BOOKS ABOUT THE PLANET EARTH
Barbary by Vonda N. McIntyre. Houghton Mifflin, 1986. AVERAGE
Rainbows to Lasers by Kathryn Whyman. Watts, 1989. AVERAGE
This Place Has No Atmosphere by Paula Danziger. Delacorte, 1986. AVERAGE

SELECTION SUMMARY
In this excerpt from *Seeing Earth from Space*, Patricia Lauber begins with the now familiar view of the fragile blue globe adrift in a sea of blackness, but she quickly moves on to startling images the naked eye cannot record. She describes false-color pictures made possible by remote sensors using infrared wavelengths and radar. Seeing these pictures of our land and seas and learning of the pictures' uses, readers feel as though they are touring some fabulous, futuristic museum.

LESSON PLANNER

		Materials	Integrated Curriculum	Meeting Individual Needs
1	**READING LITERATURE** pp. 405B–421	Student Anthology pp. 406–421 Transparency 23 Second-Language Support Manual Practice Book p. 121 Integrated Spelling p. 59 Integrated Spelling T. E. pp. 80–81	Spelling Spelling Pretest Spelling-Vocabulary Connection (long *i* sound)	Second-Language Support Vocabulary 405C Strategic Reading 405D Cooperative Reading 406, 420
2	**RESPONDING TO LITERATURE** pp. 421A–421D	Writer's Journal p. 75 Practice Book p. 122 Integrated Spelling p. 60 Integrated Spelling T. E. pp. 80–81	Vocabulary Workshop Reviewing Key Words Extending Vocabulary Writing About the Literature Speaking/Listening Spelling Review	Cooperative Learning 421B, 421C
3	**LEARNING THROUGH LITERATURE** pp. 421E–421J	Second-Language Support Manual Writer's Journal pp. 76–77 Practice Book pp. 123–125	Social Studies Science Art Multicultural	Reteach 421F Challenge 421F, 421G, 421H Second-Language Support 421F Cooperative Learning 421F

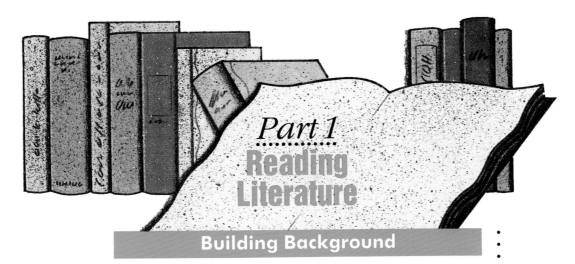

Part 1
Reading Literature

Building Background

Access prior knowledge and develop vocabulary concepts.

Tell students that they will be reading a nonfiction selection about observing Earth from space. Remind students that reviewing what they know about a subject can help them understand what they read. On the board, draw a diagram such as the one below, and ask students to fill in specific examples.

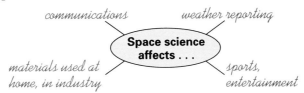

communications   weather reporting

Space science affects . . .

materials used at home, in industry   sports, entertainment

Have students quickwrite sentences.

Ask students to choose one of the areas above and write a sentence or two about how space science has touched them personally. Encourage volunteers to share their responses.

Vocabulary Strategies

Introduce Key Words and strategies.

Tell students that they may encounter some unfamiliar words in "The Planet Earth." Display Transparency 23, or write the paragraph on the board. Have students read the paragraph silently, using phonics, structural analysis, and context clues to figure out the meanings of the underlined words. Call on a volunteer to read the paragraph aloud, and help with pronunciation if necessary.

Transparency 23   Key Words

Juan was surprised at the picture on the computer screen. The sea didn't look like water but like soil left <u>fallow</u>, unsown with seed. A curvy line through the sea—he guessed a reef—resembled a stream that <u>meanders</u> through fields. These pictures made by <u>microwaves</u>, shortwaves sent by radar, were strange. Would those who study the sea, the <u>oceanographers</u>, be as surprised as he was, perhaps? New theories were <u>colliding</u> with old, and the impact would shake scientists' views.

KEY WORDS DEFINED

fallow   untilled, uncultivated

meanders   winds

microwaves   short electromagnetic waves

oceanographers   scientists who study the sea

colliding   hitting head-on

Check students' understanding.

Read the sentences below. Ask students to determine whether the Key Word is used correctly or incorrectly in each sentence and to explain why. STRATEGIES: DEFINITION/PRIOR KNOWLEDGE

1. **The corn stood high in the *fallow* field.** (Incorrectly. Fallow fields have no crops.)
2. **Rapids rush downstream, but slowly flowing water *meanders*.** (Correctly. Slowly flowing water often winds aimlessly.)
3. **In some ovens, food is cooked by heat produced when *microwaves* penetrate the food.** (Correctly. This is a common use of the word.)
4. **The *oceanographers* were busy putting the finishing touches on the chart of the southern stars.** (Incorrectly. Oceanographers study the seas, not the stars.)
5. **The crashing sound came from a single truck *colliding* by itself.** (Incorrectly. It takes two things to make a collision.)

After discussing the Key Words with students, encourage them to relate some of the words to their discussion of space science in Building Background. For example, students might suggest the sentence "*Oceanographers* use pictures taken from space to study the oceans."

Integrate spelling with vocabulary.

SPELLING-VOCABULARY CONNECTION *Integrated Spelling* page 59 reinforces spellings of the **long *i* sound** in the following Key Words: *colliding, microwaves.* The spelling of the Key Word *meanders* is also included.

SECOND-LANGUAGE SUPPORT Have students work in groups to review the Key Words, pantomiming the meaning of the word *meanders.* (See Second-Language Support Manual.)

PRACTICE BOOK
page 121: Reinforcing Key Words

INTEGRATED SPELLING
page 59: Writing and spelling words with the long *i* sound

NOTE: These pages may be completed now or after students have read the selection.

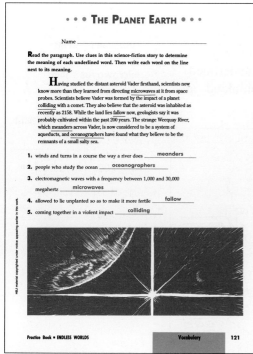

Practice Book

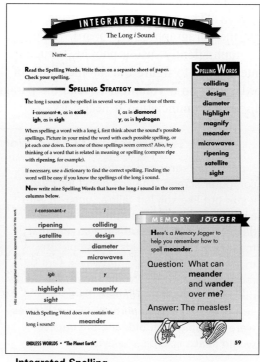

Integrated Spelling

Using the K-W-L Strategy

Have students review the K-W-L strategy.

Remind students that when they read expository, or informational, nonfiction, it is especially important to use what they already know about a topic in order to understand what they are reading. Write the K-W-L headings on the board—*What I Know, What I Want to Know, What I Learned.* Call on a volunteer to explain how to use the K-W-L strategy. (List what you know about a topic, ask questions about what you want to find out, and note the information you learn as you read.)

What I Know	What I Want to Know	What I Learned

Help students preview the selection.

Have students preview the nonfiction selection by using the title, the name of the book from which the selection was taken, and the photographs and captions to get a general idea of the information covered.

Point out that the section headings provide clues about the information in the selection. Suggest that students turn each heading into a question. Because the material covered is technical, you may want to help students formulate questions.

PERSONAL JOURNAL Have students copy the K-W-L headings in their personal journals, or have them use *Practice Book* page 122. (See page 421B in this Teacher's Edition.) Have students fill in the first two columns. Students can complete the chart as they read the selection or after they finish. (Students will return to the chart after reading, in Summarizing the Literature.)

Setting a Purpose

Have students set purposes.

Remind students that setting a purpose for reading can help them read alertly. Have students use the questions they have written to set a purpose for reading the selection.

Model purpose-setting, if necessary.

If students have difficulty setting a purpose for reading, model the thinking process:

> **I already know that this selection is about seeing Earth from space. My purpose for reading will be to find out how remote sensors can be used to increase our knowledge of Earth and to improve our lives.**

OPTIONS FOR READING

Independent Reading
Have students read the selection silently with their purpose for reading in mind.

Guided Reading
Follow the Guided Reading suggestions that appear on pages 406, 407, 412–413, and 420. These suggestions model strategic reading.

Cooperative Reading
Suggestions for Cooperative Reading appear on pages 406 and 420.

Numbered Annotations
Use the numbered annotations beside the Student Anthology pages to heighten students' appreciation of the selection.

BACKGROUND INFORMATION
The photographs in this selection were taken by Landsat and Seasat satellites. Countries and corporations spend millions of dollars every year sending satellites into space: weather satellites, communications satellites, and observation satellites. The first satellite specifically designed to photograph the earth was *ERTS 1*, launched into polar orbit on July 23, 1972. *ERTS 1*, which stands for *Earth Resources Technology Satellite 1*, was later renamed *Landsat 1*. Five Landsats were launched between 1972 and 1984. Landsat photographs have been used to forecast crop production, monitor fires and storms, identify mineral deposits, and benefit humanity in many other ways. Seasat photographs of the oceans are similar to Landsat photographs of the continents.

CHILDREN'S CHOICE

SEEING EARTH FROM SPACE

BY PATRICIA LAUBER

406

Guided Reading

SET PURPOSE/PREDICT: PAGES 406–407 Have students predict what question will be answered by the introductory part of the selection. (Accept reasonable responses: How is technology used for observing Earth?) Have students read pages 406–407 to check their predictions.

Cooperative Reading

SET PURPOSE/PREDICT: PAGES 406–421 Have students work in small groups. For each part of the selection, group members should read silently and agree on information to look for in response to each purpose-setting question.

THE PLANET EARTH

On their way to the moon, Apollo 8 Astronaunts looked back and saw a bright blue globe, partly masked by white clouds and set against the black of space. At that moment they became the first people ever to see the Earth as a planet. Their photographs and others show us Earth as we can never see it for ourselves. They also show us something we know but find hard to believe: We are all flying through space. Our space ship is the earth, whirling around the sun at 67,000 miles an hour.

Other new views come from photographs taken by astronauts orbiting a few hundred miles above Earth's surface. These astronauts are too close to see the full face of the earth. But they see large pieces of it at one time, something we cannot do. Trying to see the earth from its surface is like looking at a large painting while standing up against it. We see only details. To see the picture, we must back off.

Astronauts in orbit have backed off from Earth. They see the full length of rivers, the folds of the mountains, the birth of hurricanes, the straight lines of roads and bridges that mark the cities of the world. Their photographs give us a space tour of our home planet.

Still different pictures of Earth come from satellites carrying sensors, radar, and other instruments. They show us things that the human eye cannot see for itself.

Together, all these views of Earth teach us much about our planet, whether by showing us the unseen or by taking us sight-seeing with the astronauts.

from
SEEING EARTH FROM SPACE
by Patricia Lauber

407

1 TEXT STRUCTURE
Why does this piece begin with the *Apollo 8* launch? *(These astronauts were the first human beings to see the earth as a planet; their journey was an important milestone in our efforts to understand the earth.)*
INFERENTIAL: DRAWING CONCLUSIONS

2 FIGURATIVE LANGUAGE
Find the simile, or comparison, that expresses the difference between the perspective of an ordinary person and that of the astronauts. *(Trying to see the earth from its surface is like looking at a large painting while standing up against it.)*
LITERAL: MAKING COMPARISONS

What is the point of the simile? *(The astronauts see the whole picture because they have "backed off" a sufficient distance from Earth.)*
INFERENTIAL: DRAWING CONCLUSIONS

Guided Reading

MONITOR COMPREHENSION: PAGES 406–407
How is technology used for observing Earth?
(Satellites circle the earth carrying sensors, radar, and other instruments.) STRATEGIC READING: RETURNING TO PURPOSE

How does technology provide us with more-than-human vision? (It enables us to see the otherwise unseen and to see the world from a new perspective.) STRATEGIC READING: SUMMARIZING

SET PURPOSE/PREDICT: PAGES 408–413 Remind students that their purpose for reading is to find the answers to the questions they wrote on their K-W-L charts. Have students predict what questions they will find answers to in the first part of the selection. (Accept reasonable responses: What is remote sensing? How does it "see" or help us to see?) Have students read through page 413 to find the answers.

REMOTE SENSING

3 Space photography is called remote sensing because it is a way of learning about a target, such as the earth, without touching it. There are many kinds of remote sensing. Among them are ones found in the human body. You use yours every day of your life.

Is a radiator hot? To find out, you don't touch it. You hold your hands out toward it. If there is heat, nerve endings in your skin will sense it. That is one kind of human remote sensing.

Eyesight, or vision, is a much more important kind. To use it, you need light.

White light is a mixture of colors. You see this when the sun's white light breaks up into a band of colors and makes a rainbow in the sky. You see it when white light passes through a prism. The light breaks up into a band of colors known as a spectrum.

4 Light travels in waves, and each color has its own wavelength. When the sun's white light shines on a buttercup, the flower absorbs most of the wavelengths, but it reflects the yellow ones. And so you see a yellow flower. A purple plum is reflecting a mixture of red and violet wavelengths. A brown dog is reflecting a mixture of red, orange, and yellow ones.

408

Like the human eye, a camera takes in reflected light. Used with black-and-white or color film, a camera records the kinds of things that the eye sees.

Red wavelengths are the longest that the human eye can detect. So red is the last color we see in the spectrum. But there is color beyond red, color with longer wavelengths. It is in the part of the spectrum called the infrared, meaning "below red." If we could see in the infrared, we would see color beyond red in every rainbow, color we cannot even imagine.

If we could detect even longer infrared wavelengths, we would see something else. After sunset, we would see a dim glow, the glow of heat being given off.

Sunlight warms the earth's surface by day. The heat is absorbed by oceans, deserts, rocks, trees, and everything else on the surface. Some of the heat is radiated back into the atmosphere as infrared energy. If we could see these infrared wavelengths, the landscape would glow at night.

Although human eyes cannot sense infrared, there are ways of detecting it. One is to use film that senses infrared. There are also electronic sensors that detect infrared. They are carried on satellites—the Landsat series launched by the United States and satellites launched by other countries. The sensors scan the earth beneath them. They measure the light reflected by the earth, both the wavelengths we see and the infrared. The sensors are another kind of remote sensing.

Sensors record their measurements as numbers, using a scale of 0 to 255. The numbers are radioed to Earth, where computers put them together and make pictures. Bright false colors are added to make details stand out and to let us see what was recorded in infrared.

Some of the pictures, or images, look like photographs; some don't. But all provide far more information than the eye alone could do.

This Landsat picture was made using information sensed and recorded in green, red, and infrared wavelengths. It shows California's Salton Sea, which looks like a big footprint, and the Imperial Valley, which stretches southward. In the valley's warm, dry climate crops grow year-round, irrigated with water from the Colorado River. Healthy green plants reflect infrared strongly; they appear as bright red in this false-color image. Thinner vegetation is pink. Clear water is black. Windblown sand from the neighboring desert is white. The checkerboard pattern shows that some fields have ripening crops (red and pink) and some are lying fallow, or resting (blue-gray).

Because of a difference in the way farming is done, the border between the United States and Mexico appears as a straight line across the Imperial Valley. It is one of the few national boundaries on Earth that can be seen from space.

The Mississippi River twists and turns—it meanders—as it flows through its lower valley toward the Gulf of Mexico.

409

5 EXPOSITORY TEXT: CAUSE-EFFECT
Why can't the human eye see infrared? *(Infrared waves are too long for the eye to detect.)*
INFERENTIAL: DRAWING CONCLUSIONS

Why does the author add that if we could see infrared, we would see unimaginable colors in the rainbow? *(Accept reasonable responses: She wants to spark a sense of wonder in the reader.)*
CRITICAL: SPECULATING

6 EXPOSITORY TEXT: DETAILS
How do remote sensors help us see infrared? *(They detect the infrared light reflected by the earth. Special film records infrared, or electronic sensors measure it numerically. These numbers are relayed to computers, which turn them into pictures.)*
LITERAL: RECOGNIZING SEQUENCE

Sometimes it changes course, leaving behind the loop- and crescent-shaped lakes that now mark its earlier paths. Because of its meanderings, the lower Mississippi is longer than its valley. It travels one-and-a-half times the length of the valley from Cairo, Illinois, to New Orleans.

In this false-color image the floodplain of the river appears pinkish. Much of it is covered with farms that raise cotton, soybeans, rice, wheat, and oats. On bluffs along the borders of the flood plain, forests of oak, hickory, and pine grow.

Looking like a scar on the face of the earth, the Grand Canyon twists its way across Arizona in this Landsat picture. This part of the canyon is about a mile

410

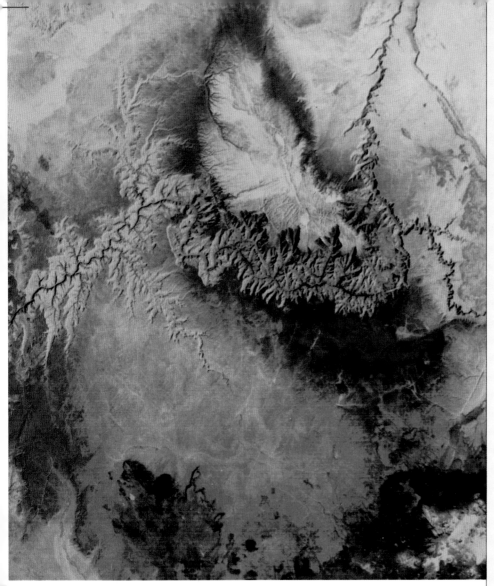

7 EXPOSITORY TEXT: MAIN IDEA
How does the Landsat view of the Grand Canyon both resemble an astronaut's view and differ from it? *(The picture is taken from far up, so the perspective is the same. The colors, however, are false ones, whereas an astronaut sees the true colors.)*
INFERENTIAL: COMPARING AND CONTRASTING

8 EXPOSITORY TEXT: MAIN IDEA
How does radar differ from the Landsat infrared detectors? *(Radar sends out radio waves or microwaves toward a target and detects their echoes. Because radar does not use light, it can be used at night or during the daytime to penetrate cloud cover.)*
LITERAL: COMPARING AND CONTRASTING

deep and 12 miles wide from rim to rim. Its layered rock walls reveal some 2 billion years of Earth's history. The racing Colorado River, which carves the canyon deeper and deeper, is later stopped and pooled by Hoover Dam and Lake Mead.

Radar is still another kind of remote sensing. Unlike the Landsat sensors, it **8** does not measure light reflected from the earth. Instead, it sends out its own radio

411

waves and microwaves. It beams them toward its target and detects their echoes. The strength of the echoes is recorded and used to make maps or pictures. Because it does not use light, radar works both day and night. And because its waves pass through clouds, it can be used when skies are overcast.

One of the space shuttles flew over Montreal, Quebec, at a time when most of the city was covered by clouds. Information from its radar was used to make this false-color image. The St. Lawrence River, at right, is shown in black, as are the smaller rivers. You can see the bridges that cross them. Buildings and pavements appear pink and blue. Land that is being cultivated is dark green. Plant life that grows wild is lighter green. The big green oval to the left of the St. Lawrence is Mount Royal.

The same shuttle flew over the high plateau of northern Peru (below). Its radar showed these folded, layered rocks, some 70 million years old. False colors have been used to highlight different kinds of rock. The wormlike black line in the center of the picture is a river that feeds into the Amazon.

9 Remote sensing shows us the earth in new and often surprising images. For scientists who use the images, they open up ways of studying the earth that have never existed before.

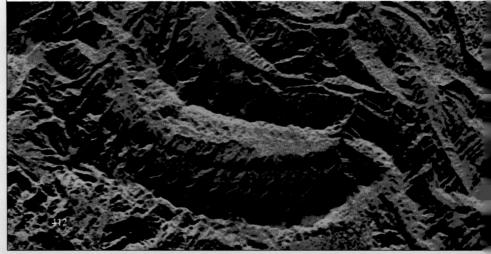

112

SET PURPOSE/PREDICT: PAGES 414–421 Ask
students which questions they might find answers to
in the rest of the selection. Suggest that as they read
they look for practical or real-life applications of
remote-sensor technology.

Oral Rereading   Have students reread a
description of one of the Landsat photos or another
key portion of the text. Encourage students to decide
on their tone of voice before reading aloud. Will it
be curious? Excited? Informative? You may want to
read a few sentences aloud using different tones to
give students an idea of their options. Allow
students time to practice silently before they read
aloud.

How have remote sensors helped geographers and oceanographers?
(Geographers have discovered mountains, lakes, and an island. They have also been able to map unreachable places. Oceanographers are now able to study the sea as a whole. They can track currents and the movements of tiny plants, called plankton, that are eaten by fish.)
INFERENTIAL: SUMMARIZING

USING REMOTE SENSING

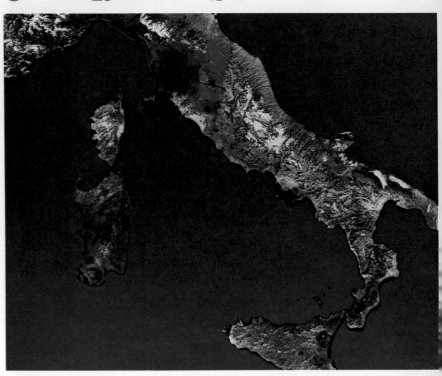

As it orbits, a satellite regularly passes over the same parts of Earth. And so its images let scientists trace what happens as the seasons change. They can, for example, predict flooding by studying winter snowfalls and spring meltings. And they can make cloud-free pictures of any region by piecing together images from different times of year. That was how they obtained this false-color image of Italy. In it, plant life appears in shades of red. Cities and barren areas are blue-gray. Mountains stand out clearly. And the volcano Mount Etna, its sides dark with lava, can be seen on the island of Sicily, off the toe of the boot.

The view from space helps many kinds of scientists. Geographers have discovered mountains and lakes that did not appear on their maps. They have found a previously unknown island off the coast of Labrador and a reef in the Indian Ocean. They have mapped mountain ranges, deserts, and Arctic lands.

In earlier times, oceanographers could only study the oceans from ships. It was

414

long, slow work. The oceans were huge, covering more than 70 percent of Earth's surface, and the ships were small. Now these scientists can also study the oceans through pictures from space. They can see large features that they could not see from ships. They can track currents, such as the Gulf Stream, that play a major part in climate. They can track the masses of tiny plants that form the base of food chains in the oceans. They can see and follow details in ways that used to be impossible.

They can, for example, follow the swirling rings of water thrown off by currents, such as these eddies in the Mediterranean Sea. Eddies can be 200 miles in diameter and travel hundreds of miles over several years. By stirring up the water, eddies speed up the spread of heat from tropical areas. They are also important to the life of the sea, because they carry minerals used by plants in making their food.

Seasat was a United States satellite that

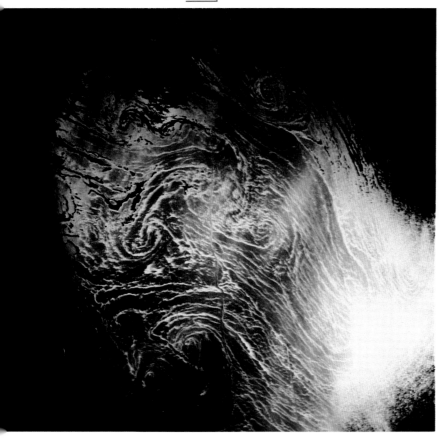

415

Vocabulary Strategy Ask students how context clues can help them figure out the meaning of *eddies* (column 2, line 3). (The author provides a very precise definition, "swirling rings of water thrown off by currents.") STRATEGY: CONTEXT CLUES

What surprising fact did the Seasat satellite record about the ocean?
(The surface of the sea rises and falls with its floor. Even without waves, the ocean's surface has hills and valleys.)
LITERAL: NOTING IMPORTANT DETAILS

How does the author develop this idea in the rest of the paragraph?
(She explains the cause of this surprising feature of the ocean's surface.)
INFERENTIAL: SUMMARIZING

failed after a few months. It was designed to study the oceans—roughness, the patterns of currents, water temperature, the speed of surface winds, sea ice. One of its instruments was a radar altimeter, which measured the height of the satellite above the ocean. Seasat sent out a beam of radio waves. When they hit the surface of the water, they were reflected back to the altimeter and recorded.

The results were a surprise: The surface of the ocean rises and falls with the rise and fall of the seabed beneath it. If you could smooth out all the waves, you would see that the ocean surface has hills and valleys. They mark places where there are undersea mountains and trenches. Where there is a big seamount, for example, there is extra gravity. The seamount pulls a little extra water toward itself. The extra water makes a gentle hill a few feet high. Above a valley or a trench, there is a dip in the surface. And so a map of the ocean

11

416

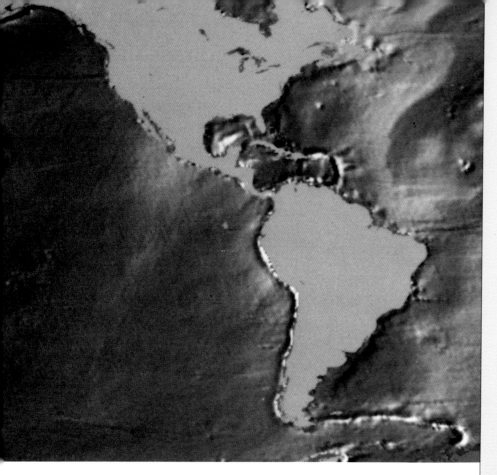

12 **FIGURATIVE LANGUAGE**
**What simile, or comparison, does
the author use to describe the
undersea mountains of the
Mid-Atlantic Ridge?** *(She says the
ridge runs down the ocean "like
the seam on a baseball.")*
LITERAL: NOTING IMPORTANT DETAILS

Why does she use this image?
*(Accept reasonable responses: She
wants to help us grasp unfamiliar
phenomena by using familiar
comparisons.)*
CRITICAL: SPECULATING

surface is also a map of the ocean floor.

This map shows several deep ocean trenches. They are places where plates of the earth's crust are colliding. The leading edge of one plate slides under the other and turns down, creating a trench.

The map also shows the Mid-Atlantic Ridge, a range of undersea volcanic mountains. The range runs down the middle of the Atlantic Ocean and continues around **12** the world, like the seam on a baseball. Here molten rock wells up from inside the

earth and is added to the trailing edges of plates.

In many Landsat images all thick, healthy plant life appears bright red, while thinner vegetation is lighter. But images can also be used to find out what kinds of plants are growing. Every kind of plant reflects sunlight in its own way; it has its own place in the spectrum, which is called its spectral signature. A spectral signature is like a fingerprint. Just as no two people have the same fingerprints, so no two

417

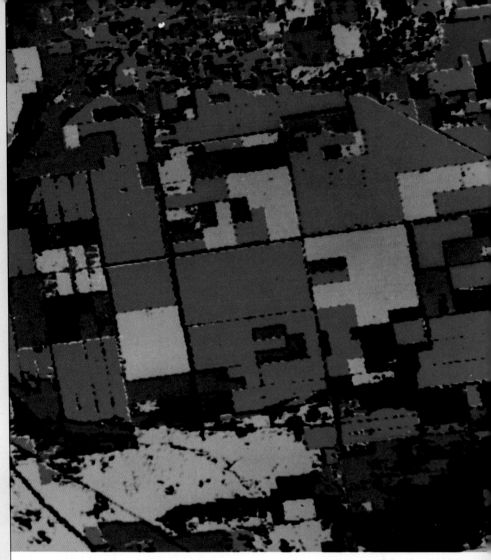

kinds of plant have the same spectral signature. Plant scientists have learned the signature of oats, for example, by studying images of fields where they know oats are growing. When they find the same signature in another place, it tells them the crop is oats. A different signature tells them the crop is wheat. By giving each signature a false color, they can see which fields are planted to oats and which are planted to wheat. In this image of the San Joaquin Valley in California, fields of cotton are red. Yellow shows safflower, while dark green shows

418

Informal Assessment Informally assessing whether students are fulfilling the established purpose for reading involves asking questions such as the following:

- Has this selection told you what you need to know to fulfill your purpose for reading it?
- If so, what ideas and details have been the most important in helping you do that?
- If not, what has the selection failed to tell you that you needed or wanted to know?

This assessment will serve important instructional purposes: It will indicate how well students are focusing as they read, and it will encourage them to watch for and select details that fulfill their purpose for reading.

wheat stubble. Fields lying fallow are blue.

Shuttle astronauts photographed this strange scene while passing over the Saudi Arabian desert. The pattern of perfect circles told them they were seeing something man-made. It turned out to be farmland. Each circle marked a piece of desert irrigated by a sprinkler that pumped water from underground and broadcast it in a circle.

The astronauts' film showed all plant life in one color. Landsat detected far more when it passed over Garden City, Kansas. Here, too, are the circles that tell how the crops are watered. But the Landsat image also tells what the crops are. The time of year is December. White shows where corn has been harvested and its stubble left on the ground. Red shows that healthy winter wheat is growing. Fields that are black and white have been left fallow to build moisture in the soil.

By noting small differences in spectral signatures, plant scientists can tell a newly planted crop from a ripe crop. They can tell whether plants are healthy. They can even tell if unhealthy plants are suffering from a disease or being attacked by pests.

13 EXPOSITORY TEXT: MAIN IDEA
What advantage does the Landsat film have over the astronauts' film? *(The astronauts' film shows all plant life in one color; the Landsat film distinguishes types of plants.)*
LITERAL: COMPARING AND CONTRASTING

14 EXPOSITORY TEXT: MAIN IDEA
In addition to identifying types of plants, what other information do spectral signatures provide? *(They tell scientists which plants are new, which are ripe, and which are suffering from blight or are under attack by pests.)*
INFERENTIAL: SUMMARIZING

Why might scientists want to know this? *(Accept reasonable responses: The information helps them keep track of harvests and predict how much grain there will be; it also helps them trace the path of plant-eating insects or plant disease.)*
INFERENTIAL: DRAWING CONCLUSIONS

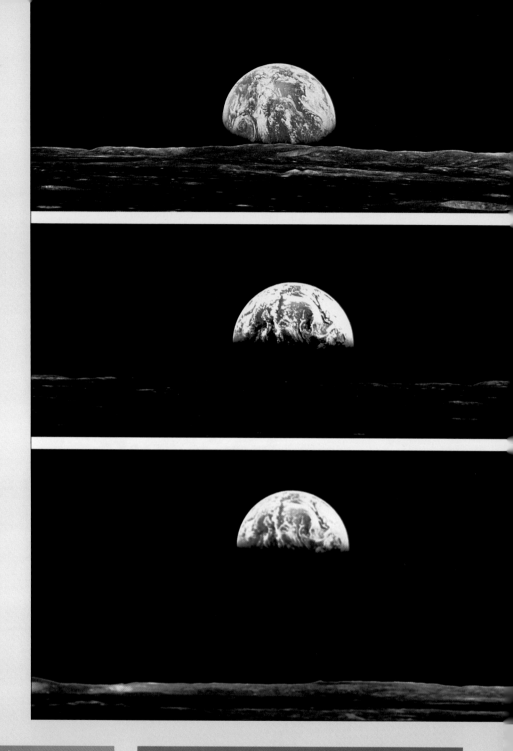

Cooperative Reading

MONITOR COMPREHENSION: PAGES 406–421
Have students discuss the end of the selection by asking each other questions such as "How might remote sensing affect everyday life?"

Guided Reading

MONITOR COMPREHENSION: PAGES 414–421
How can remote sensors be used to increase our knowledge? (They can tell us things we did not know about the earth's surface and about the seas.) **How can these findings be used to improve our lives?** (The author suggests that weather prediction, mapmaking, and control of plant pests and disease are areas that may be improved.) STRATEGIC READING: SUMMARIZING/RETURNING TO PURPOSE

SPACESHIP EARTH

The Apollo astronauts who landed on the moon found themselves in a strange new world. No one had walked this ground before; the only footprints were their own. Nowhere was there a trace of life other than their own, only craters, seas of hardened lava, hills, and rocks. Above them stars and planets shone with a brilliance never seen on Earth, for the moon has no atmosphere to dim their light. Yet for the astronauts the most exciting sight was Earth. It was more than home.

Seen from the surface of the airless, barren moon or from the orbiting spacecraft, Earth was an island of life in the black sea of space, the only outpost of life to be seen.

15

THINK IT OVER

1. *In what ways does remote sensing help us to understand the world in which we live?*
2. *What is a spectrum?*
3. *How are infrared sensors different from film that senses infrared?*
4. *How do pictures from space help oceanographers study the ocean?*

16

WRITE

Select a Landsat photograph in the selection, and write a caption that explains the illustration.

17

421

15 AUTHOR'S VIEWPOINT
Why does the author conclude that, to the first people to reach the moon, the most exciting sight was Earth? *(Accept reasonable responses: They were viewing their home planet from a distance of millions of miles. Earth, compared with the moon, is a place of richness and variety.)*
INFERENTIAL: SPECULATING

16 THINK IT OVER
1. *Remote sensing allows us to see what the eye cannot see on Earth's surface and below it.*
INFERENTIAL: SUMMARIZING
2. *A spectrum is the band of colors produced when white light is broken up by a prism.*
LITERAL: NOTING IMPORTANT DETAILS
3. *Infrared film records light wavelengths below red, whereas infrared sensors measure the wavelengths as numbers, which are then relayed to computers.*
INFERENTIAL: COMPARING AND CONTRASTING
4. *Pictures from space give oceanographers information about currents and about the movements of small plants and animals. They also help map the ocean floor.*
INFERENTIAL: SUMMARIZING

17 WRITE
Remind students that the purpose of a caption is to explain an illustration and to point out what is important about it in a limited number of words. Suggest that as a prewriting exercise, students use a "What-How-Why" box such as the one below:

What	How	Why
Photo Shows	Viewer Reads It	It's Interesting

Accept responses that provide "What-How-Why" information.
CREATIVE: WRITING CAPTIONS

NOTE Additional writing activities appear on page 421D.

Returning to the Purpose for Reading Invite students to review the questions that they wrote before reading and that they may have written in their personal journals. Have them discuss the questions for which they found answers. Also, ask students to share questions they added to their K-W-L charts as they read.

Part 2
Responding to Literature

Summarizing the Literature

Have students retell the selection and write a summary.

Ask students to summarize "The Planet Earth," using the chart they completed as they read. If students did not complete the chart, have them do so now. (See *Practice Book* page 122, on 421B.) Students may use their completed charts to retell the selection and write a brief summary statement.

What I Know	What I Want to Know	What I Learned
Scientists observe Earth and other planets in many ways.	How is technology used for observing Earth?	Satellites circle the earth, carrying sensors, radar, and other instruments.
They use space probes such as Voyager.	What is remote sensing? How does it see or help us see?	Instruments in space record what the eye cannot: infrared and radio waves.

Appreciating Literature

Have students share personal responses.

Invite students to discuss the selection in small groups. Provide a general question such as the following to get the groups started:

- **Does the author's treatment of remote sensing make you interested in this technical subject? Why or why not?**

PERSONAL JOURNAL Encourage students to use their personal journals to write about ideas and feelings that are expressed in the groups.

STRATEGY CONFERENCE

Discuss how the students' K-W-L charts helped them understand, remember, and appreciate the selection. Invite volunteers to share other reading strategies, such as studying illustrations, rereading, and visualizing, that helped them understand the selection.

Encourage both cooperative and individual responses.

FORMULATE QUESTIONS Suppose you were taken on a tour of a space-photography laboratory. Now that you know something about space pictures, what questions would you ask that were not dealt with in the selection? Suggest that students work in pairs to formulate questions that do not appear on their K-W-L charts. CRITICAL: SPECULATING

DRAW A SPACE PICTURE Imagine that remote sensors were turned on a planet called "Xelt" (a planet you make up). Have students draw a space picture of the planet's surface and write a caption explaining what the picture shows. CREATIVE: INVENTING ILLUSTRATIONS AND CAPTIONS

WRITE AND ILLUSTRATE AN ESSAY Many astronauts have remarked that Earth looks intensely beautiful from space. Why do you think people find the sight of Earth from space so moving? Invite students to write brief essays that answer this question. Encourage them to illustrate their essays with realistic or abstract images of Earth as seen from space. Display students' work. CRITICAL: MAKING JUDGMENTS

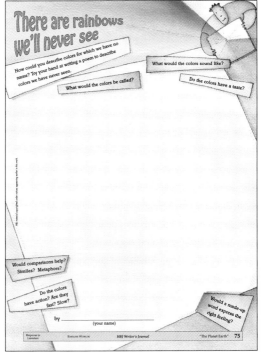

Writer's Journal

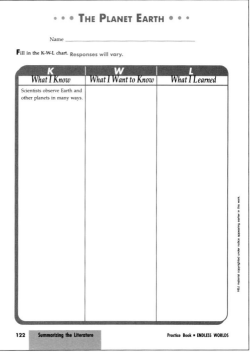

Practice Book

WRITER'S JOURNAL
page 75: Writing a creative response

PRACTICE BOOK
page 122: Summarizing the selection

VO·CAB·U·LAR·Y Workshop

Reviewing Key Words

To review how the new vocabulary is used in this selection, display the Key Words. Read each sentence below, and have students name the word or phrase that is the synonym for the Key Word. Ask them to name both the synonym and the Key Word.

1. *meanders*   The Mississippi River, which winds through the valley, makes a squiggly black line on space photographs. *(winds/meanders)*
2. *fallow*   Because healthy plants reflect infrared strongly, they appear bright red on space pictures, whereas untilled land appears blue. *(untilled/fallow)*
3. *microwaves*   Radar sends out radio waves and shortwaves toward faraway targets and then detects their echoes. *(shortwaves/microwaves)*
4. *colliding*   Trenches on the ocean floor are caused by the crashing together of the plates of the earth's crust. *(crashing together/ colliding)*
5. *oceanographers*   Scientists who study the sea have learned many important facts from remote sensors. *(scientists who study the sea/oceanographers)*

Extending Vocabulary

CONTENT-AREA WORDS   Explain that words like *microwaves* and *oceanographers* are called content-area vocabulary because they relate to a specific subject area—in this case, science. A few terms that have made their way into common speech are *clone,* an identical twin; *disk,* a plate on which computer data is stored; and *black hole,* a collapsed star from which matter and even light cannot escape.

COOPERATIVE LEARNING   Divide students into groups. Have students scan the selection and create a web with terms that relate to science. (Accept reasonable responses: *sensors, radar, infrared, wavelengths, ocean trenches, spectral signature, prism, spectrum.*) Then have students write paragraphs using the words. Students may refer to a dictionary. Have a spokesperson for each group read the paragraph to classmates. Then invite students to brainstorm other words relating to space technology and to find the meaning of those words.

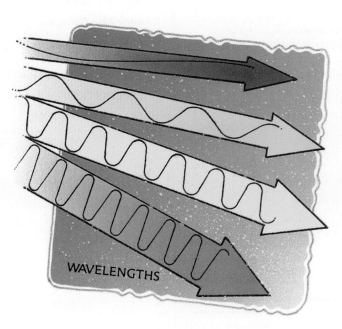

WAVELENGTHS

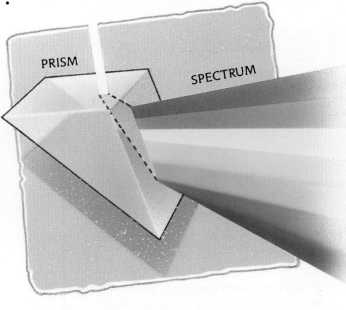

PRISM

SPECTRUM

Language Arts

Writing About the Literature

CREATIVE: DESCRIPTIVE LETTER Have students pretend they are extraterrestrials seeing Earth from a spaceship. Ask them to write a letter describing their observations. WRITING

CRITICAL: EXPOSITORY ESSAY Have students write a brief essay titled "The Advantages and Disadvantages Of Space Exploration," giving a balanced presentation of both sides of the issue. Remind students that their purpose in writing is simply to inform, not to persuade the reader to take a position for or against space exploration. Suggest that students use a graphic such as the one below. WRITING

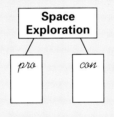

```
          Space
        Exploration
        /        \
    ┌──────┐  ┌──────┐
    │ pro  │  │ con  │
    └──────┘  └──────┘
```

NOTE: An additional writing activity appears on page 421.

SPEAKING/LISTENING

Live from Cape Canaveral
AVAILABLE ON PROJECT CARD

Have small groups of students create "You Are There" skits on great moments in space exploration. Have group members choose roles, such as astronaut and NASA spokesperson, and rehearse their parts as a group. Skits may be presented to classmates.
LISTENING/SPEAKING/READING/WRITING

SPELLING

Spelling Review

SPELLING WORDS: *colliding, design, diameter, highlight, magnify, meander, microwaves, ripening, satellite, sight*

Have students write the Spelling Words as you dictate them. Then have a volunteer write them on the board. Have students read each word aloud in unison, listening for words with the long *i* sound. Have another volunteer circle the letter or letters that represent the long *i* sound. The volunteer should underline the word that does not have a long *i* sound. LISTENING/WRITING/SPELLING

INTEGRATED SPELLING

page 60: Writing words with the long *i* sound

INTEGRATED SPELLING
The Long *i* Sound

Name _____

WORD PLAY

The numbers in each item below stand for sounds given in the Sound Key. Add the sounds together to write Spelling Words.

1. 4 + 18 + 11 = _microwaves_
2. 9 + 13 + 5 = _colliding_
3. 25 + 3 + 23 = _magnify_
4. 12 + 2 = _highlight_
5. 21 + 10 + 2 = _satellite_
6. 20 + 1 + 5 = _ripening_
7. 7 + 16 = _design_
8. 8 + 19 + 14 = _meander_
9. 15 + 24 + 10 + 22 = _diameter_

SOUND KEY

1.	pən	14.	dər
2.	līt	15.	dī
3.	na	16.	zīn
4.	mī	17.	ī
5.	ing	18.	krə
6.	sīt	19.	an
7.	di	20.	rī
8.	mē	21.	sat
9.	kə	22.	tər
10.	ə	23.	fī
11.	wāvz	24.	am
12.	hī	25.	mag
13.	līd		

SPELLING DETECTIVE

Rebecca enjoyed reading "The Planet Earth." She decided to write about her hobby, astronomy. When she proofread her first draft, she found five spelling errors in one paragraph. Find each error and circle it. Write the word correctly above the misspelled word.

design
The (desine) of my telescope allows me to see things that are very far away. It brings
sight
things very close and improves my (site) a lot. It
magnify
allows me to (magnifigh) even the most distant
satellite
planets and stars. Once I even saw a (satellight)
as it passed overhead. Sometimes, too, I can
colliding
see objects (collyding) way out in space!

60　　　　"The Planet Earth" • ENDLESS WORLDS

Integrated Spelling

COMPREHENSION
INTRODUCE

Comparing and Contrasting

OBJECTIVE: *To use comparison and contrast to better understand facts and concepts*

1	**Focus**

Explain the value of comparing and contrasting.

Explain that writers sometimes help us understand difficult facts or concepts by pointing out how they are like or unlike things we know. Ask students if they can recall an instance in which Patricia Lauber does this in "The Planet Earth." (Accept reasonable responses: She tells us how remote sensors are like and unlike those in the human body.)

2	**Teach/Model**

Teach the skill.

Tell students that when you compare things, you tell how they are alike. When you contrast things, you tell how they are different. Words that sometimes signal that items will be compared are *another, like, also,* and so on. Words that signal contrast are *unlike, instead, although,* and so on.

Model the thinking.

Have students reread page 408 of the selection. Model how you would compare and contrast:

> **The author explains remote sensors by comparing those in satellites to those of the human body. She provides a familiar example. I can tell a radiator is hot by holding out my fingers toward it and feeling the heat from a distance. Remote sensors in space also feel, or sense, heat from a distance.**

Have students identify examples.

COOPERATIVE LEARNING Invite students to work in groups to find selection passages in which the author compares and contrasts different types of remote sensors.

| 4 | **Summarize** |

Informally assess the learning.

Check students' understanding by having them summarize what they learned. (We sometimes grasp facts and concepts by thinking how they are like or unlike something else.)

READER ↔ WRITER CONNECTION

Comparing and Contrasting

▶ **Writers** use comparisons and contrasts to establish a relationship between objects, facts, and ideas or to make a point clearer.

▶ **Readers** use comparisons and contrasts to refine their own thinking and to understand the material.

WRITE DIALOGUE Have students imagine that two hosts of a radio program, "Buzz and Buzz Off," are reviewing two movies that have some common elements. Have students choose a pair of movies and write dialogue for Buzz and Buzz Off as they review the two films. Students should point out similarities and differences between the movies and have Buzz and Buzz Off tell why they liked one movie better than the other.

RETEACH Follow the visual, auditory, and kinesthetic/motor models on page R49.

CHALLENGE Have students write a simile in which they compare two unlike objects or activities. Ask them to attach a Venn diagram in which they show how the two things are alike and how they are different.

SECOND-LANGUAGE SUPPORT Students may demonstrate their understanding by comparing and contrasting their first language to English. (See Second-Language Support Manual.)

WRITER'S JOURNAL pages 76–77: Writing dialogue

PRACTICE BOOK page 123: Comparing and contrasting

Writer's Journal

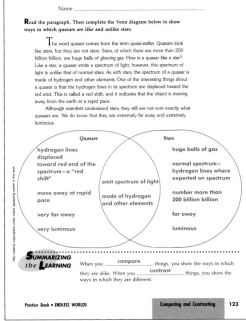

Practice Book

Structural Analysis

OBJECTIVE: *To use structural analysis to determine the meanings of unfamiliar words*

Review

Review structural analysis.

Ask students to name some word parts that are clues to meaning. (prefixes, base words, suffixes) Write on the board the word *altimeter* from "The Planet Earth" (page 416, line 5). Model how to use structural analysis:

The parts of the word look familiar. The word part *alt* in *altitude* means "high." A *meter* measures something. So an *altimeter* must measure height.

Practice/Apply

Have students use structural analysis.

Ask students to use their knowledge of word parts to define *wavelength*, *infrared*, *seabed*, and *crescent-shaped*. Discuss students' definitions.

Summarize

Informally assess the learning.

Check students' understanding by asking them to summarize what they learned. (Readers can often define a new word by analyzing its structure, or its parts.)

PRACTICE BOOK
page 124: Using structural analysis

Practice Book

Reference Sources

OBJECTIVE: *To maintain reference skills and to find information in an encyclopedia*

Review

Review reference skills.

Remind students that *The Readers' Guide to Periodical Literature* can help them find magazine articles. To check the meanings of words, they can use a dictionary.

> **I have to write a report on the first moon landing. Magazines may not help since it happened some time ago. An encyclopedia might. I don't see an entry for "Moon Landing," but under "Moon," there is a section about it.**

Practice/Apply

Have students use reference books.

Have students use reference sources to find an interesting fact about the moon. Ask them to report their findings.

Summarize

Informally assess the learning.

Ask students to summarize what they learned. (For definitions, see a dictionary; for general information, an encyclopedia; for magazine articles, *Readers' Guide*.)

CHALLENGE Ask students to find the name and author of a recent book about the moon that might be appropriate for teenagers. Suggest they consult the card catalogue of the school or local library.

PRACTICE BOOK
page 125: Using reference sources

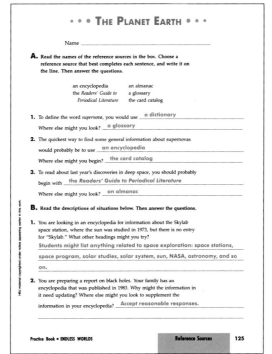

Practice Book

• • • THE PLANET EARTH • • •

Name _____

A. Read the names of the reference sources in the box. Choose a reference source that best completes each sentence, and write it on the line. Then answer the questions.

an encyclopedia   an almanac
the *Readers' Guide to*   a glossary
Periodical Literature   the card catalog

1. To define the word *supernova*, you would use __a dictionary__
   Where else might you look? __a glossary__

2. The quickest way to find some general information about supernovas would probably be to use __an encyclopedia__
   Where else might you begin? __the card catalog__

3. To read about last year's discoveries in deep space, you should probably begin with __the Readers' Guide to Periodical Literature__
   Where else might you look? __an almanac__

B. Read the descriptions of situations below. Then answer the questions.

1. You are looking in an encyclopedia for information about the Skylab space station, where the sun was studied in 1973, but there is no entry for "Skylab." What other headings might you try?
   Students might list anything related to space exploration: space stations, space program, solar studies, solar system, sun, NASA, astronomy, and so on.

2. You are preparing a report on black holes. Your family has an encyclopedia that was published in 1983. Why might the information in it need updating? Where else might you look to supplement the information in your encyclopedia? __Accept reasonable responses.__

Practice Book ■ ENDLESS WORLDS   Reference Sources   125

Integrated Curriculum

SOCIAL STUDIES

Spacey Geography

Ask students to pretend they are social studies teachers about to teach a lesson on Peru. How would they use the radar image mentioned in the selection or one like it to enrich their teaching? Have students prepare a list of features they would call attention to and, next to each feature, write the reason it is important or interesting. Suggest that students first read a chapter on Peru in a social studies text or look up the country in an encyclopedia. READING/WRITING

SCIENCE

The Proof of the Prism

Invite a group of students to bring a prism to class and demonstrate how it works. Ask students to explain the range of colors the human eye can see and what lies beyond the range at both ends of the spectrum. Patricia Lauber reveals some uses of infrared wavelengths, but students might round out the selection by reading about and explaining some practical uses of ultraviolet wavelengths. LISTENING/SPEAKING/READING

ART

But Is It Art?

Students interested in art might bring to school some reproductions of modern works that resemble false-color pictures, or a student who can paint might try a Landsat-style study. Ask students to explain how modern artists use color to convey meaning, indicating that the resemblance between false-color photography and some modern art is not purely coincidental. LISTENING/SPEAKING

SCIENCE

Color by Computer

AVAILABLE ON PROJECT CARD

Ask students interested in computers to explain how computers translate numbers into color graphics. What is the process? How is it used in such down-to-earth fields as home entertainment? Invite interested students to explain how these computers work and to give demonstrations, if possible. LISTENING/SPEAKING/READING

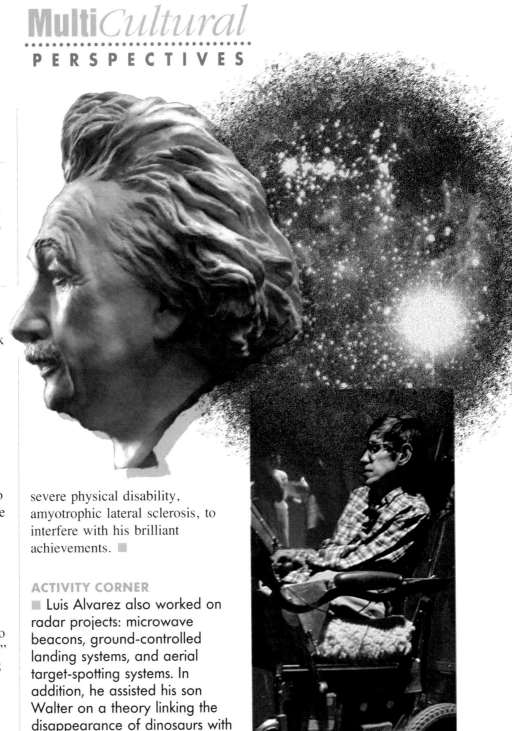

MultiCultural
PERSPECTIVES

A Science Ahead of Its Time

LONG BEFORE THEY DEVELOPED THE TECHNOLOGY TO PROVE IT, PHYSICISTS THOUGHT THAT INFRARED LIGHT EXISTED.

In the same way, the theory behind atomic energy dates back to 1905, when Albert Einstein originally published his ideas on relativity. He theorized that mass converts to energy when accelerated to extremely high speeds. To test Einstein's ideas, however, scientists had to be able to split the invisible atom and to accelerate its particles to or near to the speed of light, which they were not able to do until the 1940s.

After World War II, the American physicist Luis Walter Alvarez continued the exploration of the atom by building the first particle accelerator. This machine enabled him and other physicists to detect as many as 100 "subatomic" particles for the first time. In 1968 Alvarez won the Nobel Prize for his work.

Among current theorists whose ideas will take many years to realize experimentally is Stephen Hawking, who was born in 1942. The British physicist's mathematical explanations of black holes and the big bang theory of the universe have earned him praise as the greatest theoretical physicist since Einstein. Hawking also is admired for his personal courage: he has not allowed his severe physical disability, amyotrophic lateral sclerosis, to interfere with his brilliant achievements. ■

ACTIVITY CORNER

■ Luis Alvarez also worked on radar projects: microwave beacons, ground-controlled landing systems, and aerial target-spotting systems. In addition, he assisted his son Walter on a theory linking the disappearance of dinosaurs with meteor showers. Suggest that students prepare a one-page report on one of these topics.

■ Invite a physics teacher to your class to explain the structure of the atom, the functioning of a particle accelerator, the big bang theory, or black holes. Suggest that he or she use illustrations and diagrams in the presentation, if possible.

Physicists Albert Einstein (1879–1955), and Stephen Hawking (1942–)

An Interview with the Author: Patricia Lauber

An Interview with the Author:

PATRICIA LAUBER

AWARD-WINNING AUTHOR

ABOUT THE INTERVIEW

In this interview Patricia Lauber describes how she became a science writer, why she decided to write *Seeing Earth from Space,* and how she feels about writing fiction and nonfiction.

1 NARRATION: EVENTS

What qualities did Patricia Lauber demonstrate by accepting a job as editor of a science magazine when she did not know or like science?
(Accept reasonable responses: Her acceptance showed she has an open mind and the self-confidence to tackle new challenges.)
INFERENTIAL: DRAWING CONCLUSIONS

2 AUTHOR'S COMMENTARY

Why won't Patricia Lauber write about things that don't interest her? What does this tell you about her?
(Accept reasonable responses: Lauber feels that if she isn't enthusiastic about a topic, she can't expect her readers to be. This attitude shows that she cares about her writing and respects her readers.)
INFERENTIAL: DRAWING CONCLUSIONS

Writer Ilene Cooper had the opportunity to discuss writing with Patricia Lauber.

Ms. Cooper: You've written so many books about science. What's the attraction?
Ms. Lauber: Well, that's funny. In school I was the sort of person who never met a science course she liked. I didn't get into science until I had decided to become a free-lance writer. I had quit my job editing at a magazine; things were getting very tight financially; and I was wondering what I should do next.

Then a publisher called to ask me if I'd like to be the editor of a new science magazine for young people. I went to talk with them, and in a burst of honesty, I said I didn't know much about science. They said that would probably keep the magazine from being too technical.

I gave myself a crash course, with books and teachers, and I discovered that when I got into science at the idea level rather than the school level, I found it extremely interesting. So, after working at the magazine for a while, I began to write books.

Ms. Cooper: Who comes up with the ideas for topics for your books, you or your publisher?
Ms. Lauber: Either or both, but I won't write about things that don't interest me. If I'm not enthusiastic about a topic, I can't expect my readers to be. I'm very interested in all aspects of the natural world, especially in what we as a species are doing to our planet. We're changing it without knowing what the end result will be. Also I've always been interested in the work of scientists who dig up the past, archaeologists or paleontologists.

Ms. Cooper: How did you get the idea for Seeing Earth from Space?
Ms. Lauber: I had written a book called *Journey to the Planets,* which starts with a chapter about Earth. It has photographs of Earth from space as well as from closer, raising the question of how close you would have to get before you knew there was intelligent life on this planet, or on any

422

Reading the Interview

Ask students to share what they know about Patricia Lauber. Discuss where they have heard her name and in what connection. Then have students draw on their knowledge of Lauber's ''The Planet Earth,'' from *Seeing Earth from Space,* to think of some questions they would like to ask Lauber. Invite them to read the interview to see whether any of their questions are answered.

Teaching Tip Explain that an *archaeologist* is a scientist who studies the people, customs, and life of ancient times by excavating the ruins of ancient cities and examining the artifacts. Then define *paleontologist* as a scientist who studies the fossil remains of plants and animals that were buried and preserved in layers of rock. Point out that by studying fossils, a paleontologist can figure out what life existed during the different periods of Earth's history.

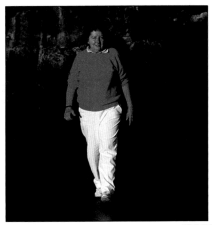

planet. People seemed fascinated by the pictures, so I got the idea of doing a whole book about Earth, based on this new way **3** of obtaining information about our planet when seen from space.

Ms. Cooper: How do you write about complex subjects so that young people will be able to understand them?
Ms. Lauber: Well, first I have to understand the information myself. Once I've digested it, I decide what really important parts have to be covered. I write for different age groups, and some topics just aren't suitable for younger children. You'll never be able to do an accurate, interesting job with material that is too difficult for your audience.

Ms. Cooper: You've written both fiction and nonfiction. Do you prefer one more than the other?
Ms. Lauber: I was the sort of child who loved the words *Once upon a time*. I still

do. The child in me would much rather write only fiction, but right now my career is centered around nonfiction. When writing nonfiction, I can see the book in my mind's eye. I'll soon know if it's possible or not possible, if I want to do it or not do it. With fiction, I never know how it's going to come out. Before I submit a fiction book to a publisher, I have to finish it, or at least have a first draft of the entire book. I have several half-finished books of fiction in my cabinet now because, for one reason or another, I can't finish them.

Ms. Cooper: Do you see any similarities between writing fiction and writing nonfiction?
Ms. Lauber: Definitely. No matter what you're writing, there should be a story line and some suspense. Whether it's fiction or nonfiction, the reader has to want to turn the page.

423

3 AUTHOR'S COMMENTARY
How does Lauber's book about Earth differ from most other books on the subject? *(It is based on information gathered by looking at Earth from space.)*
CRITICAL: MAKING COMPARISONS

Second-Language Support
Students acquiring English may be unfamiliar with the expression *mind's eye* in the right column, line 5. Explain that it is the mental ability to visualize scenes that are imaginary or recollected.

(MEETING INDIVIDUAL NEEDS)

Responding to the Interview
Invite students to use what they learned from the interview and from "The Planet Earth" to discuss the qualities and characteristics that they think make Patricia Lauber an excellent writer, particularly of nonfiction. Be sure students support their ideas with specific quotations or examples.

Gnats, Mammoths, and Saber-toothed Tigers

ABOUT THE AUTHOR

Patricia Lauber (1924–   ) is often asked where she gets the ideas for her many books and articles. "My ideas come from everywhere," she explains, "from things I read, from things people tell me about, from things I see around me, from things I experience. The important aspect is that they must interest me very much."

SELECTION SUMMARY

"Gnats, Mammoths, and Saber-toothed Tigers" explores various ways in which animals from the past were preserved as fossils. The selection also explains how paleontologists use layers of rock and the fossils in them to determine the changes that have taken place in the landforms and the climate of a region.

GNATS, MAMMOTHS, AND SABER-TOOTHED TIGERS

from
*DINOSAURS WALKED HERE
AND OTHER STORIES
FOSSILS TELL*
by Patricia Lauber

424

Building Background

Begin a discussion by asking students to define *fossil*. ("the hardened remains of an animal or plant from another geological age") Then ask what they know about how fossils were formed in the earth. You may wish to have students describe any fossils they have seen.

Strategic Reading

Informational Nonfiction   Ask students to preview the illustrations and read the captions to predict the significance of the title "Gnats, Mammoths, and Saber-toothed Tigers" and to predict the kind of information the selection contains.

STUDENT-SET PURPOSE   Ask students to use their predictions to decide what they want to learn from the selection.

*Two **Grallator** footprints.*

One day, forty million years ago, a gnat was crawling over the bark of a pine tree. It became trapped in a sticky flow of sap, or resin. Once the gnat was covered with resin, no other animal could eat it. The soft parts of the body did not decay, because bacteria could not feed on them. The gnat was quickly preserved. Much later, the resin hardened into the kind of fossil called amber, which looks something like yellow glass. Inside the amber was another fossil, the gnat. The gnat is one of many fossil insects that have been found in amber.

425

1 AUTHOR'S CRAFT
This paragraph begins a chapter in Lauber's book. **Is this an effective opening for a piece of informational writing on the subject of fossils? Explain.** *(Accept reasonable responses: Yes; it sounds like a story and draws the reader in, and the narrative details make clear how one type of fossil is formed.)*
CRITICAL: MAKING JUDGMENTS

Second-Language Support
Suggest that students look up the definitions of *gnat, mammoth,* and *saber-toothed tiger* in an illustrated dictionary if they are unfamiliar with these animals.

2 IMAGERY

The author says that thick sheets of ice "crept" out from the polar region. **What image does the verb *crept* help to create?** *(Accept reasonable responses: It tends to portray the ice as some sort of monstrous creature.)*

INFERENTIAL: DRAWING CONCLUSIONS

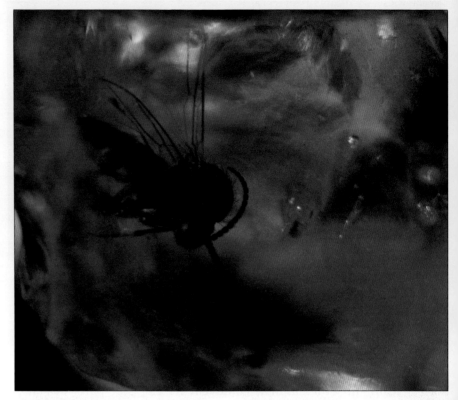

Forty-million-year-old gnat is embedded in amber. Green is caused by the breaking up of white light as it passes through tiny cracks in the amber.

Quick freezing preserved the bodies of some woolly mammoths. Mammoths were relatives of today's elephants. They were able to live through a time of great changes in the earth's climate—through an ice age. They lived through times when mile-thick sheets of ice crept out from the polar regions and down from mountains to cover once-green lands. They lived through times when the ice melted and shrank back, releasing floods of melt-water. Then, when the ice last shrank back to the polar regions and mountaintops, about 9,000 to 12,000 years ago, the woolly mammoths died out, for reasons no one knows.

We know about woolly mammoths from the cave drawings of Stone Age people. We also know about them because whole frozen mammoths have been found in the ground of Alaska and Siberia. One of these was a baby mammoth that

426

somehow lost its mother 27,000 years ago and fell into an icy pit, where it died. Bacteria had little chance to feed on the body because it soon froze and became covered with ice. The sides of the pit caved in and buried the baby mammoth **3** under six feet of earth. At that depth, the summer sun could not melt the ice or thaw the body. The body of the baby mammoth was preserved. It was discovered in <u>1977</u> by Soviet gold prospectors working in northeastern Siberia. The body was so well preserved that scientists could even find traces of its mother's milk in the mammoth's stomach.

The bones of animals have been found preserved in still another way. These are the bones of animals that were trapped in places where oil was oozing out of the ground as thick, sticky asphalt. One of these places is now known as the La Brea tar pits, in Los Angeles. Scientists suppose the animals were trapped in ways like this:

Thousands of years ago, a ground sloth the size of an elephant was being chased by a saber-toothed tiger. Lumbering across the valley as fast as it could, the sloth glimpsed a shining surface that looked like a pond. It plunged in, hoping to escape the tiger. The big saber-tooth sprang after it. But the water was only a thin layer that had collected on

When the ice age ended, large mammals, such as mastodons died out.

427

3 NARRATION: EVENTS
Point out that the author provides a sequence of causes that led to one effect—the frozen baby mammoth. **What are the events in this causal chain?** *(The mammoth fell into an icy pit and soon froze; it became covered with ice; the sides of the pit caved in and buried the mammoth so it could not thaw.)*
LITERAL: RECOGNIZING CAUSE-EFFECT

Second-Language Support
Explain that asphalt is a tarlike substance that occurs naturally in underground beds. Point out that this substance is mixed with sand or crushed stone to form asphalt for paving roads.

MEETING INDIVIDUAL NEEDS

Call students' attention to the title "Gnats, Mammoths, and Saber-toothed Tigers," and ask how these three animals exemplify the three methods of fossilization described thus far. *(Accept reasonable responses: The gnat was fossilized in amber; the mammoth was preserved in ice; the saber-toothed tiger was fossilized in asphalt.)*
INFERENTIAL: SUMMARIZING

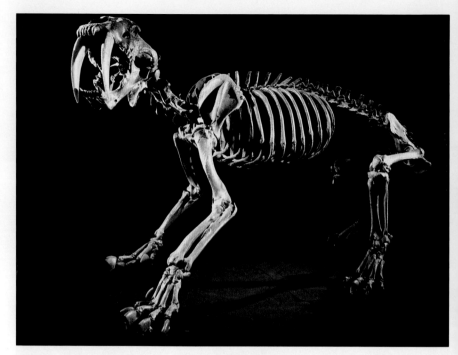

The saber-toothed tiger is one of many animals, known from their fossils, that lived and flourished in North America and then died out for reasons no one knows.

4 top of asphalt, and both animals were trapped in the sticky ooze. As they died, giant vultures dived from the sky to feed on them. One came too close to the surface, dragged its feet in the asphalt, and could not free itself.

At other times animals may have waded in to drink, only to discover they could not get out. Sometimes plant-eating animals may have scattered and fled from a meat eater. Some ran across what looked like solid ground, but an asphalt pool lay under the leaves or dirt. And so over the years many animals were trapped. Among them were camels, mammoths, bears, wolves, lions, bison, antelope, geese, and eagles. Long afterward their bones were discovered at La Brea, preserved as fossils in the asphalt. The bones told a story of animals that used to live in North America and of some that died out as mysteriously as the woolly mammoths.

Fossils tell much about plants and animals of the past. The study of fossils also tells of changes in the face of the earth and of changes in the earth's climate.

428

LAYERS OF FOSSILS

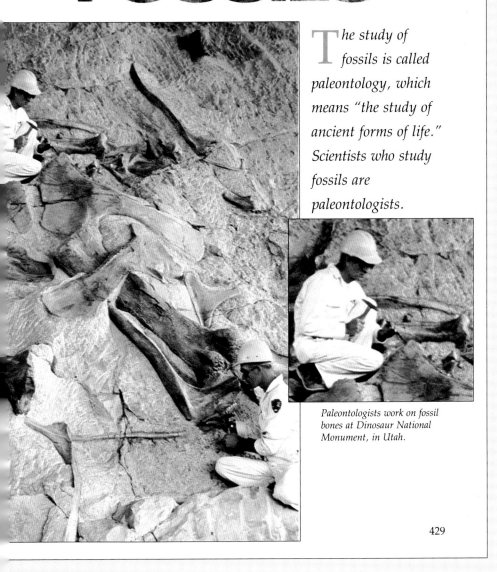

The study of fossils is called paleontology, which means "the study of ancient forms of life." Scientists who study fossils are paleontologists.

Paleontologists work on fossil bones at Dinosaur National Monument, in Utah.

429

Vocabulary Strategy Point out the suffix *-logy* in *paleontology*, elicit that it means "study of," and have students suggest other words formed with it. Also point out the suffix *-ist* in *paleontologist*, elicit that it means "one who," and have students cite other words formed with this suffix. You may also wish to tell students that *paleo* comes from the Greek word *palaios,* meaning "ancient," and that *ontos* comes from another Greek word meaning "a being."

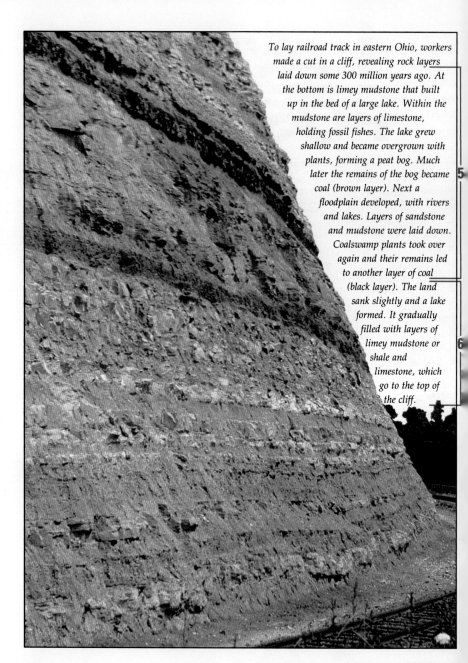

To lay railroad track in eastern Ohio, workers made a cut in a cliff, revealing rock layers laid down some 300 million years ago. At the bottom is limey mudstone that built up in the bed of a large lake. Within the mudstone are layers of limestone, holding fossil fishes. The lake grew shallow and became overgrown with plants, forming a peat bog. Much later the remains of the bog became coal (brown layer). Next a floodplain developed, with rivers and lakes. Layers of sandstone and mudstone were laid down. Coalswamp plants took over again and their remains led to another layer of coal (black layer). The land sank slightly and a lake formed. It gradually filled with layers of limey mudstone or shale and limestone, which go to the top of the cliff.

430

Paleontologists are often the finders of fossils. But many times they first hear of a find from other people—from rock collectors who came upon fossils, from miners or construction workers who found fossils while digging. Amateur fossil hunters may report a find. Sometimes someone simply sees a bone sticking out of the ground. This happens because sedimentary rocks are fairly soft and crumbly. They are easily worn away by wind and water. Fossils long buried in the rock may then be exposed. **7**

Some finds tell of great changes in the face of the earth. Climbers, for example, may come upon seashells in rocks near the

7 EXPOSITORY TEXT: CAUSE-EFFECT
How are fossils frequently exposed?
(Fossils are often found in soft sedimentary rocks; wind and water can wear away this rock easily, exposing fossils.)
LITERAL: RECOGNIZING CAUSE-EFFECT

If you look closely, you will see that this slice of rock has pairs of thin layers, one dark and one light. The sediments forming the dark layers were laid down in a lake during summer and fall. The light layers were laid down in winter and spring. The summer-fall layers are darker because the sediments were discolored by rotting leaves, dust, pollen, and soot from forest fires. Each pair stands for one year. The dark spots you see are fossils. The wide, light-colored bands occur about every hundred years. They mark a change in sediments that was probably caused by a change in climate.

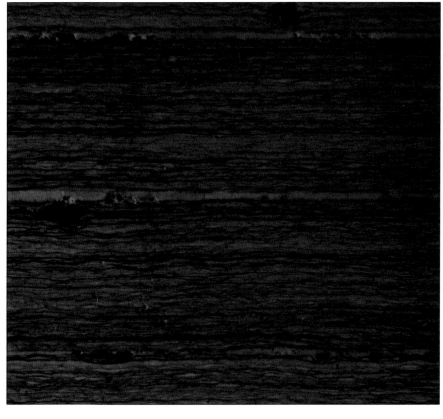

431

How was the northeastern part of Yellowstone National Park different fifty million years ago? *(The climate was warmer and wetter; there were no steep mountains; there were more leafy trees.)*
LITERAL: COMPARING AND CONTRASTING

Edmontosaurus was one of the duck-billed dinosaurs.

tops of mountains. The fossil shells are a sign that the rocks formed from sediments at the bottom of an ancient sea. At a later time mountains crumpled up out of the earth's crust. The seabed and its fossils were carried skyward.

Fossils also tell of changes in climate. Today, for example, the northeastern part

of Yellowstone National Park has rugged mountains and a climate that is cool in summer and very cold in winter. It has forests of firs and other evergreens that grow well in a cold climate. About fifty million years ago, it was very different. In place of the mountains there were broad, flat river valleys separated by rolling hills.

8

432

Vocabulary Strategy   Have students indicate the base word of *sedimentary*. *(sediment)* Elicit a definition of *sediment*. ("something that settles to the bottom of a liquid") Elicit that *-ary* is an adjective-forming suffix, and then have students suggest how sedimentary rock might be formed. (Sedimentary rock is formed from layers of sediment that pile up at the bottom of a body of water.)
STRATEGY: STRUCTURAL ANALYSIS

huge volcanic eruptions that buried them in ash and rocks. After each big eruption, new forests took root on top of the old ones. Over many, many years, minerals from moving water turned the buried tree trunks to stone. Now, millions of years later, the volcanic material around the tree trunks has weathered away. The petrified remains of ancient trees can be seen standing upright exactly where the trees used to grow.

In one area, forests were buried many times. Wind, rain, and melting snow have worn away the side of a steep bluff, exposing more than twenty layers of petrified trees. They formed over some 20,000 years, as volcanic eruptions buried a forest, a new forest grew, and eruptions buried it. The result is like a giant layer cake. Each layer of forest—of tree trunks and imprints of leaves—tells its own story about plants and climate. Each is like a page in the earth's diary.

Sedimentary rock also forms in layers. Each new layer marks a change in the sediments that were being laid down. A river, for example, might flow slowly for years, carrying along only very fine sediments and dropping them in a bay. Then a huge storm strikes upstream. Water pours into the river and the river's flow speeds up. The faster flow means that the river picks up coarse sediments as well as fine. Now it drops sand and gravel in the bay. Later the river goes back to carrying only fine sediments. The sand and gravel mark the end of one layer of fine sediment and the start of another.

The climate was mild in the hills and hot in the valleys.

We know about this change in climate because paleontologists have found forests of fossil trees in this part of the park. These were leafy trees that grow in mild to hot climates.

The forests were preserved because of

9 EXPOSITORY TEXT: CAUSE-EFFECT
Ask students to recall what the terrain of Yellowstone National Park looked like fifty million years ago. **How were the forests preserved?** *(Volcanic eruptions buried the forests, and the tree trunks became petrified.)*
LITERAL: RECOGNIZING CAUSE-EFFECT

10 FIGURATIVE LANGUAGE
What are the two similes that the author uses to describe the layers here? *(She compares the earth to a giant layer cake; she describes each layer as "a page in the earth's diary.")*
How do these similes help you understand the author's meaning? *(Accept reasonable responses: The layer-cake simile helps us visualize the layers of petrified forests in the earth; the diary simile helps the reader understand how each layer provides specific information.)*
INFERENTIAL: MAKING COMPARISONS

Vocabulary Strategy Have students identify the context clues that allow them to determine the exact meaning of *petrified*. ("minerals from moving water turned the buried tree trunks to stone") STRATEGY: CONTEXT CLUES

Oral Rereading Ask students to practice rereading page 433 until they are quite familiar with its content. Then ask them to imagine that they are science teachers explaining the layers of fossils in Yellowstone National Park. Have them consider how they would vary their tone of voice and rate of speaking in order to maintain their listeners' interest in the subject. Then call on volunteers to read paragraphs of the passage aloud.

11 THINK IT OVER

1. *Animals from the past have been preserved in resin that turned into amber, in ice, and in tar. Other animals have been preserved in layers of mud and sediment.*
INFERENTIAL: SUMMARIZING

2. *Paleontologists study fossils to learn about ancient forms of life.*
LITERAL: RECOGNIZING MAIN IDEA

3. *the remains of a giant ground sloth, a saber-toothed tiger, vultures, and many other animals*
LITERAL: NOTING IMPORTANT DETAILS

4. *Like a diary page, each layer shows what was happening at a certain time in earth's history.*
INFERENTIAL: MAKING COMPARISONS

12 WRITE

You may want to have students begin by looking at pictures of fossils in an encyclopedia or another nonfiction book. Have them make notes about the name of the plant or animal, the method of fossilization, and the fossil's age, size, and appearance.

Accept reasonable responses. Students should include specific details.
CREATIVE: DESCRIBING

WRITER'S JOURNAL page 78: Writing a creative response

Writer's Journal

You have probably seen such layers. They often appear where the sea has eaten away at a cliff or a river has carved a deep valley. They are seen where wind and rain have worn down hills and mountains. They are also seen in quarries and where road cuts pass through hills.

Paleontologists find the layers useful because they are like time capsules. Plants and animals that appear as fossils in the same layers must have lived at the same time. That is how paleontologists have learned about the world of the dinosaurs. They know what kinds of plants grew in that world. They know what the climate was like. They know what other kinds of animals shared that world. The layers, like the fossils themselves, fill out our picture of dinosaurs and how they lived.

THINK IT OVER

11
1. *Explain the different ways in which animals from the past have been preserved.*
2. *What do paleontologists do?*
3. *What was discovered at the La Brea tar pits?*
4. *How are fossils like "pages in the earth's diary"?*

WRITE

12 *Imagine that you are a paleontologist. Write a description of a particularly interesting fossil that you have discovered.*

Returning to the Predictions Invite students to discuss the predictions they made before reading and tell whether those predictions changed as they read.

Returning to the Purpose for Reading Ask students to discuss what they learned about the ways in which gnats, mammoths, and saber-toothed tigers have been found preserved or fossilized. (Gnats have been found fossilized in amber; mammoths have been preserved by sudden freezing and burial in Siberian ice; saber-toothed tigers have been trapped and fossilized in the asphalt of the La Brea tar pits.)

Earth

THEME WRAP-UP

EARTH

"The Planet Earth" and "Gnats, Mammoths, and Saber-toothed Tigers" reveal buried secrets from the earth's past. Do you agree that it is important to discover what lies under the oceans and beneath the earth's surface? Explain your answer.

• •

Would you rather be an astronaut looking for new opportunities for the future in space or a paleontologist uncovering the secrets of the earth's past? Explain your choice.

• •

WRITER'S WORKSHOP Imagine that a paleontologist and an astronaut meet. Write a conversation they could have, discussing such things as the exciting aspects of each of their jobs, new discoveries they have made, and how their jobs are alike and different.

435

Remind students that the selections in this theme show different ways of observing Earth. Help students recall what they have read about space-age sensors and prehistoric fossils. Suggest that both old bones and computer photographs tell stories about our planet. Explain that the activities on page 435 ask students to evaluate some of these different ways of observing the earth.

Note that pages 435A–435B provide support for applying the writing process to the last question.

1 Have students first think about what secrets of Earth's past have been revealed in these articles and then decide why they are important. *(Accept reasonable responses: Knowledge is important for its own sake as well as for its practical uses.)*
CRITICAL: MAKING JUDGMENTS

2 Access students' prior knowledge about each profession to help them make a choice. *(Responses will vary.)*
CRITICAL: EXPRESSING PERSONAL OPINIONS

Writer's Workshop

See pages 435A–435B for suggestions for applying the writing process. Responses should include evidence from "The Planet Earth" and from "Gnats, Mammoths, and Saber-toothed Tigers." You may prefer to allow students to respond to the theme in their own way. WRITING PROCESS: A DIALOGUE

Writer's Workshop

Before students begin, you may want to discuss the qualities that make a dialogue, or conversation, interesting and stimulating. Point out that students should concentrate on a conversational tone and avoid making speeches. Review punctuation and paragraph indentation. Students also may want to write various tag lines to add variety to their writing. Suggest that students refer to the Handbook in the *Writer's Journal* as they write, revise, and proofread their dialogues.

Prewriting

Before they begin writing,

- have students brainstorm what they know about astronauts and paleontologists.
- use a web to organize the information. Encourage students to use their webs as the basis of their imaginary conversation in which an astronaut and a paleontologist compare and contrast their work. Their completed web for the paleontologist might look something like the following:

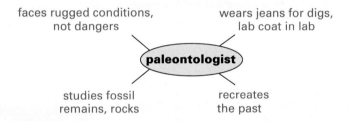

faces rugged conditions, not dangers

wears jeans for digs, lab coat in lab

paleontologist

studies fossil remains, rocks

recreates the past

Drafting

Have students write a draft of their conversations. Suggest that students

- give the speakers two or three subjects to compare and contrast.
- have the speakers stick to one subject before they move on to another.
- make sure the conversation clarifies for the reader the similarities and differences in their work.
- write without worrying about spelling, punctuation, or grammar.

COMPUTER CONNECTION   Students may want to use a computer during the revising stage of the writing process so they can easily delete unimportant details, add missing information, or rearrange sentences in their dialogues.

Responding and Revising

Suggest that students trade drafts with a partner. Have the pair discuss the drafts for clarity and interest. Offer these tips for revising:

- Is it clear what the speakers are comparing and contrasting? If not, clear up any confusion.
- Is the speaker recognizable? Will the reader know who is speaking? If not, add a tag line.
- Do the speakers wander from the topic? Make sure they stick to the subject. (See the Language/Literature Link below.)

STUDENT SELF-ASSESSMENT OPTION Students may use the Writing Self-Assessment Checklist in the *Portfolio Teacher's Guide*. Suggest that as they use the checklist, they focus on the organization and the tone of the dialogue.

Proofreading

Offer these tips:

- Be careful not to misspell names of animals or scientific concepts. When in doubt, check a dictionary or other reference source.
- Remember *Earth* is capitalized when the word refers to the planet, but not when it means *soil*.

Publishing

Some students may wish to make posters of their work, illustrating them with drawings of fossils and photographs of outer space and save them in their reading/writing portfolio. Others may wish to role-play the conversation with partners.

LANGUAGE/LITERATURE LINK
Keeping to the Topic

Explain to students that when comparing and contrasting, it is important to keep to the topic, both in writing and in speaking. Illustrate this point by reviewing Patricia Lauber's comparison and contrast of remote sensors in "The Planet Earth." Note that first she tells us about heat sensors, then about radar. Instruct students to review their work to be sure that they have not strayed from the topic.

Speaking Option

PANEL DISCUSSION The *Writer's Workshop* can be adapted to allow students to plan a panel discussion using their dialogues. Have students follow the guidelines offered for Prewriting, Drafting, and Responding and Revising. Then have small groups work together to prepare a panel discussion, with one student as moderator, the rest as scientists. Ask the moderator to prepare some questions beforehand concerning the scientists' work. Suggest these rules for discussion:

- Scientists should not use jargon that may be unfamiliar to the general audience.
- Each speaker should limit his or her responses to a specified length of time.
- They should speak clearly and speak to the audience.
- The moderator should keep the discussion moving and give everyone a chance to talk.

Have the groups hold panel discussions in front of their classmates.

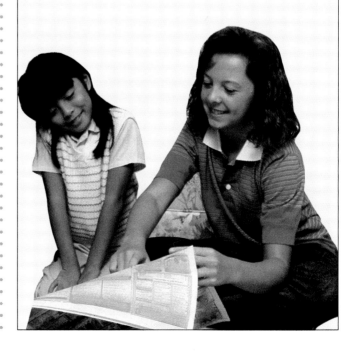

Survival

Have students look at the illustration on page 439 and explain what they would do if they found themselves in this situation. Have them discuss elements that can threaten survival. Then have them read the selection titles and speculate on their meaning. Ask why time might be "the missing element" in a scheme for survival and why a place might be "the right place" in which to stay alive.

PACING   This theme has been designed to take about two weeks to complete, depending on your students' needs.

436

Management Options

THE LITERATURE-BASED CLASSROOM   Providing a literature-rich curriculum creates unique classroom management challenges. Some management options for the selections in this theme follow.

STUDENT EVALUATION   As your students complete a major activity, a project, or even a unit, you may wish to have them summarize what they have learned, share their reactions—positive and negative—and offer suggestions for improving the activity, project, or unit. Students can share their comments orally, or you may prefer to create an evaluation form for them to fill in.

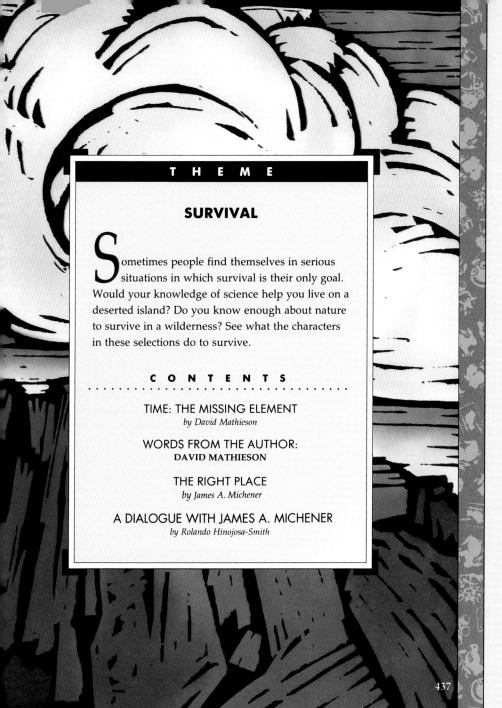

THEME

SURVIVAL

Sometimes people find themselves in serious situations in which survival is their only goal. Would your knowledge of science help you live on a deserted island? Do you know enough about nature to survive in a wilderness? See what the characters in these selections do to survive.

CONTENTS

437

STUDENTS AT RISK
Provide additional background information about the selection settings. Invite students to locate on a map British Columbia and the Eastern Shore of Chesapeake Bay. Display photographs, a filmstrip, or a video of each area and discuss the possible problems a person might have trying to survive in these environments.

GIFTED AND TALENTED
Invite students to create a crossword puzzle using clues about the settings, plots, characters, and authors of selections in this theme. Students can then exchange puzzles. Also see the *Challenge Cards.*

SPECIAL EDUCATION STUDENTS
Students with dyslexia whose perceptual difficulties interfere with their ability to read aloud will need special help with the suggested oral rereading activities. You may want to set aside time for them to practice when you can listen and offer the encouragement and assistance they may need.

LIMITED ENGLISH PROFICIENT STUDENTS
Some students who have difficulty writing in English may be unable to complete the Writer's Workshop activity on Student Anthology page 473. You may wish to have them create a poster with one or two survival tips instead.

PARENT PROGRESS REPORT You may wish to alert parents to any problems their son or daughter is experiencing and to offer suggestions for additional practice at home. A form letter that can be duplicated and filled in as needed will save you time. Be sure to inform the student that you are sending the letter and tell what specific suggestions you have made.

READING/WRITING PORTFOLIO Instruct students to keep in their portfolios their writing responses to the theme selections. Remind them also to add to their personal journals notes on their independent reading.

TIME: THE MISSING ELEMENT

by David Mathieson

DAVID MATHIESON once experienced firsthand some of the challenges faced by the hero of this selection. At the age of seventeen, he spent a year living alone in a cabin of driftwood on the coast of Oregon. He also has visited, by sailboat, the very shores that serve as the setting of this selection. Mathieson is now a writer and artist living in Port Townsend, a small town in northwest Washington. Advising young people who want to write, he says, "If you want to write about anything, don't let anyone stop you."

OTHER BOOKS ABOUT WILDERNESS SURVIVAL

Catch a Sunbeam: A Book of Solar Study and Experiments by Florence Adams. Harcourt Brace Jovanovich, 1978. AVERAGE

The Conquest of Everest by Mike Rosen. Bookwright, 1990. AVERAGE

The Place of Lions by Erik Campbell. Harcourt Brace Jovanovich, 1991. AVERAGE

A Rumour of Otters by Deborah Savage. Houghton Mifflin 1986. AVERAGE

Take a Hike! The Sierra Club Kid's Guide to Hiking and Backpacking by Lynne Foster. Little, Brown, 1991. AVERAGE

> "If you want to write about anything, don't let anyone stop you."

SELECTION SUMMARY

This excerpt from a novel titled *Trial by Wilderness* describes a teenage girl's fight for survival. Stranded on the remote British Columbian coast by an airplane crash, Elena Bradbury works to survive with salvaged items. She fashions a reflecting device to start a fire, devises a shelter, and gathers berries, clams, ferns, and buds to eat. Although secure for the moment, she realizes that she cannot survive a winter; she would need a cabin, fuel, and food, and she lacks time to prepare.

LESSON PLANNER

		Materials	Integrated Curriculum	Meeting Individual Needs
1	**READING LITERATURE** pp. 437B–455	Student Anthology pp. 438–455 Transparency 24 Second-Language Support Manual Practice Book p. 126 Integrated Spelling p. 61 Integrated Spelling T.E. pp. 82–83 Response Card 2: Setting	Spelling Spelling Pretest Spelling-Vocabulary Connection (words from Latin)	Second-Language Support Vocabulary 437C Strategic Reading 437D, 443, 445 Cooperative Reading 438, 445, 454
2	**RESPONDING TO LITERATURE** pp. 455A–455D	Writer's Journal p. 79 Practice Book p. 127 Integrated Spelling p. 62 Integrated Spelling T.E. pp. 82–83	Vocabulary Workshop Reviewing Key Words Extending Vocabulary Writing About the Literature Speaking/Listening Spelling Review	Cooperative Learning 455B, 455D
3	**LEARNING THROUGH LITERATURE** pp. 455E–455J	Second-Language Support Manual Writer's Journal pp. 80–81 Practice Book pp. 128–129	Math Science Social Studies Multicultural	Cooperative Learning 455F, 455H, 455I Reteach 455F, 455H Challenge 455F, 455H Second-Language Support 455F, 455H

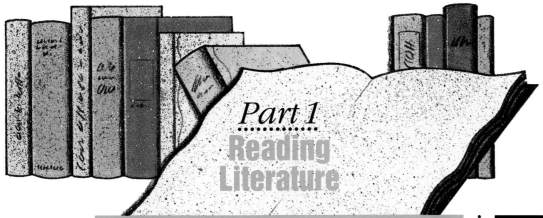

Part 1
Reading Literature

Building Background

Access prior knowledge and develop vocabulary concepts.

Tell students that the story they are about to read comes from a book titled *Trial by Wilderness*, which is about survival in the wilderness. Write *survival* in the center of a web on the board, and invite students to suggest some elements that are necessary for survival.

clothing   shelter

survival

water   food

Have students quickwrite sentences.

Ask students to choose three things they would need if they were stranded in the wilderness. Have them write a sentence about each choice. They can share sentences with a partner.

Vocabulary Strategies

Introduce Key Words and strategies.

Tell students that they may find some unfamiliar words in "Time: The Missing Element." Display Transparency 24, or write the paragraph on the board.

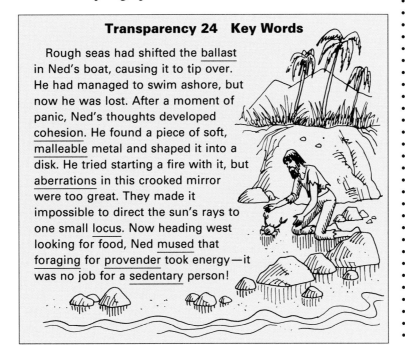

Transparency 24   Key Words

Rough seas had shifted the ballast in Ned's boat, causing it to tip over. He had managed to swim ashore, but now he was lost. After a moment of panic, Ned's thoughts developed cohesion. He found a piece of soft, malleable metal and shaped it into a disk. He tried starting a fire with it, but aberrations in this crooked mirror were too great. They made it impossible to direct the sun's rays to one small locus. Now heading west looking for food, Ned mused that foraging for provender took energy—it was no job for a sedentary person!

CULTURAL AWARENESS

To help students appreciate the cultural background and setting of "Time: The Missing Element," share with them the information under Cultural Background/Setting on page 438.

KEY WORDS DEFINED

ballast   weight to stabilize or steady something

cohesion   unity, orderliness

malleable   capable of being hammered or shaped

aberrations   defects

locus   area, place, center

mused   thought

foraging   searching for food

provender   food

sedentary   remaining in one area

Have students read the paragraph silently and use context clues, phonics, and structural analysis to figure out the meanings of the underlined words. Ask a volunteer to read the paragraph aloud. Help with pronunciation as needed.

Check students' understanding. Read aloud each word below. Have students identify the Key Word that means nearly the same thing. STRATEGY: SYNONYMS

1. **bendable** *(malleable)*
2. **searching** *(foraging)*
3. **weight** *(ballast)*
4. **food** *(provender)*
5. **faults** *(aberrations)*
6. **area** *(locus)*
7. **thought** *(mused)*
8. **inactive** *(sedentary)*
9. **unity** *(cohesion)*

Encourage use of the Glossary. **GLOSSARY** Point out that this story may contain other unfamiliar words, such as *arc* or *siege,* that students can look up in the Glossary or in a dictionary. Remind students that they can also use the Glossary to confirm or clarify their understanding of the Key Words.

Integrate spelling with vocabulary. **SPELLING-VOCABULARY CONNECTION** *Integrated Spelling* page 61 reinforces spellings of **words from Latin,** including the following Key Words: *aberrations, cohesion, locus,* and *sedentary.*

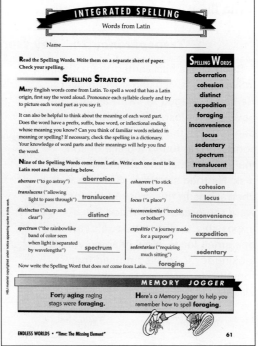

Practice Book

Integrated Spelling

Strategic Reading: Novel Excerpt

Preview and Predict

Have students use prior knowledge about previewing fiction.

Have a volunteer suggest ways of previewing an excerpt from a novel in order to make predictions. (reading and thinking about the excerpt title and the title of the novel, scanning the illustrations, reading the introduction, reading the information about the author)

Encourage predictions.

Have students preview the illustrations and read the introduction. Ask them what they learned that can help them predict what will happen next.

Introduce the problem-solution chart.

Write the headings below on the board. Have students use the problem-solution chart to predict what "Time: The Missing Element" will be about.

PROBLEM-SOLUTION CHART

Title: "Time: The Missing Element"	
Problem	**Solution**
plane crashes no food or water	get to shore on raft

PERSONAL JOURNAL Have students copy the problem-solution chart in their personal journals, or have them use *Practice Book* page 127. (See page 455B in this Teacher's Edition.) Have them complete the chart as they read the story or afterward. (Students will return to the chart after reading, in Summarizing the Literature.)

Setting a Purpose

Have students set purposes.

Tell students to use the predictions they have just made to develop questions that they would like answered by the end of the story. Invite volunteers to share their questions with the group.

Model purpose-setting, if necessary.

If students have difficulty setting a purpose for reading, model the thinking process:

> **I already know from previewing that Elena has a lot of spunk and ingenuity. But because she is alone in the wilderness with no supplies, she is going to have tremendous problems. My purpose for reading will be to find out what problems Elena encounters and how she tries to solve them.**

SECOND-LANGUAGE SUPPORT Students may benefit from the Guided Reading activities and from the additional guidance under the Student Anthology pages. (See *Second-Language Support Manual.*)

OPTIONS FOR READING

Independent Reading
Have students read the story silently with their purpose for reading in mind.

Guided Reading
Follow the Guided Reading suggestions that appear on pages 438, 444, 452, and 454. These suggestions model strategic reading.

Cooperative Reading
Reader response strategies appear on pages 438, 445, and 454.

Numbered Annotations
Use the numbered annotations beside the Student Anthology pages to heighten students' appreciation of the story.

This story takes place on the coast of British Columbia, Canada. Dotted with islands, the northern coast is separated from the nearest road or town by more than 200 miles of the Coast Mountains, which have peaks rising to 16,000 feet. Summer temperatures on the coast average around 60° Fahrenheit. It is one of the wettest places in the world, with more than 80 inches of rainfall a year.

A small plane crashes off the rugged coast of British Columbia, and one lone survivor, Elena Bradbury, a teenage girl, fights her way to shore on a makeshift raft. Her survival and eventual escape depend entirely on her courage, ingenuity, and understanding of nature.

During her first week, she locates a source of fresh water and eats berries, barnacles, and clams. She also finds some materials, including an empty paint-thinner can and some rope, that have washed ashore.

Guided Reading

SET PURPOSE/PREDICT: PAGES 438–444 Have students read to the break on page 444 to find out what problems Elena encounters and how she tries to solve them. As students read, you may wish to suggest that they keep adding problems and solutions to their problem-solution charts.

Cooperative Reading

READER RESPONSE STRATEGY: PAGES 438–444
Form groups of three to five students, and have each group select a leader. Ask group members to read pages 438–444 silently, and then encourage the leader to use dialogue questions such as those below to ensure that all members participate in the discussion. (Response Card 2: Setting, on page R63, offers a variety of dialogue questions.)

- Where does the story take place?
- When does the story take place—long ago, in the future, or in the present?

Time:
The Missing Element

from
TRIAL BY WILDERNESS
by
David Mathieson

By morning, the sky had changed. Instead of a deck of gray stratus, there came a rushing mass of cumulus clouds. They bumbled along at low altitude like a **1** herd of cotton elephants, stampeded by the wind. Patches of early morning sunlight swept across the mountains and along the beach. Shadow one moment, sun the next.

She had awakened with a feeling of hope. Although the experiments with firemaking had come to naught, she was still better off than before, thanks to the **2** empty thinner can. Properly used, the tin could increase her chance of being rescued, for even if the shipping lanes were too distant, a beam of reflected sunlight could hardly be missed by someone a short distance off in a low-flying plane.

The can would have to be modified, however.

She took one of her salvaged nails—it was almost heavy enough to be called a spike—and with repeated blows from a stone, she shaped its malleable iron into a chisel point. With this, she removed the bottom of the can, driving her makeshift chisel centimeter by centimeter around the edge, using a piece of root as a mallet. She ended up with a flat, rectangular mirror measuring perhaps fifteen centimeters by

illustrations by Patrick Soper

439

1 FIGURATIVE LANGUAGE
What comparison does the author use to describe the clouds? *(He says they look like "a herd of cotton elephants, stampeded by the wind.")*
LITERAL: MAKING COMPARISONS

Is this comparison effective? Explain. *(Accept reasonable responses: Yes, the comparison creates a vivid mental image that helps readers visualize the setting and realize that the clouds are not threatening.)*
CRITICAL: MAKING JUDGMENTS

2 CHARACTER'S TRAITS
What do you learn about Elena in the second paragraph? *(Accept reasonable responses: She seems very self-reliant, creative, and optimistic. She is hopeful even though she has not been able to make a fire, and she sees possibilities for rescue in a paint-thinner can that others might have discarded as junk.)*
METACOGNITIVE: DRAWING CONCLUSIONS

3 PLOT: ACTIONS/EVENTS

Describe how Elena hopes to use the mirror to save herself. *(She thinks she can use it to flash a distress signal to a passing ship or plane. She hopes to aim light reflected off the mirror by sighting her finger through a hole in the mirror.)*

INFERENTIAL: SUMMARIZING

4 PLOT: COMPLICATION

What problems does Elena encounter with her signaling device? What is their significance? *(The device works only within a limited range of the sun, which means that she can use it only to signal a plane that is flying near the sun. Also, she can use it only when the sun makes one of its infrequent appearances. The device probably will not help her.)*

INFERENTIAL: DRAWING CONCLUSIONS

ten. The mirror was stiffened at its edge by the remnant of a seam where the sides of the can had been attached.

Again using her chisel, she punched a hole two centimeters across exactly in the center of the mirror. The hole was for sighting; if the mirror was to be a reliable signaling device, the narrow beam of reflected sunlight had to be aimed.

While waiting for the sun to make one of its random appearances, she practiced the technique. Holding the mirror to her eye with one hand and extending the other hand in front of her, she could look through the hole and see her upraised forefinger. The idea was to tilt the mirror so that a patch of brightness lighted the end of your finger. This told you precisely where the beam was going. To signal in Morse, you simply nodded your head. This brought the spot of reflected sunlight down where you could see it on your arm—away from the target—thus creating the interval between flashes.

3

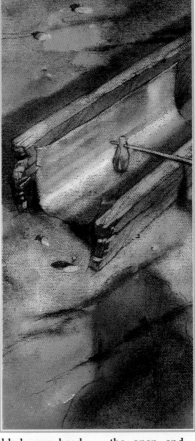

The device had a limited arc of effectiveness, as she soon discovered during a break in the clouds. The quivering rectangle of light was quite distinct whenever she chose a target within a hundred and twenty degrees of the sun. If the angle grew much greater than that, however, the beam was narrow and weak.

She noticed something else, whenever the bright patch of light touched her hand. The metal mirror was handling more than just the visible spectrum of the sun's rays. It was reflecting heat as well.

The idea hit her so suddenly it was like a jolt of electricity.

Solar oven.

Fire wasn't the only way food could be cooked! She should have thought of it earlier. It was such an obvious use of the can's gleaming interior!

Looking in through the open end, she began to visualize how the thing might be done. First the top would have to be cut off, then the seam along the side. The resulting sheet of metal could then be

440

Teaching Tip You may wish to explain that Morse code (near the bottom of column 1) is a system of communication in which letters and numbers are represented by patterns of short and long signals. These may be conveyed as flashes of light, sounds, or written dots and dashes. The system was invented by Samuel F. B. Morse for use on the telegraph.

shaped into a smooth curve.

The device was completed in record time. Two sections of plank held the sheet, top and bottom, the whole affair being supported by a mound of sand and oriented toward the point in the sky where the sun would next appear. "The Pig Trough Oven," she chuckled, giving the metal a last polish with her shirt sleeve. On impulse, she went to the clam reserve, smashed open several shells, wrapped what she could around a stick, and ran back to the reflector with it.

The beach was beginning to brighten. She held the stick crossways to the device. When the sun came, extremely brilliant slashes and stars of light appeared along the sides of the stick. The clam flesh became translucent, glowing like a strip of film in a projector. She moved the stick up and down to locate the mirror's focal point. The effect was spotty and uneven. At the center of one of the star-shaped areas, where the light was brightest, there was enough heat to bring water to a boil. She could hear an occasional hiss, and from time to time a small bubble appeared. But the areas of greatest heat made up only a small fraction of the total area. Elsewhere, there was only enough **5** heat to make things warm—too warm for her hand, but not hot enough for cooking. The aberrations of the mirror were too great. Exact focusing was impossible.

There was no method of containing the heat radiated away, either.

She experimented with the signal mirror, holding it above the stick and trying to reflect a few of the scattered rays back on their target.

No dice.

The thing couldn't be done. The reflective area was too small for cooking. In addition, the single sheet of metal could only be deformed along one axis at a time. The reflector was, in effect, part of a cylinder and was focused along an extended locus rather than upon a single point. What she needed was a reflector shaped something like the end of an egg.

A paraboloid.

She sat contemplating the device. "Useless pig trough!" she said. She dug the stick into the sand. "Science triumphs again!"

"Well," commented the voice of Reason, "what did you expect? Things are always more complex than they **6** look. And that goes for the simple technologies also."

It would have been more satisfying just to throw the thing away, as she had the bow. But instead, she lifted the piece of metal carefully from the sand. She took it over to a flat plank, and hammered a notch in the edge of the metal, using the chisel point of the nail. She positioned the sheet so the notched edge was even with the side of the plank before placing a piece of board on top.

She stood on the board.

Gripping the protruding flap of sheet metal with a folded piece of cedar bark—to protect her fingers from the razorlike edge—she gave a hard, upward pull, tearing the sheet in half.

441

5 PLOT: ACTIONS/EVENTS
Why does "The Pig Trough Oven" fail to work? *(Only small areas get hot enough for cooking, because of the aberrations of the mirror.)*
INFERENTIAL: DETERMINING CAUSE-EFFECT

6 AUTHOR'S CRAFT
Where does the "voice of Reason" come from? How do you think this "voice" might help Elena? *(It comes from Elena's mind. Accept reasonable responses: Her rational thinking encourages her to keep searching for solutions to her problems and not give up when something goes wrong.)*
INFERENTIAL: DRAWING CONCLUSIONS

Vocabulary Strategy You may want to explain that a *focal point* (column 1, middle of the second complete paragraph) is the point at which rays of light or heat meet, or come into focus. The heat or light is most intense at the focal point. STRATEGY: EXPLANATION

Teaching Tip You may wish to point out that because this is a novel excerpt, there are occasional unexplained references, such as that to "the bow" (column 2, sixth complete paragraph). When students come to a reference they do not recognize, they can ask themselves whether it is central to the story. If not, they should go on. If the answer is yes, they can check back over what they have read to see whether they have missed something. If they are still confused, they might note the reference and discuss it at the Guided Reading break.

7 PLOT: ACTIONS/EVENTS

What is Elena making? What clues help you arrive at your conclusion? *(She is making a device to focus the rays of the sun. Accept reasonable responses: She realizes that she needs a paraboloid, which is curved. She cannot mold the single sheet of metal into a paraboloid, so she tears the sheet into smaller pieces, fastens them together, and shapes the pieces into a curve.)*
METACOGNITIVE: DRAWING CONCLUSIONS

8 PLOT: ACTIONS/EVENTS

How does Elena hope to use her "tulip"? How can you tell? *(She hopes to make a fire. Accept reasonable responses: She has been experimenting all along with ways to create a fire.)*
METACOGNITIVE: DETERMINING MAIN IDEA

9 PLOT: ACTIONS/EVENTS

What causes the sizzle and "poof" Elena hears? *(The sliver has caught fire from the heat generated by the focused light in the "tulip.")*
INFERENTIAL: DETERMINING CAUSE-EFFECT

The newly shorn edge, as expected, began at the place where she'd notched the sheet. It followed the contour of the board she'd been standing on for most of its length, curving outward only at the end.

7 Ignoring the imperfection of it, she took the two half sheets and tore each of them into six smaller pieces, using the same technique as before. When she was done, there were twelve long triangles.

The pointed ends curled, like springs. She straightened these out, and punched a single hole in each of the twelve triangles, right at the apex.

With the chisel nail, she drilled a hole into the end grain of a branch and pinned all twelve of the metal triangles in place, driving a tapered twig through the twelve openings in the metal and down into the single hole at the end of the branch.

She hammered the twig deeper into the hole. This held everything tight. Then she arranged the triangles in a pinwheel. Taking this somewhat bizarre creation into the middle of the beach, she planted it firmly in the sand. It stood shoulder high, looking like a small windmill, except the blades were tilted toward the sun.

Bending each blade into a smooth curve with her fingers, she soon destroyed all resemblance to a windmill. The thing now looked like a large metal flower: a tulip. The petals of the tulip were silvery inside; they glinted in the sun. The outside was a patchwork of lettering, left over from the tulip's former existence as a container. Across one

442

petal, in large red letters, was the word DANGER!

Smiling at this, she went to find a wooden sliver of the correct size.

8 The sun was still shining when she returned. With the splinter, she began probing the reflector's interior. As it approached the center, the little spear of cedar glowed with concentrated light. The glare was so intense she had to slit her eyes against it, and even then it was painful.

Other than this, nothing happened.

Perhaps the main area of focus was farther down.

She probed deeper, squinting against the light. It happened so quickly she had no time to react. As the point of the sliver descended, there came a sizzling sound, and the inside of the reflector filled with smoke. Instinctively, she shut her eyes, for in the center the smoke glowed with a ferocious white light. There was a hollow *poof.* An instant later she felt a stinging sensation on the tip of her finger where it held the sliver.

"Ouch!"

The remains of the sliver now lay on the sand, blackened and smoking.

9 Save for the portion held between her fingers, ignition had evidently been instantaneous along its entire length. Which was understandable. All of the wood inside the reflector had been preheated, and the explosive puffing sound must have been what firemen refer to as flashover: particles of smoke catching all at once.

443

10 PLOT: RISING ACTION

What does Elena succeed in doing with the reflector? Why is this important to her? *(She succeeds in making a fire. It means she can cook and stay warm.)*

INFERENTIAL: DRAWING CONCLUSIONS

11 FIGURATIVE LANGUAGE

What figurative language does the author use to personify fire? *(He compares fire to a spouse and to a child.)*

LITERAL: MAKING COMPARISONS

"I'm going to have to find a longer sliver," she mused.

10 It was difficult to believe—this silly-looking tulip actually worked!

She was collecting the kindling and the firewood when she had to stop, look back, and assure herself that the thing truly existed.

Out on the sand, the reflector seemed more like a tulip than ever, swaying on the end of its stalk in the wind.

* * * * *

As must have occurred thousands of years before, when the first hearth-keeper tended the first fire, there came a new cohesion to the various tasks of the day. **11** Her interactions with this creature called fire were akin to those of a marriage—at least in some ways. In others, it was like caring for a child. She made offerings of dry wood, and in return the fire cooked her food, helped in making tools, kept rain and cold and darkness at bay. But a fire needed more than fuel. It needed guarding, and this confined most of her other activities to one location. No longer was it possible for her to sleep in one place, store food in another, keep salvage in a third, and do her crafting of tools and artifacts in yet another spot a hundred meters away. Fire was a magnet to all of these things. There was a reason why the word "hearth" was a synonym for "home." Fire demanded that it be the focus of all activity. Not only that; it was sedentary. You couldn't pick it up and carry it around with you, as you could a child. And you could never, never allow it to walk on its own.

That was another of its demands. The selection of a *place* had to be made with the requirements of fire in mind.

She chose the ledge at the base of the pinnacle, which proved to be nearly ideal. Burning on a rocky surface, her fire could never creep out of control. It was also above the level of the sand, which had been a constant nuisance before, always showing up where it wasn't wanted. A meter and a half away stood the divan-shaped rock. The pool of water at its lower end now did double duty: she could keep clams in it as before or, by dropping in fire-heated stones, convert the hollow in the rock into a cauldron of boiling water.

Even when the tide was in, and cold salt water filled the space between her cooking rock and the pinnacle, there was no inconvenience. She could hop from rock to ledge and back again with little risk. Access to the mainland was along the ledge and through the arching tunnel of logs. The tunnel was much too drafty and damp to convert into a shelter for herself, but it made a good shelter for the main supply of firewood. The larger chunks weren't hurt by an occasional drop of water; only the tinder and kindling needed to be kept completely dry.

Her primary shelter was constructed to seaward of the fire, where the ledge was at its widest. Here, the wall of the pinnacle was slightly concave, providing an

444

Guided Reading

MONITOR COMPREHENSION: PAGES 438–444

What problems does Elena encounter, and how does she solve them? (She is stranded on a rocky coast. She has to find food, shelter, and a way to get off the island. Her first success is solving the problem of making a fire. She finally is able to do so by making a reflector out of an old can.) STRATEGIC READING: RETURNING TO PURPOSE

What steps does she take in order to make a fire? (First, she makes a chisel. Then she cuts the can apart. She tears the metal into twelve even triangles. She makes a hole in each triangle and fastens the triangles together. She bends the triangles upward so the pieces form a tulip-shaped cup. She uses the cup to focus sunlight on a sliver of wood and thus starts a fire.) STRATEGIC READING: SUMMARIZING

SET PURPOSE/PREDICT: PAGES 444–452 Ask students to predict what new problems will complicate Elena's situation. Remind students to enter their predictions on their problem-solution charts. Then have them read to the break on page 452 for confirmation.

overhanging roof. Between the roof and the ledge she erected a palisade of branches, wedging them in place, top and bottom. Crossways to the vertical branches, she interlaced a set of horizontal ones, to form a grille. To this she secured an overlapping thatch of umbrella leaves from the marsh, starting at the bottom, as in shingling a roof, and tying the leaves stem uppermost to the frame with strips of cedar bark.

When they were all in place, the leaves looked like the scales of a large green fish.

Not long after, a brief but torrential rain disclosed a flaw in her arrangements. The rain, driven against the cliff by the wind, flowed down the rock and under **12** the moss caulking she'd used, relentlessly cascading along the inside of the frame.

The remedy came about through the kindly assistance of the fire. She took a flat stone, heated it, and placed lumps of pitch on top. When melted, the pitch ran like honey, and she was able to glue strips of umbrella leaf directly to the rock with it. The pitch also made a watertight seal. The strips of leaf overlapped the shelter wall like lengths of flashing[1] at the peak of a roof, and when the next rainstorm came, the shelter proved at last to be worthy of the name.

Still, refinements were needed. Her little house gaped at both ends. When the wind was from the wrong direction, smoke from the fire poured through the structure as if it were a chimney. She put

---

[1] flashing: sheet metal used to waterproof roof valleys or hips

> There was a reason why the word "hearth" was a synonym for "home." Fire demanded that it be the focus of all activity.

445

12 PLOT: CONFLICT
What is Elena's next problem, and what is its cause? *(Her shelter leaks. The rain flows under the moss she has stuffed between the branches and the rock.)*
INFERENTIAL: DETERMINING CAUSE-EFFECT

Cooperative Reading

READER RESPONSE STRATEGY: PAGES 444–455
Groups should continue reading silently, pausing periodically to discuss how their opinions change as they read.

Second-Language Support
Be sure students understand that *pitch* (third complete paragraph, line 3) is the sap of a pine tree. It is both sticky and water-repellent.

Informal Assessment   You can informally assess your students' appreciation of setting and mood. On occasion, ask questions like these:

- Can you give a brief description of where this story takes place? What is it like there?
- Is it important that this happened where it did? Could it have happened somewhere else? If so, where?
- Does the author's description of the place make you feel a certain way? How does it make you feel? What does the author say that makes you feel this way?

ARTIST'S CRAFT

How does this illustration help the reader understand the story?

(Accept reasonable responses: The illustration shows the reader what Elena's shelter looks like and helps the reader understand what Elena is working on.)

LITERAL: NOTING IMPORTANT DETAILS

13 PLOT: CONFLICT

What conclusion does Elena draw about the missing food? What leads her to this conclusion? *(She concludes that it is being stolen by raccoons. The food is being stolen at night and the thieves are leaving small, handlike footprints, like a raccoon's.)*
INFERENTIAL: DRAWING CONCLUSIONS

14 CHARACTER'S MOTIVATIONS

Why do you think Elena names the big raccoon? *(Accept reasonable responses: She is alone, and even though the raccoons are a problem, they are a kind of company.)*
INFERENTIAL: DRAWING CONCLUSIONS

Would you have done the same in her situation? *(Responses will vary.)*
CRITICAL: EXPRESSING PERSONAL OPINIONS

an end to this by building a removable hatch to block off the southern end of the shelter. This cut down on the draft, allowing her to enjoy the heat of the fire through the opening on the landward side without suffering the smoke. Having designed the hatch so it would open easily, she retained access to the area beyond, even during those times when the beach was under water.

Access was important, for her supplies of food were stored along the outer ledge—or, more accurately, above the ledge. At first glance it would have seemed a curious arrangement, this net of woven vines hanging against the cliff. It was her larder, held in place with strips of bark which had been glued directly to the rock with pitch. A bonnet of leaves protected her <u>provender</u> from sun and rain, and the whole affair was reachable only by standing on tiptoe.

The animals responsible for these elaborate precautions had made their presence known during the first week. Her inventory of clams in the storage pool kept running short, and at first she suspected the gulls of gliding in and stealing from her when she wasn't looking. **13** It soon became apparent, however, that the clams were disappearing only at night, when the gulls weren't flying. This coincided with the time when small, handlike prints were being left in the sand. There were new ones each morning.

Evidently, she was dealing with a family of raccoons.

It was probably more of a game for

448

them in the beginning. Had the animals been able to open the shells on their own, they would have cleaned her out then and there, instead of contenting themselves with two or three a night.

With the appearance of *cooked* clams, however—clams that had been steamed, taken from their shells, dehydrated, and smoked—the game began to be played in earnest. There were four of these bandits, and they grew amazingly bold. Even in daylight, she saw rounded, bearlike forms the size of a terrier ghosting about. She felt under siege. She couldn't let anything edible out of her sight; either it would be gone when she turned around, or else she'd find herself facing an obstinate raccoon—eye on food and reluctant to **14** give ground. There was a large one in particular, whom she named Scipio Africanus, after an ancient Roman general. Scipio would hiss and emit throaty, quacking sounds. But he was not a very brave general, and always led the retreat whenever she advanced and used her voice.

What was puzzling was that the raccoons continued to steal, even after the meaty items were placed beyond their reach. She'd dug up a number of sword ferns, washed the roots, sliced them into chunks, and roasted the chunks like potatoes, in jackets of seaweed. Cooked in this way, the root of the sword fern was perfectly good to eat. It had a pleasant, nutty flavor, and was a welcome addition to a diet that had formerly consisted of almost pure protein.

Cultural Awareness Students might like to know that Scipio [sip'ē·ō], mentioned in the first complete paragraph of the second column, lived between 236 and 183 B.C. He was called "Africanus" because he conquered the North African city of Carthage.

For some reason, the normally carnivorous raccoons seemed to have a taste for it also; as a result, the pieces of broiled sword fern root soon joined the smoked clams in the aerial larder.

After a week of privation, the act of storing food was a marvel to her. Fire, shelter, food—all were luxuries now. True, she'd have given almost anything for a set of fresh clothing, a hot bath, a clean towel, or a hairbrush. But for all that, her spirits rose. Even the onset of rainy weather had little effect on her growing optimism. She had her umbrella-leaf hat to protect her head against the rain, and she had her warm jacket, and her fire, and plenty to eat, and a dry place to sleep. And sooner or later, help would come.

In the middle of the second week, when the shelter was finished, she went and retrieved the raft at the western end of the beach. Ever since that frustrating afternoon of the broken cord, it had lain undisturbed beneath a pile of stones—a crude method of mooring, but effective. Off-loading the stone ballast, she took the raft and made a voyage with it to Whale Rock.

It was eerie, setting foot on that fateful chunk of stone for the second time. She found the scraped place among the acorn barnacles where the little death trap of a raft had been launched ten days before. Higher up, where there were no barnacles, the marks left by the plane were more difficult to see, having been darkened by repeated lavings of the tide.

The shards of metal, however, were still bright. She recovered every scrap, and when she was through, the pocket of the jacket had a definite heft to it. Last of all, she took the board she was using as a paddle and pried the aluminum cap from its knob of rock. Holding the metal shell up to the light, she could see no openings. It would make a good cup.

The purpose of the expedition had been to gather aluminum scrap. With a hundred grams or so at her disposal, she might be able to melt the aluminum down and cast herself a spoon or a fork. The idea had a certain elegance. Imagine having such an artifact! It would be a fascinating memento, and would prove just how much a person could do under primitive conditions.

Her mind was filled with pleasant speculation about this. First, she imagined an open mold of fired clay, within which the aluminum could be melted. Then another idea attracted her. If the mold itself could be placed in the fire to melt down the chips of metal, wouldn't it also be possible to make a *crucible*[2] of clay? There would be a crust of oxide and other impurities floating on the surface of the molten metal. If one used a separate container for the melting, all the dross could be removed first, and only the pure metal would go into the mold.

With great enthusiasm, she searched the face of the bluff for a usable deposit of

---

[2] crucible: a vessel used for melting substances that won't melt without a high degree of heat

449

15 DESCRIPTION
How has Elena's experience changed her outlook? Compare the way she looks at things now with her viewpoint prior to the plane crash. *(Accept reasonable responses: Things that she took for granted, like food, fire, and shelter, she now sees as luxuries.)*
INFERENTIAL: COMPARING AND CONTRASTING

16 PLOT: ACTIONS/EVENTS
Why is going to Whale Rock "eerie" for Elena? *(It is where the plane crashed and others died.)*
INFERENTIAL: DRAWING CONCLUSIONS

When were you able to guess what Elena is making? Why do you think the author describes the process before saying what the object is? *(Accept reasonable responses: Withholding identification builds interest by enticing the reader to add up the details and make a guess.)*
METACOGNITIVE: MAKING PREDICTIONS

clay. The project, however, went no further than this, for during her search she uncovered something far more valuable than potter's clay.

It was a stone. A fairly average stone, perhaps two kilograms in weight: flat and more or less trapezoidal in shape. The thing was valueless by itself, but over the years it had managed to stay in precisely the right position while the root of a tree grew around it. She worked with her chisel nail to cut the root at the treeward end, leaving a handle still attached to the stone.

It was a Neanderthal's dream—the perfect implement for bashing things.

Stone and root were united inseparably. The hatchet-shaped head was not the right material for fashioning an edge, but this didn't matter. She used the thing as a maul for making firewood, and in this role alone, the Bashing Tool, as she came to call it, saved her hours of work every day. The time spent in food gathering was also shortened. Instead of using a stick to laboriously scrape a trench around the base of a sword fern, and then severing the innumerable rootlets from the main root with a small, hand-held stone, she could now flail away with Bashing Tool, accomplishing as much in ten minutes as had taken forty, earlier.

She had by now decided that the making of an aluminum artifact could not be justified, however appealing the idea might be. She didn't need a spoon. The energy spent in making such a thing would be an investment in pride, not in

450

practicality. It would be a foolish bauble for show and tell: a waste of valuable time.

Rather than experiment with crucibles and molds, she built a squat framework of wood. It was shaped like a bird cage. The rounded dome reached no higher than her knee, but it still took a great deal of work. The interlaced branches had to be securely lashed together, for if the device were to function, the joins needed to resist a crushing action similar to that of a powerful vise.

Beneath the dome went a stout, removable floor, also made of branches. None of the openings in either the dome or the floor of the cage was large enough to permit the escape of anything larger than a table tennis ball.

17 Next, she cut a doorway in the side of the structure, about twenty centimeters in width. Across the opening she suspended a small door, hinged at the top with loops made from a scrap of barbed wire. The door was counterbalanced. When pushed from the outside, the door opened inward and one could reach inside the cage. Withdraw the hand, and the stone weight of the counterbalance automatically swung the door shut.

A creature pushing from the inside would not be able to get out.

There remained one problem: What would be the best way of lowering the trap into the water?

In the end she gave up the idea of a line entirely. Crab fishermen used a line because they needed an up-haul adaptable to various depths. If she decided on a

---

Vocabulary Strategy If students do not know the shape of a *trapezoid* (column 1, line 7), have a volunteer look up the word in a dictionary and sketch a trapezoid on the board. STRATEGY: DEFINITION/EXAMPLE

Teaching Tip Point out the reference to *Neanderthal* in column 1, paragraph 2. You may wish to explain that the Neanderthals were prehistoric people. They lived during the Stone Age, a time when many tools and weapons were made of stone. Have students discuss why a Neanderthal would have been delighted with the tool Elena found.

Why do you think the author tells us about Elena's dream? What mood does the dream create? *(It is a threatening dream. It suggests that something bad may happen.)*
INFERENTIAL: SPECULATING

What threat might standing a cabin on pilings protect against? *(a bad storm that causes high waves)*
INFERENTIAL: DETERMINING CAUSE-EFFECT

depth in advance, she could then use a rigid up-haul, such as a long branch. This could be fastened securely to the top of the cage and would float upright in the water, with the top just below tide level. In this way, the action of the waves wouldn't be transmitted to the tethered structure on the bottom. A wooden bobber could be tied to the end of the branch with a length of vine. The bobber would then serve to mark the position of the trap.

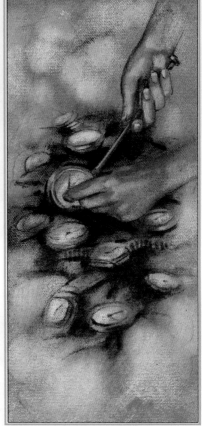

She chose a depth of three fathoms (three times the length of her outstretched arms) and once the trap was in place, the wooden marker appeared on the surface of the bay at every low tide. Daily, she paddled out, positioned the raft above the bobber, and reached down into the water to grasp the end of the submerged pole. Pulling in the trap, hand over hand, was always a time of suspense. Ashore, there was water in the cooking pool, and a pile of stones ready to heat, and a large reserve of firewood—all in the hope of finding a Dungeness crab in the trap. She could see

the way it would happen, down below. The creature would sidle into the current, following the scent of the bait inside the cage. He would crawl up the framework, exploring here and there. Gripping with his pincers. Pushing. Until at last a section of the barrier gave way. . .

But the trap continued to come up empty, except for the ballast of stones and the bait of crushed barnacles. Every day she went out in the raft to check the trap. Disappointed, she would replace the old bait with freshly broken barnacles and return the cage to the bottom.

* * * * *

She dreamt of a cabin built of logs. It rested on pilings, sunk vertically into the marsh so that the cabin stood high in the air, as if on stilts. This was a protection against . . . some threat or other. She couldn't remember what.

From the front door, a gangway angled toward the beach, and in the dream she walked down the gangway. Winter had

452

MONITOR COMPREHENSION: PAGES 444–452
What new problems does Elena encounter? What are her solutions? (She needs a shelter, which she builds. It leaks; she fixes it with pitch. She has to make her food supplies safe from raccoons; she weaves a larder of vines and hangs it up. She needs to vary her diet, so she builds a crab trap.)
STRATEGIC READING: RETURNING TO PURPOSE

The "voice of Reason" tells Elena that things are more complex than they look. How have these words proved to be true, and how do you think they may have helped Elena so far? (Accept reasonable responses: Some things she has made have not worked, at least at first. Expecting difficulties has kept Elena from looking for easy answers or giving up when she has a setback.)
STRATEGIC READING: SUMMARIZING

SET PURPOSE/PREDICT: PAGES 452–455 Remind students of the title, "Time: The Missing Element." Ask them to predict what further problem Elena will face and what time will have to do with it. Remind students to enter their predictions on their charts. Then invite them to read the rest of the story.

come, and it was cold. She had to push her way through heavy snow as she went, and the gangway rebounded underfoot like a weighted trampoline. When she got to the beach, she began digging for clams. The sand underneath the snow was hard with frost and mixed with the ashes of an ancient fire. Clams were nowhere to be found. There were only the clocks. Hundreds upon hundreds of rusted clocks.

She was awakened from the dream by the sniffing of an animal. Opening her eyes, she found Scipio Africanus peeking in at her, his masked face appearing just above the contour of the ledge.

"Good morning, Scipio," she said.

At the sound of her voice, the raccoon vanished. There was a scurrying noise from below, and after a moment, Scipio Africanus could be seen galumphing along the beach, followed by two of his cohorts. They presently disappeared among the driftwood.

Raccoons were mostly nocturnal, but there was only an hour or two of true darkness here during the summer solstice. They wouldn't have enough darkness in which to do their foraging and would have to go out whether it was daytime or not.

The sky, she noted, was its customary gray this morning. But at least it wasn't raining. She got up and removed the small lean-to of planks that sheltered the fire. There was nothing showing on the surface; only a fine powder of ash, holding the shape of what had been pieces of firewood hours earlier. She held out a hand to find the warmth, then bent over and breathed on it. The ash disintegrated to reveal a bed of coals below. She tucked a few wisps of dry grass among the coals and, when this flared, added a handful of twigs. Broken pieces of stick followed the twigs, then still larger pieces, until a merry blaze licked upward against the rock.

She warmed herself, and steam rose from her clothing as the dampness of the night was driven off. The process was speeded by taking off the jacket and drying it separately. The same for the shoes and stockings. She sat and toasted the soles of her feet before the fire while the stockings hung on a stick nearby. For perhaps the fourth time in as many days she considered finding a block of wood, so she'd be able to sit at the fire with greater dignity and comfort. And just as she had on the other occasions, she decided against it. The ledge was already crowded; a stool-sized block would merely be another thing for her to trip over. She'd fall in the drink some evening when the tide was in—though, come to think of it, the possibility that this would happen over the next few days was exactly zero. The neaps[3] had arrived: the tides were neither very high nor very low. If she'd tumbled off the ledge last night she would have hit dry sand, for at high tide the water hadn't even gone as far as the foot of Cooking Rock.

Her mind shifted from the trivial to the practical. The subject of the tide had

---

[3] neaps: tides of minimal range that occur at the first and third quarters of the moon

453

Teaching Tip   You may want to explain that the *summer solstice* (fourth complete paragraph) is the time when the sun is farthest north of the equator. On the summer solstice, which occurs around June 22, the days begin to get shorter.

Oral Rereading   Invite students to read the end of the selection aloud, beginning with the sentence *And there it was again* (page 454, column 2), or have them read from some other passage of their choosing. Remind students that punctuation and paragraphing provide clues to pauses and emphasis for oral reading. Encourage them to practice silently and then in pairs until they can read the passage fluently and with expression. Remind them to read slowly enough that listeners can take in and appreciate the author's language. After they have practiced, ask volunteers to read portions of the passage for classmates.

19 PLOT: CONFLICT

How does Elena interpret her dream? Do you agree? *(She thinks it reflects her awareness that the neap tide means she will not be able to dig clams. Accept reasonable responses: No; winter, the cabin, and the clocks are not explained in Elena's version, and they are strong elements of the dream.)*
CRITICAL: MAKING JUDGMENTS

20 CHARACTERIZATION

What does Elena decide is important about the recipe for dandelion omelette? *(The most important thing is that dandelions can be eaten.)*
LITERAL: RECOGNIZING MAIN IDEA

What does this reveal about her character and personality? *(It shows that she is able to think analytically and pick out what is important. It also suggests that instead of focusing on what she does not have, as many people might, she relentlessly focuses on what she has.)*
INFERENTIAL: DRAWING CONCLUSIONS

21 FORESHADOWING

Why do you think the author brings up the dream again? What purpose does it serve in telling the story? *(The dream is still bothering Elena. It creates a somber, worried mood that foreshadows a coming problem.)*
INFERENTIAL: MAKING PREDICTIONS

brought up a matter of more immediate concern. For the next several days she'd have to depend entirely on the reserves of meat in the larder. (Unless, of course, a crab turned up in the trap.) The clam beds would still be covered at low tide, so she wouldn't be able . . .

So *that* was it!

19 Her memory of the dream had begun to fade, but she could still remember the essentials. Winter, a cabin on stilts, no clams. There were a few disturbing elements, but these were illogical and could be dismissed. The source of the whole thing was the fact that the neaps had arrived and she wouldn't be digging any more clams for a while. That was all the dream was saying. The brooding, frightening aspects had no meaning. None at all.

"And anyway," she reminded herself, "I've got a treat for breakfast this morning." The evening before, she'd picked a handful of dandelion buds—not the flowers themselves, but the small, soft lumps that showed just before the flowers opened. The recipe for dandelion omelette involved such things as eggs, milk, onions, butter, salt, pepper—and an omelette pan—none of which she **20** possessed. The important thing to note, of course, was that dandelion buds were *edible*. She would just have to do without the rest of it.

In preparation, she scooped a mound of coals into a hollow in the rock. She poured a little water into her aircraft-aluminum cup, then bedded the cup

among the coals. When the water boiled, she dumped in the buds and covered the cup with a lid of bark to trap the steam. The cup simmered atop the coals.

It would have been pleasant to be able to brew some tea. She knew where there was a stand of Labrador tea—at least the plants *looked* like Labrador tea. But that was the problem. There was a variety known as false Labrador tea, very similar in appearance. Make an infusion of one, and you had an enjoyable drink with breakfast. Brew up with the leaves of the other and you had a cup of poison.

She improvised a song about it:

Poison, poison, drink it up!
Chill of winter in the cup!

21 And there it was again. That silly dream about clocks and winter! What was the matter with her? The whole thing had been ridiculous. A cabin on *stilts*, for heaven's sake!

Irritated with herself, she put on her shoes and went to get a leaf-wrapped breakfast ration from the larder. When she returned, she lifted the piece of bark to see how the dandelions were doing. The water had turned slightly greenish, but when she prodded the buds with a splinter they still seemed underdone. She put the cover back and chewed on a piece of dehydrated clam.

Snow on the ground and nothing to eat.

Dreams had a crazy logic of their own at times. Take the idea of a cabin. If she

454

Cooperative Reading

READER RESPONSE STRATEGY: PAGES 444–455

After group members have finished reading the selection, the group leader may use dialogue questions such as the following to help members interact with the text. (Response Card 2: Setting, on page R63, offers a wide range of dialogue questions.)

- How does the setting affect what happens in the selection?
- If you could visit the setting for this selection, would you go there? Why or why not?

Guided Reading

MONITOR COMPREHENSION: PAGES 452–455

What further problem does Elena face in this part of the story, and what does time have to do with it? (Elena faces the problem of approaching winter. She lacks the time to prepare for it.)
STRATEGIC READING: RETURNING TO PURPOSE

What personality traits help Elena survive?

(Accept reasonable responses: She does not give up easily; she is clever; she does not feel sorry for herself; she uses what she knows to good advantage.) STRATEGIC READING: SUMMARIZING

were to stay here through the winter, that was what she would need: a small cabin. A rocky ledge and a campfire wouldn't do—not at fifty-three degrees north latitude—not with twenty hours of darkness out of every twenty-four during the months of December and January. In addition to the cabin she'd need enormous supplies of firewood, properly broken up. She'd need winter clothing. Bedding. Food—four or five months' worth of food.

It was quite impossible. She lacked the resources, the equipment, the knowledge. Above all, she lacked the *time*.

A solitary human equipped with Stone Age tools would not be able to accomplish all that needed to be done. A group of people might succeed. A dozen pairs of hands: chopping, clearing, carrying, weaving, fishing, trapping, skinning, tanning, smoking, digging, building.

Eighteen, twenty hours a day.

A dozen pairs of hands to raise the shelter and break up fuel for the fire—and all would share the shelter and the fire. With only one person, there would be

22

nearly as much work, as far as shelter and heating were concerned, but only one pair of hands, not twelve.

Survive the winter alone? She wouldn't have a chance. The clams were only going to last through September, maybe into October, but after that?

She lifted the cover of bark from the aluminum cup. The water had mostly evaporated, leaving the dandelions lying dark and limp at the bottom. She speared one of them with her sliver, and blew on it. The yellow part of the flower could be seen inside.

Not too bad, she concluded, taking a bite.

Tangy.

They had a flavor similar to that of spinach . . . could have used a little salt. She'd try simmering them in sea water next time.

* * * *

To escape before the winter comes, Elena decides to construct a boat. After experiencing several unfortunate accidents while designing and building the boat, Elena eventually paddles back to safety.

THINK IT OVER

1. *Explain how Elena Bradbury is able to survive.*
2. *Describe or draw a diagram of Elena's solar oven.*
3. *What are some of the decisions Elena has to make after she has fire?*
4. *Explain the importance of time in Elena's plans for survival.*

23

WRITE

Make a list of the five most important things that help Elena to survive. Compare your list with those of your classmates.

24

455

Returning to the Predictions Invite students to review the predictions that they made before reading and that they may have written in their personal journals. Ask whether students changed their predictions while reading, and if so, why.

Returning to the Purpose for Reading Have students tell what problems Elena faced and how she solved them. (Accept reasonable responses: She was alone, without supplies, in an isolated place. She solved her problems by using available resources, thinking creatively, and remaining hopeful.)

22 PLOT: RISING ACTION
What makes Elena's new problem more serious than those she has already faced? *(She does not have enough time to prepare for winter; it is impossible for her to survive the winter alone in this place.)*
INFERENTIAL: DRAWING CONCLUSIONS

23 THINK IT OVER
1. *She is able to meet her basic needs for food, water, and shelter; she is able to put her scientific knowledge to work to make fire, to devise tools, and to use resources; she is able to keep a level head.*
INFERENTIAL: DETERMINING CAUSE-EFFECT
2. *It is a simple flat piece of metal, curved and positioned to catch the sunlight, propped up by sand.*
LITERAL: NOTING IMPORTANT DETAILS
3. *She has to decide where to put the fire so it will be safe and where to put her shelter and supplies in relation to it.*
INFERENTIAL: SUMMARIZING
4. *Given sufficient time, Elena could provide for her basic needs. However, she realizes that winter is coming and that she does not have enough time to get together all the things she will need to survive it.*
INFERENTIAL: DRAWING CONCLUSIONS

24 WRITE
To help students get started, you may want to suggest a prewriting graphic such as the following:

Things That Help Elena Survive	How They Help

Accept reasonable responses. Students may mention her ability to find water and food; fire; the chisel and the bashing tool; her understanding of science and simple technologies; her attitude.
CRITICAL: MAKING JUDGMENTS

NOTE Additional writing activities appear on page 455D.

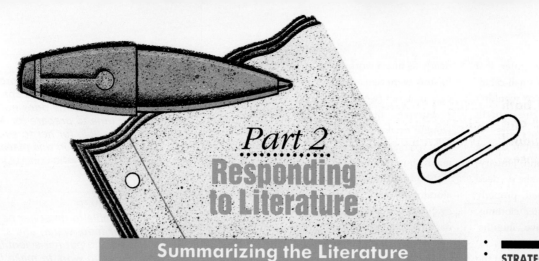

Part 2
Responding to Literature

Summarizing the Literature

Have students retell the selection and write a summary.

Invite students to summarize the selection using the chart they completed as they read. If they have not yet completed the chart, have them do so now. (See *Practice Book* page 127, on 455B.) Students may use their completed charts to retell the selection and write a brief summary statement.

PROBLEM-SOLUTION CHART

Title: "Time: The Missing Element"	
Problem	**Solution**
plane crashes	get to shore on raft
no food or water	find water, clams, roots
no way to cook	build solar oven (fails); build reflector to start fire (works)
shelter	build into rock with branches
shelter leaks	fix with pitch
raccoons steal food	hang up food
approaching winter	

Appreciating Literature

Have students share personal responses.

Divide students into small groups to discuss the story. Provide a general question such as the following to help the groups get started:

- **Would you like to read the rest of this novel? Why or why not?**

PERSONAL JOURNAL Encourage students to use their personal journals to write about ideas and feelings that are expressed in the groups. You may also wish to refer students to their personal journals after they complete the Critical Thinking Activities.

STRATEGY CONFERENCE

Discuss the problem-solution chart, asking students whether it helped them understand and enjoy the novel excerpt. Invite students to share other strategies they used, such as paying special attention to details.

INFORMAL ASSESSMENT

Having students order the details of a selection in this way will help you informally assess how well they understood key relationships. Ask yourself: Did students grasp **time relationships**? Did students recognize the **causes of effects** and the **effects of causes**? Can students tell which **details** are more important than others?

Encourage both cooperative and individual responses.

DISCUSS CHARACTER TRAITS **What character trait of Elena's do you think is most important in her survival? What evidence supports your choice?** Invite students to discuss the questions in small groups. Encourage them to agree on one trait and identify supporting facts and reasons. Each group may present its choice orally to the others and defend it in a discussion. CRITICAL: MAKING JUDGMENTS

HOLD A DEBATE **In general, do you think what Elena does would be possible for most people? Why or why not?** Encourage students with similar views to form pairs and outline supporting arguments for their opinion. Then have them debate with pairs who hold the opposite opinion. CRITICAL: MAKING GENERALIZATIONS

DESIGN A CABIN **If you could design a cabin in the wilderness, what would it look like?** Have students design a cabin, taking care to include all the features they would need to survive. Remind them that they would need to go without electricity and plumbing or improvise their own. Display students' designs. CREATIVE: SOLVING PROBLEMS

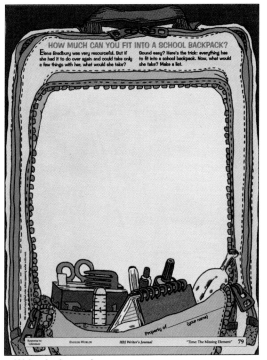

Writer's Journal

• • • TIME: THE MISSING ELEMENT • • •

Name _____

Complete the problem-solution chart.
Responses will vary.

PROBLEM	SOLUTION
plane crash	gets to shore on raft
no food or water	finds water, clams, roots
no way to cook	builds solar oven (fails); builds reflector to start fire (works)
no shelter	builds into rock with branches
shelter leaking	fixes shelter with pitch
raccoons	hangs up food
approaching winter	Solution not presented in this excerpt.

Practice Book • ENDLESS WORLDS   Summarizing the Literature   127

Practice Book

WRITER'S JOURNAL
page 79: Writing a creative response

PRACTICE BOOK
page 127: Summarizing the selection

Reviewing Key Words

To review how the new vocabulary was used in this selection, have students answer each question.

1. *malleable*   Which is more malleable, clay or stone? (clay) STRATEGY: PRIOR KNOWLEDGE

2. *foraging*   Which word means the same as *searching*? *(foraging)* STRATEGY: SYNONYMS

3. *ballast*   What would happen to a hot-air balloon if you threw the ballast overboard? (It would rise.) STRATEGY: PRIOR KNOWLEDGE

4. *provender*   Which word is a general term for things like rice, wheat, and fruit? *(provender)* STRATEGY: EXAMPLES

5. *aberrations*   Would you rather use a camera lens with or without aberrations? Why? (without; aberrations might distort the picture) STRATEGY: PRIOR KNOWLEDGE

6. *locus*   Which word means the same as *place*? *(locus)* STRATEGY: SYNONYMS

7. *mused*   Which word is similar to the word *thought*? *(mused)* STRATEGY: SYNONYMS

8. *cohesion*   Which word means the opposite of *falling apart*? *(cohesion)* STRATEGY: ANTONYMS

9. *sedentary*   If your life-style is too sedentary, what do you need more of? (exercise) STRATEGY: PRIOR KNOWLEDGE

Extending Vocabulary

STRUCTURAL ANALYSIS: ROOTS   Write *aberrations* on the board. Explain that the meaning of the word can be figured out by recognizing its parts. *Aberration* has Latin roots: its prefix *(ab-)* means "away from." Its Latin base word *(errare)* means "to wander or to err." Its English suffix *(-ation)* means "state, quality, or condition of." *Errare* is also the root of the words *aberrant, error, erroneous,* and *erratic.* Point out that words that have the same root are in the same word family and share the root's meaning. The roots of an unfamiliar word can be an important clue to its meaning.

Suggest that students find two or three words in the story that have a base word that can be combined with other prefixes and suffixes to make other words. Then have them find out each word's roots and its meaning. Ask students where to locate this information. (in a dictionary)

Integrated Language Arts

WRITING

Writing About the Literature

CREATIVE: JOURNAL ENTRY   Ask students to imagine that they are alone in an isolated place where no one can find them. They have a journal and a pen. Ask them to write a three-day journal entry describing their experience. WRITING

AVAILABLE ON PROJECT CARD

CRITICAL: EXPOSITORY PARAGRAPH   Briefly discuss the role science played in Elena's survival. Have students write expository paragraphs about making science more attractive to teenagers. They may want to outline their ideas before writing. LISTENING/ SPEAKING/WRITING

> **How to Make Science Interesting**
> **I.** Practical subjects
>   **A.** Computers
> ————————————

NOTE: An additional writing activity appears on page 455.

SPEAKING/LISTENING

Creative Dramatics

COOPERATIVE LEARNING   Ask students to imagine that they will do a talk-show interview with a survivor of a wilderness experience. Have students work with partners to create the interview. Suggest that they write questions to bring out important details. Then have them take turns role-playing the two parts to create the interview.
LISTENING/SPEAKING/WRITING

SPELLING

Spelling Review

SPELLING WORDS   *aberration, cohesion, distinct, expedition, foraging, inconvenience, locus, sedentary, spectrum, translucent*

Have students write the Spelling Words as you dictate them. Then have a volunteer write them on the board. Have students read each word aloud in unison, listening for Latin word roots. Have another volunteer circle each Latin word root and share its meaning. LISTENING/SPEAKING/WRITING/SPELLING

INTEGRATED SPELLING

page 62: Writing words from Latin

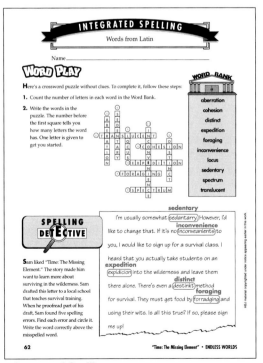

Integrated Spelling

COMPREHENSION
INTRODUCE

Making Judgments

OBJECTIVE: *To make critical judgments about literature*

1	Focus

Discuss making judgments.

Remind students that Elena has to choose where to keep her fire and where to build a shelter. In order to choose, she has to make a judgment about which places will be best. Point out to students that they, too, often need to make judgments in order to evaluate whether something is good or bad, wise or foolish, objective or biased, accurate or inaccurate, valid or invalid. Knowing how to make judgments about the decisions of story characters can help students judge wisely in their own lives.

2	Teach/Model

Model the thinking.

Model making a judgment about Elena's initial decision to make a spoon:

> **When Elena decides to make a spoon, I ask myself whether her decision can be backed up with good reasons. Making a spoon will take time and effort that I think would be better spent on things that she needs to survive. My judgment is that making a spoon would be a mistake, and I am relieved when she changes her mind.**

Have students discuss judgments.

Copy on the board the diagram given below, and have a volunteer explain the process. Then have students use the diagram to discuss how they make judgments.

Information from Story $+$ Prior Knowledge $+$ Reason and Logic

3 · Practice/Apply

Have students make judgments.

COOPERATIVE LEARNING Invite students to work in groups to make judgments about passages in the story. Have them use the diagram as a model.

4 · Summarize

Informally assess the learning.

Have students summarize what they learned. (Readers judge the value or appropriateness of something by thinking about what they know and by reasoning about it.)

READER ↔ WRITER CONNECTION

Making Judgments

▶ **Writers** make judgments about their readers and their subject matter in order to choose material and details.

▶ **Readers** make judgments about the truth, wisdom, or validity of what they read.

WRITE A CHARACTER SKETCH Have students imagine that while exploring a rain forest, they encounter a person who has never seen or heard a person from outside. Have them decide what this person is like and write a descriptive paragraph that helps the reader judge the person's character.

RETEACH Follow the **visual, auditory,** and **kinesthetic/motor** models on page R50.

CHALLENGE Have a group of students use their judgment-making skills to write short reviews of television programs, using examples and their reasoning processes to defend their judgments.

SECOND-LANGUAGE SUPPORT Students can work with a peer tutor to name some things that they think are good, bad, true, or false, and to explain why they think as they do. (See *Second-Language Support Manual.*)

WRITER'S JOURNAL
page 80: Writing a character sketch

PRACTICE BOOK
page 128: Making judgments

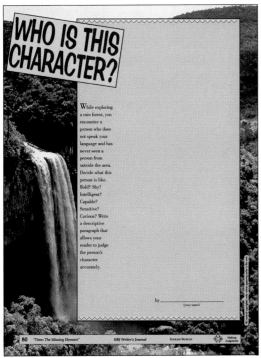

Writer's Journal

Practice Book

Directions

OBJECTIVE: *To follow and give directions accurately*

1	Focus

Explain the value of following directions accurately.

Ask students whether they have ever filled out a form incorrectly or gotten lost because they didn't read or listen to the directions carefully enough. Explain that knowing how to follow directions makes all new tasks easier.

2	Teach/Model

Model the thinking.

Model some basic strategies that help people understand and follow directions accurately:

> **When I have to follow directions, I pay special attention. If the directions are oral, I listen for clue words that indicate sequence and direction—*first, next, one, two, over, under*—and I ask questions if I'm not sure about the steps. If the directions are written, I first read them all the way through, looking for sequence and direction words. I read them a second time to be sure I have any materials or supplies needed. Then I follow the steps one at a time.**

Have students discuss directions.

Have students turn to pages 439–440 and read the steps Elena goes through to make the reflector. Ask students to identify the essential steps and materials.

3 | Practice/Apply

Have students write directions.

COOPERATIVE LEARNING Invite students to work in groups to write directions for simple activities, such as making a paper airplane or filling out a form. Then have the groups exchange directions and try to follow them. Have students discuss their success in following the directions and why they think they succeeded or failed.

4 | Summarize

Informally assess the learning.

Provide oral directions for students to follow. Ask them to fold a sheet of paper in a particular way, write information in a particular order, or draw a geometric figure with several parts. Call on volunteers to show how they interpreted the directions. Then have students summarize what they learned. (Oral directions: listen for clue words; ask questions to clarify. Written directions: read all directions; look for clue words; follow step by step.)

Writer's Journal

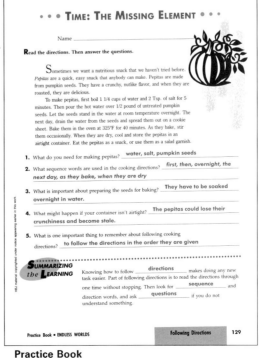

Practice Book

MEETING INDIVIDUAL NEEDS

RETEACH Follow the **visual, auditory,** and **kinesthetic/motor** models on page R51.

CHALLENGE Have a small group of students use what they have learned to write directions for a treasure hunt. Invite them to set up the treasure hunt for their classmates.

SECOND-LANGUAGE SUPPORT Students can demonstrate their understanding by orally reviewing directions they encounter for math, science, or social studies activities. (See *Second-Language Support Manual.*)

WRITER'S JOURNAL page 81: Writing directions

PRACTICE BOOK page 129: Following directions

Integrated Curriculum

Measure Up!

AVAILABLE ON PROJECT CARD

Ask students to imagine that they are editors preparing an edition of "Time: The Missing Element" for people who prefer the system of measurement used in the United States to the metric system. Have students find the references to metric measures in the story and convert them to feet, inches, or other equivalents. Invite students to present their findings in an oral report with a chart to help the audience understand the information. LISTENING/SPEAKING/READING/WRITING

SOCIAL STUDIES

Northern Neighbor

COOPERATIVE LEARNING   Ask a group of students to research the province of British Columbia. Suggest that they divide the subject into topics, such as history, geography, climate, and industry, for individual group members to examine. When group members have completed their research, they can combine their information and form a panel to report their findings to their classmates. Require students in the audience to take notes and write a summary of the presentation. LISTENING/SPEAKING/READING/WRITING

SCIENCE

Untamed Edibles

Point out to students that wild plants were an important source of food for Native Americans and settlers alike. Invite students to research edible wild plants to find out about the many common "weeds" that can be eaten or used for seasoning. Suggest that they make up a notebook of edible plants, with short descriptions and drawings of the plants and ways to use them. READING/WRITING

SCIENCE

New Under the Sun

Invite interested students to find out about modern uses for solar energy, such as heat, hot water, and water purification. Suggest that they prepare a written report that includes drawings or models as graphic aids. When the reports are finished, students may elect to present them orally, displaying their graphics. LISTENING/SPEAKING/READING/WRITING

Native American Foods

READ ALOUD TO STUDENTS:

MOST OF US TAKE FOR GRANTED THE FOODS WE EAT.

We tend to assume that people have been eating the same dishes for thousands of years. Yet many of the foods we eat most often, such as potatoes, beans, tomatoes, and corn, were known only to Native Americans before Columbus and Spanish explorers began expeditions to the "New World" in the 15th century. The explorers came seeking exotic spices, but they returned with vegetables no European had tasted before.

The food crops Native Americans had cultivated changed the diet of Europe, which had consisted mainly of wheat, rye, barley, and red meat. The potato, which grew well in northern climates, became a staple of European and Russian diets. Corn became the chief feed crop for livestock. In fact, the English soon began to use the word *corn* for any grain. Tomatoes grew particularly well in Italy's sunny climate and became a major ingredient of that country's cuisine.

Native Americans also introduced the world to such delicacies as bell and chili peppers, arrowroot, vanilla, chocolate, pumpkin, avocados, peanuts, pecans, pineapple, and blueberries. ■

Native Americans relied on an impressive variety of grains, fruits and vegetables for a balanced diet.

ACTIVITY CORNER

■ Have students search for unusual recipes using one or more of these Native American foods: corn, potato, tomato, arrowroot, bell pepper, chili pepper, chocolate, vanilla, squash, lima beans, navy beans, kidney beans, pumpkin, manioc, avocado, peanut, pecan, cashew, pineapple, blueberry, sunflower. If possible, ask each student to cook one dish and bring it to class for a tasting party. Instruct them to bring a copy of the recipe with the food. Use the recipes to compile a class cookbook.

■ Arrange a field trip to a farm to allow students to harvest, if possible, a Native American food. Depending on your location, they may pick blueberries, corn, tomatoes, pumpkins, and so on. Ask the farmer to explain the growing cycle from planting seeds and fertilization to harvest time.

An Interview with the Author: David Mathieson

ABOUT THE INTERVIEW

Writer Ilene Cooper interviews David Mathieson about writing in general and about Mathieson's novel *Trial by Wilderness* in particular. Mathieson explains why he created a female hero for his novel and why he believes young people are interested in survival stories even when they have not had related experiences.

1 AUTHOR'S COMMENTARY

Why does David Mathieson consider "cultural expectation" to be a "deadly barrier" for his character Elena? *(Accept reasonable responses: If she had believed that she could not survive in the wilderness because she was not a male, she probably would have died.)*

INFERENTIAL: DRAWING CONCLUSIONS

An Interview
DAVID MATHIESON

Writer Ilene Cooper had the opportunity to discuss writing with David Mathieson.

Ms. Cooper: *Since you have experienced circumstances similar to those Elena experienced, why did you use a girl for a hero and a third-person narrator rather than a first-person narrator in the novel?*

Mr. Mathieson: In telling the story, a writer sometimes doesn't know why things are being done a certain way until afterwards. At the start, I just thought I was helping to redress the disparity between the number of male Crusoes in fiction and the number of female Crusoes. But of course it goes deeper than that. My hero has more obstacles to overcome than the average Crusoe—no tools, no food, not even any water to begin with—plus another and more deadly barrier the males do not have to face: that of cultural expectation. A young woman is not "supposed" to be as good as a man in making tools and building a boat and surviving in the wild. Elena Bradbury must violate this expectation just to stay alive. And having done so, she is able to see her own life pattern and her culture with new eyes. It is a useful insight. It gives her the chance to save herself a second time, after returning to civilization. In truth, it just felt better, somehow, to write of Elena as "she" rather than as "I."

456

---

with the Author:

Ms. Cooper: Why do you think young people enjoy reading realistic novels concerning people in conflict with nature since so few of them will ever face such circumstances? What do you think young people can learn from reading Trial by Wilderness?

Mr. Mathieson: Personally, I think one's interest in a story has little to do with the likelihood of experiencing the thing itself. A child of five can often enjoy a story about rabbits. Older people still like to read about spies and youthful romance and, sometimes, even about dragons. Yet the notion persists that a story, in order to interest a teenager, has to be about high school. On the contrary! That period in a person's life is more, not less, oriented toward the game of "What If."

A word about humans in conflict with nature. One way of looking at *Trial by Wilderness* is to see it in terms of a hero struggling against a single adversary: the nonhuman universe. This is the viewpoint of our culture. Nature is perceived as being in a power struggle with us. As if nature cared!

For Elena, transported back into the Stone Age, nature wears another face—that of indifference. Far from being a malevolent opponent, nature, except for an occasional creature, doesn't even know we're there. Elena survives her trial not because she "wins" against a cunning adversary, but because she's bright enough **2** to face things as they are, not as they are culturally perceived. The threat is impersonal, if deadly. By facing that, Elena, Modern Teenager, becomes Elena, Savage of the Stone Age. Thereafter, she has the fun of putting her intelligence to work in a good cause: that of survival. And that is what I hope a young reader might take from this book. The heroine learns to use a kind of thinking that was needed in the Stone Age—and is needed still. The real wilderness is the one to which Elena **3** Bradbury returns, the one she has lived in all her life.

Ms. Cooper: What advice do you have for young people who want to write about their experiences "in the wilderness"?

Mr. Mathieson: If you want to write about anything, don't let anyone stop you.

457

2 AUTHOR'S COMMENTARY
How does David Mathieson view the conflict between man and nature? *(Accept reasonable responses: Nature is indifferent; it does not engage in a power struggle with people.)*
INFERENTIAL: SUMMARIZING

Do you agree with him? Explain. *(Responses will vary.)*
CRITICAL: MAKING JUDGMENTS

3 METAPHOR
David Mathieson says that Elena "has lived in [the wilderness] all her life." What does he mean? *(Accept reasonable responses: Living in society is like trying to survive in the wilderness because there are so many things to overcome, including cultural expectations.)*
INFERENTIAL: MAKING COMPARISONS

Vocabulary Strategy Ask students how they can use structural analysis to determine the meaning of *adversary*. Students might recognize the base word *adverse*, meaning "acting against, hostile," and the suffix *-ary*, meaning "person or thing engaged in," to figure out that an *adversary* is "one who acts against," or an enemy. STRATEGY: STRUCTURAL ANALYSIS

Responding to the Interview

Remind students that David Mathieson does not agree with the notion that a story has to be about high school in order to be of interest to teenagers. Invite students to discuss their views on the matter and to tell why they enjoy or do not enjoy reading adventure stories, citing specific examples from their reading experience.

The Right Place

ABOUT THE AUTHOR

James A. Michener (1907–) was raised by a Quaker woman in Pennsylvania after he lost his parents. He served with the United States Navy in the Pacific during World War II. Michener is famous for fictional works that also document the history of places such as Hawaii, Israel, and the Chesapeake Bay. His first novel, *Tales of the South Pacific,* won a Pulitzer Prize in 1948 and became the hit Broadway musical *South Pacific.*

SELECTION SUMMARY

In 1583, Pentaquod, a peace-loving Susquehannock, leaves his warlike tribe to explore an island in the Chesapeake Bay, where he hopes to settle. He finds the place abundant in food and other resources, but after a storm washes away part of the shoreline, he decides to move farther inland.

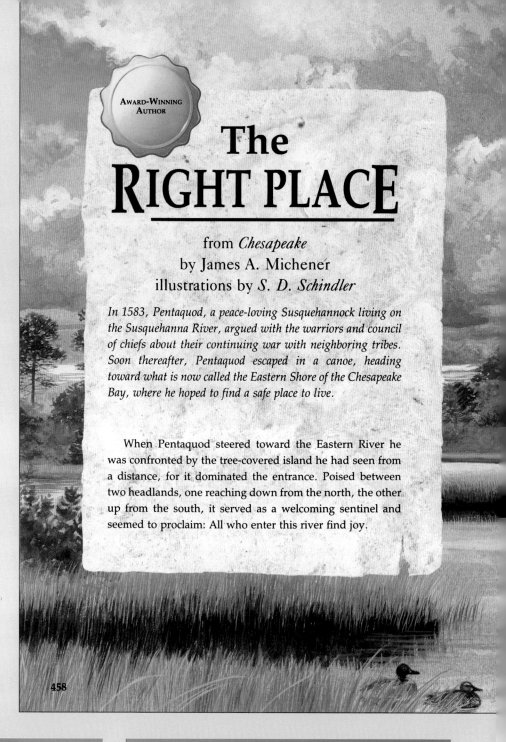

AWARD-WINNING AUTHOR

The RIGHT PLACE

from *Chesapeake*
by James A. Michener
illustrations by *S. D. Schindler*

In 1583, Pentaquod, a peace-loving Susquehannock living on the Susquehanna River, argued with the warriors and council of chiefs about their continuing war with neighboring tribes. Soon thereafter, Pentaquod escaped in a canoe, heading toward what is now called the Eastern Shore of the Chesapeake Bay, where he hoped to find a safe place to live.

When Pentaquod steered toward the Eastern River he was confronted by the tree-covered island he had seen from a distance, for it dominated the entrance. Poised between two headlands, one reaching down from the north, the other up from the south, it served as a welcoming sentinel and seemed to proclaim: All who enter this river find joy.

458

Building Background

Help students locate the Susquehanna River and the Chesapeake Bay on a map of the United States. Explain that hundreds of years ago, these areas of Pennsylvania and Maryland were wilderness. Ask students to name some ways in which a writer might learn about a place as it existed in the past in order to re-create it in a work of fiction.

Strategic Reading

Novel Excerpt   Point out that this is an excerpt from a novel. Have students read the introduction and the first four paragraphs. Then have them predict what challenges Pentaquod may face.

STUDENT-SET PURPOSE   Ask students to use their predictions to decide on a purpose for reading.

TEACHER-SET PURPOSE   If students have difficulty setting a purpose, offer this suggestion: **I'm going to read to find out whether or not Pentaquod will decide to stay on the island and why.**

459

Teaching Tip   Tell students that the Susquehannock Indians lived along the Susquehanna River in New York, Pennsylvania, and Maryland. The Susquehannock were often at war with the Iroquois, and their numbers dwindled rapidly. By 1763 there were only twenty members left, and none remain today.

1 POINT OF VIEW

Why doesn't the narrator reveal the common name by which this bird is known today? *(because the story is told in third-person limited point of view; that is, the reader is told only what Pentaquod knows)*
What are the advantages and disadvantages to this point of view? *(Accept reasonable responses: Advantages—makes us feel we are exploring with Pentaquod; heightens suspense. Disadvantage—sometimes we have to guess or fill in facts not available to him.)*
CRITICAL: MAKING JUDGMENTS

2 CHARACTER'S MOTIVATIONS

Why do you think Pentaquod observes the bird so long and carefully? *(Accept reasonable responses: He has fond memories of such birds; he is curious about the natural world; he wants to see how many fish are in the waters.)*
INFERENTIAL: DRAWING CONCLUSIONS

The island was low-lying, but its stately trees rose so high and so unevenly that they created an impression of elevation. Oak, maple, sweetgum, chestnut, birch, towering pines and iridescent holly grew so thickly that the earth itself could scarcely be seen, and it was these trees which protected Pentaquod after he dragged his canoe ashore and collapsed from lack of food and sleep.

When he awoke he became aware of one of earth's most pleasing sensations: he was lying on a bed of pine needles, soft and aromatic, and when he looked upward he could not see the sky, for the pines grew so straight and tall that their branches formed a canopy which sunlight could not penetrate. The covering gave him confidence, and before he resumed his sleep he muttered, "This is a good place, this place of trees."

He was awakened by a sound he could not immediately identify. It was warlike and terrifying, coming at him from a spot directly overhead. It echoed ominously: *"Kraannk, kraannk, kraannk!"*

In fear he leaped to his feet, but as he stood there under the tall trees, preparing to defend himself, he burst into laughter at his foolishness, for when he listened to the cry again, he remembered where he had heard it. *"Kraannk, kraannk!"* It was Fishing-long-legs, one of the most ingratiating birds of the rivers and marshlands.

1 There it stood, knee-deep in water: tall, thin, awkward, many hands high, with extremely long legs and rumpled white head. Its most prominent feature was a long yellowish bill, which it kept pointed downward at the water. Infrequently, when Pentaquod was young, this voracious fisherman had visited the Susquehanna to feed, wading tiptoe among the reeds, and often Pentaquod, while playing, had tried to imitate its movements.

2 Now Pentaquod stood silent, watching the bird with affection as it stalked slowly, clumsily along the muddy shore, and out into the water until its bony knees were submerged. Then, with a dart of its long neck so swift that Pentaquod could not follow, it speared its sharp beak into the water and caught a fish. Raising its head, it tossed the fish in the air, catching it as it descended. With a gulp, it swallowed the fish, and Pentaquod could see the progress of the meal as it slowly passed down the extended gullet. For some time he stayed in the shadows, watching as the bird caught fish after fish. He must have made some sound, for the bird turned suddenly toward him, ran a few ungainly steps along the

460

Vocabulary Strategy Have students identify a word they know that is part of the word *aromatic* in the second paragraph. *(aroma)* Then have them guess the meaning of *aromatic*, based on its root and the context. ("fragrant; sweet-smelling") Help them practice pronouncing the two words, noting how the accented syllable changes. STRATEGY: STRUCTURAL ANALYSIS/CONTEXT CLUES

Second-Language Support Point out to students that *bill* (paragraph 5) is a word that has many different meanings in English. Here it refers to a bird's beak. Have peer tutors provide an illustrated guide to other meanings of the word.

shore, then rose in slow, extended, lovely flight. *"Kraannk, kraannk!"* it cried as it passed overhead.

Knowing that there would be ample food, if he could but catch it, Pentaquod pulled his canoe farther inland, hiding it among the oaks and maples which lined the shore, for he knew that he must explore this island quickly. And as he moved among the trees and came to a meadow, he heard the comforting cry so familiar in his days along the great river. *"Bob-white! Bob-white!"* Now the call came from his left, then from a clump of grass to his right and sometimes from a spot almost under his feet, but always it was as clear and distinct as if an uncle who could whistle had been standing at his side. *"Bob-white!"* It was the call of the quail, that sly bird with the brown-and-white head. Of all the birds that flew, this was the best eating, and if this island held a multitude, Pentaquod could not only survive on his fish but eat like a chieftain with his quail.

With extreme caution, he started inland, noticing everything, aware **3** that his life might depend upon the carefulness of his observation. With every step he found only reassurance and never a sign of danger: nut trees laden with midsummer shells not yet ripe; droppings of rabbits, and the signs that foxes lived here, and the location of brambled berry bushes, and the woody nests of eagles, and the honeysuckle twisting among the lower branches of the cedar trees.

It was an island rich in signs and promises. On such an island a man with intelligence could live well, if he worked many hours each day, but in spite of its favorable omens Pentaquod was not ready to commit **4** himself to it, for he could not tell whether it was populated by other people, or what its temperament might be in a storm.

He kept probing, and satisfied himself that it was more extensive west to east than it was north to south. A deep bay cutting in from the east almost met a stream in the south, nearly severing the island; the eastern portion of this division was markedly richer than the western. He walked beneath majestic oaks until he reached the eastern tip, and there he stood, dumbfounded, for wherever he looked he saw a grand expanse of water forming itself into bays and creeks and coves and even small rivers for as far as he could see. And along the shores of these varied waters rose land of the most inviting nature: at times broad fields, at other times gently rising land covered with trees even taller than those

461

---

3 CHARACTERIZATION
What details convince Pentaquod that there is an ample food supply on the island? *(the cry of the quail, the nut trees and berry bushes, the signs of rabbits and foxes)*
LITERAL: NOTING IMPORTANT DETAILS

What does Pentaquod's observation of these details tell you about him? *(He is a careful observer of nature, well acquainted with its creatures, and knows how to survive in the wilderness.)*
INFERENTIAL: DRAWING CONCLUSIONS

---

4 FORESHADOWING
What hints tell you that Pentaquod may encounter some difficulty on the island? *(He puts off his decision to stay until he can learn whether there are other people on the island and how the island fares in a storm.)*
INFERENTIAL: DRAWING CONCLUSIONS

Teaching Tip The largest bay in the eastern United States, the Chesapeake, is bordered by Maryland and Virginia. About 200 miles long and 3 to 25 miles wide, the bay is created by the Susquehanna, Potomac, and other rivers that flow into it. Captain John Smith of the Jamestown colony was an early explorer of the bay, and his discoveries led to European settlements. Known for its abundant fish and shellfish, the bay now suffers from pollution by sewage and industrial wastes, which threaten its wildlife.

on the island, and everywhere the impression of opulence, and quietness, and gentle living.

It was the most congenial place he had ever seen. He judged that in a storm this sleeping body of water might have the capacity for considerable turbulence, and he was certain that before he could possess any part of this wonderland he would have to contend with its present owners, who might be just as cantankerous as the Susquehannocks, but of one thing he was certain: along this splendid river he wished to spend the rest of his life.

He had no sooner come to this decision than a snorting kind of sound attracted his attention, and he turned to look behind him, among the trees, and there stood a huge-eyed doe with two brown-speckled fawns. The three dear halted in rigid attention, staring at this stranger. Then the inquisitive doe cocked her head, and this almost undetectable action released the fawns, and they began to move cautiously toward Pentaquod, little deer on unsteady legs exploring their new world.

When they had moved quite close to Pentaquod their suspicious mother gave a cough, and the babies leaped sideways, ran in distracted circles, then stopped. Seeing that nothing harmful had happened, they moved back toward Pentaquod, lifting their spindly legs in delightful awkwardness, probing with their great eyes.

"Heh!" Pentaquod whispered. The fawns stared at him, and one moved closer.

"Heh!" The foremost fawn cocked its little head, waited, then resumed its approach. When it had come so close that Pentaquod could have reached out and touched it, the doe gave a warning snort, leaped aside, raised her white tail and darted back into the woods. The trailing fawn did likewise, but the one closest to Pentaquod became confused, or stubborn, and did not follow the others to safety. It simply stood there, staring at this stranger, and after a moment the mother returned in a series of fine leaps, swept past the inquisitive fawn and lured it into the trees.

Fish and quail and deer! Pentaquod thought. And if one finds seed, maize and probably pumpkins. Turkeys too, if I guess right. And not many people, judging so far. This is the right place.

He returned to his canoe, caught some fish for supper, made a small fire and, with a large handful of blackberries to accent the smoking fish,

462

463

ARTIST'S CRAFT

How does the illustration help you to put yourself in Pentaquod's place as he explores the island? *(Accept reasonable responses: The three deer appear to be looking at me just as they look at Pentaquod; I see the scene as Pentaquod sees it).*
CRITICAL: MAKING JUDGMENTS

5 PLOT: COMPLICATION

What clues does Pentaquod observe that suggest there may be some problems involved in living on the island? *(no signs of habitation, no signs that people had ever grown crops there)*
LITERAL: NOTING IMPORTANT DETAILS

Why does he decide to ignore these signs? *(He understands why most people would prefer safer areas inland, but he is willing to accept the risk of storms to have the island to himself.)*
INFERENTIAL: SUMMARIZING

6 CHARACTER'S EMOTIONS

Did you find Pentaquod's feelings about the smell of skunk surprising? Explain your answer. Why might his opinion of the smell be different from ours? *(Most students probably find a skunk odor unpleasant. They may speculate that someone who lives close to nature and is used to natural smells might find such smells comforting.)*
INFERENTIAL: COMPARING AND CONTRASTING

fed well. He slept well, too, except that long before dawn he heard in the sky overhead the cry he would always associate with his first exploration of this river: *"Kraannk, kraannk!"* It was Fishing-long-legs coming back to patrol the shore.

5 In the days that followed, Pentaquod explored every corner of the island and concluded that whereas others might know of it, they certainly did not think enough of it to build their homes here, for he could find no sign of habitation. And so far as he could ascertain, not even the meadows that appeared at curious intervals among the trees had ever grown corn or squash, and on none of the headlands facing the island could he detect any indication of either homes or cultivated fields.

This did not disturb him. If land as congenial as this existed upriver, there would be no reason for people to settle near the mouth; it would be much safer inland. Storms coming off the bay would be diminished and distances across water shortened. Perhaps the land would be richer, too, and there might be other advantages which he could not envisage. But on one point he was satisfied: life here would be good.

For the time being he quit his speculations, accepting the boon he had been granted. He built himself a small, well-hidden wigwam inland from the northern shore, using bent saplings for the frame and abundant river grasses for the roof. He found it so easy to catch fish that he did not even have to go after them in his canoe: the large brown-speckled ones with the blunt snouts swam up to him determined to be caught, and whereas he had been unable yet to trap any of the numerous bob-whites, he had shot one deer, which would feed him for some time. A fox strolled by one afternoon, and one night a skunk made things odorous.

6 He rather liked the smell of skunk, if it didn't come too close. It reminded him of the woods which he had trailed as a boy, of cold autumn nights, and the snugness of winter. It was the smell of nature, heavy and pervasive: it assured him that life in all its complexity was thriving. He had rarely seen a skunk, and he saw none now, but he was pleased that they shared the island with him.

It was his friend Fishing-long-legs who introduced him to one of the strangest experiences of the eastern shore. The blue-feathered bird with the long beak had flown in one evening with its accustomed croaking cry and was now probing the shallow waters along the shore, ignoring the man to whom it had become accustomed. Suddenly it shot its fierce bill

464

deep into the water and came up with a struggling something Pentaquod had not seen before.

It was larger than a man's hand, seemed to have numerous legs that squirmed in the fading sunlight and was brown-green in color. The bird was obviously pleased with its catch, for it threw it in the air, severed it with one snap of its beak, gulped down one half, allowing the other to fall into the water. The swallowed portion was so big and with so many **7** protruding legs that it required time and effort to maneuver it down the long gullet, but once this was accomplished, the bird retrieved and ate the other half. Having enjoyed a feast of this kind, it did not bother with mere fish. With a short run it rose in the air, uttered its mournful croaking and soared away.

Pentaquod went to where the bird had feasted, searching for clues. There were none. The bird had eaten everything. Next day he went there with his fishing line, but caught nothing. However, some days later he watched as Fishing-long-legs caught another of these morsels, enjoying it even more than before, and Pentaquod crept close to see if he could determine what it was that the bird was eating. He discovered nothing he had not seen before: bigger than a man's hand, many legs, brown-green in color, so soft that it could easily be bitten in half.

He was determined to solve this mystery, and the first clue came one day while he walked along the southern shore of his island: washed up on the beach and obviously dead lay a creature much like the one the bird had been catching. It was the right size; it had many feet, or what passed **8** for feet; and it was brown-green, with touches of blue underneath. But there the similarity stopped, for this dead animal was encased in a shell so hard that no bird could eat it. Also, its two front legs had formidable jaws with serrated, heavy teeth which could, if the animal were alive, inflict substantial harm.

How could the bird cut this shell in half? Pentaquod asked himself, and then, an even more perplexing question: And how could he swallow it if he did? He tapped the hard substance and knew there was no possible way for that bird to swallow that shell.

For ten days he tried to catch one of these strange creatures on his line and failed, and yet twice in that period he saw Fishing-long-legs catch one, cut it in half and force the food down its long neck. In frustration, he realized that this was a mystery he was not destined to solve.

465

7 HUMOR
How does the author's use of details create a humorous effect in his description of the bird eating?
(The details help readers picture how ridiculous the bird must have looked trying to maneuver the large creature with protruding legs down its long gullet.)
CRITICAL: MAKING JUDGMENTS

Based on the details the author gives, can you guess the mystery creature the bird is eating? *(Accept reasonable responses: crab, lobster.)*
INFERENTIAL: SPECULATING

Teaching Tip If students do not figure out the identity of the mysterious sea creature, tell them that it is the blue crab, the shellfish delicacy most identified with Chesapeake Bay. In the summer, the crabs lose their shells and are marketed as "softshell crabs." Blue crabs are most common in shallow waters and are a favorite food of the great blue heron, the long-legged bird mentioned in the selection.

9 MOOD

How does the mood, or feeling, of the selection begin to change here? *(Up until now, the mood has been optimistic, peaceful. At this point, it becomes ominous.)*
INFERENTIAL: COMPARING AND CONTRASTING

10 METAPHOR

Why do you think the author describes the clouds as "galloping"? *(By comparing them to a galloping horse, he suggests their speed and power and gives the impression that they have a life of their own.)*
INFERENTIAL: MAKING COMPARISONS

He did, however, discover two facts about his home that disturbed him. The more he explored the two deep cuts which came close to bisecting the island, the more he realized that some day the arms must meet, cutting the island in half, and if this could be done, why might there not evolve other cuts to fragment it further?

9 His second discovery came as the consequence of a sudden and devastating storm. The midpoint of summer had passed and life on the island had been a growing joy; this was really an almost ideal place to live, and he supposed that later on, when he had traveled upriver to establish contact with whatever tribes occupied the area, he would become a member of their unit. But for the time being he was content with his solitary paradise.

It had been a hot day, with heavy moist air, and in the late afternoon a bank of towering clouds gathered in the southwest, on the opposite side of the bay. With a swiftness that he had never witnessed in the north this congregation of blackness started rushing eastward, and even though the sun remained shining over Pentaquod's head, it was obvious that a storm of some magnitude must soon break.

Still the sun shone; still the sky remained clear. Deer moved deeper into the forest and shore birds retreated to their nests, although the only **10** sign of danger was that galloping cloud bank approaching the bay.

Pentaquod watched its arrival. It struck the distant western shore with enormous fury, turning what had been placid water into turbulent, crested waves leaping and tossing white spume into the air. The clouds moved so swiftly that they required only moments to cross the bay, their progress marked by the wildly leaping waves.

With the storm came an immense amount of rain, falling in sheets slanting eastward. For it to speed over the last portion of the bay took only a fragment of time, and then the storm was striking Pentaquod, descending on him in a fury he had not witnessed before. Great jagged flashes of lightning tore through the sky, followed almost instantly by shattering claps of thunder; there was no echo, for the world was drowned in rain. Winds of extraordinary power ripped along the surface of the bay, lashing it into waves of pounding force.

But Pentaquod was not afraid of the storm, and next morning, when it had passed and he surveyed his island, he did not find the damage extensive. He had seen storms before, rather violent ones which swept

466

Second-Language Support

Point out to students that *bank* is another English word that has several very different meanings. Tell them that some of these meanings include "business that lends money," "small container for saving money," "place where supplies are kept in reserve," "a pile or heap," and "the land bordering a river." Ask which meaning seems to apply to the use of the word in the fourth paragraph.

down the river valley of his home, and although this one had been swifter and more thunderous, it was merely an exaggeration of what he had long known. The trees knocked down were larger than any he had seen go down in the north, and that was about it. If storms on the island were no worse than this, he could abide them.

What was it, then, that disturbed him, causing him to wonder about his new home? After his cursory inspection of the island, and after satisfying himself that his yellow canoe had survived, he behaved like any prudent husbandman and started checking the general situation, desiring to see if any animals had been killed or streams diverted, and as he came to a spot on the northwestern tip of the island, he noticed that the storm, and more particularly the pounding waves, had carried away a substantial portion of the shore. Tall pines and oaks which had marked this point had been undercut and now lay sprawled in the water side by side, like the bodies of dead warriors after battle.

Wherever he went along the western shore he saw this same loss of land. The tragedy of the storm was not that it had knocked down a few trees, for more would grow, and not that it had killed a few fish, for others would breed, but that it had eaten away a substantial edge of the island, and this was a permanent loss. Pentaquod, looking at the destruction, decided that he would abandon this island, congenial **11** though it was, and look farther inland.

THINK IT OVER

1. *What are some of the things that Pentaquod discovered that make him think "this is the right place"?*
2. *What mystery is Pentaquod determined to solve?*
3. *Why do you think Pentaquod decided to abandon the island?*

12

WRITE

Design and write an advertisement encouraging tourists to visit Pentaquod's island.

13

467

Returning to the Predictions Invite students to discuss the predictions they made before reading and tell whether those predictions changed as they read.

Returning to the Purpose for Reading Ask students to discuss why Pentaquod's reason for leaving the island outweighed all his reasons for staying. (Though food was abundant, the destruction of a piece of the island by the storm was permanent. Pentaquod probably felt that storms of greater force would cause worse damage and would be a constant threat to a peaceful existence.)

11 PLOT: RESOLUTION
Were you surprised that Pentaquod decided to leave? Would you have made the same decision? *(Responses will vary.)*
CRITICAL: MAKING JUDGMENTS

12 THINK IT OVER
1. *Accept reasonable responses: plentiful food, beautiful land, no people.*
LITERAL: NOTING IMPORTANT DETAILS
2. *to figure out how to eat a hard-shelled creature he's seen a heron eat*
LITERAL: NOTING IMPORTANT DETAILS
3. *He saw that storms were wearing away the coastline, and he wanted a permanent home.*
INFERENTIAL: DRAWING CONCLUSIONS

13 WRITE
To help students get started, you may want to suggest that they list features that would make the island a good place to visit.

Accept reasonable responses. Students should use descriptive details appealing to tourists.
CREATIVE: DESCRIBING

WRITER'S JOURNAL page 82: Writing a creative response

Writer's Journal

Conversation with James A. Michener

ABOUT THE AUTHOR

Rolando Hinojosa-Smith (1929–), Michener's interviewer, is a Mexican American novelist who grew up near the Texas-Mexico border. He has captured the history of this region in his novels.

SELECTION SUMMARY

Hinojosa-Smith questions Michener about the techniques of observation that have enabled Michener to portray settings vividly. The two writers discuss how students can become better observers and writers.

1 INTERVIEW: MAIN IDEA
What is Michener's secret to writing well about places? *(He says to visit or revisit them so you know them well and they are fresh in your mind.)*
INFERENTIAL: SUMMARIZING

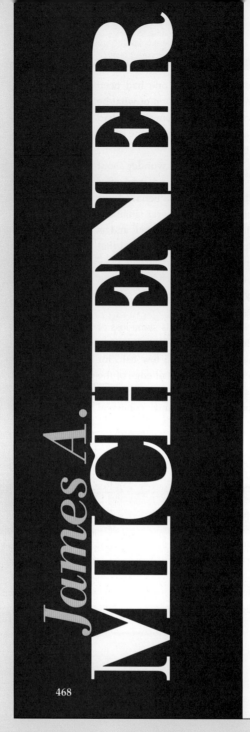

James A. MICHENER

468

Conversation with James A. Michener

by Rolando Hinojosa-Smith

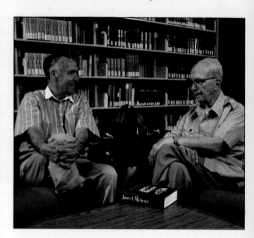

Novelist Rolando Hinojosa-Smith, right, Director of the Texas Center for Writers at the University of Texas, and best-selling author James A. Michener discuss important aspects of writing.

Mr. Hinojosa-Smith: An outstanding feature of your writing is the sense of place and time, the specifics and the details. Let me ask you this: did you visit or revisit the area before you wrote *Chesapeake*, and did you take the route that Pentaquod took?

Mr. Michener: Yes. I can say specifically that, except for my writing about the moon and the men on the moon, I have been to every place that I have written about. I have gotten to know the places very well. Rolando, if you wanted me to write **1** about the little town in which I grew up, which I know intimately, I wouldn't dare do it unless I went back—to remind myself of how much I don't

---

Building Background

Encourage students to evaluate Michener's writing in "The Right Place," paying particular attention to his use of details of setting. Discuss how writers might get ideas for places in which to set stories and novels, and ask volunteers to name some places they have lived in or visited that would make interesting settings for a story.

Strategic Reading

Interview Based on students' discussion of Michener's writing, have them predict what types of questions an interviewer might want to ask him.

STUDENT-SET PURPOSE Ask students to use their predictions to frame a question they hope Michener will answer in the interview.

TEACHER-SET PURPOSE If students have difficulty setting a purpose independently, offer this suggestion: **What will Michener say about the art of writing, especially the art of describing places?**

remember. I never write without going back to places I already know.

Mr. Hinojosa-Smith: There is something about going back that I also find necessary. I need to be there to trigger this mechanism for details. How do you collect details about a place?

Mr. Michener: When I decide to write about an area, my wife goes ahead of me to find a place to live. Then I go there, and we maintain a very low profile for the first five or six months. I want to be there, I want to read the morning papers, I want to listen to the weather reports. I want to find out what's happening in politics. I want to go to the local grocery store and to the local restaurant so that I get a complete feel of the place. My wife is a very gregarious person—she loves people and she loves to talk, converse. And during that time she's making friends, so that by the time the six months is up, we are as ingrained in that situation as if we'd lived there for the last ten years.

Mr. Hinojosa-Smith: That's an interesting process.

Mr. Michener: And it works. She meets people and brings them home. She tells me I ought to talk with this person or that person. We go out, we go to the restaurants, we meet strangers who become friends. We find out what it's really like.

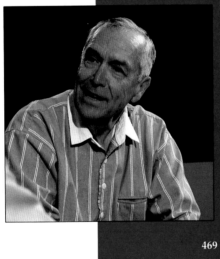

2 INTERVIEW: DETAILS
Which details show that Michener really wants to get to know the places he visits? *(He and his wife live in a place for at least five or six months; he reads the local newspapers, listens to weather reports, goes to the local restaurant and grocery, and meets people in the community.)*
LITERAL: NOTING IMPORTANT DETAILS

Vocabulary Strategy Help students determine the meaning of the word *gregarious* ("enjoying the company of other people, sociable") from the context of Michener's remarks on page 469.
STRATEGY: CONTEXT CLUES

3 Mr. Hinojosa-Smith: You learn specific details—weather, travel, living conditions, people's thinking. So when natives of an area read about the area, they say, "Well, this person really knows what he's talking about."

Mr. Michener: That is what I try to get. I would hate for anybody to say that Jim Michener flew in on an airplane and stayed one weekend and then wrote about us. They cannot say that, ever.

Mr. Hinojosa-Smith: Unfortunately, not all writers are that accurate. Scientists look at specific details and have to be accurate, and as writers we have to be just as careful. I don't think we're so different as observers. One has to be correct about the details.

Mr. Michener: That is true. I myself relate most often not to scientists but to geographers. We have that type of mind, for collecting and codifying and organizing.

4 Mr. Hinojosa-Smith: I wonder how we can talk to young people about becoming better observers. They can stop and smell the roses, but they should also look at them in some detail.

Mr. Michener: I would want them to remember the most important thing I said: that I could not write about a place without going back to look—to see how the streets run, what

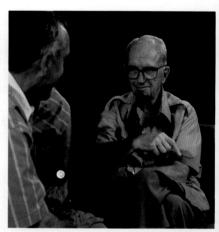

470

the houses look like, where the morning papers are delivered. All of that is the body of work that writers deal with, and they had better know what they're writing about. If there were a young person listening to us today who wanted to write a short story about a schoolroom in which a class is taking place, I would advise that girl or boy to look around that schoolroom very carefully, maybe spend twenty minutes. Where is the blackboard? What does it look like? How does the light fall on it? Where does your teacher sit? What is your desk like? Are there initials carved in it from former students? To a large degree that is what writing is made up of.

Mr. Hinojosa-Smith: Setting is what makes the act of writing easier and more difficult at the same time. When you fail to create a complete, accurate setting, then you lose the reader's credibility.

Mr. Michener: If the setting is flabby or uninteresting or nonspecific, I think you lose the reader.

5

Mr. Hinojosa-Smith: I think young people reading this will realize the importance of specifics and details. They will begin to notice shades of difference in people, places, things. That's important. Details, I think, are what we need to begin writing.

Mr. Michener: If a young person writes a story that is read to the

5 INTERVIEW: MAIN IDEA
Do you agree with what the two writers say about the importance of "a complete, accurate setting"? Explain your answer. *(Responses will vary.)*
CRITICAL: EXPRESSING PERSONAL OPINIONS

471

Second-Language Support
Students may not understand the phrase *shades of difference*. Tell them that the phrase refers to small differences among things that might seem similar at first glance. The meaning of *shades* in this context is taken from art, where it refers to variations of a single color, such as sky blue, navy blue, and royal blue.

MEETING INDIVIDUAL NEEDS

Oral Rereading Pairs of students may enjoy role-playing what they consider the most important part of the interview. Have them reread the interview silently to choose the part they want to read. Then have one partner read Michener's words and the other partner read Hinojosa-Smith's. Give the partners time to rehearse, and then have them present their readings to the class.

6 THEME/MESSAGE
What connection is there between being a good reader and being a good writer? *(Accept reasonable responses: A good reader becomes familiar with the techniques of good writers and may be inspired to do as good a job.)*
INFERENTIAL: DRAWING CONCLUSIONS

7 THINK IT OVER
1. *Accept reasonable responses: Like geographers, writers must observe, categorize, and describe details of places.*
INFERENTIAL: MAKING COMPARISONS
2. *Accept reasonable responses: Most students will acknowledge the influence of reading on writing.*
CRITICAL: EXPRESSING PERSONAL OPINIONS
3. *Accept reasonable responses: Details of setting are readily observable to anyone, but describing them exactly is difficult.*
INFERENTIAL: DRAWING CONCLUSIONS

8 WRITE
To help students get started, you may want to suggest that they use a prewriting chart like the following:

What I See	How It Looks

Accept reasonable responses. Students should include many precise details.
CREATIVE: DESCRIBING

class, and the class hears familiar facts and realizes, "Yes, she had that right, that's just the way it is" or "I hadn't thought about that, but that's the way Miss Kinderkleine sits when she's reading to us" or "That's where the bookcase is," then the writer gains credibility with the very people he or she's writing for.

Mr. Hinojosa-Smith: That's important. Once you establish credibility with a small group, it can also be done with a wider audience.
Mr. Michener: And I would suppose that anyone listening to what you and I are saying would be able to describe the classroom in a very real way.

Mr. Hinojosa-Smith: Perhaps even better than two old pros! There's something about writing that young people should also remember. In addition to having an attention to details, they have to have a love for reading. They should avail themselves of books in school and in public libraries, the way we did. We had a fine lending library in my hometown.
6 Mr. Michener: As I said once, a young person who really wanted to be a writer would have no chance of being successful unless by the age of twenty-two he or she wore glasses. If you haven't read enough, you haven't used your eyes enough! That was a joke, but do remember it. You have to read in order to know how to write.

Think It Over

7
1. *Why do you think Mr. Michener said that good writers have to have some of the same skills as geographers?*
2. *Do you agree with Mr. Michener when he jokingly said that in order to be a successful writer, one should wear glasses by the age of twenty-two?*
3. *What do you think Mr. Hinojosa-Smith meant when he said, "Setting is what makes the act of writing easier and more difficult at the same time"?*

Write

8 *Follow Mr. Michener's directions to write a description of your classroom.*

472

Returning to the Predictions Invite students to discuss the predictions they made before reading and tell whether those predictions changed as they read the interview.

Returning to the Purpose for Reading Ask students to discuss whether the interview helped them understand Michener's views on writing, especially the importance of observing in person the places he describes. Also, ask whether the interview answered their own questions about Michener.

SURVIVAL

What do Elena from "Time: The Missing Element" and Pentaquod from "The Right Place" have in common that helps them to be survivors?

· ·

If you had to trade places with either Elena or Pentaquod, which environment would you choose? Why?

· ·

WRITER'S WORKSHOP Imagine that you are Pentaquod or Elena and you meet someone who needs information about how to survive where you do. Write a how-to paragraph giving suggestions and guidelines for survival in that particular place.

473

Survival

Remind students that they have read about the hardships two characters encountered while trying to survive in primitive environments. Help them recall how and why each character was prepared to meet this challenge. Explain that the activities on page 473 will help them think further about ideas that were addressed in these selections.

Note that pages 473A–473B provide support for applying the writing process to the last question.

---

1 Have students first identify the traits that helped each character survive and then point out the traits that both characters have in common. *(Accept reasonable responses: good knowledge of nature, strong powers of observation, self-reliance)*
INFERENTIAL: SYNTHESIZING

---

2 Have students consider each environment before making a choice. *(Responses will vary.)*
CRITICAL: MAKING JUDGMENTS

Writer's Workshop
See pages 473A–473B for suggestions for applying the writing process. Students may choose to be either character. Responses should draw on only one story. You may prefer to allow students to respond to the theme in their own way. WRITING PROCESS: A HOW-TO PARAGRAPH

Writer's Workshop
A HOW-TO PARAGRAPH

Before students begin, ask them what is most important to them when trying to follow instructions or directions. Point out that when they explain a process, their explanation should be clear, complete, accurate, and useful to the people who will be using it. Ask students to give examples of directions or instructions that they have found useful. Suggest that students refer to the Handbook in the *Writer's Journal* as they write, revise, and proofread their how-to paragraphs.

Prewriting

Before they write, have students
- choose a setting, either an island in the Chesapeake Bay or on the British Columbian seacoast.
- think about their purpose for writing and their audience.
- use a list to collect information they might include. Encourage students to include facts and details from the selection they chose. The list might cover these elements:

---
1. finding food
2. building or finding shelter
3. examining the environment for threats
4. keeping warm
5. avoiding poisonous plants
6. coping with fear and loneliness

Suggest students arrange the list items in order of importance.

Drafting

Ask students to write a draft of their how-to paragraphs. Remind them to
- use a specific title such as "How to Survive in (place name)."
- write the steps in order of importance.
- write clear and smooth transitions between the most to least important steps.
- write freely without worrying about spelling, punctuation, or grammar.

COMPUTER CONNECTION Students may want to use a computer during the responding and revising stage. Partners can type in comments and questions they may have about the how-to paragraphs, using a different font, and the writers can clarify their paragraphs and then erase the queries.

Responding and Revising

Have each student read his or her draft aloud to a partner. Encourage the pair to discuss the overall clarity of the draft, using the following tips. Then, have students revise their work.

- Does the draft describe the process step by step? If not, add time words or phrases such as *first, next,* and *then.*
- Are the steps presented clearly enough so a reader can follow them? If not, replace weak, vague words with precise ones. (See the Language/ Literature Link below.)

STUDENT SELF-ASSESSMENT OPTION   Students may use the Writing Self-Assessment Checklist in the *Portfolio Teacher's Guide.* Suggest that as they use the checklist, they focus on the order of the paragraph and the preciseness of the language.

Proofreading

Offer these tips for proofreading their work:
- Check for correct punctuation and capitalization.
- Mark any words that may be misspelled. Find out in a dictionary the correct spellings.

Publishing

Discuss with students various publishing options. Some students may wish to read their how-to paragraphs aloud to classmates and then save them in their reading/writing portfolio. Others may wish to collect them in a class survival manual.

LANGUAGE/LITERATURE LINK

Using Precise Language

Review the meaning of precise language by offering a negative example. Write a vague direction on the board, such as "Find something to eat." Ask students why this advice would not be helpful to someone stranded in the wilderness. Then have them suggest alternatives. For an example of a precisely described meal, turn to page 465, paragraph two, of "The Right Place." Ask students to point to examples of exact words and phrases. *(squirmed, severed, gulped, protruding legs, gullet)* Have students review their paragraphs for vague or imprecise words and check a thesaurus for substitutes.

Speaking Option

PROCESS SPEECH   You may wish to adapt the *Writer's Workshop* to allow students to present their how-to paragraphs orally. Have students follow the guidelines for Prewriting, Drafting, and Responding and Revising. Offer these speaking tips to help students deliver their speeches:

- Speak clearly and loudly, without shouting.
- If necessary, paraphrase or repeat complicated steps so that your audience understands them.
- Sketch a map or a diagram to help your audience visualize the process.

Have students give their speeches to small groups of classmates.

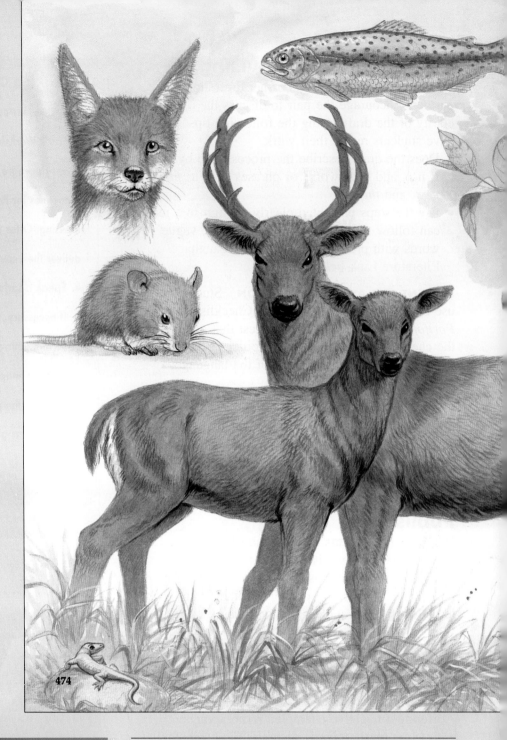

Watching Nature

Have students look at the illustration and read the theme introduction on Student Anthology page 475. Elicit from volunteers what they know about animals in the wild and about hawks and cranes in particular. Ask why these birds might be the focus of the theme "Watching Nature." Give students a moment to read and think about the selection titles. Encourage speculation on the meaning of "Free Flight" and "First Sighting."

PACING This theme has been designed to take about two weeks to complete, depending on your students' needs.

474

Management Options

THE LITERATURE-BASED CLASSROOM Providing a literature-rich curriculum creates unique classroom management challenges. Some management options for the selections in this theme follow.

PROOFREADING CONFERENCE When students reach the proofreading stage of the writing process and begin to check grammar, punctuation, spelling, and capitalization, have them work with a partner to review their writing. Provide students with a checklist. If a student needs individual help, arrange a conference. Discuss the piece, and make corrections on a separate sheet of paper.

THEME

WATCHING NATURE

The soaring flight of a sparrow hawk . . . the hidden nest of a sandhill crane . . . the trumpeting cry of a startled bird. . . . Discover the thrill of observing nature in the following selections.

CONTENTS

475

STUDENTS AT RISK

You may wish to display pictures of the birds and other animals described in the theme selections. Write their names on the board. Challenge students to match the name with the picture of the correct bird or animal.

GIFTED AND TALENTED

Challenge students to take the point of view of the sparrow hawk in "Free Flight" or the porcupine in "First Sighting" and write a description of its experiences with humans. Also see *Challenge Cards*.

SPECIAL EDUCATION STUDENTS

You may wish to provide a copy of each graphic aid you will be using throughout the unit theme to students with low vision who may not be able to see the board clearly.

LIMITED ENGLISH PROFICIENT STUDENTS

Some students may misplace adjectives when writing their descriptions of an animal for the Writer's Workshop activity on Student Anthology page 501. Review the use and placement of adjectives in English.

PARENT-TEACHER CONFERENCE SUGGESTIONS

- Give parents time to share their questions and concerns about their child's progress.
- Use samples from the student's portfolio to point out strengths and weaknesses. Share with parents your strategies for ensuring the student's progress and suggest ways they might help their child at home.
- End the conference on a positive note.

READING/WRITING PORTFOLIO
Instruct students to keep in their portfolios their writing responses to the theme selections. Remind them also to add to their personal journals notes on their independent reading.

FREE FLIGHT

by Loren Eiseley

LOREN EISELEY (1907–1977) was born in Lincoln, Nebraska. Even when he was young, he was very interested in fossils and in writing. In a high school English essay, he declared, "I want to be a nature writer." He became, along the way, a poet, a traveler, and an anthropology professor. In 1948, during a six-month attack of deafness, Eiseley began writing personal nature essays, but *The Immense Journey*—from which "Free Flight" has been taken—was not published until 1957. Eiseley was the author of several inspirational nature books and the subject of the film *Cosmos, The Universe of Loren Eiseley.*

OTHER BOOKS ABOUT BIRDS AND NATURE
Birds of Prey by Jill Bailey. Facts on File, 1988.
AVERAGE
An Owl in the House: A Naturalist's Diary by Bernd Heinrich, adapted by Alice Calaprice. Little, Brown, 1990. CHALLENGING

"**I** want to be a nature writer."

SELECTION SUMMARY
In this excerpt, Eiseley describes his assignment to capture live birds for a zoo. Arriving in the high country before his crew, he entered a dilapidated cabin where he knew birds would roost. Using a ladder and a spotlight, Eiseley climbed toward a shelf where sparrow hawks were sleeping. When he seized a female bird, her mate attacked him, lacerating his hand. The female escaped, but Eiseley captured the attacking male. Next morning, Eiseley had a change of heart and freed the male hawk, which flew skyward to join his mate.

LESSON PLANNER	Materials	Integrated Curriculum	Meeting Individual Needs
1 **READING LITERATURE** pp. 475B–481	Student Anthology pp. 476–481 Transparency 25 Second-Language Support Manual Practice Book p. 130 Integrated Spelling p. 63 Integrated Spelling T.E. pp. 84–85 Response Card 7: Free Response	Spelling Spelling Pretest Spelling-Vocabulary Connection (the /əl/ sound)	Second-Language Support Vocabulary 475C Strategic Reading 475D Cooperative Reading 476, 480
2 **RESPONDING TO LITERATURE** pp. 481A–481D	Writer's Journal p. 83 Practice Book p. 131 Integrated Spelling p. 64 Integrated Spelling T.E. pp. 84–85	Vocabulary Workshop Reviewing Key Words Extending Vocabulary Writing About the Literature Speaking/Listening Spelling Review	Cooperative Learning 481B, 481C
3 **LEARNING THROUGH LITERATURE** pp. 481E–481J	Practice Book pp. 132–134	Science Ecology Art Multicultural	Challenge 481E, 481F, 481G, 481H Cooperative Learning 481G, 481H

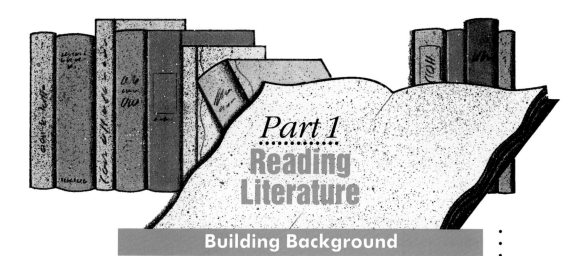

Part 1
Reading Literature

Building Background

Access prior knowledge and develop vocabulary concepts.

Tell students that they will be reading an autobiographical excerpt titled "Free Flight." It is a true account of a scientist's experience with wildlife. Ask students to share what they know about the lives of wild birds and of birds in captivity. Remind students that by recalling what they already know, they will prepare themselves to understand and enjoy "Free Flight."

captive — **Birds** — wild

Have students quickwrite a response.

Ask students whether they think some birds and animals should be captured for zoos. Have students write an immediate response and a reason.

Vocabulary Strategies

Introduce Key Words and strategies.

Tell students that "Free Flight" contains some words that may be unfamiliar. Display Transparency 25, or write the paragraph on the board.

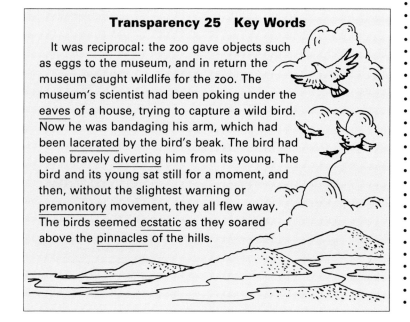

Transparency 25   Key Words

It was reciprocal: the zoo gave objects such as eggs to the museum, and in return the museum caught wildlife for the zoo. The museum's scientist had been poking under the eaves of a house, trying to capture a wild bird. Now he was bandaging his arm, which had been lacerated by the bird's beak. The bird had been bravely diverting him from its young. The bird and its young sat still for a moment, and then, without the slightest warning or premonitory movement, they all flew away. The birds seemed ecstatic as they soared above the pinnacles of the hills.

KEY WORDS DEFINED

reciprocal   done or given in return, mutual

eaves   overhanging lower edge of a roof

lacerated   cut jaggedly, tore

diverting   distracting, deflecting

premonitory   giving warning

ecstatic   joyous, happy and excited

pinnacles   peaks or highest points

Have students read the paragraph silently using context clues, phonics, and structural analysis to figure out the meanings of the underlined words. Then ask a volunteer to read the paragraph aloud. Provide help with pronunciation if necessary.

Check students' understanding.

Have students demonstrate their understanding of the Key Words by using them to answer the following questions and riddles:

1. **I am underneath a roof, but I'm not a ceiling. What am I?** *(eaves)* STRATEGY: PRIOR KNOWLEDGE
2. **I am happy, but I'm not calm. What am I?** *(ecstatic)* STRATEGY: ANTONYMS
3. **If you climb to the top of one of me, you can't climb any higher. What am I?** *(pinnacles)* STRATEGY: EXPLANATION
4. **If something is unbroken and uncut, it is not this.** *(lacerated)* STRATEGY: ANTONYMS
5. **I can describe something that gives you a warning. What am I?** *(premonitory)* STRATEGY: EXPLANATION
6. **I am a word that means the opposite of** *focusing.* **What am I?** *(diverting)* STRATEGY: ANTONYMS
7. **If you give someone something and get nothing back, you cannot call the arrangement this.** *(reciprocal)* STRATEGY: EXPLANATION

Integrate spelling with vocabulary.

SPELLING-VOCABULARY CONNECTION *Integrated Spelling* page 63 reinforces spellings of the /əl/ sound in the following Key Words: *reciprocal, pinnacles.*

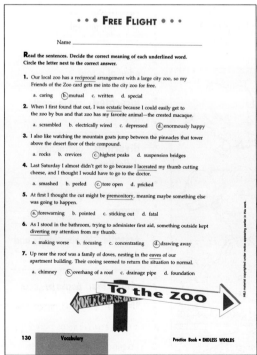

Practice Book

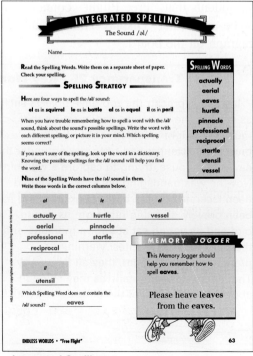

Integrated Spelling

PRACTICE BOOK
page 130: Reinforcing Key Words

INTEGRATED SPELLING
page 63: Writing and spelling words with the /əl/ sound

NOTE: These pages may be completed now or after students have read the selection.

Preview and Predict

Help students use prior knowledge and preview the selection.

Ask students to recall what they know about autobiography from reading excerpts such as "Mister Kinte!" and "The Platoon System." Point out that an autobiographical excerpt is a true story about something important in the writer's life. Then have students preview the selection.

Introduce the prior knowledge–prediction chart.

Remind students that before they start to read, they can focus their reading by thinking about what they already know and about what might happen. Have them record their prior knowledge and predictions on a chart like the one below.

PRIOR KNOWLEDGE–PREDICTION CHART

Prior Knowledge	Predictions	Actual Outcomes
Birds in the wild fly free.	*The birds Eiseley caught did not want to be confined. They escaped.*	
An autobiography tells about important experiences in the author's life.	*The experience in "Free Flight" was important to Eiseley. He stopped capturing animals.*	

PERSONAL JOURNAL Have students copy the chart in their personal journals, or have them use *Practice Book* page 131. (See page 481B in this Teacher's Edition.) Students can complete the chart as they read the story or afterward. (Students will return to the chart in Summarizing the Literature, after reading the selection.)

Setting a Purpose

Have students set purposes.

Have students use the second column of their charts to set a purpose for reading "Free Flight."

Model purpose-setting if necessary.

If students have difficulty setting a purpose for reading, model the thinking process:

> **I have already made some predictions about this selection. To set a purpose for reading, I will think about what will happen in the selection as a whole; for example, I will read to find out how the experience described in "Free Flight" affects Loren Eiseley.**

SECOND-LANGUAGE SUPPORT   Students may benefit from the Guided Reading activities and the additional guidance under the Student Anthology pages. (See *Second-Language Support Manual.*)

OPTIONS FOR READING

Independent Reading
Have students read the selection silently with their purpose for reading in mind.

Guided Reading
Follow the Guided Reading suggestions that appear on pages 476, 478–479 and 480. These suggestions model strategic reading.

Cooperative Reading
Reader response strategies appear on pages 476 and 480.

Numbered Annotations
Use the numbered annotations beside the Student Anthology pages to heighten students' appreciation of the selection.

Birds like the sparrow hawks in this excerpt are found in most parts of the world. (The general term *sparrow hawk* refers to a number of different species, some of which are technically falcons rather than hawks.) Sparrow hawks prey mainly on small birds, including sparrows, although the female, which is larger than the male, sometimes attacks birds as large as pigeons. The sparrow hawk generally stalks its prey before taking it by surprise.

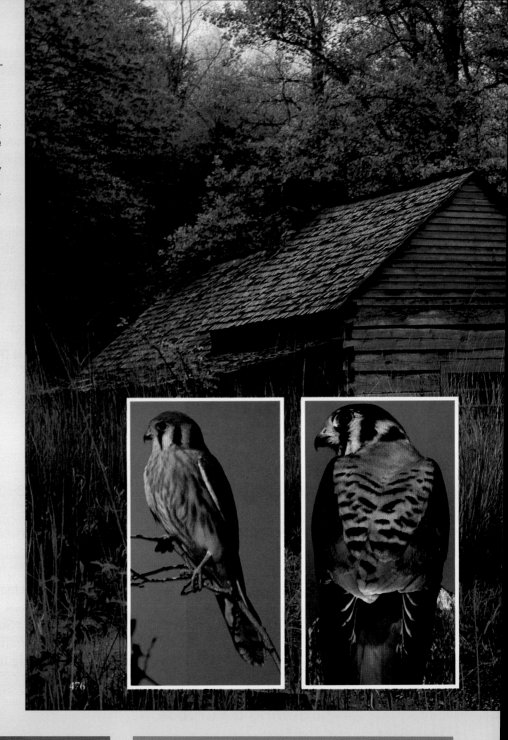

476

Guided Reading

SET PURPOSE/PREDICT: PAGES 476–479 Have students read to the bottom of page 479 to find out what happened when Eiseley set out to capture wild birds.

Cooperative Reading

READER RESPONSE STRATEGY: PAGES 476–481
Have students work in pairs. Ask each pair to decide whether to read silently or aloud and how frequently to stop. At designated stopping points, the members of each pair should respond freely to what they have read so far. Have pairs continue the procedure until they reach the end of the selection. (Response Card 7: Free Response, on page R68, gives complete directions for using the strategy.)

FREE FLIGHT

from *THE IMMENSE JOURNEY*
by Loren Eiseley

The word had come through to get them alive—birds, reptiles, anything. A zoo somewhere abroad needed restocking. It was one of those reciprocal matters in which science involves itself. Maybe our museum needed a stray ostrich egg and this was the payoff. Anyhow, my job was to help capture some birds and that was why I was there before the trucks.

The cabin had not been occupied for years. We intended to clean it out and live in it, but there were holes in the roof and the birds had come in and were roosting in the rafters. You could depend on it in a place like this, where everything blew away, and even a bird needed some place out of the weather and away from coyotes. A cabin going back to nature in a wild place draws them till they come in, listening at the eaves, I imagine, pecking softly among the shingles till they find a hole and then suddenly the place is theirs and man is forgotten.

477

1 POINT OF VIEW
What clues in the first paragraph tell you that this is an autobiography rather than a biography? *(The narrator uses words such as* our, my, *and* I.*)*
METACOGNITIVE: DRAWING CONCLUSIONS

2 SETTING
Where did the events take place? *(at a cabin in a wilderness)*
LITERAL: NOTING IMPORTANT DETAILS

Informal Assessment Informally assessing whether students are fulfilling the established purpose for reading involves asking questions like the following:

- Has this excerpt told you what you need to know to fulfill your purpose for reading?
- If so, what ideas and details have been the most important in helping you fulfill your purpose?
- If not, what has the excerpt failed to tell you that you needed or wanted to know?

This assessment will serve important instructional purposes: it will indicate how well students are focusing as they read, and it will encourage them to watch for and select details that fulfill their purpose for reading.

478

3 NARRATION: ACTIONS/EVENTS
What is the narrator "coming back" from? *(From a digression, or brief departure, from the main narrative; the digression is about events at a later time in his life.)*
What is he coming back to? *(to the main narrative and chronological sequence of events)*
INFERENTIAL: DETERMINING SEQUENCE

4 NARRATION: CHARACTER'S TRAITS
Do you think Eiseley should have been better prepared for his task? *(Accept reasonable responses: Yes; he ought to have anticipated that the birds might fight back; he ought to have worn heavy gloves.)*
CRITICAL: MAKING JUDGMENTS

Sometimes of late years I find myself thinking the most beautiful sight in the world might be the birds taking over New York after the last man has run away to the hills. I will never live to see it, of course, but I know just how it will sound because I've lived up high and I know the sort of watch birds keep on us. I've listened to sparrows tapping tentatively on the outside of air conditioners when they thought no one was listening, and I know how other birds test the vibrations that come up to them through the television aerials.

"Is he gone?" they ask, and the vibrations come up from below, "Not yet, not yet."

3 Well, to come back, I got the door open softly and I had the spotlight all ready to turn on and blind whatever birds there were so they couldn't see to get out through the roof. I had a short piece of ladder to put against the far wall, where there was a shelf on which I expected to make the biggest haul. I pushed the door open, the hinges squeaking only a little. A bird or two stirred—I could hear them—but nothing flew and there was a faint starlight through the holes in the roof.

I padded across the floor, got the ladder up and the light ready, and slithered up the ladder till my head and arms were over the shelf. Everything was dark as pitch except for the starlight at the little place back of the shelf near the eaves. With the light to blind them, they'd never make it. I had them. I reached my arm carefully over in order to be ready to seize whatever was there and I put the flash on the edge of the shelf where it would stand by itself when I turned it on. That way I'd be able to use both hands.

4 Everything worked perfectly except for one detail—I didn't know what kind of birds were there. I never thought about it at all, and it wouldn't have mattered if I had. My orders were to get something interesting. I snapped on the flash and sure enough there was a great beating and feathers flying, but instead of my having them, they, or rather he, had me. He had my hand, that is, and for a small hawk not much bigger than my fist he was doing all right. I heard him give one short metallic cry when the light

Cultural Awareness The sparrow hawk is sometimes used for hunting quail, especially in the Middle East. The bird's courage and speed inspired an ancient Persian proverb: "The sparrow hawk's body is small, but its heart is great." You may wish to discuss how this proverb applies to the selection after students have finished reading.

Guided Reading

MONITOR COMPREHENSION: PAGES 476–479
What happened when Eiseley set out to capture birds? (He caught a sparrow hawk with great difficulty, after it had wounded him in order to free its mate.) STRATEGIC READING: RETURNING TO PURPOSE

What have we learned about Eiseley so far?
(Accept reasonable responses: He had a genuine respect for animals; he didn't really want to capture them, but this was his job.) STRATEGIC READING: SUMMARIZING

went on and my hand descended on the bird beside him; after that he was busy with his claws, and his beak was sunk in my thumb. In the struggle I knocked the lamp over on the shelf, and his mate got her sight back and whisked neatly through the hole in the roof and off among the stars outside. It all happened in fifteen seconds and you might think I would have fallen down the ladder, but no, I had a professional reputation to keep up, and the bird, of course, made the mistake of thinking the hand was the enemy and not the eyes behind it. He chewed my thumb up pretty effectively and lacerated my hand with his claws, but in the end I got him, having two hands to work with.

He was a sparrow hawk and a fine young male in the prime of life. I was sorry not to catch the pair of them, but as I dripped blood and folded his wings carefully, holding him by the back so that he couldn't strike again, I had to admit the two of them might have been more than I could have handled under the circumstances. The little fellow had saved his mate by diverting me, and that was that. He was born to it, and made no outcry now, resting in my hand hopelessly, but peering toward me in the shadows behind the lamp with a fierce, almost indifferent glance. He neither gave nor expected mercy and something out of the high air passed from him to me, stirring a faint embarrassment.

I quit looking into that eye and managed to get my huge carcass with its fist full of prey back down the ladder. I put the bird in a box too small to allow him to injure himself by struggle and walked out to welcome the arriving trucks. It had been a long day, and camp still to make in the darkness. In the morning that bird would be just another episode. He would go back with the bones in the truck to a small cage in a city where he would spend the rest of his life. And a good thing, too. I sucked my aching thumb and spat out some blood. An assassin has to get used to these things. I had a professional reputation to keep up.

* * * * *

479

---

5 NARRATION: ACTIONS/EVENTS
What does the narrator imply was the bird's real enemy? *(the eyes behind the hand)* **In your own words, explain what the narrator means by that.** *(Accept reasonable responses: The man's eyes, and the brain behind them, catch the bird; if the bird attacked the eyes, it would stay free.)*
INFERENTIAL: PARAPHRASING

6 TONE
What is the narrator's attitude toward the hawk at this point? *(Accept reasonable responses: admiring and respectful; the narrator is a little ashamed and ill at ease at having captured such a fine competitor.)*
INFERENTIAL: DRAWING CONCLUSIONS

7 TONE
What is the narrator's attitude toward himself at this point? What clues tell you this? *(He feels ashamed of himself; he calls himself an assassin and seems to be ironic about his "professional reputation"; he thinks his work is not worth the pain it causes the hawk.)*
INFERENTIAL: DETERMINING MAIN IDEA

SET PURPOSE/PREDICT: PAGES 480–481 Have students read the rest of the selection to find out how Loren Eiseley's experiences in trying to capture the bird were important to him.

Oral Rereading   Invite students to reread aloud the ending of "Free Flight," beginning with the last paragraph on page 480. Guide students to read the passage in a way that conveys the mood, or emotional content, without overexpression. Encourage students to practice reading silently before reading aloud.

What clues have there been that point to what the narrator will do next? *(Accept reasonable responses: Earlier, when the narrator noticed the wind stirring, he thought that it was "a fine day to be alive"; when he again felt the breeze, he may have thought that the hawk, half-dead in captivity, should be allowed to live free. In addition, before he opened the box, he looked all around "secretively.")*
METACOGNITIVE: MAKING PREDICTIONS

In the morning, with the change that comes on suddenly in that high country, the mist that had hovered below us in the valley was gone. The sky was a deep blue, and one could see for miles over the high outcroppings of stone. I was up early and brought the box in which the little hawk was imprisoned out onto the grass where I was building a cage. A wind as cool as a mountain spring ran over the grass and stirred my hair. It was a fine day to be alive. I looked up and all around and at the hole in the cabin roof out of which the other little hawk had fled. There was no sign of her anywhere that I could see.

"Probably in the next county by now," I though cynically, but before beginning work I decided I'd have a look at my last night's capture.

Secretively, I looked again all around the camp and up and down and opened the box. I got him right out in my hand with his wings folded properly and I was careful not to startle him. He lay limp in my grasp and I could feel his heart pound under the feathers but he only looked beyond me and up.

8 I saw him look that last look away beyond me into a sky so full of light that I could not follow his gaze. The little breeze flowed over me again, and nearby a mountain aspen shook all its tiny leaves. I suppose I must have had an idea then of what I was going to do, but I never let it come up into consciousness. I just reached over and laid the hawk on the grass.

He lay there a long minute without hope, unmoving, his eyes still fixed on that blue vault above him. It must have been that he was already so far away in heart that he never felt the release from my hand. He never even stood. He just lay with his breast against the grass.

In the next second after that long minute he was gone. Like a flicker of light, he had vanished with my eyes full on him, but without actually seeing even a premonitory wing beat. He was gone straight into that towering emptiness of light and crystal that my eyes could scarcely bear to penetrate. For another long moment there was silence. I could not see him. The light was too intense. Then from far up somewhere a cry came ringing down.

480

Cooperative Reading

READER RESPONSE STRATEGY: PAGES 476–481
After the students read the selection, have each one respond to it freely as a whole. Remind students to draw from their previous discussions about the selection as they participate in the Responding to Literature activities on pages 481A–481D.

Guided Reading

MONITOR COMPREHENSION: PAGES 480–481
What happened to the bird after its capture?
(The narrator freed the bird. At first the hawk lay lifeless, but then he flew off to rejoin his mate; they flew together and called to each other.) STRATEGIC READING: RETURNING TO PURPOSE

Why did Eiseley feel good about his decision to let the bird go free? (Accept reasonable responses: because the bird would never experience life in captivity.) STRATEGIC READING: SUMMARIZING/ DETERMINING CAUSE-EFFECT

I was young then and had seen little of the world, but when I heard that cry my heart turned over. It was not the cry of the hawk I had captured; for, by shifting my position against the sun, I was now seeing farther up. Straight out of the sun's eye, where she must have been soaring restlessly above us for untold hours, hurtled his mate. And from far up, ringing from peak to peak of the summits over us, came a cry of such unutterable and ecstatic joy that it sounds down across the years and tingles among the cups on my quiet breakfast table.

I saw them both now. He was rising fast to meet her. They met in a great soaring gyre that turned to a whirling circle and a dance of wings. Once more, just once, their two voices, joined in a harsh wild medley of question and response, struck and echoed against the pinnacles of the valley. Then they were gone forever somewhere into those upper regions beyond the eyes of men.

Think It Over

1. Several times Loren Eiseley mentions his professional reputation. What clues help you know how he really feels about his job?
2. How does Eiseley capture the sparrow hawk?
3. Do you approve or disapprove of what Eiseley does with the bird? Give reasons for your answer.

Write

Suppose that Eiseley had not freed the bird. Write a summary of how the ending of the selection would have changed.

Returning to the Predictions Invite students to discuss the predictions that they made before reading and that they may have written in their personal journals. Encourage students to talk about how those predictions changed as they read the selection.

Returning to the Purpose for Reading Have students explain how the experiences described in "Free Flight" affected Eiseley. (Accept reasonable responses: The experiences made him respect the right of wild animals to be free.)

---

9 **NARRATION: RESOLUTION**
Do you think his encounter with the two hawks changed the narrator's attitudes? How? *(Accept reasonable responses: Yes; the encounter changed his attitudes toward wildlife and toward his work. At the beginning of the selection, he was willing to capture the birds; by the end, he preferred to leave them free.)*
INFERENTIAL: DETERMINING MAIN IDEA

10 **THINK IT OVER**
1. Accept reasonable responses: The fact that he lets the bird go free, the ironic tone he uses to describe his job, and the word assassin *are clues that he is having doubts about capturing animals.*
METACOGNITIVE: SYNTHESIZING
2. He climbs a ladder and tries to blind the birds with a light; the light is knocked over in the struggle and the female gets away. Then Eiseley catches the male with both hands.
LITERAL: NOTING IMPORTANT DETAILS
3. Responses will vary.
CRITICAL: EXPRESSING PERSONAL OPINIONS

11 **WRITE**
Encourage students to brainstorm independently or in small groups. To help students get started, you may want to suggest a prewriting graphic such as the following:

	Cause	Effect
1.	Eiseley does not free bird.	
2.		
3.		

Accept reasonable responses. Students should display an understanding of how keeping the bird caged would have affected not only the bird but also the bird's mate and Eiseley.
CREATIVE: INVENTING NEW ENDINGS

NOTE Additional writing activities appear on page 481D.

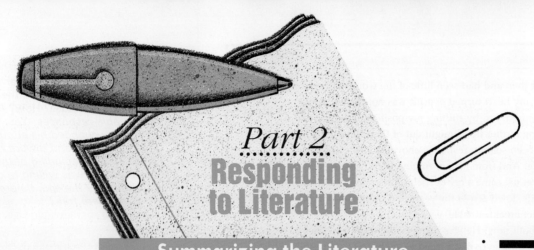

Part 2
Responding to Literature

Summarizing the Literature

Have students retell the selection and write a summary.

Have students summarize "Free Flight," using the chart they completed as they read. If they did not complete the chart, have them do so now. (See *Practice Book* page 131, on 481B.) Students may use their completed charts to retell the selection and write a brief summary statement.

PRIOR KNOWLEDGE–PREDICTION CHART

Prior Knowledge	Predictions	Actual Outcomes
Birds in the wild fly free.	The birds Eiseley caught did not want to be confined. They escaped.	Eiseley set the bird free.
An autobiography tells about important experiences in the author's life.	The experience in "Free Flight" was important to Eiseley. He stopped capturing animals.	The experience did have an important effect on Eiseley. He gained a deeper appreciation of nature and felt good about himself.

Appreciating Literature

Have students share personal responses.

Assign students to small groups to discuss the selection. Provide a general question such as the following to help the groups get started:

- **What did you learn about the narrator as a person from this autobiographical selection?**

PERSONAL JOURNAL   Encourage students to use their personal journals to write about ideas and feelings that are expressed in the groups. You may also wish to refer students to their personal journals after they complete the Critical Thinking Activities.

STRATEGY CONFERENCE

Discuss the prior knowledge-prediction chart, asking students whether it helped them understand and enjoy "Free Flight." Invite students to share other reading strategies, such as empathizing with the wild creatures or the narrator, that helped them enjoy the selection.

Encourage both cooperative and individual responses.

HOLD A DEBATE   Now that you have read the selection, do you think it is right for people to keep wildlife in captivity? What would be lost and what would be gained if there were no wildlife in captivity? Defend your position with reasons based on your personal knowledge and on what you learned from reading "Free Flight." You may wish to have students debate the question. Have them form two teams and build arguments to support their views. CRITICAL: EXPRESSING PERSONAL OPINIONS

DISCUSS OPINIONS   Do you think Eiseley did the right thing? What evidence can you find in the selection for your view? Encourage students to discuss the question in small groups and then write their answers. CRITICAL: MAKING JUDGMENTS

WRITE AND ILLUSTRATE A SCENE   What do you think probably happened to Eiseley when his colleagues learned that he had freed the bird? Have individual students write and illustrate a scene in which Eiseley confronts other scientists. CREATIVE: INVENTING NEW SCENES

INFORMAL ASSESSMENT

Few types of activities offer a better chance for informal assessment than do those that require making judgments or expressing opinions. This kind of activity incorporates and integrates (1) **noting important details**, (2) considering **cause and effect** as well as other types of thinking, and (3) **classifying** characters, events, and other textual features.

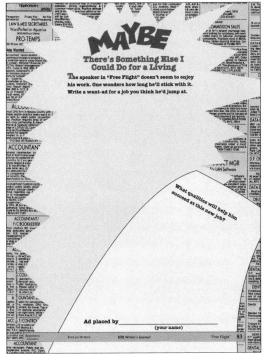

Writer's Journal

Practice Book

WRITER'S JOURNAL
page 83: Writing a creative response

PRACTICE BOOK
page 131: Summarizing the selection

VO·CAB·U·LAR·Y Workshop

Reviewing Key Words

To review how the new vocabulary is used in this selection, display the Key Words. Read each sentence below, and ask students to tell which word or phrase is a synonym for a Key Word. Have them name both the synonym and the Key Word.

1. *diverting* **The bird tried distracting the man's attention from its mate.** *(distracting)*
2. *premonitory* **The male bird did not give any warning movement before it took off.** *(warning)*
3. *reciprocal* **The male and female sparrow hawks' concern for each other was mutual.** *(mutual)*
4. *eaves* **Looking under the edge of the roof, the scientist discovered birds roosting.** *(edge of the roof)*
5. *pinnacles* **The birds circled joyously above the peaks of the hills.** *(peaks)*
6. *ecstatic* **Rejoining each other in flight, the two birds gave joyful cries.** *(joyful)*
7. *lacerated* **The hawk cut the scientist's thumb.** *(cut)*

Extending Vocabulary

PRECISE AND DESCRIPTIVE LANGUAGE Challenge students to list as many adjectives as they can that describe happiness, starting with *ecstatic*. They may use a dictionary or a thesaurus. (Accept reasonable responses: *pleased, overjoyed, rapturous, glad, delighted, elated, exultant.*) Discuss the different shades of meaning among these synonyms. Have students place their findings on a gradient such as the one below:

Happy				More Happy
pleased	glad	delighted	overjoyed	ecstatic

COOPERATIVE LEARNING Assign students to small groups. Have groups prepare similar gradients for other descriptive adjectives, such as *wet, tired, angry, hot, peaceful.*

Once they have completed their gradients, instruct groups to exchange papers. Each group should then use the other's synonyms to write sentences that reveal the differences in meaning. Then have volunteers read the sentences. Discuss with students how word choice can help them express a precise meaning.

Integrated Language Arts

WRITING

Writing About the Literature

AVAILABLE ON PROJECT CARD

CRITICAL: COMPARISON-CONTRAST ESSAY
Ask students to compare and contrast Loren Eiseley's feelings before he freed the hawk with his feelings afterward. Suggest that they use a prewriting chart such as the following. LISTENING/SPEAKING/READING/WRITING

Before	After

CREATIVE: DESCRIPTION   Invite students to reread "Free Flight" to notice how integral the wild-nature setting is to the author's theme. Then have students think of a different type of setting—for example, a small town, a large city, or an empty room—and have them write a paragraph or two that develops the mood of that setting. READING/WRITING

NOTE: An additional writing activity appears on page 481.

SPEAKING/LISTENING

Oral Reading

Invite students to find other descriptions of natural areas and to choose interesting passages to read aloud to other students. Students listening should attempt to make a drawing of the setting from the description. LISTENING/SPEAKING/READING

SPELLING

Spelling Review

SPELLING WORDS   *actually, aerial, eaves, hurtle, pinnacle, professional, reciprocal, startle, utensil, vessel*

Have students write the Spelling Words as you dictate them. Then have a volunteer write them on the board. Have students read each word aloud in unison, listening for the /əl/ sound in nine of the words. Have another volunteer circle the letters in the nine words that represent the /əl/ sound. Point out the fact that the /əl/ sound always falls in an unaccented syllable. Then have a volunteer name a word that has the long *e* sound spelled as in *eaves*. (leaves, each) LISTENING/SPEAKING/READING/WRITING/SPELLING

INTEGRATED SPELLING

page 64:   Writing words with the /əl/ sound

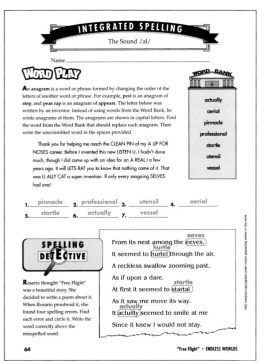

Integrated Spelling

STUDY SKILLS REVIEW

Book Parts

OBJECTIVE: *To locate and use various parts of a book*

Review

Review the parts of a book.

Remind students that all books contain some front matter and that most contain back matter as well. Review with them that front matter may include a title page, a copyright page, a dedication page, a table of contents, a foreword, a preface, and an acknowledgments page. Model finding the acknowledgments in the Student Anthology:

> **I need a publisher's name in order to find the book from which an excerpt was taken. At the front of the Student Anthology, I find the acknowledgments page, which lists the selections and includes the name of the original publishers. However, in this book there are so many acknowledgments that they are continued in the back matter.**

Practice/Apply

Have students identify various book parts.

Have students examine a book of factual information to find the following: title, author, copyright date, whether the author has thanked anyone or has dedicated the book, the organization of the book as shown in the table of contents, and the significance of the book as outlined in the preface or the foreword. Also have students list the parts of the back matter.

Summarize

Informally assess the learning.

Ask students to summarize what they reviewed. (The various parts of a book in the front matter and back matter provide useful information.)

CHALLENGE Invite students to plan and prepare a booklet showing the various parts of a hypothetical book.

Comparing-Contrasting/ Making Judgments

OBJECTIVE: *To use comparison and contrast in forming a judgment*

Review

Review the process of making judgments.

Remind students that making a judgment often involves comparison (noting similarities) and contrast (noting differences). Model making a judgment about Eiseley:

He did what he thought was right when he freed the hawk. It would have been easier to keep it. This contrast helps me judge that Eiseley had integrity.

Practice/Apply

Have students make judgments.

Ask students to compare and contrast two selections they have read and to make a judgment about which is better.

Summarize

Informally assess the learning.

Ask students to summarize what they reviewed. (Comparing and contrasting are important in making judgments.)

CHALLENGE Ask students to examine the judgments they made in Practice/Apply from the viewpoint of someone who disagrees. Do the comparisons and contrasts they made between the two selections hold up? Could someone make a different judgment by using different comparisons and contrasts?

PRACTICE BOOK

page 132: Comparing and contrasting/making judgments

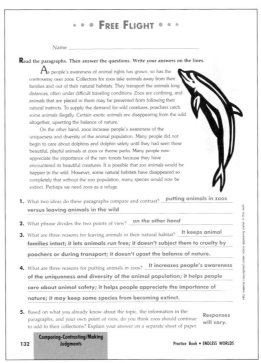

Practice Book

On the practice book page:

• • • FREE FLIGHT • • •

Name _____

Read the paragraphs. Then answer the questions. Write your answers on the lines.

As people's awareness of animal rights has grown, so has the controversy over zoos. Collectors for zoos take animals away from their families and out of their natural habitats. They transport the animals long distances, often under difficult traveling conditions. Zoos are confining, and animals that are placed in them may be prevented from following their natural instincts. To supply the demand for wild creatures, poachers catch some animals illegally. Certain exotic animals are disappearing from the wild altogether, upsetting the balance of nature.

On the other hand, zoos increase people's awareness of the uniqueness and diversity of the animal population. Many people did not begin to care about dolphins and dolphin safety until they had seen these beautiful, playful animals at zoos or theme parks. Many people now appreciate the importance of the rain forests because they have encountered its beautiful creatures. It is possible that zoo animals would be happier in the wild. However, some natural habitats have disappeared so completely that without the zoo population, many species would now be extinct. Perhaps we need zoos as a refuge.

1. What two ideas do these paragraphs compare and contrast? __putting animals in zoos__ __versus leaving animals in the wild__

2. What phrase divides the two points of view? __on the other hand__

3. What are three reasons for leaving animals in their natural habitat? __It keeps animal__ __families intact; it lets animals run free; it doesn't subject them to cruelty by__ __poachers or during transport; it doesn't upset the balance of nature.__

4. What are three reasons for putting animals in zoos? __It increases people's awareness__ __of the uniqueness and diversity of the animal population; it helps people__ __care about animal safety; it helps people appreciate the importance of__ __nature; it may keep some species from becoming extinct.__

5. Based on what you already know about the topic, the information in the paragraphs, and your own point of view, do you think zoos should continue to add to their collections? Explain your answer on a separate sheet of paper. __Responses will vary.__

132 Comparing-Contrasting/Making Judgments

Practice Book • ENDLESS WORLDS

Structural Analysis

OBJECTIVE: *To use structural analysis to understand word meanings*

Review

Review different types of word parts.

Remind students that major word parts are prefixes, suffixes, and base words. Model analyzing *premonitory* in "Free Flight":

Pre- means "before," -y usually forms adjectives, and to monitor means to watch. Could *premonitory* mean "watching beforehand"?

Practice/Apply

Have students analyze word structure.

COOPERATIVE LEARNING Have groups of students choose one Key Word, analyze its parts, and check their analysis in a dictionary.

Summarize

Informally assess the learning.

Check understanding by having students summarize what they reviewed. (Analyzing the parts of a word helps you understand its meaning.)

CHALLENGE Invite students to perform a structural analysis of the words *structure, structural, analysis,* and *analyze.* Ask them to report their findings to classmates.

PRACTICE BOOK
page 133: Using structural analysis

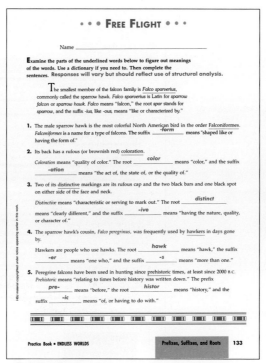

Practice Book

Reference Sources

OBJECTIVE: *To use reference sources to find information*

Review

Review major reference sources.

Remind students that *Books in Print* lists titles and authors of books about many subjects and that *Readers' Guide to Periodical Literature* can help them find magazine articles. Model how to find information about hawks:

> **I can look in the *Subject Guide to Books in Print* to find books on birds of prey. *Readers' Guide* can direct me to articles in magazines.**

Practice/Apply

Have students plan research.

COOPERATIVE LEARNING   Have small groups of students plan a hypothetical research project on current practices of zoos or on Loren Eiseley. Groups should list entries on their topic from *Books in Print* and from *Readers' Guide*.

Summarize

Informally assess the learning.

Check students' understanding by having them summarize what they reviewed. (*Books in Print* and *Readers' Guide* can provide helpful information.)

CHALLENGE   Challenge students to investigate critics' opinions of Loren Eiseley and to prepare a bibliography of books and articles written about him.

PRACTICE BOOK

page 134: Using reference sources

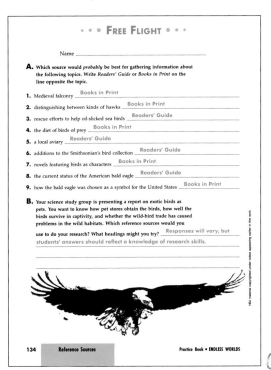

• • • FREE FLIGHT • • •

Name _____

A. Which source would *probably* be best for gathering information about the following topics. Write *Readers' Guide* or *Books in Print* on the line opposite the topic.

1. Medieval falconry __Books in Print__
2. distinguishing between kinds of hawks __Books in Print__
3. rescue efforts to help oil-slicked sea birds __Readers' Guide__
4. the diet of birds of prey __Books in Print__
5. a local aviary __Readers' Guide__
6. additions to the Smithsonian's bird collection __Readers' Guide__
7. novels featuring birds as characters __Books in Print__
8. the current status of the American bald eagle __Readers' Guide__
9. how the bald eagle was chosen as a symbol for the United States __Books in Print__

B. Your science study group is presenting a report on exotic birds as pets. You want to know how pet stores obtain the birds, how well the birds survive in captivity, and whether the wild-bird trade has caused problems in the wild habitats. Which reference sources would you use to do your research? What headings might you try? __Responses will vary, but students' answers should reflect a knowledge of research skills.__

134   Reference Sources   Practice Book ▪ ENDLESS WORLDS

Practice Book

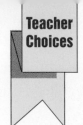

Integrated Curriculum

SCIENCE

Don't Fence Me In!

Have students research and report on new zoo-keeping practices that have made the environments of zoo animals less artificial in recent years. If possible, invite a local zookeeper to address the students. LISTENING/SPEAKING/READING/WRITING

ECOLOGY

Eiseley and I

Encourage students to write personal essays based on their own observations of nature. They may wish to do field work in their communities before writing and then check their observations with library research. Emphasize that even urban and suburban areas have distinct, interesting flora and fauna—there are hawks in New York City and peregrine falcons in both New York City and Boston. Collect students' essays into a volume or magazine to distribute to other groups. READING/WRITING

ART

In Audubon's Society

AVAILABLE ON PROJECT CARD

Invite students to show what a sparrow hawk and other birds of prey look like by drawing or painting pictures. Display students' work on a bulletin board or in another suitable place. Invite the artists to give talks explaining the details of the birds' appearance and the drawing or painting techniques they used. LISTENING/SPEAKING

SCIENCE

What Is a Hawk?

Invite students to research and report on hawks. Have them describe the kinds, the habits, and the habitats of these birds. Remind students to bring in photographs to accompany their oral or written reports. LISTENING/SPEAKING/READING/WRITING

Life, Liberty, and the Pursuit . . .

THE HAWKS IN "FREE FLIGHT" SHOW GREAT DEVOTION TO EACH OTHER.

Similarly, many individuals have felt a loyalty to their own people, a desire to help them escape their bonds and soar to freedom. Among these individuals are the African American entrepreneur Paul Cuffe and the Cherokee leader John Ross.

Paul Cuffe, born in Massachusetts in 1759, became a rich and influential merchant shipowner. He used his wealth to help others by building a schoolhouse on his farm to educate the children of the town, both black and white, and by speaking up for voting rights for African Americans. Finally, Cuffe launched his most ambitious dream: to build a homeland for African Americans in Sierra Leone, West Africa. He partly realized this last dream before he died in 1817.

John Ross was born in 1790 in what is now Tennessee. A member of the Cherokee people and their principal chief for forty years, Ross negotiated tirelessly with the United States government to defend his nation's rights to its homeland. However, he faced an uphill struggle against the white settlers' desire for land. In 1838 the Cherokee Nation was forced to leave its homeland in the southeast and move west to what is now Oklahoma. ■

Multi*Cultural* PERSPECTIVES

ACTIVITY CORNER

■ Have a group of students research Freetown, Paul Cuffe's settlement in Sierra Leone. Ask them to write a brief presentation. Recommend that they use illustrations.

AVAILABLE ON PROJECT CARD

■ Suggest that students read about the Cherokees' "Trail of Tears" and write a diary entry from the point of view of one of the Cherokees who participated in it.

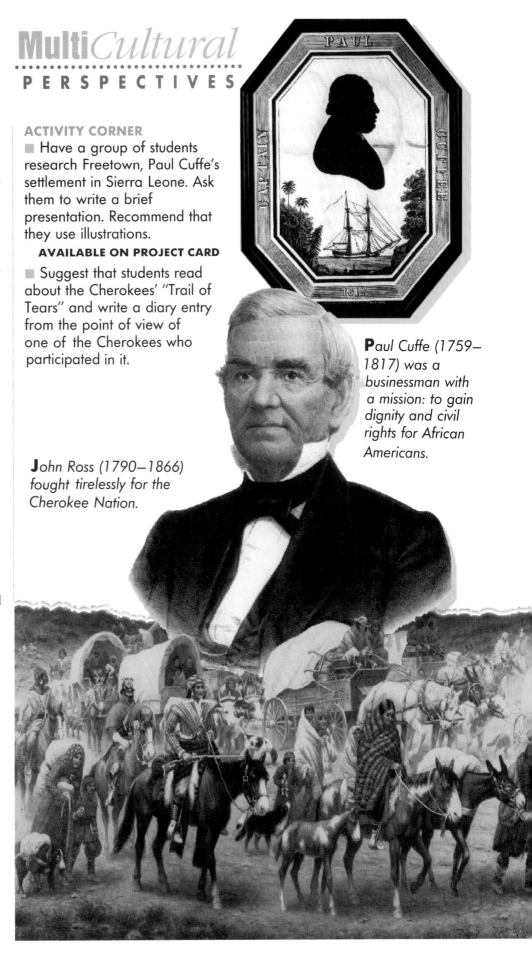

Paul Cuffe (1759–1817) was a businessman with a mission: to gain dignity and civil rights for African Americans.

John Ross (1790–1866) fought tirelessly for the Cherokee Nation.

The Sparrow Hawk

ABOUT THE POET

Russell Hoban (1925–) began writing and illustrating children's books in 1959. Many of the ideas for his books came from his own seven children. About his writing he says, "My working rule is just to try to keep going—to do a little if I can't do a lot, and to keep looking and listening for the story that wants to be written."

ABOUT THE POEM

After comparing the sparrow hawk to an armed, freewheeling outlaw, Russell Hoban then describes a small fieldmouse hiding from danger after seeing the shadow of an enemy.

482

Reading the Poem

Invite students to close their eyes while you read the poem aloud. Encourage them to visualize the hawk and the mouse. Then have partners read the poem to each other as though they were actually watching the hawk and the mouse in the meadow.

The Sparrow Hawk

by Russell Hoban

Wings like pistols flashing at his sides,
Masked, above the meadow runway rides,
Galloping, galloping with an easy rein.
Below, the fieldmouse, where the shadow glides,
Holds fast the small purse of his life, and hides.

1

2

White Bird, 1950, Milton Avery, gouache on paper, 16 ½" X 21 ½". Collection of The University of Arizona, Museum of Art, Tucson, Arizona. Gift of Edward J. Gallagher, Jr.

483

Responding to the Poem

Ask students to quickwrite their responses to the poem in their personal journals. In their writing they might consider what the hawk may represent or symbolize and how people are in some ways like the mouse.

1 FIGURATIVE LANGUAGE
What comparison helps you picture the hawk? *(Accept reasonable responses: By comparing the hawk's wings to pistols and using the words* masked, galloping, *and* rein, *the poet creates a picture of the hawk as a robber or a Western outlaw planning a holdup.)*
INFERENTIAL: MAKING COMPARISONS

2 IMAGERY
What impression of the mouse does the poet give you by using the image of the purse? *(Accept reasonable responses: that the mouse is small and nervous, clinging to life, which could easily be stolen from him.)*
CREATIVE: VISUALIZING

WRITER'S JOURNAL page 84: Writing a creative response

The Small, Unnoticed Thing

When the hawk is flying overhead, we might not notice the fieldmouse. We might not see the seed pod burst in the path of a blazing forest fire or the cocoon curled within the dying leaf. Think of a small, unnoticed thing and describe it in prose or poetry.

by _____
(your name)

84   "The Sparrow Hawk"   HBJ Writer's Journal

Writer's Journal

FIRST SIGHTING

by Keith Robertson

KEITH ROBERTSON (1914–) wanted to be a writer even as a boy, but people discouraged him. Instead, he went to the U.S. Naval Academy and studied science. He worked briefly as an engineer but returned to the navy during World War II as an officer aboard destroyers. He wrote his first book for young people almost by accident: he was selling children's books and decided to try writing one. After that, he was hooked. "The letters an author gets from young readers are enough to make his labors eminently worthwhile and enjoyable," says Robertson.

MORE BOOKS BY KEITH ROBERTSON
Henry Reed, Inc. Viking, 1958. EASY
Henry Reed's Big Show. Viking, 1970. AVERAGE
Henry Reed's Think Tank. Viking, 1986. AVERAGE

OTHER BOOKS ABOUT WATCHING NATURE
Bird Watch: A Book of Poetry by Jane Yolen. Philomel Books, 1990. AVERAGE
Drawing from Nature by Jim Arnosky. Lothrop, Lee, and Shepard, 1982. AVERAGE
Storm Bird by Elsie McCutcheon. Farrar, Straus and Giroux, 1987. AVERAGE

"The letters an author gets from young readers . . . make his labors eminently worth-while."

SELECTION SUMMARY
Link Keller is spending the summer with his aunt Harriet in the woods of Michigan. Link, a city boy, is bored by the rustic scene. There are tensions with his aunt, whom he barely knows, but he agrees to stay until he has snapped a photo of the rare sandhill crane. Link finds no crane, but he does discover the joy of watching wild creatures. After Link has a mishap with a porcupine, his aunt removes the quills deftly and sympathetically, and the two begin to like each other better.

LESSON PLANNER			
	Materials	**Integrated Curriculum**	**Meeting Individual Needs**
1 **READING LITERATURE** pp. 483B–499	Student Anthology pp. 484–499 Transparency 26 Second-Language Support Manual Practice Book p. 135 Integrated Spelling p. 65 Integrated Spelling T.E. pp. 86–87	Spelling Spelling Pretest Spelling-Vocabulary Connection (the /k/, /ks/, and /kw/ sounds)	Second-Language Support Vocabulary 483C Strategic Reading 483D, 495
2 **RESPONDING TO LITERATURE** pp. 499A–499D	Writer's Journal p. 85 Practice Book p. 136 Integrated Spelling p. 66 Integrated Spelling T.E. pp. 86–87	Vocabulary Workshop Reviewing Key Words Extending Vocabulary Writing About the Literature Speaking/Listening Spelling Review	Cooperative Learning 499B, 499C
3 **LEARNING THROUGH LITERATURE** pp. 499E–499J	Second-Language Support Manual Writer's Journal p. 86 Practice Book pp. 137–138	Science Art Social Studies Multicultural	Challenge 499F, 499G, 499H Second-Language Support 499F Cooperative Learning 499H

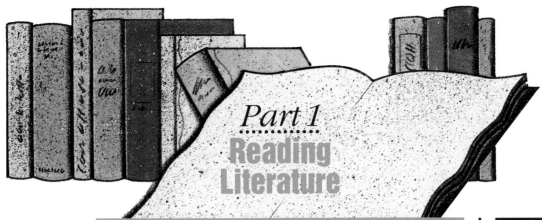

Part 1
Reading Literature

Building Background

Access prior knowledge and develop vocabulary concepts.

Tell students that they will be reading a story titled "First Sighting," about a teenager from the city who must spend a summer in the country. Explain that the teenager prefers city life and that he experiences internal conflicts, struggles within himself. Write *City Person* in a web, and ask students to suggest why a girl or boy might prefer city life.

likes noise and action   has city friends

involved in activities — **City Person** — cares little about wildlife

enjoys comforts and conveniences

Have students quickwrite phrases.

Ask students to quickly write several phrases about being somewhere new and different. Students might share their ideas in small groups.

Vocabulary Strategies

Introduce Key Words and strategies.

Tell students that they may encounter some unfamiliar words in "First Sighting." Display Transparency 26, or write the paragraphs on the board. Let students read the paragraphs silently.

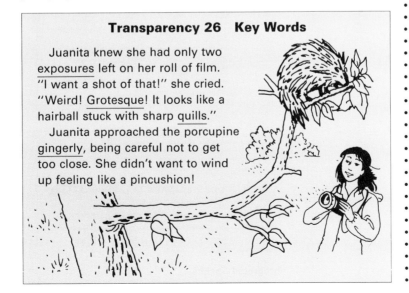

Transparency 26 Key Words

Juanita knew she had only two exposures left on her roll of film. "I want a shot of that!" she cried. "Weird! Grotesque! It looks like a hairball stuck with sharp quills."

Juanita approached the porcupine gingerly, being careful not to get too close. She didn't want to wind up feeling like a pincushion!

CULTURAL AWARENESS

To help students appreciate the cultural background and setting of "First Sighting," share with them the information under Cultural Background/Setting on page 484.

KEY WORDS DEFINED

exposures sections of film that make photographs; one section, or exposure, makes a single photograph

grotesque outlandish, strange, ugly

quills sharp spines on a porcupine

gingerly cautiously, carefully

Encourage students to use phonics, structural analysis, and context clues to determine the meanings of the underlined words. Call on a volunteer to read the paragraphs aloud. Offer help with pronunciation if necessary.

Check students' understanding.

Have students use a predict-o-gram to classify the new words according to how the author might use them in "First Sighting." Save the chart for use in Reviewing Key Words.
STRATEGY: PRIOR KNOWLEDGE

PREDICT-O-GRAM

Discovering Country Life	Character's Reactions
quills	grotesque
exposures	gingerly

Integrate spelling with vocabulary.

SPELLING-VOCABULARY CONNECTION *Integrated Spelling* page 65 reinforces spellings of words with the **/k/, /ks/,** and **/kw/ sounds,** including the following Key Words: *quills, exposures,* and *grotesque.*

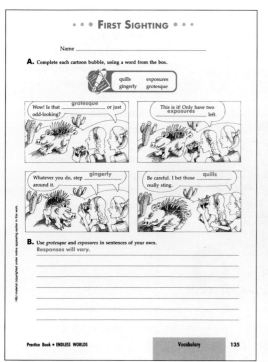

Practice Book

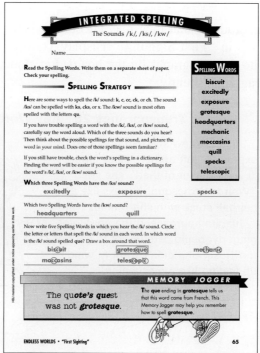

Integrated Spelling

Preview and Predict

Have students preview the literature.

Remind students that episodes from a novel can frequently stand alone. Such episodes are often excerpted in magazines and books. Call on volunteers to suggest ways of previewing this excerpt in order to make predictions about it. (Read the title and the title of the novel, look at the illustrations, read the introduction and the first few paragraphs.) Have students follow these suggestions. Point out that the introduction sets the scene and tells something about the characters. Ask students what they learn here about Link and his aunt Harriet and how the information foretells Link's internal conflicts.

Introduce the character conflict chart.

Write the chart headings on the board to encourage students to predict what the conflicts are and how they will be resolved.

CHARACTER CONFLICT CHART

Conflict	Predicted Resolution	Actual Resolution

PERSONAL JOURNAL Have students copy the chart in their personal journals, or have them use *Practice Book* page 136. (See page 499B in this Teacher's Edition.) You may wish to have students complete the first two columns before they read the story and the last column after they finish. (Students will return to the chart after reading, in Summarizing the Literature.)

Setting a Purpose

Have students set purposes.

Have students use the predictions they have just made to set a purpose for reading, or have them formulate questions they would like to have answered by the end of the story. Invite volunteers to share their questions with the group.

Model purpose-setting, if necessary.

If students have difficulty setting a purpose for reading, model the thinking process:

> **I know from previewing that Link doesn't like the idea of vacationing in the wild with an aunt he hardly knows. But he has a job to do there: to photograph a rare bird. My purpose for reading will be to find out whether Link's search for the bird changes his feelings about living in the country and about his aunt.**

SECOND-LANGUAGE SUPPORT Students may benefit from participating in the Guided Reading activities and from the additional guidance under the Student Anthology pages. (See Second-Language Support Manual.)

OPTIONS FOR READING

Independent Reading
Have students read the story silently with their purpose for reading in mind.

Guided Reading
Follow the Guided Reading suggestions that appear on pages 484, 491, and 498. These suggestions model strategic reading.

Numbered Annotations
Use the numbered annotations beside the Student Anthology pages to heighten students' appreciation of the story.

The story takes place in the woods in Michigan, an area rich in wildlife, including birds. Link Keller is supposed to find and photograph a sandhill crane for his uncle. The sandhill crane is a large bird with long legs and a long neck. Its wingspread is six to seven feet. It is gray and, as Link notes in the story, has a bald, red crown. The rare bird can be found in the northwestern, north-central, and southeastern United States, as well as parts of Alaska and Canada, inhabiting prairies, grainfields, and marshes, where Link looks for one.

The woods in the story were once the home of the Chippewa people, a nation of Native Americans sometimes also called the Ojibwa. The Chippewa used the bark of birch trees to make beautiful canoes, dishes, and baskets. They fished and hunted, and they gathered the wild rice that grows near the lakes. Today, most of the wild rice consumed in the United States is still harvested by Chippewa Indians.

484

Guided Reading

SET PURPOSE/PREDICT: PAGES 484–491 Have students read through the first five lines on page 491 to find out what the differences are between Link's life in the city and his life in the country.

FROM

IN SEARCH OF A SANDHILL CRANE

BY

KEITH ROBERTSON

When Lincoln Keller's mother decides to take a computer course in another state, Link agrees to spend the summer in Michigan with his aunt Harriet, whom he hardly knows. With some reluctance, he takes his uncle Albert's expensive camera in order to get pictures of the rare sandhill crane. Soon after getting to Michigan, Link goes with his aunt Harriet to her log cabin in the wilderness. When Link sees the isolated cabin with no modern conveniences, he is afraid he is going to have a very boring vacation.

The cabin had only three rooms. Most of the space was taken up by one large room that served as the kitchen, dining, and living area. An old-fashioned kitchen range stood near one corner, and a big stone fireplace occupied the middle of the opposite wall. There was a cedar plank table, four straight chairs, several easy chairs that looked worn but comfortable,

illustrations by Richard Cook

485

1 SETTING
Why do you think the author gives such a detailed description of the cabin? *(Accept reasonable responses: He wants the reader to be able to imagine the simplicity of the cabin in which Link will be living.)*
INFERENTIAL: DRAWING CONCLUSIONS

2 CHARACTER'S TRAITS
What does the cabin tell the reader about Aunt Harriet? *(She enjoys living close to nature. She does not care about luxury, though she does care about cleanliness.)*
INFERENTIAL: DRAWING CONCLUSIONS

3 HUMOR
Why does Link think his aunt is joking when he hears the Chippewa's name? *(A charley horse is a type of muscle cramp.)*
INFERENTIAL: DRAWING CONCLUSIONS

some built-in cupboards, and a worktable near the stove. Two doors led to the two smaller rooms. Each contained a bed, with what appeared to be a new mattress, a straight chair, an old bureau, and a small closet.

The floors were of worn planks, and the inside of the log walls had been paneled with boards. Inside, the cabin was much cozier and more inviting than Link had expected. It was clean and had none of the musty smell that houses usually have after being closed for a long time.

"Charley and his wife did a good job cleaning the place," Harriet said approvingly. "He has looked after the cabin for years—kept the roof tight, repaired the windows, things like that. When I wrote him that I was coming up this summer, he said that the squirrels and mice had got in and had ruined the mattresses. So I sent up two new ones. He's put new screens on the windows, and I noticed before we came in that he'd set out some tomato plants for us. He's a wonderful man. You'll like him."

"What is Charley's last name?" Link asked.

"Horse."

"You're not serious?"

"His real name is Running Horse," Harriet said. "He's a Chippewa Indian. He used to work in the lumber camps as a young man, and someone called him Charley Horse and he's kept the name ever since. He knows more about the woods than anyone I've ever known. He's an expert guide."

Link unloaded the station wagon while his aunt put things away. Then he went to the pile of wood that Charley Horse had left near the edge of the clearing and brought in wood for the kitchen stove.

"We used to have an outdoor fireplace," Harriet said. "It was built of stones stacked together. If we can find the metal grill, we can rebuild it. Then we can cook out of doors part of the time. In the middle of the summer it's too hot to build a fire in the stove. We usually didn't unless it rained."

"What about a refrigerator?" Link asked, looking at the cases of ginger ale he had carried in from the car.

"I've talked about getting one of those gas refrigerators for

486

years," Harriet said. "But I just haven't bothered. There's a spring not very far away. We used to use it for our drinking water when your father and I were children. Later we drilled a well. But I still use the spring to keep things cold, like butter. We put whatever we want in one of those metal pails and put the pail in the water. As for the bottles of soda, just tie a string around the necks and lower them into the water. You'll be surprised how cold they'll get."

They had lamb chops, canned peas, and baking powder biscuits for dinner. Then Harriet got her cane, and with Link carrying the large metal pail full of perishables, they walked through the gathering gloom down an overgrown path to the spring. It was not far. The trail sloped downward for a short distance and then wound around a small hillock. Water gushed out of a low ledge of rock and trickled down into a pool about ten feet in diameter. A tiny stream led the overflow away into the darkness of the woods.

"I think the water is perfectly safe to drink," Harriet said. "The real reason Dad had the well put in was that he and your father liked to come down here to take baths. Mother objected to that. She said she wasn't going to drink bathwater even if it was running."

Link leaned over and put his hand in the water. "It's ice cold," he said.

"Much too cold to bathe in, I always thought," she agreed. "Mother and I carried water and took a bath with warm water in a tub."

Link found a flat rock ledge in the pool, placed the pail on it, and then weighted it down with another rock.

"That will do fine unless some bear gets too inquisitive," Harriet said. "One year I had real trouble. Charley put a rope up over that limb, and I suspended the pail out in the middle of the pool. I had to use a long stick with a hook on the end to reach out and get it."

"Are there many bears around here?" Lincoln asked, looking back into the thick depths of the woods.

"Lots of them. But if you leave them alone, they'll usually leave you alone."

It was dark by the time they returned to the cabin. Harriet lighted a kerosene lamp and showed Link how it worked. "I imagine you're tired," she said. "Up here you'll find you just

487

4 CHARACTER'S MOTIVATIONS
Why do you think that Aunt Harriet has never bothered to get a gas refrigerator? *(Accept reasonable responses: She can keep things cold in the spring; she prefers going without modern appliances in the country; she likes to keep things the way they were when she was a child.)*
INFERENTIAL: DRAWING CONCLUSIONS

5 CHARACTERIZATION
When Link puts his hand in the stream, he remarks, "It's ice cold." Does Aunt Harriet catch his meaning? *(She does, and she agrees with him that it is too cold to bathe in.)* **What does her remark tell you about her?** *(Accept reasonable responses: She is sensitive. She doesn't take living simply to unreasonable extremes.)*
INFERENTIAL: DRAWING CONCLUSIONS

Vocabulary Strategy Ask students how structural analysis and context clues can help them figure out the meaning of *perishables* (line 10). (The base word *perish* means "to spoil or die," the suffix *-able* means "capable of," and the *-s* ending signals a plural. Context clues tell us the word applies to food that must be kept cold. By using both strategies, students can determine that *perishables* are food items likely to spoil.) STRATEGY: STRUCTURAL ANALYSIS/CONTEXT CLUES

Oral Rereading Have students perform a Readers Theatre by reading part of the selection dramatically. Invite volunteers to begin at paragraph 2 on page 487 and read through the first line on page 488. Assign the parts of Link, Aunt Harriet, and the narrator. Ask those reading dialogue to try to convey Link's and Aunt Harriet's feelings through their voices. Point out that Aunt Harriet talks a lot. Is she nervous or just chatty? Allow students to practice reading their parts silently before reading aloud for the class. After the performance, ask the rest of the group how the oral rereading enhanced their understanding of the text.

6 CHARACTERIZATION

How does the contrast between the country's animal sounds and the noises of city machinery help you understand Link? *(Accept reasonable responses: Link fears the unknown. He is familiar and comfortable with the loud city noises and they lull him to sleep, but the animal sounds make him nervous because he cannot identify them and does not know whether they are made by dangerous animals.)*
INFERENTIAL: COMPARING AND CONTRASTING

7 FORESHADOWING

What clues does the author give that a porcupine will play a role in this story? *(The animal is intrusive and already causing trouble.)*
METACOGNITIVE: NOTING IMPORTANT DETAILS

naturally get up with the light and go to bed with the dark."

Link went outside and brushed his teeth at the pump and then went to bed. When he blew out the lamp, complete darkness descended. There were no distant street lights outside his window and no occasional flash of headlights. The room was so totally black that it bothered him. He glanced at his watch just to be certain that nothing had happened to his eyes. After about ten minutes he was able to make out the square of his window, a slightly grayer shade of black in the black wall.

6 Suddenly he heard something rustling around outside. It sounded enormous. Charley Horse had put new screens on the windows, but would a screen discourage a bear? He tried to convince himself that if iron bars had been needed, they would have been put on. The rustling was suddenly replaced by a gnawing sound as though a rat the size of a bear were gnawing down a big tree. There were lots of trees, he decided, one or more less would make no difference as long as it didn't fall on him. He had just become resigned to the gnawing, when suddenly the night was pierced with a blood-chilling screech: "*Ooииοοоииииοο, oh oh oh!*" This brought him bolt upright in bed. Then he lay back down again. He'd read of screech owls. The screech was repeated, and then in the distance he heard a high-pitched barking, like a dog but still not a dog. The peace and quiet of the deep woods! he thought disgustedly. What he needed was a few trucks or cement mixers driving down the street so he could get to sleep. He covered his ears with his pillow and closed his eyes.

He drifted off to sleep in spite of the strange noises, and the next thing he knew it was light and he was awake. He could smell coffee. He got dressed, went out to the pump, and sloshed cold water over his face. On his way back he noticed the broom that had been left beside the door. It had fallen to the ground, and something had gnawed the handle half through. He carried it inside and held it up for Harriet to see.

7 "Porcupine," she said with a laugh. "I think it's the salt in the perspiration from your hands that they're after. They'll sometimes gnaw a hoe handle in two in a night. Did you hear that owl screeching last night?"

488

489

Informal Assessment You can informally assess your students' abilities to identify cause and effect and causal chains in stories that they read. On occasion, ask questions such as these:

- Why did this character do what he or she did? Are there any other reasons for the character's actions?
- What do you think will happen because this character did what he or she did? Why?

This informal assessment can also be accomplished by establishing a brief scenario. Have specific students imagine that they are the main character in this story. Ask the students to explain why they did what they did, said what they said, or thought what they thought.

Why doesn't Link get out of the spring when the water makes his feet numb? *(He recalls that his father used to swim there. He thinks that if his father could do it, he can, too.)*
INFERENTIAL: DETERMINING CAUSE-EFFECT

What does Link's decision to stay in the spring tell the reader about him? *(He has determination. He is willing to give things a try.)*
INFERENTIAL: DRAWING CONCLUSIONS

"I heard lots of animals, and I see signs of them, but I don't see them," Link objected.

"Once in a while you will just stumble onto an animal, but usually they are very wary and cautious. So you have to be even more wary and quiet. If you stand quietly any place long enough, you'll be surprised at what you'll see."

While they ate breakfast, Harriet drew a rough map of the surrounding area, pointing out what she thought might interest him.

"It's always a good idea to carry a compass if you go very far into the woods," she cautioned. "It's not so much that a compass will keep you from getting lost, but if you do get lost, you can then keep going in one direction. Eventually, even up here, you will come to a road."

She produced a small compass, which Link stuck in his pocket before he went exploring. He found the swamp that Harriet had indicated, and the sizable stream of dark-brown water that led away from it through the trees to the Manistique River. He located the old beaver dam and a pond above it. And he visited the remains of what Harriet had said was an old stagecoach station. They were interesting, he admitted, but you couldn't stand around for hours and look at a beaver dam or a tumbledown log cabin. By the middle of the afternoon he had seen practically everything on Harriet's crude map. He was on his way back to the cabin when he passed by the spring. Walking through the woods was much warmer work than he had expected, and the water looked inviting. He stripped off his clothes and stepped into the edge of the pool.

8 The water was icy. It was so cold that his feet felt numb in a matter of seconds. He looked out at the center of the pool. The water was at least four feet deep. His father used to take a bath here, he told himself. He could at least take a quick dip. Holding his breath, he made a shallow dive toward the center. The water was deeper than he had expected; when he stood up it came to his chin. He had never been so cold in his life. With his teeth chattering he waded as quickly as possible to the edge and climbed out.

He found a spot of sunshine and stood shivering in it for several minutes while he tried to brush off some of the water from his body.

490

He was covered with goose pimples. He put on his clothes and then sat down by the pool for a while. He felt wonderful. That quick dip had been the most fun of anything since his arrival in Michigan. But that was only a minute. What was he going to do with an entire summer?

The next day he went into Germfask with his aunt to buy some **9** milk and a few other staples. They visited the Seney Wildlife Refuge Headquarters, looked at the exhibits, and Link watched some Canada geese on the pond just outside the main building. When they returned to the cabin, he wrote several letters and took several short, aimless walks into the woods. The following morning he weeded the area around the tomato plants and then thumbed aimlessly through one of his aunt's bird books.

"You're bored, aren't you?" Harriet asked in the middle of lunch. **10**

The sudden question caught Link unprepared. "Well, I don't know what you find to do all summer up here," he admitted finally. "What did my dad do when he was a boy?"

"He was like me. He could lie hidden in the underbrush and watch a beaver or a heron all day long. You have to love the creatures of the wild to like it here, I guess. I find New York City terribly dull." She reached out a hand and touched him on the arm. "I suppose in a way the whole idea of coming up here was selfish. Now that I am partially crippled I don't feel up to staying here alone the way I once did. So I told myself that you would enjoy it so that I could come. I love it here. I can hobble outside and just sit watching and have a wonderful time. And of course there *was* the chance that you might like it too. Would you like to leave?"

"Well, I haven't really given it a trial yet," Link said, reluctant to hurt her by saying that he would.

"You've run out of things to do," Harriet observed. "I suppose you ought to try to get that picture your uncle wanted before you leave."

"Yes, I'd forgotten that," Link agreed. "Where would I go to find sandhill cranes?"

"Lakes, marshes, wet areas," Harriet said. "There are a number of these around within a few miles. Why don't we leave it that

491

9 SETTING
How do you know that some time has passed? *(The words* next day *signal a change in time.)*
METACOGNITIVE: DETERMINING SEQUENCE

How much time has passed since the excerpt began? *(two days and two nights)*
INFERENTIAL: DETERMINING SEQUENCE

10 PLOT: CONFLICT
Why is Link taken aback when Aunt Harriet asks him whether he's bored and would like to leave? *(Accept reasonable responses: He is surprised that she has noticed. He is a little embarrassed to admit boredom when she is so content. He doesn't want to hurt her feelings.)*
INFERENTIAL: DRAWING CONCLUSIONS

Guided Reading

MONITOR COMPREHENSION: PAGES 484–491
What are the differences between Link's life in the city and his life in the country? (Link had modern conveniences and entertainments in the city. He can identify city noises, but he is fearful of the animal noises in the country.) STRATEGIC READING: RETURNING TO PURPOSE

How does Link feel about the country after his swim? (The dip in the ice-cold water, though it gives him goose bumps, makes him feel wonderful.

Link is learning that there are appealing aspects to country life.) STRATEGIC READING: SUMMARIZING

SET PURPOSE/PREDICT: PAGES 491–499 Ask students to predict how Link's willingness to give things a try will help resolve his conflicts. Have them read the rest of "First Sighting" to confirm their predictions.

Why is Link now feeling that he would be willing to stay another week in the woods? *(because he knows he does not have to stay the entire summer)*
INFERENTIAL: DETERMINING CAUSE-EFFECT

What does this reveal about him? *(Accept reasonable responses: He is sensitive to other people's needs and desires; he cares about his aunt.)*
INFERENTIAL: DRAWING CONCLUSIONS

you will stay long enough to get your pictures. Then we'll pack up and leave."

"That's fair enough," Link said, feeling much better.

"I want to go pay Charley Horse for his work here and see several other people," Harriet said, getting up from the table. "You don't mind being left here alone?"

"Not at all," Link said.

He went to his room, got out his uncle Albert's camera, and picked a 105 mm. lens. There were only four exposures left on the roll of film, so he went outside and used them up taking pictures of the cabin. Then he reloaded the camera, tucked his aunt's bird guide in his pocket, and started off through the woods. There might be a sandhill crane at the old beaver pond. "Wet areas," Harriet had said. He might be lucky and get his pictures right away. If he did, he wouldn't say anything but wait until he got the developed slides

11 back. He could put up with another week or so buried in the woods. Then Harriet wouldn't feel she had completely wasted her money having the cabin repaired.

He spent the next hour crouched beside the pond, trying to sit quietly, but it was almost impossible. Tiny insects buzzed around his face, crawled down his collar, and generally made him miserable. At first he tried to swat them but decided this was a waste of time. Finally he crawled underneath a low shrub and, with the leaves almost brushing his face, managed to find a little peace.

He waited as patiently as he knew how, but he saw nothing that either resembled a crane or a crane's nest. According to his bird book they didn't build much of a nest—just a shallow cluster of sedge grass and twigs on the ground. The trouble was that the edges of the pond were thick with sedges, reeds, and cattails, and it would have been difficult to see a standing crane, much less a nest. He was about to give up and move on, when suddenly, almost in front of him in the middle of the pond, there was a floating bird. It looked slightly like a small duck with a long, slender neck. Its back was gray-brown and it had a white bill. Link raised his camera to his eyes and looked through the telescopic lens. There was a black band around the whitish bill. He snapped pictures and then put his camera down gently. He began thumbing through the book trying

492

Teaching Tip Explain to students that a 105 mm. lens (paragraph 4, line 2) is a telephoto lens. Based on the same principle as a telescope, the telephoto lens makes distant objects appear closer.

493

ARTIST'S CRAFT
You may wish to point out to students that the bird in the painting is the one described in the last six lines of page 492. The pied-bill grebe, an excellent diver, lives in still, fresh water in areas throughout most of North and South America. The artist's rendition of the bird is painstakingly accurate.
How do you think the artist, Richard Cook, knew exactly what this type of bird looks like? *(Cook did research in books about birds.)*
Do you think it is important for an artist to be accurate in illustrating a selection like this? Explain. *(Accept reasonable responses: Yes; the appreciation of wildlife is an important part of the selection, so it is important that the wildlife be illustrated accurately.)*
CRITICAL: MAKING JUDGMENTS

12 PLOT: TURNING POINT

What fascinates Link about the ducklike bird that appears? *(The bird can remain underwater for some time and pop up in a different place. It can sink and surface slowly, rather like a submarine.)*

LITERAL: NOTING IMPORTANT DETAILS

Why is the sight of this bird a turning point in the story? *(Link begins to understand why his aunt is fascinated by wildlife and living in the country.)*

INFERENTIAL: DRAWING CONCLUSIONS

to find a picture of the floating bird. He made a slight sound as he turned the pages and when he looked up the bird was slowly sinking into the water. It sank lower and lower until finally just its eyes were above the water. He watched fascinated as it disappeared entirely. He waited and waited until he decided that something must have pulled it under and eaten it. Then suddenly it popped to the surface about twenty feet farther away. Link watched as the bird dived several times. It could disappear in a flash or sink slowly and then reappear fifteen or twenty feet away. He wished that he could swim like that underwater. Finally it disappeared for a much longer period of time. His eyes searched the surface of the pond looking for it. Then, entirely by chance, he saw its head slowly emerging in the reeds, not very far from where he sat. It came up slowly, its neck turning cautiously like a submarine periscope. Suddenly it hopped onto what seemed to be a floating pile of reeds. It scratched away some covering reeds and sat down on a nest.

Slowly and cautiously, Link raised his camera and took several pictures. He had been sitting within a few yards of the nest for some time without seeing it. He understood now what Harriet had meant when she said if he sat still long enough he would see things.

After ten minutes of thumbing through his book, he decided that the strange bird that could impersonate a submarine was a pied-bill grebe. He sat quietly for another hour. He saw blue jays and several songbirds that he could not identify and then—for a few hopeful minutes—he thought he saw a sandhill crane. An enormous bird flew high overhead on slow, flapping wings. Link looked at it through his camera lens. It was blue-gray, but it had no red crown on its head. His uncle Albert had warned him not to confuse the great blue heron with the sandhill crane.

"A crane flies with his neck stretched out straight and a heron curves his in an *S* curve," Albert had said.

He was growing stiff and restless, and buzzing insects continued to plague him, so he decided to call it a day, go back, and have a quick dip in the spring. He took a slightly different route and passed through a small natural clearing that he had not visited before. He was partway across when he realized that several birds, including a particularly noisy blue jay, were screaming excitedly about

494

something. He stopped and looked around carefully, searching for the cause of all the fuss. He looked first at the ground and then at the lower branches of the trees. Suddenly he saw an animal about eighteen inches long up in a maple tree at the edge of the clearing. Whether it was the cause of the birds' alarm or not he had no idea, but it was so <u>grotesque</u>-looking that he forgot about the birds. He raised his camera to use the lens as his binoculars. The animal had sort of yellowish-tinged hair and a back and tail covered with white spikes. It was a porcupine! It seemed to be staring straight at him.

He moved slowly toward the tree. The porcupine made no move to run away or even to hide behind the tree trunk.

That would make quite a picture, he thought, as he watched the animal with its ratlike face and eyes. The trouble was that a branch partially blocked his view. He circled, trying to get a clear shot. Either maple leaves or the feathery branches of a nearby spruce kept him from getting a good picture. The porcupine still showed no sign of being afraid.

He looked at a low branch thoughtfully. If he climbed up about level with the animal he could get a beautiful shot. There would be nothing in the way, and he could take the picture from the correct angle as far as the light was concerned. What a story that would make when he got back home! "I was in the same tree as the porcupine when I took this shot," he would say casually.

He slung the camera over his shoulder so that it hung against his back. Then he reached up, grabbed the lowest limb, and began climbing. It was not difficult but he went slowly and cautiously, keeping a wary eye on the porcupine. He got up about ten feet, just slightly below the porcupine, propped himself in a reasonably secure position, and got his camera. He took several shots and then moved a trifle closer. The porcupine began to show the first signs of nervousness. It retreated along its branch, moving about three feet farther out. The fact that it seemed frightened of him gave Link more courage. He climbed one branch higher and leaned over to get at just the right angle. He snapped one picture and then leaned farther to the left. He was too intent on getting the picture, and his right foot slipped. He began to topple. He grabbed frantically for the nearest branch—which was the one on which the porcupine was

13

495

perched. He caught it. The sudden weight on the small branch shook the porcupine off. Link was too busy to notice or care what happened to the porcupine. His right foot slipped off the branch completely, throwing most of his weight on his left foot. The branch on which it was resting was small, and it snapped. That left him with only his right hand grasping one branch. His left hand still held the precious camera. The branch was too big around to hold properly, and it was doubtful if he could have held himself by one hand anyway. He did manage to hold on long enough to allow his feet to swing over so that he was dangling upright. Then he let go and dropped.

It was not a long drop, and he landed on his feet on soft ground. Slightly off balance, he stumbled backward and sat down heavily. There was an instant searing pain. He let out a yelp of agony and dropped the camera. It fell only a few inches to the ground, which was carpeted with leaves and pine needles. Link was not much interested whether the camera was safe or not. He was in too much agony. He felt as though he were sitting on a red-hot stove. He rolled over until he was on his hands and knees. Then he reached back and felt the seat of his pants with his hand, half expecting to feel blood. Instead he felt what seemed to be stiff needles. He looked around suddenly for the porcupine. It was gone, but it had left plenty to remember it by. The entire seat of his pants was filled with quills! He had either landed on or beside the porcupine when he sat down.

Slowly and gingerly he got to his feet. Each movement was painful. He reached around and carefully took hold of the nearest quill he could see. He gave a yank. Nothing happened except he felt a sharp pain in his behind.

He picked up the camera and slowly started toward the cabin. Each step was torture. He paused every few feet, but he couldn't sit down. There was nothing to do but to plod onward, trying to move with the least amount of pain. About two thirds of the way he leaned against a tree, sort of half lying on his stomach, and examined the camera. It seemed unharmed. He blew away a few specks of dirt on the lens and got the lens cap from his pocket and put it on. At least he had got some good shots before he fell. And

496

497

ARTIST'S CRAFT
How do you think the artist is trying to make you feel with this painting? Does the painting help you appreciate the story? Why or why not? *(Accept reasonable responses: Excited, nervous for Link; yes, it helps me visualize what is happening and appreciate Link's feelings.)*
INFERENTIAL: DRAWING CONCLUSIONS

What is Link most afraid of when he lies on his bed? *(that he will have to go to a hospital, where the doctors and nurses will laugh at him)*
LITERAL: RECOGNIZING MAIN IDEA

15 **CHARACTERS' TRAITS**

Why do you think Link might appreciate Aunt Harriet's reaction to his predicament? *(Accept reasonable responses: She is sympathetic, but not overly so. She is honest about the fact that removing the quills will hurt. Above all, she doesn't laugh at him.)*
INFERENTIAL: DRAWING CONCLUSIONS

---

what a story he would have to tell now when he showed the family those slides!

He reached the cabin, went to his room, and lay face down on his bed. Once more he tried pulling a quill. He had no more success than before. Those things were in there to stay! He could see himself being wheeled into a hospital, face down on the stretcher. The doctor would operate while the nurses and everyone stood around laughing.

He was wondering how he would ever get to the hospital when he heard his aunt drive in. He waited until she had entered the cabin.

"Would you come in here, Aunt Harriet?" he called. "I had an accident!"

Harriet came into the room. Link turned to look at her. She glanced at him without changing her expression and said, "Yes, you certainly did. And I'll bet it's painful! What did you do, sit on him?"

"I guess," he said. "I climbed a tree to take his picture and we both fell."

"Hurt yourself otherwise?" she asked.

"Nope. It was rough walking home, though."

"I'll bet it was," she said. "Well, we have to get those quills out. Each quill is covered with dozens of little barbs. That makes them hard to pull out. But if you don't pull them out they work deeper. You can't possibly take off your pants. I'll have to pull the quills out through the cloth. The best way is to take a pair of pliers and give a quick yank. I've got some antiseptic that has sort of a chilling effect, and I'll try to spray you thoroughly with that. Maybe it will soak through your trousers and deaden the pain a little. But I warn you it will hurt."

"Go ahead," Link said, relieved that he wouldn't have to go to the hospital.

Harriet left and returned a few minutes later with a pair of pliers from the car and a can of antiseptic spray. She sprayed Link's posterior thoroughly and then asked, "Ready?"

"I guess as ready as I'll ever be," Link said. He pressed his lips together.

There was a sudden stab of pain, and Harriet said, "That's one!

498

Guided Reading

MONITOR COMPREHENSION: PAGES 491–499

How does Link's willingness to give things a try help resolve his conflicts? (It keeps him in the country and also by the pond long enough to discover that life in the country can be as interesting and as satisfying as his life in the city.) STRATEGIC READING: RETURNING TO PURPOSE

How is this summer vacation helping Link grow? (Accept reasonable responses: It is helping him become more open-minded and less self-centered. It is opening his eyes to the world around him.)
STRATEGIC READING: SUMMARIZING

There's quite a few to go!"

"Don't count them," Link said. "I don't want to know how many until it's all over."

"The Indians dyed porcupine quills and used them to decorate deerskin shirts and pouches and moccasins," she said some time later as she yanked out the fifteenth quill.

"I'm going to save these and use them to decorate a poster that says 'Beware of Porcupines,'" Link said. He clenched his teeth as she gave another yank.

She pulled out twenty-two quills altogether. Link was sore and he knew he would be unable to sit comfortably for several days, but at least he could walk without pain.

"You'd better take off your clothes and examine yourself closely **16** to be certain we haven't missed any. And then spray yourself with disinfectant again."

Link followed her suggestion and then dressed. "I'm going down to the spring," he announced as he walked into the main room of the cabin. "The other day when I waded in, my feet were numb by the time I'd gone three feet. Maybe if I sit down for fifteen minutes I can get the same results."

Harriet gave a slight chuckle. "I don't blame you." He had reached the door when she said, "Link."

He turned.

"I want you to know that I realize how painful that was," she said, almost shyly.

She was much more sympathetic than he had thought, he decided, as he went on toward the spring. But she didn't know how to express it. He was beginning to understand her a little, and the more he understood her the better he liked her. She was really quite a good egg.

THINK IT OVER

1. Soon after Link arrives in the woods, he begins learning about the different forms of wildlife that live **17** there. Discuss the animals he meets and what he learns about them.

2. How did Charley Horse get his name?

3. What does Link find interesting about the pied-bill grebe?

4. In this excerpt from the novel, what indications are there that Link will become interested in observing the wildlife in the Michigan woods?

WRITE

Write a journal entry that Link might **18** have written about his experience with the porcupine.

499

16 PLOT: RESOLUTION
How do Link's efforts at humor indicate a change in attitude?
(Instead of looking at his accident as another negative aspect of the country, Link views it with humor. He has also become comfortable enough with his aunt to make jokes.)
INFERENTIAL: DRAWING CONCLUSIONS

17 THINK IT OVER
1. Link watches a grebe and learns about its odd swimming habits. He meets a porcupine and learns, the hard way, that it is dangerous.
INFERENTIAL: SUMMARIZING
2. Charley Horse is a Chippewa whose real name is Running Horse. Some joker in a lumber camp started calling him Charley, and he kept the name.
LITERAL: NOTING IMPORTANT DETAILS
3. Link is interested in the grebe's ability to swim underwater and surface in unexpected places—like a submarine.
LITERAL: NOTING IMPORTANT DETAILS
4. Link spends two hours watching birds by the pond, and he climbs a tree to get pictures of a porcupine. Although the quills hurt, Link seems exhilarated rather than discouraged.
INFERENTIAL: DRAWING CONCLUSIONS

18 WRITE
Remind students that Link likes a good story, so he might exaggerate a bit. You may wish to suggest that students begin with a "vivid language" chart:

Describing	Verbs	Adjectives	Nouns
the porcupine the fall the pain the walk home Link's feelings			

Responses will vary.
CREATIVE: VISUALIZING

NOTE Additional writing activities appear on page 499D.

Returning to the Predictions Invite students to review the predictions that they made before reading and that they may have written in their personal journals. Encourage them to say whether their predictions changed while reading, and if so, why.

Returning to the Purpose for Reading Ask students whether Link's search for the crane changed his feelings about the country and about his aunt. (Accept reasonable responses: Yes; the search for the crane helped him to appreciate nature and to come to know and respect his aunt.)

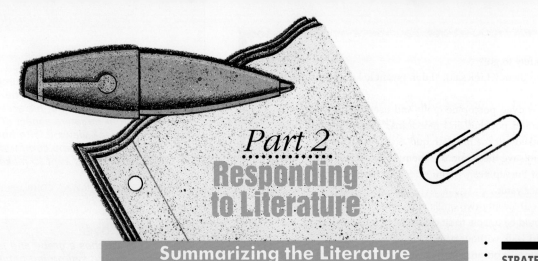

Part 2
Responding to Literature

Summarizing the Literature

Have students retell the story and write a summary.

Invite students to summarize "First Sighting" by using the character conflict chart. If they have not yet completed the chart, have them do so now. (See *Practice Book* page 136, on 499B.) Students may use their completed charts to retell the story and write a brief summary statement.

CHARACTER CONFLICT CHART

Conflict	Predicted Resolution	Actual Resolution
Link prefers city life but has promised to try to photograph a sandhill crane.	He tries to find the crane, can't, and decides to go home.	Link decides to stay and finds things to enjoy in the country.
Link doesn't know his aunt well.	He gets to know her a bit better after a few days.	After he sees a grebe and is stuck full of porcupine quills, Link begins to appreciate his aunt.

Appreciating Literature

Have students share personal responses.

Divide students into small groups to discuss the story. Provide a question such as the following to help the groups get started:

- **Did the author succeed in making the main character's change of heart believable to you? Why or why not?**

PERSONAL JOURNAL Encourage students to use their personal journals to write about ideas and feelings that are expressed in the groups.

STRATEGY CONFERENCE

Discuss the character conflict chart, asking students how it helped them understand and enjoy "First Sighting." Invite volunteers to share other reading strategies they used, such as identifying with the character.

INFORMAL ASSESSMENT

Having students summarize in this way will help you informally assess how well they comprehended the **main conflicts** in the selection. It also will help you see how well they recognized the importance of particular details in contributing to the story's **resolution**.

Critical Thinking Activities

Encourage both cooperative and individual responses.

WRITE A SCENE **Aunt Harriet and Link seem to be understanding each other better at the end of "First Sighting." Write a scene that describes what they do together the next day.** Have students write a new scene with a partner. Encourage them to write dialogue and story action that shows Link is still unsure of himself in the country but is willing to try new things. CREATIVE: INVENTING NEW SCENES

IMPROVISE A MONOLOGUE **Suppose Link had left the country when his aunt first suggested it. How do you think he might have felt about his decision?** Have students improvise a monologue that conveys Link's thoughts on his way back to the city. CREATIVE: INVENTING NEW ENDINGS

WRITE AN ESSAY **Aunt Harriet brought Link to the country on the chance he might like it, despite his obvious reluctance. Do you believe it's wise to force new experiences on people? Why or why not?** Ask students to write brief essays in response to this question. Suggest that they first list arguments both for and against. CRITICAL: MAKING JUDGMENTS

Link might decide to keep himself busy during his stay at the cabin by keeping a nature journal. Write entries for two or three days. If you like, include drawings of the animals or plants sighted.

Thursday, July 14

by _____
(your name)

Writer's Journal

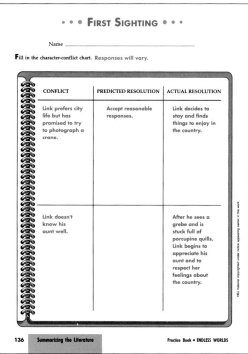

• • • FIRST SIGHTING • • •

Name _____

Fill in the character-conflict chart. Responses will vary.

CONFLICT	PREDICTED RESOLUTION	ACTUAL RESOLUTION
Link prefers city life but has promised to try to photograph a crane.	Accept reasonable responses.	Link decides to stay and finds things to enjoy in the country.
Link doesn't know his aunt well.		After he sees a grebe and is stuck full of porcupine quills, Link begins to appreciate his aunt and to respect her feelings about the country.

136 Summarizing the Literature

Practice Book • ENDLESS WORLDS

Practice Book

WRITER'S JOURNAL
page 85: Writing a creative response

PRACTICE BOOK
page 136: Summarizing the selection

VO·CAB·U·LAR·Y
Workshop

Reviewing Key Words

Have students review the predict-o-gram they completed before reading and confirm or modify their predictions. As they discuss the revised charts, students should support their choices with evidence from the story.

PREDICT-O-GRAM

Discovering Country Life	Character's Reactions
quills	*grotesque* *gingerly*

Point out that *exposures* does not fit well in the final predict-o-gram. Ask students to tell how *exposures* was used in the story. (to describe the film Link was using to take photographs of the animals) Then discuss how the other words were used.

Extending Vocabulary

CLASSIFYING AND CATEGORIZING   Remind students that Link encounters some fairly strange animals in the country—one of them called a pied-bill grebe. From context clues, we know that a grebe is a water bird that resembles a duck. Explain that by calling a grebe a *bird* and noting its resemblance to a *duck,* we are classifying and categorizing it. We are putting the creature under a general heading and then saying that it is like another animal we know.

COOPERATIVE LEARNING   Have pairs of students look up *boar, condor, dromedary,* and *porpoise* in a dictionary or a guide to wild animals. Ask them to label each animal as a mammal or a bird, and then to name a more familiar animal that each one resembles.

Integrated Language Arts

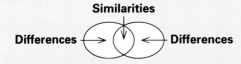

WRITING

Writing About the Literature

CREATIVE: DESCRIPTIVE POEM Invite students to write poems in which they contrast the area where they live with a place they've seen or read about that is very different. Suggest that they use a Venn diagram in planning their poems. WRITING

Similarities

Differences → ⟨⟩ ← Differences

AVAILABLE ON PROJECT CARD

CRITICAL: SELF-HELP ESSAY Explain to students that they are going to write a short self-help book for teenagers on how to get along with other people. Spark a group discussion by asking for some *do*s and *don't*s on the subject. Direct students to choose one of the *do*s or *don't*s and then write a page-length section of the book, with reasons and examples. LISTENING/SPEAKING/WRITING

NOTE: An additional writing activity appears on page 499.

SPEAKING/LISTENING

Recommended Readings

Have students imagine that they are taking a vacation in the wild. Ask them to list three books they would take along to entertain themselves. Have students work in small groups to try to convince the others of the validity of their choices.
LISTENING/SPEAKING/WRITING

SPELLING

Spelling Review

SPELLING WORDS: *biscuit, excitedly, exposure, grotesque, headquarters, mechanic, moccasins, quill, specks, telescopic*

Have students write the Spelling Words as you dictate them. Then have a volunteer write them on the board. Have students read each word aloud in unison, listening for the /k/, /ks/, and /kw/ sounds. Have another volunteer circle the letter or letters in each word that represent the /k/, /ks/, or /kw/ sounds. LISTENING/WRITING/SPELLING

INTEGRATED SPELLING

page 66: Writing words with the /k/, /ks/, and /kw/ sounds

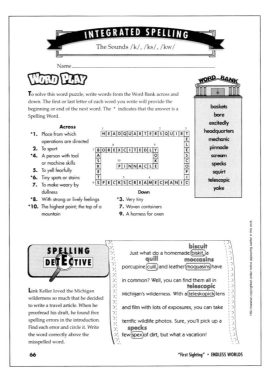

Integrated Spelling

LITERARY APPRECIATION
INTRODUCE

Point of View

OBJECTIVE: *To identify first- and third-person points of view*

1	Focus

Explain the importance of point of view.

Ask students to imagine how "First Sighting" would be different if the same events were written in the form of a diary kept by Aunt Harriet. (Accept reasonable responses: Readers would learn more about what she thinks and does and less about Link's actions and thoughts.) Explain that the point of view a writer uses to tell a story determines how much information a reader gets and how the story develops.

2	Teach/Model

Teach the skill.

Tell students that in the third-person point of view the narrator is someone outside the story who refers to all of the characters as *he, she,* or *they*. Point out that a third-person narrator can be either omniscient (capable of telling what every character thinks and feels) or limited (capable of telling the feelings and thoughts of only one character).

Model the thinking.

Have students read paragraph 7 on page 486. Then model identifying clues to point of view:

> **The story is told from the third-person point of view by an outside observer. If Link were telling the story, he would say, "I unloaded the station wagon. . . ." If Aunt Harriet were telling the story, she would say, "while I put things away."**

Explain to students that the story is told from a limited third-person point of view. If the story were told from an omniscient point of view, the reader would know Aunt Harriet's thoughts and feelings as well as Link's.

3   Practice/Apply

Have students apply the learning.

Ask students to identify clues to the point of view in paragraph 1 on page 498. Ask volunteers to share their clues.

4   Summarize

Informally assess the learning.

Ask students to summarize what they learned. (A story written in the third-person point of view is told by an outside observer. A story written in the first person is told by a character in the story.)

READER ⟷ WRITER CONNECTION

Point of View

▶ **Writers** use point of view to define a story's perspective and to control the way it unfolds.

▶ **Readers** use point of view to understand how much information to expect from a character.

WRITE FIRST- AND THIRD-PERSON REPORTS   Have students imagine that a crime has been committed, and all the relevant information needs to be recorded. Have students write two reports, one from the point of view of the victim, the other from the point of view of the first police officer on the scene.

CHALLENGE   Challenge students to write a mystery story, using the first-person point of view. Suggest that they use this point of view to help the reader unravel the mystery and understand the central character.

SECOND-LANGUAGE SUPPORT   Pair students with peer tutors to discuss point of view in "First Sighting." (See *Second-Lanugage Support Manual*.)

Writer's Journal

Practice Book

WRITER'S JOURNAL
page 86: Writing from first- and third-person points of view

PRACTICE BOOK
page 137: Identifying point of view

Comparing-Contrasting/Making Judgments

OBJECTIVE: *To make judgments about characters or events in a story by comparing and contrasting*

Review

Review making judgments by comparing and contrasting.

Model how you would consider the views of the characters and the story events.

Aunt Harriet seems to think the country is peaceful, but Link is disturbed by the strange noises at night. Comparing these views to judge who is right, and thinking of the story events, I note that Link does sleep soundly, so Aunt Harriet seems to be right.

Practice/Apply

Have students make judgments.

Have students judge whose idea of the country the story supports.

Summarize

Informally assess the learning.

Ask students to summarize what they reviewed. (To make judgments about characters or events in a narrative, readers compare and contrast actions and attitudes.)

CHALLENGE Ask students to compare and contrast Link's and Aunt Harriet's ideas about bears. Then have them invent a new episode that would prove Link's fears were justified.

PRACTICE BOOK
page 138: Comparing and contrasting to make judgments

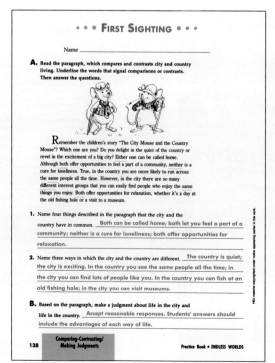

• • • FIRST SIGHTING • • •

Name _____

A. Read the paragraph, which compares and contrasts city and country living. Underline the words that signal comparisons or contrasts. Then answer the questions.

Remember the children's story "The City Mouse and the Country Mouse"? Which one are you? Do you delight in the quiet of the country or revel in the excitement of a big city? Either one can be called home. Although both offer opportunities to feel a part of a community, neither is a cure for loneliness. True, in the country you are more likely to run across the same people all the time. However, in the city there are so many different interest groups that you can easily find people who enjoy the same things you enjoy. Both offer opportunities for relaxation, whether it's a day at the old fishing hole or a visit to a museum.

1. Name four things described in the paragraph that the city and the country have in common. _Both can be called home; both let you feel a part of a community; neither is a cure for loneliness; both offer opportunities for relaxation._

2. Name three ways in which the city and the country are different. _The country is quiet; the city is exciting. In the country you see the same people all the time; in the city you can find lots of people like you. In the country you can fish at an old fishing hole; in the city you can visit museums._

B. Based on the paragraph, make a judgment about life in the city and life in the country. _Accept reasonable responses. Students' answers should include the advantages of each way of life._

138 Comparing-Contrasting/
Making Judgments   Practice Book ■ ENDLESS WORLDS

Practice Book

Fact-Opinion/Viewpoint

OBJECTIVE: *To identify an author's purpose and viewpoint by distinguishing fact from opinion*

Review

Review identifying author's viewpoint.

Remind students that readers can often identify an author's viewpoint on a subject by separating opinions from facts. Readers can then go on to identify the author's purpose for writing. Model how to identify viewpoint:

> **Link finds the woods dull at first but later becomes fascinated by animals. It is a *fact* that the woods have not changed. I see that the author's viewpoint is that nature is fascinating. His purpose is to convince readers of that through Link's change of opinion.**

Practice/Apply

Have students identify fact and opinion.

COOPERATIVE LEARNING Have small groups of students discuss how Aunt Harriet's opinions reflect those of the author. Ask them to find facts to support Aunt Harriet's opinions.

Summarize

Informally assess the learning.

Have students summarize what they reviewed. (Readers sift fact from opinion to learn an author's viewpoint and purpose.)

CHALLENGE Ask students to imagine they have been sent to a new school to which they want to convince a friend to go. Challenge them to write a letter to the friend, describing the school and slanting the information to express a favorable opinion.

Integrated Curriculum

SCIENCE

Craning Your Neck

Link isn't the only person to have trouble spotting cranes. Some cranes are hard to find because they are endangered species. Invite a group of students to choose an endangered species and to report to their classmates on why it is in peril and how scientists are trying to help it survive. Likely sources of information are magazines such as *Audubon, Zoo, Wildlife Conservation,* and *Science World.* If students have trouble selecting a species, suggest one of the following: the whooping crane, the African elephant, the panda.

LISTENING/SPEAKING/READING/WRITING

SOCIAL STUDIES

The Chippewa Way of Life

CULTURAL AWARENESS Ask interested students to research the Chippewa, Charley Horse's people, who lived in the woods of Michigan before white people came. As a helpful hint, tell students that the Chippewa are also known as the Ojibwa, a name under which they are sometimes described in encyclopedias. An artistic student might provide a drawing of a traditional Chippewa costume. Such costumes, according to Aunt Harriet, were often decorated with porcupine quills. READING

ART

Passenger Pigeon Portraits

Explain to students that John James Audubon was a famous birdwatcher and artist. Ask interested students to research Audubon's work and art for presentation to the group. Students might enjoy drawing or painting pictures of unusual birds for display in the classroom.

LISTENING/SPEAKING/READING/WRITING

SCIENCE

Great Observers

AVAILABLE ON PROJECT CARD

In "First Sighting," Link discovers the rewards of observing nature. Suggest to students that our ability to observe hidden natural phenomena, such as distant stars, microscopic animals, or even the bones of our own bodies, is the result of inventions by great observers, some famous, some not so famous. Ask students to look up one of the following inventions in a science book or an encyclopedia: the telescope, the microscope, the X-ray machine. Encourage students to find out how the instrument works, who invented it, and what interesting stories there are about the invention or the inventor. Call on volunteers to give oral reports, and invite other students to ask questions or to supply missing details. LISTENING/SPEAKING/READING/WRITING

A Life's Calling

OBSERVING ANIMALS IN THE WILD IS CALLED FIELD RESEARCH.

The famous paleoanthropologist Louis Leakey believed that a good field researcher is patient, a close observer, systematic but not rigid, and resolute enough to stay with a tough job. Leakey found these qualities in Jane Goodall and Dian Fossey.

Jane Goodall, a native of England, has been studying the family life and habits of chimpanzees in Tanzania since 1957. Dian Fossey, an American, had no field experience when, in 1960, Leakey hired her to observe the African gorilla. Fossey gained the trust of a gorilla family by lying down in a passive pose when observing them. In time she grew fiercely protective of the apes.

Both Goodall and Fossey wrote about their observations for the general public. Many field observations, however, reach us through the work of nature writers, such as Barry Lopez. He traveled across the Arctic to observe its landscape and animals. Then, in his book *Arctic Dreams*, he described the playful harp seals, the wavy-coated musk ox, and the ivory-tusked narwhal that few Americans have ever seen. ■

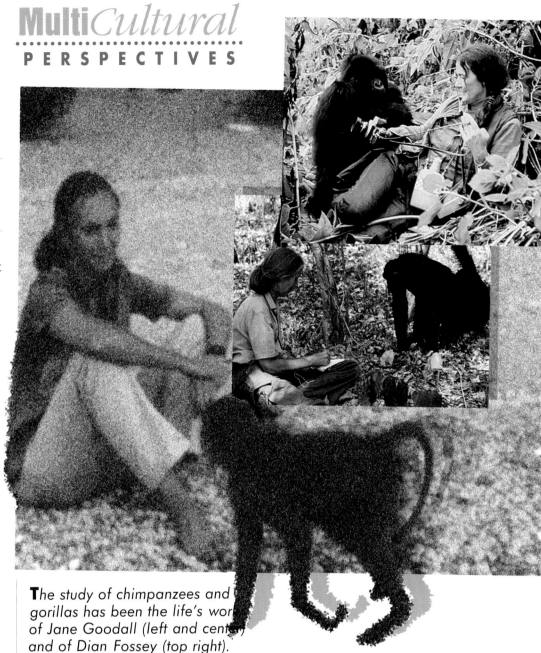

The study of chimpanzees and gorillas has been the life's work of Jane Goodall (left and center) and of Dian Fossey (top right).

ACTIVITY CORNER

■ Ask students to conduct field research on a pet or on another animal for several days, using an observation log to record their findings. When their research is complete, ask: What can you infer about this animal from your observations? What questions remain unanswered?

■ Read aloud a passage from Lopez's *Arctic Dreams* about the polar bear, often called "the great wanderer." Ask students to record any questions they may have about the bear as you read. Then invite them to find out the answers by writing to a zoo or wildlife organization.

AVAILABLE ON PROJECT CARD

■ Suggest that students read more about Jane Goodall, Dian Fossey, or field researchers in other parts of the world and write a brief report based on what they learn.

Be Like the Bird

ABOUT THE POET

Victor Hugo (1802–1885) was a French poet and novelist who experimented with dialect and rhythm, creating what was considered revolutionary lyric poetry. He believed, however, that writers should lead people morally. Therefore, in his novels, especially *Les Misérables,* he tried to arouse concern for poor people.

1 POETIC STRUCTURE

How are the short lines appropriate to the poem's subject? *(Accept reasonable responses: The short lines give the poem a choppy rhythm, perhaps like that of a bird hopping from branch to branch.)*

CRITICAL: MAKING JUDGMENTS

2 THEME

What is the poet suggesting that his readers do? *(Accept reasonable responses: They should take risks with confidence.)*

INFERENTIAL: DETERMINING MAIN IDEA

WRITER'S JOURNAL page 87: Writing a critical response

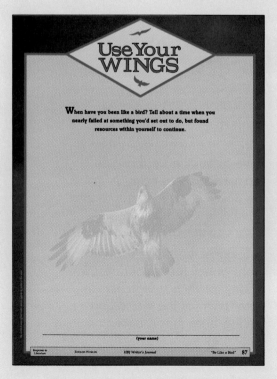

Use Your WINGS

When have you been like a bird? Tell about a time when you nearly failed at something you'd set out to do, but found resources within yourself to continue.

(your name)

Response to Literature   ENDLESS WORLDS   HBJ Writer's Journal   "Be Like a Bird" **87**

Be Like the Bird

by Victor Hugo

Be like the Bird, who
Halting in his flight
On limb too slight
Feels it give way beneath him,
Yet sings
Knowing he hath wings.

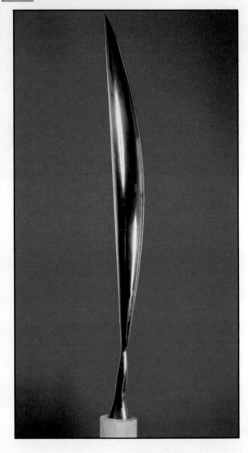

L'Oiseau, 1940, Constantin Brancusi, Musée National d'Art Moderne, Paris, France.

Reading the Poem

Read the poem aloud for students, encouraging them to listen to the rhythm and the pauses. Then invite small groups of students to practice and present a choral reading of the poem.

Responding to the Poem

Ask students if they agree with or would like to follow the poet's suggestion. Discuss what it means to have the self-confidence to try something that is new or a little risky. Ask them how self-confidence helps people try again after a first attempt fails.

WATCHING NATURE

Think about the different birds mentioned in each selection. Compare these birds to the description presented in Victor Hugo's poem "Be Like the Bird." What does Victor Hugo think people can learn from birds? Do you agree?

. . . .

As Lincoln in "First Sighting" spends more time in the woods, he learns more about nature and begins to appreciate it. Do you think he would enjoy a job similar to Loren Eiseley's in "Free Flight"?

. . . .

WRITER'S WORKSHOP Reread Russell Hoban's poem "The Sparrow Hawk." Write a poem or a short essay describing one of the animals from the selections or an animal that you have observed in nature.

501

Watching Nature

Remind students that the prose selections in this theme dealt with encounters between birds and human beings. Help them recall what the people in each selection learned from the encounter about nature and themselves. Point out that the sense of watching and learning is conveyed in the poems in another way, through sound effects and imagery. Turn to page 501 for theme wrap-up activities.
  Note that pages 501A–501B provide support for applying the writing process to the last question.

1 First have students decide what the speaker in Victor Hugo's poem thinks we can learn from birds. Then ask them to agree or disagree by citing birds in the prose selections. *(Accept reasonable responses: Hugo's bird can teach us courage in the face of adversity. So can Eiseley's hawk.)*
CRITICAL: SYNTHESIZING

2 Tell students to consider what Link would and would not like about Eiseley's job. *(Accept reasonable responses: Link would enjoy working with animals, but he might have qualms about keeping wild creatures in cages, as Eiseley himself does.)*
INFERENTIAL: SPECULATING

Writer's Workshop
See pages 501A–501B for suggestions for applying the writing process. Responses may draw on the reading or on students' own experience. You may prefer to allow students to respond to the theme in their own way. WRITING PROCESS: A DESCRIPTIVE POEM OR ESSAY

Writer's Workshop

Review the elements of description. Remind students that a good description, whether in a poem or an essay, contains the writer's observations. The writer observes and then identifies details by using the five senses: sight, hearing, touch, smell, and taste. The writer then translates these sensory images into appropriate words and phrases. Suggest that students refer to the Handbook in the *Writer's Journal* as they write, revise, and proofread their descriptive poems or essays.

Prewriting

The first task for students is to decide whether to write a poem or an essay. If they select a poem, suggest that they examine the imagery and sound effects in "The Sparrow Hawk" before writing. Whichever genre they choose, have students

● think about the animals from the selections or animals they have seen in nature.

● use a web to gather descriptive details. Encourage students to include details about the animal's appearance, sounds, and behavior. Their web might look like the following:

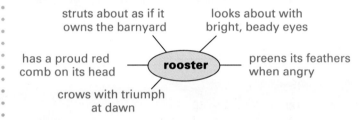

Drafting

Ask students to compose a draft of their descriptive poem or essay. Encourage them to

● use vivid details, sensory images, and comparisons.

● use vivid verbs to describe the animal's movements.

● write the description from a single point of view.

● write freely without regard to spelling, punctuation, or grammar.

COMPUTER CONNECTION   Students may want to use a computer during the revising stage so that they may easily insert strong adjectives and adverbs to strengthen their descriptions.

Responding and Revising

Have students work in small groups to respond to one another's poems or essays. Offer these guidelines for evaluation and revision:

- Does the writer use the five senses in the description? Can a reader use sensory images to understand the piece? If not, use the senses to replace fuzzy images.
- Would well-chosen adjectives or adverbs help the piece? Look for opportunities to add them. (See the Language/Literature Link below.)

STUDENT SELF-ASSESSMENT OPTION   Students may use the Writing Self-Assessment Checklist in the *Portfolio Teacher's Guide*. Suggest that as they use the checklist, they focus on the sensory images in their descriptions and their use of adjectives and adverbs.

Proofreading

Offer these proofreading tips:
- Check for pronoun consistency. If you call your animal *it* in one place, don't use *he* or *she* in another.
- If you decided to capitalize the first word of each line of your poem, check to see if you followed your choice consistently.

Publishing

If you wish, discuss with students options for publishing. Some students may wish to illustrate their poems or essays and save them in their reading/writing portfolio or bind them into a class booklet about animals.

LANGUAGE/LITERATURE LINK

Expanding Sentences

Remind students that adjectives and adverbs are modifiers. Explain that good writers use modifiers with care. Illustrate the point by turning to page 479, paragraph two, of "Free Flight." Have students find examples of effective adjectives and adverbs. *(hopelessly, fierce, indifferent)* Discuss how these modifiers help the reader grasp the hawk's predicament and respond emotionally to its proud resignation. Have students revise their work by using strong adjectives and adverbs.

Speaking Option

ORAL DESCRIPTION   The *Writer's Workshop* can be adapted to allow students to present their poems or essays as an oral description. Have students follow the guidelines for Prewriting, Drafting, and Responding and Revising. Offer these tips for oral reading of a descriptive poem or essay:

- Introduce your subject in a way that sparks audience interest.
- Adjust reading speed and tone of voice to suit your poem or essay.
- If possible, use visual aids to enhance your oral description.

Have students give their oral readings to a small group of classmates.

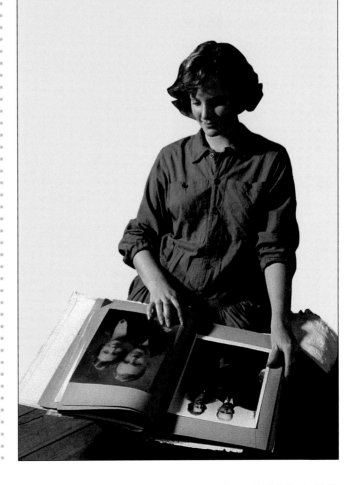

Connections

The Connections activities on Student Anthology pages 502–503 guide students to synthesize multicultural and content-area information with the unit theme. Before students begin, ask them to review quickly the purpose-setting paragraph on page 400. Then ask students which of the selections in Unit 5 they liked best and why. Invite them to discuss what they learned from reading about observation, and ask them to explain its importance in their own lives.

To prepare students for the Multicultural Connection, you may wish to give them background on Chinese landscape painting.

Explain that the art of landscape painting flowered in China in the tenth century, more than a thousand years ago. Its masters wandered through the countryside and painted the scenes that filled their hearts. Traditional Chinese landscape painters did not paint realistic representations of nature, but a higher truth they saw beyond it. Sometimes they added lakes and trees that weren't really there to give the picture a sense of harmony. Sometimes they made a mountain huge and a human figure tiny to convey the grandeur of nature.

CONNECTIONS

MULTICULTURAL CONNECTION

YOUTHFUL ARTIST

When she was only three years old, Wang Yani amazed her family and friends with her wonderful pictures of animals. Born in Gongcheng, China, in 1975, this creative young girl has had her pictures in major exhibits and museums since she was four years old.

When she was young, her paintings were often of monkeys and cats. Now the landscape around her home and her family and friends are her favorite subjects.

Wang Yani has had little instruction in how to paint, but she has a wonderful imagination and a good memory, two important characteristics for an artist. When you look at her paintings, you can imagine the movements she made with her paint brushes when she was creating her delightful animals.

In 1985, thousands of visitors came to see her paintings at the Smithsonian Institution in Washington, D.C. Titled "Yani: The Brush of Innocence," the exhibition featured her paintings of animals, birds, and landscapes.

■ *For many centuries the Chinese have painted beautiful pictures of people, animals, and landscapes. They are also famous for intricate jade carvings and woven fabrics. Bring photographs of Chinese arts and crafts to class. Contrast the arts and crafts of China with those of the United States. Discuss the likenesses and differences between the arts of these two cultures.*

502

Multicultural Connection

YOUTHFUL ARTIST   Before students begin the activity, remind them to look at the artwork. Ask what feelings Wang Yani's animals and landscapes arouse in them. You might want to refer to the book on Wang Yani, *A Young Painter* by Theng Yhensun (Scholastic, 1991). Encourage students to bring photos of Chinese arts and crafts to class, and discuss their responses to them. Suggest that students work in small groups to research the arts and crafts of the two cultures before they do a comparison study.

PICTURES OF PICTURES

Create a poster about a painter whose work you admire. Design your poster any way you like, but be sure to include information about the painter's life, sample pictures of paintings with captions, and an analysis of his or her work. Display your poster on a wall or bulletin board in the classroom, and give a short presentation on the painter.

ART/SOCIAL STUDIES/SCIENCE CONNECTION

PAINTING PROJECT

Think of a feature of the natural world that you would like to paint. Then fill out a web like the one below, explaining why you would choose that subject, how you would paint the picture, and what impact you would like your painting to have on an audience. Summarize your thoughts in a short essay, and then explain your project to a small group.

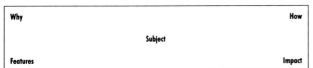

Why		How
	Subject	
Features		Impact

503

Art Connection

PICTURES OF PICTURES Guide students to sources that can help them complete this project, such as museum card shops and art books in the school or local library. You may wish to offer students a list of artists whom they might appreciate and enjoy. Encourage students to collaborate in small groups to plan a presentation on the painter of their choice.

Art/Social Studies/Science Connection

PAINTING PROJECT Students may profit from a discussion before they begin this activity. Decide on a subject from nature, such as a storm. Discuss how hail, lightning, or swollen rivers, painted realistically, might arouse fear or awe in a viewer. Then have students proceed with their own projects.

Integrated Language Arts

Reviewing Vocabulary—Make Up a Story

1. On the board, write six Key Words or other vocabulary words that might be used in a coherent story. For example:

Key Words

fallow	provender
meanders	eaves
foraging	diverting

2. Ask successive students to use a Key Word in a sentence. Remind the students that the sentences have to connect to form a story.

3. Continue the game with a new set of Key Words and the same or a different story.

4. Have students work in groups to make up stories from other Key Words. Groups might compare stories to see which is the funniest or the most interesting.

Reviewing Spelling Words

Integrated Spelling page 67 provides a review of the Spelling Words from Unit 5. *Integrated Spelling* page 68 provides practice with commonly confused words.

Writing About "Observations"

You may wish to have students respond to the Unit focus by writing a travel article about a place they have visited or would like to have visited. Or students may respond by writing original poetry or choosing poetry that appeals to them. Both or either of these assignments can be added the magazine in their *Writer's Journal*. (See *Writer's Journal* pages 88–89.)

INTEGRATED SPELLING

pages 67–68: Reviewing unit words and commonly confused words

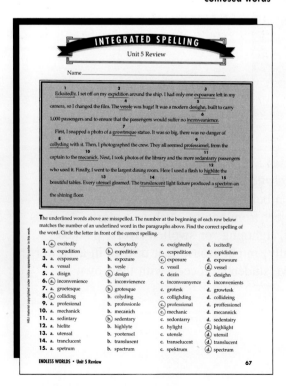

WRITER'S JOURNAL

pages 88–89: Making Your Own Magazine

Assessment Options

Informal Assessment

See the suggestions below to informally assess students' progress in Unit 5.

INFORMAL ASSESSMENT NOTES AND CHECKLISTS

If you used the informal assessment notes in the lesson plans to evaluate students' reading and writing behaviors, you may now want to update your Running Records. You may wish to have students complete the Self-Assessment checklist in the *Portfolio Teacher's Guide*.

PORTFOLIO CONFERENCE

The Portfolio Conference provides you with an opportunity to learn about each student's

- preference for fiction or nonfiction.
- general writing development.
- understanding of comparing/contrasting and making judgments.

Discuss the reading selections in Unit 5, focusing on whether the student likes them. Ask about similar works of fiction or nonfiction the student has read.

Have the student choose from the reading/ writing portfolio he or she enjoyed working on. The different ending to "Free Flight" might be interesting to discuss. Ask the student to comment on what he or she liked about the piece. Offer positive feedback and encouragement.

Formal Assessment

The formal assessment tools described below may be found in the *Teacher's Resource Bank*.

SKILLS ASSESSMENT

The Unit 5 *Skills Assessment* provides the teacher with feedback about students' mastery of the specific skills and strategies taught in Learning Through Literature. Skills tested in this unit are Structural Analysis and Compare-Contrast/Making Judgments. If students had difficulty, refer to pages R35–R52 for visual, auditory, and kinesthetic/motor models that may be used to reteach skills tested in this unit.

HOLISTIC ASSESSMENT

The *Holistic Assessment* for Unit 5 may be used to assess a student's ability to understand passages written at the same level as the selections in the Student Anthology. If students have difficulty, refer them to the appropriate lessons in the Handbook for Readers and Writers: Active Reading Strategies, Reading Nonfiction, Vocabulary Strategies.

INTEGRATED PERFORMANCE ASSESSMENT

The *Integrated Performance Assessment* for Unit 5 provides you with a profile of how well each student uses reading, writing, listening, and speaking strategies to read and respond to a piece of literature. Assessment results reflect how well students employ the strategies modeled and practiced in the classroom.

Be a Teacher-Researcher

It's been said that every teacher is a researcher in his or her own classroom. Keeping tabs on a class of middle schoolers can be a formidable task. Test your observation skills by constructing a profile for each student, based on questions such as these:

- Does the student wear eyeglasses?
- Is the student left- or right-handed?
- Does the student have brothers or sisters?
- What are the student's favorite hobbies and pastimes?
- What was the last book the student was excited about?
- What seems to be the student's best time of day?
- Does the student wear orthodontic braces?

- What are the student's strengths in reading/writing activities?
- Is the student a leader or a follower within his or her group?
- Does the student participate in after-school activities?

You may wish to use this profile to begin a portfolio for each student. Other items that might be added to the portfolio include

- occasional photographs
- significant anecdotal events
- representative samples of the student's best work

The portfolio might be useful in preparing for appropriate instruction or for parent-teacher conferences.

SOARING STUDIES

Whether it is observing pigeons in a city park or hawks in a rural habitat, birdwatching not only introduces students to a fascinating hobby, but leads to a greater awareness of the environment. These resources may help get your fledgling birders off the ground.

■ *Field Guide to the Birds* by Roger Tory Peterson (Houghton Mifflin). Peterson's guide features color paintings and maps of habitats.

■ *The Birder's Handbook* by Paul Ehrlich, David Dobkin, and Darryl Wheye (Simon and Schuster). This reference contains useful information that builds upon the typical facts and charts found in most field guides.

■ Check with local offices of your state's wildlife management agencies or Audubon Society.

Survival Arts for Students

Most educators consider that higher-order thinking strategies such as visualizing, representing, and problem-solving are powerful tools that enable students to adapt to change. Here are some reasons to make creative expression a part of your language arts program:

1. Art projects enhance students' ability to concentrate and stay focused on tasks.
2. Artwork helps students set standards and goals and establish plans for achieving them.
3. Art can affect the way children perceive objects and relationships.
4. Dramatics enable students to adopt multiple points of view.
5. Composing helps students identify and use patterns.
6. Art reinforces the idea that communication requires clarity.

UNIT

SOLUTIONS

SIX

Planning Center

What's Ahead in "Solutions"?

LOOKING TOWARD OTHERS: PAGES 508–539B   Your students may discover something about themselves when they meet a fictional character and a real person who use their skills and inventiveness to improve the lives of others.

INNOVATIONS: PAGES 540–559B   What are the qualities of an inventor? Your students will discover the answer as they read "Innovations." Perhaps they will also discover that they have what it takes.

SPACE: PAGES 560–579B   Is there life elsewhere in the universe? Challenge your students to think about the possibility as they read a short story, an excerpt from a nonfiction article, and a poem.

Pacing

This unit is designed to take approximately five or six weeks, depending on your students' needs.

Assessment and Evaluation

ASSESSMENT OPTIONS		
Title	Description	When and How It's Used
INFORMAL ASSESSMENT OPTIONS (Ongoing)		
Reading/Writing Portfolio	Contains samples of students' literacy development.	Collect samples of personal journals and writing throughout the unit. Hold periodic Portfolio Conferences.
Informal Assessment Notes	Appear throughout the *Teacher's Edition*.	Observe students' reading, writing, listening, and speaking behaviors. Complete checklists on an ongoing basis.
Student Self-Assessment Notes	Appear throughout the *Teacher's Edition*.	Students monitor their use of reading and writing strategies.
Running Records	Ongoing assessment of students' reading skills and strategies as they read both fiction and nonfiction.	Record periodically to track students' progress.
FORMAL ASSESSMENT OPTIONS (End of Unit)		
Skills Assessment	Assesses mastery of strategies and skills taught in Learning Through Literature.	Administer at end of the unit.
Holistic Assessment	Evaluates students' ability to read and understand excerpts from literature.	Administer at end of the unit.
Integrated Performance Assessment	Assesses use of reading and writing strategies modeled and practiced in the classroom.	Administer at end of the unit.

Literature Cassette 2

Recordings of some of the selections in "Solutions" may be used for instruction or students' listening enjoyment:

- "Little Green Men"
- "The First"

Audiovisual Materials and Software

Alexander Graham Bell: The Voice Heard 'Round the World. Aims Media. Follow the life of one of the most famous American inventors, who was also a teacher and a poet. INTERACTIVE VIDEODISC

Chicano Park. Cinema Guild, 1990. This film highlights artists, musicians, and activists who were key to the creation of a park in the heart of a barrio in San Diego. FILM OR VIDEO

The Friends by Rosa Guy. Media Guild, 1987. A mix of acted vignettes and an author interview in a story about a Caribbean immigrant girl developing new friendships in Harlem during the 1950s. FILM OR VIDEO

The Halley Project: A Mission in Our Solar System. Mindscape, 1986. Students become space navigators while they learn about the solar system. COMPUTER SOFTWARE

Spaceborne. Pyramid. The best moments from a decade of discovery transformed into one spectacular journey in this "space ballet". FILM OR VIDEO

Toni Cade Bambara. American Audio Prose Library. An interview with the author touches on many topics. AUDIOCASSETTE

"These men and women have through their creativity, ingenuity, and knowledge, brought about changes that have been of enormous benefit to all mankind."

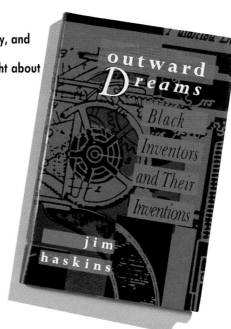

HBJ Treasury of Literature Library

Here are some of the options you will find in the *HBJ Treasury of Literature Library Guide* for *Outward Dreams: Black Inventors and Their Inventions:*

- **Reading Cooperatively** in response groups
- **Reading Independently** during sustained silent reading periods
- **Directing the Reading** through questioning strategies
- **Reading Aloud** to encourage literature appreciation

Bulletin Board Idea

On the bulletin board labeled "What's the Problem?" put up four general words such as *red, seven, congress,* and *water.* Explain that these words are answers or solutions to questions or problems that the class is to provide. Invite students to tack up questions that will help their classmates learn or review interesting information. An example of a question answered by *red* might be: "What is the lowest color in the spectrum that the human eye can see?" Tell students to use note cards for writing out their questions. Invite them to suggest other general words that can serve as answers to questions their classmates formulate.

Solutions

Ask students for different meanings of the word *solutions*. You may wish to write these on the board: *answers, clarifications, explanations.* Ask them to read the unit introduction and preview the theme titles on page 505 to help them set a purpose for reading the unit. Then have students speculate about which meaning of *solutions* might apply to "Looking Toward Others," "Innovations," and "Space." Ask students to think about how people of different cultures might react to these titles. CULTURAL AWARENESS

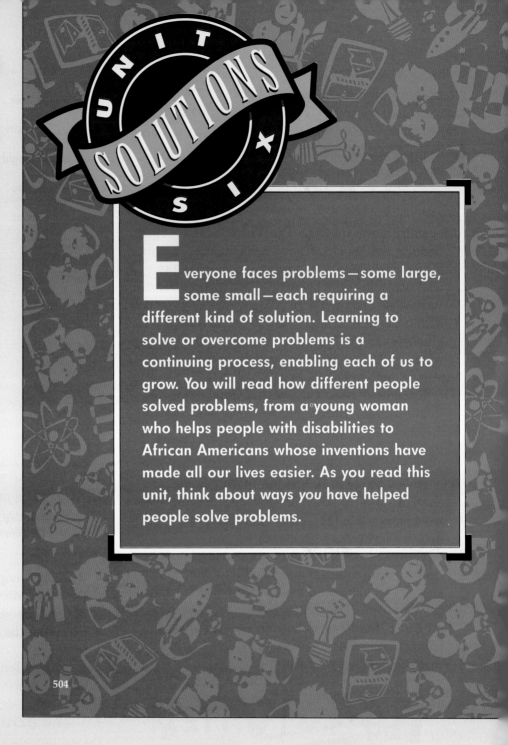

UNIT SIX
SOLUTIONS

Everyone faces problems—some large, some small—each requiring a different kind of solution. Learning to solve or overcome problems is a continuing process, enabling each of us to grow. You will read how different people solved problems, from a young woman who helps people with disabilities to African Americans whose inventions have made all our lives easier. As you read this unit, think about ways *you* have helped people solve problems.

504

THEMES

LOOKING TOWARD OTHERS
· ·
508

INNOVATIONS
· ·
540

SPACE
· ·
560

505

Focus on Literary Genre

If you wish to have students focus on literary genre, or form, as they read the selections in "Solutions," refer to the Literary Genre list. (A complete Table of Contents classified by literary genre appears on pages R98–R101.) The labels on the numbered annotations beside the reduced student pages will help you guide students to note and analyze the literary elements and characteristics of each genre.

BOOKSHELF

OUTWARD DREAMS: BLACK INVENTORS AND THEIR INVENTIONS
BY JIM HASKINS

Few of the people in this book appear in history books, but all of these inventors were heroic in their struggles to overcome prejudice to gain patents and recognition.

HBJ LIBRARY BOOK

THE WRIGHT BROTHERS: HOW THEY INVENTED THE AIRPLANE
BY RUSSELL FREEDMAN

Freedman tells how these self-taught bicycle mechanics solved the problems that had baffled generations of scientists and engineers. Photographs illustrate this vivid account of the lives of these two young men. ALA NOTABLE BOOK

506

HBJ Library Book

Have students read the information about *Outward Dreams: Black Inventors and Their Inventions* and look at the cover illustration. Have them discuss what they know about the book so far. Page 503F provides a preview of the lesson plans that can be found in the *HBJ Treasury of Literature Library Guide*.

THE BROOKLYN BRIDGE: THEY SAID IT COULDN'T BE BUILT

BY JUDITH ST. GEORGE

This fascinating account describes the major contributions of John A. Roebling and his son to the design and construction of one of the world's most famous bridges.

THE WAY THINGS WORK

BY DAVID MACAULAY

This book is an overview of the technology of some of the inventions that shape our lives. Macaulay not only illustrates how machines work, he also shows how inventions are linked to others. ALA NOTABLE BOOK, SCHOOL LIBRARY JOURNAL BEST BOOK

MORE THAN A FRIEND: DOGS WITH A PURPOSE

BY MARY ELLEN SIEGEL AND HERMINE M. KOPLIN

In this book you can read the true stories of remarkable dogs trained to help people in special ways.

507

WRITER'S JOURNAL pages 90–92:

Reading and writing about "Solutions"

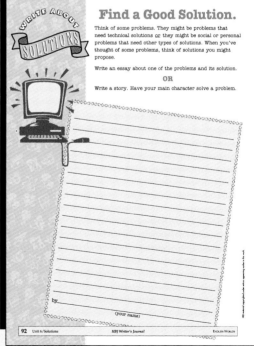

Writer's Journal

**Read aloud
to students.**

Barrio Boy

by Ernesto Galarza

Miss Hopley joined us with a large book and some papers in her hand. She, too, sat down and the questions and answers began by way of our interpreter. My name was Ernesto. My mother's name was Henriqueta. My birth certificate was in San Blas. Here was my last report card from the Escuela Municipal Numero 3 para Varones of Mazatlán,[1] and so forth. Miss Hopley put things down in the book and my mother signed a card.

As long as the questions continued, Doña[2] Henriqueta could stay and I was secure. Now that they were over, Miss Hopley saw her to the door, dismissed our interpreter and without further ado took me by the hand and strode down the hall to Miss Ryan's first grade.

Miss Ryan took me to a seat at the front of the room, into which I shrank—the better to survey her. She was, to skinny, somewhat runty me, of a withering height when she patrolled the class. And when I least expected it, there she was, crouching by my desk, her blond radiant face level with mine, her voice patiently maneuvering me over the awful idiocies of the English language.

During the next few weeks Miss Ryan

[1]**Escuela Municipal Numero 3 para Varones of Mazatlán**
es·kwä′ lə mōō·nē·sē·päl′nōō·mē·rō träs pä′rä vä·rō näs mä·sät·län′: Municipal School Number 3 for Boys of Mazatlán.
[2]**Doña** (dô′nyä): A Spanish title of respect meaning "lady" or "madam."

overcame my fears of tall, energetic teachers as she bent over my desk to help me with a word in the pre-primer. Step by step, she loosened me and my classmates from the safe anchorage of the desks for recitations at the blackboard and consultations at her desk. Frequently she burst into happy announcements to the whole class. "Ito can read a sentence," and small Japanese Ito, shy, slowly read aloud while the class listened in wonder: "Come, Skipper, come. Come and run." The Korean, Portuguese, Italian, and Polish first graders had

And when I least expected it, there she was, crouching by my desk, her blond radiant face level with mine, her voice patiently maneuvering me over the awful idiocies of the English language.

SELECTION SUMMARY Enrolling in a new school is an adventure for Ernesto because he does not understand English. Young Ernesto soon realizes that many of the children attending Lincoln School are also struggling to learn the language. Through the understanding of one very special teacher, Ernesto learns to read. More importantly he learns that he does not have to forget his roots or be ashamed of his heritage.

ABOUT THE AUTHOR Ernesto Galarza (1905–1984) was not only a writer, but a Mexican American historian and civil rights leader. Born in Mexico, he came to the United States when he was six years

old. Throughout his life, Galarza worked to improve the conditions of Mexican Americans.

Strategies for Listening

LISTENING/THINKING STRATEGY—IDENTIFYING PROBLEMS AND SOLUTIONS Remind students that both nonfiction and fiction often relate the attempts of a person to find a solution to a problem. Explain to students that listening carefully to identify the problems and how they are resolved will help them to understand and appreciate the story.

SET A PURPOSE FOR LISTENING Explain that this excerpt from *Barrio Boy* is the author's own story.

similar moments of glory, no less shining than mine the day I conquered "butterfly," which I had been persistently pronouncing in standard Spanish as boo-ter-flee. "Children," Miss Ryan called for attention. "Ernesto has learned how to pronounce *butterfly*!" And I proved it with a perfect imitation of Miss Ryan. From that celebrated success, I was soon able to match Ito's progress as a sentence reader with "Come, butterfly, come fly with me."

Like Ito and several other first graders who did not know English, I received private lessons from Miss Ryan in the closet, a narrow hall off the classroom with a door at each end. Next to one of these doors Miss Ryan placed a large chair for herself and a small one for me. Keeping an eye on the class through the open door, she read with me about sheep in the meadow and a frightened chicken going to see the king, coaching me out of my phonetic ruts in words like *pasture, bow-wow-wow, hay,* and *pretty,* which to my Mexican ear and eye had so many unnecessary sounds and letters. She made me watch her lips and then close my eyes as she repeated words I found hard to read. When we came to know each other better, I tried interrupting to tell Miss Ryan how we said it in Spanish. It didn't work. She only said "oh" and went on with *pasture, bow-wow-wow,* and *pretty.* It was as if in that closet we were both discovering together the secrets of the English language and grieving together over the tragedies of Bo-Peep. The main reason I was graduated with honors from the first grade was that I had fallen in love with Miss Ryan. Her radiant, no-nonsense character made us either afraid not to love her or love her so we would not be afraid, I am not sure which. It was not only that we

sensed she was with it, but also that she was with us.

Like the first grade, the rest of the Lincoln School was a sampling of the lower part of town where many races made their home. My pals in the second grade were Kazushi, whose parents spoke only Japanese; Matti, a skinny Italian boy; and Manuel, a fat Portuguese who would never get into a fight but wrestled you to the ground and just sat on you. Our assortment of nationalities included Koreans, Yugoslavs, Poles, Irish, and home-grown Americans.

At Lincoln, making us into Americans did not mean scrubbing away what made us originally foreign. The teachers called us as our parents did, or as close as they could pronounce our names in Spanish or Japanese. No one was ever scolded or punished for speaking in his native tongue on the playground. Matti told the class about his mother's down quilt, which she had made in Italy with the fine feathers of a thousand geese. Encarnación acted out how boys learned to fish in the Philippines. I astounded the third grade with the story of my travels on a stagecoach, which nobody else in the class had seen except in the museum at Sutter's Fort. After a visit to the Crocker Art Gallery and its collection of heroic paintings of the golden age of California, someone showed a silk scroll with a Chinese painting. Miss Hopley herself had a way of expressing wonder over these matters before a class, her eyes wide open until they popped slightly. It was easy for me to feel that becoming a proud American, as she said we should, did not mean feeling ashamed of being a Mexican.

He describes his experiences as a new student. Encourage students to note the author's problems, how they are resolved, and who helps him.

Responding to Literature

1. **Why were Ernesto's early school experiences so important?** (Accept reasonable responses: He learned to speak and read English; he learned that he did not have to feel ashamed of being a foreigner, nor did he have to forget his heritage and roots to become an American citizen.) INFERENTIAL: SUMMARIZING

2. **How would you characterize Miss Ryan as a teacher?** (Accept reasonable responses: Miss Ryan was a good teacher because she went out of her way to help students who could not read or speak English to feel successful and good about themselves.) CRITICAL: MAKING JUDGMENTS

SPEAKING   Have students form groups to discuss what problems a new foreign student might have adjusting to life in their school and community.

Looking Toward Others

Ask students what sort of stories they expect to find under the theme "Looking Toward Others." Then have them read the selection titles on page 509 of the Student Anthology. Invite students to speculate about what the titles, such as "Helping Hands," may mean and how they might relate to the theme on looking toward others.

PACING   This theme has been designed to take about two weeks to complete, depending on your students' needs.

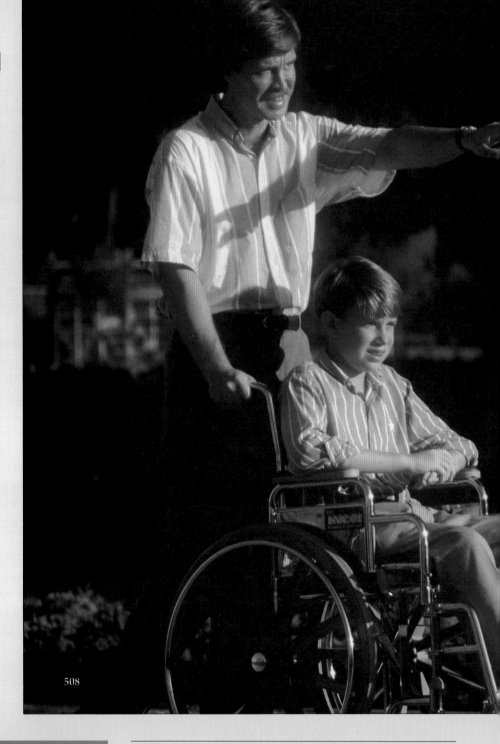

508

Management Options

THE LITERATURE-BASED CLASSROOM   Providing a literature-rich curriculum creates unique classroom management challenges. Some management options for the selections in this theme follow.

TAP ORGANIZATIONS AND COMMUNITY SERVICES
This theme offers an excellent opportunity for students to learn more about people who help those who are disabled. Research and contact organizations and nearby facilities that provide care, training, rehabilitation, and education for disabled persons. Invite specialists to visit your classroom to talk about what they do.

THEME

LOOKING TOWARD OTHERS

For some people, finding solutions that help others is a lifetime goal. Discover how these people use their skills and inventiveness to improve the lives of others.

CONTENTS

509

STUDENTS AT RISK
You may wish to have students work with a partner to complete the suggested prewriting graphic for the Write activity following each selection. Students can then exchange drafts and make suggestions for improvements.

GIFTED AND TALENTED
Have students list all the facts they learned from reading "Helping Hands" and then use the facts to make up a quiz for their classmates to take for fun. Suggest that they include true/false, multiple choice, and fill-in-the-blank questions. Also see the *Challenge Cards.*

SPECIAL EDUCATION STUDENTS
As you work through the Learning Through Literature lesson on imagery, invite students to identify the senses they depend upon and how they envision imagery from "Raymond's Run."

LIMITED ENGLISH PROFICIENT STUDENTS
Some students may have difficulty recalling the correct subject-verb-object order when speaking and writing in English. Have students play sentence games such as unscrambling sentences to reinforce correct sentence structure.

LITERATURE RESPONSE GROUPS Have students form groups to discuss each selection and the suggested questions. Then have one member from each group share the group's conclusions. A variety of conclusions could be a source for additional discussion and debate.

READING/WRITING PORTFOLIO Instruct students to keep in their portfolios their writing responses to the theme selections. Remind them also to add to their personal journals notes on their independent reading.

RAYMOND'S RUN

by Toni Cade Bambara

TONI CADE BAMBARA (1939–) grew up in New York City and in neighboring New Jersey. She credits her mother with treating her and her brother the same—expecting both of them to develop their talents and also to be caring and responsible. Many of the stories in Bambara's collection *Gorilla, My Love,* from which "Raymond's Run" is taken, feature confident African American young people expressing themselves in vivid language as they face the challenges of their world. Bambara has also written a novel, but she prefers short stories. "Temperamentally, I move toward the short story because I am a sprinter rather than a long-distance runner," she says.

OTHER BOOKS ABOUT LOOKING TOWARD OTHERS
Badger on the Barge by Janni Howker. William Morrow, 1984. CHALLENGING

Hank by James Sauer. Delacorte, 1990. AVERAGE

"**I** move toward the short story because I am a sprinter rather than a long-distance runner."

SELECTION SUMMARY
Squeaky, a self-reliant, self-absorbed girl living in Harlem, doesn't like or trust other girls; instead, she lives for running. On her daily runs, she takes along Raymond, her disabled older brother, who is her responsibility. As Squeaky runs the May Day race, Raymond runs beside her outside a fence. Raymond "wins, too," breaking through Squeaky's self-interest to make her feel that, with her help, he also can become a champion runner.

LESSON PLANNER	Materials	Integrated Curriculum	Meeting Individual Needs
1 READING LITERATURE pp. 509B–521	Student Anthology pp. 510–521 Transparency 27 Second-Language Support Manual Practice Book p. 139 Integrated Spelling p. 69 Integrated Spelling T. E. pp. 92–93 Response Card 1: Characters	Spelling Spelling Pretest Spelling-Vocabulary Connection *(the /j/ sound)*	Second-Language Support Vocabulary 509C Strategic Reading 509D, 512, 517 Cooperative Reading 510, 516, 520
2 RESPONDING TO LITERATURE pp. 521A–521D	Writer's Journal p. 93 Practice Book p. 140 Integrated Spelling p. 70 Integrated Spelling T. E. pp. 92–93	Vocabulary Workshop Reviewing Key Words Extending Vocabulary Writing About the Literature Speaking/Listening Spelling Review	Cooperative Learning 521B, 521C
3 LEARNING THROUGH LITERATURE pp. 521E–521L	Second-Language Support Manual Writer's Journal pp. 94–95 Practice Book pp. 141–142	Social Studies Physical Education Math Multicultural	Challenge 521F, 521H, 521I, 521J Second-Language Support 521F, 521H Cooperative Learning 521H

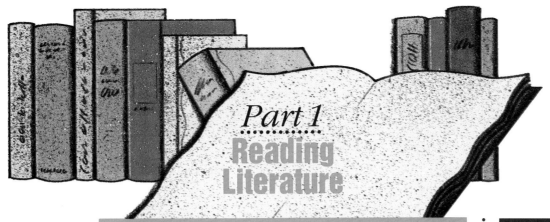

Part 1
Reading Literature

Building Background

Access prior knowledge and develop vocabulary concepts.

Remind students that thinking about what they already know can help them understand a story. Tell students that "Raymond's Run" is about a girl who is an excellent runner. Have students brainstorm about running.

determination
speed
must train daily
stiff competition — **Running** — promotes fitness
run laps
good running form
endurance

Have students quickwrite sentences.

Ask students to quickly write a few sentences about how it might feel or does feel (if the student is a runner) to be a competitive runner. Invite volunteers to share their writing.

Vocabulary Strategies

Introduce Key Words and strategies.

Tell students that "Raymond's Run" may contain unfamiliar words. Display Transparency 27, or write the paragraph on the board. Have students read silently and use context clues, phonics, and structural analysis to figure out the meanings of the underlined words. As a volunteer reads the paragraph aloud, help with pronunciation if necessary.

Transparency 27   Key Words

In a book of amazing facts, I read of a violin <u>prodigy</u>, an extraordinary child who began playing at age three with no training. I found an item about a <u>ventriloquist</u> who made his voice seem to come from darkened places in a theater. I read about runners who won every race by <u>psyching</u> out their opponents, destroying their confidence through psychological tricks. Most amazing were mice taught to <u>prance</u> in lively, high steps, pulling a tiny wagon.

CULTURAL AWARENESS

To help students appreciate the cultural background and setting of "Raymond's Run," share with them the information under Cultural Background/Setting on page 510.

KEY WORDS DEFINED

prodigy   child or young person with extraordinary talent

ventriloquist   one who speaks so that the sounds seem to come from a source other than the speaker, as from a dummy

psyching   undermining the confidence of a competitor by using psychology

prance   to move with high steps, to move in a lively manner

Check students' understanding.

Have students demonstrate their understanding by answering the following questions either orally or in writing:

1. *prance* **What might cause someone to prance happily down the street?** (Accept reasonable responses: being proud of an accomplishment; wanting attention.) STRATEGIES: PRIOR KNOWLEDGE/EXAMPLE

2. *prodigy* **Why would the violin prodigy still practice each piece of music?** (Accept reasonable responses: to improve technique; because he or she enjoys playing; to play even harder pieces.) STRATEGY: EXPLANATION

3. *ventriloquist* **Where does the voice of a ventriloquist seem to be coming from?** (Accept reasonable responses: from across the room; from a "dummy.") STRATEGY: PRIOR KNOWLEDGE

4. *psyching* **Why might an athlete plan a strategy for psyching out an opponent?** (to beat the opponent; to undermine his or her confidence) STRATEGIES: PRIOR KNOWLEDGE/DEFINITION

Encourage use of the Glossary.

GLOSSARY Point out that this story may contain other unfamiliar words, such as *pageant* or *periscope*, that students can look up in the Glossary or in a dictionary. Remind students that they can also use the Glossary to confirm or clarify their understanding of the Key Words.

Integrate spelling with vocabulary.

SPELLING-VOCABULARY CONNECTION *Integrated Spelling* page 69 reinforces spellings of words with the **/j/ sound,** including the Key Word *prodigy*. The spelling of the Key Word *psyching* is also included.

SECOND-LANGUAGE SUPPORT Encourage students to work with a peer tutor to practice pronouncing the Key Words. Have the tutor point out silent letters and help divide words into syllables. (See *Second-Language Support Manual*.)

PRACTICE BOOK
page 139: Reinforcing Key Words.

INTEGRATED SPELLING
page 69: Writing and spelling words with the /j/ sound

NOTE: These pages may be completed now or after students have read the story.

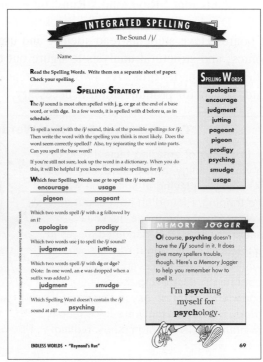

Practice Book

Integrated Spelling

Strategic Reading: Short Story

Preview and Predict

Discuss the value of previewing and predicting.

Remind students that making predictions about a story can help them become more involved in their reading. Have a volunteer suggest ways of previewing a short story in order to make predictions. (reading and thinking about the title, reading part of the story, scanning illustrations, reading information about the author)

Have students preview and predict.

Have students read the first two paragraphs of the story. Then ask questions such as the following to help students make predictions:

- **What challenges will Squeaky face?**
- **What is the relationship between Squeaky and Raymond?**

Introduce the character map.

Use the character map to encourage students to predict what kind of person the narrator will be and how she will demonstrate her personal qualities.

CHARACTER MAP

PERSONAL JOURNAL Have students copy the character map in their personal journals, or have them use *Practice Book* page 140. (See page 521B in this Teacher's Edition.) Have them complete it as they read the story or afterward. (Students will return to the map after reading, in Summarizing the Literature.)

Setting a Purpose

Have students set purposes.

Remind students that making predictions about what will happen in the story or posing a question they would like to have answered can help them set an individual purpose for reading. Have students use predictions or questions to set a purpose for reading. Invite volunteers to share their purposes with classmates.

Model purpose-setting if necessary.

If students have difficulty setting a purpose for reading, model the thinking process:

> **From previewing, I already know that Raymond isn't the narrator of the story, even though the story's title is "Raymond's Run." My purpose for reading will be to find out what part Raymond plays in the story.**

SECOND-LANGUAGE SUPPORT Students may benefit from the Guided Reading activities and the additional guidance under the Student Anthology pages. (See *Second-Language Support Manual.*)

OPTIONS FOR READING

Independent Reading
Have students read the selection silently with their purpose for reading in mind.

Guided Reading
Follow the Guided Reading suggestions that appear on pages 510, 515, and 520. These suggestions model strategic reading.

Cooperative Reading
Reader response strategies appear on pages 510, 516, and 520.

Numbered Annotations
Use the numbered annotations beside the Student Anthology pages to heighten students' appreciation of the story.

This story takes place in Harlem, a section of New York City whose population is predominantly African American. Situated in the northern part of Manhattan, Harlem has been a center of African American culture for decades.

510

Guided Reading

SET PURPOSE/PREDICT: PAGES 510–516 Have students read through the first two lines on page 516 to determine how the narrator feels about her brother Raymond. You may wish to suggest that students keep adding to their character maps as they read.

Cooperative Reading

READER RESPONSE STRATEGY: PAGES 510–516 Form groups of three to five students, and have each group select a leader. Ask group members to read pages 510–516 silently, and then encourage the leader to use dialogue questions such as those below to ensure that all members participate in the discussion. (Response Card 1: Characters, on page R62, offers a wide variety of dialogue questions.)

- Who are the main characters?
- Which characters do you like or dislike? Explain your opinion.

Raymond's Run

by Toni Cade Bambara

I don't have much work to do around the house like some girls. My mother does that. And I don't have to earn my pocket money by hustling; George runs errands for the big boys and sells Christmas cards. And anything else that's got to get done, my father does. All I have to do in life is mind my brother Raymond, which is enough.

Sometimes I slip and say my little brother Raymond. But as any fool can see he's much bigger and he's older too. But a lot of people call him my little brother cause he needs looking after cause he's not quite right. And a lot of smart mouths got lots to say about that too, especially when George was minding him. But now, if anybody has anything to say to Raymond, anything to say about his big head, they have to come by me. And I don't play the dozens or believe in standing around with somebody in my face doing a lot of talking. I much rather just knock you down and take my chances even if I am a little girl with skinny arms and a squeaky voice, which is how I got the name Squeaky. And if things get too rough, I run. And as anybody can tell you, I'm the fastest thing on two feet.

There is no track meet that I don't win the first place medal. I used to win the twenty-yard dash when I was a little kid in

illustrations by Jerry Pinkney

511

1 POINT OF VIEW
Who is telling the story? *(Squeaky)*
What can you tell about her from the way she describes herself? *(Accept reasonable responses: She is tough and confident; she is protective of her brother; she seems fearless.)*
INFERENTIAL: DRAWING CONCLUSIONS

Teaching Tip You may want to tell students that the story is told in a conversational style and that there is much use of idiomatic informal language. For example, *they have to come by me* (paragraph 2, line 7) means that anyone who makes remarks about Raymond will have to answer to the narrator. Suggest that students try to "hear" the narrator's voice in their head as they read; in doing so, the expressions will often become clear.

kindergarten. Nowadays it's the fifty-yard dash. And tomorrow I'm subject to run the quarter-meter relay all by myself and come in first, second, and third. The big kids call me Mercury cause I'm the swiftest thing in the neighborhood. Everybody knows that—except two people who know better, my father and me.

He can beat me to Amsterdam Avenue with me having a two fire-hydrant headstart and him running with his hands in his pockets and whistling. But that's private information. Cause can you imagine some thirty-five-year-old man stuffing himself into PAL shorts to race little kids? So as far as everyone's concerned, I'm the fastest and that goes for Gretchen, too, who has put out the tale that she is going to win the first place medal this year. Ridiculous. In the second place, she's got short legs. In the third place, she's got freckles. In the first place, no one can beat me and that's all there is to it.

2 I'm standing on the corner admiring the weather and about to take a stroll down Broadway so I can practice my breathing exercises, and I've got Raymond walking on the inside close to the buildings cause he's subject to fits of fantasy and starts thinking he's a circus performer and that the curb is a tightrope strung high in the air. And sometimes after a rain, he likes to step down off his tightrope right into the gutter and slosh around getting his shoes and cuffs wet. Or sometimes if you don't watch him, he'll dash across traffic to the island in the middle of Broadway and give the pigeons a fit. Then I have to go behind him apologizing to all the old people sitting around trying to get some sun and getting all upset with the pigeons fluttering around them, scattering their newspapers and upsetting the wax-paper lunches in their laps. So I keep Raymond on the inside of me, and he plays like he's driving a stagecoach, which is O.K. by me so long as he doesn't run me over or interrupt my breathing exercises, which I have to do on account of I'm serious about my running and don't care who knows it.

3 Now some people like to act like things come easy to them, won't let on that they practice. Not me. I'll high prance down 34th Street like a rodeo pony to keep my knees strong even if it does get my mother uptight so that she walks ahead like she's not with me, don't know me, is all by herself on a shopping trip, and I am somebody else's crazy child.

Now you take Cynthia Procter for instance. She's just the opposite. If there's a test tomorrow, she'll say something like, "Oh I guess I'll play handball this afternoon and watch television tonight," just to let you know she ain't thinking about the test. Or like last week when she won the spelling bee for the millionth time, "A good thing you got 'receive,' Squeaky, cause I would have got it wrong. I completely forgot about the spelling bee." And she'll clutch the lace on her blouse like it was a narrow escape. Oh, brother.

But of course when I pass her house on my early morning trots around the block, she is practicing the scales on the piano over and over and over and over. Then in music class, she always lets herself get bumped around so she falls accidently on purpose onto the piano stool and is so surprised to find herself sitting there, and so decides just for fun to try out the ole keys and what do you know—Chopin's waltzes just spring out of her fingertips and she's the most surprised thing in the world. A regular prodigy. I could kill people like that.

I stay up all night studying the words for the spelling bee. And you can see me anytime of day practicing running. I never walk if I can trot and shame on Raymond if he can't keep up. But of course he does, cause if he hangs back someone's liable to walk up to him and get smart, or take his allowance from him, or ask him where he got that great big pumpkin head. People are so stupid sometimes.

So I'm strolling down Broadway breathing out and breathing in on counts of seven, which is my lucky number, and here comes Gretchen and her sidekicks—Mary Louise, who used to be a friend of mine when she first moved to Harlem from Baltimore and got beat up by everybody till I took up for her on account of her mother and my mother used to sing in the same choir when they were young girls, but people ain't grateful, so now she hangs out with the new girl Gretchen and talks about me like a dog; and Rosie, who is as fat as I am skinny and has a big mouth where Raymond is concerned and is too stupid to know that there is not a big deal of difference between herself and Raymond and that she can't afford to throw stones. So they are steady coming up Broadway and I see right away that it's going to be one of those Dodge City scenes cause the street

4 **AUTHOR'S CRAFT**
Why do you think the author has Squeaky provide such a complete description in one long sentence?
(Accept reasonable responses: She is showing that Squeaky's character is outspoken, straightforward, and prone to exaggeration. She is also showing that Squeaky dislikes pretentious people. The style is conversational and reflects the first-person narrative.)
METACOGNITIVE: DRAWING CONCLUSIONS

5 **ALLUSION**
What does Squeaky mean when she says that Rosie "is too stupid to know that there is not a big deal of difference between herself and Raymond and that she can't afford to throw stones"? *(Squeaky is referring to the proverb "People who live in glass houses shouldn't throw stones." Unless a person has no faults or weaknesses, that person shouldn't find fault with others.)*
INFERENTIAL: DETERMINING MAIN IDEA

6 FIGURATIVE LANGUAGE
Why does Squeaky describe the conversation with the girls as a "ventriloquist-dummy routine"? *(because Gretchen is Squeaky's competitor, but Mary Louise and Rosie are doing all the talking for Gretchen)*
INFERENTIAL: MAKING COMPARISONS

7 CHARACTER'S TRAITS
How do you know that Squeaky will probably be the winner in this confrontation? *(She has shown herself to be tough, fearless, and fiercely protective of her brother; the other girls have not demonstrated similar qualities.)*
METACOGNITIVE: MAKING PREDICTIONS

ain't that big and they're close to the buildings just as we are. First I think I'll step into the candy store and look over the new comics and let them pass. But that's chicken and I've got a reputation to consider. So then I think I'll just walk straight on through them or over them if necessary. But as they get to me, they slow down. I'm ready to fight, cause like I said I don't feature a whole lot of chit-chat, I much prefer to just knock you down right from the jump and save everybody a lotta precious time.

"You signing up for the May Day races?" smiles Mary Louise, only it's not a smile at all.

A dumb question like that doesn't deserve an answer. Besides, there's just me and Gretchen standing there really, so no use wasting my breath talking to shadows.

"I don't think you're going to win this time," says Rosie, trying to signify with her hands on her hips all salty, completely forgetting that I have whupped her many times for less salt than that.

6 "I always win cause I'm the best," I say straight at Gretchen, who is, as far as I'm concerned, the only one talking in this <u>ventriloquist-dummy routine</u>.

Gretchen smiles but it's not a smile and I'm thinking that girls never really smile at each other because they don't know how and don't want to know how and there's probably no one to teach us how cause grown-up girls don't know either. Then they all look at Raymond, who has just brought his mule team to a standstill. And they're about to see what trouble they can get into through him.

"What grade you in now, Raymond?"

"You got anything to say to my brother, you say it to me, Mary Louise Williams of Raggedy Town, Baltimore."

"What are you, his mother?" sasses Rosie.

7 "That's right, Fatso. And the next word out of anybody and I'll be *their* mother too." So they just stand there and Gretchen shifts from one leg to the other and so do they. Then Gretchen puts her hands on her hips and is about to say something with her freckle-face self but doesn't. Then she walks around me looking me up and down but keeps walking up Broadway, and her sidekicks follow her. So me and Raymond smile at each other and he says "Gidyap" to his team and I continue with my breathing exercises, strolling down

514

515

Guided Reading

MONITOR COMPREHENSION: PAGES 510–516

What do you know about Squeaky's attitude toward her brother? How do you know this? (She is very protective of him. She watches after him and takes him out with her. She does not let people tease him.) STRATEGIC READING: RETURNING TO PURPOSE

What problem is Squeaky facing? (She is going to race at a track meet. She wants to win first place as she has in the past, but Gretchen appears to have a chance to win.) STRATEGIC READING: SUMMARIZING

SET PURPOSE/PREDICT: PAGES 516–521 Ask students to predict whether Squeaky will win the race and what Raymond will have to do with the outcome. You may want to have students record their predictions on their character maps. Then have students read the remainder of the story.

Broadway toward the ice man on 145th with not a care in the world cause I am Miss Quicksilver herself.

I take my time getting to the park on May Day because the track meet is the last thing on the program. The biggest thing on the program is the May Pole dancing, which I can do without, thank you, even if my mother thinks it's a shame I don't take part and act like a girl for a change. You'd think my mother'd be grateful not to have to make me a white organdy dress with a big satin sash and buy me new white baby-doll shoes that can't be taken out of the box till the big day. You'd think she'd be glad her daughter ain't out there prancing around a May Pole getting the new clothes all dirty and sweaty and trying to act like a fairy or a flower or whatever you're supposed to be when you should be trying to be yourself, whatever that is, which is, as far as I am concerned, a poor black girl who really can't afford to buy shoes and a new dress you only wear once a lifetime cause it won't fit next year.

I was once a strawberry in a Hansel and Gretel pageant when I was in nursery school and didn't have no better sense than to dance on tiptoe with my arms in a circle over my head doing umbrella steps and being a perfect fool just so my mother and father could come dressed up and clap. You'd think they'd know better than to encourage that kind of nonsense. I am not a strawberry. I do not dance on my toes. I run. That is what I am all about. So I always come late to the May Day program, just in time to get my number pinned on and lay in the grass till they announce the fifty-yard dash.

I put Raymond in the little swings, which is a tight squeeze this year and will be impossible next year. Then I look around for Mr. Pearson, who pins the numbers on. I'm really looking for Gretchen if you want to know the truth, but she's not around. The park is jam-packed. Parents in hats and corsages and breast-pocket handkerchiefs peeking up. Kids in white dresses and light-blue suits. The parkees unfolding chairs and chasing the rowdy kids from **8** Lenox as if they had no right to be there. The big guys with their caps on backwards, leaning against the fence swirling the basketballs on the tips of their fingers, waiting for all these crazy people to clear out the park so they can play. Most of the kids in my class are carrying bass drums and glockenspiels and flutes. You'd think they'd

516

Cooperative Reading

READER RESPONSE STRATEGY: PAGES 516—521
Groups should continue reading silently, pausing periodically to discuss how their predictions and conclusions change as they discover more about the characters.

Cultural Awareness Explain that the May Pole dance (line 5) is a festive folk dance performed by young girls, who dance around a tall pole draped with flowers and ribbons. Each dancer takes the end of a ribbon and, in a complex dance, the dancers weave the ribbons into patterns. Such dances are found all over the world.

put in a few bongos or something for real like that.

Then here comes Mr. Pearson with his clipboard and his cards and pencils and whistles and safety pins and fifty million other things he's always dropping all over the place with his clumsy self. He sticks out in a crowd cause he's on stilts. We used to call him Jack and the Beanstalk to get him mad. But I'm the only one that can outrun him and get away, and I'm too grown for that silliness now.

"Well, Squeaky," he says checking my name off the list and handing me number seven and two pins. And I'm thinking he's got no right to call me Squeaky, if I can't call him Beanstalk.

"Hazel Elizabeth Deborah Parker," I correct him and tell him to write it down on his board.

"Well, Hazel Elizabeth Deborah Parker, going to give some-one else a break this year?" I squint at him real hard to see if he is seriously thinking I should lose the race on purpose just to give someone else a break.

"Only six girls running this time," he continues, shaking his head sadly like it's my fault all of New York didn't turn out in sneakers. "That new girl should give you a run for your money." He looks around the park for Gretchen like a periscope in a submarine movie. "Wouldn't it be a nice gesture if you were . . . to ahhh . . ." **9**

I give him such a look he couldn't finish putting that idea into words. Grownups got a lot of nerve sometimes. I pin number seven to myself and stomp away—I'm so burnt. And I go straight for the track and stretch out on the grass while the band winds up with "Oh the Monkey Wrapped His Tail Around the Flag Pole," which my teacher calls by some other name. The man on the loudspeaker is calling everyone over to the track and I'm on my back looking at the sky trying to pretend I'm in the country, but I can't, because even grass in the city feels hard as sidewalk and there's just no pretending you are anywhere but in a "concrete jungle" as my grandfather says.

The twenty-yard dash takes all of the two minutes cause most of the little kids don't know no better than to run off the track or run the wrong way or run smack into the fence and fall down and cry. One little kid, though, has got the good sense to run straight for the white ribbon up ahead, so he wins. Then the second-graders line up for the thirty-yard dash and I don't even bother to turn my head to

517

Teaching Tip Point out to students that "Oh the Monkey Wrapped His Tail Around the Flag Pole" (paragraph 6, lines 4–5) is really a traditional piece for marching bands, often played at events such as this one. Its true title is "National Emblem," and it was written by E. E. Bagley.

Second-Language Support
Students may not be familiar with the story of "Jack and the Beanstalk" or the word *stilts* (paragraph 1, lines 4–5). Briefly retell the story about the beanstalk that grew to the sky. Then explain the meaning of *stilts*. These two pieces of information will help students understand the significance of the nickname *Beanstalk*. Be sure they understand that Mr. Pearson is not literally walking on stilts but is simply very tall.

10 DESCRIPTION

Tell in your own words what Raymond is doing. *(On the other side of the fence, he has lined himself up with Squeaky at the starting line, in the posture of a runner ready to begin the race.)*
LITERAL: RECOGNIZING MAIN IDEA

11 FLASHBACK

What scene from the past does the author insert into the story at this point? *(a scene of Squeaky as a young child running through fields of corn and up a hill to an orchard, pretending she is a choo-choo train)*
LITERAL: NOTING IMPORTANT DETAILS

Why do you think this reliving of the past is happening in Squeaky's mind at this moment? *(Accept reasonable responses: To help her run better and faster, Squeaky has created for herself a peaceful, dreamlike feeling and an image of herself as being swift, happy, and light.)*
INFERENTIAL: DRAWING CONCLUSIONS

watch cause Raphael Perez always wins. He wins before he even begins by psyching the runners, telling them they're going to trip on their shoelaces and fall on their faces or lose their shorts or something, which he doesn't really have to do since he is very fast, almost as fast as I am. After that is the forty-yard dash, which I used to run when I was in first grade. Raymond is hollering from the swings cause he knows I'm about to do my thing cause the man on the loudspeaker has just announced the fifty-yard dash, although he might just as well be giving a recipe for angel food cake cause you can hardly make out what he's saying for the static. I get up and slip off my sweat pants and then I see Gretchen standing at the starting line kicking her legs out like a pro. Then as I get into place I see that

10 ole Raymond is in line on the other side of the fence, bending down with his fingers on the ground just like he knew what he was doing. I was going to yell at him but then I didn't. It burns up your energy to holler.

Every time, just before I take off in a race, I always feel like I'm in a dream, the kind of dream you have when you're sick with fever and feel all hot and weightless. I dream I'm flying over a sandy

11 beach in the early morning sun, kissing the leaves of the trees as I fly by. And there's always the smell of apples, just like in the country when I was little and use to think I was a choo-choo train, running through the fields of corn and chugging up the hill to the orchard. And all the time I'm dreaming this, I get lighter and lighter until I'm flying over the beach again, getting blown through the sky like a feather that weighs nothing at all. But once I spread my fingers in the dirt and crouch over for the Get on Your Mark, the dream goes and I am solid again and am telling myself, Squeaky, you must win, you must win, you are the fastest thing in the world, you can even beat your father up Amsterdam if you really try. And then I feel my weight coming back just behind my knees then down to my feet then into the earth and the pistol shot explodes in my blood and I am off and weightless again, flying past the other runners, my arms pumping up and down and the whole world is quiet except for the crunch as I zoom over the gravel in the track. I glance to my left and there is no one. To the right a blurred Gretchen, who's got her chin jutting out as if it would win the race all by itself. And on the other

518

Oral Rereading Have students prepare to read aloud the long paragraph that begins on page 518 and ends on page 520. The paragraph begins with the peaceful scene that Squeaky imagines before the race, continues with the excitement of the race, and ends with Squeaky's apparent victory. Discuss the changing mood of the passage, and suggest that students try to show the mood changes with their voices. Have volunteers practice and then read the passage aloud. Students may wish to read aloud other story sections showing contrasting moods.

519

Informal Assessment You can informally assess your students' abilities to identify cause and effect in stories. On occasion, ask questions such as these:

- Why did this character do what she/he did? Are there any other reasons for the character's actions?
- What do you think will happen because of this character's actions?

Alternatively, tell students to pretend that they are the main character and to explain the reasons for their actions.

12 side of the fence is Raymond with his arms down to his side and the palms tucked up behind him, running in his very own style and the first time I ever saw that and I almost stop to watch my brother Raymond on his first run. But the white ribbon is bouncing toward me and I tear past it racing into the distance till my feet with a mind of their own start digging up footfuls of dirt and brake me short. Then all the kids standing on the side pile on me, banging me on the back and slapping my head with their May Day programs, for I have won again and everybody on 151st Street can walk tall for another year.

"In first place . . ." the man on the loudspeaker is clear as a bell now. But then he pauses and the loudspeaker starts to whine. Then static. And I lean down to catch my breath and here comes Gretchen walking back for she's overshot the finish line too, huffing and puffing with her hands on her hips taking it slow, breathing in steady time like a real pro and I sort of like her a little for the first time. "In first place . . ." and then three or four voices get all mixed up on the loudspeaker and I dig my sneaker into the grass and stare at Gretchen, who's staring back, we both wondering just who did win. I can hear old Beanstalk arguing with the man on the loudspeaker and then a few others running their mouths about what the stop watches say.

Then I hear Raymond yanking at the fence to call me and I wave to shush him, but he keeps rattling the fence like a gorilla in a cage like in them gorilla movies, but then like a dancer or something he starts climbing up nice and easy but very fast. And it occurs to me, watching how smoothly he climbs hand over hand and remembering how he looked running with his arms down to his side and with the wind pulling his mouth back and his teeth showing and all, it occurred to me that Raymond would make a very fine runner. Doesn't he always keep up with me on my trots? And he surely knows how to breathe in counts of seven cause he's always doing it at the dinner table, which drives my brother George up the wall. And I'm smiling to beat the band cause if I've lost this race, or if me and Gretchen tied, or even if I've won, I can always retire as a **13** runner and begin a whole new career as a coach with Raymond as my champion. After all, with a little more study I can beat Cynthia and her phony self at the spelling bee. And if I bugged my mother,

520

I could get piano lessons and become a star. And I have a big rep as the baddest thing around. And I've got a roomful of ribbons and medals and awards. But what has Raymond got to call his own?

So I stand there with my new plan, laughing out loud by this time as Raymond jumps down from the fence and runs over with his teeth showing and his arms down to the side, which no one before him has quite mastered as a running style. And by the time he comes over I'm jumping up and down so glad to see him—my brother Raymond, a great runner in the family tradition. But of course everyone thinks I'm jumping up and down because the men on the loudspeaker have finally gotten themselves together and compared notes and are announcing "In first place—Miss Hazel Elizabeth Deborah Parker." (Dig that.) "In second place—Miss Gretchen P. Lewis." And I look over at Gretchen wondering what the P stands for. And I smile. Cause she's good, no doubt about it. Maybe she'd like to help me coach Raymond; she obviously is serious about running, as any fool can see. And she nods to congratulate me and then she smiles. And I smile. We stand there with this big smile of respect between us. It's about as real a smile as girls can do for each other, considering we don't practice real smiling every day you know, cause maybe we too busy being flowers or fairies or strawberries instead of something honest and worthy of respect . . . you know . . . like being people.

THINK IT OVER

1. At the end of the story, why does Squeaky feel that winning the race isn't the most important thing anymore? What is important to her? Why?
2. Why does Squeaky always arrive late at the May Day program?
3. Who is the one person Squeaky says can beat her in a race?
4. Do you think Squeaky will be a good coach for Raymond? Give several reasons to support your opinion.

WRITE

Squeaky says that girls don't practice real smiling because they are "too busy being flowers or fairies or strawberries instead of something honest and worthy of respect . . . ." Is Squeaky honest and worthy of respect? Explain what you think in several written paragraphs.

521

Returning to the Predictions Invite students to review the predictions that they made before reading and that they may have written in their personal journals. Ask students how their predictions changed as they read.

Returning to the Purpose for Reading Have students discuss why the story is titled "Raymond's Run" and what part Raymond played in the story. (Squeaky learned to see potential in Raymond's ability to run. He helped her become less self-centered.)

14 PLOT: RESOLUTION
How do you know that Gretchen and Squeaky are probably going to be friends? *(Squeaky respects Gretchen as a competitor. Gretchen graciously congratulates Squeaky. They smile almost-real smiles at each other.)*
METACOGNITIVE: MAKING PREDICTIONS

15 THINK IT OVER
1. *Squeaky realizes that, even if she's lost the race, she can "retire" to coach Raymond. Helping Raymond be the best he can be has become more important to her than her own winning.*
INFERENTIAL: DETERMINING MAIN IDEA
2. *She comes only to run and thinks the other May Day activities are foolish.*
LITERAL: RECOGNIZING CAUSE-EFFECT
3. *Only Squeaky's father can beat her in a race.*
LITERAL: NOTING IMPORTANT DETAILS
4. *Accept reasonable responses: Yes, because she has a good relationship with Raymond and has a lot to teach him; no, because she will be too tough with Raymond.*
CRITICAL: MAKING JUDGMENTS

16 WRITE
To help students get started, you may want to suggest a prewriting graphic such as the following:

Traits That Show Honesty/ Respectability	Does Squeaky Have These Traits?

Accept reasonable responses: Students may feel that Squeaky is honest and deserves respect because of her unswerving determination as well as her constant care of Raymond. Some students may feel that Squeaky is honest but guilty of rash judgments.
CRITICAL: MAKING JUDGMENTS

NOTE Additional writing activities appear on page 521D.

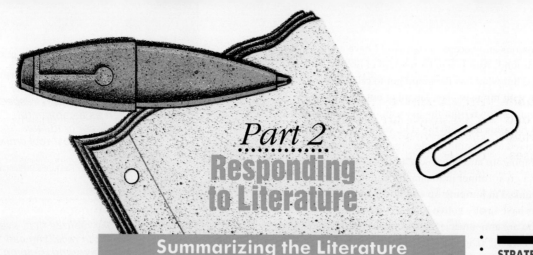

Part 2
Responding to Literature

Summarizing the Literature

Have students retell the story and write a summary.

Invite students to summarize "Raymond's Run" using their character maps. If they did not complete the map, have them do so now. (See *Practice Book* page 140, on 521B.) Students may use their completed maps to retell the story and write a brief summary statement.

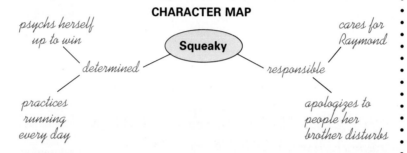

CHARACTER MAP

psychs herself up to win

determined

Squeaky

responsible

cares for Raymond

practices running every day

apologizes to people her brother disturbs

Appreciating Literature

Have students share personal responses.

Divide students into small groups to discuss the story. Provide general questions such as the following to help the groups get started:

- **Which of Squeaky's qualities strikes you as a good characteristic to develop within yourself? Why? How does Squeaky demonstrate this quality?**

PERSONAL JOURNAL Encourage students to use their personal journals to write about ideas and feelings that are expressed in the groups.

STRATEGY CONFERENCE

Discuss the character map, asking students how it helped make the story's events clearer. Encourage students to tell about other reading strategies they used, such as giving special attention to details and visualizing.

Encourage both cooperative and individual responses.

HOLD A DEBATE **Do you think Squeaky's opinions of other people are justified? Why or why not?** Invite students to skim the story to help them recall Squeaky's opinions of different people or types of people. Encourage them to carefully study factual evidence as well as her reasoning to decide whether or not her opinions are based on solid reasons and facts. Should students disagree in their judgments of Squeaky, suggest that they form teams and debate their ideas. CRITICAL: MAKING JUDGMENTS

ROLE-PLAY CONVERSATIONS **How do you think other people might feel about Squeaky? What might they say about her?** Have volunteers role-play conversations among various characters: Gretchen, older people on the street, Cynthia Proctor, Mr. Pearson. Remind students not to "gossip" and to support their character's opinion of Squeaky with evidence: what she says and how she acts. CREATIVE: INVENTING NEW SCENES

WRITE AN ESSAY **How do you think Squeaky may change in the future? Why?** Invite students to think about Squeaky's realization at the story's end and how her new awareness will change her opinions of—and her behavior toward—other people. Have students write short essays giving their predictions and supporting their reasoning. CRITICAL: EXTENDING A STORY

INFORMAL ASSESSMENT

Few types of activities offer a better chance for informal assessment than do those that require making judgments or expressing opinions. This kind of evaluating incorporates and integrates (1) noting **important details**, (2) considering **cause and effect,** as well as other types of thinking, and (3) **classifying** characters, events, and other story features.

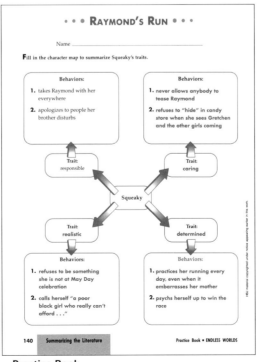

Writer's Journal

Practice Book

WRITER'S JOURNAL
page 93: Writing a creative response

PRACTICE BOOK
page 140: Summarizing the selection

VO·CAB·U·LAR·Y Workshop

Reviewing Key Words

To review how the new vocabulary was used in this selection, display the Key Words. Then have students help you complete a map like the following for as many words as they can. Each map should include the headings *What is it? What is it like?* and *What are some examples?* For Key Words such as *psyching* and *prance,* which do not fit well in this type of web, ask students to list synonyms.

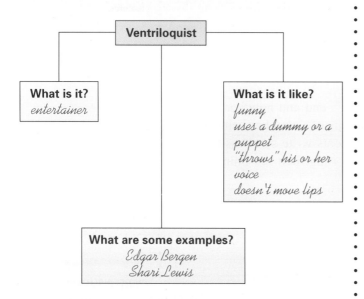

Ventriloquist

What is it?
entertainer

What is it like?
funny
uses a dummy or a puppet
"throws" his or her voice
doesn't move lips

What are some examples?
Edgar Bergen
Shari Lewis

Extending Vocabulary

DESCRIPTIVE LANGUAGE/IDIOMS   Remind students that one way authors make characters seem real is to have them use the language such a person would use in real life. Point out that Squeaky says one of the runners is "psyching" his opponents; that is, trying to make them nervous before the race so they won't perform well. Ask students whether they would use the same word or a different word to describe a similar situation. Explain that people in different parts of the country and in different groups often use different words to describe the same situation. Also, point out that informal language changes quickly—a popular expression today may be out of date next year.

COOPERATIVE LEARNING   To reinforce these ideas, have pairs of students reread Squeaky's thoughts on pages 513 (paragraph 4) through 514 (paragraph 3) of the story and then work together to "translate" her thoughts twice, first replacing such words and phrases as *sidekicks, took up for her, hangs out, talks about me like a dog, that's chicken, I don't feature a whole lot of chit-chat, right from the jump, trying to signify, all salty,* and *whupped* with the words and phrases they would use if they were telling the story informally, and then replacing them with formal language. Ask volunteers to read their versions aloud.

I DON'T FEATURE A WHOLE LOT OF CHIT-CHAT.

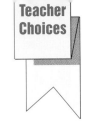

Language Arts

WRITING

Writing About the Literature

CREATIVE: FIRST-PERSON NARRATIVE Suggest students rewrite the race from Gretchen's point of view. As a prewriting activity, have them imagine how Gretchen is probably feeling at the beginning of the race, in the middle, and at the end. Then have them consider Gretchen's "voice" as a narrator.

Beginning	Middle	End
confident	wary	disappointed

Have students form small groups and read their narratives aloud to the group.
LISTENING/SPEAKING/WRITING

CRITICAL: EXPOSITORY PARAGRAPH Ask students to discuss whether or not Squeaky's way of handling people who bother her brother is the most effective way. Have students write paragraphs stating their opinions of her methods and their reasons for those opinions.
LISTENING/SPEAKING/WRITING

NOTE: An additional writing activity appears on page 521.

SPEAKING/LISTENING

Creative Role-Playing

AVAILABLE ON PROJECT CARD

Have partners role-play a conversation between Squeaky and Gretchen some time in the future when they are friends. The girls should compare and contrast their earlier perceptions of each other with their current perceptions. LISTENING/SPEAKING

SPELLING

Spelling Review

SPELLING WORDS: *apologize, encourage, judgment, jutting, pageant, pigeon, prodigy, psyching, smudge, usage*

Have students write the Spelling Words as you dictate them. Then have a volunteer write them on the board, underlining the word that has no /j/ sound. Have students read the other words aloud in unison, listening for the /j/ sound. Have another volunteer circle the letter or letters that represent the /j/ sound. LISTENING/SPEAKING/SPELLING

INTEGRATED SPELLING

page 70: Writing words with the /j/ sound

INTEGRATED SPELLING
The Sound /j/

Name

WORD PLAY

Circle the three words from the Word Bank used in this sentence:

Its neck (jutting) out proudly, the (pigeon) was preparing for the (pageant).

Now write three sentences of your own. Use at least three words from the Word Bank in each sentence. Your sentences can be silly or serious.
Answers will vary.

WORD BANK
apologize
encourage
judgment
jutting
pageant
pigeon
prodigy
psyching
smudge
usage

SPELLING DETECTIVE

After the May Day track meet, Squeaky and Gretchen became good friends. Squeaky hadn't seen Gretchen for a while, so she decided to write her a note. As usual, she was in a rush when she wrote it. Then, when Squeaky proofread the note, she found six spelling errors. Find each error and circle it. Write the word correctly above the misspelled word.

Hi, Gretch,
apologize
I (apolojize) for not stopping by lately. (Oh, no!
smudge
I've got a (smuge) on this note already.) Are you
pageant   psyching
going to be in the (padgent) next week? I'm (syching)
myself for it. I don't really want to dress up, but I
encourage
will if you will. Now, I don't want to (encouraje) you
or anything. Just let me know. (Maybe I could dress
pigeon
as a (pidgin) and give everyone a laugh!)

70   "Raymond's Run" • ENDLESS WORLDS

Integrated Spelling

Part 3
Learning
Through Literature

LITERARY APPRECIATION
INTRODUCE

Characterization

OBJECTIVE: *To understand how writers develop characters*

| 1 | Focus |

Explain how writers develop characters.

Explain to students that writers use three methods to develop a character: the character's words and actions, the words of other characters in the story, and the writer's description of the character.

Explain to students that sometimes characters are described very broadly to fit a certain type of person, such as a bully, a hero, and so on. These are called flat characters, or stereotypes. Most often, however, characters are more realistic, or rounded, such as those in "Raymond's Run."

| 2 | Teach/Model |

Model the thinking.

Model how you would identify Squeaky's character:

I notice in the story that Squeaky tells us many things about herself and shows her character in her actions. Other people show what they think of her by their actions—her parents trust her, Raymond loves her, Gretchen comes to respect her.

| 3 | Practice/Apply |

Have students identify characterization.

Ask students to look for passages in the story that describe Squeaky and other characters. Have them point out which method the author uses to develop the character.

Informally assess the learning.

Check students' understanding of the lesson by having them summarize what they learned. (Writers use several different methods to develop characters in a story.)

READER ↔ WRITER CONNECTION

Characterization

▶ **Writers** develop a character through the character's words and actions, the words of other characters in the story, and descriptions of the character.

▶ **Readers** enjoy the feeling of wholeness that results when the characters in a story are fully developed.

WRITE A CHARACTER DESCRIPTION Have students develop a character of their choice by writing one or two paragraphs that include at least two of the following: a regional dialect, several of the character's actions, a description of the character's appearance, a description of the character's room or office, and revealing dialogue with another character.

CHALLENGE Have students write a short sequel to the story in which Raymond enters a race and wins. Remind them to include a description of how Raymond's character develops and grows.

SECOND-LANGUAGE SUPPORT Students can demonstrate their understanding of characterization by listing the personal qualities that Squeaky reveals by her actions. (See *Second-Language Support Manual.*)

Writer's Journal

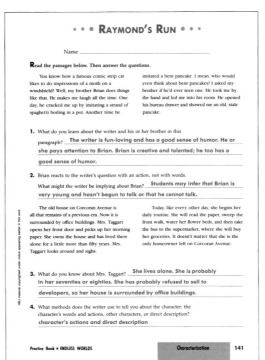

Practice Book

WRITER'S JOURNAL
page 94: Writing a character description

PRACTICE BOOK
page 141: Understanding characterization

Imagery

OBJECTIVE: *To appreciate an author's use of imagery*

1	Focus

Introduce the concept of imagery.

Tell students that the author of "Raymond's Run" uses imagery extensively in the story. Remind students that imagery is strong, vivid language that describes people, places, things, or ideas by appealing to the senses or by using comparison (figurative language). Ask students to name words that appeal to the senses of sight, sound, smell, taste, and touch. Then ask them to suggest some common uses of comparisons, or figurative language; for example, *light as a feather*.

2	Teach/Model

Model the thinking.

Explain to students that they can recognize imagery by finding words or phrases that describe something so well that they can form a mental picture of it. Have students turn to page 512 and read the two paragraphs beginning *I'm standing on the corner*. Model the thinking:

> **The details in these paragraphs are so specific and so sense-appealing that I can see the scene as if it were on a movie or television screen. I can see Raymond pretending he's on a tightrope, and then sloshing and dashing and scaring the pigeons. I can see people getting all upset as the pigeons flutter, newspapers scatter, and wax-paper lunches get spilled.**

Have students discuss imagery.

Have students discuss which senses the author appeals to in the passage described above. (mostly sight, though the word *slosh* also suggests the sound and the feel of the water; and the repetition of *breathing exercises* helps the reader feel Squeaky's controlled breathing) Then ask students to find figurative language in the passage. (simile: *I'll high prance . . . like a rodeo pony,* in lines 4–5 from bottom)

3   Practice/Apply

Have students identify imagery.

COOPERATIVE LEARNING   Have students form small groups. Then let each group choose a passage from the story and analyze its imagery. Encourage students to read the passage aloud and examine the words and phrases to determine which senses they appeal to. Also have students find examples of figurative language.

4   Summarize

Informally assess the learning.

Ask students to summarize what they learned. (Imagery is the use of strong, vivid language that appeals to the senses.)

READER ↔ WRITER CONNECTION

Imagery

▶ **Writers** use imagery to make their settings, characters, and plots more real, and thus more interesting, to their readers.
▶ **Readers** appreciate imagery because it helps them imagine what is going on in a story.

WRITE WITH IMAGERY   Have students think of a memorable scene, not too complicated, but rather limited and crisp. It might be tranquil, noisy, silly, or scary. Then have students write a three-line haiku or free verse poem that creates a single image for the reader.

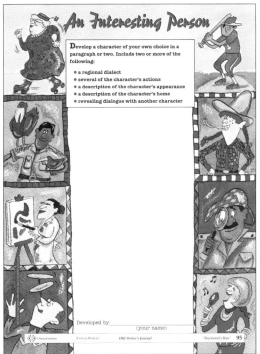

Writer's Journal

CHALLENGE Suggest that students write a description that relies heavily on imagery. Before they write, have them brainstorm moments when they saw, heard, smelled, tasted, or touched something memorable.

SECOND-LANGUAGE SUPPORT Ask students the words for *see, hear, smell, taste,* and *touch* in their first language. Have them keep these words in mind as they search for imagery. (See *Second-Language Support Manual.*)

WRITER'S JOURNAL page 95: Writing with imagery

RAYMOND'S RUN / **521H**

Point of View

OBJECTIVE: *To determine point of view in a first-person or third-person narrative*

Review

Review point of view.

Remind students that a first-person narrative is told by a story character using the pronoun *I*, whereas a third-person narrative is told by an outside observer who refers to all story characters as *he* or *she*. A third-person narrator may be omniscient (all-knowing) or limited.

Practice/Apply

Have students identify other first-person narratives.

Have students recall other first-person narratives they have read. Have them discuss why an author might choose to tell a story in the first person instead of the third person.

Summarize

Informally assess the learning.

Ask students to summarize what they reviewed. (A first-person narrative is told by a character using the pronoun *I;* a third-person narrative is told by an outside observer who refers to the characters as *he* or *she*.)

MEETING
INDIVIDUAL
NEEDS

CHALLENGE Have students find a story written in the third person and rewrite one of its scenes from the first-person point of view. When they finish, have them compare and contrast the two versions, telling which they prefer and why.

PRACTICE BOOK
page 142: Identifying point of view

Practice Book

Comparing-Contrasting/ Making Judgments

OBJECTIVE: *To review how comparing and contrasting persons, places, or events can help readers make judgments about them*

Review

Review comparing and contrasting to make judgments.

Ask students to tell one way in which Squeaky was different at the end of "Raymond's Run" than she was at the beginning. Model how comparing and contrasting can help you make judgments:

At the beginning of the story, Squeaky thought mostly about winning the May Day race. I thought she was a bit self-absorbed and egotistical. At the end of the story, she is thinking about helping her brother Raymond become a runner. I think she's become more mature and better able to think unselfishly about other people.

Practice/Apply

Have students apply the skills.

Have students compare and contrast their feelings about Raymond at the beginning of the story and at its end. Did they feel more hopeful about Raymond's future at the end? Why or why not? Did their judgment of him change?

Summarize

Informally assess the learning.

Have students summarize what they learned. (Comparing and contrasting characters, places, or events in a story can help readers make judgments.)

CHALLENGE Invite students to write a list comparing and contrasting their own skills and accomplishments as a fourth grader and as a seventh grader. Then have them make a judgment about their own development.

Integrated **Curriculum**

SOCIAL STUDIES

Harlem Had a Renaissance

AVAILABLE ON PROJECT CARD

CULTURAL AWARENESS Have students research, in books and periodicals, Harlem's history, especially its 1920s renaissance of the arts. Encourage students to draw a poster map of Harlem. They can then present their research by numbering sites on the map and writing descriptions of what happened or who lived at each site, much as a "walking tour" brochure of any historical place would do. Students can display their posters and invite classmates to "tour" Harlem; to enhance the atmosphere, students could obtain recordings of Duke Ellington and Cab Calloway to play in the background. Other students might read aloud poems by Langston Hughes.
LISTENING/SPEAKING/READING/WRITING

PHYSICAL EDUCATION

Running Fun

Encourage students to research the sport of running. They may look into the different kinds of races, running equipment, and training for running. Suggest that they present their information on a poster decorated with pictures or drawings of great runners. READING/WRITING

SOCIAL STUDIES

American Talk

CULTURAL AWARENESS Have students research regional variations in language, using such books as Stuart Berg Flexner's *I Hear America Talking* and William Safire's books on language. Have them compare and contrast the words that Americans in different parts of the country use for such food-related items as pancakes, submarine sandwiches, and soft drinks. Students can then role-play speakers from the Northeast, South, Midwest, and West describing a visit to a restaurant.
LISTENING/SPEAKING/READING/WRITING

MATH

Fast Footwear

Have students compare prices of different brands and styles of running shoes and rank them from least expensive to most expensive. Suggest that they present their findings in a graph. Then have students tell which shoes they would choose for running and why. LISTENING/SPEAKING/READING/WRITING

Harlem on Their Minds

READ ALOUD TO STUDENTS:

HARLEM WAS BUILT IN THE LATE 1800s AS A MIDDLE-CLASS SUBURB OF NEW YORK CITY.

The area contains some of the finest examples of row houses in the city. Harlem's name comes from a Dutch city, Haarlem, and is part of New York's heritage from its earliest Dutch settlers. In the early 1900s, commercial development in midtown New York forced many black people to move north to Harlem.

In the 1920s, Harlem became famous as a center of African American culture. An important person in the "Harlem Renaissance," or flowering of the arts, was Langston Hughes, the first black American who made a living from writing and lecturing. Hughes wrote poems, stories, novels, and plays. He was criticized by some for concentrating on the everyday lives of ordinary people, but his work won fame because it celebrated the beauty, strength, and spirit of African Americans.

Another leader to emerge from Harlem was Herman Badillo, who came to the United States from Puerto Rico as a young orphan and graduated with honors from the City College of New York. Elected to the United States House of Representatives in 1970 with 85 percent of the vote, Badillo was the first person of Puerto Rican birth to serve in Congress. ■

ACTIVITY CORNER

■ Have students do research on other figures of the Harlem Renaissance and make a poster about the artists, musicians, and writers who brought excited New Yorkers flocking to Harlem.

AVAILABLE ON PROJECT CARD

■ Have students read Langston Hughes's poetry and choose a favorite poem to read or recite to classmates.

Herman Badillo was the first United States Congressman of Puerto Rican birth.

Langston Hughes is a major American writer whose work celebrates Harlem life.

■ Ask students to identify other political leaders who have come from Harlem or from the African American and Hispanic American communities in general. Have them make a list of these individuals and their major achievements.

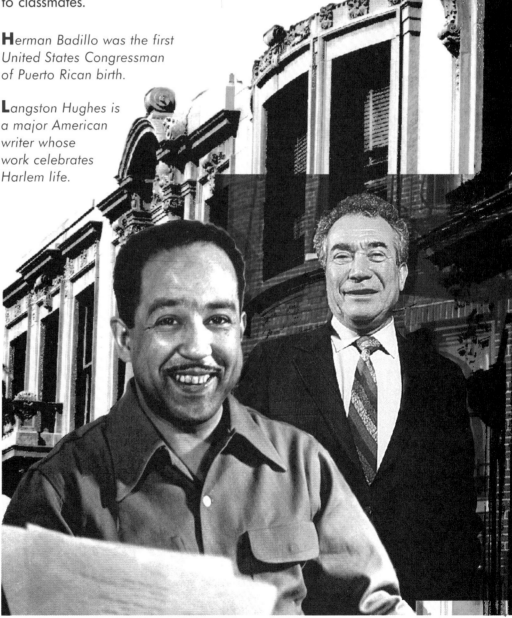

HELPING HANDS

by Brent Ashabranner

BRENT ASHABRANNER (1921–), a native Oklahoman, was teaching at Oklahoma State University and writing about the West when the U.S. Agency for International Development offered him a job in Africa. Ashabranner's experiences there and in the Peace Corps made him a close observer of other cultures. Since his return to the United States, he has applied his skill in observing cultural differences to the problems of underrepresented groups: He writes about Native Americans, migrant workers, immigrants, and the disabled. The title of the book from which this selection is excerpted is *People Who Make a Difference*.

MORE BOOKS BY BRENT ASHABRANNER
Into a Strange Land: Unaccompanied Refugee Youth in America, with Melissa Ashabranner. Dodd, Mead, 1987. AVERAGE
The Times of My Life. Dutton, 1990. AVERAGE

OTHER BOOKS ABOUT MAKING A DIFFERENCE
Dreams into Deeds: Nine Women Who Dared by Linda Peavy and Ursula Smith. Scribner, 1985. AVERAGE
Teacher: Anne Sullivan Macy by Helen Keller. Greenwood, 1985. CHALLENGING

- **SELECTION SUMMARY**
- This nonfiction
- excerpt describes the
- work of Helping
- Hands: Simian Aides
- for the Disabled, an
- organization founded
- by Mary Joan Willard
- that trains monkeys
- to do simple tasks for
- quadriplegics. In the
- program, a female
- baby monkey lives
- with a human family
- for about three years.
- Then trainers teach
- her commands like
- "off," "on," "bring,"
- and "open." Finally
- she is placed with
- someone whose
- needs match her
- skills and personality.
- The monkey not only
- carries out tasks
- for its owner but
- also provides
- companionship.

LESSON PLANNER			
	Materials	**Integrated Curriculum**	**Meeting Individual Needs**
1 READING LITERATURE pp. 521N–535	Student Anthology pp. 522–535 Transparency 28 Second-Language Support Manual Practice Book p. 143 Integrated Spelling p. 71 Integrated Spelling T.E. pp. 94–95	Spelling Spelling Pretest Spelling-Vocabulary Connection (noun suffixes: *-ity, -ment*)	Second-Language Support Vocabulary 521O Strategic Reading 521P, 526 Cooperative Reading 522, 534
2 RESPONDING TO LITERATURE pp. 535A–535D	Writer's Journal p. 96 Practice Book p. 144 Integrated Spelling p. 72 Integrated Spelling T.E. pp. 94–95	Vocabulary Workshop Reviewing Key Words Extending Vocabulary Writing About the Literature Speaking/Listening Spelling Review	Cooperative Learning 535B, 535C
3 LEARNING THROUGH LITERATURE pp. 535E–535J	Second-Language Support Manual Writer's Journal p. 97 Practice Book pp. 145–147	Science Social Studies Health Multicultural	Reteach 535F Challenge 535F, 535G, 535H Second-Language Support 535F Cooperative Learning 535F, 535G

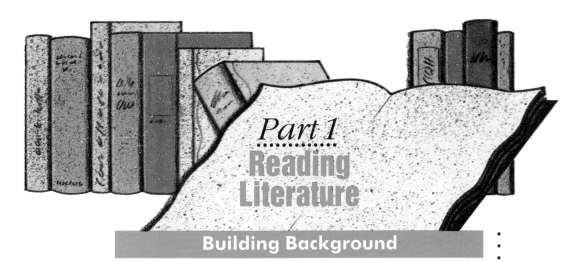

Part 1
Reading Literature

Building Background

Access prior knowledge and develop vocabulary concepts.

Tell students that the selection they are about to read is "Helping Hands." Write the words *Helpful People* on the board, and have students complete a Frayer Model:

Essential Characteristics	Nonessential Characteristics
willingness to work	*cheerfulness*
ability to do simple tasks	*thoughtfulness*

Helpful People

Examples	Nonexamples
cleaning up	*refusing to help*
responding to requests	*talking back*

Have students quickwrite.

Ask students to describe one helpful act in a few sentences. Students can share their ideas in small groups.

Vocabulary Strategies

Introduce Key Words and strategies.

Tell students that some words in "Helping Hands" may be unfamiliar. Display Transparency 28, or write the paragraph on the board. Have students read the paragraph silently and use context clues, word structure, and phonics to figure out the meanings of the underlined words. As a volunteer reads the paragraph aloud, help with pronunciation if necessary.

Transparency 28 Key Words

When a philanthropic organization offered Jay a free monkey, he worried that having a monkey helper care for him might be demeaning. After his primate friend arrived, though, he was glad that the rehabilitative hospital where he went for therapy had advocated monkey helpers. The dexterity of the monkey's tiny hands amazed him. Showing her off was the motivation he needed to start inviting people in. Jay and his simian friend both enjoyed the opportunity for socialization that company provided.

KEY WORDS DEFINED

philanthropic charitable

demeaning degrading

primate of an order of mammals that includes apes, monkeys, and human beings

rehabilitative restoring to health

advocated supported

dexterity skillfulness

motivation something that provides a reason to act

simian having to do with a monkey

socialization process of taking part in social activities

Check students' understanding.

Have students demonstrate their understanding by predicting how the Key Words will be used in "Helping Hands." Tell them to categorize the words under the headings below and to explain to you why each word belongs in its group. If students feel that some words don't fit, have them explain why. STRATEGY: PRIOR KNOWLEDGE

PREDICT-O-GRAM

Therapy	About Monkeys	Animal Training	Spokesperson for Charity
rehabilitative dexterity	simian primate	motivation socialization	advocated philanthropic

Integrate spelling with vocabulary.

SPELLING-VOCABULARY CONNECTION *Integrated Spelling* page 71 reinforces spellings of words with the **noun suffix -ity** or **-ment,** including the Key Word *dexterity.* The spelling of the Key Word *demeaning* is also included.

• • • HELPING HANDS • • •

Name _____

A. Read the sentences. Circle the letters next to the *two* words or phrases that together define each underlined word.

1. People who work for philanthropic agencies often get as much as they give.
(a.) benevolent   (b.) charitable   c. international   d. stamp-collecting

2. Although their motivation is to help others, in return, they feel good about themselves.
a. negative part   b. positive part   (c.) incentive   (d.) desire to accomplish something

3. Some people have actually advocated helping others as a means of improving one's own quality of life.
a. denounced   (b.) argued for   (c.) recommended   d. argued against

4. Some people find some forms of work demeaning, but I feel all work is worthwhile.
(a.) degrading   b. proud   c. easy   (d.) belittling

5. When people are in need of rehabilitative exercise, they can often obtain physical therapy in a clinic or hospital.
a. professional   (b.) restorative   c. easy   (d.) helping

6. The tables could turn at any moment; the physical therapist could lose her dexterity, and she'd be the one in need of help.
(a.) ability   (b.) skill in using hands   c. desire to help   d. training

7. Perhaps part of socialization is learning that we are all in this together.
a. growing up   (b.) becoming civilized   c. defining goals   (d.) living in society

B. Use the word *primate* or *simian* to fill in each blank. Use a dictionary to help you with the correct meanings.

Every ___simian___ is a ___primate___, but every
___primate___ is not a ___simian___.

Practice Book ▪ ENDLESS WORLDS   Vocabulary   143

Practice Book

INTEGRATED SPELLING

Noun Suffixes *-ity, -ment*

Name_____

Read the Spelling Words. Write them on a separate sheet of paper. Check your spelling.

━━ SPELLING STRATEGY ━━

Nouns can be formed by adding suffixes to other parts of speech. The suffix **-ity,** for example, can be added to an adjective to form a noun. The suffix **-ment** forms a noun when it is added to a verb. Here are some rules for making these nouns.

Adding -ity: You can usually just add the suffix **-ity** to the adjective (**personal + ity = personality**). However, to add **-ity** to a word that ends in **e,** drop the final **e** (**pure + ity = purity**). When you add **-ity** to a word that ends in **ble,** insert an **i** between **b** and **l** (**able + ity = ability**).

Adding -ment: This suffix is usually added without changes to base words. When adding **-ment** to **argue, acknowledge,** and **judge,** though, you must drop the final **e** (**acknowledge + ment = acknowledgment**).

Which *-ity* Spelling Word was made from a Latin root and is related to the word *dexterous?*   ___dexterity___

Which Spelling Word was formed by changing its prefix, dropping its final e, and adding an i?   ___inability___

Which three Spelling Words were made into nouns simply by dropping the final e before adding the noun suffix?
___acknowledgment___   ___argument___   ___purity___

Which four words weren't changed when the suffix was added?
___encouragement___   ___personality___   ___placement___   ___publicity___

Which Spelling Word has the inflectional ending *-ing?*   ___demeaning___

SPELLING WORDS
acknowledgment
argument
demeaning
dexterity
encouragement
inability
personality
placement
publicity
purity

━ MEMORY JOGGER ━

Dean's meaning was **demeaning**.

Here's a Memory Jogger to help you remember how to spell **demeaning**.

ENDLESS WORLDS • "Helping Hands"   71

Integrated Spelling

INTEGRATED SPELLING
page 71: Writing and spelling words with the noun suffixes: *-ity, -ment*

NOTE: These pages may be completed now or after students have read the selection.

Using the K-W-L Strategy

Have students review the K-W-L strategy.

Remind students that the K-W-L strategy can help them understand expository, or informational, nonfiction. Write the K-W-L headings on the board: *What I Know, What I Want to Know, What I Learned.* Allow a volunteer to explain the use of the K-W-L strategy. (List what you know about the subject, form questions about what you want to find out, and write the answers you learn as you read.)

Help students preview the selection.

Invite students to preview the selection by looking at the illustrations and by reading the title of the excerpt, the title of the book from which it comes, and the first four paragraphs.

PERSONAL JOURNAL Have students copy the headings of the chart in their journals, or have them use *Practice Book* page 144. (See page 535B in this Teacher's Edition.) Instruct students to brainstorm what they know about monkeys, animal training, and the needs of paralyzed people to fill in the first column. Help them form questions for the second column. Students can complete the chart as they read. (They will return to the chart after reading, in Summarizing the Literature.) Their K-W-L charts might begin like this:

K-W-L CHART

What I Know	What I Want to Know	What I Learned
People who are paralyzed can't move and can't do some things for themselves.	How do people who are paralyzed manage everyday chores?	

Setting a Purpose

Have students set purposes.

Have students use the questions in the second column of their K-W-L charts to set a purpose for reading. Invite volunteers to share their purposes with classmates.

Model purpose-setting, if necessary.

If students have difficulty setting a purpose for reading, model the thinking:

> **What I know, I list in the first column. What I want to know, I list as questions in the second column. My purpose for reading will be to answer these questions.**

SECOND-LANGUAGE SUPPORT Students may benefit from the Guided Reading and Cooperative Reading activities and the additional guidance under the Student Anthology pages. (See *Second-Language Support Manual.*)

OPTIONS FOR READING

Independent Reading
Have students read the selection silently with their purpose for reading in mind.

Guided Reading
Follow the Guided Reading suggestions that appear on pages 522, 528–529, and 534. These suggestions model strategic reading.

Cooperative Reading
Suggestions appear on pages 522 and 534.

Numbered Annotations
Use the numbered annotations beside the Student Anthology pages to heighten students' appreciation of the selection.

Helping Hands

by Brent Ashabranner

You are thirsty. A cold drink is in the refrigerator ten feet away, but it might as well be ten miles away. You can't move a muscle to reach it. Your nose itches until your eyes water, but you can't lift a hand to scratch. You want to watch a videotape, but all you can do is look helplessly at your VCR across the room and wait until someone comes to put in the cassette.

522

Guided Reading

SET PURPOSE/PREDICT: PAGES 522–528 Have students read to the end of paragraph 4 on page 528 to find out how monkeys can be used as "helping hands." As students read, remind them to add notes and questions to their K-W-L charts.

Cooperative Reading

SET PURPOSE/PREDICT: PAGES 522–535 Have students form pairs and share the questions they want answered in the excerpt. Then have partners read the selection silently, pausing periodically to discuss what they have learned, to fill in their charts, and to revise their questions as needed.

Your name is Mitch Coffman, and you are a prisoner in your own body. Your mind is clear and sharp; you can talk and move your head, but you can't move any other part of your body. Like almost a hundred thousand other men and women in the United States, you are a quadriplegic, totally paralyzed from the neck down.

Mitch Coffman's entry into the world of the quadriplegic came on a day that should have been a happy one. He was returning from a party to celebrate his thirtieth birthday when his car skidded on a bridge and went into a spin. Mitch was thrown out with an impact that broke his neck.

When Mitch regained consciousness, he came instantly face-to-face with a terrible reality: he had suffered permanent damage to his spine between the third and fifth cervical vertebrae. He would be paralyzed for the rest of his life.

After months of physical therapy, Mitch regained enough movement in his left hand to operate the control for an electric wheelchair. And he was more fortunate than most quadriplegics because he was able to move into a government-subsidized apartment building especially equipped for people with severe physical disabilities. The building has ramps instead of stairs, roll-in showers, light switches and other electrical and kitchen equipment that are easy to reach and operate. Attendants are also on duty at all times. Still, there were endless hours every day and night when Mitch was alone in his apartment waiting, waiting for the simplest tasks to be performed for him.

And then one day a stranger arrived in Mitch's little apartment. She was only eighteen inches tall, weighed but a furry six pounds, and communicated in excited squeaks and endless trills. But she could open the refrigerator door and bring Mitch a cold drink or a sandwich. She could scratch his nose with a soft cloth when it itched. She could put a videotape in the VCR. She could do dozens of other things for him that he could not do for himself.

523

1 EXPOSITORY TEXT: MAIN IDEA AND DETAILS
Explain how Mitch's apartment building is designed to help people with disabilities. **What is the purpose of these design features?**
(The entire building is accessible to people in wheelchairs, and attendants are there to help. These features help people with disabilities do more for themselves.)
INFERENTIAL: DRAWING CONCLUSIONS

2 EXPOSITORY TEXT: MAIN IDEA
How much of a difference do you think it made in Mitch's life to have someone around to do these things for him? Why do you think so?
(Accept reasonable responses: It made a huge difference, because he didn't feel so alone and frustrated.)
INFERENTIAL: DETERMINING CAUSE-EFFECT

Vocabulary Strategy Draw students' attention to the word *quadriplegic* (line 5). Divide the word in half and explain that *-plegic* refers to paralysis. To help students figure out the meaning of *quadri-* ("four"), ask them to name other words they know with the same root. (Accept reasonable responses: quadruple, quadrangle, quadruped.) STRATEGY: STRUCTURAL ANALYSIS

3 LITERARY FORMS: EXPOSITORY NONFICTION
What clues tell you that this is expository, or informational, nonfiction? *(Accept reasonable responses: The selection explains and gives information. Although it begins with a narrative, the narrative is used as an example.)*
METACOGNITIVE: CLASSIFYING

4 EXPOSITORY TEXT: MAIN IDEA
As a psychologist, Mary Joan felt that Joe needed to be more independent in spite of his physical limitations. What do you think is the psychological effect of dependence? Of independence? *(Accept reasonable responses: Being dependent usually makes people unhappy. People are generally happier when they can make choices and do things for themselves.)*
INFERENTIAL: MAKING GENERALIZATIONS

The stranger was a black and brown capuchin[1] monkey, and her improbable name was Peepers. Almost as important as what she could do for him was the fact that she was there, a companion, a constant presence in the apartment where, for most of the long hours of long days, there had been only Mitch.

"It took us months to learn to live together," Mitch explains as Peepers sits quietly in his lap. "Now I can't imagine living without her."

3 The modest quarters of Helping Hands: Simian Aides for the Disabled are on the fourth floor of an office building on Commonwealth Avenue in Boston. On my first visit there I could hear monkeys chattering in the training room. I was eager to watch the training, but before that I wanted to talk to Mary Joan Willard, the educational psychologist who started and is director of Helping Hands.

Quantum leaps of the imagination have always fascinated me, and I opened our conversation on that point. "How did you get the idea that monkeys might be trained to do things for paralyzed human beings?" I asked. "What made you think it was possible?"

Mary Joan explained that after receiving her doctorate in educational psychology from Boston University, she began a postdoctoral fellowship in 1977 at Tufts New England Medical Center in Boston. The fellowship was for rehabilitative study and work with persons who had suffered severe physical injury. In her daily rounds she soon came to know Joe, a patient at the center. One minute he had been a happy, healthy twenty-three-year-old. The next minute, because of a diving accident, he was a quadriplegic, paralyzed from the neck down. His story was an all-too-familiar one, but he was the first quadriplegic Mary Joan had ever known.

4 "I was shocked," she said. "I found it inconceivable that someone so young, so full of life was going to spend the rest of his days completely dependent on other people, dependent for a drink of water, for a bite of food, dependent on someone to bring him a book or turn out a light. I am a psychologist, and I kept thinking, there has to be some way to make him more independent.

"I couldn't get him out of my mind. I would sit in my room and

---

[1]capuchin [kap′yə·shən]

524

Oral Rereading   Invite students to read aloud the last two paragraphs on page 523 and the first two on page 524 or another passage in which the author makes his point through describing what something is like rather than stating it directly. Suggest that students work in pairs to practice reading the passage until they can read fluently and with expression. Then ask volunteers to read their passages aloud.

Mary Joan Willard enjoys her capuchin friend.

525

Vocabulary Strategy   Point out the phrase *quantum leaps* (paragraph 4, line 1, on page 524), and ask students to identify the author's example of a quantum leap. (the idea that monkeys might be trained to do things for paralyzed human beings) Invite a volunteer to look up *quantum leap* in a dictionary and share its meaning with classmates. ("an abrupt major change, especially in knowledge") Discuss how the phrase applies to this situation. (Willard was not building on the ideas of others. No one had ever expressed this idea before.)
STRATEGY: CONTEXT CLUES/DEFINITION

think about him lying there in his room, helpless. And then one night it hit me out of the blue. Chimps! Why couldn't chimpanzees be trained to do things for quadriplegics like Joe? I kept thinking about it, and I didn't get much sleep that night."

The next day Mary Joan went to see B. F. Skinner, the famous Harvard psychologist who has done extensive pioneering research with animals, using reward and punishment techniques to alter their behavior. Mary Joan had worked three years for Skinner as a part-time assistant. He might not think her idea was workable, but she knew he would not scoff at it.

Skinner was amused at his assistant's excitement over her new idea; he pointed out that chimpanzees grow to be almost as big as humans, are stronger than humans, and often are bad-tempered. Chimpanzees would be too risky. But Mary Joan was right; Skinner did not laugh. The idea intrigued him.

5 Why not, he asked, think about using capuchins, the little creatures traditionally known as organ-grinder monkeys? They are small, usually no more than six or seven pounds and seldom more than eighteen inches tall. They are intelligent, easy to train, and form strong bonds of loyalty to their human masters. Furthermore, they have a long life expectancy, an average of about thirty years.

That was all the encouragement Mary Joan needed. She did some reading about capuchins, found out where they could be purchased, then went to the director of postdoctoral programs at Tufts and asked for money to start an experimental capuchin training program.

"He nearly fell off his chair laughing," Mary Joan said, remembering the director's first reaction to her proposal.

But Mary Joan was persistent and persuasive. When the director stopped laughing, he came through with a grant and some training space. The grant was just two thousand dollars, but it was enough for Mary Joan to buy four monkeys, some cages, and hire student trainers at one dollar an hour.

"I thought we could train them in eight weeks," Mary Joan recalled. "I had never touched a monkey! It took us eight weeks just to coax them out of their cages. The monkeys I was able to buy had had some pretty hard treatment. They weren't in a mood to trust any human being."

526

Second-Language Support
Help students understand that *extensive pioneering research* (line 6) means that Skinner was one of the first to do experiments showing which ways of teaching worked best.

But a beginning had been made, and patience and dedication paid off in training the monkeys in an astonishing variety of tasks: taking food from a refrigerator and putting it in a microwave oven; turning lights on and off; doing the same with a television set, stereo, heater, air conditioner; opening and closing curtains; setting up books, magazines, and computer printouts on a reading stand.

One piece of equipment essential to most quadriplegics is a mouthstick, which is used for turning pages, dialing a phone, typing, working a computer, and many other actions which improve the quality of a quadriplegic's life. One problem is that the mouthstick often falls to the floor or onto the wheelchair tray. The monkey helper is quickly taught to pick up the stick and replace it correctly in its master's mouth.

"The capuchins have great manual dexterity, greater than a human adult's," Mary Joan said, "and they're very bright. But we don't try to train them to do tasks where they have to think."

Judi Zazula, an occupational therapist, has been with Helping Hands almost from the beginning. Her title is program director, but Mary Joan describes her as a partner. Judi makes the same point about not putting a monkey in a situation where it has to think about the right way to do something. "Everything," she says, "is planned so that the monkey has just one way to respond if it does the task right."

The basic motivation for a monkey to perform a task correctly is a simple reward system. When it carries out a command as it is supposed to—turning on a VCR or bringing a drink—the trainer, and later the quadriplegic owner, praises the monkey for doing a good job and at the same time gives it a treat, usually a few drops of strawberry-flavored syrup. The quadriplegic releases the syrup by means of a wheelchair control.

There is also a system of punishment because capuchins are endlessly curious and occasionally mischievous. One monkey, for example, began dimming the lights when its owner was reading so that it would get a reward when it was told to turn them up again. More often, however, misbehavior is likely to be opening a drawer without being asked to or throwing paper out of a wastebasket in the hope of finding something interesting.

527

6 EXPOSITORY TEXT: CAUSE-EFFECT
Why do you think Mary Joan and the trainers chose these particular tasks? *(These would be the kinds of tasks that quadriplegics would most often need help with.)*
INFERENTIAL: DRAWING CONCLUSIONS

7 EXPOSITORY TEXT: MAIN IDEA
Why do you think it is important to train the monkeys in a way that does not require them to think? *(Accept reasonable responses: If there is just one way to do a thing, the monkey will succeed most of the time. If it has to decide for itself, it will often fail. It is fairer to the monkey and to the handler if the monkey succeeds.)*
INFERENTIAL: DRAWING CONCLUSIONS

Teaching Tip You may want to explain that one of the jobs of an occupational therapist (paragraph 4, line 1) is to show persons who have disabilities how to do things that make them more independent of others' help, such as using a mouthstick to dial a telephone. In this role, the occupational therapist works closely with a physical therapist, who uses exercise and massage to help people regain use of their muscles.

8 EXPOSITORY TEXT: CAUSE-EFFECT
Do you think the method used to train the monkeys is a good one? Explain your answer. *(Accept reasonable responses: It seems good because it works; the monkeys receive rewards for doing the job right and are punished only if they misbehave.)*
CRITICAL: MAKING JUDGMENTS

9 NARRATION: ACTIONS/EVENTS
Contrast Robert's life before Hellion came to live with him with his life now. *(Before Hellion came, Robert was helpless for many hours a day. Now he can read, watch television, see a movie, use the phone or computer, and have food or a drink when he needs it. His life with Hellion is obviously much better.)*
INFERENTIAL: COMPARING AND CONTRASTING

8 The monkeys are taught that anything with a white circular sticker pasted on it—such as a medicine cabinet—is off limits. If a monkey violates the off-limits rule, it is warned with a buzz from a small battery-operated device that it wears on a belt around its waist. If it doesn't obey the warning, the quadriplegic master can use remote controls to give the monkey a tiny electric shock. The warning buzz is usually sufficient.

Late in 1979 Robert Foster, a twenty-five-year-old quadriplegic living near Boston, became the first person to take part in a pilot project to test the feasibility of using a capuchin monkey aide. Robert, paralyzed from the shoulders down as the result of an automobile accident at the age of eighteen, had been living by himself for several years with the help of a personal care attendant. The attendant lived in the apartment with Robert but worked full time in a nearby hospital. That meant that Robert was alone in the apartment for nine hours or more at least five days a week.

Robert's new helper, a six-pound capuchin female named Hellion, helped to fill the long hours and continues to do so eight years after the experiment began. Robert communicates with Hellion—who deserves a nicer name—by aiming a small laser pointer at what he wants the monkey to bring or do. The laser is mounted on the chin control mechanism of his wheelchair. He also gives her a voice command such as "Bring" or "Open."

9 Hellion feeds Robert, brushes his hair, tidies up his wheelchair tray, brings him books, and carries out a whole range of other helpful tasks. For his part Robert dispenses strawberry-syrup rewards and tells Hellion how nice she is. Hellion is close by Robert's wheelchair all day, but when he tells her it is time for bed, she will go into her cage and lock the door.

As publicity about simian aides has spread across the country, Helping Hands has been swamped with requests for monkeys. Mary Joan and Judi are proceeding slowly with placements, however, still treating each case as an experiment. A number of additional capuchins have been placed with quadriplegics, and there have been no failures.

Mary Joan has had to spend an increasing amount of her time in fund raising and in administrative details of making Helping Hands a smoothly functioning nonprofit organization. "For the first two

528

Guided Reading

MONITOR COMPREHENSION: PAGES 522–528

How can monkeys be used as "helping hands"?
(They can be trained to do a variety of tasks to help quadriplegics, such as feeding them; turning lights, television, and other electronic equipment on and off; retrieving a mouthstick; setting up books; and so forth.) STRATEGIC READING: RETURNING TO PURPOSE

Why are monkeys good companions for quadriplegics? (They are intelligent and gentle, have nimble fingers, and can easily be trained to do simple tasks.) STRATEGIC READING: SUMMARIZING/DETERMINING CAUSE-EFFECT

What differences does having a Helping Hands monkey make in the life of a quadriplegic?
(Accept reasonable responses: With a monkey, a quadriplegic is no longer unable to satisfy basic needs. With the monkey's help, she or he can eat, take a drink, and so on. Being able to exercise control makes the person feel better about herself or himself.) INFERENTIAL: COMPARING AND CONTRASTING

years we had to get along on three thousand dollars a year," Mary Joan said. "Fortunately, we don't have to pay student trainers much, and they love the experience."

Several major organizations and agencies concerned with severely disabled persons were interested, but all were skeptical. In the early stages Mary Joan wrote thirty-nine grant proposals and sent them to philanthropic foundations and government agencies, but not one was approved. But she persisted and, as evidence mounted that the capuchins could do the job, a trickle of financial support began. Now the Veterans Administration, National Medical Enterprises, the Educational Foundation of America, and the Paralyzed Veterans of America give some financial help to Helping Hands. Money is also received through private contributions, but fund raising still requires time that Mary Joan would rather be giving to other parts of the program.

Lack of money was not the only problem in the early days of the program. Some critics said that the idea of monkeys serving as helpers was demeaning to the quadriplegics as human beings. Some medical authorities said that mechanical equipment—robotics is the technical term—could be developed to do a better job than monkeys.

10

To the first criticism, Mary Joan points out that no one thinks it is beneath the dignity of a blind person to have a dog serve as a guide. As to robotic equipment, she agrees that for some quadriplegics mechanical tools may be best. But she points out that no piece of equipment can provide the companionship and sheer pleasure that an affectionate capuchin can.

"A robot won't sit in your lap and put its arms around you," Mary Joan said.

Trial-and-error testing proved to the Helping Hands crew that early socialization was necessary to train a monkey that would be affectionate and happy when it became part of a human household. The answer has been the creation of a foster home program. When the monkeys are young babies, six to eight weeks old, they are placed with foster families. These volunteer families agree to raise the monkeys in their homes for about three years and then turn them over to Helping Hands to be trained as aides to quadriplegics.

The carefully selected volunteer families agree to spend ten hours a day with their primate babies for the first six months—ten

529

10 EXPOSITORY TEXT: ARGUMENT
If you were in need of help, which do you think you would rather have, a Helping Hands monkey or robotic equipment? Why?
(Responses will vary.)
CRITICAL: SPECULATING

SET PURPOSE/PREDICT: PAGES 528–535 Ask students to predict what happens to the Helping Hands organization after the placement of the first monkey. Remind them to jot down new questions and answers on their K-W-L charts.

Judi Zazula teaches one of her
bright pupils to place a tape in a
cassette player.

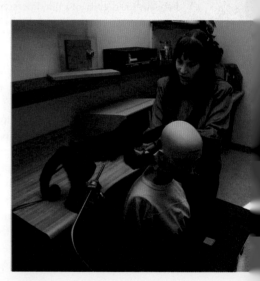

Practice makes perfect.
Someday this monkey will
gently rub a quadriplegic's
itching nose or cheek.

530

Informal Assessment   You can informally assess
your students' ability to summarize by setting up the
following scenario:

> Pretend that this selection is a documentary you
> are watching on television. There is a
> commercial break right now, and someone
> comes into the room and asks you what the
> show is about. What can you explain while the
> commercial is still on?

Judi Zazula studying the record of one of the monkeys in training.

531

ARTIST'S CRAFT

How do the photographs on pages 530–531 help the reader understand the selection? *(Accept reasonable responses: The reader doesn't have to use imagination to visualize how the monkeys and their trainer interact; the photographs add information to the selection.)*

METACOGNITIVE: DETERMINING CAUSE-EFFECT

What do you think would be the advantages and disadvantages of having a monkey to raise? *(Accept reasonable responses: advantages—it would probably be fun and make the owner "special" by attracting attention; disadvantages—a demanding, mischievous pet would be a heavy responsibility.)*
INFERENTIAL: MAKING GENERALIZATIONS

hours with the monkey outside its cage. This means that the foster mother and father and older children are actually carrying the baby monkey as they go about their household routines. Older monkeys require less time, but members of the household still must spend at least four hours daily with the young capuchin if it is to become a truly "humanized" primate.

11 Being a foster parent to a young monkey may sound like fun, and in many ways it can be a delightful experience. But it is time-consuming and demanding, and the time inevitably comes when the monkey must be given over to Helping Hands. "Everyone knows this moment of parting is coming, and most people handle it well," Mary Joan said, "but for some it is very hard. We have been offered as much as five thousand dollars to let a family keep a monkey. But, of course, we can't do that."

If for any reason a monkey does not successfully complete its training at Helping Hands, it is offered to its foster care family as a pet. Should the foster care family be unable to take it, Helping Hands maintains a carefully screened list of other families who have applied for a monkey pet. The "unsuccessful" monkey will be placed in the kind of human home environment to which it is accustomed.

Over sixty-five monkeys are now living with foster families. More than a hundred additional families have passed the screening test and are waiting to receive their foster "children."

Judi Zazula is a rehabilitation engineer. Together with Doug Ely, a solar research specialist for Arthur D. Little, Inc., she has designed most of the special equipment needed in the Helping Hands program: the laser pointer, chin and other wheelchair controls, and equipment that the capuchin's tiny hands can hold and manipulate.

"One of the first things I was asked to design was the nose scratcher," Judi told me and added, "The monkeys helped design a lot of the equipment."

She explained that by watching the monkeys as they carried out their tasks, she and Doug Ely could tell when a piece of equipment needed changing or when some new device was necessary.

The training of a monkey usually takes about eight months. A session with the student trainer may last from half an hour to an hour, but it might be as short as ten minutes depending upon the

532

monkey's personality. There may be several training sessions a day.

"Every monkey is different," Judi said. "Every one has her own personality and her own strengths and weaknesses."

Judi's biggest job within Helping Hands is to match the right monkey with the right quadriplegic who is being considered to receive one. A training log is kept on each monkey, and Judi pores over every page until she knows everything that can be known about a particular capuchin's personality and about her strengths and weaknesses.

Then Judi visits the quadriplegic. She stays at least two days and gets to know as much about the person as she can and about the environment where the monkey is going to live and work for the rest of her life. Judi even makes a video of the quadriplegic's living quarters so that they can be duplicated in the final training of the monkey the quadriplegic will receive.

"I am totally consumed with getting the right monkey in the right place," Judi said to me. "By the time they leave this training room, they are my children. I always think, what kind of life will **12** they have out there? I want to make sure it will be the best and most useful life possible."

Judi has come to know dozens of quadriplegics very well, and she has thought a great deal about the total loss of hope that they suffer. "A spinal cord injury is an especially terrible thing," Judi said, "because it usually happens to young people, and it usually occurs at a happy moment in life—a car accident after a junior-senior prom or having fun diving into a swimming pool or playing football. Then everything is lost in a split second. The person comes to and his or her world has collapsed and a nightmare begins.

"Most people thinking about something like that happening to them say, 'I wouldn't want to live; I'd rather be dead.' But these people aren't dead. Slowly, if they begin to believe that they can do things and affect things, they begin to think that it is worth hanging around."

Both Mary Joan and Judi know very well that the success of Helping Hands depends upon how effective simian aides are in performing tasks that help quadriplegics lead better and more pro-ductive lives. But they also believe passionately that having a capuchin helper adds an interest and spice to quadriplegics' lives

533

12 AUTHOR'S CRAFT

What does the use of dialogue contribute to this nonfiction selection? *(Accept reasonable responses: Dialogue creates authenticity and believability; it characterizes Judi as being dedicated, caring, and compassionate.)*
CRITICAL: MAKING JUDGMENTS

534

13 EXPOSITORY TEXT: CAUSE-EFFECT

What effect does having a monkey create for a quadriplegic in public? *(The monkey attracts people and encourages them to talk to the quadriplegic.)* **How do you think quadriplegics with monkeys feel about the way people approach them?** *(Accept reasonable responses: They are probably pleased to be approached and asked about something they can do—control the monkey—rather than be noticed only for what they cannot do.)*

INFERENTIAL: DRAWING CONCLUSIONS

Judi Zazula rewards a capuchin trainee.

that can make a huge psychological difference. The companionship is important, but beyond that their ability to control the monkey makes them special. They can do something few other people can do.

As part of her master's degree work, Judi made a study of how people react to a quadriplegic with and without a monkey helper. When one quadriplegic she was using in her study was at a shopping center without his monkey, only two strangers stopped to talk with him in the course of an hour. When the monkey was sitting beside him on the wheelchair, seventy-one people took time from their shopping to speak to the quadriplegic during the same amount **13** of time.

"The quadriplegic who can control a monkey is an expert in a very unusual way," Judi said, "and that makes him interesting to other people."

One quadriplegic had this to say: "When I go outdoors in my wheelchair, all that people see is the wheelchair. But when I go out with my monkey, the only thing they see is the monkey. Nobody notices the chair at all."

Mary Joan Willard has a sense of history and a vision of the future. In terms of need and demand, Helping Hands may seem slow in getting trained monkeys to the thousands of quadriplegics who want them. But she points out that the possibility of training dogs to guide the blind had been debated and advocated for a century before the Seeing Eye program began early in this century.

534

Cooperative Reading

MONITOR COMPREHENSION: PAGES 522–535

When partners have finished reading, have them discuss the selection by asking each other questions from their K-W-L charts.

Guided Reading

MONITOR COMPREHENSION: PAGES 528–535

What happened to Helping Hands after it began placing monkeys? (It was swamped with requests for more monkeys. Mary Joan spends more time on fund-raising.) STRATEGIC READING: RETURNING TO PURPOSE

What training stages does a monkey go through? (A family raises a monkey for three years; then it is trained for eight months at Helping Hands; after being matched to the right person, it gets final training.) STRATEGIC READING: SUMMARIZING

"Compared to that, we are doing all right," Mary Joan said to me.

Mary Joan's immediate goal for Helping Hands is to place forty simian aides a year and to move beyond that as fast as the job can be done properly. Costs for training, equipment, and placement are approximately nine thousand dollars for each Helping Hands monkey. If a recipient is able to meet these costs from insurance payments or other personal resources, he or she is expected to do so; however, no one selected to receive a monkey is refused for inability to pay. For most quadriplegics, costs are met from U.S. Veterans Administration and state rehabilitation program funds or from private research or charitable organizations.

Of one thing Mary Joan Willard is sure. "I see this as a life's work," she told me.

Judi Zazula feels the same way. "I can't imagine getting the satisfaction out of anything else that I get from this work," she said.

Judi was recently married to Doug Ely, her long-time partner in equipment development. Instead of a flower girl, Judi decided to have a flower primate. Hellion, the first monkey to become a simian aide in the Helping Hands program, carried a little bouquet of flowers.

THINK IT OVER

1. What are some of the arguments against using capuchins to help quadriplegics? Do you think any of these arguments are valid? Explain your answer.
2. How long do young capuchins stay with foster families before they start training at Helping Hands?
3. What is the usual reward given a capuchin when it carries out a command?
4. Why are capuchins more useful as "helping hands" than chimpanzees would be?

WRITE

Imagine that you are a foster parent for a capuchin. Write a letter telling about the personality of the monkey to the quadriplegic who will have it as a helper.

---

14 THINK IT OVER
1. *Using a monkey is demeaning to the quadriplegic; mechanical aids can do the job better. Accept reasonable responses: The success of Helping Hands seems to invalidate these criticisms.*
CRITICAL: MAKING JUDGMENTS
2. *about three years*
LITERAL: NOTING IMPORTANT DETAILS
3. *strawberry syrup*
LITERAL: NOTING IMPORTANT DETAILS
4. *Chimpanzees are large, often unreliable, and hard to manage. Capuchins are small, intelligent, easily trained, loyal to humans, and have long lives.*
INFERENTIAL: COMPARING AND CONTRASTING

---

15 WRITE
You may want to help students get started with a prewriting graphic such as the following:

Our Monkey	
Its Strengths	*Its Weaknesses*

Accept reasonable responses: Each monkey is an individual, but strengths will probably be intelligence, affection, loyalty, and perhaps obedience; weaknesses may be mischievousness or wanting to play in the middle of the night.
CREATIVE: WRITING A DESCRIPTIVE LETTER

NOTE Additional writing activities appear on page 535D.

Returning to the Purpose for Reading   Have students discuss the questions they wrote on their K-W-L charts and that they may have written in their personal journals. Encourage students to talk about the way those questions changed as they read.

Part 2
Responding to Literature

Summarizing the Literature

Have students retell the selection and write a summary.

Invite students to summarize "Helping Hands" using the K-W-L chart. If they have not yet completed the chart, have them do so now. (See *Practice Book* page 144, on 535B.) Students may use their completed charts to retell the selection and write a brief summary statement.

K-W-L CHART

What I Know	What I Want to Know	What I Learned
People who are paralyzed can't move and can't do things for themselves.	How do people who are paralyzed manage everyday chores?	Even with special equipment, quadriplegics must depend on others.
Monkeys are agile, intelligent, and fun to watch.	Why are monkeys suitable for helping people who are paralyzed?	Capuchin monkeys are small, smart, easy to train, loyal to humans, have dexterity, and have long lives.

Appreciating Literature

Have students share personal responses.

Divide the class into small groups to discuss the selection. Provide a general question to help the groups get started:

- **What do you think was the most important idea that you got out of this selection? Why is it important to you?**

PERSONAL JOURNAL Encourage students to use their personal journals to write about ideas and feelings that are expressed in the groups. You may also wish to refer students to their personal journals after they complete the Critical Thinking Activities.

STRATEGY CONFERENCE

Discuss the K-W-L chart, asking students whether it helped them understand and appreciate the selection. Invite students to share other reading strategies, such as using prior knowledge, that helped them enjoy the selection.

INFORMAL ASSESSMENT

Having students summarize in this way will help you informally assess how well they comprehended the **main ideas** of the selection. It will also help you see how well they recognized the importance of particular **details** in contributing to these main ideas.

Encourage both cooperative and individual responses.

DISCUSS NAMES Why is Helping Hands a good name for this organization? Give as many reasons as you can think of to explain why the name is suitable, or else suggest a better name. Allow pairs of students to discuss this question and to share their ideas with classmates. CRITICAL: MAKING JUDGMENTS

DESIGN AN APARTMENT What kinds of household devices make everyday chores easier for a person who uses a wheelchair? Invite students to design an apartment that meets the needs of a differently abled, or disabled, person. Display students' drawings. CREATIVE: SOLVING PROBLEMS

WRITE AN ESSAY The title of Brent Ashabranner's book is *People Who Make a Difference*. What kinds of people make a difference? Have students write a short essay responding to this question. Remind them to support their arguments with reasons and examples. CRITICAL: EXPRESSING PERSONAL OPINIONS

Writer's Journal

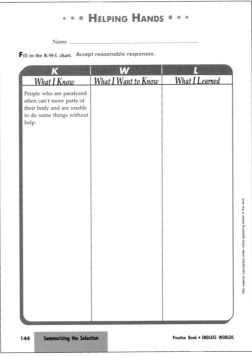

Practice Book

WRITER'S JOURNAL
pages 96–97: Writing a creative response

PRACTICE BOOK
page 144: Summarizing the selection

VO·CAB·U·LAR·Y
Workshop

Reviewing Key Words

To review how the new vocabulary was used in this selection, display the predict-o-gram students completed earlier. Discuss whether students' predictions were correct and why. Also discuss any words that students feel do not fit in the predict-o-gram.

PREDICT-O-GRAM

Therapy	About Monkeys	Animal Training	Spokesperson for Charity
rehabilitative dexterity	simian primate	motivation socialization	advocated philanthropic

Extending Vocabulary

SIGNALS, SIGNS, AND NONVERBAL COMMUNICATION   Ask students to recall what a white circular sticker means to a Helping Hands monkey. (off limits) Then ask them what other signs or signals mean "no" or "stop." (stop sign, red traffic light, upraised palm, head shake, diagonal line through a circle) Point out that signs, signals, and gestures are a kind of international language that communicates ideas even when people cannot talk directly to one another.

COOPERATIVE LEARNING   Suggest that students brainstorm lists of nonverbal signals and signs that they recognize and use, such as road and highway signs, gestures, and sounds such as sirens. Then have them form groups to create an illustrated dictionary of signs, signals, and nonverbal communication.

Integrated Language Arts

Writing About the Literature

AVAILABLE ON PROJECT CARD

CREATIVE: MYSTERY STORY Ask students to work in small groups to invent a mystery that involves a quadriplegic detective with an animal helper. Encourage them to build a mood of mystery and suspense. They might find an outline helpful to organize their ideas.
LISTENING/SPEAKING/WRITING

Setting:
Characters:
Plot: *Introduction of the mystery or puzzle* *Complications* *Resolution*

CRITICAL: PERSUASIVE LETTER Ask students to write a letter presenting themselves as candidates for raising a baby monkey for three years. Remind them to give reasons why they consider themselves qualified. WRITING

NOTE: An additional writing activity appears on page 535.

SPEAKING/LISTENING

Exclusive!

Suggest that students work in pairs to role-play a dialogue between an interviewer and the owner of a Helping Hands monkey. Encourage volunteers to present their interview. LISTENING/SPEAKING/READING/WRITING

SPELLING

Spelling Review

SPELLING WORDS: *acknowledgment, argument, demeaning, dexterity, encouragement, inability, personality, placement, publicity, purity*

Have students write the Spelling Words as you dictate them. Then have a volunteer write them on the board. Have students read each word aloud in unison, listening for the noun suffix *-ity* or *-ment* in nine of the words. Have another volunteer circle the *-ity* and *-ment* suffixes. Then ask students to divide the word *demeaning* into a base word and an ending. *(demean + -ing)* LISTENING/READING/WRITING/SPELLING

INTEGRATED SPELLING

page 72: Writing words with noun suffixes: *-ity, -ment*

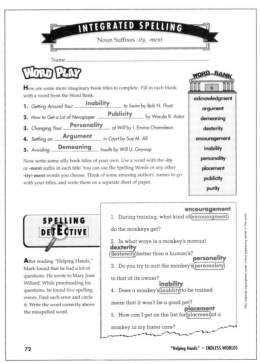

Integrated Spelling

COMPREHENSION
INTRODUCE

Summarizing

OBJECTIVE: *To summarize all or part of a literature selection*

1	Focus

Explain the value of summarizing.

Tell students that summarizing is a tool that they can use to check their comprehension. For example, if they can summarize "Helping Hands," it means that they understand the main points the author presents.

2	Teach/Model

Teach the skill.

Explain to students that a summary gives the essential ideas of a longer passage or selection. A good summary includes major ideas or details and omits unimportant ones. It is shorter than the original and is given in the summarizer's own words. Often, a summary can be a single sentence.

Model the thinking.

Have students turn to page 526 and read the first six complete paragraphs. Model how you would summarize the information:

> To summarize this passage, I focus on the most important ideas in each paragraph and try to state them in my own words. First, Mary Joan took her idea to B. F. Skinner. He suggested capuchin monkeys instead of chimpanzees. Mary Joan did some research on capuchins and then asked for money to start a program. The director laughed at first but finally provided money and a training space. I can reduce this summary to one sentence: *On B. F. Skinner's advice, Mary Joan decided to use capuchin monkeys and began an experimental training program with them.*

3   Practice/Apply

Have students write summaries.

Have students read one or more of the following passages from the selection and discuss the main ideas: page 523, paragraphs 1–4; page 527, paragraphs 5 and 6; and page 532, last paragraph, through page 533, fourth complete paragraph.

COOPERATIVE LEARNING   Invite students to work in groups to write summaries for the passages they just read. Encourage them to describe their thinking process as they summarize. You may wish to have students reduce longer summaries to a single sentence.

4   Summarize

Informally assess the learning.

Have students summarize what they learned. (A summary is a statement of the most important information in a passage.)

READER ↔ WRITER CONNECTION

Summarizing

▶ **Writers** can summarize their ideas before they begin writing to make sure their work is organized.

▶ **Readers** can summarize what they read to remember main ideas.

WRITE A SUMMARY   Have students imagine they are writing a book review of "Helping Hands." Have them summarize the main ideas in six to eight lines.

RETEACH Follow the visual, auditory, and kinesthetic/motor models on page R52.

CHALLENGE Encourage students to use the *Readers' Guide to Periodical Literature* or the card catalog to find more information on ways to help people with disabilities. Have them summarize their findings.

SECOND-LANGUAGE SUPPORT Have students identify main ideas in their first language. Then have them translate and discuss the main ideas with a peer tutor. (See *Second-Language Support Manual*.)

WRITER'S JOURNAL
page 98: Summarizing for a book review

PRACTICE BOOK
page 145: Summarizing

Writer's Journal

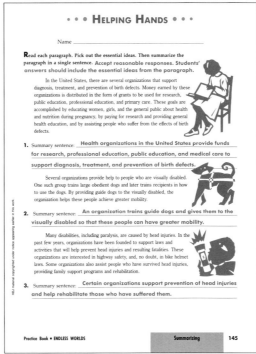

Practice Book

Directions

OBJECTIVE: *To follow directions*

Review

Review following directions.

Remind students of the steps to take in following directions. Model how to follow directions:

First, I read or listen to all the directions carefully and make sure I understand what I have to do. When I am sure, I follow the directions step by step. I do exactly what the directions say to do.

Practice/Apply

Have students follow directions.

COOPERATIVE LEARNING   Have pairs of students take turns giving and carrying out simple directions for such tasks as taking notes or using reference sources.

Summarize

Informally assess the learning.

Have students summarize what they reviewed. (Following directions accurately and in the right order ensures that a job will be done right.)

CHALLENGE   Have individual students use what they have learned to write directions for something they know how to make or do, such as how to cover a book or make cookies. Suggest that they swap directions and try to follow each other's directions.

PRACTICE BOOK
page 146: Following directions

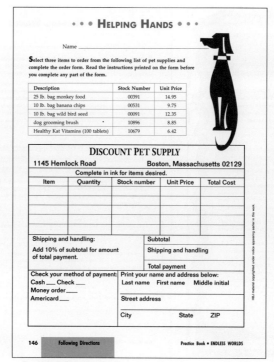

• • • HELPING HANDS • • •

Name _____

Select three items to order from the following list of pet supplies and complete the order form. Read the instructions printed on the form before you complete any part of the form.

Description	Stock Number	Unit Price
25 lb. bag monkey food	00391	14.95
10 lb. bag banana chips	00531	9.75
10 lb. bag wild bird seed	00091	12.35
dog grooming brush	10896	8.85
Healthy Kat Vitamins (100 tablets)	10679	6.42

DISCOUNT PET SUPPLY
1145 Hemlock Road   Boston, Massachusetts 02129

Complete in ink for items desired.

Item	Quantity	Stock number	Unit Price	Total Cost

Shipping and handling:	Subtotal
Add 10% of subtotal for amount of total payment.	Shipping and handling
	Total payment

Check your method of payment: Print your name and address below:
Cash ___ Check ___   Last name   First name   Middle initial
Money order ___
Americard ___   Street address

                                  City   State   ZIP

146   Following Directions   Practice Book ■ ENDLESS WORLDS

Practice Book

Graphic Aids

OBJECTIVE: *To use graphic aids to gain information*

Review

Review types of graphic aids.

Remind students that graphic aids present information visually. Have them name types of graphic aids, and list them on the board. (maps, diagrams, graphs, charts, schedules, time lines) Model the use of a graphic aid:

When I look at a map, I first read its title to find out what information it shows. I read the map key to learn about the symbols it uses. Then I can use the map to find exactly what I am looking for.

Practice/Apply

Have students use a graphic aid.

Have students use a classroom graphic aid, such as a map, to locate specific information that you name.

Summarize

Informally assess the learning.

Ask students to summarize what they learned about graphic aids. (Graphic aids, such as maps, graphs, charts, or diagrams, present information visually.)

CHALLENGE Invite students to find examples of different kinds of graphic aids in current newspapers or magazines. Have them write a paragraph explaining the information each graphic aid displays. Post examples of different graphic aids and students' explanations on the bulletin board.

PRACTICE BOOK
page 147: Using graphic aids

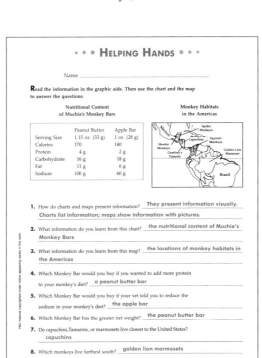

Practice Book

Integrated Curriculum

SCIENCE

Monkey Business

AVAILABLE ON PROJECT CARD

Point out that monkeys, chimpanzees, and other primates have long been the subject of observation in the wild. Invite interested students to find out about one scientific study of primates, such as the study of chimpanzees initiated by Jane Goodall, and write a report about it. Volunteers may share their findings with classmates by reading their reports aloud. LISTENING/SPEAKING/READING/WRITING

SOCIAL STUDIES

Ought There to Be a Law?

Suggest that students form groups to research the development of the federal law requiring that buildings be accessible to people who have disabilities. As part of their research, encourage them to write to their senators and representatives requesting information. Suggest that they prepare a chart showing the steps the bill went through before becoming law. As an extension students could debate the question of whether the federal government should or should not interfere with a building owner's decisions about how to design a building. LISTENING/SPEAKING/READING/WRITING

HEALTH

Safety First

Point out that many accidents that cause spinal cord injuries are avoidable. Suggest that students do research to find out the main causes of spinal cord injuries. Then have them work in groups to prepare a safety manual giving simple precautions for avoiding such accidents.

LISTENING/SPEAKING/READING/WRITING

SCIENCE

The Rehab Team

Invite students to form groups to find out more about rehabilitative medicine. Suggest that they contact a veterans' group or a nearby hospital for the names of institutes that specialize in rehabilitation. Tell students to contact those places for more detailed information. Encourage them to learn what medical specialties are involved in rehabilitating patients with spinal injuries and what each specialist does. Students may be interested in setting up a "rehab fair" in which individuals or pairs present information about a particular specialty.

LISTENING/SPEAKING/READING/WRITING

Lending a Hand

READ ALOUD TO STUDENTS:

MANY AMERICANS HAVE USED THEIR EXPERTISE TO AID THOSE WITH PHYSICAL DISABILITIES.

Newton Wesley, a Japanese American optometrist, theorized that gentle, constant pressure from a contact lens might prevent the blindness caused by keratoconus, a corneal disease. Working with a European American partner, Dr. George Jessen, Wesley invented a small plastic contact lens that did prevent keratoconus blindness. Ultimately, Wesley and Jessen's techniques also led to the manufacture of the first contact lenses for the general public.

In 1926 Alice Fong Eu became the first Chinese American teacher in the San Francisco public schools. Eu specialized in teaching children with cerebral palsy. Realizing that many people with cerebral palsy are hindered in school by speech difficulties, Eu worked to institute a district-wide speech therapy program. She directed the program until her retirement. ▪

Alice Fong Eu taught school children with cerebral palsy.

The work of Drs. Newton Wesley and George Jessen led to the manufacture of today's contact lenses.

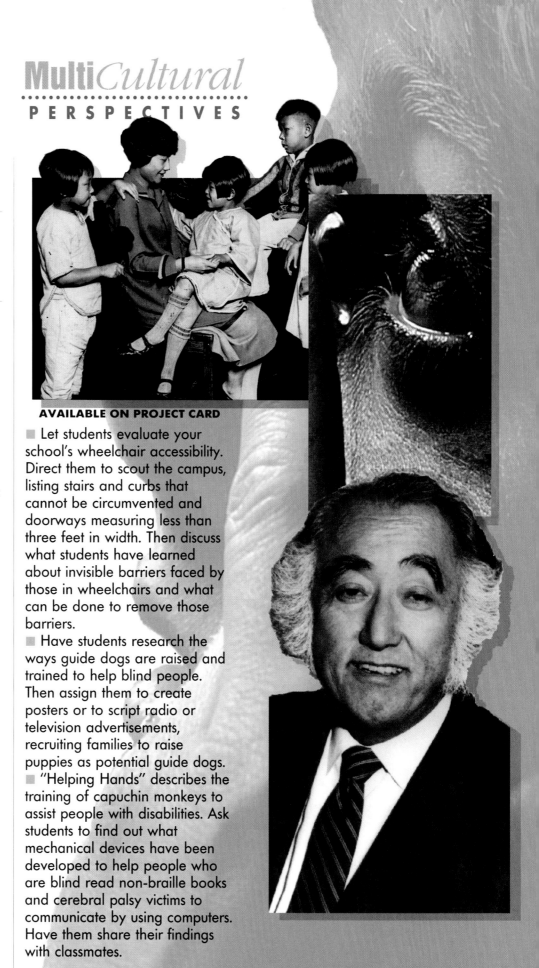

AVAILABLE ON PROJECT CARD

▪ Let students evaluate your school's wheelchair accessibility. Direct them to scout the campus, listing stairs and curbs that cannot be circumvented and doorways measuring less than three feet in width. Then discuss what students have learned about invisible barriers faced by those in wheelchairs and what can be done to remove those barriers.

▪ Have students research the ways guide dogs are raised and trained to help blind people. Then assign them to create posters or to script radio or television advertisements, recruiting families to raise puppies as potential guide dogs.

▪ "Helping Hands" describes the training of capuchin monkeys to assist people with disabilities. Ask students to find out what mechanical devices have been developed to help people who are blind read non-braille books and cerebral palsy victims to communicate by using computers. Have them share their findings with classmates.

Words from the Author: Brent Ashabranner

Words from Brent Ashab

ABOUT THE AUTHOR FEATURE

Brent Ashabranner discusses his career, his views on writing nonfiction, and the selection "Helping Hands" from his book *People Who Make a Difference.* He explains his purposes for writing and discusses the importance of his audience.

---

1 AUTHOR'S COMMENTARY

According to Ashabranner, one purpose of writing nonfiction is "to correct distorted ideas." In your opinion, why is that so important? *(Accept reasonable responses: If you want to have a true understanding of an individual, a group, an event, or an idea, it is crucial that you have all the facts to examine.)*
CRITICAL: MAKING JUDGMENTS

---

2 AUTHOR'S COMMENTARY

In your opinion, what qualities make Ashabranner a good writer? Explain. *(Accept reasonable responses: Even when writing nonfiction, he tries to find the "story" in his material; stories encourage readers' involvement.)*
CRITICAL: EXPRESSING PERSONAL OPINIONS

Everything I write flows out of my life interests. Many of my books deal with the interaction of different cultures. That interest came from my years of living in Ethiopia, Libya, and India when I was in the Peace Corps. One of the reasons I've written so frequently about the immigrant experience is that, to a small extent, I have been an immigrant myself, trying to adjust to a different culture, a different world. Also, I've seen those people—the ones who become immigrants here—in their native lands, and so I have a special interest in watching how they make the adjustment to a new culture.

1 One of the purposes of writing nonfiction is to correct distorted ideas by letting a person examine an issue or an idea more fully. By the same token, nonfiction also gives the reader new ideas. Imagine that you see something on television that interests you. A news clip is only a minute or two long, so if you want to learn more about that topic, you go to a book on the subject. You can really pursue your interests with nonfiction.

536

I think a great deal about my readers when I write. Based on my own experience, I've been firmly convinced for a long time that the most important reading we do is when we're young. The experiences that I had overseas, what I was learning about other cultures and how they relate to each other, seemed important to share with my young readers.

2 I understand from many teachers and librarians that there is a special interest in nonfiction these days. That gratifies me, even though I started my career as a fiction writer. For many years I just wrote short stories, and I've written two fiction books for young people. It's funny, though, I still think of myself as a storyteller. I've never lost the tools I learned writing fiction. I always look for the "story," and until I find it, I can't write a word. I see everything as a story or a series of stories.

In an odd way, the idea for my book *People Who Make a Difference* came out of my other books. My photographer, Paul Conklin, and I are constantly

---

Reading the Author Feature

Invite students to share what they know about Brent Ashabranner. Discuss where they have heard his name and in what connection. Then ask students to predict, based on their reading of Ashabranner's "Helping Hands," what the author might be like, what inspired him to write this book, and what he likes to write about.

Teaching Tip Explain to students that the Peace Corps, established by the United States government in 1961, is an independent program in which volunteers serve overseas at the request of the host country. The volunteers are trained to live with the residents and to work with them on improving food production, health care, housing, education, and so on.

the Author: ranner

3 NARRATION: EVENTS
Why do you think Mary Joan Willard was happy to be a part of Ashabranner's book _People Who Make a Difference_? *(Accept reasonable responses: The book would be one way to create interest, understanding, and acceptance of her idea of using monkeys to aid the disabled.)*
INFERENTIAL: SPECULATING

traveling around, gathering information. In our journeys, we've heard of or met people who in one way or another have made a difference. We decided someday we would do a book about these people.

Mary Joan Willard, the woman in "Helping Hands," came to my attention while I was in Boston working on another book. I was reading the newspaper and saw a small feature about her work. I called her, and she was happy to become a part of the book. It was an affecting experience to interview her. I've always been fascinated by quantum leaps of the human imagination, and her idea of using monkeys to aid the disabled certainly is one. She told me that it took one hundred years for the idea of guide dogs for the blind to gain any credence, but I hope monkeys for the disabled will take off faster than that.

537

Responding to the Author Feature

Have students discuss Brent Ashabranner's belief that "the most important reading we do is when we're young." Ask them why this might be so. Encourage them to draw from their own experiences by naming memorable books they've read and explaining why these books are memorable or what they learned.

I May, I Might, I Must/I Watched an Eagle Soar

ABOUT THE POETS

Marianne Moore (1887–1972) wrote witty poems in a precise, compact form. In 1952 she won the Pulitzer Prize for poetry.

A South Dakota Sioux, Virginia Driving Hawk Sneve (1933–) uses her writing to "present an accurate portrayal of American Indian life as I have known it."

1 CHARACTERIZATION

What is the speaker's attitude toward the impossible? *He or she believes that all things are possible if you try hard enough and believe in yourself.)*
INFERENTIAL: DRAWING CONCLUSIONS

2 THEME

What is the message of this poem? *(Accept reasonable responses: An inspiring event stays with you.)*
INFERENTIAL: DETERMINING MAIN IDEA

WRITER'S JOURNAL page 99: Writing a creative response

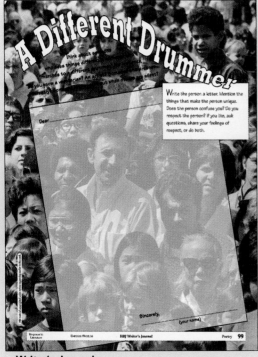

Writer's Journal

I May, I Might, I Must

by Marianne Moore

AWARD-WINNING AUTHOR

1 | If you will tell my why the fen
appears impassable, I then
will tell you why I think that I
can get across it if I try.

I Watched an Eagle Soar

by Virginia Driving Hawk Sneve

2 | Grandmother, I watched an eagle soar
high in the sky
until a cloud covered him up.
Grandmother,
I still saw the eagle
behind my eyes.

Plains tribes eagle dancer

538

Reading the Poems

Invite students to take turns reading each poem aloud, expressing the somewhat defiant tone of the first poem and the feeling of amazement in the second poem. Then ask students whether or not they feel oral reading makes the poems easier to understand.

Responding to the Poems

Ask students to discuss whether or not they agree with the messages of the poems.

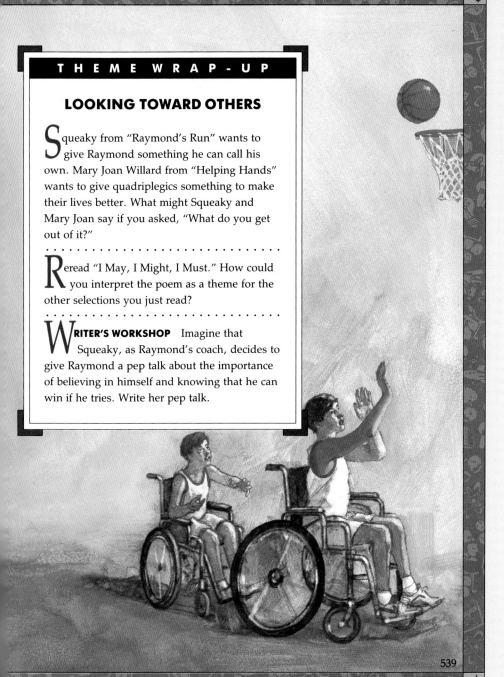

LOOKING TOWARD OTHERS

Squeaky from "Raymond's Run" wants to give Raymond something he can call his own. Mary Joan Willard from "Helping Hands" wants to give quadriplegics something to make their lives better. What might Squeaky and Mary Joan say if you asked, "What do you get out of it?"

· ·

Reread "I May, I Might, I Must." How could you interpret the poem as a theme for the other selections you just read?

· ·

WRITER'S WORKSHOP Imagine that Squeaky, as Raymond's coach, decides to give Raymond a pep talk about the importance of believing in himself and knowing that he can win if he tries. Write her pep talk.

539

Looking Toward Others

Guide students in recalling how the people they have read about in this theme shared a desire to help others. Remind them of Squeaky's love for her brother Raymond and of Mary Joan Willard's persistence in training monkeys. Explain that the activities on page 539 will help them think further about giving to others.

Note that pages 539A–539B provide support for applying the writing process to the last question.

---

1 Suggest that students answer the question separately for each character. *(Accept reasonable responses: Squeaky might say that she finds the idea of coaching Raymond exciting. Mary Joan Willard might say that helping quadriplegics gives her a fulfilling career.)*
INFERENTIAL: SPECULATING

---

2 Ask students to first decide on the poem's message and then see how that message applies to Squeaky and Mary Joan Willard. *(Accept reasonable responses: Both Squeaky and Mary Joan Willard are taking on a task that some might consider impossible.)*
INFERENTIAL: SYNTHESIZING

Writer's Workshop
See pages 539A–539B for suggestions for applying the writing process. Responses should draw on the information about the characters in "Raymond's Run." You may prefer to allow students to respond to the theme in their own way. WRITING PROCESS: A PERSUASIVE ESSAY

Writer's Workshop

Remind students that in persuasion they are trying to convince others to agree with them. In their pep talks, they will use a classic approach, which is to state a proposition and then give the audience reasons to support it. Have students recall when they received a pep talk from a parent, teacher, or coach. Ask them if that person's approach worked. Tell that they will first think of a proposition. Then they will think of valid reasons to get someone to support it. Suggest that students refer to the Handbook in the *Writer's Journal* as they write, revise, and proofread their persuasive paragraphs.

Prewriting

Before they write, have students
- think about their audience and purpose.
- imagine the reasons Squeaky might give Raymond for trying out her plan.
- use a chart to organize material for Squeaky's pep talk. Encourage students to include in the chart Squeaky's reasons and her "back-up" explanations. The chart might look something like this:

> **Position Statement:** You have got to learn to run.
> **1. Reason:** You need to be good at something.
> **Explanation:** The kids will respect you.
> **2. Reason:** You know you can do it if you try.
> **Explanation:** You keep up with me, and I'm the fastest thing on Broadway.
> **3. Reason:** You've got assets.
> **Explanation:** You can breathe in counts. I've seen you do it at the dinner table.
> **Conclusion:** Let's get to work.

Drafting

Have students write a draft of their persuasive essays. Remind them to
- state Squeaky's opinion clearly.
- give her reasons in order of importance.
- use language that reflects Squeaky's manner of speaking.
- write their first drafts without worrying about spelling, punctuation, or grammar.

COMPUTER CONNECTION Students may want to use a computer during the drafting and revising stages so that they may easily rearrange the order of their persuasive arguments.

Responding and Revising

Ask each student to read his or her essay aloud to a partner, and have each pair discuss how effectively the draft fulfills its goals. Suggest these tips for evaluation and revision:

- Are the reasons strong enough to overcome Raymond's reluctance? If not, brainstorm stronger ones.
- Does the pep talk end with a call to action? If not, provide a stirring one.
- Have you used words and phrases that would have a strong impact on Raymond rather than those that are overused and trite? Try to avoid clichés. (See the Language/Literature Link below.)

STUDENT SELF-ASSESSMENT OPTION   Students may use the Writing Self-Assessment Checklist in the *Portfolio Teacher's Guide*. Suggest that as they use the checklist, they focus on the position statement and supporting reasons and also on including original ideas and avoiding clichés.

Proofreading

Offer these tips to help students proofread and correct their work:

- Look for errors in capitalization and punctuation, especially in street names.
- Correct any misspelled words, but keep the dialect spellings that reflect Squeaky's speech.

Publishing

Invite students to discuss the best audience for their pep talks. Some students may wish to read aloud their pep talks to a classmate who is playing the role of Raymond and then save them in their reading/writing portfolio. Others may want to submit their essays to the advice column of a school newspaper.

LANGUAGE/LITERATURE LINK

Avoiding Clichés

Remind students that persuasive writing is geared to a specific audience. Point out that Toni Cade Bambara's Squeaky punctures clichés like balloons. Tell students to try to think like Squeaky and present their arguments in an original and convincing way.

Speaking Option

PEP TALK   You may wish to adapt the *Writer's Workshop* to allow students to give oral pep talks. Have students follow the guidelines offered for Prewriting, Drafting, and Responding and Revising. Make these suggestions to help students deliver their pep talk effectively:

- Rehearse your pep talk beforehand, so your talk sounds spontaneous.
- Imagine Raymond standing in front of you and talk *to* him.
- Sound strong and sure of yourself. Use nonverbal skills to enhance your words.

Have each student deliver his or her pep talk to a small group of classmates.

Innovations

Make sure that students understand what the word *innovations* means. Ask them to name a synonym, such as *novelties* or *inventions.* Then have the students tell how the invention in the illustration probably works. Have them read the introductory paragraph on Student Anthology page 541. Encourage a discussion of inventors and inventions. Invite students to suggest the traits that might lead someone to become a successful inventor.

PACING   This theme has been designed to take about two weeks to complete, depending on your students' needs.

Management Options

THE LITERATURE-BASED CLASSROOM   Providing a literature-rich curriculum creates unique classroom management challenges. Some management options for the selections in this theme follow.

WRITER'S WORKSHOP PUBLISHING ALTERNATIVE
Invite interested students to produce a program called "Inventors and Inventions" in which the host interviews inventors. After students select an everyday item and research the inventor, have them develop a script with questions and answers. Allow the group members sufficient time to practice their roles before presenting the program to classmates.

THEME

INNOVATIONS

Have you ever picked up a simple gadget and wondered how it came to be? Keep your inventive mind alert as you read about a variety of inventions and their creators.

CONTENTS
. . . .

STUDENTS AT RISK
To help motivate students before they begin reading "Be an Inventor," invite them to think about something they would like to invent. Have them explain how their invention would benefit the user.

GIFTED AND TALENTED
Challenge students to do some research to find out what the inventors of Braille (Louis Braille, 15 years old), synthetic dye (William Perkin, 18 years old), and earmuffs (Chester Greenwood, 15 years old) had in common. (They were quite young when they developed their inventions.) Also see the *Challenge Cards.*

SPECIAL EDUCATION STUDENTS
Suggest that students who use special equipment such as a hearing aid or a brailler find out more about the inventors who developed them. Invite students to share their knowledge with classmates and to demonstrate their use.

LIMITED ENGLISH PROFICIENT STUDENTS
Pair students with English-fluent students to complete the Practice/ Apply portion of the Learning Through Literature lesson on following directions. Students may want to write the directions in their first language and work with a partner to write them in English.

FORMS AND APPLICATIONS To reinforce the Learning Through Literature lesson on forms and applications, provide students with actual samples to examine, such as catalog order forms, school registration forms, standardized test answer sheets, applications for employment or insurance, and medical forms. Students can practice filling them out.

READING/WRITING PORTFOLIO Instruct students to keep in their portfolios their writing responses to the theme selections. Remind them also to add to their personal journals notes on their independent reading.

BE AN INVENTOR

by Barbara Taylor

BARBARA TAYLOR has written several books for young people and has worked as an editor at *Weekly Reader* for more than twenty years. Taylor has also taught in elementary schools in France, Germany, Japan, and the United States.

MORE BOOKS BY BARBARA TAYLOR
Bouncing and Bending Light. Franklin Watts, 1990.
   AVERAGE
Color and Light. Franklin Watts, 1990. AVERAGE

OTHER BOOKS ABOUT INVENTIONS
Before the Wright Brothers by Don Berliner. Lerner,
   1990. AVERAGE
Experimenting with Inventions by Robert Gardner.
   Franklin Watts, 1990. CHALLENGING
Famous Experiments You Can Do by Robert Gardner.
   Franklin Watts, 1990. CHALLENGING
Guess Again: More Weird and Wacky Inventions by Jim
   Murphy. Bradbury, 1986. AVERAGE

SELECTION SUMMARY

In this nonfiction selection, the author recounts the true stories of some famous inventions and their inventors. The stories of how Velcro, the safety line for space walks, and the computer chip came into being show that inventors are curious, imaginative problem solvers. The author then discusses how inventors get ideas. She describes the invention of the Frisbee, chewing gum, and the safety hood that led to gas masks. Finally, she advises readers how to get started on one of their own inventions.

LESSON PLANNER			
	Materials	**Integrated Curriculum**	**Meeting Individual Needs**
1 READING LITERATURE pp. 541B–557	Student Anthology pp. 542–557 Transparency 29 Second-Language Support Manual Practice Book p. 148 Integrated Spelling p. 73 Integrated Spelling T. E. pp. 96–97	Spelling Spelling Pretest Spelling-Vocabulary Connection (career words)	Second-Language Support Vocabulary 541C Strategic Reading 541D, 544, 556
2 RESPONDING TO LITERATURE pp. 557A–557D	Writer's Journal p. 100 Practice Book p. 149 Integrated Spelling p. 74 Integrated Spelling T. E. pp. 96–97	Vocabulary Workshop Reviewing Key Words Extending Vocabulary Writing About the Literature Speaking/Listening Spelling Review	Cooperative Learning 557B
3 LEARNING THROUGH LITERATURE pp. 557E–557J	Transparency 30 Second-Language Support Manual Practice Book pp. 150–152	Science/Math Science Social Studies Social Studies/Art Multicultural	Challenge 557F, 557G, 557H Second-Language Support 557F Cooperative Learning 557G

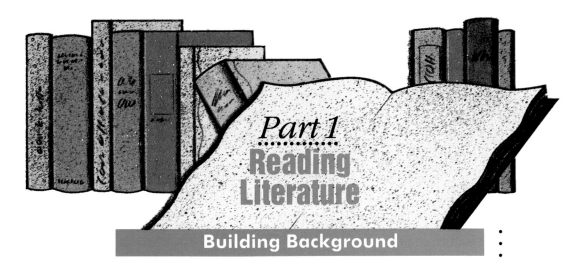

Part 1
Reading Literature

Building Background

Access prior knowledge and develop vocabulary concepts.

Write the word *inventor* on the board. Ask students to share thoughts that come to mind when they see this word. Encourage them to brainstorm qualities of inventors, as well as names of famous inventors and inventions.

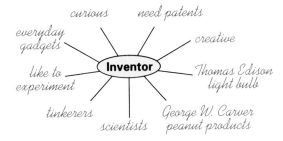

Have students quickwrite a description.

Ask students to write a brief description of their mental picture of an inventor and an invention. Suggest that students compare their ideas with the author's after they have finished reading the selection.

Vocabulary Strategies

Introduce Key Words and strategies.

Tell students that "Be an Inventor" may contain unfamiliar words. Display Transparency 29, or write the paragraph on the board. Have students read silently and use context clues, phonics, and structural analysis to figure out the meanings of the underlined words. As a volunteer reads the paragraph aloud, help with pronunciation if necessary.

Transparency 29   Key Words

Sold for profit, some commercially available inventions benefit everyone! Shoebox-size generators produce electricity for a home. Pocket-size televisions are possible because miniature transistors and resistors control the flow and voltage of electricity. Electrical circuits fit on tiny chips of a tough element, silicon. Luminous plastic panels enable radiologists to read X-ray film.

KEY WORDS DEFINED

commercially   in a way that allows someone to profit

generators   machines that convert mechanical energy into electricity

transistors   tiny electronic devices that control the flow of electricity

resistors   devices used to offer resistance in an electrical circuit

silicon   element used in making transistors and chips

luminous   giving off light

radiologists   those who work with X rays

Check students' understanding. Have students demonstrate their understanding by classifying the words on the following chart. STRATEGY: CLASSIFYING

INVENTIONS

Famous Invention	People Who Use an Invention	Natural Element Used in an Invention	A Quality of an Invention	How an Invention Is Used
generators transistors resistors	radiologists	silicon	luminous	commercially

Integrate spelling with vocabulary.

SPELLING-VOCABULARY CONNECTION *Integrated Spelling* page 73 reinforces spellings of **career words,** including the Key Word *radiologists*. The spelling of the Key Word *luminous* is also included.

SECOND-LANGUAGE SUPPORT Have students work with a peer tutor and use an encyclopedia to find words related to electronics and to study the accompanying pictures. (See *Second-Language Support Manual*.)

PRACTICE BOOK
page 148: Reinforcing Key Words

INTEGRATED SPELLING
page 73: Writing and spelling career words

NOTE: These pages may be completed now or after students have read the selection.

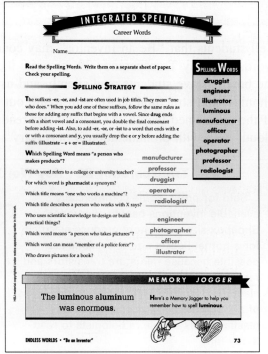

Practice Book

Integrated Spelling

Using the SQ3R Strategy

Discuss the SQ3R strategy.

Write *SQ3R* on the board. Ask a volunteer to explain how to use the SQ3R strategy. (*S—Survey* the material to determine what it is about. *Q*—Use the headings to ask *questions* and make predictions. *R—Read* to find answers. *R—Recite* answers to questions. *R—Review* by rereading the headings to see if you remember the answers to your questions.)

Have students survey the selection.

Have students survey the nonfiction article by looking at the illustrations and reading the title, the headings, and the first four paragraphs. Tell students to turn each major heading into a question they would ask themselves.

Begin the SQ3R chart.

Write the headings on the board:

SQ3R CHART

S—Survey *This article discusses four traits of inventors: curiosity, imagination, willingness to work hard, and confidence.*		
Q—Question *Why is curiosity an important trait for inventors?*	**[Predicted Answer]** *Curiosity leads inventors to notice new things.*	**R—Read**
R—Recite		**R—Review**

PERSONAL JOURNAL Have students copy the SQ3R chart headings in their personal journals, or have them use *Practice Book* page 149. (See page 557B in this Teacher's Edition.) Have them fill in the first two columns. They can check their predicted answers after they read each section or after they read the entire article. (Students will return to the chart after reading, in Summarizing the Literature.)

Setting a Purpose

Have students set purposes.

Have a volunteer state his or her purpose for reading. (to find out whether the answers predicted on the SQ3R chart are correct)

Model purpose-setting, if necessary.

If students have difficulty setting a purpose for reading, model the thinking process:

> **I have already turned the headings in this article into questions, and I have predicted the answers to those questions. Now I will read to find out whether my predictions are correct.**

OPTIONS FOR READING

Independent Reading
Have students read the selection silently with their purpose for reading in mind.

Guided Reading
Follow the Guided Reading suggestions that appear on pages 542, 544–545, 553, and 556. These suggestions model strategic reading.

Numbered Annotations
Use the numbered annotations beside the Student Anthology pages to heighten students' appreciation of the selection.

▼▼▼▼▼▼▼ BE AN ▼▼▼▼▼▼▼
INVENTOR

BY BARBARA TAYLOR

1 WHAT MAKES A PERSON INVENTIVE?

When many people hear the word *inventor*, they picture a mad scientist with fuzzy hair surrounded by bubbling test tubes and generators crackling with electricity.

But, in fact, inventors are very much like the rest of us. They may be old or young, male or female, postgraduate students or kindergartners. They may work in multimillion-dollar laboratories or in family kitchens.

2 Yet inventors do have qualities in common that set them apart from other people. They are curious about the world around them. They have active imaginations. They are willing to work at solving problems. They have the confidence to make their inventions successful, regardless of what others think or say.

Let's take a closer look at some well-known inventors of the past and present to see what role these four factors played in their work.

illustrations by Clarence Porter

542

INVENTORS ARE CURIOUS

Ever hear the saying "Necessity is the mother of invention"? If that's true, then curiosity might well be the father of invention. It is curiosity that sets the spark of creativity in the inventor's mind and starts him or her on the path to a new invention.

Think about Velcro®, the popular, lightweight, washable fastener that keeps your coat and book bag closed.

George de Mestral had just returned from a walk with his dog in the Swiss mountains near his home when he noticed his pet's fur was thick with burrs.

As de Mestral struggled to pull off the burrs, he wondered what made them cling so stubbornly to his dog. He looked at the burrs under a microscope and saw that they had tiny hooks that snagged onto the dog's fur. It suddenly occurred to de Mestral that if he could copy the hooks of the burr, he could invent the perfect fastener.

It wasn't until years later that the inventor got around to working on his fastener. After many experiments with different materials, de Mestral found a way to copy nature's hooks and loops and attach them to strips of cloth. In 1957 he patented his invention.

Today the Velcro fastener is used on everything from children's shoes to spacecraft supplies. It can withstand the heat of the tropics and the freezing cold of the Arctic. And we can thank a curious man out for a stroll for this popular product.

543

INVENTORS ARE ImAgiNaTiVE

It takes imagination to find the answer to a puzzling problem, even though that answer may be right under the inventor's nose.

In 1960, scientist Theodore Marton was looking for a way to bring an astronaut in space back safely into a spacecraft. A safety line to do the job had to be both flexible and rigid. It had to be flexible so that the astronaut could move about freely in space. But it also had to be rigid to keep the weightless person from drifting about while being drawn back into the spacecraft.

Marton couldn't figure out how to make a line both rigid and flexible. Then one day, as he was watching his son play with a toy dog, he noticed something he hadn't really noticed before. When the boy pushed a button on the toy, the dog collapsed.

Examining the toy, Marton saw that the dog was made of small segments and was kept erect by a tight string inside it. When the button was pushed, the string relaxed and the dog collapsed.

Marton used this idea in designing his safety line. The line is relaxed and flexible when an astronaut walks in space but it can be tightened, or made rigid, when the astronaut is towed back into the spacecraft. By using his imagination, Marton was able to apply the workings of a simple children's toy to create an important tool for space travel.

544

Second-Language Support

Students who are not familiar with idiomatic and figurative expressions in English may interpret what they read literally, especially in nonfiction selections. Clarify the figurative meaning of the phrase *right under the inventor's nose* in the first paragraph. (something so obvious you can't miss it)

MEETING INDIVIDUAL NEEDS

Guided Reading

MONITOR COMPREHENSION: PAGES 542–545 **Why is curiosity an important trait for an inventor?** (Curiosity sets the spark of creativity.) **What other important qualities do inventors need?** (They must be imaginative and they must enjoy solving problems.) STRATEGIC READING: RETURNING TO PURPOSE

INVENTORS ARE PROBLEM SOLVERS

While working on a new invention, an inventor may face a number of different problems. The inventor's success or failure depends on how hard he or she is willing to work at solving these problems.

Jack St. Clair Kilby, an engineer working for Texas Instruments, is one inventor whose solution to a tough problem resulted in a revolution in the field of electronics.

Kilby's problem was parts—tens of thousands of them. In the mid-1950s, he and other electrical engineers were struggling to build an electric circuit. This circuit would have to perform the big jobs needed in the new electronic age of communications and space travel.

An electric circuit for such tasks had to hold hundreds of thousands of transistors, resistors, and capacitors. All these parts had to be connected in one unbroken path along which current could flow. To wire and solder all these parts together would be a nightmare. One mistake, and the path would be broken; current would not flow. And even if such a circuit could be designed, it would be so gigantic it could never fit in a newsroom or a rocket going to the moon.

Many engineers believed such a circuit could never be built, but Jack Kilby disagreed. He took fresh approaches to solving this difficult problem. One approach was to think in miniature. Why not put an entire electric circuit together on a single chip of silicon? The silicon would conduct electric charges to all parts of the circuit at once so there would be no need to wire or solder the parts. And the parts could **5** be squeezed onto a space no larger than a fingernail.

In 1958 Kilby made his idea a reality. He built the first integrated circuit, or chip, as it came to be called. Today, the chip is the heart of every computer.

545

5 AUTHOR'S CRAFT
How does the author create suspense in the "story" of Jack Kilby's invention? *(She doesn't tell us what the invention is until the end.)*
METACOGNITIVE: DRAWING CONCLUSIONS

What role do these qualities play in the work of inventors? (Accept reasonable responses: Curiosity sparks creativity; imagination helps inventors find answers to problems; the enjoyment of problem solving gives inventors the willingness to work hard at new approaches.) STRATEGIC READING: SUMMARIZING

SET PURPOSE/PREDICT: PAGES 546–553 Point out that the next spread (pages 546–547) is a sort of "break" in the article. Have students read the spread to answer a question such as "What are some strange and unusual inventions and the purpose of each one?" (Responses will vary. Encourage students to guess at the purpose of each invention shown.)

Next, have students read through page 553 to answer another question on their SQ3R charts, for example: "How do the lives of inventors illustrate the importance of the qualities discussed earlier?"

6 TEXT STRUCTURE

Why do you think the author inserted these "mystery" Inventions here? *(Accept reasonable responses: to give the reader a short "break" from absorbing information; to make the reader curious enough to read further.)*

CRITICAL: SPECULATING

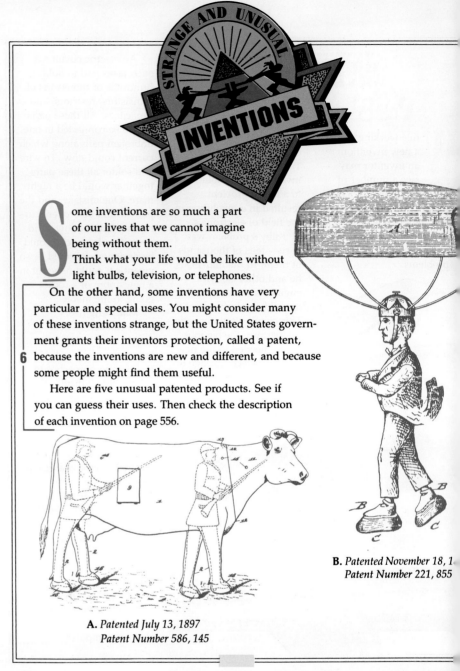

Some inventions are so much a part of our lives that we cannot imagine being without them. Think what your life would be like without light bulbs, television, or telephones.

On the other hand, some inventions have very particular and special uses. You might consider many of these inventions strange, but the United States government grants their inventors protection, called a patent, because the inventions are new and different, and because some people might find them useful.

Here are five unusual patented products. See if you can guess their uses. Then check the description of each invention on page 556.

A. *Patented July 13, 1897*
Patent Number 586, 145

B. *Patented November 18, 1*
Patent Number 221, 855

546

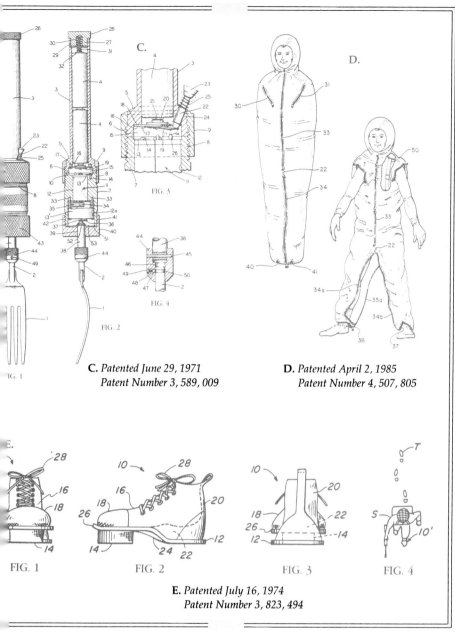

FIG. 3

FIG. 4

FIG. 2

FIG. 1

C.

D.

C. *Patented June 29, 1971*
Patent Number 3, 589, 009

D. *Patented April 2, 1985*
Patent Number 4, 507, 805

E.

FIG. 1   FIG. 2   FIG. 3   FIG. 4

E. *Patented July 16, 1974*
Patent Number 3, 823, 494

547

Informal Assessment   You can informally assess
whether your students can identify an author's
purpose for writing nonfiction. On occasion, ask
questions like these:

- Why did the author write this article? Does the
  author expect you to do anything special with this
  information? What?
- What about the article makes you think this was
  the author's purpose?
- How well does the author succeed in fulfilling this
  purpose? Is there anything else the author should
  have done?

What motivated Garrett Morgan to invent the things he did? *(He was concerned about others' safety; he saw a need for improved safety for firefighters, who rescue people from smoke-filled places.)*
INFERENTIAL: DETERMINING CAUSE-EFFECT

A BEHIND-THE-SCENES LOOK AT SOME INVENTIONS

Why does one person think of the idea for an invention before anyone else does? Let's take a behind-the-scenes look at how some inventions came to be. There may be lessons to learn from these stories.

HERO OF THE SAFETY HOOD

Some people create inventions that make life safer for others. They get their ideas by thinking of other people's welfare instead of their own needs or comforts.

Garrett Morgan was granted a patent in 1912 for the Morgan Safety Hood, a special breathing helmet that pumped air directly into a mask that fitted over a person's face. The air was stored in a bag attached to the mask. There was enough air in the bag for 15 to 20 minutes of breathing—enough time for a firefighter to enter a smoke-filled burning building and rescue people inside.

Morgan was awarded the grand prize at the Industrial Exposition of Safety in New York in 1914, but it wasn't until an unexpected disaster in 1916 that Morgan and his invention became famous.

One night a tunnel collapsed 250 feet below the surface of Lake Erie in Morgan's hometown of Cleveland, Ohio. Workers from the Cleveland Waterworks were overcome by deadly gas fumes and trapped in the tunnel. Poisonous gas drove back firefighters who tried to reach the trapped men. But someone at the scene of the disaster remembered seeing Morgan give a demonstration of his safety hood some weeks before.

Police quickly located the inventor and asked him to come to their aid. Morgan, accompanied by his brother, arrived at the scene of the disaster with safety hoods. The two entered the clouded tunnel to rescue the helpless workers inside.

Garrett Morgan, pioneer in safety

548

Cultural Awareness You may want to tell students that Garrett Morgan (1877–1963) is included in many collections of autobiographies of famous African Americans. His first job was fixing sewing machines. His first invention was a belt fastener for sewing machines, which he sold for fifty dollars in 1901. He opened his own tailoring business in 1907 and earned enough money in his first year to buy a home for his family.

Morgan and his brother succeeded in carrying all 32 trapped workmen from the tunnel. Fortunately, many were still alive and the inventor was proclaimed a hero. As news spread of the daring rescue, his safety hood became a great success. Soon it was standard equipment in fire departments across the nation.

When the United States entered World War I, Morgan adapted his safety hood into a gas mask that was worn by American soldiers fighting in Europe. The masks protected them from deadly chlorine fumes on the battlefield.

Garrett Morgan continued to invent, keeping other people's welfare in mind. He designed the first three-way traffic signal, making roadways safer for millions of motorists. Before he died in 1963 at the age of 86, Garrett Morgan had lived to see the United States a safer country, thanks to his inventions.

8

INVENTOR'S
IDEA BOX

Getting an Idea

- What products do I or my friends use that could work better? Be more appealing? Be made to do more? Be made for less?
- Is there something that would make a person's job easier?
- What particular problem would I like solved?

9

549

8 NARRATION: ACTIONS/EVENTS
How did an unexpected disaster make people appreciate Garrett Morgan and his invention? *(He was able to use his invention to rescue thirty-two workers trapped in a tunnel.)*
INFERENTIAL: DETERMINING CAUSE-EFFECT

9 TYPOGRAPHICAL CUES
Why do you think authors of nonfiction sometimes isolate information in a box like this? *(Accept reasonable responses: They think the information is important; the information doesn't exactly fit in with the rest of the article; the boxed information provides a summary of or handy reference to main ideas in the article.)*
INFERENTIAL: SPECULATING

Why did the author set off the terms *invisible wire* and *free* in quotation marks? *(The reader is supposed to understand that the author doesn't mean these things literally but that these are the terms Walter Fred Morrison used to lure people.)*

INFERENTIAL: DRAWING CONCLUSIONS

The FABULOUS FRISBEE

Some inventors take a common item already in existence and find an entirely new use for it. That's how the popular toy the Frisbee came to be.

One day in 1948, Walter Fred Morrison happened to be driving past the Frisbie Pie Company in Bridgeport, Connecticut, when he saw two truck drivers tossing empty pie pans back and forth in the parking lot.

It reminded Morrison of his childhood, when he'd thrown pie pans with his playmates. Returning home to Los Angeles, California, Morrison went to work designing a disc that could be thrown back and forth like the pie pans. The disc had to be light enough not to hurt someone who got in its flight path and still heavy enough to fly a good distance. He found the right material for his toy—a soft plastic that was bouncy but tough. He called his invention "Morrison's Flyin' Saucer" and took two cartons of his toys to a nearby county fair to sell.

Morrison thought of a gimmick to make people want to buy his flying saucers. He told the crowds at the fair that there was an "invisible wire" stretched between him and a friend. When Morrison threw the saucer, he

10

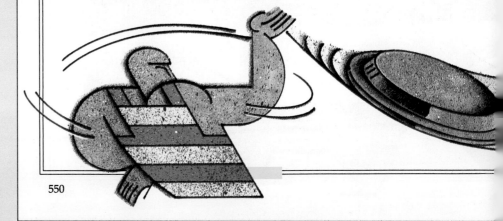

550

claimed it flew along the wire directly to his friend's waiting hand. Morrison charged one cent per foot for the invisible wire and threw in a "free" Flyin' Saucer with every 100 feet of wire a customer bought. The gimmick worked and soon Morrison had sold out his supply of saucers and invisible wire.

But Morrison still wasn't satisfied. He improved the design and gave the toy a new name—the Pluto Platter. In 1957, the Wham-O Toy Company of San Gabriel, California, saw the Pluto Platter, liked it, and bought it from Morrison.

Sales of Pluto Platters were steady among beachgoers, who loved playing catch with them, but were slow among the general public. Then one day, Wham-O owner Rich Knerr saw some college students throwing the Platters at Harvard University in Cambridge, Massachusetts. The students told him how they used to throw pie pans from the Frisbie Pie Company. Knerr remembered Morrison's story about the same pie company and decided that a change of name would make the toy more popular. The Pluto Platter became the Frisbee (an unintentional misspelling) and the rest is history.

The Frisbee remains popular with people of all ages and athletic abilities. And it all started with an empty pie pan and an inventor with imagination.

11

11 EXPOSITORY TEXT: MAIN IDEA
How would you rate Garrett Morgan's invention in comparison with that of Walter Fred Morrison?
(Accept reasonable responses: Compared to Morgan's invaluable, lifesaving invention, Morrison's device was unnecessary and frivolous, yet the Frisbee brings a lot of pleasure to many people and is not expensive.)
CRITICAL: MAKING JUDGMENTS

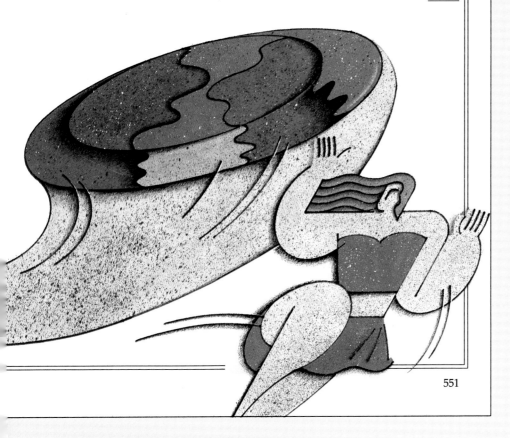

551

Oral Rereading   Have students reread "The Fabulous Frisbee" section silently. Then have them imagine they are people from the future and that the Frisbee has been discovered in a ruin by archaeologists. Invite volunteers to read this report to their classmates as though they are newscasters explaining to viewers just what a Frisbee is. Alternatively, invite volunteers to select their favorite passage from the selection to read aloud.

Is the main idea of this section stated in the subheading or in the first sentence? *(first sentence)* **What seems to be the purpose of the subheading?** *(to arouse readers' curiosity through clever use of language)*
INFERENTIAL: DRAWING CONCLUSIONS

13 EXPOSITORY TEXT: DETAILS

The author states that Indians had been chewing chicle for over a thousand years. Do you think this is a fact or an opinion? How can you decide? *(The statement is factual because its accuracy can be checked through research.)*
CRITICAL: DISTINGUISHING FACT FROM OPINION

FROM CHICLE ▼▼▼▼ TO ▼▼▼▼ CHEWING GUM

12

What is worthless to one person may be valuable to someone else. And when that someone else happens to be an inventor, the results can be spectacular.

Take the case of Thomas Adams of New Jersey. Adams turned a supply of apparently useless tree sap sitting in his warehouse into a new product—chewing gum.

The dried sap Adams had is called *chicle.* It comes from the wild sapodilla tree of Central America. Adams had spent two years trying to make a substitute for rubber from the chicle but his efforts had failed. Then Adams noticed his young son chewing chicle in imitation of the Indians who had chewed it for over a thousand years. What was good for the Indians, thought Adams, might just be enjoyable to the folks at home. At that time, Americans were chewing less tasty materials such as spruce resin and paraffin.

13

So Adams and his sons, Horatio and Thomas, went to work. They mixed chicle with water, rolled it into balls, and sold it to druggists along the East Coast. Customers welcomed the flavorless chewing gum and, by 1872, Adams was operating his own chewing-gum factory with 250 workers.

Despite teachers who outlawed it in schools and doctors who mistakenly warned that it would make the intestines stick together if swallowed, chewing gum became a worldwide success.

Adams constantly improved his product. He changed the packaging, sold it in vending machines, and added numerous flavors. You can still buy his licorice-flavored Black Jack in stores today.

552

Teaching Tip You may want to point out that on page 553 the section title "Glow, Little Glow Sheet" is a parody of the song title "Glow, Little Glow Worm."

GLOW
Little Glow Sheet

Some inventors adapt their inventions to meet the needs of others.

Rebecca Schroeder was only nine when she invented the glow sheet. She went for a drive with her mother and sat in the car doing homework while her mother went shopping. Soon it began to grow dark and Rebecca could no longer see well enough to write. As the light grew dimmer, another kind of light lit up in Rebecca's brain. Why not make a board or panel, she thought, that would light up so that people could write in the dark?

It was a great idea, but how was she going to turn it into a practical invention? Rebecca asked her father, a patent attorney and an inventor himself, to buy her some luminous paint. Then one night, after experimenting with the paint in her bedroom, she came running out to tell her surprised parents, "It works! It works!"

Rebecca's invention, which she calls the "Glow Sheet," consists of a sheet of special luminous paper embedded in a plastic clipboard. When a sheet of writing paper is placed over the clipboard, it lights up. The darker it is, the brighter the paper glows. When she found that the glow sheet began to lose its glow after 15 minutes, Rebecca found a way to lengthen the glow's life. She wired the clipboard with electricity and attached a battery-operated button. To "turn" the glow sheet on, a person only had to push the button.

Today, in her mid-20s, Rebecca heads her own company. She works at trying to get her glow sheets produced as inexpensively as possible so that many people will be able to afford to buy them.

And she's busy promoting her glow sheet idea to various groups and individuals. She is always thinking up new ways to make her invention useful. For example, with the glow sheet, hospital nurses could write their reports without turning on the lights and disturbing a sleeping patient. Police officers could fill out reports in emergencies or at the darkened scene of a crime. Radiologists and photographers, who must develop their X rays and photographs in darkened rooms, could take notes without damaging their work. And customers in dimly lit restaurants could read the menu more easily.

Finally, Rebecca's invention could help other inventors. When an idea for a new invention comes in the middle of the night, an inventor could just reach for the glow sheet on the bedside table and jot down the idea. In the morning, the inventor would be ready to start working on that midnight inspiration!

15

553

14 AUTHOR'S PURPOSE
What purpose do you think the author had for including a nine-year-old inventor in her article? *(to show that anyone, regardless of age, can be an inventor)*
INFERENTIAL: DRAWING CONCLUSIONS

15 NARRATION: CHARACTERIZATION
What qualities does Rebecca Schroeder show in developing, improving, and promoting her invention? *(Accept reasonable responses: imagination, determination, initiative, practicality, perseverance.)*
INFERENTIAL: DRAWING CONCLUSIONS

Guided Reading

MONITOR COMPREHENSION: PAGES 546–553 **How did the lives of the inventors mentioned in this section (Garrett Morgan, Walter Fred Morrison, Thomas Adams, and Rebecca Schroeder) demonstrate the importance of the qualities mentioned earlier in the selection?** (Accept reasonable responses: Students should mention the importance of curiosity, imagination, and problem solving in connection with each inventor.)
STRATEGIC READING: RETURNING TO PURPOSE

How were these four inventors alike? How were they different? (Accept reasonable responses: All found a creative way to satisfy a need or desire that people had; only Garrett Morgan invented something that has benefited humanity in a significant way.)
STRATEGIC READING: SUMMARIZING

SET PURPOSE/PREDICT: PAGES 554–557 Have students turn the heading *Getting Started* (on page 554) into a question and use it to establish a purpose for reading the rest of the selection. If students have difficulty, suggest they read the rest of the selection to find out how to begin to think like an inventor.

16 EXPOSITORY TEXT: MAIN IDEA AND DETAILS
Why was Clarence Birdseye a good example for the author to use in the section "Ask Around"? *(To get his idea, he asked the people of Labrador what they needed most.)*
CRITICAL: SYNTHESIZING

17 NARRATION: ACTIONS/EVENTS
How did Birdseye get his idea for quick-freezing foods? *(He watched how the Labradorean people froze fresh fish, he admired the results, and he applied the idea to commercial frozen foods.)*
LITERAL: NOTING IMPORTANT DETAILS

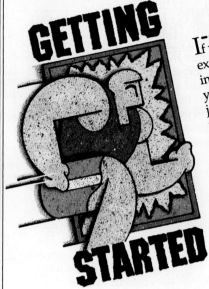

GETTING OF STARTED

If you're inspired by the example of other inventors and you think you have what it takes to join their ranks, how do you get started? Every invention begins with an idea. But where does the all-important idea come from? It comes from you or the people you know———

Ask Around.

Every successful invention fulfills a need. Sometimes it's a personal need, sometimes it's a need shared by many people.

You know what you need. The way to find out about the needs of others is to ask questions. Talk to your friends, neighbors, classmates, and family members. Ask them what would make their jobs easier or their lives more fun.

16 Clarence Birdseye, a member of a U.S. government survey team in Labrador in 1915, asked the local people what they needed most. The answer he got was fresh foods. Few vegetables or meats could be produced in such a cold, northern land and there was no way to transport foods there without spoilage.

Frozen foods had been available commercially in the United States since 1865, but they had little flavor when they were thawed. Birdseye noticed that fish frozen very quickly by the Labradorean natives retained all its flavor after being thawed. It occurred to him that the **17** problem with commercial freezing was that it was done too slowly. The food spoiled partially during the long freezing process and food cells were damaged.

After several years of experimenting, Birdseye developed a process to quick-freeze foods and came to be known as the "Father of Frozen Foods."

But Clarence Birdseye never stopped asking questions. He surveyed his customers regularly to see what new kinds of frozen foods they wanted. Today you

554

Teaching Tip You may want to point out Labrador (third paragraph) on a map or a globe. If no map or globe is available, tell students that Labrador is a large peninsula in northeastern Canada. The winters are severe, with snow on the ground from September through June in some places. Agriculture is nearly impossible.

can still buy Birds Eye® frozen foods, named after the inventor of modern quick-freezing.

Birdseye did not only ask questions; he set out to improve something that already existed—frozen foods. Not every invention needs to be new. There's always room for taking an old idea and making it better.

INVENTOR'S IDEA BOX

Getting the Facts

- What subject areas should I read about and study before going ahead with my invention?
- What specific information will I need to know to make my invention work?
- What books or periodicals might add to my knowledge of my subject?
- What persons or organizations might be of help?

GET THE FACTs

Inventors need more than original ideas to develop an invention. They need to learn everything they can about the subject areas related to their ideas. This information helps them plan, design, and refine their inventions. Clarence Birdseye had to learn all about ice crystals before he could successfully freeze food. Marconi took physics courses to find out how sound travels. George Eastman learned about chemicals and early photography before he invented film and the Kodak camera. And Melville Bissell, inventor of the carpet sweeper, had to become an expert on a subject as simple as brushes to help him with his famous invention.

18

You, too, will need to become an expert on your subject. Read all you can about it—in books, magazines, and journals—and add constantly to your collection of information. If possible, contact manufacturers and organizations specializing in your subject.

555

18 EXPOSITORY TEXT: MAIN IDEA AND DETAILS
How does the author use details to support the main idea of the section "Get the Facts"? *(The author tells how Birdseye, Marconi, Eastman, and Bissell all gathered information before developing their inventions.)*
LITERAL: NOTING IMPORTANT DETAILS

19 NARRATION: CHARACTERIZATION

What do the words on Gail Borden's tombstone say about his character? *(that he was patient and persistent)*
INFERENTIAL: DRAWING CONCLUSIONS

What other expressions or stories do you know that express the same idea? *(Accept reasonable responses: the expression "If at first you don't succeed, try, try again"; the story of the little engine that could.)*
INFERENTIAL: MAKING COMPARISONS

▼▼▼▼▼
T·A·K·E
Y·O·U·R
T·I·M·E

You've probably heard the old saying "Rome wasn't built in a day." The same could be said for a successful invention. Asking questions, researching facts, and thinking your invention through in every detail all take time. If you rush past any step, you may overlook something important.

Gail Borden spent years inventing a way to preserve milk. In the 1800s, there was no refrigeration, and milk often went bad before consumers drank it. Many people became sick drinking this contaminated milk; some even died.

Borden believed that if he could remove the water from milk—condense it—it could be canned and remain safe for long periods of time. He tested and retested many methods for condensing. He checked and rechecked each step in his process. But when he succeeded and applied for a patent on his condensing method, the U.S. Patent Office turned him down. They claimed his process showed "nothing new."

But Gail Borden did not give up. He kept working at his invention. Finally, in 1856, he proved his condensing method new and workable and was granted a patent.

He was soon operating the world's first condensed-milk factory. Today the Borden Company still turns out millions of cans of condensed milk, as well as many other dairy products, for people everywhere.

Borden had a saying that was later engraved on his tombstone, words that every inventor should keep in mind, especially when things are going wrong: *I tried and failed; I tried again and again, and succeeded.*

ANSWERS to "STRANGE and UNUSUAL INVENTIONS"
PAGES 546–547.

A. Hunting Decoy. Designed to help hunters outsmart ducks and other flying game, this grazing cow is actually camouflage for two hunters. When the hunters are ready to fire, they lower the neck of the decoy or open a panel on its side.

B. Improvement in Fire Escapes. This invention helps people save themselves from burning buildings. A person attaches the five-foot-wide parachute to his or her head, neck, or arms before leaping from the burning building. With the parachute, the person can land safely, while pads on the soles of the shoes cushion the shock.

C. Spaghetti Fork. This spinning fork is intended to make a favorite food easier to eat. The diner turns on the switch and a motor spins the tines, wrapping strands of spaghetti neatly around the fork.

D. Ambulatory Sleeping Bag. This unique sleeping bag is called ambulatory because it lets a camper move about. It has openings for arms and legs, allowing a camper, while snug inside the bag, to scratch an itchy nose or to take off in a hurry from a wandering bear.

E. Footwear with Heel and Toe Positions Reversed. The toes of these soldier's boots point in the opposite direction from that in which they're actually moving. Because the boots point backward when the soldier walks forward, they give the enemy the impression that its foe is headed another way.

556

Second-Language Support

If students do not understand the saying *Rome wasn't built in a day* (lines 2–3), help them understand that it means that worthwhile things usually cannot be accomplished quickly. Call attention to the use of quotation marks to set off a popular expression.

MEETING INDIVIDUAL NEEDS

Guided Reading

MONITOR COMPREHENSION: PAGES 554–557 **What have you learned about beginning to think like an inventor?** (Accept reasonable responses: ask around to discover people's needs; be sure your idea is really new; research; take your time.) STRATEGIC READING: RETURNING TO PURPOSE

What are the reasons for keeping a notebook? (Accept reasonable responses: to think, to plan, to provide proof for the U.S. Patent Office if necessary, to record test results.) STRATEGIC READING: SUMMARIZING

Make a Notebook

Before you go to work on your invention, get a notebook and keep it handy. Inventors say their notebooks are their most valuable tools. They fill them with notes on their ideas and the materials they use, test results, progress reports, and things they learn while working on their inventions.

As you fill up your notebook, get witnesses—friends or family members—to sign some dated entries. This is valuable proof that your invention is your idea and no one else's. You might need to present these witnessed records to the U.S. Patent Office if someone else claims to have invented the same invention before you did.

Daniel Drawbaugh learned this lesson the hard way. If he had kept a notebook containing witnesses' signatures, he might today be honored as the inventor of the telephone. Witnesses claimed they had heard him talk over his telephone long before Alexander Graham Bell even filed a

patent application for the same invention in 1876. But their words weren't good enough in a court of law. The law wanted written, dated testimony and that was the one thing Drawbaugh couldn't produce.

To avoid cases like Drawbaugh's, patent officials stress the importance to inventors of notebooks to show when their work on an invention began and how they followed through on the idea.

Thomas Edison, inventor of the phonograph, the electric lamp, and the kinetoscope, among other things, called the work he did in his notebooks "thinking on paper." He filled hundreds of notebooks and sketchbooks with notes, diagrams, and drawings. For the electric lamp alone, he wrote more than 40,000 pages of notes!

You, too, will come to value your notebooks. These written records of your invention's progress will help you plan, think through your ideas, and solve problems. You will want to share them with experts and fellow inventors.

THINK IT OVER

1. What characteristics did the inventors in the selection have in common? Why are these qualities important to inventors?

2. Which of the inventions was based on an idea the inventor got from a child's toy?

3. Who is the "Father of Frozen Foods"?

4. Which of the stories behind an invention surprised you most? Explain what made the story so interesting.

5. What are several reasons that inventors say their notebooks are their most valuable tools?

WRITE

Think of a "strange and unusual" invention. Draw a diagram of your invention and write a description of its purpose and how it is used.

557

Returning to the Purpose for Reading Have students check the answers that they wrote in the "Read" column of the SQ3R charts and that they may have written in their personal journals. Have one volunteer read each question aloud; have another volunteer answer.

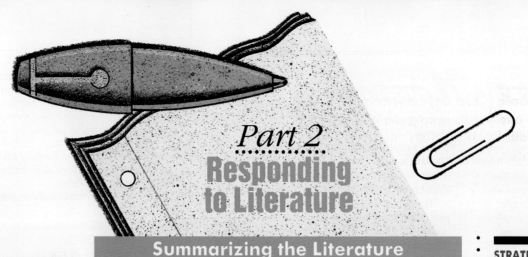

Part 2
Responding to Literature

Summarizing the Literature

Have students retell the selection and write a summary.

Invite students to summarize the information in the selection, using the SQ3R chart. If they have not yet completed the chart, have them do so now. (See *Practice Book* page 149, on 557B.) Students may use their completed charts to retell the selection and write a brief summary statement.

SQ3R CHART

S—Survey *This article discusses four traits of inventors: curiosity, imagination, willingness to work hard, and confidence.*		
Q—Question *Why is curiosity an important trait for inventors?*	**Predicted Answer** *Curiosity leads inventors to notice new things.*	**R—Read** ✓
How does imagination help inventors?	*Inventors need imagination to solve problems in new ways.*	✓
R—Recite		**R—Review**

Have students recite their answers and then review the headings in the selection.

Appreciating Literature

Have students share personal responses.

Organize students into small groups to discuss the selection. Provide a general question such as the following to help the groups get started:

- **What do you feel is the most important paragraph or passage in this article? Explain why you think it is important.**

PERSONAL JOURNAL Encourage students to use their personal journals to write about ideas and feelings that are expressed in the groups. You may also wish to refer students to their personal journals after they complete the Critical Thinking Activities.

STRATEGY CONFERENCE

Discuss the SQ3R chart, asking students how it helped make the information clearer. Encourage students to tell other strategies they used, such as recognizing main ideas and noting important details.

STUDENT SELF-ASSESSMENT

To help students self-assess their listening, write a list of good-listening skills on the board:

An effective listener
- pays attention
- does not interrupt
- thinks about and builds on other people's ideas
- argues with ideas, not with people

Encourage both cooperative and individual responses.

DISCUSS OPINIONS   Do you agree with the author concerning the qualities that inventive people possess? Why? Can you think of any other qualities inventive people have? Invite students to discuss their agreement or disagreement with the author and to cite qualities of inventive people they know. Encourage students to add to or to change the author's list of "inventive" characteristics. CRITICAL: EXPRESSING PERSONAL OPINIONS

ROLE-PLAY AN INTERVIEW   If you could meet one of the inventors discussed in this selection, what questions would you ask? Have students work in pairs to role-play an interview between a reporter and an inventor. CREATIVE: CONDUCTING AN INTERVIEW

WRITE AN ESSAY   The author states, "Every invention fulfills a need." Is this statement fact or opinion? Give reasons for your answer. Invite students to apply the author's statement to the inventions presented in the selection and to inventions they use in their everyday lives. Have students write short essays telling whether the author is stating a fact or an opinion and present reasons for their choice. CRITICAL: DISTINGUISHING FACT FROM OPINION

Writer's Journal

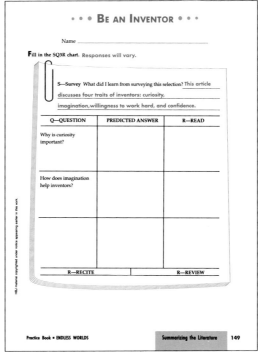

Practice Book

WRITER'S JOURNAL
page 100: Writing a creative response

PRACTICE BOOK
page 149: Summarizing the selection

VO·CAB·U·LAR·Y Workshop

Reviewing Key Words

To review how the new vocabulary was used in this selection, display the Key Words. Read each question below, and have students answer.

1. *generators* **Where might you find a generator?** (in any machine where mechanical energy must be changed into electricity: cars, power plants)

2. *transistors* **How did transistors revolutionize electronic equipment?** (Their small size and light weight made large tubes and electronic circuits unnecessary; equipment using such materials became smaller and more efficient.)

3. *luminous* **What is the advantage of having equipment with luminous dials, numbers, faces, and so on?** (Such equipment can be seen and read in dim light or in the dark.)

4. *silicon* **What is one use of silicon in computers?** (It is used in making computer chips.)

5. *resistors* **Where would you find resistors?** (in an electrical circuit)

6. *radiologists* **Why would you visit a radiologist?** (to have an X ray; to find out if you had a broken bone)

7. *commercially* **Which inventions in the selection were commercially successful?** (most of them, with the possible exceptions of the glow sheet and the "strange and unusual inventions")

Extending Vocabulary

COINED WORDS Tell students that people are often creative in making up new words to fit new situations. For example, when transistors were invented, so was their name. The word *transistor* was formed by combining the words *transfer* and *resistor*. When doctors began using radiation, the word *radiologist* was coined. Have students think of other modern inventions and brainstorm words that were coined to name them or their parts or functions or people involved with that invention. They might start with *telephone, telegraph,* and *television.* Have them write their ideas in a concept map that shows the relationship among ideas.

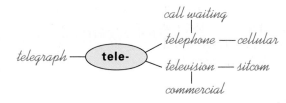

Writing About the Literature

AVAILABLE ON PROJECT CARD

CREATIVE: FIRST-PERSON NARRATIVE   Have students choose one invention and rewrite the story of its creation in the first person. Encourage students to have the inventor tell the story in a suspenseful way, building up to the moment of success. READING/WRITING

CRITICAL: CAUSE-AND-EFFECT ESSAY   Have students write an essay evaluating the effects of one invention, such as television or the computer. They should classify the effects as beneficial or harmful, using an outline. WRITING

Effects of _____
  I. Beneficial
     A.
     B.
  II. Harmful
     A.
     B.

  _____

NOTE: An additional writing activity appears on page 557.

SPEAKING/LISTENING

Role-Playing

Suggest that each student research an inventor. After students have read an encyclopedia article or two, suggest they find a biography or an autobiography and become informed about the inventor's work. Have students role-play the part of the inventor and give a speech titled "Secrets of My Success." Encourage other students to ask questions.
LISTENING/SPEAKING/READING

SPELLING

Spelling Review

SPELLING WORDS: *druggist, engineer, illustrator, luminous, manufacturer, officer, operator, photographer, professor, radiologist*

Have students write the Spelling Words as you dictate them. Then have a volunteer write them on the board and circle the word that is not a career word. Have students read each word aloud in unison, listening for the affixes in the career words. Have another volunteer identify each career word and give a brief definition of it.
LISTENING/SPEAKING/READING/WRITING/SPELLING

INTEGRATED SPELLING

page 74:   Writing career words

INTEGRATED SPELLING
Career Words

Name _____

WORD PLAY

Play a game of "What's My Job Title?" Guess the job titles of the nine speakers below. Write their titles on the blanks. Choose your titles from the Word Bank.

WORD BANK

druggist
engineer
illustrator
manufacturer
officer
operator
photographer
professor
radiologist

1. "I'm on the teaching staff at Harvard University. I'm a
   professor ."

2. "I answer incoming calls at the phone company. I'm an
   operator ."

3. "I use X rays to diagnose diseases. I'm a   radiologist ."

4. "I use film to record people, places, and events. I'm a
   photographer ."

5. "I produce goods sold around the world. I'm a   manufacturer ."

6. "I run the bank. I'm the bank's   officer ."

7. "I make drawings to explain things in textbooks. I'm an   illustrator ."

SPELLING DETECTIVE

Akasa invented a great new product and jotted down some notes about possible users for it. When she proofread her notes, she found six spelling errors. Find each error and circle it. Write the word correctly above the misspelled word.

- Useful to someone who measures things,
  druggist   radiologist
  such as a druggist or a radiologyst

- Handy for someone who draws, such
  illustrator   engineer
  as an illustrater or an enginier

- Great for someone who frames things,
  photographer
  such as a photographor or a window
  manufacturer
  manufactureer

74   "Be an Inventor" • ENDLESS WORLDS

Integrated Spelling

STUDY SKILLS
INTRODUCE

Forms and Applications

OBJECTIVE: *To understand the process involved in completing a form or an application*

1   Focus

Explain the value of knowing how to complete forms and applications.

Point out to students that forms and applications are an important part of life. For example, inventors must apply to the U.S. Patent Office to protect their ideas. Ask students to name situations in which they filled out a form or an application. (They may recall school registration forms, standardized test answer sheets, or catalog order forms.) Ask them what consequences may result when forms or applications are filled out incorrectly.

2   Teach/Model

Display forms.

Display Transparency 30, or write the following form parts on the board. Have students study them silently for a moment, looking for similarities and differences.

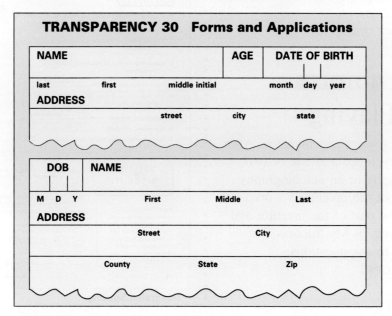

TRANSPARENCY 30   Forms and Applications

NAME			AGE	DATE OF BIRTH
last	first	middle initial		month day year
ADDRESS				
	street	city	state	

DOB	NAME			
M D Y	First	Middle	Last	
ADDRESS				
	Street	City		
	County	State	Zip	

Model the thinking. Fill out the top form, explaining each step as you go. When you have completed the top one, model how you would approach the next one.

> No two forms and applications are exactly alike, so the first thing I do when I'm filling one out is to read it. Although most require my name, address, and birth date, the order of the information requested is rarely the same.

| 3 | Practice/Apply |

Have students compare and contrast forms and applications. Have students study a variety of forms and applications, pointing out likenesses and differences. You may suggest that students actually fill out individual forms and applications, copying them, if necessary, to save the originals.

| 4 | Summarize |

Informally assess the learning. Have students generalize about the likenesses and differences of the forms and applications with which they have worked. Then have students summarize what they have learned. (No two forms or applications are the same, and each one requires careful reading to be completed correctly.)

CHALLENGE Encourage students to apply for membership in local organizations or for prizes based on student achievement. If possible, have these forms available or tell students how they may obtain them.

SECOND-LANGUAGE SUPPORT Students can work with peer tutors to prepare the personal data that is commonly required on applications and forms. (See *Second-Language Support Manual.*)

PRACTICE BOOK page 150: Completing forms and applications

• • • BE AN INVENTOR • • •

Name _____

A patent gives an inventor the sole right to make and sell a new invention for a set number of years. Suppose that you have invented something and want to apply for a patent. Read the directions on this patent application. Then complete the form. Responses will vary.

INTERNATIONAL APPLICATION UNDER THE PATENT COOPERATION TREATY REQUEST	(The following is to be filled in by the receiving Office) INTERNATIONAL APPLICATION No:
	INTERNATIONAL FILING DATE:
THE UNDERSIGNED REQUESTS THAT THE PRESENT INTERNATIONAL APPLICATION BE PROCESSED ACCORDING TO THE PATENT COOPERATION TREATY	(Stamp) Name of receiving Office and "PCT International Application"
	Applicant's or Agent's File Reference (indicated by applicant if desired).

I. TITLE OF INVENTION

II. APPLICANT   Additional information is contained in supplemental box. ☐
Name

Address (including postal code and country)

Nationality (country)   Residence (country)

Telephone number (if any)   Telegraphic address (if any)   Teleprinter address (if any)

III. INVENTOR   (Applicant is also the inventor ☐   Additional information is contained in supplemental box. ☐
Name

Address (including postal code and country)

IV. PURPOSE OF INVENTION

V. BRIEF DESCRIPTION OF INVENTION

Drawings attached ☐   No drawings ☐

| 150 | Forms and Applications | Practice Book ▪ ENDLESS WORLDS |

Practice Book

Summarizing/Generalizing

OBJECTIVE: *To review how summarizing can help a reader make valid generalizations*

Review

Review summarizing and generalizing.

Remind students that a summary is a brief restatement of important points. Generalizations are statements with broad applications. Model how to use a summary to generalize:

> **To summarize how Velcro was invented, I would say that a man's curiosity about how burrs clung to his dog led him to invent a new fastener. A generalization based on this summary might be "Inventors are curious people."**

Practice/Apply

Have students apply the skills.

COOPERATIVE LEARNING   Have student groups work together to summarize the stories of other inventors and then have them make valid generalizations.

Summarize

Informally assess the learning.

Have students summarize what they learned. (A valid generalization may be based on a summary.)

CHALLENGE   Invite students to look through their science or social studies books for sections on people: scientists, colonists, pioneers, leaders, and so on. Suggest that they read a section that appeals to them, summarize the section, and then write a generalization based on the summary.

PRACTICE BOOK
page 151:
Summarizing/generalizing

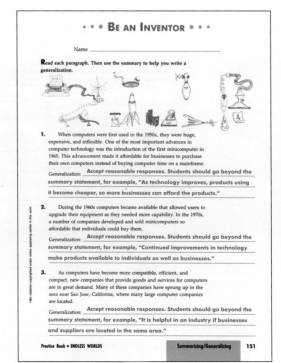

Practice Book

Directions

OBJECTIVE: *To review how to follow and give directions*

Review

Review following and giving directions.

Remind students that having clear directions to follow can make a task easier. Have students brainstorm activities that require directions. Model how to give directions:

> **When I give oral directions, I give the steps in order. I'll say, "Put your math books away, and then get out your science folders." When I write directions, I first visualize the process and think out the steps; then I write the steps in order.**

Practice/Apply

Have students write directions.

Tell students to write a set of directions for getting from one place to another, checking for clarity and for accuracy.

Summarize

Informally assess the learning.

Ask students to summarize what they learned. (In giving directions, I visualize the process while I think out the steps. Then I write or tell the steps in order.)

CHALLENGE Invite students to write a set of directions for a favorite hobby, sport, or cooking activity. When students have finished, suggest that they either follow the directions themselves or exchange them with a partner.

PRACTICE BOOK
page 152: Following directions

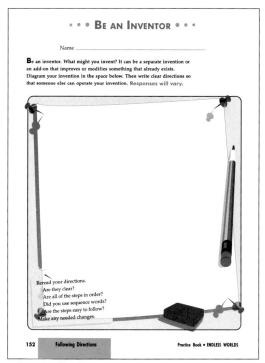

Practice Book

Integrated Curriculum

SCIENCE/MATH

What a Chip!

Suggest that students research the silicon computer chip that replaced the big, bulky electronic circuits of the 1950s. Have them use graph paper to draw a computer chip to a larger scale. Under their scale drawing, have students indicate the scale of the drawing (for example, 10 times actual size), as well as how much information one chip can store. Encourage students to look through personal-computer magazines to find pictures of computer circuits that they can display with their drawings. READING/WRITING

SCIENCE

Wacky Inventions

Have students research patented inventions that never became commercially successful. Suggest that they present pictures of the inventions and have their classmates guess the purposes of the devices. Afterwards, have students discuss possible reasons for the failure of each invention. LISTENING/SPEAKING/READING/WRITING

SOCIAL STUDIES

It's All in the Game

AVAILABLE ON PROJECT CARD

Have students research the history of such popular toys and games as the yo-yo, Slinky, Silly Putty, Rubik's Cube, and Scrabble. Then have volunteers invent their own toy or game and test its appeal to children of different ages. LISTENING/SPEAKING/READING

SOCIAL STUDIES/ART

What Are You Saying, Rube Goldberg?

Invite students to become acquainted with the cartoonist Rube Goldberg. Students can research Goldberg's early cartoon strips and his cartoon creation "The Inventions of Professor Lucifer K. Butts, A.K." Encourage them to analyze Goldberg's cartoons to determine his opinions about inventors, inventions, and society's views of the inventor. Students might then enjoy creating a Goldberg-type cartoon of their own to demonstrate their ideas for ridiculous inventions. READING/WRITING

HOW TO WATER YOUR FAVORITE PLANT

Multi*Cultural*
PERSPECTIVES

Sweet Beginnings

READ ALOUD TO STUDENTS:

THE PROCESS OF EXTRACTING MAPLE SUGAR WAS A REMARKABLE DISCOVERY.

Early in America's history, Iroquois Indians taught the colonists in New England how to gash the bark of sugar maple trees when the sap was flowing, collect the sap, and boil it down to make sugar crystals. For sustenance on long journeys, warriors and hunters often carried a nutritious mixture of sugar, dried venison or bear meat, and berries. The northeastern Indians enjoyed pouring hot syrup over popped corn, just as we do today. Maple sugar was an essential food in the colonies until refined cane sugar became widely available. Pure maple syrup, a popular part of our heritage from Native American cultures, is now an expensive luxury.

The climate of the southern states was well suited for growing sugarcane, another source of sugar. Norbert Rillieux, a black engineer born in Louisiana and educated in France, revolutionized the sugar industry and gained international recognition for his 1846 improvement of the vacuum pan. Rillieux's ideas made it possible to get a finer grade of sugar faster and at half the cost of the older method. His contributions to the sugar-manufacturing process have been compared with George Washington Carver's contributions to the peanut industry. ■

ACTIVITY CORNER

■ Have students working in small groups choose a common item or product and develop a "Believe It or Not" invention history for the item. (Possibilities: safety pins, zippers, permanent waves, bicycles, plastic, light bulbs)

■ Ask students to interview adults about recent inventions that they use in their work and daily lives. Students should ask how each invention saves the worker time and effort over an older process.

■ Suggest that students investigate the amount and kinds of sweeteners used in the United States and in other parts of the world. They may prepare a graph comparing their findings.

The sugar industry honored Norbert Rillieux with this commemorative plate, now at the Louisiana State Museum.

The Iroquois taught the colonists how to make sugar crystals from the sap of maple trees.

The Microscope

ABOUT THE POET

Maxine Kumin (1925–) is a novelist as well as a poet. She has published several books of poetry, and in 1973 she won the Pulitzer Prize for her poetry book *Up Country*. Kumin feels that the job of a poet is "bringing things back to the world's attention and dealing with things small and overlooked."

1 IRONY

Who turned out to be "dumkopf," Anton Leeuwenhoek or the townsfolk? Explain. *(Accept reasonable responses: the townsfolk, because things they considered impossible were proven true by Leeuwenhoek's microscope.)*
CRITICAL: MAKING JUDGMENTS

2 THEME

What is the theme of this poem? *(Accept reasonable responses: It is human nature to scoff at ideas or inventions that one does not understand; therefore, geniuses must ignore criticism.)*
INFERENTIAL: DETERMINING MAIN IDEA

WRITER'S JOURNAL page 101: Writing a creative response

Writer's Journal

The Microscope

by Maxine Kumin

Anton Leeuwenhoek was Dutch.
He sold pincushions, cloth and such.
The waiting townsfolk fumed and fussed
As Anton's dry goods gathered dust.

He worked instead of tending store,
At grinding special lenses for
A microscope. Some of the things
He looked at were:
                        mosquitoes' wings,
the hairs of sheep, the legs of lice,
the skin of people, dogs and mice;
ox eyes, spiders' spinning gear,
fishes' scales, a little smear
of his own blood.
                        and best of all,
the unknown, busy, very small
bugs that swim and bump and hop
inside a simple water drop.

1 Impossible! Most Dutchmen said.
This Anton's crazy in the head.
We ought to ship him off to Spain.
He says he's seen a housefly's brain.
He says the water that we drink
Is full of bugs. He's mad, we think!

2 They called him dumkopf, which means dope.
That's how we got the microscope.

Accent in Rose, Wassily Kandinsky, 1926. Musée National d'Art Moderne, Paris, France.

Reading the Poem

Have students read the poem silently. Then invite individual students to read the first four stanzas. Ask students to read the fifth stanza in unison; then recite the final stanza yourself, emphasizing the first line and understating the last.

Responding to the Poem

Encourage students to discuss why Leeuwenhoek's contemporaries might have considered him insane. Students may then research other discoveries or inventions that people initially ridiculed.

Innovations

Remind students that they have read about inventors and inventions in this theme. Invite them to name some reasons why an inventor's work might be rewarding. Explain that the activities on page 559 will help them compare the poetry to the nonfiction in this theme.

Note that pages 559A–559B provide support for applying the writing process to the last question.

---

1 Suggest that students review the subheads of "Be an Inventor" to find traits or qualities important to inventors and then decide which traits Leeuwenhoek shares. *(Accept reasonable responses: The Dutch inventor clearly has curiosity and imagination, too much of both to simply mind the store.)*
INFERENTIAL: SYNTHESIZING

---

2 Tell students to think about the ways in which people they know react to new ideas and to use this knowledge in answering the question. *(Accept reasonable responses: The Dutch mock Leeuwenhoek's microscope because they don't understand it. Many people today respond in a similar way to new things they don't understand.)*
CRITICAL: MAKING GENERALIZATIONS

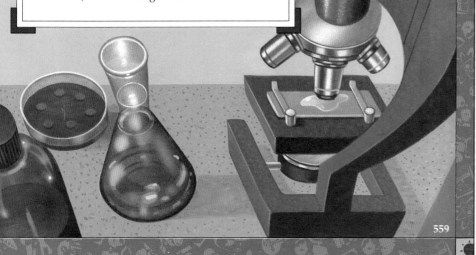

THEME WRAP-UP

INNOVATIONS

How can reading "Be an Inventor" help you to better understand Anton Leeuwenhoek from "The Microscope"? Do you think Anton might have some of the qualities that "Be an Inventor" says are important?

. . . .

Reread "The Microscope." Why do you think the Dutchmen ridicule Anton for his microscope and the discoveries he makes with it? Do you think there are people today who would make fun of something just because it is new? Explain your answer.

. . . .

WRITER'S WORKSHOP   Think of an everyday item that you use, and investigate it. Write a research report in which you present such information as who invented or discovered the item, what earlier versions were like, and how long it has been in use.

559

Writer's Workshop
See pages 559A–559B for suggestions for applying the writing process. Responses should draw on information found in reference books. You may wish to allow students to respond to the theme in their own way. WRITING PROCESS: A RESEARCH REPORT

Writer's Workshop

Have students recall how they have gone about finding information for previous research reports. Review reference sources and the procedures for looking up information in the school or community library, including the card catalog, microfilm or microfiche, and a computer database. Have students determine which reference sources they will need for their reports. Suggest that students refer to the Handbook in the *Writer's Journal* as they write, revise, and proofread their research reports.

Prewriting

Before they write, have students

- choose an everyday object they would like to investigate before researching.
- write a list of questions they would like their research to answer. The questions and answers might be set up in a chart like the following:

What I Want to Know	What I Learned
Who invented the telephone?	Alexander Graham Bell
When and where was it invented	in Boston in the mid-1870s
What led to the discovery?	Bell's work in teaching deaf children to talk
What were earlier versions like?	There were none. People called in person or wrote letters.
Are there any interesting stories connected with the discovery?	Someone else invented the telephone at the same time.

Advise students to complete their research before they begin drafting.

Drafting

Ask students to write a draft of their research reports. Remind them to

- organize the information in a way that is clear to the reader.
- explain why the object was invented and what purpose it serves.
- write in formal English but not in a stiff or stilted style.
- avoid worrying about spelling, punctuation, or grammar.

COMPUTER CONNECTION Students may want to use a computer during the prewriting stage to help them with their research. They can access the latest information available by using databases and on-line services.

Responding and Revising

Suggest that each student read his or her draft aloud to a partner. Have the pair review the draft for clarity and coherence. Offer the following tips, and then have students revise their work:

- Are the details included appropriate and relevant? Delete any extraneous material.
- Has the writer included quotations to add interest to the report? If so, do they fit in with the flow of the prose and has the writer identified the source? (See the Language/Literature Link below.)

STUDENT SELF-ASSESSMENT OPTION Students may use the Writing Self-Assessment Checklist in the *Portfolio Teacher's Guide.* Suggest that as they use the checklist, they focus on the organization of the research report and the inclusion of quotations from oral or written sources.

Proofreading

Offer these tips to help students proofread their work:

- The proper form for citing dates is month, day, year. For example: July 16, 1993.
- If you mention a reference book, underline the title.

Publishing

Students may wish to illustrate and collect their reports into a booklet called "Great Inventions," which the class might use for reference in history or science classes. Or they might save them in their reading/writing portfolio.

LANGUAGE/LITERATURE LINK

Using Quotations

Point out that quotations add authority and human interest to research reports and that quotations can be obtained from an oral source. Discuss the quotation Barbara Taylor uses on page 553 of "Being an Inventor." No doubt she asked the parents what their daughter had said when she invented the glow sheet: "It works! It works!" Point out that quotations also can come from written sources. For instance, students may find an apt sentence in a book they want to include in their reports. Tell them they can do so, but they must put the sentence in quotation marks and also identify the source of their quoted material.

Speaking Option

INFORMATIVE SPEECH The *Writer's Workshop* can be adapted to allow students to plan an informative speech from their research reports. Have students follow the guidelines for Prewriting, Drafting, and Responding and Revising. Offer these tips to help students deliver their speeches:

- Practice your speech thoroughly. Use note cards instead of your full-length report as prompters.
- Start off by relating your topic to your audience's experience: for example, "Can you imagine a world without a telephone?"
- Avoid pretentious words, which obviously are taken from an encyclopedia.
- Use audiovisual aids to help your audience remember information.

Have each student deliver his or her speech in front of a small group of classmates.

THEME OPENER

Space

Have students look at the photograph and read the introduction about space on Student Anthology page 561. Invite them to air their views on extra-terrestrials. Do they think there is someone or something out there? Ask the class to read the selection titles and speculate on their meaning. How seriously do they take the title "Little Green Men"? If necessary, explain that E.T. is a famous movie extraterrestrial popularized by the filmmaker Steven Spielberg.

PACING This theme has been designed to take about two weeks to complete, depending on your students' needs.

560

Management Options

THE LITERATURE-BASED CLASSROOM Providing a literature-rich curriculum creates unique classroom management challenges. Some management options for the selections in this theme follow.

A CLASS POLL Before students begin reading the selections in "Space," conduct a class poll to determine how many believe there is other intelligent life in the universe and how many do not. Post the results on the bulletin board. After completing the selections and the Writer's Workshop activity on Student Anthology page 579, poll students again to see if the results have changed.

THEME

SPACE

When you look up at the stars, do you ever wonder whether someone out there is looking back at you? For generations, people have been wondering whether there is life elsewhere in the universe and have been searching for evidence of it. Perhaps the following selections will help you make up your own mind.

CONTENTS

LITTLE GREEN MEN
by Barry B. Longyear

LOOKING FOR E.T.
by Larry Kelsey and Darrel Hoff

THE FIRST
by Lilian Moore

561

STUDENTS AT RISK

Encourage students to explain the steps they follow when evaluating two opposing points of view. Suggest that they follow the steps as they read the selections and decide whether or not there is life elsewhere in the universe.

GIFTED AND TALENTED

As an alternative to the Write activity on Student Anthology page 577, invite students to make a model of a starship that could be used to transport a space colony to Alpha Centauri. Students may then wish to write a science fiction adventure. Also see the *Challenge Cards.*

SPECIAL EDUCATION STUDENTS

To help students participate in the Learning Through Literature review lesson on summarizing and generalizing, you may wish to tape-record sections of "Looking for E.T." Students can listen and orally summarize the section.

LIMITED ENGLISH PROFICIENT STUDENTS

When you refer to the SQ3R strategy, be sure students understand what each of the letters means. It may be helpful to create a chart with the English word for each letter and its equivalent in each of their first languages.

YEAR-END READING TRIVIA CONTEST Assign a number of selections from Units 1 through 6 to each student. Have students write questions about each selection on one side of an index card and the answer on the reverse side. Suggest that they include questions about character, plot, and setting, as well as about the author. Then use the questions for a trivia quiz.

READING/WRITING PORTFOLIO Instruct students to keep in their portfolios their writing responses to the theme selections. Remind them also to add to their personal journals notes on their independent reading.

Little Green Men

ABOUT THE AUTHOR

Barry B. Longyear (1942–), noted science fiction writer, received the Nebula, Hugo, and Lucas awards in 1980 for his novella *Every Mine* and the John W. Campbell Award for best new science fiction writer. He has also written several novels. Some of his stories, poems, and articles have been published under pseudonyms.

SELECTION SUMMARY

Three days after a reported UFO sighting, Jhanni searches on his own for "little green men" from outer space, for his father has forbidden him to search with the other Star Scouts. What Jhanni finds is not a "little green man" but Frank Gambino, Captain, United States Air Force, a creature no taller than one of Jhanni's fingers.

562

Building Background

Explain that this story is about a boy's search for evidence of a UFO that had reportedly landed during a dust storm. Ask what *UFO* means, and then access students' prior knowledge about UFOs. (Accept reasonable responses: *UFO* is an abbreviation for "**u**nidentified **f**lying **o**bject"; some believe UFOs are spacecraft from other planets, while others believe they have more ordinary explanations.) Explain that there has been considerable controversy concerning their existence and that there have been sightings for hundreds of years.

Strategic Reading

Science Fiction   Review the idea that science fiction is a kind of fantasy with scientific elements. Have students read the first three paragraphs and predict whether Jhanni will find a UFO and an alien.

STUDENT-SET PURPOSE   Ask students to use their predictions to set a purpose for reading the story.

TEACHER-SET PURPOSE   If students have difficulty setting a purpose, offer this suggestion: **I'm going to read to discover how Jhanni will react if he does find a UFO and an alien.**

BY BARRY B. LONGYEAR

Jhanni caught his breath and rested in the shade of a boulder; he had found nothing. His father had forbidden him to search with the other Star Scouts for the UFO reported three days ago, and he wouldn't think of disobeying his father. Still, I said nothing about searching on my own, thought Jhanni.

"All this about 'invaders from outer space' is nonsense." His father had been unshakable on the subject, and nearly everybody thought the same way since the probe to Venus had reported no detectable life on the planet. *Adventurer 7* had met with a mishap on its way to Saturn, and Jhanni's father had been furious. "More taxpayers' money thrown away on foolishness! We should spend the money to take care of problems here." Evidently the government felt the same way. When Jhanni turned thirteen the space program was canceled. Along with the program, the Star Scouts were officially scrapped.

Still, Jhanni's friends, and Star Scouts from all over, kept their squadrons alive to search for evidence—proof that would rekindle the space program and put them back on their road to the stars. Every time a UFO was reported, the squadron in that area would turn out and search for evidence—disturbed soil, burn marks, abandoned equipment —anything. But two years of searching had turned up nothing.

ILLUSTRATIONS BY FRANKLIN HAMMOND

563

2 PLOT: CONFLICT

Why, for the first time in his life, does Jhanni argue with his father? *(Jhanni's father has forbidden him to waste study time by searching for spaceships and aliens, which Jhanni believes in deeply.)*
INFERENTIAL: DRAWING CONCLUSIONS

3 CHARACTER'S MOTIVATIONS

Why does Jhanni search the boulder field instead of the hills to the north? What does this show you about Jhanni? *(Jhanni's father has forbidden him to search with the Star Scouts, who are in the hills. Besides, Jhanni thinks the UFO might have been blown south to the boulder field because the wind was blowing in that direction on the day the UFO was seen; Jhanni is logical, imaginative, and very observant.)*
INFERENTIAL: DRAWING CONCLUSIONS

"Someday," Jhanni had told his squadron, "someday we'll find the proof we need, but until then we have to keep on trying." Nevertheless, one by one, the Star Scouts were leaving the squadron. Some, like Jhanni, were forbidden to waste good study time on such foolishness; others were discouraged; and still more had come to believe as their parents believed: Space travel costs too much to spend for uncertain returns. Jhanni's father had pulled him out of the squadron when his grades began to drop.

"We've had UFO reports for years. Spaceships, death rays and little green men from outer space, and it's always been something that could be explained. I don't want you ruining your education by wasting your time with it."

2 Jhanni loved his father, but he had argued with him for the first time in his life. "How do you know there's no life on other planets? Isn't it possible?"

"No one knows for sure, Jhanni, but I'll tell you this: Before I believe it, someone's going to have to show me one of those little green men."

And that's what we're looking for, thought Jhanni, one of those little green men. He pushed away from the boulder and stepped into the sunlight. Shielding his eyes, he looked around. The squadron was searching the hills north of the development where the "object" was reported to have come down during the dust storm three days ago. His father wouldn't give his permission to join the search in the hills, and Jhanni was so angry it took him three tries to properly cycle the airlock on his home before stepping out into the desert.

3 He went south from the development to search the boulder field, although the "object" was reported north. The wind storm was blowing south that day, thought Jhanni. It's possible; not probable, but possible.

As he looked out over the boulder-strewn desert floor, the evening shadows grew long. Soon it would be dark and the desert cold. He checked the light buckle and heater in his belt and headed for his favorite boulder. At every turn he strained to glimpse the spaceship he hoped would be there. He knew he could get a better view from his boulder, the largest one in the field. It was pockmarked with great

564

Teaching Tip You may wish to point out to students that the description of aliens as "little green men" with "death rays" is a common stereotype that has been fostered over the years in books, movies, and the comics.

holes bored there by the action of the wind and sand, and Jhanni hadn't been there since he was a child playing with the friends who later became his mates in the Star Scouts.

Sometimes he would take one of his mother's blankets and some extra power cells and spend most of an icy night on his boulder, looking at the stars and dreaming of traveling among them. But the dreams became fewer as he grew older. There was no official interest anymore in moons, planets, stars or anything else that might cost the taxpayers more money.

As the sun dropped below the horizon, the stars appeared, and Jhanni watched them as he reached his boulder and climbed to the top. As he watched the countless pinpricks of light from unknown and unexplored stars, he let himself dream again of flying among them. His eyes glistened and he looked down. Maybe it is childish, he thought. The road to the stars is closed unless people can see the little green men in the flesh. And maybe . . . maybe the little green men don't exist after all.

Jhanni thought he heard a sound, and he looked over his shoulder. Seeing nothing unusual, he crawled over and around the boulder, looking into the tiny, wind-blown caves. There was nothing. He shrugged and stood atop the boulder, looking toward the development and his home. The outside light was on at his house, and his mother would scold him if he were late for dinner. He shook his head when he remembered he still had a tough stretch of homework to do and a math test in the morning. He knew he'd better pass this one. Too much imagination and not enough perspiration, his father would say if he failed. Taking one last look at the stars, Jhanni sighed and began to climb down from the boulder.

PING.

Jhanni froze. Slowly he turned his head in the direction of the sound. Deep in the shadow of a wind hole, a tiny light danced back and forth. Warily he crept toward the hole.

"HEY!"

Jhanni picked himself off the ground, knocked there by the suddenness of the sound. He reached to his belt and turned on his light buckle, aiming it at the hole. Inside there was a small, white

565

Why does Jhanni say, "The road to the stars is closed unless people can see the little green men in the flesh"? *(Accept reasonable responses: The space program has been canceled, as well as the Star Scouts; unless there is proof—little green men—that there is life on other planets, the government does not want to spend any more money on a space program.)*
INFERENTIAL: DETERMINING CAUSE-EFFECT

5 FORESHADOWING
What clue tells you that something is going to happen? As you think back over the story, what other clues did the author give you? *(Jhanni thought he heard a sound; the fact that Jhanni went south to the boulder field instead of searching north was another clue.)*
METACOGNITIVE: SYNTHESIZING

Second-Language Support
Students may need help understanding the meaning of the expression "Too much imagination and not enough perspiration." Explain that Jhanni's father thinks he spends too much time daydreaming about outer space and thinking about UFOs—*imagination*—and not enough time working on his school studies—*perspiration*. Invite students to share similar expressions in their first language.

MEETING INDIVIDUAL NEEDS

6 CHARACTERS' EMOTIONS
Why do you think Jhanni and the creature are not frightened of each other? *(Accept reasonable responses: This is what Jhanni has been hoping for; the creature is small and friendly and does not seem to be a threat to Jhanni; the creature might be too concerned about running out of oxygen to worry about Jhanni.)*
INFERENTIAL: DRAWING CONCLUSIONS

cylinder propped up on spindly legs supported by round pads. The cylinder was dented, and its legs looked bent and battered.

"Turn off the light! I can't see."

Jhanni turned off his light buckle, and as his widening eyes adjusted again to the dark, tiny lights on the cylinder appeared and illuminated the hole. On one side of the object a tiny door opened, and a small, white-clad creature emerged, looked around and climbed down a tiny built-in ladder to the bottom of the wind hole. Jhanni peered closely as the creature lifted something and aimed it in Jhanni's direction.

"Can you hear me?"

"Uh . . ."

"Hold it." The creature adjusted a knob on its chest. "Had to lower the volume a bit. Good thing you dropped by; I only have a day's life support left."

6 "Uh . . .," Jhanni tried to untie his tongue, a million questions in his mind competing for the first answer. "Are you . . . are you from up there?" He pointed up. "How can you talk to me, and where . . . ?"

"One thing at a time. That's where I come from, and I'm talking to you through a universal translator. I rigged it up with a speaker from the lander console in case anyone came by."

"What happened?"

The creature threw up its tiny arms. "What didn't? I've been out of touch with my base ever since the wind blew me into this hole three days ago, damaging my oxygen regulator and radio. I'm running a little short. Can you get me to an oxygen-enriched atmosphere?"

"Well . . . there's my gas box. I raise tropical insects, and they're oxygen absorbing. I did it for a school project in biochem once, and . . ."

"Do the bugs eat meat?"

"Oh. Well, I can put them in another container. Can you fly or anything? My home's quite a walk from here."

"I guess you better carry me, but take it easy."

"I will." Jhanni picked up the little creature and held it in his hand, surprised at its weight. It was only as tall as one of Jhanni's fingers. He could just barely see the creature shaking his head inside his tiny helmet.

"I can't get over how big you Martians are. Wait until Houston hears about this!"

Teaching Tip   You may wish to explain that there have been no actual manned flights to Mars, the fourth planet from the sun. However, unmanned United States spacecraft approaching and orbiting the planet have provided photos of the planet and its two moons. In 1976 the U.S. spacecraft *Viking I* and *Viking II* landed on Mars with instruments that analyzed the atmosphere and the soil, but scientists have not yet determined whether there is life on Mars.

Second-Language Support
Students may not know that Houston is a city in Texas. Point out Houston on a map. Explain that the National Aeronautics and Space Administration's (NASA's) Lyndon B. Johnson Space Center is located in Houston and that space flights are directed from this center.

Jhanni laughed. "If you think I'm big, wait until you see my father!" And wait until my father gets a load of you, thought Jhanni. "By the way, creature, what color are you under that suit?"

"My name's Frank Gambino, Captain, United States Air Force. I'm sort of brown; why?"

"No special reason." Jhanni slipped the tiny creature into his pocket and began climbing down from the boulder. The little man isn't green, thought Jhanni, but he'll do. As he reached the desert floor and started to run home, he stopped himself just in time from patting his pocket.

THINK IT OVER

1. *How does the setting of the story make it more interesting than a science fiction story set on Earth?*
2. *What is Jhanni's father's main reason for being opposed to space exploration?*
3. *Why does Jhanni have to drop out of his Star Scout squadron?*
4. *What are some of the clues that the author uses to reveal the identities of Jhanni and the alien?*

7

WRITE

List questions that you think Jhanni and Frank Gambino would want to ask each other.

8

Returning to the Predictions Invite students to discuss the predictions they made before reading and to tell whether those predictions changed as they read the story.

Returning to the Purpose for Reading Ask students to discuss how Jhanni reacts to the alien and how the alien reacts to him. (Jhanni seems shocked at first but helps the tiny alien; the Captain is frustrated by his situation and is preoccupied with running out of oxygen, but he does not seem to be upset by Jhanni's size.)

---

7 THINK IT OVER
1. *Accept reasonable responses: An unfamiliar setting adds suspense and provides a surprise ending.*
CRITICAL: MAKING JUDGMENTS
2. *He believes the space program wastes taxpayers' money, which should be spent to solve problems where they live.*
LITERAL: NOTING IMPORTANT DETAILS
3. *because of the decline in his grades*
LITERAL: RECOGNIZING CAUSE-EFFECT
4. *Accept reasonable responses: The author refers to the airlock outside Jhanni's home, the dust storms, the light buckle and heater in his belt; the alien's need for oxygen and the reference to Houston are strong clues that the alien is from Earth.*
METACOGNITIVE: SYNTHESIZING

---

8 WRITE
You may want to suggest that students begin by listing questions that start with the following words: *who, what, when, where, why,* and *how.*

Accept reasonable responses. Students should try to imagine themselves in each character's place.
CREATIVE: SPECULATING

WRITER'S JOURNAL pages 102–

103: Writing a creative response

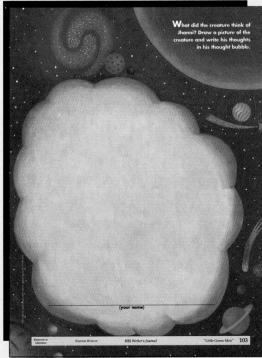

Writer's Journal

LOOKING FOR E. T.

by Larry Kelsey and Darrel Hoff

LARRY KELSEY and **DARREL HOFF** teach astronomy in the Department of Earth Sciences at the University of Northern Iowa in Cedar Falls, Iowa. This selection is an excerpt from their book *Recent Revolutions in Astronomy*. The book presents complex scientific ideas in an organized, simplified format for laypersons.

OTHER BOOKS ABOUT SPACE

Astronomy by Dennis B. Fradin. Children's Press, 1987.
 AVERAGE

The Boy Who Reversed Himself by William Sleator. Dutton, 1986. AVERAGE

Could You Ever Build a Time Machine? by David Darling. Macmillan, 1991. AVERAGE

The Day We Walked on the Moon: A Photo History of Space Exploration by George Sullivan. Scholastic, 1990. AVERAGE

Radio Astronomy by Alan Nourse. Franklin Watts, 1989.
 CHALLENGING

Sweetwater by Laurence Yep. HarperCollins, 1973.
 AVERAGE

- **SELECTION SUMMARY**
- This nonfiction
- excerpt discusses
- ways in which the
- scientific community
- is studying whether
- there is other
- intelligent life in the
- universe. The findings
- of space probes
- indicate that our own
- Solar System seems
- unlikely to contain
- any other intelligent
- life. However, other
- space probes have
- been launched in
- hopes of contacting
- aliens beyond our
- Solar System. The
- selection points out
- that the existence of
- extraterrestrial life
- has not been proven.

LESSON PLANNER			
	Materials	**Integrated Curriculum**	**Meeting Individual Needs**
1 READING LITERATURE pp. 567B–577	Student Anthology pp. 568–577 Transparency 31 Second-Language Support Manual Practice Book p. 153 Integrated Spelling p. 75 Integrated Spelling T.E. pp. 98–99 Response Card 8: Written Conversation	Spelling Spelling Pretest Spelling-Vocabulary Connection (adjective suffixes: -able, -ible, -ous)	Second-Language Support Vocabulary 567C Strategic Reading 567D, 570 Cooperative Reading 568, 576
2 RESPONDING TO LITERATURE pp. 577A–577D	Writer's Journal p. 102 Practice Book pp. 154–155 Integrated Spelling p. 76 Integrated Spelling T.E. pp. 98–99	Vocabulary Workshop Reviewing Key Words Extending Vocabulary Writing About the Literature Speaking/Listening Spelling Review	Cooperative Learning 577B, 577C
3 LEARNING THROUGH LITERATURE pp. 577E–577J	Practice Book pp. 156–157	Math Science Social Studies Art/Literature Multicultural	Challenge 577E, 577F, 577G, 577H Cooperative Learning 577H

567A

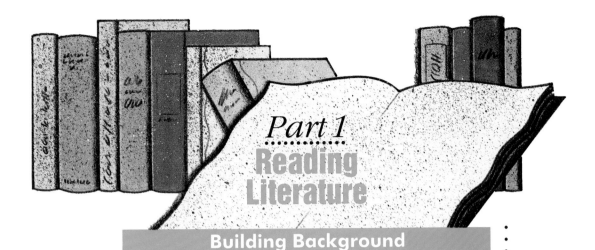

Part 1
Reading Literature

Building Background

Access prior knowledge and develop vocabulary concepts.

Tell students that they will be reading a nonfiction excerpt titled "Looking for E.T." Ask how many of them have seen the movie *E.T.*, and ask what it is about. Write the word *extraterrestrial* on the board, and give its meaning. ("beyond the Earth" or "an alien creature not of this Earth") Have students list on the board ways scientists might search for extraterrestrials.

Looking for Extraterrestrials

1. send robots into space
2. send humans into space
3. take photos of planets
4. listen for radio messages from space
5. look for signs of UFOs on Earth

Have students quickwrite a paragraph.

Have students quickly write a brief paragraph about the possibility of other intelligent life in the universe. Ask volunteers to share their writing.

Vocabulary Strategies

Introduce Key Words and strategies.

Tell students that they may come across unfamiliar words in "Looking for E.T." Display Transparency 31, or write the following paragraph on the board. Have students silently read it, using context clues, phonics, and structural analysis to decode each underlined word and to figure out its meaning. As a volunteer reads the paragraph aloud, help with pronunciation.

Transparency 31   Key Words

Science fiction writers hypothesize about the existence of extraterrestrial life. They argue that another planet could be an abode for aliens. Some write of aliens visiting Earth, citing manifestations that people claim to have seen. But scientists think such sightings are improbable, not likely to be accurate. Pessimistic about life "out there," they argue that such phenomena are seldom seen clearly and remain ambiguous, and often proving to be hoaxes by practical jokers.

KEY WORDS DEFINED

hypothesize to propose an idea that seems a true explanation

extraterrestrial from outside Earth's atmosphere

abode dwelling place

manifestations signs or evidence of something

improbable not likely

pessimistic not hopeful

phenomena occurrences observed by the senses

ambiguous having more than one possible meaning

hoaxes tricks, deceptions

Check students'
understanding.

Have students select the vocabulary word that is a synonym for each pair of words. STRATEGY: SYNONYMS

1. *home, dwelling, ____ (abode)*
2. *uncertain, unclear, ____ (ambiguous)*
3. *evidence, signs, ____ (manifestations)*
4. *deceptions, tricks, ____ (hoaxes)*
5. *events, occurrences, ____ (phenomena)*
6. *doubtful, unlikely, ____ (improbable)*
7. *propose, speculate, ____ (hypothesize)*
8. *unearthly, alien, ____ (extraterrestrial)*
9. *hopeless, gloomy, ____ (pessimistic)*

Integrate spelling
with vocabulary.

SPELLING-VOCABULARY CONNECTION *Integrated Spelling* page 75 reinforces spellings of words with the **adjective suffixes -able, -ible,** and **-ous,** including the following Key Words: *ambiguous, improbable.* The spelling of the Key Word *phenomena* is also included.

• • • LOOKING FOR E.T. • • •

Name _____

Read the sentences. Decide on the correct meaning of each underlined word. Circle the letter in front of the correct answer.

1. In old-fashioned novels, people often referred to where they lived as their abode.
   (a.) home   b. school   c. bedroom   d. walls of mud and straw

2. People in authority often show manifestations of their power by making rules and expecting everyone to obey them.
   a. reversals   b. tricks   c. mistakes   (d.) evidence

3. If you are unsure about something and the meaning is ambiguous, you should ask for help.
   a. long   b. clear   (c.) unclear   d. scary

4. Today, young people seem to be enthralled by stories of outer space and extraterrestrial beings.
   a. underwater   (b.) not of Earth   c. of the ground   d. above ground

5. Because of advances in science and technology, what were once considered strange phenomena are now easily explained.
   a. languages   b. creatures   (c.) events   d. sounds

6. We no longer hypothesize about every strange thing that happens; we can go to a book and find out the answer.
   a. imaging   b. cry out   c. picture   (d.) guess

7. I am no longer pessimistic about the state of the universe; I have much more hope for the future.
   (a.) worried   b. excited   c. encouraging   d. quiet

8. Although it is not impossible that great changes will happen in the next few years, it is improbable.
   a. sure thing   (b.) unlikely   c. likely   d. possible

9. In all areas of life, people should be on guard against hoaxes and should concentrate on important matters.
   a. balancing acts   b. special events   c. songs   (d.) tricks

Practice Book • ENDLESS WORLDS   Vocabulary   153

Practice Book

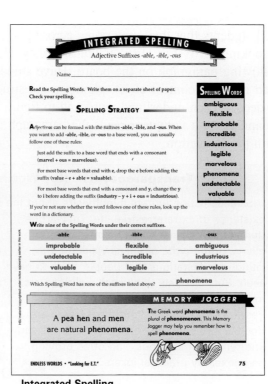

INTEGRATED SPELLING
Adjective Suffixes *-able, -ible, -ous*

Name _____

Read the Spelling Words. Write them on a separate sheet of paper. Check your spelling.

— SPELLING STRATEGY —

Adjectives can be formed with the suffixes *-able, -ible,* and *-ous.* When you want to add *-able, -ible,* or *-ous* to a base word, you can usually follow one of these rules:

Just add the suffix to a base word that ends with a consonant (**marvel + ous = marvelous**).

For most base words that end with **e**, drop the **e** before adding the suffix (**value – e + able = valuable**).

For most base words that end with a consonant and **y**, change the **y** to **i** before adding the suffix (**industry – y + i + ous = industrious**).

If you're not sure whether the word follows one of these rules, look up the word in a dictionary.

Write nine of the Spelling Words under their correct suffixes.

-able	-ible	-ous
improbable	flexible	ambiguous
undetectable	incredible	industrious
valuable	legible	marvelous

Which Spelling Word has none of the suffixes listed above? ____ phenomena

SPELLING WORDS
ambiguous
flexible
improbable
incredible
industrious
legible
marvelous
phenomena
undetectable
valuable

MEMORY JOGGER

A **pea hen** and **men** are natural **phenomena.**

The Greek word **phenomena** is the plural of **phenomenon**. This Memory Jogger may help you remember how to spell **phenomena.**

ENDLESS WORLDS • "Looking for E.T."   75

Integrated Spelling

Using the SQ3R Strategy

Review the SQ3R strategy.

Draw a chart like the following on the board:

SQ3R CHART

S—Survey *"Looking for E.T." is about how scientists are working to discover whether intelligent life exists beyond Earth.*		
Q—Question *Might life exist on other planets in our Solar System?*	**Predicted Answer**	**R—Read**
What have scientists learned about other planetary systems?		
R—Recite		**R—Review**

Ask volunteers to explain how to use the SQ3R strategy. (*S*—Survey to get an idea of the article's content; *Q*—Use the headings to form questions and predict the answers; *R*—Read to find the answers; *R*—Recite the answers from memory; *R*—Review by rereading the headings to see if you remember the answers to your questions.)

Help students preview the selection.

Encourage students to survey the excerpt by looking at the illustrations and by reading the title of the excerpt, the title of the book from which it came, the introduction, and the section headings. Invite discussion of what students learned from the survey.

Next, ask volunteers to suggest ways of turning the first heading into a question, and have them predict the answer. Then have students turn the other headings into questions and predict the answers.

PERSONAL JOURNAL Have students start a chart by copying a short form of the first three SQ3R headings and their questions into their personal journals, or have them use *Practice Book* page 154. (See page 577B in this Teacher's Edition.) Have students complete the chart as they read the excerpt or afterward. (Students will return to the chart after reading, in Summarizing the Literature.)

Setting a Purpose

Have students set purposes.

Remind students to use the questions they have written on their SQ3R charts to set a purpose for reading the selection. Suggest that as they read they take notes about the answers to their questions in the *R—Read* column of their chart.

OPTIONS FOR READING

Independent Reading
Have students read the selection silently with their purpose for reading in mind.

Guided Reading
Follow the Guided Reading suggestions that appear on pages 568, 570–571, and 576. These suggestions model strategic reading.

Cooperative Reading
Reader response strategies appear on pages 568 and 576.

Numbered Annotations
Use the numbered annotations beside the Student Anthology pages to heighten students' appreciation of the selection.

The earliest astronomers—from Native Americans to Egyptians to Greeks—studied the night sky and speculated about life on other planets. None had the technological ability to prove if life existed elsewhere. Eventually, the invention of the telescope made the study of objects in space easier. Then, in 1877, Giovanni Schiaparelli, an amateur astronomer, claimed that the faint lines he saw on Mars ("canali," or grooves) proved there was life there. This was the beginning of the search for further evidence.

Guided Reading

SET PURPOSE/PREDICT: PAGES 568–571 Have students read through the end of page 571 to learn what is known about the possibility of life on other planets in our Solar System.

Cooperative Reading

READER RESPONSE STRATEGY: PAGES 568–577 Have students work in pairs. Ask each student to read pages 568–577 silently and then use the written conversation strategy. (Response Card 8: Written Conversation, on page R69, gives complete directions for using this strategy.)

1. Each student writes a comment and a question.
2. Students pass their papers to their partners.
3. Each student writes the answer, adds a question, and passes the paper back.
4. Each student answers the new question.

LOOKING FOR E.T.

from
RECENT REVOLUTIONS IN ASTRONOMY
by Larry Kelsey and Darrel Hoff

1 LITERARY FORMS: EXPOSITORY NONFICTION
How do you know that this selection is nonfiction, even though the title might suggest fiction?
(Students should note that the source of the selection, Recent Revolutions in Astronomy, *and the style of the first section, the questions it raises, and its heading clearly mark this as nonfiction. No elements of fiction appear.)*
METACOGNITIVE: SYNTHESIZING

For several million years, our ancestors have looked upward, wondering about the nature of the lights visible in the night sky. Gradually, during the last 2,000 years, we have come to understand that we are looking at planets, stars, galaxies, and other objects in the heavens. But with this understanding has come a new question: Are we alone? Do intelligent creatures exist on those planets, near those stars, or within those galaxies?

This is a question that we finally have the ability to try to answer. A growing number of scientists are working on the problem in a variety of ways.

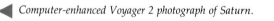

Our Solar System

We began the search by looking in our own backyard—the other planets and moons of our Solar System. All scientists agree that the most similar environment to Earth (within our Solar System) is found on Mars. It may not be the best place to spend a summer vacation, but with a little fixing up, human beings could live there.

Viking 1 and 2 were sent to Mars in 1976 to look for possible life. Although no obvious life forms were photographed, life still might exist in the form of microorganisms in the soil, or traces of previous life might be detected. As a result, a series of experiments involving Martian soil, water, and nutrients was performed.

False-color closeup of the B and C rings of Saturn

◀ *Computer-enhanced Voyager 2 photograph of Saturn.*

569

Informal Assessment You can informally assess whether your students understand the authors' viewpoint and can identify the authors' purpose for writing nonfiction. On occasion, ask questions like these:

- Why did the authors write this selection? What do they think about this topic? What about the excerpt makes you think this was the authors' purpose?
- How well do the authors succeed in fulfilling this purpose? Is there anything else the authors should have done or told?

Teaching Tip You may want to supply additional information about *Viking 1* and 2 (last paragraph). Both were U.S. space probes. *Viking 1* was launched August 20, 1975, and landed on Mars on July 20, 1976. Though it was designed to operate only ninety days, it relayed photos and other information about the planet for almost six and a half years before going silent in November 1982. *Viking 2* was launched September 9, 1975, and landed September 3, 1976. It functioned for three and a half years.

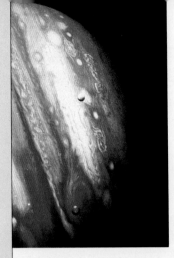
Voyager I approaches Jupiter with Moons Io and Callisto in foreground.

Today, most scientists agree that the *Viking* spacecraft detected no signs of life on Mars, though it did find some unusual soil chemistry. This does not mean that life does not or did not exist anywhere on Mars. But it makes us rather pessimistic. Our best candidate for life within the Solar System seems unpromising.

Some scientists claim that we have only scratched the surface. Carl Sagan[1] points to the clouds of Jupiter as a possible abode for airborne life. The famous British astronomer Fred Hoyle claims that the cores of comets might be warm enough to melt, creating lakes in which simple life might exist. Other scientists want to examine the oceans of Jupiter's moon Europa or Saturn's moon Titan for possible life.

2 Though these places, and others, are worthy of consideration, it is becoming apparent that any life found elsewhere in our Solar System is likely to be simple life—not intelligent. What about life on objects beyond our Solar System?

[1]Carl Sagan: U.S. astronomer, author, and educator

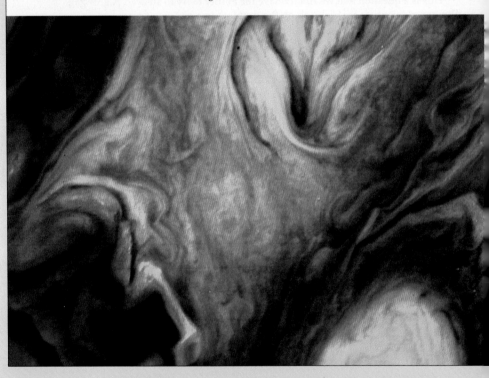

Other Planetary Systems

Astronomers have been hunting for planets orbiting other stars for more than a century. Unfortunately, they have met with little success. The reason can be seen from the following.

Pluto, the farthest known planet, is visible only when viewed through a large telescope under normal conditions. The nearest stars are tens of thousands of times farther away than Pluto. **3** Imagine the difficulty of looking for a faint planet at these distances, especially when a fairly bright star is close to the planet and you are looking through our own shimmering atmosphere. With current ground-based telescopes, catching a view of planets in another star system is impossible.

However, there are other ways to search. The American astronomer Peter van de Kamp announced after a decade-long study of several nearby stars that a few show a wobble in their motions as they move through space. This could be caused by orbiting planets. Although his findings have been questioned, other astronomers have been encouraged to seek new methods to detect planets.

The infrared satellite IRAS has located several nearby stars surrounded by infrared emission.[2] Astronomers believe that this emission comes from dust and gas clouds that surround these stars. These clouds are material left over from the star's formation. Astronomers <u>hypothesize</u> that such clouds will form (or in some cases have already formed) planetary systems.

A group of astronomers at the University of Arizona used a new technique to carefully search the area around the nearby star Beta Pictoris in 1984. They discovered a disk of material seen nearly edge-on. They believe this is dust left over after planets formed around Beta Pictoris.

It is beginning to appear that other stars (perhaps many other stars) have planetary systems. If this is so, we have our possible abodes for life. But how might we detect such possible life?

---

[2]Infrared emissions cannot be detected by the human eye.

◀ *Closeup of Jupiter's cloud movement.*

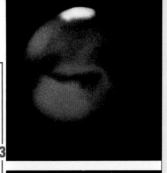

Top right, Ground-based telescope photo of Mars. Center, A part of the Milky Way in the constellation Aquila. Bottom right, Artist's impression of the Planet Pluto and its moon Charon.

571

3 EXPOSITORY TEXT: CAUSE-EFFECT
Why is it difficult to see planets in other star systems through ground-based telescopes? *(The other star systems are very far away, and their planets are faint. Nearby bright stars and our own shimmering atmosphere block them out.)*
INFERENTIAL: SUMMARIZING

According to the authors, what evidence have scientists found that suggests other star systems might have planets? (stars that show a wobble, stars surrounded by infrared emissions, a disk that may be made of dust around Beta Pictoris)
STRATEGIC READING: SUMMARIZING

SET PURPOSE/PREDICT: PAGES 572–577 The question at the bottom of this page, together with the heading at the top of page 573, suggests a purpose for reading the next section. Have students state this purpose for reading as a question. (Accept reasonable responses: "How can we probe space for other planets and for possible life?")

572

Vocabulary Strategy   Point out the abbreviation *IRAS* in the fourth paragraph of page 571. Ask students to use context clues to help them figure out what the letters might stand for. *(Infrared Astronomical Satellite)* STRATEGY: CONTEXT CLUES/EXPLANATION

Space Probes?

Space is a big place. Sending a space probe out into this dark ocean is a lot like dropping a note in a bottle into the sea. The fastest space probe we have ever launched was the *Pioneer 10* probe in 1972, and seventeen years were needed for it to reach the orbit of Pluto. To reach even the nearest of stars would take tens of thousands of years.

Yet scientists did attach messages to *Pioneer 10* and its sister probe *Pioneer 11*. The small plaques, which look like metal postcards, show a man and woman standing in front of a drawing of the spacecraft. There is also a drawing of our Solar System and some data about where we are located and when the probe was launched.

Five years later, the messages placed on the *Voyager 1* and *2* probes were a bit more sophisticated. Each contained a gold video disk along with instructions on how to use it to reproduce the sights and sounds of earth.

In all likelihood the spacecraft and their messages will never be found by aliens. If anyone does find them, it may be our own descendants overtaking them as they journey outward. (Remember the movie *Star Trek I—The Motion Picture*?) Perhaps the craft and plaque will wind up in some twenty-fourth-century museum as relics of a nearly forgotten past.

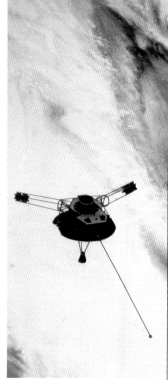

Artist's conception of Pioneer 10 and Jupiter

Interstellar Travel

A better way to contact extraterrestrial life may be for humans to make the journey themselves. Here there are two options: a slow, inexpensive trip, or a quick, expensive trip.

The slow, inexpensive option would involve launching a traveling space colony. (Here we use the term "inexpensive" to refer to the fuel requirements. In truth, the undertaking would be financially quite expensive.) A huge starship, containing hundreds if not thousands of people, would be launched on a leisurely flight toward Alpha Centauri. At 30 miles per second (50 kilometers per second), the escape velocity for our Solar System, the trip would take about 27,000 years. Obviously, the people who began the journey would not arrive at their destination,

p. 572 Top, Voyager Spacecraft

Bottom, Jupiter with moons

573

4 FIGURATIVE LANGUAGE
What point are the authors making by comparing sending out a space probe with dropping a note in a bottle into the sea? *(that the chances are slim that something so small would ever be discovered in such a vast space)*
INFERENTIAL: MAKING COMPARISONS

5 EXPOSITORY TEXT: MAIN IDEA
What was the purpose of sending the messages carried by the space probes? *(The messages were designed to give information about our planet to whoever might find them.)*
INFERENTIAL: DETERMINING MAIN IDEA

6 AUTHORS' VIEWPOINT
How optimistic do you think the authors are about the chances of the slow, inexpensive option's success? Explain your answer. *(Not very; they emphasize the time the trip would take and hint at the problems involved.)*
METACOGNITIVE: DRAWING CONCLUSIONS

Vocabulary Strategy Help students determine the meaning of *interstellar* (second heading) by analyzing its parts: *inter-* means "between," and *-stellar* means "having to do with stars." Interstellar travel is travel between stars. STRATEGY: STRUCTURAL ANALYSIS

How optimistic do the authors seem about the possibility of a quick, expensive probe of other star systems? How can you tell? *(Not very; they say it will remain "an invention of science fiction for the foreseeable future," and they mention problems of lethal radiation.)*

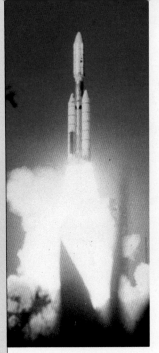

Jupiter liftoff

Voyager I composite image of Saturn and six of its moons superimposed on a painted starry sky background

574

but their descendants just might—that is, if all the engineering and social problems along the way could be solved.

The other option, that of a quick flight, would be unbelievably expensive in terms of the energy required. The quickest way to get from one place to another is to accelerate halfway there and to decelerate the last halfway. This is like saying the quickest way to get from one stoplight to the next is to "floor" the accelerator and then jam on the brakes as you get to your stop.

Suppose we accelerate a small spaceship at 32 feet per second per second (9.8 meters per second per second) toward Alpha Centauri. Its maximum velocity would be about 90 percent of the speed of light. Halfway there we begin decelerating by the same amount. We could make the round trip within a person's lifetime, but the amount of fuel required would be enormous. Such a journey probably will remain an invention of science fiction for the foreseeable future. Another problem is gamma and X-ray radiation[3] created by the impact of the spaceship with interstellar gas at greater than half the speed of light. Their radiation is lethal.

[3]Gamma and X-ray radiation are undetectable by humans.

Oral Rereading Have students reread a part of the selection that they may initially have found confusing or difficult to understand, perhaps the one on interstellar travel (pages 573–574). Suggest that they reread it silently to identify the main ideas and supporting details and to make certain they clearly understand it. Encourage them to rehearse their reading aloud with a partner, emphasizing the main ideas they want the partner to remember.

Searching by Radio

Perhaps the best, if not the only, option we have for finding life elsewhere is something we are already trying—looking by radio. We have been listening to the stars for more than half a century. Although we have learned a lot about the universe, so far we have not overheard anyone from another world.

More than a dozen studies have been made since the first modern attempt in 1960 by the American astronomer Frank Drake, who pointed an 86-foot (26-meter) radio dish in Green Bank, West Virginia, toward two nearby stars for 150 hours. Although these searches have failed, only a few hundred stars have been examined. The problem is not only picking the right star, but also finding the right radio frequency and the right time. The negative findings are not too surprising.

Although it is more practical for us to listen for signals than to send them (for the same reason that it is cheaper to make a **8** radio receiver than to build a radio station), occasionally radio signals have been beamed to the stars. One time was in 1974 when the huge radio telescope in Arecibo, Puerto Rico, was resurfaced to improve its sensitivity. At that time, a powerful signal was beamed toward the globular cluster of stars (M13) in the constellation Hercules. The message was a series of dots and dashes that could be reconstructed into a picture. It showed the human form, the DNA molecule, the Solar System, the radio dish, and other data.

If anyone out there was listening, they might have noticed a three-minute blast of radio energy containing the message coming from our area of the sky. But we'll have to be patient for any possible reply: the cluster is 24,000 light-years away. That means that if we do get an answer, it should be about the year A.D. 0,000.

Martian sunset, computer-enhanced, taken by Viking I

Callisto taken from 1,438,000 miles

575

*Comet West, showing its
dust trail (white)
and its gas trail (blue)*

*False-color image of
the Pleiades*

9 EXPOSITORY TEXT: MAIN IDEA
**Which sentence states the main
idea of the authors' argument about
UFOs?** (The scientific community is
solidly in favor of the view that
there is no good evidence that UFOs
are extraterrestrial spacecraft.)
LITERAL: RECOGNIZING MAIN IDEA

Has E.T. Already Been Here?

The subject of UFOs is one that tends to polarize people.
Either you believe they represent visits by extraterrestrials or
you believe they are hoaxes or misidentified natural or human-
made phenomena. Few people have no opinion on the subject.

The scientific community is solidly in favor of the view that
there is no good evidence that UFOs are extraterrestrial spacecraft. This is not to say that these same scientists do not believe
in the likelihood of extraterrestrials. Many insist that the universe is so vast that it seems highly improbable that we are the
only intelligent species that exists.

All too often, UFO reports can be readily attributed to bright
stars, meteors, clouds, ball lightning, flocks of birds, helicopters,
balloons, or satellites, to name a few phenomena. The few cases
that do not fall into these categories usually happen in peculiar
circumstances. They never occur in broad daylight with
hundreds of witnesses. Usually there are only one or two observers in poor lighting, and the only proof is an ambiguous
photograph.

It seems incredible that among the one group of people
trained to observe the skies, there has never been a reported
sighting of an alien spacecraft. Thousands of professional and
amateur astronomers study the heavens each night without any
such sightings. Thousands of amateur radio operators are constantly scanning all radio frequencies 24 hours a day. They have

576

Cooperative Reading

READER RESPONSE STRATEGY: PAGES 568–577
Have pairs discuss the selection by asking questions
such as these:

- Do you agree with the authors about the
likelihood of extraterrestrial beings? Explain your
answer.
- What are the most important ideas in this
selection? Explain your answer.

(Response Card 8: Written Conversation, on page
R69, offers a wide variety of questions.)

Guided Reading

MONITOR COMPREHENSION: PAGES 572–577
How have we probed for life in space? (We have
sent probes to take pictures and carry messages,
beamed radio messages, and listened for radio
signals.) STRATEGIC READING: RETURNING TO
PURPOSE

**How do the authors support their view about
UFOs?** (They argue that the "evidence" for UFOs
is ambiguous and unscientific.) STRATEGIC
READING: SUMMARIZING

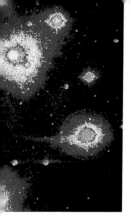

The Orion Nebula

heard nothing from an extraterrestrial spacecraft. This strongly argues that UFOs are not the products or <u>manifestations</u> of extraterrestrial intelligence.

The universe is a huge and marvelous place. Events considered part of the realm of fantasy a generation ago are being witnessed today; objects unimaginable then have become accepted as reality today. As yet, however, extraterrestrial life has not been found.

THINK IT OVER

1. *Summarize the reasons given in the selection to show that extraterrestrial life does not exist.*
2. *Where in our Solar System is the environment most similar to Earth's?*
3. *How long would it take a space colony to reach Alpha Centauri?*
4. *Summarize the attempts that have been made to determine if intelligent creatures exist somewhere other than Earth.*
5. *List several reasons why it is unlikely that extraterrestrials have visited Earth.*

10

WRITE

Describe a starship that could be used as a space colony to Alpha Centauri.

11

577

10 THINK IT OVER
1. *No obvious life forms have been found on any planet or in its surrounding atmosphere by satellites or space probes. We have received no answers to any messages we have sent through space. Most UFO reports are found to be related to natural phenomena.*
INFERENTIAL: SUMMARIZING
2. *on Mars*
LITERAL: NOTING IMPORTANT DETAILS
3. *27,000 years, for a slow trip; less than a person's lifetime, for a quick trip*
LITERAL: NOTING IMPORTANT DETAILS
4. *Searches have been made with large telescopes, with satellites, and with remote-controlled space probes. Radio dishes have been set to receive transmissions from outer space.*
INFERENTIAL: SUMMARIZING
5. *No report of a UFO has been proven to be true. Trained observers have never sighted an alien spacecraft. Amateur radio operators have heard nothing.*
INFERENTIAL: DRAWING CONCLUSIONS

11 WRITE
To help students get started, you may want to suggest a prewriting list such as the following:

Relocation to Alpha Centauri
1. Trip will take _____ years.
2. Problems to be accounted for during trip:

   food supplies   recreation
   living quarters   medical facilities
   sanitation   water

Accept reasonable responses. Students should account for both the physical and the mental needs of the space travelers.
CREATIVE: VISUALIZING

NOTE Additional writing activities appear on page 577D.

Returning to the Predictions Invite students to discuss the predictions they made in response to the questions on the SQ3R chart before reading and that they may have written in their personal journals. Encourage them to talk about whether their predictions changed as they read the selection.

Returning to the Purpose for Reading students exchange SQ3R charts with classmates in order to check the answers they wrote in the *R—Read* column.

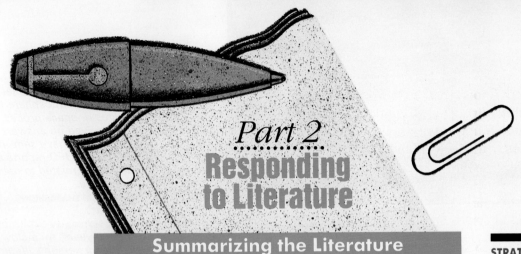

Part 2
Responding to Literature

Summarizing the Literature

Have students retell the selection and write a summary.

Invite students to summarize the information in the selection, using the chart. If they have not yet completed the chart, have them do so now. (See *Practice Book* page 154, on 577B.) Students may use the completed chart to retell the selection and to write a brief summary statement.

SQ3R CHART

"Looking for E.T." is about how scientists are working to discover whether intelligent life exists beyond Earth.		
Q—Question Might life exist on other planets in our Solar System?	**Predicted Answer**	**R—Read** Viking 1 and 2 found no life on Mars. Any life elsewhere in our Solar System is likely to be simple.
What have scientists learned about other planetary systems?		The wobbly motion of some stars and the dust clouds around some stars suggest the presence of planets.
R—Recite		**R—Review**

Appreciating Literature

Have students share personal responses.

Divide students into small groups to discuss the selection. Provide a general question such as the following to help the groups get started:

- **What do you feel is the most important paragraph or passage in this excerpt? Explain.**

PERSONAL JOURNAL Encourage students to use their personal journals to write about ideas and feelings that are expressed in the groups. You may also wish to refer students to their personal journals after they complete the Critical Thinking Activities.

STRATEGY CONFERENCE

Discuss the chart, asking students how it helped make the selection's information clearer. Encourage students to tell other reading strategies they used, such as noting main ideas and important details.

INFORMAL ASSESSMENT

Having students summarize in this way will help you informally assess how well they comprehended the **main idea** of each section of the selection. It also will help you see how well they recognized the **importance of particular details** in contributing to each main idea.

Encourage both cooperative and individual responses.

DISCUSS COSTS AND BENEFITS Do you think the expense involved in continuing to probe the universe for signs of intelligent life is justified? Explain your answers. Encourage students to work in small groups to weigh the possible advantages of space exploration against its costs. Have each group elect one member to present its opinion and its supporting reasons. CRITICAL: EXPRESSING PERSONAL OPINIONS

DISCUSS A HYPOTHETICAL JOURNEY Would you volunteer to join a space colony traveling to a distant star system, knowing that you would not live to see the final destination? Explain your answer. Encourage small groups of students to discuss how the rewards and demands of such a journey would fit their own values. Tell them to consider whether they would be adventurous, tolerant, optimistic, and future-oriented enough to endure such a journey and whether they would consider the purpose worthwhile. CRITICAL: MAKING JUDGMENTS

DESIGN A PLAQUE What would you put on a plaque that is being sent to the stars? Invite students to design a plaque to let civilizations on other planets know about Earth and the people who live here. First, have them review the content of other messages that have been sent to the stars; then, encourage them to be original in their designs. CREATIVE: SOLVING PROBLEMS

Writer's Journal

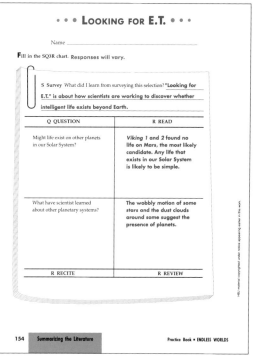

Practice Book

WRITER'S JOURNAL

page 104: Writing a creative response

PRACTICE BOOK

page 154: Summarizing the selection

VO·CAB·U·LAR·Y Workshop

Reviewing Key Words

To review how the new vocabulary was used in this selection, display the Key Words, and have students answer the following questions orally or in writing:

1. *pessimistic* **Because space probes have found no trace of other intelligent life in the universe, should people be pessimistic about the possibility?** *(Accept reasonable responses: Yes, this proves there is life only on Earth; no, space probes are too limited, so we can still hope to find life elsewhere.)*

2. *abode* **What kind of abode might a person live in?** *(Accept reasonable responses: a house, an apartment.)*

3. *hypothesize* **Can scientists accurately hypothesize what an alien might look like?** *(no, since none have ever been seen)*

4. *extraterrestrial* **Where would extraterrestrial life come from?** *(from outer space, beyond our Solar System)*

5. *hoaxes* **Some UFO sightings are hoaxes. Why might people report such a sighting?** *(to attract attention to themselves; to fool the public; because they were fooled by the hoax)*

6. *phenomena* **Give examples of natural phenomena.** *(Accept reasonable responses: thunder, lightning, earthquakes, rainbows.)*

7. *improbable* **Give an example of an improbable situation.** *(Accept reasonable responses.)*

8. *ambiguous* **Why are UFO sightings ambiguous evidence that extraterrestrial life exists?** *(UFO sightings have usually been disproved. No trained observers have ever seen a UFO.)*

9. *manifestations* **What would you consider unmistakable manifestations of extraterrestrial life?** *(Accept reasonable responses.)*

Extending Vocabulary

ACRONYMS Remind students of the abbreviation *IRAS* in the selection (page 571). Point out that this type of abbreviation can be read as a word. Such words are known as acronyms; other acronyms include *radar* (*r*adio *d*etecting *and r*anging), and *sonar* (*s*ound *n*avigation *and r*anging).

COOPERATIVE LEARNING Have small groups of students look up the meaning of each of these acronyms: *NASA, ROM, RAM, NATO, NOW, UNICEF, GIGO, laser*. Have groups classify the terms as the names of organizations or as computer and science terms.

PRACTICE BOOK
page 155: Identifying acronyms

• • • LOOKING FOR E.T. • • •

Name _____

A. Read the following paragraph. Pay attention to the acronyms and abbreviations. Then list each, along with its meaning, under the appropriate heading on the chart.

Although the first minicomputer was introduced in 1965, computer technology exploded in the 1980s. Disks were introduced that permanently store data so that it cannot be erased. These disks (called WORMs, for "write once, read many") can be used in library archives and anyplace else where one wants to be sure the data remains unchanged. As ICs, or integrated circuits, became more dense and CPUs (central processing units) smaller, laptops, or small portable computers, became available and computers became more powerful and faster. Computer users might have become faster too if computers had switched to a newly designed keyboard, but so many people had learned to type on the qwerty keyboard that computer companies chose not to change it. Computers, like CD players, VCRs and many other innovations of the 1970s and '80s are destined to be used extensively in the next century, not only in the United States and the EEC (European Economic Community), but throughout the world.

Abbreviations	Acronyms
ICs integrated circuits	WORMS write once, read many
CPU Central Processing Unit	QWERTY the first 5 letters on a
CD compact discs	standard keyboard
EEC European Economic Community	

B. Select four acronyms or abbreviations from the paragraph. Use each one in a sentence.

1. Answers will vary.
2. _____
3. _____
4. _____

Practice Book ■ ENDLESS WORLDS   Abbreviations and Acronyms   **155**

Practice Book

Integrated Language Arts

Writing About the Literature

AVAILABLE ON PROJECT CARD

CREATIVE: POEM Invite students to write a short poem about exploring for extraterrestrial life in space. Urge them to use figurative language. Suggest they use a chart to create similes or metaphors.

Object	Quality	Compare to
moon	shimmering	white satin

You may wish to have students illustrate their poems. WRITING

CRITICAL: LETTERS TO THE EDITOR Have students imagine that "Looking for E.T." appeared in their local paper. Have them write a letter to the editor praising or criticizing it. Remind them to cite specific examples from the excerpt to support their opinions.
READING/WRITING

NOTE: An additional writing activity appears on page 577.

SPEAKING/LISTENING

Viking, Pioneer, Voyager

Have students work in groups to prepare a discussion on the findings of the *Viking*, *Pioneer*, and *Voyager* explorations. Ask groups to use photos taken by these probes as well as their own visual aids. LISTENING/SPEAKING/READING/WRITING

SPELLING

Spelling Review

SPELLING WORDS: *ambiguous, flexible, improbable, incredible, industrious, legible, marvelous, phenomena, undetectable, valuable*

Have students write the Spelling Words as you dictate them. Then have a volunteer write them on the board. Have students read each word aloud in unison, listening for the adjective suffix *-able*, *-ible*, or *-ous* in nine of the words. Have another volunteer circle each adjective suffix. LISTENING/WRITING/SPELLING

INTEGRATED SPELLING

page 76: Writing words with the adjective suffixes *-able*, *-ible*, *-ous*

INTEGRATED SPELLING

Adjective Suffixes *-able, -ible, -ous*

Name _____

WORD PLAY

Find and underline the two words from the Word Bank in this newspaper headline:

INDUSTRIOUS LAWYER FIGHTS AMBIGUOUS LAW

Now write three serious or silly headlines of your own. Use at least two words from the Word Bank in each one.

Answers will vary.

WORD BANK

ambiguous
flexible
improbable
incredible
industrious
legible
marvelous
phenomena
undetectable
valuable

SPELLING DETECTIVE

John really enjoyed "Looking for E.T." He thought it might be fun to write his own message to aliens from another planet. John wrote his message quickly. When he proofread it, he found five errors. Find each error and circle it. Write the word correctly above the misspelled word.

Hello! I'm John Khakuo, from Earth. I
marvelous
think it would be *marvelus* to meet someone from
improbable
another planet. Now, this might be an *improbible*
incredible
event, but it would be *incredible* if it happened!
If you can come to see me, I think we'd learn
valuable
some *valueable* information about each other.
flexible
I'm pretty *flexoble* about where you land, as
long as you're somewhere near Chicago.

76

"Looking for E.T." • ENDLESS WORLDS

Integrated Spelling

STUDY SKILLS
REVIEW

Note-Taking Strategies

OBJECTIVE: *To use note-taking skills to recall information*

Review

Have students review the note-taking process.

Remind students that taking notes is a very useful way to remember the main ideas and important details in nonfiction. Have students recall the steps in the note-taking process. Then model the note-taking process for the first two paragraphs on page 571 of the selection.

> **I write the heading *Other Planetary Systems*. Then I jot down these phrases:**
> *scientists looking for 100+ yrs*
> *little success because stars too far away*
> *Earth telescopes not strong enough*

Practice/Apply

Have students take notes.

Ask students to choose a section of the selection and to take notes on it. Then encourage them to discuss main ideas and important details, as well as any symbols or abbreviations they used.

Summarize

Informally assess the learning.

Check students' understanding by having them summarize what they learned. (Note-taking can help readers remember important information in nonfiction.)

CHALLENGE Have students practice note-taking with a science or a social studies chapter on a topic of their choice. Then have them give a short oral summary of the chapter, using only the notes they took.

Reading Rate and Method

OBJECTIVE: *To identify how and when to adjust reading rates and methods*

Review

Have students review the concept of adjusting reading rates.

Ask students how knowing that "Looking for E.T." is an informational excerpt helps them determine how fast to read it. (Since an informational selection may include technical details, reading slowly is best for comprehension.) Model how to determine an appropriate reading rate.

> **I read fiction quickly because I'm not trying to remember every detail. I read nonfiction more slowly so that I can absorb main ideas and details. I stop occasionally to review and to reread passages I don't understand so I won't get confused and give up trying to follow what the authors are saying.**

Practice/Apply

Have students practice the strategy.

Have students reread sections of the selection, adjusting their reading rate and method as needed. Encourage them to determine which paragraphs may need rereading and to explain why.

Summarize

Informally assess the learning.

Check students' understanding by having them summarize what they reviewed. (Readers should vary their rate and method, depending on the kind of material being read.)

CHALLENGE Provide students with a selection of magazines. Have students peruse the articles, determining an appropriate reading rate and method for each. Ask that they give reasons for their decisions.

Summarizing/Generalizing

OBJECTIVE: *To review how to summarize a selection and how to generalize from that summary*

Review

Have students review summarizing and generalizing.

Remind students that after summarizing a selection, they can generalize; that is, make a broad statement that applies to many different situations. Model how to summarize and generalize:

> **My summary of the first section of the excerpt is that scientists hoped to find life on Mars but failed. My generalization is that scientists revise their ideas as new evidence becomes available.**

Practice/Apply

Have students generalize.

Have students summarize each section of the selection and then make a generalization about the section.

Summarize

Informally assess the learning.

Check understanding by having students summarize what they reviewed. (Summarizing a selection can help in forming a generalization.)

CHALLENGE Have students practice by summarizing a section of a science or social studies selection on a topic of their choice. Then have them make a generalization about that summary.

PRACTICE BOOK
page 156: Summarizing and generalizing

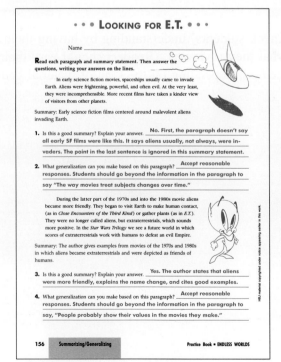

Practice Book

Test-Taking Strategies

OBJECTIVE: *To use strategies to improve test-taking performance*

Review

Have students review the concept of test-taking strategies.

Ask students what strategies can help them perform well on tests. (reading the directions thoroughly, looking for signal words, pacing) Model how you might pace yourself:

> **First, I read through a test quickly, answering those questions I know. Then, I divide the time I have left by the items I have left to answer. I spend *approximately* that amount of time on each unanswered item.**

Practice/Apply

Have students identify test-taking strategies.

COOPERATIVE LEARNING Have students discuss with a partner how they would apply test-taking strategies to a test from their math or social studies book.

Summarize

Informally assess the learning.

Have students summarize what they reviewed. (Test-taking strategies can help test-takers perform well.)

CHALLENGE Have students brainstorm problems they have faced when taking tests, such as running short on time or marking answers incorrectly. Then have students discuss how they would have solved those problems by using test-taking strategies.

PRACTICE BOOK
page 157: Identifying test-taking strategies

Practice Book

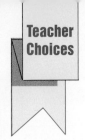

Integrated **Curriculum**

MATH

Star Trips

AVAILABLE ON PROJECT CARD

Invite students to research the distances from Earth to the ten nearest stars and to make a chart showing the distances in light-years. Then have them calculate how long it would take to reach each star if we could build spaceships that traveled at the speed of light, at one-tenth the speed of light, and at one-hundredth the speed of light. Divide students into teams to work cooperatively to solve the problems. LISTENING/SPEAKING/READING/WRITING

SCIENCE

The Martian Connection

Have students form small groups to research conditions on Mars and to design an underground colony that would allow humans to survive there. Instruct groups to take into account factors such as the temperature, the length of day and year, the atmosphere, and the resources on Mars. Some students might want to build a scale model of their colony; others may wish to draw a blueprint. LISTENING/SPEAKING/READING/WRITING

SOCIAL STUDIES

From Space to You

USE *READERS' GUIDE* The benefits from the U.S. space programs are many and varied. Encourage students to research the many conveniences as well as major changes that have become a part of our daily lives because of both the manned and the unmanned programs. Students can check the *Readers' Guide to Periodical Literature* and the card catalog and can also write to NASA for free information. Students can find out various NASA addresses at a library. Urge students to publish their discoveries in a book, citing the origins and uses of the things they learn about. READING/WRITING

ART/LITERATURE

Science Facts and Fiction

Invite students to research the novels and stories of science fiction pioneers such as Jules Verne, H. G. Wells, and Arthur C. Clarke to find out which of their imaginative ideas about future scientific advances later came true. Ask them also to identify imaginative ideas that have not yet proved true or that have turned out to be false. Students can present their findings on posters with the heading *Science Facts and Science Fiction*. READING/WRITING

Multi*Cultural*

PERSPECTIVES

Probing the Skies

READ ALOUD TO STUDENTS:

LONG BEFORE SPACECRAFT PHOTOGRAPHED VENUS AND MARS, ANCIENT CIVILIZATIONS WERE STUDYING THE STARS AND THE PLANETS.

The Maya, who developed an accurate 365-day calendar, built an observatory at Chichén-Itza, Mexico (inset). Stonehenge, built in England more than 3,500 years ago, probably served as an astronomical calendar.

Early Babylonian astronomers used the moon and the stars to develop a calendar and also identified many constellations, or patterns of stars, including some of the constellations of the zodiac. Later, Assyrian astronomers made close observations of the planets Venus, Jupiter, Saturn, and Mars, which they believed were stars of the great gods. They thought that the movement of these heavenly bodies influenced what happened on Earth. Their recordings of star and planet appearances were the first scientific study of astronomy.

The Africans in ancient Egpyt used shadow clocks, star clocks, and water clocks to determine divisions of the day and the year. They developed the 24-hour day and the 365-day year we still use to measure time. The Egyptian calendar begins on the day the Dog Star, Sirius, rises in line with the sun. It is also the day the Nile begins to rise each year. The Egyptians also used a "sun gate" to determine distance ratios from the earth to the sun and to other planets.

The Maya independently developed a 365-day calendar for the year, along with an elaborate ritual calendar of 260 days. Their day-count calendar, developed around A.D. 300, could fix dates going back to 3000 B.C. Astronomers of each culture used the instruments they had to explore the heavens and to mark the passage of time on Earth. ■

ACTIVITY CORNER

■ Have each student research an astronomical instrument, such as the Egyptian water clock, the Moorish astrolabe, or the Hubble telescope, and write a one-page report. Compile all the reports into a class book. Brainstorm as a group for an appropriate title for the book, and display it in the school library.

■ Like the ancient astronomers, the modern-day world is probing the mysteries of space. Ask students to imagine that they are scientists assigned to write a message that a space probe such as *Voyager* will carry into outer space. What would their message say?

LOOKING FOR E.T. / **577J**

The First

ABOUT THE POET

ABOUT THE POET

Lilian Moore has always considered herself a writer. As a child, she sat on a big metal box outside a local hardware store and told her friends stories. As an adult, she won the NCTE Excellence in Poetry for Children Award (1985).

1 PERSONIFICATION

In what way is the moon personified, or given human qualities, in this poem? *(The speaker addresses the moon as if it has memory ["remember"] and will ["you pulled"].)*
INFERENTIAL: MAKING COMPARISONS

2 IMAGERY

Why does the poet call the moon's dust "bleak"? *(Accept reasonable responses: It supports no life.)*
INFERENTIAL: DRAWING CONCLUSIONS

WRITER'S JOURNAL page 105: Writing a creative response

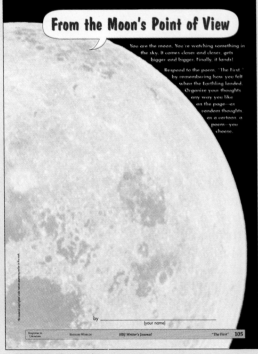

From the Moon's Point of View

You are the moon. You're watching something in the sky. It comes closer and closer, gets bigger and bigger. Finally, it lands!

Respond to the poem "The First" by remembering how you felt when the Earthling landed. Organize your thoughts any way you like — on the page — as random thoughts, as a cartoon, a poem — you choose.

by _____
[your name]

Response to
Literature ENDLESS WORLDS HBJ Writer's Journal "The First" 105

Writer's Journal

The First

by Lilian Moore

AWARD-WINNING
AUTHOR

1 Moon,
remember
how men left their
planet
in streams of
flame,
rode weightless
in the skies
till you pulled
them down,
and then
in the blinding sunlight
2 how the first shadow
of an
Earthling
lay
on your
bleak dust?

578

Reading the Poem

Read the poem aloud for students. Encourage them to listen to your pauses for commas and the rise in your voice for the question mark. Then invite volunteers to read the poem aloud.

Responding to the Poem

Invite students to imagine what the moon's response might be to the speaker's question about this brief but important moment in human history. Suggest that they write a poem about what the moon might say in response.

SPACE

"Little Green Men" and "Looking for E.T." tell about looking for intelligent life in space. Do you think such a search is worthwhile? Explain your answer.

· ·

In "Little Green Men" many people like Jhanni's father think it is foolish to look for creatures from other planets, but Jhanni and the Star Scouts keep on looking. Do you think the writer of "Looking for E.T." would agree more with Jhanni or his father? Give reasons for your answer.

· ·

WRITER'S WORKSHOP "Looking for E.T." and "Little Green Men" present different views about whether or not there is life on other planets. What do you think? Write an essay in which you try to convince someone that your opinion is the correct one.

579

Remind students that they have read a story and an article that address the question "Is there intelligent life in space?" Point out that one piece is science, while the other is science fiction. Discuss the different ways the two selections approach the question. Direct students to the activities on page 579 that will help them formulate some conclusions on the question of intelligent life in space.

Note that pages 579A–579B provide support for applying the writing process to the last question.

---

1 Ask students to weigh the arguments for and against looking for life in space in formulating their answers. *(Responses will vary.)*
CRITICAL: EXPRESSING PERSONAL OPINIONS

---

2 Have students first determine the viewpoint of the authors of "Looking for E.T." and then decide whether that viewpoint is closer to Jhanni's or to his father's. *(Accept reasonable responses: Like Jhanni's father, the authors of the article doubt that the search for life in space is worth the effort and expense.)*
INFERENTIAL: SYNTHESIZING

Writer's Workshop
See pages 579A–579B for suggestions for applying the writing process. Responses should cite evidence from the theme selections but might also draw on outside reading. You may prefer to allow students to respond to the theme in their own way. WRITING PROCESS: A PERSUASIVE ESSAY

Writer's Workshop
A PERSUASIVE ESSAY

Before students begin, review the techniques of persuasion. Point out that one way people convert others to their point of view is to provide evidence to support their facts. Remind students that corroborative evidence consists of both facts and expert opinions. Allow students to do limited research in planning their persuasive essays in order to provide the evidence they will need to bolster their arguments. Suggest that students refer to the Handbook in the *Writer's Journal* as they write, revise, and proofread their persuasive essays.

Prewriting

Before they write, have students
- consider the viewpoints presented in the reading.
- make a chart listing the arguments for and against the possibility of life on other planets. Their completed chart might look like the following:

Arguments For:	Arguments Against
1. Reputable scientists believe there may be simple life on the outer planets of the solar system. 2. Wobbles, dust, and gas clouds suggest other stars have planets. 3. Given the distance that separates the stars, messages might get lost, and travelers to Earth might not arrive for thousands of years.	1. No life was found on the likeliest place for it. 2. No voices have been heard from the stars or our own solar system. 3. If other stars have planets, these may not be life-supporting. 4. No scientist or astronomer has ever seen a UFO.

Have students review the arguments and decide which one is better supported. Suggest they keep the opposing arguments in mind while drafting.

Drafting

Ask students to write a draft of their persuasive essays. Remind them to
- take a clear position, for or against.
- refer to their charts for arguments that support their position.
- present these arguments in order of importance.
- write their drafts without worrying about spelling, punctuation, or grammar.

COMPUTER CONNECTION Students may want to use a computer during the drafting stage so that they may easily experiment with synonyms in order to make the right word choice.

Responding and Revising

If possible, pair off students who hold opposing viewpoints. Have the pair review each other's drafts for logic and persuasiveness. Offer these tips for revising:

- Does the essay flow smoothly from one point to another? Aim for effective transitions.
- Does the writer use language that is concrete and varied? When revising, try for precise words and synonyms. Use a thesaurus to help you. (See the Language/Literature Link below.)

STUDENT SELF-ASSESSMENT OPTION Students may use the Writing Self-Assessment Checklist in the *Portfolio Teacher's Guide*. Suggest that as they use the checklist, they focus on the consistency of their argument and their use of precise words.

Proofreading

Offer these tips to help students:

- Capitalize names of planets and adjectives that are formed from them. Example: Mars, Martian.
- Write out numbers below ten, except when they are part of a name, such as *Viking 2*. Use numerals for large numbers, such as 20,000 light-years.

Publishing

Discuss publishing options with students. They may wish to make posters of their essays, which might include the written text and illustrations of galaxies, spacecraft, and aliens, or they may choose to save them in their reading/writing portfolio.

LANGUAGE/LITERATURE LINK

Using a Thesaurus

Explain that a thesaurus is a useful tool. Suggest how Lilian Moore might have used a thesaurus in writing "The First." Suppose the poet wanted an adjective to describe sunlight, one that conveyed its brightness in space. Have a volunteer look up *bright* in a thesaurus and read off its possible meanings: *alert, brilliant, cheerful,* and so on. Ask students which word the poet might have looked up. Then have the volunteer turn to the number beside *brilliant* and read the synonyms given. Discuss why the poet chose *blinding*.

Speaking Option

DEBATE You may wish to adapt the *Writer's Workshop* to allow students to present their arguments in a debate. Have students follow the guidelines for Prewriting, Drafting, and Responding and Revising. Have interested students form debating teams, and offer these speaking tips:

- State your propositions formally at the start: "Proposed: There is (is not) life on other planets."
- Prepare a brief, or outline, of your case with closely reasoned arguments.
- Practice stating your case in a clear, confident voice.

You may wish to give speakers a minute each to rebut their opponent's arguments.

Connections

The Connections activities on Student Anthology pages 580–581 guide students to synthesize multicultural and content-area information with the unit theme. Before students begin, ask them to review quickly the purpose-setting paragraph on page 504. Then have them identify their favorite selections in the unit. As students mention titles, ask why each was included in a unit called "Solutions."

To prepare students for the Multicultural Connection, you may wish to share the following information on Benjamin Banneker, an early African American inventor.

Banneker was born in Maryland in 1731. His grandmother helped him learn how to read. She was a visionary white woman who freed her slaves and married one of them.

While working on the land, Banneker taught himself math and astronomy. For several years late in his life, he published an almanac. Impressed by the work, Thomas Jefferson sent a copy to the august Royal Academy of Sciences in Paris.

Tell students that the Multicultural Connection will tell them more about Banneker and other African American scientists.

CONNECTIONS

Benjamin Banneker

MULTICULTURAL CONNECTION

MAJOR CONTRIBUTORS

African American scientists and inventors have made man_ contributions to life in the United States. For example, the mathematician and inventor Benjamin Banneker helped to create the urban plan for Washington, D.C., and the chemist Percy Lavon Julian developed drugs that saved thousands of lives. Few inventors or scientists accomplished more, however, than Granville T. Woods (1856–1910).

Woods was a self-taught inventor and electrical engineer who was once called "the greatest electrician in the world." He secured more than fifty patents during his lifetime for inventions ranging from a telephone transmitter to an electrified "third rail" for subway systems.

Woods helped to revolutionize the railroad system with hi_ invention of air brakes and a telegraph system that allowed moving trains to communicate with train stations. The overa_ scope and brilliance of his inventions led some to compare Woods with a fellow inventor and contemporary, Thomas Alva Edison.

■ *Think of a current need or problem, and design an invention t_ meet that need. Share your invention with classmates, explaining how it works and why it is useful or necessary.*

580

Multicultural Connection

MAJOR CONTRIBUTORS As students read about African American inventors, encourage them to look at the photographs and illustrations. Refer students to "Getting Started" and "Inventors Idea Box" on Student Anthology pages 554–555 for help with the activity. To help them get started, tell them they might also brainstorm a "wish list" of gadgets or appliances.

AFRICAN AMERICAN SCIENTISTS

Research the life and achievements of an important African American scientist or inventor, such as Benjamin Banneker, Daniel Hale Williams, Garrett A. Morgan, or Charles Richard Drew. Prepare a written report on that person, and present an oral summary of your report in class.

Charles Richard Drew

THE ORIGINS OF THINGS

With a partner or in a small group, investigate the origins of three innovations or inventions. They may be small, simple things or great and important developments. Make a chart like the one below, listing the invention or innovation, its origins or inventor, and how it solved a problem or met a need. Add pictures or drawings to your chart, and display it for your classmates.

Daniel Hale Williams

Invention/Innovation	Invention/Innovation	Invention/Innovation
Origins/Inventor	Origins/Inventor	Origins/Inventor
Solution	Solution	Solution

581

Science/Social Studies Connection

AFRICAN AMERICAN SCIENTISTS Guide students to reference sources, such as *The Encyclopedia of American Biography*, for the information they will need. Tell them to try to include what motivated each scientist in his discovery. Suggest that students take notes on index cards, which can be used for either written or oral reports.

Science Connection

THE ORIGINS OF THINGS Have students complete this project in cooperative learning groups. Encourage students to be imaginative in their choice of invention. Remind them that somebody invented the humble pencil sharpener, and before that, the pencil.

Integrated Language Arts

Reviewing Vocabulary—Name Something (or Someone)

1. Write six Key Words or other vocabulary on the board. For example:

Key Words

prance	silicon
ventriloquist	transistors
primate	extraterrestrial

2. Give verbal clues for each Key Word, such as "Name someone who makes dummies talk" *(ventriloquist)* or "Name something used for computer chips" *(silicon).*
3. Call on students to supply the answer after each verbal clue. After one or two rounds, let students play the game by themselves.
4. Have students work in groups to create clues for other Key Words. Groups should exchange clues and supply the answers.

Reviewing Spelling Words

Integrated Spelling page 77 provides a review of the Spelling Words from Unit 6. *Integrated Spelling* page 78 provides practice with abbreviations.

Writing About "Solutions"

You may wish to have students respond to the Unit focus by having them write and illustrate an account of the latest, greatest world records. Encourage students to be creative or even outlandish. You may choose to have students use their creativity to invent things that will make the everyday lives of their classmates easier. Encourage them to use vivid descriptions of the new invention. Students can add both assignments to the magazine in their *Writer's Journal.* (See *Writer's Journal* pages 106–107.)

INTEGRATED SPELLING

pages 77–78: Reviewing unit words and abbreviations

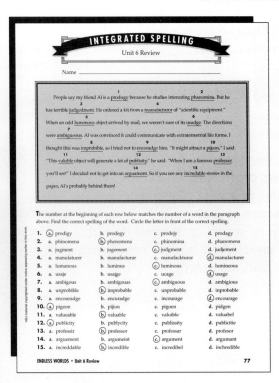

WRITER'S JOURNAL

pages 106–107: Making Your Own Magazine

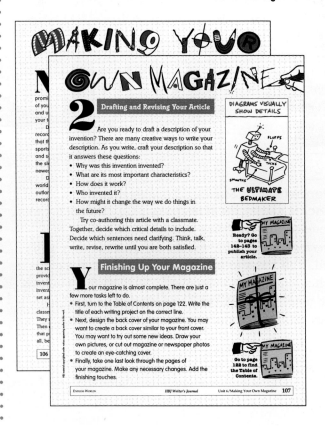

Assessment Options

Informal Assessment

See the suggestions below to informally assess students' progress in Unit 6.

INFORMAL ASSESSMENT NOTES AND CHECKLISTS

If you used the informal assessment notes in the lesson plans to evaluate students' reading and writing behaviors, you may now want to update your Running Records. You may want to have students complete the Self-Assessment Checklist in the *Portfolio Teacher's Guide*.

PORTFOLIO CONFERENCE

The Portfolio Conference provides you with an opportunity to learn about each student's

- preference for realistic fiction or fantasy.
- general writing development.
- understanding of summarizing and generalizing.

Discuss the selections that were read in Unit 6, eliciting the student's preferences. Ask about similar works the student has read. Also discuss the student's feelings about reading scientific pieces.

Have the student choose from the reading/writing portfolio a piece of writing that he or she enjoyed working on. Perhaps the description of the starship bound for Alpha Centauri ("Looking for E.T.") or the letter from the monkey's foster parent ("Helping Hands") might be shared. Ask the student what he or she liked best about the piece. Compliment the student for effective passages found in the writing.

Formal Assessment

The formal assessment tools described below may be found in the *Teacher's Resource Bank*.

SKILLS ASSESSMENT

The Unit 6 *Skills Assessment* provides the teacher with feedback about students' mastery of the specific skills and strategies taught in Learning Through Literature. Skills tested in this unit are Following Directions and Summarizing/Making Generalizations. If students had difficulty, refer to pages R35–R52 for visual, auditory, and kinesthetic/motor models that may be used to reteach skills tested in this unit.

HOLISTIC ASSESSMENT

The *Holistic Assessment* for Unit 6 may be used to assess a student's ability to understand passages written at the same level as the selections in the Student Anthology. If students had difficulty, refer them to the following sections in the Handbook for Readers and Writers: Active Reading Strategies, Reading Nonfiction, and Vocabulary Strategies.

INTEGRATED PERFORMANCE ASSESSMENT

The *Integrated Performance Assessment* for Unit 6 provides you with a profile of how well each student uses reading, writing, listening, and speaking strategies to read and respond to a piece of literature. Assessment results reflect how well students employ the strategies modeled and practiced in the classroom.

Break Time

Do Good—It's Good for You!

Scientists now tell us that people who help others experience less stress. They are happier and healthier, and live longer, too. As a teacher, you've been fortunate to enjoy the benefits of working in a helping profession. You'll be glad to know that experts have concluded that those good, rewarding feelings can have a cumulative effect that can be stored up against tough times.

You might want to introduce your students to the rewards of helping others through activities similar to the following:

- If possible, have your students act as visiting readers to children in a lower grade.
- Help students organize campaigns to gather food and clothing for needy persons.
- Help students arrange visits to a community center for senior citizens.
- Encourage clean-up or planting projects to improve the physical appearance of the school or the community.
- Encourage the development of a school welcoming committee to help new students adjust and make friends.
- Talk with students about ways they can be helpful at home.

Remind students that numerous opportunities for helping others are all around them. Let them do themselves a favor—by lending a helping hand.

PROMOTING INTEREST IN SCIENCE

Helping students develop enthusiasm for science is one of the most important tasks teachers face today. To achieve this goal, the Task Force on Women, Minorities, and the Handicapped in Science recommends the following:

■ **Emphasize science and math for educational values and career potential.**

■ **Encourage parents to set high goals for science and math achievement.**

■ **Maintain relationships with local universities and businesses that employ scientists. Invite female visitors as guest teachers or to serve as mentors.**

■ **Continue your own science and math study with workshops and retraining.**

■ **Make science a hands-on activity and provide opportunities for a variety of responses.**

PRINCIPAL

WARREN

"Your son will get better grades if you show an interest in and respect for education. Screaming and yelling will help, too."

Reprinted by permission

Creative Daydreaming

You're writing your novel—and it's going great! Your pen flies across the paper, leaving a trail of brilliant prose. You pause only to find that the page on your desk is really a student's essay titled "My Inspiration." You've been daydreaming—an activity psychologists call beneficial. Here are some tips for daydreamers:

■ Daydreaming can keep your mind active when you're doing something that doesn't take your full attention.

■ Read aloud "The Secret Life of Walter Mitty" by James Thurber. Talk with students about ways we use daydreams to work out solutions to problems or to take part in activities that would be dangerous in real life.

Handbook for Readers and Writers

CONTENTS

Handbook for Readers and Writers

The lessons on pages R3–R12 are designed to help students understand and apply the strategies outlined in the Handbook for Readers and Writers. Developing active reading strategies and related strategies for speaking, listening, writing, and research will benefit students across all areas of the curriculum.

You will notice throughout the Handbook a focus on metacognition, which encourages students to think about purpose and process and to monitor their own thinking, so that they will grow not only as readers and writers but also as thinkers.

640000

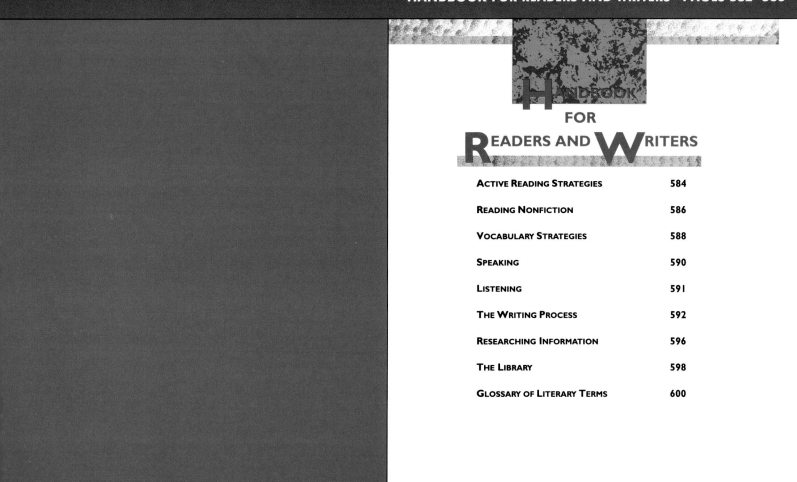

FOR

READERS AND WRITERS

583

Using the Handbook

Have students preview the Table of Contents on page 583. Point out the organizational pattern of the Handbook—reading, speaking and listening, writing, and research—and ask students to make predictions about the content of each section. Remind them that as well as introducing them to and reminding them of concepts and strategies, the Handbook is a helpful reference tool to use when they are having difficulty.

ACTIVE READING STRATEGIES

You use strategies when you are reading for your reading class, but do you think of using strategies when you are reading for your math class? Do you use what you know about reading strategies when you are studying a science textbook? Do you use strategies when you read the newspaper? You are lucky if you can answer "yes" to all of those questions. You will find that reading strategies are especially helpful when you are reading textbooks and other nonfiction materials.

Here are some ways to think about familiar strategies when you are reading nonfiction and textbooks in other classes.

Before reading

✓ **Preview** as usual, paying special attention to titles and subtitles. Think about how the chapter is organized, and look for the main ideas. *Helpful hint:* Main ideas are usually named in the main headings. Read any introductory material and the summary or conclusion, if there is one. Look at all the illustrations, graphs, and tables, and read their captions. Be sure to read the study questions and activities at the end of the chapter. Of course, you probably can't answer the questions yet, but knowing what they are can help you get an idea of what the chapter is about.

✓ **Think about the topic.** Get your mind in gear by remembering what you already know about what you are going to read, whether it's about the Civil War or the process of photosynthesis. Scientists who study thinking processes point out that your brain will receive new information more efficiently if it's already "in the groove," just as a warmed-up car engine runs better than a cold one.

✓ **Predict** what the chapter is about. This is easy when you have already previewed it, but you should also add your previous knowledge about the topic to your predictions. For example, think about what the chapter will tell you that you don't already know.

✓ **Determine your purpose for reading.** You might think that you are reading the chapter only because your teacher assigned it. But your real purpose is to learn something. Ask yourself what you expect to learn. Use what you have gained from previewing, thinking about the topic, and predicting to establish your purpose. You'll discover a real benefit from this process—you'll understand what you read much better.

During reading

✓ **Check your predictions** as you read, and revise them to match what you are reading.

✓ **Monitor your own understanding.** Occasionally, stop and ask yourself if you really are understanding what you are reading. If not, try these ideas to help yourself figure it out:
- reread
- stop and think
- visualize, or picture in your mind, how something works
- compare what you are reading to what you already know
- write some notes
- write a short summary of the main points you have read so far

One way to take notes or summarize what you are reading is to try to make a chart or a graph for yourself. Here are some examples.

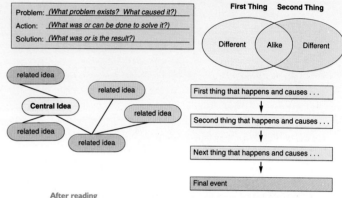

After reading

✓ **Summarize** again. Remember the main ideas. Answer the questions at the end of the chapter.

✓ **Compare** what you have read to what you knew earlier. Think about how your reading has changed your understanding.

✓ **Evaluate** your reading. Think how you can use what you have learned.

Active Reading Strategies

Exploring the Strategies After students have read the strategies, you may want to discuss with them ways that they could apply the strategies to reading for math class, studying a science textbook, or reading a newspaper. The same approach can carry over to the sections on strategies to use during and after reading. You may want to give students an opportunity to study and comment on the examples of charts and graphs shown on page 585 and discuss how they could use each type.

Following Up You may want to use these suggestions with all or some of your students.

- Choose several short, diverse pieces of text, and have small groups of students discuss how they apply active reading strategies to each of them.
- Encourage students to write notes about how they apply active reading strategies to their reading in subject areas such as math, science, and social studies.

READING NONFICTION

You can benefit from using reading strategies with everything you read. When you are studying or reading nonfiction, some special strategies can be useful. One is known as **SQ3R**, which stands for Survey, Question, Read, Recite, and Review. Here's how Rita used SQ3R to read "Astronaut Training."

SURVEY: Preview the selection. Read all the titles and subtitles, look at the illustrations, and think about the topic.

I can tell from reading the title and subtitles that this is about the training that people go through to become astronauts. I've always wondered what they have to do, but I don't know much about it.

QUESTION: Predict what the selection is about by making up questions it should answer. Use what you found in your survey. You might try turning the titles and subtitles into questions. Then predict the answers. Finding the answers can be your purpose for reading.

1. What kind of training do astronauts need?
2. Do they need to be trained pilots?
3. What is survival training?
4. What does classroom training mean? Do astronauts actually go to school? Why?

READ: Read the selection with your questions in mind. As you read, check your predictions and revise them to fit what you learn.

Astronaut Training
from *The Astronaut Training Book for Kids*
by Kim Long

Nobody knew exactly what to expect when the first astronauts were chosen to go into space. These astronauts were picked very carefully for their excellent physical condition, ability to work under unknown conditions and stress, and their past experience in piloting aircraft.

Many of the tests for selecting astronauts are no longer used. Although an astronaut candidate must still be in good physical and mental condition, extreme physical tests have proven to be unnecessary.

Pilot Training

It is no longer necessary for all astronauts to be pilots. Some candidates might be sent to flight school after selection if they do not already have piloting experience. Flight training has proven to be effective in preparing space shuttle passengers for the sensations of riding in a vehicle that is maneuvered into many unusual positions.

In the past, NASA gave preference to scientists who had valuable skills if they were also pilots. This situation is changing, however, as the space program becomes more complex and more people are needed to carry out new assignments. For instance, the simulator for the MMU is a complex machine that requires dexterity and good hand-eye coordination. But experienced pilots who have good dexterity and coordination usually take longer to get the hang of this device than nonfliers.

RECITE: Monitor your understanding by putting what you learn from each part in your own words.
- Rita started a web diagram when she surveyed the selection. Here's how the diagram looked after she finished reading the Pilot Training section.

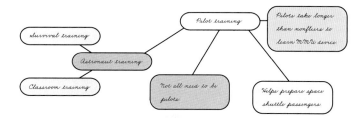

Survival Training

The U.S. astronaut corps uses the space shuttle as its only form of transportation to space and back. Because something could go wrong during the launch or reentry phase of a mission, the space shuttle might not be able to land at its designated spot. A forced landing at sea or in a remote area makes survival training a necessity for all astronauts.

This training involves demonstrations and practice. Emergency exits from shuttle mock-ups are practiced on dry land and in the water. Methods of using rafts and helicopter retrievals are part of this program. Astronauts who take flight instruction must also learn ejection techniques and the use of parachutes.

Classroom Training

Most of the astronaut's time during the first year is spent in classrooms, learning new material. Astronauts must learn how the shuttle is constructed, how it works, and how to operate the life-support systems, as well as the complex flight controls and many console monitors, equipment controls, and computers. They must also study ground-control operations.

Astronauts must be familiar with every aspect of the system that runs each spaceflight. Even though astronauts have already become experts in specialized fields before being accepted into the space program, they must also learn about other subjects. In space, astronauts have to do many things, and understanding different sciences and procedures ensures that they will be able to do the job.

REVIEW: Summarize by answering the questions you asked earlier.

1. Astronauts need some flight training, survival training, and classroom training.
2. Astronauts do not have to be pilots, though they may be sent to flight school as preparation for the sensations of space travel.
3. Survival training prepares astronauts for a forced landing at sea or in remote areas.
4. Astronauts go to a special school to learn about the equipment and operations so they can do their job.

Reading Nonfiction

Exploring SQ3R   You may want to point out to students the headings *Survey, Question, Read, Recite,* and *Review* in the side notes and the italic paragraphs of Rita's thoughts that correspond to the *Survey, Question,* and *Review* steps, as well as the web that follows the *Recite* step. After students have completed their reading, they might want to discuss Rita's use of the strategies. Emphasize that their own thoughts and approaches while reading might differ from Rita's somewhat, as they apply SQ3R to meet their own needs.

Following Up   You might want to use these supplementary activities with some or all of your students.

- Have students work cooperatively to apply SQ3R as they read a chapter in their science or social studies book. Encourage them to share their thoughts during each stage of the process.
- Some students might like to create posters or other visual displays to help remind readers of the steps in the SQ3R strategy.

VOCABULARY STRATEGIES

Language is always evolving. Words change in length, their meanings change, they are combined to form new words, and they come into common use or disappear. Shortened for simplicity, *laboratory* became *lab*, *bicycle* became *bike*, and *moving picture* became *movie*. *Cool* is an example of a word that has changed its meaning. Not too long ago, it meant only "cold," not "unconcerned and self-confident." Compound words, like *weekend* and *homemade*, are constantly being formed. They may combine the meanings of the original words or take on unique meanings of their own. For example, *footloose* doesn't mean "having loose feet," but rather "free to travel or move around." The word *groovy* was commonly used in the late sixties and early seventies. Nowadays, to describe something as *groovy* is outdated.

STRUCTURAL ANALYSIS: Many English words have been taken from roots in other languages, particularly Greek and Latin. Words are built by adding prefixes and suffixes to roots. If you encounter an unfamiliar word, see if you can figure out its meaning by looking at its parts. This strategy is known as **structural analysis.** The chart lists some common roots and prefixes.

Latin				Modern English	
Prefix	Meaning	Root	Meaning	Prefix + Root	Meaning
inter	"between"	*ject*	"throw"	*interject*	"insert abruptly"
pre	"before"	*dict*	"say, speak"	*predict*	"foretell"
trans	"across"	*port*	"carry"	*transport*	"carry from one place to another"

CONTEXT: As you read, you will come across many unfamiliar words. Even experienced readers with very large vocabularies regularly encounter words they don't know. Often it is possible to determine the meaning of a word by looking at **context,** or the surrounding text.

If you can't figure out a word's meaning from its context, you can use the book's **glossary** or a **dictionary** to look it up. However, keep in mind that you will frequently encounter words you don't know and that sometimes it's better not to interrupt yourself to look up each one.

Sometimes a word's **denotation,** or basic dictionary definition, doesn't convey its full meaning. Think of words as colors. Blue is a color with many different shades: midnight blue, sky blue, navy blue, royal blue, and so on. Each shade of blue has a distinctly different quality, yet it is still called *blue*. Words also have shades of meaning, or **connotations,** that convey different ideas or feelings. For example, *quiet* and *dull* are synonyms, or words that mean close to the same thing. However, *quiet* suggests "peaceful," while *dull* suggests "boring." Looking at context can help you understand a word's connotations.

Use vocabulary strategies to figure out the underlined words in this paragraph.

> The Aztec Indian empire <u>extended</u> beyond the central valley of Mexico, as far south as Guatemala. Aztec government was <u>theocratic</u>: its rulers claimed they were guided by the will of the gods. The Aztecs were a <u>militaristic</u>, or warlike, people that <u>dominated</u> peaceful neighboring tribes. Such tribes were frequently forced to pay tribute to their Aztec rulers. It isn't surprising that these tribes eventually joined forces with the <u>invading</u> Spanish to defeat the Aztecs in 1521.

Theocratic is explained by the context clue in the second half of the sentence. Knowing that *theos* was the Greek word for "god" would help, too. A synonym for *militaristic* gives you a context clue to its meaning. Here are some other Latin prefixes and roots that can help you understand the underlined words.

ex- = out
in- = in
tendere = to stretch
dominus = master
vadere = to go

Vocabulary Strategies

Exploring the Strategies After students have read and discussed the strategies on page 588, you may want to have them work cooperatively to apply the strategies to the underlined words in the paragraph on page 589. Encourage them to combine strategies as much as possible. You might want to have students identify other words they know that share the roots and prefixes defined in this lesson.

Following Up You may want to use these activities with all of your students or with selected groups.

- Encourage students to read with a partner or in small groups, discussing and applying the vocabulary strategies to unfamiliar words.
- Students may be interested in keeping lists of Greek and Latin roots and prefixes. They may meet in groups to discuss how they can organize their lists, what kinds of information and examples to include, and so on.

SPEAKING

Expressing your ideas and feelings can be highly rewarding or downright frustrating, depending on how well others understand and respond to you. Whether you plan to be a politician or a carpenter, the ability to communicate is one of the most important skills you can have. Effective speaking is at the heart of successful communication. The best strategies to help yourself become a good speaker are to identify your purpose, know your audience, prepare, and practice.

IDENTIFY YOUR PURPOSE: Ask yourself what you want to say and why you want to say it. In general, people make a speech in order to **share information, give directions, entertain, or persuade.**

KNOW YOUR AUDIENCE: Plan your speech with your listeners in mind. The way you address first-graders, for example, should be different from the way you address adults.

PREPARE: Prepare by researching your subject and making notes. If you're expressing an opinion, make sure you support your opinion with facts. Find examples that will keep your audience interested. Study your notes so you know your subject thoroughly.

PRACTICE: By yourself or with a partner, give your speech a few times. Practice looking at your audience and speaking loudly and clearly.

Mr. Perez has asked his students to give oral presentations about life in the future. Nina and Carlos are practicing together.

- Nina's purpose is to **persuade** her classmates to help prevent problems in the future. Nina will **share information** about problems such as pollution and energy shortages. Carlos suggests that she use as examples the transportation and smog problems in Mexico City, where Nina grew up. Nina practices using examples from her own experience.
- Carlos has written a story about computer-driven machines that will make life different in the year 2500. By writing an **entertaining** story, Carlos hopes to **persuade** his classmates to be concerned about the future. Nina suggests that Carlos tell his story in a more dramatic style. Carlos practices adding more emotion and excitement as he speaks.

590

LISTENING

Successful communication depends on good listening as much as it does on effective speaking. No matter how well you express your ideas, effective communication cannot occur unless listeners understand. As with reading, writing, and speaking, listening is an important skill that takes practice. Here are some useful strategies.

IDENTIFY YOUR PURPOSE: Just as setting a purpose for reading makes you a better reader, identifying your purpose for listening can help you become a better listener. Are you listening **for information, for appreciation,** or **for directions**?

THINK CRITICALLY: Thinking critically doesn't mean criticizing; it means carefully evaluating what the speaker is saying, thinking about why he or she is saying it, and then forming your own opinion. Try to determine whether the speaker is stating a fact or expressing an opinion. Ask yourself what motives or attitudes may be influencing what the speaker is saying. Decide whether or not you agree with the speaker and why.

- Nina's classmates are **listening for information,** but they also know Nina wants to **persuade** them to agree with her. They are **thinking critically** about what she is saying, and they are forming their own opinions.

RESPOND APPROPRIATELY: Give the speaker your full attention. When the speaker is finished, you may ask questions or offer your own ideas. If you disagree with the speaker, don't just criticize; explain why you disagree, and defend your opinion.

- Carlos's classmates are **listening for appreciation.** They are fascinated by his story about how computers will affect everyday life in the future. They respond appropriately by paying attention and smiling and clapping at the end. When Carlos finishes reading, his classmates discuss his story and share their own ideas about technology in the future.

591

Speaking

Exploring Speaking Strategies You may want to ask students to recall occasions when they gave oral presentations. Students may comment on speaking strategies they used or wish they had used, or they might want to tell how a partner helped them. You might point out that some speaking situations do not allow time for much preparation or practice. Discuss with students which strategies or parts of strategies they can adapt to such situations, such as when they are called upon in class or want to obtain information.

Listening

Exploring Listening Strategies While discussing with students the three general purposes for listening, you might refer them to the four general purposes for speaking, listed on page 590. Have students comment on how their purpose for listening relates to the speaker's purpose. They may give examples of occasions when they have listened for information, for appreciation, or for directions. As students discuss the section on thinking critically, you may want to help them focus on how they can distinguish fact from opinion as they listen.

THE WRITING PROCESS

Although your main purpose for writing is to communicate with others, writing may also help you clarify your own thoughts and feelings. No matter what your intent is, the writing process can be an effective blueprint.

Elvia's class has been reading about setting personal goals. The teacher, Mr. Alvarez, asks the students to write essays about their goals. He suggests that they include any events that led to their selecting goals—"sort of an autobiography that concentrates on the development of your goals," he says. As they brainstorm more specific topic ideas, Mr. Alvarez and the class decide that the students will write about career goals (What will I be when I grow up?), family goals (What kind of family life do I see for myself?), or character goals (What kind of a person do I want to be?).

PREWRITING

Elvia is eager to start. She is almost sure she wants to be an architect. This assignment will be a good chance for her to think more about that goal.

In the first part of her essay, she will write about personal experiences that made her think about being an architect. She remembers being amazed by a green glass skyscraper near the Chicago River. To refresh her memory, she looks through her journal and finds some details about what she saw and how she felt at the time. She makes some notes about the details she will include.

In the second part of her essay, Elvia will write about what she must do to reach her goal. As she considers this, she doodles a picture of an imaginary skyscraper. Suddenly she sees that planning a career is something like constructing a building: You make a plan and then work up from the foundation. She decides to use her drawing as a graphic organizer—a sort of a time line—for her essay.

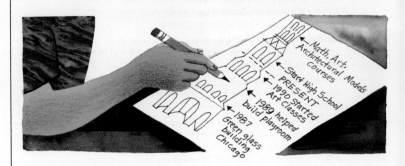

DRAFTING

Elvia likes the way she has organized her ideas, so she goes on to the drafting stage. If she hadn't liked her planning and ideas, she could have started over. With the writing process, you are always able to go back and make a new beginning. As Elvia writes her first draft, she states her ideas as clearly as possible without worrying about errors. When Elvia has completed her draft, she rereads it to decide whether she is satisfied. She is, so she moves ahead.

The Writing Process

Stages of the Process As you review and discuss the stages of the writing process with students, you may want to emphasize the flexibility of the process as it is applied to different purposes and different types of writing. Students might address the question of how Elvia would have applied each stage of the writing process differently if, for instance, she was writing a letter to obtain information about studying architecture or writing an imaginative story about a fictional architect.

Drafting You may want to point out that Elvia is satisfied with her first draft because she has stated her ideas and included everything she wants to say. At this stage in the writing process, she has not yet addressed the question of whether she is satisfied with the way she has expressed her ideas.

RESPONDING AND REVISING

Elvia's next step is to ask her partner, Ted, to respond to her writing. He uses these questions to help think of ways to improve Elvia's draft.

- Does the writer present events that pointed her toward her goal?
- Does the writer tell how her plans will help her achieve her goal?
- Is everything presented in order?
- Are there any details that should be left out?
- Does the writer use vivid words to help the writing come alive?

After deciding which of Ted's suggestions she likes, Elvia uses editor's marks to make these changes in the beginning of her essay.

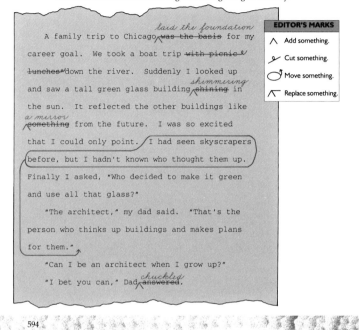

PROOFREADING

Elvia checks her capitalization, punctuation, grammar, and spelling and makes corrections using these editor's marks.

EDITOR'S MARKS

☰ Capitalize.	Transpose.
⊙ Add a period.	Spell correctly.
∧ Add a comma.	Indent paragraph.
⌄⌄ Add quotation marks.	/ Make a lowercase letter.

Even though my real training to be an architect will come in colledge there are some things I can do now and in High School I can keep studying art and alot of math. my sister knows a boy who take a High School course in architectural models. I will investgate that.

PUBLISHING

Elvia can't make up her mind how to publish her essay. Her friend Michiko notices the building she has drawn. Before Elvia can stop her, Michiko snatches up the picture.

"This is gorgeous!" she exclaims. "Here's how you can publish your writing. Make this picture bigger, and put it up on the board beside your essay." Elvia is pleased that her friend likes her picture, and she decides to follow her suggestion.

Later, Elvia and some classmates present their career goal essays orally in an assembly for other seventh-graders. Elvia shows her drawing, reads her essay, and answers questions about architecture.

At the end of the year, Elvia takes her drawing home. She hangs it on her closet door and draws the unfinished parts of her building as she takes steps toward her goal.

The Revising and Proofreading Samples

Have students discuss and evaluate the revisions and corrections shown in red on the samples on pages 594 and 595. You may want to emphasize that, though the two samples may look similar at first glance, the changes on the first sample are made to improve the content, while those on the second sample correct the mechanics. Ask students to offer reasons for each of the revisions on page 594. Remind students to refer to the boxed Editor's Marks as necessary.

Following Up

Encourage students to think about the stages of the writing process and how applying the process will help them in their writing.

- Students might work in pairs to complete a writing assignment, discussing each stage of the process as they go along. Writing partners may ask another pair of writing partners to respond to their first draft.
- Challenge students to explore different and unusual ways to publish their writing. Encourage them to consult with others and to share their ideas.

RESEARCHING INFORMATION

Research is a valuable learning tool that you can use for many different purposes, both in school and on your own. Whether you're studying for an exam on Greek mythology, writing a research paper about Mayan civilization, or teaching yourself basic carpentry, research is the first step. Skimming, scanning, and taking notes are three useful skills that will help you become a more effective researcher.

SKIMMING means quickly looking over a book or a reference source to identify its subject and to find out how it is organized. The purpose of skimming is to help you locate sections that you want to go back to and read carefully. Skimming saves time because it shows you which sections do not relate to your topic. If you were doing research on the Aztecs, you would see by the title of the chapter below that you should look at that chapter. If your research was on the Incas, you could skip it.

SCANNING means looking quickly through a passage to find key words or phrases. Scanning is a fast way to locate specific information. Scanning for the word *Aztec* will tell you quickly that the second paragraph is the only one you need to read carefully in this part of the chapter.

Mayans, Toltecs, and Aztecs

Chichén Itzá was founded by the Mayans about 1,200 years ago. This city and its ruins are the work of two of Mexico's great Indian civilizations. First built by the Mayans, whose empire once covered much of southern Mexico and parts of Guatemala and Honduras, the city was conquered by the Toltec Indians. The Toltecs added buildings or changed the style of some of the Mayan temples.

The Mayan and Toltec empires covered much of southern Mexico. The Aztecs later developed their civilization in the *altiplano*. Their cities were thriving when the Spaniards arrived in the sixteenth century.

Today there are over two million Indians in Mexico and Central America who are descendants of the once-great Mayans. The Mayan story began over three thousand years ago. But it was from about A.D. 250 until A.D. 1000 that these remarkable builders flourished. The Mayans learned how to make paper and evolved a system of writing; and Mayan astronomers developed a calendar of 365.2420 days in a year. This was a remarkable feat when we realize that modern astronomers with many scientific instruments at their disposal calculate the year at 365.2422 days!

Aztec calendar

596

Many books contain sections that provide specialized information or help you locate the information you need. Use your skimming and scanning skills on these pages to find key chapters, sections, or words that relate to your topic.

TITLE AND COPYRIGHT PAGES: The **title page** appears at the beginning of the book and lists the title, the author, the publisher, and the city in which the book was published. The **copyright page** shows the year when the book was published. This should indicate how up-to-date the information in the book is.

CONTENTS: The **table of contents** appears after the title page and lists the sections of the book and the numbers of the pages where they begin. Use it to find the parts that you need.

GLOSSARY: A **glossary** appears at the back of some books. It provides the meanings of words as they are used in the book.

INDEX: The **index** appears after the glossary and lists important names or topics and the numbers of the pages on which they appear in the book. An index can help you find the specific topics you need.

Taking notes is a quick way to record the results of your research. You can take notes in a notebook or on index cards, depending on what method you find most convenient. Remember to write only what you need to remember, and use your own words. Use short phrases instead of sentences. Be sure to write down the source of your information.

It is important to look at several different sources of information when you are doing research. Be sure to use your own words when you write your report.

597

Researching Information

Exploring the Strategies You might want to have students identify some of the specific items they would look for in skimming a book or a reference source, such as chapter titles, divisions, and headings. In discussing the parts of a book, listed on page 597, you may have students locate each part in their own books and perhaps in several different types of books that you provide for this purpose.

Following Up You may want to use these activities with some or all of your students.

- Students might work in pairs or in small groups to apply the strategies to a research project in science or in social studies. Encourage them to discuss what they learn as they skim and scan, and to take notes cooperatively as they read.
- Students may work independently to practice research strategies by using nonfiction books rather than textbooks or encyclopedia articles.

THE LIBRARY

Human beings are always collecting knowledge. To store our ideas, our literature, and the facts we've gathered about the world, we've created special places called *libraries*. Libraries enable us to share our knowledge with one another and with future generations. Whatever your topic, your local library will have information about it or will be able to direct you to a place that does.

Libraries hold many kinds of materials, from books and newspapers to government documents and videodiscs. To make it easy to find what you want, most libraries have separate rooms or sections for fiction, nonfiction, juvenile books, periodicals, and reference sources. The first time you visit a library, spend a few minutes finding out where each kind of material is located.

NONFICTION: Nonfiction books are organized alphabetically in the card catalog. Each book is listed on three different cards that begin with the title, the author, and the subject.

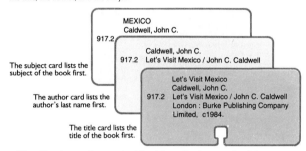

The subject card lists the subject of the book first.

The author card lists the author's last name first.

The title card lists the title of the book first.

Many libraries now keep card catalog information in computer data bases because computers are easier and faster for you to use and for libraries to keep up to date. Computerized card catalogs are also organized by title, author, and subject. Although each library may have a different system, all systems will provide printed instructions that explain the options and the steps on the screen for finding information.

Suppose you want to find information about Mexico. You would type your system's subject command first and then the word *Mexico*, following the instructions given you. The computer would respond to the command by displaying a list of books about *Mexico*. It would give you the **call number** for each book.

A call number is assigned to every nonfiction book in the library. This number appears on the three cards or the computer screen, on the library shelf, and on the spine of the book itself. Based on the **Dewey Decimal System**, call numbers are used to arrange nonfiction books by subject area. As you can see on the chart below, *Let's Visit Mexico* falls under travel and geography within the subject area of History.

000–099	General works (encyclopedias, atlases, newspapers)
100–199	Philosophy (ideas about the meaning of life)
200–299	Religion (world religions, myths)
300–399	Social Science (government, law, business, education)
400–499	Language (dictionaries, grammar books)
500–599	Pure Science (mathematics, chemistry, plants, animals)
600–699	Applied Science (how–to books, engineering, radio)
700–799	Arts and Recreation (music, art, sports, hobbies)
800–899	Literature (poems, plays, essays)
900–999	History (travel, geography, biography)

(Note: In some libraries, biographies are located in a separate section, alphabetized by the name of the subject.)

FICTION: Fiction is listed in the card catalog in alphabetical order according to the author's last name. Fiction books do not have call numbers.

PERIODICALS: Magazine and newspaper articles are listed by subject and author in a reference source called the *Readers' Guide to Periodical Literature*. Many libraries store information about periodicals in computer data bases, too.

REFERENCE SOURCES: Libraries have a great variety of reference sources. In addition to encyclopedias, there are specialized dictionaries, atlases, indexes, maps, and files. For example, if you want to read about one of your favorite authors, you can look that person up in *Something About the Author*, a collection of short biographies of writers of young people's books. Often the most difficult thing about using reference materials is knowing what's available. If you're not sure where to begin, ask your librarian. Chances are good that there are reference materials that can help you.

The Library

Exploring the Information   You might want to provide some nonfiction books from the library, with call numbers on the spines. Encourage students to examine the title, the table of contents, and the call numbers to see how each book is classified according to the Dewey Decimal System. You may also want to expand upon the use of the *Readers' Guide to Periodical Literature* by providing examples and demonstrating how you would go about using the *Readers' Guide* to find the information.

Following Up   You may want to provide additional opportunities for students to learn about the library.

- Set aside time for students to find materials in the school library for projects or for independent reading, using the card catalog or computerized catalog and perhaps the *Readers' Guide*. Pairs of students might work together to formulate and carry out research plans.
- Students might work independently or in groups to draw up a floor plan of your school library or local library, showing where materials are located.

GLOSSARY OF LITERARY TERMS

Alliteration The close repetition of consonant sounds, usually at the beginning of words, as in "the bee buzzed busily."

Allusion A reference to a work of literature or art, or to a person, place, or event, that a writer expects a reader to recognize, as in "he has the Midas touch."

Analogy A comparison made between two things to show their similarities.

Character A person or animal in a story, poem, or play. *Main*, or *major*, *characters* are central to the action. *Minor characters* help advance the action or reveal the qualities of a main character.

Characterization The way a writer portrays or develops a character through various techniques (such as describing what the character says, thinks, or does, or showing how others respond to the character).

Conflict A struggle between characters or opposing forces in a story, play, or narrative poem. (See also **Plot**.)

Connotation The meaning that a word implies or suggests, usually by the ideas or feelings associated with the word. (See also **Denotation**.)

Denotation The dictionary definition of a word, or its literal meaning. (See also **Connotation**.)

Dialect The characteristic way of speaking belonging to a particular region or group. Dialect may differ from standard English in vocabulary, pronunciation, and sentence structure.

Essay A brief composition in which the writer expresses personal views on a particular subject.

Expository writing Writing that presents, explains, and often evaluates information. Expository writing is used mainly in nonfiction works.

Fiction Writing that comes from the author's imagination and that is intended mainly to entertain.

Figurative language Language that uses imagery and such figures of speech as similes, metaphors, personification, and hyperbole. (See also **Imagery, Metaphor, Personification, Simile, Hyperbole**.)

Flashback The technique of interrupting the action in a story or play to explain something that has happened earlier.

Folklore Traditional literature, first handed down orally and later in writing, with no known author. Folklore includes ballads, folktales, myths, legends, tall tales, fables, and proverbs.

Foreshadowing The technique of giving clues early in a story, play, or poem to hint at what is to happen later.

Free verse Poetry that follows no regular stanza or rhythm pattern and has irregular rhyme or no rhyme.

Genre The form or type of a literary work, such as biography, novel, short story, poem, play, essay, or mystery.

Hyperbole A figure of speech using extreme exaggeration for emphasis, as in "I reminded her a million times."

Imagery The use of vivid description, usually rich in sensory words, to create pictures, or images, in the reader's mind. (See also **Figurative language**.)

Irony A contrast or difference between what is stated and what is really meant, or between what is expected to happen and what actually happens. Two kinds of irony are 1) verbal irony, in which a writer or speaker says one thing and means something entirely different; and 2) dramatic irony, in which a reader or an audience knows something that a story character does not know.

Lyric poetry A poem, usually brief, that expresses thoughts and feelings.

Metaphor A figure of speech that suggests a comparison between things that are not alike, as in "life is a long road" or "life is but a dream." (See also **Figurative language**.)

Mood The emotional atmosphere or effect of a story, poem, or play, often produced by the writer's use of language. (See also **Tone**.)

Narrative poetry A poem, usually long, that tells a story.

Narrative writing Writing that tells a story or gives events in sequence; it may be fiction or nonfiction.

Narrator The person or character who tells the story or, in a play, describes or explains what is happening.

Nonfiction Writing that is about real life, rather than about imaginary people and events.

Onomatopoeia The use of words whose sounds suggest or imitate their meaning, such as *buzz, clang,* and *hiss*.

Parody An imitation, often humorous or witty, of a serious literary work or of another author's characteristic style of writing.

Personal narrative A person's written account of an episode or experience in his or her own life.

Personification A figure of speech in which ideas or inanimate objects are given human qualities, as in "the wind bellowed and roared." (See also **Figurative language**.)

Persuasion A type of writing or speech whose purpose is to convince its audience to accept a certain opinion, to do or not do something, or to do both.

Plot The sequence of events in a work of fiction or narrative poetry that follows a five-part structure: exposition, rising action, climax, falling action, and resolution.

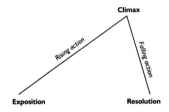

Point of view The position from which an author tells a story. There are two basic points of view. In the *first-person* point of view, the story is told by one of the characters, using "I." In the *third-person* point of view, the narrator is not a character in the story. Third-person point of view is further broken down into 1) *limited third person*, in which the narrator tells the story but the focus is on the thoughts and actions of one character more than any others, and 2) *omniscient third person*, in which the narrator can tell what all the characters are thinking and doing.

Rhyme The repetition of vowel sounds and ending sounds in words that appear close together, as at the ends of lines of poetry.

Rhythm The sense of movement or pattern in an arrangement of accented and unaccented words or syllables, especially in poetry.

Satire Writing that pokes fun at people, things, ideas, or subjects, often using humor or wit.

Setting The time and place in which the events of a story, play, or poem happen.

Simile A figure of speech that makes a comparison between two things that are not alike, using words such as *like* or *as*, as in "a smile as bright as a sunbeam." (See also **Figurative language**.)

Stanza A group of lines forming a division of a poem and often having a particular pattern of rhyme and rhythm.

Style A writer's characteristic way of expressing ideas, usually shaped by his or her choice of words, arrangement of words in sentences, and patterns of sentences.

Symbolism A writer's use of a person, object, or event to suggest or stand for something else, such as the use of an eagle to symbolize America.

Theme The central idea or message, stated or implied, in a story, play, or poem.

Tone The attitude or feeling a writer expresses toward his or her subject, characters, or even readers, often conveyed through the style of writing. (See also **Mood**.)

Viewpoint An author's opinion about his or her subject, often implied rather than stated.

600

601

Glossary of Literary Terms

Explain to students that literary terms are words or phrases that we use when we speak about literature. Encourage them to scan the Glossary of Literary Terms and pick out a term with which they are familiar. You might want to point out that entries are in alphabetical order, and ask students to find and read the definitions for one or more terms.

You may also want to discuss briefly with students the idea that some terms, such as *style* or *tone*, might have other meanings in other contexts, but this glossary gives the specific meaning of each term when it is applied to literature. Encourage students to refer to this glossary as needed when they are reading about literature.

Introducing the Glossary

Explain to students that a glossary is often included in a book to make it convenient for readers to find the meaning and pronunciation of words used in that book. You might remind students that they can look up words in a glossary the same way they do in a dictionary, using alphabetical order and guide words. You might want to model using the Pronunciation Key on page 607 to determine the correct pronunciation of a word.

As students look over the Glossary, you may want to point out that illustrations accompany some definitions, such as those of *colander* and *concave* on page 606. Point out on the same page that an expanded explanation and background information about some words, such as *commercial,* are presented in the margin.

You may wish to have students look up several words in the Glossary, identifying the correct page number and guide words and noting illustrations or additional information in the margin. Students may recall that a vocabulary strategy given on page 588 called for using a dictionary or a glossary.

GLOSSARY

The **pronunciation** of each word in this glossary is shown by a phonetic respelling in brackets; for example, [ab'ə·rā'shən]. An accent mark (') follows the syllable with the most stress: [kə·lĭd']. A secondary, or lighter, accent mark (') follows a syllable with less stress: [pes'ə·mis'tik]. The key to other pronunciation symbols is below. You will find a shortened version of this key on alternate pages of the glossary.

Pronunciation Key*

a	add, map	m	move, seem	u	up, done
ā	ace, rate	n	nice, tin	û(r)	burn, term
â(r)	care, air	ng	ring, song	yōō	fuse, few
ä	palm, father	o	odd, hot	v	vain, eve
b	bat, rub	ō	open, so	w	win, away
ch	check, catch	ô	order, jaw	y	yet, yearn
d	dog, rod	oi	oil, boy	z	zest, muse
e	end, pet	ou	pout, now	zh	vision, pleasure
ē	equal, tree	ŏŏ	took, full	ə	the schwa,
f	fit, half	ōō	pool, food		an unstressed
g	go, log	p	pit, stop		vowel representing
h	hope, hate	r	run, poor		the sound spelled
i	it, give	s	see, pass		a in *above*
ī	ice, write	sh	sure, rush		e in *sicken*
j	joy, ledge	t	talk, sit		i in *possible*
k	cool, take	th	thin, both		o in *melon*
l	look, rule	th	this, bathe		u in *circus*

*Adapted entries, the Pronunciation Key, and the Short Key that appear on the following pages are reprinted from *HBJ School Dictionary*. Copyright © 1990 by Harcourt Brace Jovanovich, Inc. Reprinted by permission of Harcourt Brace Jovanovich, Inc.

A

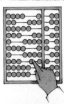

abacus

ab·a·cus [ab'ə·kəs] *n.* A computation instrument made of a frame, rods, and movable beads: **Huang's *abacus* had been used by his grandfather when he was a schoolboy.**

ab·a·lo·ne [ab'ə·lō'nē] *n.* A type of shellfish enclosed in a flat shell: **The diver searched underwater for *abalone*.**

ab·er·ra·tion [ab'ə·rā'shən] *n.* 1 Any departure from what is correct or natural. 2 The failure of a lens or mirror to focus light rays at a single point.

a·bode [ə·bōd'] *n.* The place where a person or animal lives: **The dark cave was an *abode* for bats.** *syns.* home, residence

abode

aftermath *Math* in this word comes from the Old English *mæth*, which meant "mowing." In Britain the growing season was short. When farmers harvested two crops of hay in the same season, the second mowing or harvest was often inferior to the first. So an *aftermath* is often a bad outcome of an event.

ac·a·dem·ic [ak'ə·dem'ik] *adj.* Scholarly, as opposed to commercial or artistic: **Sophia had always enjoyed sculpting and oil painting, but she disliked her *academic* art history course.**

ac·cord [ə·kôrd'] *v.* **ac·cord·ed, ac·cord·ing** To give or grant what is due or earned: **When she became the mayor, she was *accorded* a city car and a spacious office.**

ac·cost [ə·kôst' *or* ə·kost'] *v.* **ac·cost·ed, ac·cost·ing** To stop a person and talk to him or her. *syns.* approach, greet

ad·ren·a·line [ə·dren'ə·lin] *n.* A substance produced in the body to prepare a person to respond to difficult situations: **Victor felt his *adrenaline* rush when he saw a barking dog running toward him.**

anemone

ad·vo·cate [ad'və·kāt] *v.* **ad·vo·cat·ed, ad·vo·cat·ing** To say or write that one supports or is in favor of something. *syns.* endorse, recommend

af·ter·math [af'tər·math] *n.* An effect or result of a traumatic or disastrous event. *syn.* consequence

a·gape [ə·gāp'] *adv., adj.* With amazement.

a·loof [ə·lōōf'] *adj.* Uninterested or distant in behavior or character; not warm or friendly: **Many parents at the school picnic were offended by the *aloof* new principal.**

am·big·u·ous [am·big'yōō·əs] *adj.* Unclear; having the possibility of more than one meaning. *syns.* fuzzy, unfocused

an·a·lyt·i·cal [an'ə·lit'ə·kəl] *adj.* Having the tendency to examine the structures of issues, events, or objects critically, by breaking them into their separate elements: **Harry enjoys science labs when he solves problems in an *analytical* way.**

a·nem·o·ne [ə·nem'ə·nē] *n.* A brightly colored sea animal whose body is shaped like a flower: **At the aquarium Toyo saw *anemones* and other sea creatures with unusual shapes.**

ap·pre·ci·a·tion [ə·prē'shē·ā'shən] *n.* Awareness or sensitivity; recognition of value and significance: **After watching the group, Josef has an *appreciation* of the discipline of ballet.**

a·que·duct [ak'wə·dukt'] *n.* A human-made channel for transporting water over a great distance.

arc [ärk] *n.* A section of a curve, particularly of a circle: **The path of the rising airplane was an *arc*.**

ar·cade [är·kād'] *n.* A row of arches and columns: **The director of the play decided to limit the set to two *arcades* and a fountain.**

a·stride [ə·strīd'] *adv.* With one leg on each side.

B

bal·last [bal'əst] *n.* Heavy material placed in a ship or boat to keep it steady: **Maria and her father were eager to fish, but Pedro said he was going along in the boat just to provide *ballast*.**

bard [bärd] *n.* A poet; a singer of poems: **His folk songs were so poetic that he became known as the *Bard* of Madison Junior High.**

bar·na·cle [bär'nə·kəl] *n.* A shellfish that attaches to docks and the bottoms of ships.

bat·ten [bat'(ə)n] *n.* A strip of wood used to stiffen the edge of a canvas sail: **The sailor inserted *battens* along the edge of the sail.**

ba·zaar [bə·zär'] *n.* A marketplace; a row of shops.

be·calm [bi·käm'] *v.* **be·calmed, be·calm·ing** To make motionless due to a lack of wind: **Elena was unable to return to the harbor before dark because her sailboat had been *becalmed* for several hours.**

bod·ice [bod'is] *n.* The upper portion of a dress: **The skirt of the ugly dress was black with white polka dots, and the *bodice* was pink with red stripes.**

boom [bōōm] *n.* A pole that extends horizontally from a mast and is used to expand a sail: **When the wind turned, the *boom* swung and knocked him off the boat.**

bow·sprit [bou'sprit'] *n.* A pole that extends from the front of a sailboat and is used to brace the mast: **During the storm, the *bowsprit* of one boat pierced the hull of another.**

bron·co [brong'kō] *n.* A wild horse of the western U.S.: **Dale wanted to ride a *bronco* in the rodeo.**

C

ca·coph·o·ny [kə·kof'ə·nē] *n.* A harsh combination of sounds: **The small child was frightened by the *cacophony* of police sirens, screeching tires, and beeping car horns.**

can·o·py [kan'ə·pē] *n.* An overhead covering: **Because it was about to rain, Carlos made a *canopy* with sheets to protect the food for the picnic.**

car·niv·o·rous [kär·niv'ə·rəs] *adj.* Meat-eating: **All members of the cat family, from lions to house cats, are *carnivorous*.**

ca·vort [kə·vôrt'] *v.* **ca·vort·ed, ca·vort·ing** To prance about.

cha·os [kā'os] *n.* Complete disorder and confusion: **The news reporter described the *chaos* following the earthquake.** *syn.* disorder

chlo·rine [klôr'ēn'] *n.* A poisonous gaseous element with a strong odor; sometimes used as a disinfectant: **The workers coughed when they breathed in some *chlorine*.**

chron·i·cle [kron'i·kəl] *n.* A record of historical events.

cir·cum·vent [sûr'kəm·vent'] *v.* **cir·cum·vent·ed, cir·cum·vent·ing** To avoid or to find a way around.

clam·ber [klam'bər] *v.* **clam·bered, clam·ber·ing** To climb up or down using hands and feet: **Mr. Vazquez *clambered* up the tree to rescue the howling cat.**

cock·pit [kok'pit'] *n.* The sunken part of a boat deck, where the boat is steered: **From inside the *cockpit*, he didn't see the rock that damaged the ship's hull.**

co·he·sion [kō·hē'zhən] *n.* A logical connection among parts. *syn.* unity

bronco

chaos Today the word *chaos* means "extreme disorder." In Greek mythology, however, it apparently meant the emptiness that existed before the creation of the universe. Our word *chasm*, a deep, gaping canyon in the earth, is related to *chaos*. In the seventeenth century a chemist made up the word *gas* from *chaos* to name the form of matter that lacks a definite shape and volume.

a	add	ŏŏ	took
ā	ace	ōō	pool
â	care	u	up
ä	palm	û	burn
e	end	yōō	fuse
ē	equal	oi	oil
i	it	ou	pout
ī	ice	ng	ring
o	odd	th	this
ō	open	th	thin
ô	order	zh	vision

ə = { a in *above*   e in *sicken* / i in *possible* / o in *melon*   u in *circus* }

colander

commercial *Commerce*, "trading together," combines the Latin prefix *com-*, "together" and the root *merx*, "merchandise." *Merx* gave us words like *merchant* and *market*. The Roman god of commerce, Mercury, has this root in his name.

concave

co·hort [kō′hôrt] *n.* A follower or group of companions: **Juan faced the bully on the playground with several of his *cohorts* for support.**

co·in·cide [kō′in·sīd′] *v.* **co·in·cid·ed, co·in·cid·ing** To happen at the same time: **Kiko's business trip here *coincided* with my vacation, so we spent several days together.**

co·in·ci·dence [kō·in′sə·dəns] *n.* A chance occurrence of two similar or related events at the same time: **By *coincidence*, Aunt Luzanne telephoned from Europe just as we opened her letter.**

col·an·der [kul′ən·dər *or* kol′ən·dər] *n.* A bowl-like utensil with holes in it; used to drain liquids from foods: **Lemuel drained the noodles in the *colander* before he served them.** *syn.* strainer

col·lide [kə·līd′] *v.* **col·lid·ed, col·lid·ing** To crash together violently: **We saw the truck *colliding* with the train as it tried to cross the tracks.** *syn.* crash

com·mer·cial [kə·mûr′shəl] *adj.* Pertaining to business as opposed to scholarly or artistic: **In the *commercial* program, Esteban studied word processing, banking, and retailing.**

com·mer·cial·ly [kə·mûr′shəl·ē] *adv.* For sale to the public in stores: **Soda pop is a *commercially* available product that can be bought in many stores.**

com·part·ment [kəm·pärt′mənt] *n.* A separate section of an enclosed area: **The small child ran up the aisle to the front *compartment* of the plane.**

com·pound [kom′pound′] *n.* A group of buildings inside a wall or fence.

con·cave [kon·kāv′ *or* kon′kāv′] *adj.* Curved inward like the inside of a bowl: **The warrior held the shield so that its *concave* side was against his body.** *syn.* hollowed

con·ceit·ed [kən·sē′tid] *adj.* Overly impressed with oneself: **Rudy was so *conceited* that he thought his friends were admiring his clothes when actually they were laughing at his vanity.** *syn.* vain

con·fig·u·ra·tion [kən·fig′yə·rā′shən] *n.* The shape, form, or arrangement of something: **The *configuration* of the parking area made it impossible for more than three cars to fit comfortably.**

con·firm [kən·fûrm′] *v.* **con·firmed, con·firm·ing** To verify; to eliminate all doubt about something.

con·form·i·ty [kən·fôr′mə·tē] *n.* Acceptance of the ideas, behaviors, and rules established by others; going along with the wishes of others.

con·sole [kon′sōl′] *n.* The part of a spacecraft that contains the knobs, meters, speakers, and other equipment to operate the ship: **During a rocket launch, an astronaut must pay careful attention to all the dials on the *console*.**

con·tempt [kən·tempt′] *n.* A feeling of disrespect or revulsion for another person, act, or object. *syns.* disdain, scorn.

con·tour [kon′tŏŏr] *n.* The shape of something: **The *contour* of the mountains was extremely jagged.** *syns.* outline, shape

craft [kraft] *n.* Skill, occupation, or trade: **The *craft* of jewelry making is one of the world's oldest trades.**

crest [krest] *v.* **crest·ed, crest·ing** To reach the top or highest point.

crev·ice [krev′is] *n.* A narrow crack or opening in a rock or wall: **The black snake slid through the *crevice* in the wall, escaping from the garden.**

cruis·er [krōō′zər] *n.* A motorboat with a cabin: **The captain carefully steered her *cruiser* into the harbor.**

cur·ric·u·lum [kə·rik′yə·ləm] *n.* All of the courses taught in a school or particular grade: **The summer school *curriculum* included classes in water skiing, cooking, flower arranging, and pet grooming.**

cur·ry [kûr′ē] *v.* **cur·ried, cur·ry·ing** To rub down a horse.

cyn·i·cal·ly [sin′i·klē] *adv.* In a way that doubts the goodness of others: **When I said that I was mowing Mrs. Alvarez's lawn to help her and not for the money, my sister laughed *cynically*.** *syn.* sarcastically

D

dan·der [dan′dər] *n.* Temper, anger.

de·ceit·ful [di·sēt′fəl] *adj.* Conniving; misleading or lying.

def·er·en·tial·ly [def′ə·ren′shəl·ē] *adv.* With respect and consideration.

de·for·es·ta·tion [dē·fôr′is·tā′shən] *n.* The destruction and clearing of forests: **If *deforestation* continues at the current rate, soon there will be few birds in this area.**

de·hy·drate [dē·hī′·drāt′] *v.* **de·hy·drat·ed, de·hy·drat·ing** To remove the water from: **Elena's high fever *dehydrated* her body, so the doctor told her to drink lots of liquids.**

de·mean·ing [di·mēn′ing] *adj.* Making someone feel inferior: **Domingo was shorter than the other boys, and they sometimes said cruel, *demeaning* things about his height.** *syns.* degrading, insulting

de·tect·a·ble [di·tekt′ə·bəl] *adj.* Able to be measured with instruments: **Scientists do not believe that life exists on Mars because there is no *detectable* evidence.** *syns.* noticeable, measurable

de·te·ri·o·rate [di·tir′ē·ə·rāt′] *v.* **de·te·ri·o·rat·ed, de·te·ri·o·rat·ing** To diminish in value, condition, or quality: **The old photos may *deteriorate* if we leave them in the moldy trunk in the basement.**

de·vour [di·vour′] *v.* **de·voured, de·vour·ing** To consume reading material eagerly.

dex·ter·i·ty [dek·ster′ə·tē] *n.* The ability to skillfully use one's hands or body. *syn.* agility

dig·i·tal [dij′i·təl] *adj.* Presenting information with numerals: **According to the *digital* sign on the roof of the bank, it was 101°F. this afternoon.**

dig·ni·tar·y [dig′nə·ter′ē] *n.* An official in a high government or church position: **The town held a parade in honor of the foreign *dignitary*.**

dis·a·bil·i·ty [dis′ə·bil′ə·tē] *n.* A physical condition that prevents a person from being able to do certain things in a typical way: **Rolando was born blind, so he attended a special school for people with *disabilities*.** *syn.* impairment

dis·lo·cate [dis′lō·kāt′] *v.* **dis·lo·cat·ed, dis·lo·cat·ing** To put out of position: **Anita *dislocated* her knee when she scored the winning goal.**

curriculum The Latin word meaning "to run" was *currere*. From this word developed *curriculum*, a "small chariot" that the sports-loving Romans used for races. Later the word came to be used for the track where the races took place. Finally, the word was taken over by scholars to mean the "path" or "course of education" that students follow.

dander

a	add	o͝o	took
ā	ace	o͞o	pool
â	care	u	up
ä	palm	û	burn
e	end	yo͞o	fuse
ē	equal	oi	oil
i	it	ou	pout
ī	ice	ng	ring
o	odd	th	thin
ō	open	*th*	this
ô	order	zh	vision

ə = a in *above*, e in *sicken*, i in *possible*, o in *melon*, u in *circus*

eaves

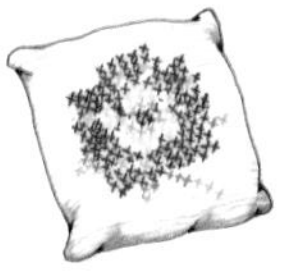

embroidery

erosion

di·verge [di·vûrj′ *or* dī·vûrj′] *v.* **di·verged, di·verg·ing** To branch off in different directions: **We all hiked together at first, but then we broke into two groups at a fork in the trail where two paths *diverged*.** *syn.* split

di·vert [di·vûrt′] *v.* **di·vert·ed, di·vert·ing** To turn something away: **Joe thought he could catch the ball by *diverting* my attention.** *syn.* distract

doc·tor·ate [dok′tər·it] *n.* An advanced degree from a university: **Most college professors have earned *doctorates* in their fields of study.**

do·mes·tic [də·mes′tik] *adj.* Pertaining to the home or family or to one's own country.

down·cast [doun′kast′] *adj.* Depressed, sad. *syn.* dejected

drone [drōn] *v.* **droned, dron·ing** To speak in a boring way, without variation in inflection: **Pat *droned* on about his favorite baseball game until his listeners started yawning.**

dys·lex·ic [dis·lek′sik] *n.* **dys·lex·i·a** A person whose brain function makes it difficult to learn to read: **The woman is a good student, even though she is a *dyslexic*.**

E

eaves [ēvz] *n. pl.* On a roof, the lower part that hangs over or extends beyond the walls of the building.

ec·sta·sy [ek′stə·sē] *n.* Great happiness, rapture: **Isabel is in *ecstasy* about her high score on the math test.**

ec·stat·ic [ek·stat′ik] *adj.* Full of great joy or happiness. *syns.* joyful, rapturous

ee·ri·ness [ir′ē·nis] *n.* A feeling of fear or strangeness.

e·lude [i·lōōd′] *v.* To escape or avoid through speed or cleverness.

em·broi·der·y [im·broi′dər·ē] *n.* Needlework decoration: **Carlita has beautiful *embroidery* on her blouse.**

en·deav·or [in·dev′ər] *n.* An attempt or struggle: **The fact that Larry is blind made his *endeavor* to climb Mt. Washington even more admirable.**

en·trance [in·trans′] *v.* **en·tranced, en·tranc·ing** To fill with wonder. *syns.* fascinate, charm

ere [âr] *prep.* Before.

e·ro·sion [i·rō′zhən] *n.* A wearing away or destruction of something by the action of wind or water.

ex·ca·vate [eks′kə·vāt′] *v.* **ex·ca·vat·ed, ex·ca·vat·ing** To uncover; to carefully dig out.

ex·er·tion [ig·zûr′shən] *n.* Great effort.

ex·po·sure [ik·spō′zhər] *n.* **1** The act of displaying or uncovering. **2** A section of film for one photograph.

ex·tra·ter·res·tri·al [ek′strə·tə·res′trē·əl] *adj.* Having to do with outer space and things not from Earth.

F

fac·tor [fak′tər] *n.* One element of a situation or one cause of a result. *syn.* consideration

fal·low [fal′ō] *adj.* Left unplanted to increase soil fertility.

fe·ro·cious [fə·rō′shəs] *adj.* Extremely intense or violent. *syns.* fierce, savage

fi·ber·glass [fī′bər·glas′] *n.* Thin, light, flexible building material made of glass fibers: **Her new *fiberglass* surfboard was much lighter than her old wooden one.**

flail [flāl] *v.* **flailed, flail·ing** To swing or beat: **The baby *flailed* his arms in the swimming pool like a bird flapping its wings.** *syn.* fling

flak [flak] *n.* Informal criticism, verbal opposition: **The committee received a lot of *flak* for inviting the boring speaker to the meeting.**

for·ag·ing [fôr′ij·ing] *n.* A search for food or supplies.

forge [fôrj] *v.* **forged, forg·ing** To shape hot metal; to create objects out of unformed metal.

fur·row [fûr′ō] *n.* A long trench dug in the ground by a plow.

fu·tile [fyōō′təl] *adj.* Useless. *syn.* ineffective

G

gen·er·a·tor [jen′ə·rā′tər] *n.* A machine that produces electricity.

ge·ner·ic [ji·ner′ik] *adj.* Occurring everywhere; not specific: **Palm trees are *generic* in Florida and on many tropical islands.** *syns.* universal, general

gim·mick [gim′ik] *n.* A feature that makes people want to buy a product: **Putting small toys in cereal boxes is a *gimmick* that influences people to buy certain kinds of cereal.**

gin·ger·ly [jin′jər·lē] *adv.* In a cautious manner. *syns.* carefully, reluctantly

glock·en·spiel [glok′ən·spēl′] *n.* A musical instrument made up of metal bars that are hit with a small hammer: **At the German festival, we heard musicians play cheerful songs on *glockenspiels*.**

gnarled [närld] *adj.* Knotty, lumpy, and twisted: **The veins on the old man's hands were *gnarled*.**

gro·tesque [grō·tesk′] *adj.* Very ugly or strange looking. *syn.* distorted

gyre [jīr] *n.* A spiraling motion: **The water in the whirlpool moved in a *gyre*.**

H

hal·yard [hal′yərd] *n.* A rope used to hoist a sail up the mast: **Both of the *halyards* snapped when the sails were halfway up the masts.**

hatch [hach] *n.* The door that covers an opening in a ship's deck: **The divers expected to find gold beneath the *hatch* of the sunken ship.**

ha·ven [hā′vən] *n.* A safe place. *syns.* shelter, refuge

heart·rend·ing [härt′ren′ding] *adj.* Causing great sadness. *syn.* heartbreaking.

helm [helm] *n.* A device used for steering a ship: **The wind was so strong that two crewmembers had to hold the *helm* to keep the ship on course.**

her·cu·le·an [hûr·kyōō′lē·ən *or* hûr′kyə·lē′ən] *adj.* Requiring superhuman strength or endurance: **Removing the fallen tree was a *herculean* task.**

hi·er·o·glyph·ics [hī′ər·ə·glif′iks *or* hī′rə·glif′iks] *n.* A method of writing using pictures or symbols.

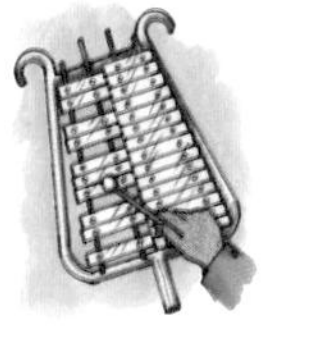

glockenspiel

hieroglyphics

a	add	o͝o	took
ā	ace	o͞o	pool
â	care	u	up
ä	palm	û	burn
e	end	yo͞o	fuse
ē	equal	oi	oil
i	it	ou	pout
ī	ice	ng	ring
o	odd	th	thin
ō	open	*th*	this
ô	order	zh	vision

ə = a in *above*, e in *sicken*, i in *possible*, o in *melon*, u in *circus*

illuminate

immersed *Immersed* comes from the Latin prefix *in-*, "into" and *mergere*, "to plunge." When you see the prefix *in-* or its variations *im-*, *il-*, and *ir-*, don't plunge to the conclusion that it means "in," "into," or "on." It certainly has this sense in words like *illuminated*, *indoctrinated*, and *inspired*. However, Latin had another prefix *in-* that meant "not." This appears in *improbable*, *inaudible*, and *irresistible*. *In-* meaning "in" goes back even further than Latin to the ancient root *en*. *In-* that means "not," however, has its origins in *ne*, which is seen in *never* and *neither*.

hoax [hōks] *n.* A trick that fools people into believing something that is not true: **Pablo convinced the crowd that he was a famous actor, but we later found out that this was another one of his *hoaxes*.** *syns.* deception, stunt

hutch [huch] *n.* A fenced place where small animals are kept: **At the farm, Pat watched the rabbits playing in the *hutches*.** *syns.* pen, coop

hy·brid [hī′brid] *n.* Someone whose background is a blend of different cultures or heritages: **Karen feels she is an unusual *hybrid*, since her mother is Irish and her father is Japanese.**

hy·poth·e·size [hī·poth′ə·sīz′] *v.* To make an educated guess: **Scientists *hypothesize* what will happen before they try to prove it.**

I

il·lu·mi·nate [i·lōō′mə·nāt′] *v.* **il·lu·mi·nat·ed, il·lu·mi·nat·ing** To light up: **When the electricity went out, Kenji *illuminated* the room with candles.**

im·merse [i·mûrs′] *v.* **im·mersed, im·mers·ing** To completely involve or absorb someone in an idea or activity.

im·pen·e·tra·ble [im·pen′ə·trə·bəl] *adj.* Not able to be solved or understood: **The complicated code was to remain an *impenetrable* mystery.**

im·prob·a·ble [im·prob′ə·bəl] *adj.* Unlikely: **Since we left so late, it is *improbable* that we will arrive at the theater on time.** *syn.* doubtful

im·pro·vise [im′prə·vīz′] *v.* **im·pro·vised, im·pro·vis·ing** 1 To create on the spur of the moment without rehearsal: **Because Nadjee had forgotten to prepare her oral report, she *improvised* one.** 2 To create out of any available materials: **Marta *improvised* a spoon out of a piece of plastic so that we could eat the yogurt.**

im·pu·dent [im′pyə·dənt] *adj.* Rude and disrespectful. *syn.* insolent

in·ad·e·qua·cy [in·ad′ə·kwə·sē] *n.* **in·ad·e·qua·cies** Being unsuccessful or lacking certain skills: **Sumi's *inadequacies* in reading music and staying on key made singing in the choir a challenge for her.**

in·au·di·ble [in·ô′də·bəl] *adj.* Unable to be heard.

in·can·des·cent [in′kən·des′ənt] *adj.* Very bright; glowing; shining: **Teresa had spent so much time waxing the car that it appeared *incandescent*.**

in·doc·tri·nate [in·dok′trə·nāt′] *v.* **in·doc·tri·nat·ed, in·doc·tri·nat·ing** To teach behavior or attitudes. *syns.* train, instruct

in·dul·gent·ly [in·dul′jənt·lē] *adv.* Giving in to someone else's wishes. *syn.* leniently

in·ev·i·ta·bil·i·ty [in·ev′ə·tə·bil′ə·tē] *n.* An event that is certain to happen: **The senator's victory in the election was an *inevitability* because she was so popular with the voters.** *syn.* certainty

in·i·ti·ate [in·ish′ē·āt′] *v.* **in·i·ti·at·ed, in·i·ti·at·ing** To introduce a person to an activity, status, or stage of life; to welcome a person to membership through a special ceremony.

in·spire [in·spīr′] *v.* **in·spired, in·spir·ing** To fill with hope, energy, or motivation: **Seeing the movie *inspired* Assunta to finish her screenplay.**

in·stan·ta·ne·ous [in′stən·tā′nē·əs] *adj.* Occurring in an instant: **Her *instantaneous* reaction to the whizzing ball was to duck.** *syn.* immediate

in·stinc·tu·al [in·stingk′chōō·əl] *adj.* Pertaining to inborn impulses and natural abilities: **She had never received any formal instruction in tennis; her success was purely *instinctual*.** *syns.* instinctive, innate

in·sur·gent [in·sûr′jənt] *adj.* Rebelling; in opposition to authority.

in·ten·sive·ly [in·ten′siv·lē] *adv.* In a thorough and complete manner: **Coach Rodriguez *intensively* prepared her field-hockey team for the state championship.**

in·ter·cept [in′tər·sept′] *v.* **in·ter·cept·ed, in·ter·cept·ing** To seize; to prevent from passing by or getting through: **The Bulldogs' halfback *intercepted* the pass, ran it down the field, and scored a goal.**

in·ter·mit·tent·ly [in′tər·mit′ənt·lē] *adv.* In a way that stops and starts or occurs from time to time. *syn.* occasionally

in·ter·stel·lar [in′tər·stel′ər] *adj.* Between stars: **The scientist was working on a spacecraft that could make the *interstellar* journey from Earth to one of the stars.**

in·tim·i·date [in·tim′ə·dāt′] *v.* **in·tim·i·dat·ed, in·tim·i·dat·ing** To frighten; to scare into submission: **The powerful current of the Colorado River can *intimidate* boaters into heading for shore.**

in·trep·id [in·trep′id] *adj.* Courageous; without fear.

in·trigue [in·trēg′] *v.* **in·trigued, in·tri·guing** To spark someone's interest: **Because Vasco enjoyed baking so much, he was *intrigued* by the idea of taking a night class in cooking.** *syn.* fascinate

in·trin·sic [in·trin′sik] *adj.* Pertaining to the real nature of something.

in·tru·sion [in·trōō′zhən] *n.* An action that invades a person's privacy.

in·vol·un·tar·i·ly [in′vol′ən·ter′ə·lē] *adv.* Done without intention or control. *syns.* accidentally, unintentionally.

ir·re·sis·ti·ble [ir′i·zis′tə·bəl] *adj.* Impossible to oppose or refuse.

i·so·late [ī′sə·lāt′] *v.* **i·so·lat·ed, i·so·lat·ing** To separate.

intercept

J

jib [jib] *n.* A triangular sail set in front of the mast of a boat: **We could always spot the Tangs' boat on the horizon because it had a bright orange *jib* blowing in the breeze.**

jounce [jouns] *v.* **jounced, jounc·ing** To bounce; to shake: **The baby *jounced* along in her stroller as her mother jogged behind.**

K

knot [not] *n.* A unit of measurement, equal to one nautical mile per hour, used to describe the speed of boats or wind: **The ship was traveling at a speed of 20 *knots*.**

a	add	**ŏŏ**	took
ā	ace	**ōō**	pool
â	care	**u**	up
ä	palm	**û**	burn
e	end	**yōō**	fuse
ē	equal	**oi**	oil
i	it	**ou**	pout
ī	ice	**ng**	ring
o	odd	**th**	thin
ō	open	**th**	this
ô	order	**zh**	vision

ə = a in *above*, e in *sicken*, i in *possible*, o in *melon*, u in *circus*

lingo Our word *language* developed from the Latin word for "tongue," *lingua*. This makes sense because the tongue is an important organ of speech. *Lingo* is slang with a somewhat negative connotation. It usually refers to speech or language that we can't understand.

locust

lorry

meander In the western part of Asia Minor settled by the early Greeks was a river called Maiandros. It didn't seem to know where it was going, but wound aimlessly back and forth as it flowed toward the ocean. That is why people who wander around without a clear destination are said to *meander*.

L

lac·er·ate [las′ər·āt′] *v.* **lac·er·at·ed, lac·er·at·ing** To wound by tearing.

la·goon [lə·gōōn′] *n.* Shallow body of water separated from the sea by a reef: **The pirates rowed the rowboat around the reef to the largest of the *lagoons*, where they dumped the trunk.**

lev·er·age [lev′ər·ij *or* lē′vər·ij] *n.* The extra power or help a person gets from using an object to lift something: **To gain *leverage*, Yumiko pulled on a tree branch to climb the steep bank.**

li·cense [lī′səns] *v.* **li·censed, li·cens·ing** To issue legal permission to do, be, or own something.

line [līn] *n.* Rope used to fasten a boat to a dock: **One of the *lines* was loose, so the boat slipped away from the dock.**

lin·e·age [lin′ē·ij] *n.* All of a person's ancestors. *syn.* ancestry

lin·go [ling′gō] *n.* A language used in a particular field of interest or by a specific group of individuals; jargon.

lin·guis·tics [ling·gwis′tiks] *n.* The study of language: **In a lesson about *linguistics*, David learned that many English words were borrowed from Greek.**

lo·cus [lō′kəs] *n.* A specific area, especially one being focused on: **A patch of white sand covered with bread scraps was the *locus* of the seagulls' diving and swooping.**

lo·cust [lō′kəst] *n.* An insect that is similar to a grasshopper and travels in swarms, destroying crops: **After the *locusts* devoured our entire crop of corn, they moved on to the next farm.** *syn.* cicada

lor·ry [lôr′ē] *n.* A sideless wagon pulled by a horse: **The farmer hitched up the horse to the *lorry* stacked with bales of hay.**

low re·lief [lō ri·lēf′] *n.* A form of sculpture in which figures are only partially carved out from the background.

lu·mi·nous [lōō′mə·nəs] *adj.* Glowing.

M

mal·le·a·ble [mal′ē·ə·bəl] *adj.* Able to be hammered, rolled, or bent without breaking. *syn.* flexible

ma·neu·ver *or* **ma·noeu·vre** [mə·n(y)ōō′vər] *n.* A procedure or planned movement.

man·i·fes·ta·tion [man′ə·fes·tā′shən] *n.* A sign that reveals the existence of something. *syn.* evidence

ma·noeu·vre [mə·n(y)ōō′vər] Maneuver.

ma·ri·na [mə·rē′nə] *n.* A docking site for sailboats and yachts: **The sailors refueled the yacht and picked up supplies at the *marina*.**

mas·o·chism [mas′ə·kiz′əm *or* maz′ə·kiz′əm] *n.* Abnormally finding pleasure in a situation that causes pain or discomfort to oneself.

mast [mast] *n.* A vertical pole from which the sails on a boat hang: **He climbed up the *mast* to try to repair the torn sail.**

me·an·der [mē·an′dər] *v.* To move in a winding path: **Some rivers flow in an almost straight line, but this one *meanders* through the fields to the sea.** *syns.* wind, wander

mes·quite [mes·kēt′] *n.* A shrub or tree common to the southwestern U.S. and Central America: **Manolo started a roaring fire with *mesquite* branches.**

mete [mēt] *v.* **met·ed, met·ing** To dole out; to distribute according to a measure or judgment: **The Red Cross volunteer carefully *meted* out three gallons of water to each family.**

mi·cro·or·gan·ism [mī′krō·ôr′gən·iz′əm] *n.* A living thing that is so small that it can only be seen by using a microscope: **The scientist was studying bacteria and other *microorganisms* by looking through her microscope.**

mi·cro·wave [mī′krə·wāv′] *n.* An electromagnetic wave with a short wavelength: ***Microwaves* are used in radar, in communication over moderate distances, and for cooking.**

mis·de·mean·or [mis′di·mē′nər] *n.* A legal offense that is not as serious as a felony: **The lawyer tried to convince the judge to rule that his client's offense was only a *misdemeanor*.**

mis·sion [mish′ən] *n.* One's role, task, or purpose in life.

mo·sa·ic [mō·zā′ik] *n.* Art consisting of tiny pieces of colored stone or glass carefully arranged: **The artist was asked to create a large *mosaic* on the side wall of the national museum.**

mo·ti·va·tion [mō′tə·vā′shən] *n.* Something that causes someone to act in a certain way. *syn.* incentive

mu·ral [myŏŏr′əl] *n.* A painting done on a wall.

muse [myōōz] *v.* **mused, mus·ing** To ponder in a thoughtful way. *syns.* consider, contemplate

mus·keg [mus′keg] *n.* A soft, moist area of land. *syns.* bog, marsh

N

ne·go·ti·ate [ni·gō′shē·āt′] *v.* **ne·go·ti·at·ed, ne·go·ti·at·ing** To give and take in order to resolve a disagreement: **My family spent a week *negotiating* vacation plans before everyone agreed to go on a camping trip.** *syn.* bargain

non·cha·lant [non′shə·länt′] *adj.* Unaffected; casual and calm.

O

ob·scu·ri·ty [əb·skyŏŏr′ə·tē] *n.* The condition of not being well known: **No one had heard of the artist, who lived in *obscurity*.**

ob·ses·sion [əb·sesh′ən] *n.* A thought or idea that constantly occupies a person's mind: **Elvira was always reading books about science because her interest in the subject had become an *obsession*.**

o·ce·an·og·ra·pher [ō′shē·ən·og′rə·fər *or* ō′shən·og′rə·fər] *n.* A scientist who studies the physical features, chemistry, and life forms of oceans.

op·tion [op′shən] *n.* A choice: **Tracy had two *options*—to join the choir or to play on the volleyball team.** *syn.* alternative

P

pag·eant [paj′ənt] *n.* A show that is put on for an audience: **Masako was not nervous about being in the play because she had been in a *pageant* last year.**

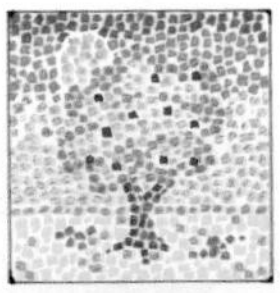

mosaic

mural

nonchalant What would you call your friends who have an air of calm and unconcerned self-confidence about them? You might say they are *cool*. Another word you could use is *nonchalant*. It came into English by way of French and goes back to the Latin *non-*, "not," and *calere*, "to be warm."

a	add	**ŏŏ**	took
ā	ace	**ōō**	pool
â	care	**u**	up
ä	palm	**û**	burn
e	end	**yōō**	fuse
ē	equal	**oi**	oil
i	it	**ou**	pout
ī	ice	**ng**	ring
o	odd	**th**	thin
ō	open	**th**	this
ô	order	**zh**	vision

ə = a in *above*, e in *sicken*, i in *possible*, o in *melon*, u in *circus*

peninsula

periscope

plagiarism The word *plagiarism* goes all the way back to the ancient Greek *plagios*, meaning "crooked." Like our word *crooked*, *plagios* also had the figurative sense "treacherous." The word passed into Latin as *plagium*, which signified a special kind of treachery—"kidnapping." People who *plagiarize* aren't just using someone else's words, they are guilty of kidnapping them!

pa·lav·er [pə·lav′ər] **1** *v.* To talk idly. **2** *n.* A discussion or conference in public, sometimes including idle chatter.

pal·i·sade [pal′ə·sād′] *n.* A barrier made of stakes set upright in the ground: **The explorers surrounded their camp with a *palisade* to keep out animals.** *syns.* fence, barricade

pal·let [pal′it] *n.* A thin mattress filled with straw: **The *pallets* the explorers slept on did not prevent the arctic ground from chilling them.**

pas·sion·ate [pash′ən·it] *adj.* Filled with intense emotion: **Sam was so *passionate* about his writing that he got a job in order to buy a typewriter.**

pen·in·su·la [pə·nin′s(y)ə·lə] *n.* A section of land that juts out and is almost completely surrounded by water: **The Iberian *Peninsula* is surrounded by the Atlantic Ocean and the Mediterranean Sea.**

Pen·ta·teuch [pen′tə·t(y)o͞ok′] *n.* The first five books of the Old Testament in the Bible: **Lola's grandmother read parts of the *Pentateuch* to her every night at bedtime.**

per·e·stroi·ka [per·i·stroi′kə] *n.* A restructuring of the Soviet Union; being connected with the time of that reconstructing: **The citizens cheered the speaker when he described the effects of *perestroika*.**

per·il·ous [per′əl·əs] *adj.* Very dangerous.

per·i·scope [per′ə·skōp′] *n.* A tube that someone who is in an underwater submarine can look through to see things on the surface of the water: **When Clara looked through the *periscope*, she could see an island in the distance.**

per·jure [pûr′jər] *v.* To make (oneself) guilty of lying: **That woman will *perjure* herself if she claims that she did not witness the accident.**

per·sis·tent [pər·sis′tənt] *adj.* Being able to stick to doing something: **Alonso wrote poetry every day, and this *persistent* practice helped him develop into a great poet.** *syn.* persevering

per·sua·sive [pər·swā′siv] *adj.* Being able to make someone do something: **Before the lecture, we didn't agree with Teresa, but she is such a *persuasive* speaker that we signed her petition.**

pes·si·mis·tic [pes′ə·mis′tik] *adj.* Expecting disappointment: **While Elena expected the team to win, Hilda was *pessimistic* and thought the team would lose.**

phe·nom·e·na [fi·nom′ə·nə′] Plural of **phenomenon.**

phe·nom·e·non [fi·nom′ə·non′] *n.* *pl.* **phe·nom·e·na** An event that can be explained scientifically.

phil·an·throp·ic [fil′ən·throp′ik] *adj.* Having to do with giving money to help people or organizations. *syn.* charitable

pho·net·ic [fə·net′ik] *adj.* Relating to the way words sound when spoken: **Poets appreciate the *phonetic* qualities of words.**

phys·i·cal ther·a·py [fiz′i·kəl ther′ə·pē] *n.* External treatment for disease or injury, as massage, exercise, or other training: **After the car accident, Lonnie had to have *physical therapy* in order to use his hand again.**

pin·na·cle [pin′ə·kəl] *n.* A tapering spire, often of rock. *syns.* turret, peak

pla·gia·rism [plā′jə·riz′əm] *n.* Stealing and presenting as one's own the ideas, writings, or work of another.

pla·toon [plə·to͞on′] *n.* A military unit within a company or troop: **Each counselor at Camp Redwood led a *platoon* of seven campers.**

plumb [plum] *adv. informal* Completely; entirely: **After pruning all the trees in the yard, Rick was *plumb* exhausted.**

pock·mark [pok′märk′] *v.* **pock·marked, pock·mark·ing** To cover with holes or scars: **In archery class, our targets are *pockmarked* with holes from our arrows.**

prance [prans] *v.* To walk in a very lively, bouncy way. *syn.* swagger

pre·cau·tion [pri·kô′shən] *n.* Measure taken to prevent injury or harm.

pre·dic·a·ment [pri·dik′ə·mənt] *n.* Difficult, embarrassing, or dangerous situation.

pre·mon·i·to·ry [pri·mon′ə·tôr′ē] *adj.* Giving a warning.

pres·tig·ious [pres·tē′jəs *or* pres·tij′əs] *adj.* Well known and well respected: **Ms. Benitez, a *prestigious* mathematician from Mexico, spoke to the students about careers in mathematics.** *syn.* esteemed

pre·sum·a·bly [pri·zo͞o′mə·blē] *adv.* Probably; according to what is believed to be true: ***Presumably*, the pep rally will be in the gym where it was last year.**

pri·mate [prī′māt′] *n.* A certain type of animal.

pri·va·tion [prī·vā′shən] *n.* The lack of essential or everyday things that make people comfortable. *syn.* deprivation

probe [prōb] *n.* A mission or a measurement device for gaining specific information: **The main purpose of the space *probe* is to get photographs of the planet's surface.** *syn.* investigation

prod·i·gy [prod′ə·jē] *n.* A child who is very talented at doing something.

prom·i·nent·ly [prom′ə·nənt·lē] *adv.* In a manner that is highly visible: ***Prominently* displayed on her mother's desk was the trophy she had won in fourth grade.** *syn.* conspicuously

prov·en·der [prov′ən·dər] *n.* Food, especially dry food for cattle.

psych [sīk] *v. informal* **psyched, psych·ing** To outguess, analyze, or make someone uneasy.

psy·chi·a·trist [sī·kī′ə·trist] *n.* A doctor who treats mental illness: **The *psychiatrist* asked Luis when his forgetfulness first began.**

ptar·mi·gan [tär′mə·gən] *n.* A plump bird with feathery legs that lives in North America: **The bird watchers gazed at a *ptarmigan* through their binoculars.** *syn.* grouse

Q

quan·tum [kwon′təm] *adj.* Abrupt or sudden; totally different or new: **The discovery was a *quantum* leap in our knowledge of disease.**

quill [kwil] *n.* A stiff, barbed spine from the hide of an animal: **The poor dog came whimpering back from its romp in the forest with a nose full of porcupine *quills*.**

quo·tient [kwō′shənt] *n.* **1** The answer to a division problem. **2** The key to solving a mystery or unfamiliar problem: **In the 1800s, a scientist found that the presence of bacteria in milk was the *quotient* for understanding the cause of certain diseases.**

prestigious The Romans combined the prefix *prae*, "beforehand," with *stringere*, "to bind." When they used *praestingere* in connection with the eyes, it meant "to dazzle." Related words came to refer to jugglers' or magicians' tricks because these performers can dazzle our eyes with their illusions.

primate

ptarmigan

a	add	ŏŏ	took		
ā	ace	o͞o	pool		
â	care	u	up		
ä	palm	û	burn		
e	end	yo͞o	fuse		
ē	equal	oi	oil		
i	it	ou	pout		
ī	ice	ng	ring		
o	odd	th	thin		
ō	open	*th*	this		
ô	order	zh	vision		

ə = a in *above*, e in *sicken*, i in *possible*, o in *melon*, u in *circus*

reciprocal If you have a *reciprocal* agreement with someone, it is a give-and-take arrangement. The word itself contains the Latin roots meaning both "back" and "forward," *re* and *pro*.

reef

R

ra·di·ol·o·gist [rā′dē·ol′ə·jist] *n.* Someone who uses X rays to study diseases: ***Radiologists* work in hospitals.**

ram·i·fi·ca·tion [ram′ə·fə·kā′shən] *n.* A result. *syns.* outgrowth, consequence

ran·dom [ran′dəm] *adj.* Without a plan or a system; chance; in any order.

rap·port [ra′pôr′] *n.* A warm or close relationship.

rav·i·o·li [rav′ē·ō′lē] *n.* Pasta filled with cheese or meat and usually smothered in tomato sauce: **Antonio's family loved his homemade *ravioli* because he stuffed it with anchovies instead of cheese.**

re·cip·i·ent [ri·sip′ē·ənt] *n.* Someone who receives something: **Marta was the *recipient* of several gifts on her birthday.** *syn.* receiver

re·cip·ro·cal [ri·sip′rə·kəl] *adj.* Given by two sides in mutual exchange. *syn.* mutual

rec·og·ni·tion [rek′əg·nish′ən] *n.* Public acknowledgment, fame: **Suzanne didn't expect to make a fortune from her car-part sculptures, but she did hope for some *recognition*.**

re·con·noi·ter [rē′kə·noi′tər *or* rek′ə·noi′tər] *v.* To survey one's position.

reef [rēf] *n.* A ridge made of sand, rocks, or coral near the surface of the water.

re·for·es·ta·tion [rē′·fôr·is·tā′shən] *n.* The replanting of trees and regenerating of forest: **More *reforestation* is needed in Brazil, where huge areas of rain forest have been destroyed.**

re·ha·bil·i·tat·ive [rē′hə·bil′ə·tāt′iv] *adj.* Having to do with helping people recover or get better at doing things.

re·ju·ve·nate [ri·jo͞o′və·nāt′] *v.* **re·ju·ve·nat·ed, re·ju·ve·nat·ing** To cause to feel younger or more lively. *syn.* enliven

re·kin·dle [ri·kin′dəl] *v.* To make active again: **Carmen noticed that her father hardly played the piano anymore, and she wanted to *rekindle* his interest in playing.** *syn.* reactivate

re·luc·tance [ri·luk′təns] *n.* Lack of eagerness: **Our cat Mabel showed her *reluctance* to go out in the rain by hiding in a closet.** *syn.* unwillingness

rem·i·nisce [rem′ə·nis′] *v.* **rem·i·nisced, rem·i·nisc·ing** To think fondly about the past. *syns.* remember, recollect

re·nal [rē′nəl] *adj.* Involving or relating to the kidneys: **When Yoko felt pain in her kidneys, she called a doctor who treats people with *renal* problems.**

res·ig·na·tion [rez′ig·nā′shən] *n.* Calm acceptance: **When she was asked to serve on another school committee, Lois smiled with *resignation*.**

re·sis·tor [ri·zis′tər] *n.* An object that provides resistance to an electrical current.

rés·u·mé [rez′o͞o·mā′ *or* rez′o͞o·mā′] *n.* A summary of one's job or educational experience and accomplishments: **Todd forgot to include his summer job on his *résumé*, so he had to type it all over again.**

rev·er·y [rev′ər·ē] *n.* Also spelled **reverie;** daydream

rid·dle [rid′(ə)l] *v.* **rid·dled, rid·dling** To affect throughout; permeate.

rig [rig] *v.* To equip a boat with sails: **She learned to correctly *rig* a boat before she ever went sailing.**

riv·et·ing [riv′it·ing] *adj.* Commanding; demanding attention.

S

sat·u·rat·ed [sach′ə·rā′tid] *adj.* Completely soaked. *syn.* drenched

saun·ter [sôn′tər] *v.* **saun·tered, saun·ter·ing** To walk slowly and casually. *syn.* stroll

schol·ar·ship [skol′ər·ship′] *n.* A money award given to a student to pay for tuition.

sec·ond·hand [sek′ənd·hand′] *adj.* Previously owned; not new.

sed·en·tar·y [sed′ən·ter′ē] *adj.* **1** Requiring or accustomed to sitting. **2** Not movable or portable. *syn.* settled

sem·blance [sem′bləns] *n.* Outward appearance; display. *syn.* impression

sheer [shir] **1** *v.* To veer off course. **2** *adv.* Very steeply; straight up.

short·hand·ed [shôrt′han′did] *adj.* Having too few employees or workers: **Because the doughnut factory was *shorthanded*, all employees had to work overtime.**

siege [sēj] *n.* A military operation against a fortified town or city: **The city was surrounded by the enemy and remained under *siege* for three months.**

sil·i·con [sil′ə·kən] *n.* An element found in the Earth's crust and often used for computer circuits.

sim·i·an [sim′ē·ən] *adj.* Having to do with monkeys or apes.

sin·ew·y [sin′yo͞o·ē] *adj.* Strong or firm. *syn.* tough, muscular

smite [smīt] *v.* **smote, smit·ten, smit·ing** To affect powerfully and unexpectedly.

smit·ten [smit′(ə)n] Past participle of **smite.**

so·cial·i·za·tion [sō′shəl·ī·zā′·shən] *n.* Experience that helps a person or animal get along with others.

sol·stice [sol′stis] *n.* Each of the two periods of time during the year when the sun is at its farthest north or south of the equator: **Rita was always glad when the winter *solstice* came because she knew that the days would begin to get longer.**

so·phis·ti·cat·ed [sə·fis′tə·kā′tid] *adj.* Having excellent equipment: **Instead of buying a plain car, Eva bought a *sophisticated* one with a stereo, air conditioning, and a burglar alarm.** *syn.* advanced

sou·ve·nir [so͞o′və·nir′] *n.* An object that serves to remind someone about the past: **Mom bought a picture of a seagull as a *souvenir* of her trip to Cape Cod.** *syn.* memento

spay [spā] *v.* **spayed, spay·ing** To perform an operation on a female animal to prevent it from having offspring: **Sue's father insisted on *spaying* the dog because he didn't want her to have puppies.**

squad·ron [skwod′rən] *n.* An organized group of people: **Each *squadron* of soldiers was made up of ten people.** *syns.* division, unit

squire [skwīr] *n.* A landowner.

staff [staf] *n.* A pole used as a cane, weapon, or symbol of authority: **Queen Valda used her golden *staff* to keep her subjects from touching her.**

stalk [stôk] *v.* **stalked, stalk·ing** To track; to sneak up on.

saturated

siege *Siege* came into English from the French *sieger*, "to sit." That is exactly what an army does when it *besieges* a town or city. It surrounds the city and sits down to wait for the inhabitants to surrender. *Sieger* itself goes back to the Latin word *sedere*, "to sit." English words such as *sedentary* bypassed French and came to us directly from this Latin root.

a	add	ŏŏ	took
ā	ace	o͞o	pool
â	care	u	up
ä	palm	û	burn
e	end	yo͞o	fuse
ē	equal	oi	oil
i	it	ou	pout
ī	ice	ng	ring
o	odd	th	thin
ō	open	*th*	this
ô	order	zh	vision

ə = a in *above*, e in *sicken*, i in *possible*, o in *melon*, u in *circus*

stoicism Zeno was a Greek philosopher who claimed that people should lead their lives unmoved by either pleasure or pain. Zeno and his pupils used to gather in the marketplace of ancient Athens at the *poikile stoa*, or "painted porch." This covered portico supported by columns was decorated with famous paintings. From this *stoa* Zeno's philosophy was named *stoicism* and his followers *stoics*.

terraced

tortilla

stam·i·na [stam'ə·nə] *n.* Strength: Ballerinas take several dance classes each day to build up their *stamina*. *syns.* vitality, endurance

stern [stûrn] *n.* The back end of a boat: The captain told the seasick passengers that the boat would feel calmer at the *stern*.

sto·i·cism [stō'ə·siz'əm] *n.* A calm mood without happiness, pain, or other feelings.

stren·u·ous [stren'yōō·əs] *adj.* Requiring a great deal of effort and energy: The climb up the steps of the ancient temple was too *strenuous* for Nell's grandfather. *syn.* rigorous

stride [strīd] *v.* strode, strid·den, strid·ing To take long steps.

strode [strōd] Past tense of stride.

stuc·co [stuk'ō] *adj.* Made of a fine plaster or cement: The *stucco* walls kept the house cool in the summer and warm in the winter.

sub·si·dized [sub'sə·dīzd'] *adj.* Aided by gifts of money: Gloria attended a *subsidized* school, which was given money by the city. *syn.* funded

suc·cumb [sə·kum'] *v.* suc·cumbed, suc·cumb·ing To give in to something: Ana *succumbed* to her exhaustion and fell asleep. *syn.* yield

suede [swād] *adj.* Made of soft, velvety leather: Her new striped *suede* shoes were ruined in the rain.

suf·fi·cient [sə·fish'ənt] *adj.* Enough: Elena thought it was *sufficient* to study only half an hour each evening.

swell [swel] *n.* The long roll of a wave: The *swells* slowly lifted the ship, carrying it farther from the coast.

T

tac·i·turn [tas'ə·tûrn'] *adj.* Not given to speaking; silent, reserved: When she heard about Chuck's visit, the usually *taciturn* Eloisa suddenly couldn't stop talking.

te·lep·a·thy [tə·lep'ə·thē] *n.* Communication through thoughts alone: Martha found a book about the *telepathy* between identical twins who seemed to sense each other's thoughts.

ten·der·foot [ten'dər·fōōt'] *n.* An inexperienced person; a beginner. *syn.* rookie

ter·raced [ter'ist] *adj.* Consisting of a series of raised, level areas, one on top of the other, creating steps: Many of the hills in southeast China are *terraced*, so that crops can easily be grown on their leveled surfaces.

teth·er [teth'ər] *v.* teth·ered, teth·er·ing To tie or fasten something with a rope or chain so it can't get away: The man *tethered* his horse to the tree. *syns.* attach, hitch

ther·a·py [ther'ə·pē] *n.* Treatment that helps someone recover from an illness or injury. *syn.* treatment

there·up·on [thâr'ə·pon'] *adv.* Then; right afterward.

the·sis [thē'sis] *n.* A statement or an opinion that can be supported with evidence.

throng [throng] *v.* thronged, throng·ing To move as a crowd: Teenagers were *thronging* to the theater to hear their favorite rock star. *syn.* crowd

tor·til·la [tôr·tē'yä] *n.* Circular, flat Mexican bread made of cornmeal or flour: Conchita and Eduardo made 300 *tortillas* for the wedding reception.

tot·ter [tot'ər] *v.* tot·tered, tot·ter·ing To walk weakly and unsteadily. *syn.* wobble

tract [trakt] *n.* A sizable area of land: The developer bought a *tract* of forest to convert into a golf course.

tran·scend [tran·send'] *v.* To go beyond the limits of everyday experience: Bernardo felt that no other experience *transcends* the thrill of mountain climbing. *syn.* exceed

tran·sis·tor [tran·zis'tər] *n.* An electronic object made of a semiconductor with at least three electrodes.

trans·lu·cent [trans·lōō'sənt] *adj.* Allowing light to pass through without allowing objects to be identified: Through the *translucent* glass of the door I could see that someone was there, but I couldn't tell who it was.

trough [trôf] *n.* A narrow valley or depression between the swells of waves: The Coast Guard lost sight of the sinking boat every time it dipped into a *trough*.

trove [trōv] *n.* Short for treasure-trove, or something valuable that was discovered.

trudge [truj] *v.* trudged, trudg·ing To walk heavily and with great effort: Loren was *trudging* across the flooded field toward home, in his boots weighted down with mud. *syn.* plod

tu·i·tion [t(y)ōō·ish'ən] *n.* The charge for school instruction.

tur·bu·lence [tûr'bya·ləns] *n.* The choppy movement of water. *syn.* agitation

tur·moil [tûr'moil] *n.* Confusion and agitation: *Turmoil* erupted in the auditorium when the principal announced that the school board was closing the school. *syns.* tumult, upheaval

U

un·de·ci·phered [un'di·sī'fərd] *adj.* Not translated or interpreted: The detective thought the *undeciphered* message was the key to solving the mystery. *syns.* uninterpreted, unexplained

un·ex·pur·gat·ed [un'eks'pər·gāt'əd] *adj.* Published whole as written, with parts that might offend some readers.

un·ob·tru·sive·ly [un'əb·trōō'siv·lē] *adv.* In a way that cannot be noticed. *syn.* unnoticeably

V

var·mint [vär'mənt] *n. informal* Rascal, scoundrel; a person or animal that is mischievous or troublesome.

ve·loc·i·ty [və·los'ə·tē] *n.* Rate of speed: The car was traveling at a *velocity* of 55 miles per hour.

ven·dor [ven'dər] *n.* A seller: At the Boston market, there was one *vendor* selling food next to another selling leather goods.

ven·geance [ven'jəns] *n.* With extreme power or violence.

ven·tril·o·quist [ven·tril'ə·kwist] *n.* A person who can speak and make it appear that his or her voice is coming from something or someone else.

Vi·et·nam [vē·et·nam'] *n.* A southeast Asian country bordering on the South China Sea: Hue located his native *Vietnam* on the world map.

vi·tal [vīt'(ə)l] *adj.* Very important. *syn.* essential

ventriloquist Ventriloquists are people who can make their voices appear to come from somewhere else. The name derives from the Latin words for "belly," *venter*, and "to speak," *loqui*. Although we associate ventriloquism with entertainment, it is still used in religious ceremonies by some Eskimos, Africans, and Polynesians.

Vietnam

a	add	ōō	took
ā	ace	ōō	pool
â	care	u	up
ä	palm	û	burn
e	end	yōō	fuse
ē	equal	oi	oil
i	it	ou	pout
ī	ice	ng	ring
o	odd	th	thin
ō	open	th	this
ô	order	zh	vision

ə = { a in *above*   e in *sicken*
      i in *possible*
      o in *melon*   u in *circus* }

W

yam

war·i·ly [wâr'ə·lē] *adv.* Suspiciously; cautiously. *syn.* carefully

warp [wôrp] *v.* warped, warp·ing To bend or twist out of shape.

whee·dle [(h)wēd'(ə)l] *v.* whee·dled, whee·dling To persuade someone by using flattery. *syn.* coax

wince [wins] *v.* winced, winc·ing To recoil or draw back from something painful or unpleasant. *syn.* flinch

with·drawn [with·drôn' or with·drôn'] *adj.* Lost in thought; quiet and reserved. *syn.* unsociable

Y

yam [yam] *n.* A type of sweet potato.

Using the Index of Titles and Authors

Explain to students that the Index in this book lists alphabetically the titles and authors of the selections. You may want to point out that authors' names are listed last name first, as they are in a library card catalog. Ask students how they can tell at a glance which entries are selection titles and which are authors' names. You will want to call attention to the references to page numbers in light type. Then you may want to select several index entries, and have students predict what they will find when they turn to the page or pages listed.

INDEX OF
TITLES AND AUTHORS

Page numbers in light type refer to biographical information.

Acknowledgments continued

Hastings House Publishers, New York, Ltd.: "Advice to Travelers" from *Come As You Are* by Walker Gibson. © 1958 by Walker Gibson.
Tim Hilderbrandt: Cover illustration by Tim Hilderbrandt from *The White Mountains* by John Christopher. Illustration © 1988 by Tim Hilderbrandt.
Holiday House: Cover illustration from *The Wright Brothers: How They Invented the Airplane* by Russell Freedman. Copyright © 1991 by Russell Freedman. Cover illustration from *Of Paul: The Mighty Logger* by Glen Rounds. Copyright 1936, 1949 by Holiday House, Inc.; copyright © 1976 by Glen Rounds. "I Watched an Eagle Soar" by Virginia Driving Hawk Sneve from *Dancing Teepees: Poems of American Indian Youth*. Text copyright © 1989 by Virginia Driving Hawk Sneve.
Houghton Mifflin Company: Cover illustration from *The Way Things Work* by David Macaulay. Illustration copyright © 1988 by David Macaulay. From pp. 70-95 in *Trial by Wilderness* (Retitled: "Time: The Missing Element") by David Mathieson. Text copyright © 1985 by David Mathieson. From pp. 25-39 in *Carlota* (Retitled: "The Secret Galleon") by Scott O'Dell. Text copyright © 1977 by Scott O'Dell. "How Winter Man's Power Was Broken" from *Tales of the Cheyennes* by Grace Jackson Penney. Text copyright 1953 by Grace Jackson Penney; copyright © renewed 1981 by Grace Jackson Penney.
Daniel F. Jaffe: "The Forecast" by Daniel F. Jaffe from *Prairie Schooner*. © 1964 by Dan Jaffe.
Alfred A. Knopf, Inc.: "Long Trip" from *Selected Poems* by Langston Hughes. Text copyright 1926 by Alfred A. Knopf, Inc., renewed 1954 by Langston Hughes. Cover illustration by Leo and Diane Dillon from *Anthony Burns: The Defeat and Triumph of a Fugitive Slave* by Virginia Hamilton. Illustration copyright © 1988 by Leo and Diane Dillon.
Little, Brown and Company: Cover illustration from *Jingo Django* by Sid Fleischman. Copyright © 1971 by Albert S. Fleischman.
Los Angeles Times: From "At Home with the Titan of the Trail" by Paul Dean from the *Los Angeles Times*. Text copyright 1990 by Los Angeles Times.
Margaret K. McElderry Books, an imprint of Macmillan Publishing Company: Cover illustration from *Frozen Fire* by James Houston. Copyright © 1977 by James Houston. From pp. 53-76 in *The Mystery of the Ancient Maya* (Retitled: "Treasure Trove") by Carolyn Meyer and Charles Gallenkamp; cover illustration by Dolana Roberts. Text and cover illustration copyright © 1985 by Carolyn Meyer and Charles Gallenkamp.
McIntosh and Otis, Inc.: From *The Secret of the Wall* by Elizabeth Borton de Treviño. Text copyright © 1966 by Elizabeth Borton de Treviño.
William Morrow & Company, Inc.: From "The Platoon System" in *A Girl from Yamhill* by Beverly Cleary. Copyright © 1988 by Beverly Cleary.
Harold Ober Associates Incorporated: "The Sparrow Hawk" from *The Pedaling Man and Other Poems* by Russell Hoban. Text copyright © 1968 by Russell Hoban.
Orchard Books, New York: From *Seeing Earth from Space* (Retitled: "The Planet Earth") by Patricia Lauber. Text copyright © 1990 by Patricia Lauber. "Lost at Sea," a version of *The Voyage of the Frog* by Gary Paulsen. Text copyright © 1989 by Gary Paulsen. Originally published in *Boys' Life* Magazine.
Pocket Books, a division of Simon & Schuster, Inc.: Cover illustration from *Tricia Zimic* from *The Ordinary Princess* by M. M. Kaye. Illustration copyright © 1986 by Tricia Zimic.
Prentice-Hall, a division of Simon & Schuster, New York: Cover illustration from *Kon-Tiki* by Thor Heyerdahl. © 1950, 1960, 1984 by Thor Heyerdahl.
G. P. Putnam's Sons: Cover illustration by Margot Tomes from *Homesick: My Own Story* by Jean Fritz. Illustration copyright © 1982 by Margot Tomes. Cover illustration from *The Brooklyn Bridge: They Said It Couldn't Be Built* by Judith St. George. Copyright © 1982 by Judith St. George.
Random House, Inc.: From "Raymond's Run" in *My Love* by Toni Cade Bambara. From "The Bird and the Machine" by Loren Eiseley. Text copyright 1970 by Toni Cade Bambara. From "The Bird and the Machine" in *The Immense Journey* by Loren Eiseley. Text copyright © 1955 by Loren Eiseley. Cover illustration by Domenick D'An-

drea from *The Black Stallion* by Walter Farley. Illustration copyright © 1991 by Domenick D'Andrea. From *Chesapeake* (Retitled: "The Right Place") by James Michener. Text copyright © 1978 by Random House, Inc.
Barrett Root: Cover illustration by Barrett Root from *Baseball in April and Other Stories* by Gary Soto.
R studio T: Cover design by R studio T from *Outward Dreams: Black Inventors and Their Inventions* by Jim Haskins. Copyright © 1991 by Jim Haskins.
Scholastic, Inc.: "The Golden Apples: The Story of Atalanta and Hippomenes" from *Favorite Greek Myths*, retold by Mary Pope Osborne. Text copyright © 1989 by Mary Pope Osborne.
The Society of Authors, as the literary representative of the Estate of John Masefield: "Sea Fever" from *Poems* by John Masefield. Text copyright 1912 by Macmillan Publishing Company, Inc., renewed 1940 by John Masefield.
Jeremy P. Tarcher, Inc., Los Angeles, CA: From "The Flood" in *The Beauty of the Beasts* by Ralph Helfer. Text copyright © 1990 by Ralph Helfer.
The University of Chicago Press and Walter Blair: From "Pecos Bill, King of Texas Cowboys" in *TALL TALE AMERICA: A Legendary History of Our Humorous Heroes* by Walter Blair. Text © 1944, 1987 by Walter Blair.
Viking Penguin, a division of Penguin Books USA Inc.: Cover illustration from *The Twenty-One Balloons* by William Pène du Bois. Copyright © 1986 by William Pène du Bois. "I May, I Might, I Must" from *The Complete Poems of Marianne Moore* by Marianne Moore. Text copyright © 1959 by Marianne Moore. "Trombones and Colleges" from *Fast Sam, Cool Clyde and Stuff* by Walter Dean Myers, cover illustration by Jerry Pinkney. Text copyright © 1975 by Walter Dean Myers; cover illustration copyright © 1988 by Viking Penguin Inc. *If You Say So, Claude* by Joan Lowery Nixon. Text copyright © 1980 by Joan Lowery Nixon. From *In Search of a Sandhill Crane* (Retitled: "First Sighting") by Keith Robertson. Text copyright © 1973 by Keith Robertson. *Three Strong Women* by Claus Stamm. Text copyright © 1962 by Claus Stamm and Kazue Mizumura, renewed 1990 by Claus Stamm and Kazue Mizumura.
Walker and Company, Inc.: Cover photograph by Stephanie M. Koplin from *More Than a Friend: Dogs With a Purpose* by Mary-Ellen Siegel and Hermine M. Koplin. Copyright © 1984 by Mary-Ellen Siegel and Hermine M. Koplin.
Franklin Watts, Inc.: "Looking for E.T." from *Recent Revolutions in Astronomy* by Larry Kelsey and Darrel Hoff. Text copyright © 1987 by Larry Kelsey and Darrel Hoff. Cover illustration from *Supernova!* by Christopher Lampton. Copyright © 1988 by Christopher Lampton.

Handwriting models in this program have been used with permission of the publisher, Zaner-Bloser, Inc., Columbus, OH.

Photograph Credits

Key: (t) top, (b) bottom, (l) left, (r) right, (c) center.

HBJ Photo, 58–61; HBJ/Black Star/Lisa Quinones, 59; Carolyn Soto, 93; HBJ Photo/Map, George Buctel, 216; Library of Congress, 217 (bl); National Archives of Canada, 218, 221, 222, 224, 225 (b), 226, 229 (r); Newell/University of Washington, 223; Photographed material courtesy of Yakima Valley Museum and Historical Association, 225 (tr); Yukon Archives/Clayton Betts Collection, 227; Library of Congress, 229 (l); Stephen J. Krasemann/DRK, 230–234; Murray & Assoc./TSW, 240; Byron Augustin/D. Donne Bryant, 242; John Phelan/D. Donne Bryant, 243; Justin Kerr, 244; Wallace Murray/DDB Stock, 245 (l); William Boehm/West Stock, 245 (r); Bob Daemmrich/Stock Boston, 246; D. Donne Bryant, 247; Edward Slater/Southern Stock, 248; HBJ/Maria Paraskevas, 266 (t); HBJ/Debi Harbin, 266 (b); Roy Morsch/Stock Market, 284; Dennis Doran/West Stock, 285; Hammond, Inc., 286; Jack W. Dykinga/Bruce Coleman, Inc., 288; Jeffry Myers/Southern Stock, 289; Roy Morsch/Stock Market, 290; Steve Vidler/Leo deWys, Inc., 291; Heinz Plenge/Peter Arnold, 294 (tl); Heinz Plenge/Peter Arnold, 294 (cl); Bloomsburg Craftsman, 302; HBJ Photo, 303; Bloomsburg Craftsman, 304–318; Jeff Schultz/Alaska Stock, 322–329; HBJ Photo, 336; Michael Mauney/People Weekly Time,

Inc., 340 (tb); Daniel B. Ecoff/Sygma, 344 (t); Steve Shapiro/Sygma, 344 (b); HBJ/Maria Paraskevas, 360 (t); HBJ/Britt Runion, 360 (b); HBJ Photo, 384–395; European Space Agency, 406; HBJ Photo, 406B; NASA, 408–420; HBJ/Rick Friedman/Black Star, 423; Western New England College, 425 (t); HBJ Photo, 425 (b); University of California, 426; Smithsonian Institution, 427–428; Donald Baird, 430–431; Smithsonian Institution, 432–433; HBJ/Debi Harbin, 474 (t); Tim Davis/Photo Researchers, 476 (l); Tom Brakefield/Bruce Coleman, Inc., 476 (r); E. R. Degginger/Color-Pic, 476–477; Robert C. Simpson/Tom Stack, Assoc., 477 (tr); B.K. Wheeler/Academy of Natural Sciences, 478–481; HBJ/Debi Harbin, 506 (t); Paul Conklin, 525–534; New York Public Library, 548; New York Public Library, 553; NASA/Photo Researchers, 568; HBJ Photo, 568 (br); Photo Researchers, 569; Courtesy KCET T.V./Photo Researchers, 570 (t); JPL, 570 (b); Dr. Robert Leighton/JPL, 571 (t); Jerry Schad/Photo Researchers, 571 (c); David A. Hardy/Photo Researchers, 571 (r); JPL, 572–573, 574 (t); NASA/Photo Researchers, 574 (b), 575 (t); JPL, 575 (b); Rev. Ronald Rover/Photo Researchers, 576 (tll); Fred Espenak/Photo Researchers, 576 (tr) (tll); U.S. Naval Observatory/Photo Researchers, 577 (tll); Historical Picture Service, 580; HBJ, 584; Robert Frerck/Odyssey, 589; Robert Frerck/Odyssey, 596.

Table of Contents Art
Key: (t) top, (b) bottom, (l) left, (r) right, (c) center.
Bill Boyko, 4–5 (c), 7 (tr), 8 (bl), 10 (tl), 11 (br), 12–13 (c), 15 (tr); Normand Cousineau, 4 (bl), 6 (tl), 7 (br), 8–9 (c), 11 (br), 12 (bl), 14 (tl), 15 (br); Ruben DeAnda, 5 (br), 8 (tl), 9 (br), 10–11 (c), 13 (tr), 14 (bl); Clarence Porter, 4 (tl), (br), 6–7 (c), 9 (tr), 10 (bl), 12 (tl), 13 (br) 14–15 (c).

Unit Opening Patterns
David Diaz

Bookshelf Art
Ray-Mel Cornelius, 112–113, 506–507; Amanda Schaffer, 212–213; Joel Spector, 402–403; James Staunton, 18–19, 298–299.

Theme Opening Art
Gary Baseman, 540–541; Linda Bleck, 70–71; Gerry Bustamante, 266–267; Normand Cousineau, 238–239; David Diaz, 427–437; Ruben DeAnda, 332–333; John Dyess, 214–215; Gene Faulkner, 560–561; Marty Gunsaulus, 300–301; Jennifer Hewitson, 20–21; Amanda Schaffer, 118–119; Walter Stuart, 474–475; Tracy Widener, 182–183.

Theme Closing Art
David Davis, 579; Rae Ecklund, 45, 147, 473; Mark Frueh, 331; Tom Leonard, 501, 559; Edward Martinez, 539; San Murata, 107; Gail Piazza, 397; Clarence Porter, 207, 237; Stacey Previn, 629; Lynn Rowe Reed, 359; Arvis Stewart, 265, 293; Walter Stuart, 435; Roxana Villa, 181.

Connections Art
David Diaz, 294–295; William Maughan, 398–399; Clarence Porter, 580–581; Tracy Sabin, 208–209, 502–503; Roxana Villa, 108–109.

Selection Art
Dan Andreasen, 252, 253, 254, 259; Charles Cashwell, 198, 199, 200, 201, 202, 203, 204, 205; Richard Cook, 484–485, 488–489, 492–493, 496–497; Greg Correll, 105; Manuel Garcia, 268–283; Ken Goldammer, 48–57; Cheryl Greisbach and Stanley Martucci, 176, 177; Franklin Hamilton, 562–567; David McCall Johnston, 171; Ross McDonald, 184, 188, 191, 193, 196; Francisco Mora, 84, 90; Paul Morin, 162, 167; David Moses, 116, 117, 123, 129; Brian Pinkney, 63, 65, 67; Jerry Pinkney, 500, 515, 519; Clarence Porter, 334–347, 543, 544, 545, 548, 549, 550, 551, 552, 554, 556–557; Muns Quan, 362, 363, 368, 371, 374, 376, 381; Scott Scheidly, 349; Dick Sakahara,

134, 135, 139, 144, 145, 146; S.D. Schindler, 458–467; Patrick Soper, 438, 440, 443, 446–447, 451, 452; J. A. White, 22, 23, 29, 37, 39; Leslie Wu, 363, 365, 368–369, 370, 373, 376–377, 378.

Integrated Instruction

We believe that through a more

holistic approach to teaching

reading and language arts, students

will discover the connection

between reading, writing, listening,

and speaking.

Why Authentic Literature Has Replaced the Old Standards

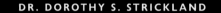

Shared Reading! Literature Response Groups! Author Studies! Genre Studies! Response Logs!

Literature-Based Reading!

DR. DOROTHY S. STRICKLAND

The State of New Jersey Professor of Reading at Rutgers University and Senior Author, HBJ Treasury of Literature

These terms are finding their way into the lesson plan books of an increasing number of teachers throughout the United States and the world. Their use is just one of the signs that literature-based reading is receiving widespread attention, acceptance, and acclaim.

Interest in the use of literature to teach reading and writing has increased as more and more teachers and administrators seek to re-examine the way literacy is taught in their schools. Many, having moved toward teaching writing as process, have sought to make their reading programs more process oriented, too. The use of strategies such as shared reading and literature response groups seemed to fit in well with their writing programs. Some were attracted to the idea by the wealth of quality books now available to children. Still others were influenced by the potential for linking content themes in social studies and science with literary studies typically associated with learning to read and write.

Children not only read and respond to a rich variety of literature, they also learn about many of the authors and poets...

The move toward literature-based reading may occur in a single classroom, a single school, or in many cases, an entire school district. Whether such a program is launched on a large scale or on a small one, certain instructional elements are evident. Each is an essential part of *HBJ Treasury of Literature*.

1. "Real literature" predominates in the reading program throughout the grade levels.

2. Reading, writing, and oral language are closely linked.

3. In-depth studies are made of authors and their craft.

4. Students respond to literature through discussion, writing, art, drama, and more reading.

5. Self-selected independent reading is valued, and student choice is respected.

6. Students read and respond to a wide variety of literary forms and genres.

7. Literature is integrated with content areas across the entire curriculum.

8. Students are helped to use their experiences with literature to learn the strategies and skills required to become competent readers, writers, and thinkers.

HBJ Treasury of Literature is filled with the works of award-winning poets and authors. Newbery and Caldecott Medal winners are represented, as are writers whose nonfiction works are listed among the Outstanding Science Trade Books.

Children not only read and respond to a rich variety of literature, they also learn about many of the authors and poets, discovering how these writers go about their craft. Through frequent discussion and daily opportunities to write, students link what they learn to their own writing development as well.

The literature selections are arranged in interesting themes that help to unify activities and to make connections with other curriculum areas such as social studies and science. This makes learning "real," the way it is outside of school.

Through varied experiences with literature, students are helped to see the naturally occurring patterns in text. It is through wide exposure to these patterns that the strategies and skills needed to read and write effectively are developed. These literacy strategies are made explicit through continued, varied exposure and through specific teacher-guided activities.

The goals of literature-based reading extend well beyond simply teaching children to read and write. As exemplified in *HBJ Treasury of Literature*, the primary goal of literature-based reading is to foster the development of *readers* and *writers*—students who are not only competent readers and writers, but who view reading and writing as an integral part of their lives. ●

Why Shouldn't Young Readers Read Great Writers?

DR. BERNICE E. CULLINAN

Professor of Early Childhood and Elementary Education at New York University and Senior Consultant, HBJ Treasury of Literature

It was survival of the greatest as books were selected for HBJ Treasury of Literature.

The foundation of any successful literature-based reading program is, of course, great literature. Great literature does many things. It enriches children's lives and makes them aware of the pluralistic nature of our world. It allows children to savor experience and to experience life. As we selected literature for *HBJ Treasury of Literature*, we looked for these qualities and more. We looked for literature that

- stimulates the reader's imagination.
- contains sparkling language and natural dialogue.
- provides heroes, role models, and memorable characters.
- evokes deep emotion, tickles the funny bone, or tingles the spine.
- gives new information and deepens understanding.
- sparks a love of reading through many literary genres.
- elicits high praise from children and adults alike.

Some people spend their entire lives collecting great works. And sometimes, we, as teachers, are fortunate to discover that someone has done the work for us—that a treasury of great literature has already been assembled—that a program like *HBJ Treasury of Literature* exists. ●

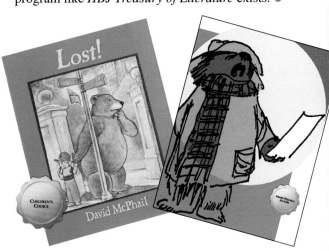

Lost!

CHILDREN'S CHOICE

David McPhail

Look for
- Authentic literature
- How the best books survive HBJ's screening process
- *HBJ Treasury of Literature* Library Books linked with every literary theme
- Numerous opportunities for self-selected independent reading
- In-depth studies of authors and their craft

Truth Is Stranger than Fiction

Or at least more interesting

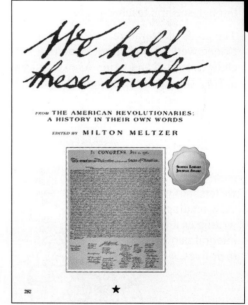

DR. RICHARD F. ABRAHAMSON

*Professor of Education at the University of Houston
and Author, HBJ Treasury of Literature*

Nonfiction's surprising appeal among young readers

Across the country, teachers of literature-based reading programs are discovering the powerful role that nonfiction plays in the reading lives of today's children and young adults—tomorrow's leaders.

America is a country of nonfiction readers. Our interest in nonfiction starts in elementary school and increases steadily as we move through middle school and high school. Within the pages of *HBJ Treasury of Literature,* our students can find some of the most interesting nonfiction pieces by the finest authors in the field.

Research tells us that between forty and fifty percent of all the books students check out of elementary and middle-school libraries are nonfiction. And they are read, often for pleasure. In a study of ten years of Children's Choice lists compiled by the International Reading Association and the Children's Book Council, forty-three percent of the titles were nonfiction.

Much has been written recently about that growing segment of the student population called aliterate readers — those youngsters who can read but choose not to. Research has shown that even readers with the most negative attitudes toward reading do read some things. What they read is nonfiction— magazine selections about natural disasters, books about sports and sports heroes, math and science games, and fascinating discoveries about dinosaurs.

> *...a special book in your life... may well have been nonfiction.*

What better way to welcome many aliterate readers back into the reading club than by using the inviting nonfiction pieces found in *HBJ Treasury of Literature*!

Good nonfiction writing is not just a collection of facts. It can move us deeply. Think back to a special book in your life, one that challenged you or even moved you to tears. It may well have been nonfiction.

Among the many quality nonfiction pieces offered in *HBJ Treasury of Literature* are selections from Alex Haley's *Roots,* Gary Paulsen's autobiographical account of competing in a grueling dogsled race, and many interviews with authors such as Chris Van Allsburg, Lois Lowry, Gary Soto, and James Michener. This is the kind of nonfiction that spells reading motivation for today's young readers. ●

Look for
- The most interesting nonfiction pieces by the finest authors in the field
- Great poetry that opens up a world of feeling for children

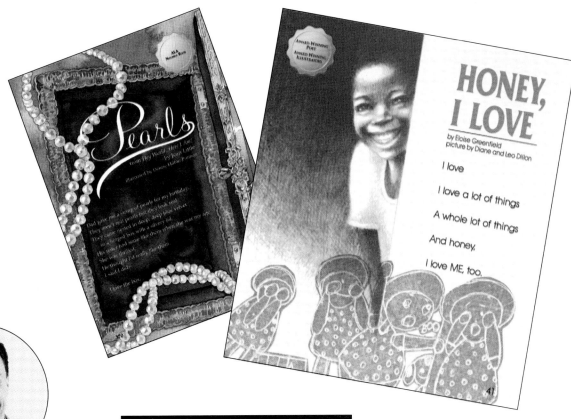

DR. LEE BENNETT HOPKINS

Poet, author, anthologist, and Consultant,
HBJ Treasury of Literature

The Gift of Poetry

Opening a world of feeling to children

I have said it many times; I shall say it again and again: Poetry should flow freely in the lives of children; it should come to them as naturally as breathing, for nothing—no thing—can ring and rage throughout hearts and minds as does this genre of literature.

As a classroom teacher, I quickly learned the value of poetry—how it can enhance every area of the curriculum—from mathematics to science. More important, I soon realized that poetry was an effective force with above-average, average, and reluctant readers on every grade level. And, oh, what poetry can do to bolster the self-esteem of children everywhere.

Every day is a great day for poetry—the kind of great poetry that can be found in *HBJ Treasury of Literature*. Poets such as Eve Merriam, Nikki Giovanni, John Ciardi, Teresa Paloma Acosta, and Aileen Fisher open up a world of feelings to children.

> *And, oh, what poetry can do to bolster the self-esteem of children everywhere.*

As educators we must lead children into poetry—ignite the spark for them to appreciate it, love it. This is one of the greatest gifts we can give to our students, whether they are pre-schoolers or young adult readers.

There is a place for poetry—every day—everywhere—all of the time.

For me, any day without a poem is just another day on the calendar. I hope it will be for you, too, and for the children you nurture, reach, touch. ●

Putting the Thinking Back into Reading

Developing strategic readers

DR. DONNA M. OGLE

Chair, Reading and Language Arts Department of National-Louis University, Evanston, Illinois, and Author, HBJ Treasury of Literature

Good readers are confident. They know they are in charge of the reading process and can adjust their reading behaviors if necessary to achieve their purpose. They have a repertoire of strategies they know will work for them in a variety of reading situations.

Reading is not a passive activity involving the eyes scanning a page. Each reading situation is an encounter between an absent author and a reader who is trying to construct a clear understanding from the available written message. Good readers, like athletes, set goals and plan for how they will achieve them. They make adjustments and alterations to their plan as necessary.

We know from much research with active readers that certain kinds of behaviors are common across all reading situations. These include anticipating meaning and linking the text to what the reader already knows, making predictions and altering them as information unfolds, constructing interpretations by making inferences

...good readers confidently adjust their reading and thinking behaviors to meet their own needs and those of the situation.

Look for

- Preview and predict strategy employed in every fiction selection
- KWL or SQ3R strategy employed in every nonfiction selection
- Strategy lessons
- Vocabulary strategies
- Strategy conferences
- Critical thinking activities

and elaborating on the ideas presented by the author, visualizing, asking questions of the text, and monitoring one's understanding so that alterations can be made and fix-up strategies employed.

DR. ROBERT J. STERNBERG

*IBM Professor of Psychology
and Education at Yale
University and Consultant,*
HBJ Treasury of Literature

New Ways of Thinking About Thinking

Building critical and creative thinking

I don't understand why Cricket is saying this. I think I'd better reread the last few paragraphs to see what's going on.

Other behaviors are more situation specific. For example, if a reader needs to retain information for a specific purpose for school or personal learning, more active retention strategies will be employed. One of these might be filling out a K-W-L chart. Another might be following the SQ3R procedure. No matter what the task or how difficult the material, good readers confidently adjust their reading and thinking behaviors to meet their own needs and those of the situation.

Reading strategies don't develop automatically. A recent study of middle-school readers (LaZansky and Tierney) revealed that there was little variety in the strategies they used.

However, students who use the kind of strategy instruction provided in *HBJ Treasury of Literature* come to realize that there are options for dealing with unfamiliar text.

Instruction in strategic reading begins early in *HBJ Treasury of Literature*. Even first-grade readers employ strategies they have learned. As readers mature, they build a rich repertoire of strategies that empowers them so that they *want* to read and *do* read successfully. The program builds an understanding of the reading process. Young readers are given clear information about active reading-thinking behavior and direct modeling of each process. This scaffolded instruction produces confident readers who choose reading for their own pleasure and learning. ●

Critical thinking involves analyzing arguments, making judgments, drawing conclusions. Creative thinking involves such activities as inventing scenes, speculating, and solving problems.

A story from *Hatchet,* by Gary Paulsen, appears in *HBJ Treasury of Literature.* The story is about a boy who flies a plane when the pilot has a deadly heart attack. A comprehension question asks:

> What are the problems that Brian Robeson faces in this story?

Note that this question measures true understanding, not merely factual recall. A Critical Thinking Activity reads:

> Think about Brian's behavior throughout the story. Write a report that praises some of his actions and criticizes others.

Here students make judgments that critically evaluate Brian's response.

Finally, consider an activity from the lesson that explores creative thinking.

> What would have helped Brian during the emergency? Write a list of the supplies, information, and skills that might have made his ordeal more bearable.

These kinds of critical and creative thinking activities are an integral part of *HBJ Treasury of Literature.* They invite children to think by presenting them with challenges that are intriguing and that touch their lives. ●

Integrating the Language Arts

DR. BARBARA BOWEN COULTER

*Director, Communication Arts for
the Detroit Public School District
and Author, HBJ Treasury of
Literature*

New insights on linking the language arts

As an information revolution sweeps us into the twenty-first century, we
realize that we are teaching more than reading, more than writing, more than listening, and more than speaking. We are teaching communication. We recognize the
need to teach skills, but we want children to do this at the same time that they are discovering the joys of reading, the power of writing, and the roles that listening and
speaking play in those processes.

HBJ Treasury of Literature...*teaches reading within the context of the integrated language arts.*

HBJ Treasury of Literature embodies a teaching approach that
contains the tools to achieve this goal. It teaches reading within
the context of the integrated language arts. As students participate in the diverse activities that are available in *HBJ
Treasury of Literature*, they build a foundation that makes
them adept communicators. The teacher is empowered to
structure their learning experience in ways that allow them
to develop the confidence,
the skills, and the knowledge to solve problems and
become independent
thinkers and learners. ●

Don't Underestimate the Power of the Pencil

DR. TIMOTHY SHANAHAN

Professor of Urban Education at the University of Illinois at Chicago and Author, HBJ Treasury of Literature

How writing builds better readers and writers

During the fifth grade, I decided to become a writer—a peculiar choice, as my school experiences offered no opportunity to put my thoughts to paper. Now, years later, it is finally widely recognized that we must provide children with an abundant heritage of literature while celebrating their voices.

We have, in *HBJ Treasury of Literature*, also a treasury of writing experiences carefully designed to help children become better readers. First, writing activities deepen their understanding of the processes of reading and the structures of text. After reading a mystery, for example, children might be asked to try their hand at creating their own mysteries—complete with suspense. Second, *HBJ Treasury of Literature* contains original interviews and specially commissioned personal reflections that reveal why authors write as they do. Throughout the program, children also use writing as a form of self-communication to help them participate in conversation with their classmates and others. Writer's Workshops involve children in the writing process. Finally, *HBJ Treasury of Literature* demonstrates how writing, when allied with reading, can become a more powerful avenue to learning. Toward this end, children are encouraged to do "quickwrites" to activate prior knowledge, to use writing to summarize and extend their understandings of text, and to write personal responses to literature.

This wonderful interplay between children's literature and the literature of children entices students to explore their world through the written word—to communicate, to create, to know. It almost makes me wish I were still in the fifth grade. ●

After reading a mystery, for instance, children might be asked to try their hand at creating their own mysteries—complete with suspense.

Look for
- Integrated Language Arts
- Reader/Writer Connections
- Writer's Workshops
- Quickwrites
- Personal journals
- Original interviews and personal reflections by authors

DR. W. DORSEY HAMMOND

Professor of Education at Oakland University in Rochester, Michigan, and Senior Consultant, HBJ Treasury of Literature

New Strategies Spell S-U-C-C-E-S-S with Students

Anything worth writing is worth spelling right.

Good readers and writers also become good spellers, or so the research indicates. However, the spelling abilities of elementary and middle school students will not develop or reach full potential if ignored or left to chance. All students, therefore, can benefit from an organized spelling curriculum.

Good spellers use strategies, conscious or unconscious. *HBJ Treasury of Literature Integrated Spelling* takes certain important strategies and makes them available to all students. Let's take a look at some of the strategies that super-spellers develop, seemingly by intuition.

Integrated Spelling teaches students to make spelling generalizations by taking key words directly from the reading selections. Students also receive explanations of unusual spellings and numerous opportunities to proofread for spelling. In addition, *Integrated Spelling* provides metacognitive strategies to help children develop their "spelling consciousness," including pattern recognition, going from the known to the unkown, and mnemonic devices. Perhaps most importantly for the concept of the reading and writing processes as systems, spelling is taught in the natural context of literature.

Most students want to be able to spell. It can be a source of pride to them as they learn other communication skills. The methods used in *HBJ Treasury of Literature Integrated Spelling* are designed to unlock the mysteries of good spelling and make the skill available to all students. ●

Integrated Spelling *provides metacognitive strategies to help students develop their "spelling consciousness"...*

PATRICIA SMITH

Adjunct Professor of Education at the University of Houston at Clear Lake and Author, HBJ Treasury of Literature

Writing with Style

Teaching students to "read with a writer's eye"

> "From that day forward, the generous king would frequently sort through the treasure chest looking for just the right jewel to offer as a gift. And they all lived happily ever after."

Just as the king in this traditional story had a cache from which to draw jewels, so, too, do the readers of *HBJ Treasury of Literature* have a source of beautifully crafted word usage. The literature serves as an exemplary language model for students. They are taught to "read with a writer's eye" in order to find and appreciate well-crafted passages.

Besides being generally immersed in a treasury of language-rich literature, students are explicitly instructed in effective language use. In each theme, Language/Literature Link offers explicit instruction on integrating language with literature. Elements of authors' craft such as elaboration through use of precise words, sensory language, examples, and

The literature serves as an exemplary language model for students.

dialogue are explained. Grammar elements such as vivid verb usage, sentences with compound predicates, and expanded sentences are integrated into the theme. Students always receive the dual invitation to return to the literature to experience the language technique and to reach forward to incorporate the language technique into their own writing.

For example, the precise word choice of Patricia MacLachlan exemplified in her *Sarah, Plain and Tall* becomes the model for student use of precise wording. The literature and language are linked together to form an integrated whole for effective reading and writing. Perhaps the result of the rich integration in *HBJ Treasury of Literature* would be this modern-day version of the traditional story ending.

> "And so…from that day forward, the students called forth from the rich language of their literary experiences just the right techniques to present their thoughts. And they all lived happily ever after." ●

Look for
- Language/Literature Link
- Spelling-Vocabulary Connection
- *HBJ Treasury of Literature* Integrated Spelling

When Does Two Plus Two Equal Five?

DR. JUDITH L. IRVIN

Director, Center for the Study of Middle Level Education and Author, HBJ Treasury of Literature

Making connections between different subjects can add up to greater learning.

Most teachers are humbled by their experience at one time or another. I was during a social studies lesson on pollution, years ago. A student asked me, "Is the environment we are studying in social studies the same environment we studied in science?"

Recent research on brain-based learning sheds valuable information on the reasons for integrating curriculum studies. It indicates that the brain recognizes, sorts, and organizes information according to large patterns. Information presented in context becomes meaningful to the learner while isolated bits of information seem to hinder this process.

...information presented in context becomes meaningful to the learner...

Set forth here are some general guidelines that *HBJ Treasury of Literature* followed to help you move toward an integrated curriculum.

- Each Anthology from grades 4 through 8 contains a unit of literature that focuses on science and a unit of literature that focuses on social studies.

- Integrated Curriculum activities appear in each lesson plan and Connections at the end of each unit.

- Within each level are eighteen themes—collections of literature related to a concept or idea.

Given these features from *HBJ Treasury of Literature* and the flexibility and ease-of-use of the program, reshaping curriculum has never been easier.

Of course, some students make connections between disciplines by themselves. For them, *HBJ Treasury of Literature* will validate these discoveries. For those who have not yet made their own internal learning "map," the cross-curricular activities in this series provide scaffolding for a skill that will serve them well throughout their lives. ●

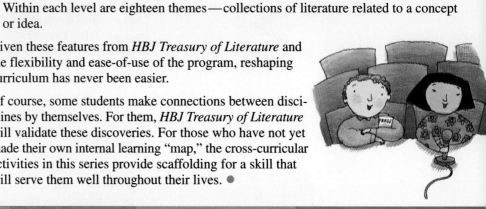

Look for
- Literature arranged by themes
- Units focusing on science and on social studies
- Integrated curriculum in each lesson plan
- Cross-curriculum connections at the end of each unit

Classroom Management

We recognize that each classroom is a unique learning environment and that effectively managing the resources within that environment is a challenge. We are committed to helping teachers meet the needs of all students in a literature-based classroom.

Making Your Classroom Reading-Friendly

DR. ROGER C. FARR

Professor of Education and Director of the Center for Reading and Language Studies, Indiana University and Senior Author, HBJ Treasury of Literature

A checklist of management strategies for the literature-based classroom

There is no one best way to manage a literature-based classroom. However, good management grows out of good organization. When planning literature-based instruction, consider which of the many techniques for organizing the classroom will work best for you. Whatever technique you choose, consider these general guidelines:

- The instructional needs and interests of students are paramount in determining effective instructional strategies.

- The organization of the classroom provides students with many opportunities to share with you and with each other the things they are reading and writing.

- A variety of books, magazines, and writing materials are easily accessible to students. The classroom has comfortable reading "corners," which become havens where students can escape with a favorite book or magazine.

- The students are empowered. They are included in the planning and share in the responsibility to ensure that learning experiences are effective.

- The management plan is flexible. It allows the teacher to take advantage of student interests and motivation and to seize upon teachable moments.

The research-tested organizational patterns below have been used effectively by many teachers in literature-based reading programs. These are just a few of the options you will find support for in *HBJ Treasury of Literature*.

Good management grows out of good organization.

Popular Organizational Patterns

Organization	What is it?	Examples
Whole Class	Teacher works with the entire class at the same time. Variations may include times when the teacher is directing the entire group and times when individual class members are doing the same task at the same time.	Shared Reading Sustained Silent Reading Direct Whole-Class Instruction
Small-Group/ Cooperative Group	Groups of children work together toward a common goal. Often, the group determines how the task is divided among its members; other times the teacher directs the activity. Sometimes, as few as two students take turns reading a story or leading an activity.	Reader Response Groups Paired/Buddy Reading Small-Group Instruction Cooperative Reading Activity/Interest Groups
Individual	Each student functions independently and is responsible for his or her own work.	Independent Reading Self-Selected Reading Independent Projects Learning Centers

As you plan instruction for each new theme in *HBJ Treasury of Literature*, you will find specific suggestions given for managing a literature-based classroom. Here are a few general tips to help you start planning:

- Consider all of the factors that enter into planning: people, time, space, facilities, materials, and organization.

- Plan ahead in combining activities. As students work on a writing activity, you might pull out students for portfolio conferences.

- Be flexible. Develop plans that follow general guidelines.

- Continuously assess, revise, and modify your plans.

A significant factor in determining the success of a literature-based program is maintaining contact with students' families. Family Involvement Activities, such as those at the beginning of each *HBJ Treasury of Literature* lesson plan, can be used by parents to reinforce important concepts and themes. In addition, when Practice Book pages are assigned independently after small-group instruction, family members can help children build responsibility in completing and returning assignments.

Making family involvement flow smoothly also requires effective communication. Suggestions that might be included in a family information letter can be found in *HBJ Treasury of Literature* Family Involvement Activities. ●

Putting Literature Up for Discussion

DR. KAREN S. KUTIPER

Assistant Professor of Education at Southeast Texas State University and Author, HBJ Treasury of Literature

Finding shared and personal meanings in reader response groups

Reader response groups—small groups of students responding independently to literature selections in a non-threatening environment—offer teachers a new alternative in classroom management. Children in response groups hold a dialogue among themselves that is focused on elements of literature.

So why would teachers use reader response groups? Are they just one more classroom management option? Reader response groups are much more than a management technique.

Children working in response groups bring literature to life, find personal meanings in literature, and share the pleasure of reading. They begin to realize that each group member might have a differ-

ent yet valid response and that listening to these shared responses often helps them clarify or enrich their own understanding.

Children who participate in reader response groups see that their ideas can be received and valued by others. They are challenged to think critically by participating in discussions that seldom stay at the literal level. They learn to function in varying group roles. The teacher becomes a facilitator of learning, encouraging children to seek new depths of understanding by developing their own avenues of discussion. The reading of literature becomes a quest to discover personal and shared meanings.

Because of their flexibility, reader response groups fit well into many classroom-management plans. *HBJ Treasury of Literature* provides the teacher with many suggestions for using reader response groups. Appropriate places for their use are suggested in the lesson plans, along with management tips. Response Cards in the Teacher Resources section of the Teacher's Editions for grades 2–8 may be used to allow students to function independently from the teacher.

Reader response groups provide a means of encouraging a love of reading and of helping children build the communication and interpersonal skills that also affect self-esteem. No wonder so many teachers use them! ●

Reader response groups allow...students to respond to literature selections in a loosely-structured, non-threatening environment.

Look for
- Options for reading
- Management strategies for a literature-based classroom
- *HBJ Treasury of Literature* Family Involvement Activities
- Suggestions for using reader response groups
- Response Cards to copy and keep

Second Language Support

DR. MARGARET A. GALLEGO

Assistant Professor of Education at Michigan State University and Author, HBJ Treasury of Literature

Tailoring teaching strategies for the linguistically diverse classroom

Millions of children are coming to school from homes where languages other than English are spoken, making it inevitable that all teachers will eventually teach students of various linguistic backgrounds. A classroom of diverse students can offer unlimited possibilities for creating a unique community of learners. However, addressing linguistically diverse students' individual reading instruction needs can be exceptionally challenging.

To meet the needs of linguistically diverse students, *HBJ Treasury of Literature* has integrated Second-Language Support throughout the program.

1. Second-Language Support notes in the Teacher's Editions are embedded throughout Vocabulary Strategies, Strategic Reading, and Learning Through Literature.

2. Suggestions for classroom management of Second-Language Support appear in each theme.

...unlimited possibilities for creating a unique community of learners.

3. Lessons in the Second-Language Support Manual give students the background and vocabulary needed to successfully participate in *HBJ Treasury of Literature*.

In addition, the *English as a Second Language (ESL) Manual* offers activities to help students develop English proficiency and the *Transition for ESL Students* provides support for those transferring into *HBJ Treasury of Literature* from Spanish or other language reading programs. ●

Are gifted children really worth all that extra attention?

Yes, but not at the expense of their classmates

An ideal reading program for gifted and talented students offers diversity and challenge, stresses critical and creative thinking and offers opportunities for students to customize activities that result in concrete accomplishments. In addition, it provides a range of assessment instruments to meet the needs of all students.

Challenge activities help you customize the lesson plans.

DR. ROBERT J. STERNBERG

IBM Professor of Psychology and Education at Yale University and Consultant, HBJ Treasury of Literature

How does *HBJ Treasury of Literature* compare to an ideal program for gifted and talented children? Meeting Individual Needs provides specific teaching strategies for gifted and talented students. Challenge activities help you customize the lesson plans. Critical and creative thinking questions and activities abound. Writer's Workshops, as well as other activities, invite students to create and customize tangible products. Also, a variety of assessment options helps teachers meet the needs of gifted and talented students. ●

Look for
- Meeting Individual Needs section in every lesson plan
- Specific support for students with limited English proficiency, students at risk, special education students, and gifted and talented students
- Self-Assessment Notes, Strategy Conferences, and Portfolio Conferences
- Critical and creative thinking questions and activities
- Projects, activities, and Writer's Workshops
- Second-Language Support notes and manual
- *English as a Second Language (ESL) Manual*
- *Transition for ESL Students*

Special Education Without Special Classrooms

Meeting the individual needs of learning-disabled and other special pupils in a mainstream setting

More and more teachers are finding themselves teaching some children who, in the past, were taught in special education classes. Most teachers agree that this is a positive step in the education of special education students; however some teachers find it frustrating to meet the needs of an even wider variety of children than before.

Ideas are included for learning-disabled students, including those with dyslexia, as well as for students with physical, visual, and auditory disabilities.

The majority of special education students placed in mainstream classrooms have been learning-disabled students. For many of them, reading is a difficult process because of problems with visual or auditory acuity or perception. To be effective today, a reading program in a mainstream classroom must meet the needs of *all* students, including those with learning disabilities or other special needs.

HBJ Treasury of Literature was developed keeping special education students in mind. Meeting Individual Needs offers teachers specific strategies to help special students. Ideas are included for working with learning-disabled students, including those with dyslexia, as well as for students with physical, visual, and auditory disabilities. Flexibility in grouping throughout the program makes it especially easy to meet the needs of special students. ●

DR. ALONZO A. CRIM

Benjamin E. Mays Professor of Urban Educational Leadership at Georgia State University, Professor of Education at Spelman College and Consultant, HBJ Treasury of Literature

No Risk of Failure

How to succeed with students at risk

There is no commonly agreed upon definition for "at risk." But although teachers may not agree on a definition, almost all will tell you they have students at risk sitting in their classrooms.

So who are students at risk? They can often be characterized by unsatisfactory academic achievement, performance below academic ability, poor self-concept, withdrawn behavior, or negative behavior not limited to a specific teacher or classroom situation.

While each student at risk would seem to have a dif-ferent profile, there are several strategies that research has shown to be effective for all students at risk.

1. Emphasize the positive.

2. Have high expectations.

3. Involve children in their own education.

4. Create opportunities for children to succeed.

Options within lesson plans allow all *students to meet common goals in a variety of ways.*

HBJ Treasury of Literature has embedded these strategies throughout the program. Meeting Individual Needs provides specific teaching strategies for students at risk. Options within lesson plans allow *all* students to meet common goals in a variety of ways. Self-Assessment Notes, Strategy Conferences, and Portfolio Conferences help students take an active part in their own education. Support, encouragement, and opportunities for individual successes fill every page of *HBJ Treasury of Literature*, and take the risk of failure out of teaching students at risk. ●

Pacing

A reading program that meets varied school schedules

A basic unit of instruction in *HBJ Treasury of Literature* takes from $4^1/_2$ to 6 weeks to complete and is comprised of three themes.

A Typical Unit of Instruction / $4^1/_2$ to 6 Weeks

Theme —	1	2	3
Weeks —	$1^1/_2 - 2$	$1^1/_2 - 2$	$1^1/_2 - 2$

While this model meets the needs of many teachers, we believe that classroom teachers must have the flexibility to make instructional pacing decisions based on their needs and the needs of their students. Special features, such as the following, have been embedded throughout the program to allow easy adjustment to meet any schedule:

- Managing the Literature-Based Classroom preceding each theme offers classroom-management suggestions that will vary the amount of time required to complete the theme. These range from the use of reader response groups for cooperative reading to suggestions for using additional literature to extend and enrich the themes.

- Sections labeled Teacher Choices are found throughout the lesson plans. Teachers will find many optional activities from which they may choose and that will help them adjust pacing.

Flexibility is the key component of the pacing of HBJ Treasury of Literature.

Reteach Lessons

When students have difficulty applying a strategy or skill, an array of multisensory teaching strategies is available to help you modify your methods and accommodate student needs.

Context/Multiple-Meaning Words

OBJECTIVE: *To use context clues to determine the meaning of a multiple-meaning word*

1. Focus

Share the following information with students:

When readers come across a word that has more than one meaning, they can use information in the sentences that surround the word to determine which meaning the author intends. Using context to determine word meaning helps readers better understand what they read.

2. Choose a Teaching Model

VISUAL MODEL Write the following chart and passage on the board (underlining words as shown):

Word	Possible Meanings
sail	large piece of cloth that catches wind to move a boat
	to move in a boat
	to float or glide through the air
vessel	hollow container
	ship or boat
	tube inside the body for carrying fluids
counter	long table or board on which to serve meals
	person or thing that counts
	in an opposite direction

   Madeline's dream was to <u>sail</u> across the Pacific Ocean by herself in a small boat. She worked for many years to save enough to buy and prepare a <u>vessel</u> to make the long sea trip. Finally, she set off. Her journey was difficult at first, because the wind blew <u>counter</u> to the way she intended to travel. However, she eventually made it, fulfilling her dream.

Have students review the chart and read the paragraph silently. Ask volunteers to come to the board and read each underlined word aloud. Have them write in colored chalk the correct meaning above each word and explain how they used context

to arrive at their answer. Next, ask students to write context sentences that use the other two meanings of each word. Have volunteers share their sentences and ask classmates to identify which meaning is being used in each sentence. Then follow the suggestions in **Summarize/Reinforce.**

AUDITORY MODEL Display the chart from the Visual Model and ask students to review it silently. Then have them listen carefully as you slowly read aloud the paragraph from the Visual Model. Pause to allow students to identify context clues for each word. Then ask volunteers to identify the correct meaning in the chart for each word and explain how the context helped them. Next, have students work in pairs to write sentences using the underlined words with the other meanings in the chart, read their sentences aloud, and have classmates identify the meaning. Then follow the suggestions in **Summarize/Reinforce.**

KINESTHETIC/MOTOR MODEL Distribute copies of the chart from the Visual Model and review it with students. Then read aloud the paragraph from the Visual Model, asking students to listen carefully for context clues to help them identify the appropriate meaning of each underlined word. Reread the paragraph and have students circle the correct meaning with pencil or pen. Then, for each word, ask them to write a sentence that demonstrates one of its other meanings. Have volunteers share their sentences, explaining how the context shows the word's meaning. Then follow the suggestions in **Summarize/Reinforce.**

3. Summarize/Reinforce

Have students summarize what they learned. (Readers can determine the appropriate meaning of multiple-meaning words by using context clues.) Reinforce the lesson by having students identify the appropriate meaning of multiple-meaning words they find in a favorite story. Remind students to use the strategies from this lesson to help them determine word meanings as they read.

Graphic Aids

OBJECTIVE: *To read and use information from maps and diagrams to visualize text content*

NOTE: You may wish to adapt this lesson for use with a map of your state.

1. Focus

Share the following information with students:

> *Maps* **show the relative shape, size, location, and importance of land areas and bodies of water. A map has such features as a compass rose, a distance scale, and place names to help readers use the information in the map.** *Diagrams* **are labeled drawings that show the parts and features of something, or show how something works. Knowing how to use these graphic aids helps readers better understand and visualize what is described in the text.**

2. Choose a Teaching Model

VISUAL MODEL Display a map of California and have volunteers point to the compass rose, distance scale, land and ocean markings, and place names. Ask two students to mark with flags the cities of Ventura and Santa Barbara on the map. Then have a volunteer use the distance scale to determine the distance between the two cities. Next, help students locate Anacapa Island on the map. Instruct another volunteer to determine how far it is from Oxnard to Anacapa Island. For diagrams, consult an encyclopedia to make a simple drawing of a flower on the board, and label a few of the most immediately recognizable parts, such as the stem. Have volunteers label as many other parts as they can. Encourage them to refer to the encyclopedia, as necessary. Then follow the suggestions in **Summarize/Reinforce.**

AUDITORY MODEL Display a map of California. Point to various features of the map, such as the compass rose and the scale of miles, and have volunteers identify and explain the function of each

one. Next, ask the following questions and have volunteers respond, demonstrating on the map how to arrive at their answers: **Where are Santa Barbara and Ventura? How far is it from Santa Barbara to Ventura? Where are Anacapa Island and Oxnard? How far is the island from Oxnard?** For diagrams, draw or display a picture of a flower. Point to various parts of the flower, such as the stem, petals, and leaves, and have students name each part as you write it on the board. Encourage students to consult an encyclopedia, if necessary. Then follow the suggestions in **Summarize/ Reinforce.**

KINESTHETIC/MOTOR MODEL Have students work in pairs. First, distribute an outline map of California with a compass rose and a distance scale. Also display a labeled map of the state. Instruct partners to add to their outline map important features, such as mountains and rivers and important place names. Next, have partners label the cities of Santa Barbara, Ventura, and Oxnard, as well as Anacapa Island. Ask them to determine the distance between Santa Barbara and Ventura and the distance between Oxnard and Anacapa Island. Have volunteers share their answers. For diagrams, have students draw a picture of a flower on a sheet of paper and label its various parts. Urge students to consult an encyclopedia, as necessary. Finally, have volunteers display their diagrams. Then follow the suggestions in **Summarize/Reinforce.**

3. Summarize/Reinforce

Have students summarize what they learned. (Maps help readers clearly see where an event is taking place. Diagrams help readers visualize something that is described in the text.) To reinforce the lesson, have students measure the distance between two places mentioned in a newspaper article and find and explain a diagram used in a newspaper. Remind them to use the strategies from this lesson to help them use maps and diagrams as they read.

Sequence

OBJECTIVE: *To use sequence clues to determine the order of events in fiction*

1. Focus

Share the following information with students:

> **Events in a story occur in a certain order, or sequence. Authors often use time-order words or phrases such as *first, next, this time, then, now,* and *before* to indicate this sequence of events. Noting the correct sequence can help readers understand how characters and events change in a story as well as predict what might happen next.**

2. Choose a Teaching Model

VISUAL MODEL   Refer students to the previous selection, "Lost at Sea," and have them read silently the first two paragraphs on page 33, beginning with "All night the *Tadpole* sat on a silent sea. . . ." Next, ask a volunteer to list on the board the time-order words in those two paragraphs. (*all night, for hours, then, one moment, the next, later*) Ask another student to write on the board a sequence chart similar to the following, listing the events in order and using the time-order words. Discuss with students the order of events in this passage, and how the time-order words help make the sequence clear. Next, ask students how being aware of the order of events helps the reader better understand Brennan's character. Then follow the suggestions in **Summarize/Reinforce.**

Sequence Chart

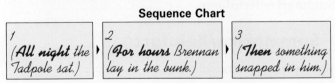

AUDITORY MODEL   Refer students to "Lost at Sea" and the paragraphs indicated in the Visual Model. Ask students to work in pairs. Have one partner read the first paragraph while the other listens for time-order words. Point out that when there are few sequence words in a passage, readers can ask themselves the questions "What happened first?" "What happened next?" and so on. Have partners reverse roles and repeat the process for the second paragraph. Ask each pair to compile a list of the sequence words in the two paragraphs and to note beside each the event that the word or phrase introduces. Have volunteers share their lists of words and events. Discuss with students how being aware of this sequence helps readers better understand Brennan's character. Then follow the suggestions in **Summarize/Reinforce.**

KINESTHETIC/MOTOR MODEL   Ask students to open their books to the passage noted in the Visual Model and follow along as you read aloud. Have students work in pairs to copy the two paragraphs onto a sheet of paper and to circle the time-order words and underline the events. Have volunteers name the sequence words and the events they introduce. Finally, discuss with students how recognizing the sequence of events and thoughts in the passage helps the reader understand Brennan's character. Then follow the suggestions in **Summarize/Reinforce.**

3. Summarize/Reinforce

Have students summarize what they learned. (Sequence means the order in which story events occur. The sequence of events is often signaled by certain time-order words or phrases.) To reinforce this lesson, have students identify time-order words in passages of other selections they have read. Remind them to use the strategies from this lesson to help them determine the sequence of events in stories they read.

Cause and Effect

OBJECTIVE: *To recognize cause-and-effect relationships in literature*

1. Focus

Share the following information with students:

A *cause* is the reason something happens in a story. An *effect* is what happens as a result of a cause. An effect may have more than one cause, and a cause may have several effects. Knowing how to recognize cause-and-effect relationships helps readers understand what events happen in a story and why they happen.

2. Choose a Teaching Model

VISUAL MODEL Have students open to the previous selection, "Lost at Sea," on Student Anthology page 23, and read the first three paragraphs of the story. Ask them to identify the cause-and-effect relationships in this passage by first asking themselves questions such as "What happened to Brennan?" (He got a boat.) Then have them ask themselves questions such as "Why did this event happen?" to determine the cause. Point out to students that when they identify the causes and effects, they will make the relationships clear if they use such words and phrases as *since, because, as a result,* and *therefore.* Have volunteers write their answers on the board in a chart similar to the one shown. Next, ask students to identify other effects Uncle Owen's death had on Brennan. Then follow the suggestions in **Summarize/Reinforce.**

AUDITORY MODEL Refer students to the previous selection, "Lost at Sea," on Student Anthology page 23. Have students work in groups of three, taking turns as they read aloud the first three paragraphs of the story. Then have group members work together to identify the cause-and-effect relationships in the passage, helping them by asking the following questions: **What happened to Brennan? Why?** Have volunteers read their answers aloud, encouraging them to use clue words to signal the cause in each case and to identify the multiple effects that Uncle Owen's death had on Brennan. Then follow the suggestions in **Summarize/ Reinforce.**

KINESTHETIC/MOTOR MODEL Have students open to "Lost at Sea." Ask students to read the first three paragraphs of the story. Then write the following incomplete sentence on the board and have students copy it onto a sheet of paper:

Brennan now owns a cruising sailboat _____.

Instruct students to complete the sentence by adding a cause; encourage them to use a clue word or phrase to signal the cause. Next, ask students to discuss other effects which the death of Brennan's uncle had on Brennan. Finally, have volunteers share their completed sentences with classmates. Then follow the suggestions in **Summarize/Reinforce.**

3. Summarize/Reinforce

Have students summarize what they learned. (A cause is the reason something happens. An effect is what actually happens. Causes are often signaled by clue words.) To reinforce this lesson, have students look for cause-and-effect relationships in other selections they have read. Remind them to use the strategies from this lesson to help them determine causes and effects as they read.

Narrative Elements

OBJECTIVE: *To identify the major narrative elements of a short story*

1. Focus

Share the following information with students:

To identify the major *narrative elements* of a story, readers must recognize the *characters*; the *setting*, or where and when the story takes place; the *plot*, or what happens in the story; and the *theme*, or the message the author is trying to convey. Recognizing these elements helps readers understand and appreciate what they read.

2. Choose a Teaching Model

VISUAL MODEL   Display the following incomplete story map:

Character(s)	*(Lonnie Jackson, Ann Taylor, Mrs. Brignole, Eddie Brignole)*
Setting	*(Afternoon at college gym, basketball court)*
Plot	*(Lonnie shoots baskets in the gym, trying to get a response from Eddie, a withdrawn child.)*
Theme	*(Insights on reaching out to other people)*

Have students open to the previous selection, "A Nice Touch," beginning on Student Anthology page 48. Point out that a story map is one way to identify the major narrative elements of the story. Ask students to think about the narrative elements in "A Nice Touch," skimming the selection if necessary. Then have volunteers fill in each entry listed on the map. Encourage students to discuss their answers to the plot and theme elements, which may vary widely. Then follow the suggestions in **Summarize/ Reinforce.**

AUDITORY MODEL   Have students open to the selection indicated in the Visual Model. Refer to the narrative elements in the story map from the Visual Model and ask the following questions, allowing time for students to respond: **Who are the characters in the story? What is the setting of the story?** Then have students form small groups. Ask them to discuss the plot and the theme, encouraging students to skim the story if necessary. Have volunteers share their answers with classmates. Then follow the suggestions in **Summarize/Reinforce.**

KINESTHETIC/MOTOR MODEL   Have students turn to the selection indicated in the Visual Model. Invite volunteers to summarize and then pantomime key events in the selection. Display the incomplete story map from the Visual Model, pointing out that a story map is one way to identify and organize a story's narrative elements. Then ask students to work in pairs, copy the story map onto a sheet of paper, and fill it in. Encourage students to reread the story if necessary. Have volunteers discuss their answers aloud. Then follow the suggestions in **Summarize/Reinforce.**

3. Summarize/Reinforce

Check students' understanding of the lesson by having them summarize what they learned. (The major narrative elements of a story are character, setting, plot, and theme.) To reinforce this lesson, have students identify the major story elements in other selections they have read. Remind them to use the strategies from this lesson to help them understand what they read.

Structural Analysis

OBJECTIVE: *To use structural analysis to determine the meanings of unfamiliar words*

1. Focus

Share the following information with students:

> **When readers come across unfamiliar words while reading, they can use what they know about prefixes, suffixes, base words, and compound words to determine the meanings of the new words.**

2. Choose a Teaching Model

VISUAL MODEL Display the following chart and passage (without underlining or circling words):

Word Part	Meaning
-logy	from Greek root for "speech, study of"
-ist	from Greek root for "agent, one that performs a specific action"
ex-	prefix meaning "out"
cave	from Latin root for "hollow"
-ator	suffix meaning "one that acts in a certain manner"

> **My grandfather tells the story of a little-known mineralogist who came to Krakow in search of riches. Using a steam-driven excavator, she dug a huge hole just outside the city. To everyone's surprise, she found gold and gemstones worth thousands of groschen. Her treasure was worth so much that she hired a bodyguard to protect her.**

Have students read the chart and the passage silently. Then ask volunteers to underline the words in the passage that are compound words and circle the ones that contain word parts from the chart. Have students use the information in the chart and their own knowledge of word meanings to figure out the meaning of each word. Ask volunteers to share their responses and explain how they figured out the meaning of each word. Then follow the suggestions in **Summarize/Reinforce**.

AUDITORY MODEL Display on the board the chart from the Visual Model. Distribute copies of the passage to pairs of students. Have students follow along as you read the passage aloud. Then ask the following questions about the passage, and have partners work together to figure out the answers: **Which word means "someone who studies minerals"? Which word means "someone who guards or protects another"? Which word means "a device for digging a hole"? Which word means "precious stones"?** Ask volunteers to share their responses and explain how they used the chart and their knowledge of word meanings to figure out the correct answers. Then follow the suggestions in **Summarize/Reinforce**.

KINESTHETIC/MOTOR MODEL Display the passage and chart from the Visual Model on the board. Have a volunteer read the passage aloud, underline the compound words, and circle the words that contain the affixes and/or base words from the chart. Then distribute nine index cards to pairs of students. Have partners write down each word part or base word on a separate card, placing the meaning on the back of the card. Then ask partners to combine their cards to help them figure out the meaning of each word. Have volunteers share their responses. Then follow the suggestions in **Summarize/Reinforce**.

3. Summarize/Reinforce

Have students summarize what they learned. (Readers can use what they know about word parts and compound words to figure out the meanings of **Reinforce the lesson by having** students find and decode compound words or words containing suffixes, prefixes, and base words in a newspaper article. Remind students to use the strategies from this lesson to determine word meanings in their readings.

Drawing Conclusions/Predicting

OBJECTIVE: *To use selection content and prior knowledge to explain what has happened in a selection or to predict what will happen*

1. Focus

Share the following information with students:

> While reading, good readers continually draw conclusions about what has already happened in the story. They add their prior knowledge to information presented in the story to arrive at these conclusions. In addition, such readers also use their own knowledge along with story information to predict what will happen next. Drawing conclusions and predicting help readers stay involved with the plot.

2. Choose a Teaching Model

VISUAL MODEL   Ask a volunteer to give a brief summary of the story "Naftali the Storyteller and His Horse, Sus." Then display on the board this excerpt from the story:

> Reb Zebulun said, "I'm liable to come to a town where there are only two or three children who want to read storybooks. It doesn't pay me to walk there for the few groschen I might earn nor does it pay me to keep a horse or hire a wagon."
>
> "What do these children do without storybooks?" Naftali asked. And Reb Zebulun replied, "They have to make do. Storybooks aren't bread. You can live without them."
>
> "I couldn't live without them," Naftali said.

After students have read the excerpt, ask them what conclusion they can draw about young readers in the towns skipped by Reb Zebulun. Help students see that their responses are likely to be based on what they know from personal experience, that children who grow up with books often learn to love reading, and on what they learned from the story, that only a few children in those towns want to read. Then ask what prediction they would make about Naftali's future job. Help students see that again their

responses are based on personal experience, that people prefer to work at jobs that interest them, and on information from the story, that Naftali loves books. Then follow the suggestions in **Summarize/Reinforce.**

AUDITORY MODEL   Ask a volunteer to give a brief summary of the story "Naftali the Storyteller and His Horse, Sus." Then have pairs of students take the parts of Reb Zebulun and Naftali, and give them copies of the excerpt from the Visual Model to read aloud. Have students tell what conclusion they can draw about the children in the towns skipped by Reb Zebulun. Then have students predict Naftali's future job. Ask students to support their responses by telling how they used prior knowledge and story information. Then follow the suggestions in **Summarize/Reinforce.**

KINESTHETIC/MOTOR MODEL   Ask a volunteer to give a brief summary of the story "Naftali the Storyteller and His Horse, Sus." Then ask students to listen closely while you read the story excerpt from the Visual Model. Have volunteers express through pantomime and body language how the two characters felt. Ask students to tell what conclusion they can draw about the children in the towns skipped by Reb Zebulun. Next, have them predict Naftali's future job. Have them give reasons for their responses. Then follow the suggestions in **Summarize/Reinforce.**

3. Summarize/Reinforce

Have students summarize what they learned. (Readers use what they already know and what they learn in a selection to draw conclusions about what has already happened and to predict what will happen next.) To reinforce the lesson, have students choose a story they have not read. Ask them to read the title and paragraph and then to draw a conclusion and make a prediction about the story's contents. Remind students to use the strategies from this lesson to draw conclusions and make predictions as they read.

Figurative Language

OBJECTIVE: *To understand figurative language and its importance in literature*

1. Focus

Share the following information with students:

> Authors use *figurative language* (language that is not supposed to be factual or taken literally) to create vivid images in the reader's mind. Figures of speech are kinds of figurative language and include *similes*, which compare two unlike things by using words such as *like, as,* or *than; metaphors,* which compare two unlike things without using *like, as,* or *than; hyperbole,* which exaggerates to add color or show humor; and *personification,* which gives human qualities to something nonhuman. Recognizing these figures of speech helps readers better understand and enjoy the author's use of language.

2. Choose a Teaching Model

VISUAL MODEL   Display the following passage (omitting the words in parentheses):

> If you go to the Luxembourg Gardens in Paris, you will find, everywhere, green metal chairs. These are the best seats in the world. (*hyperbole*) Unlike the benches in so many parks and gardens, these chairs are not bolted or chained to the ground like dogs on short leashes. (*simile*) One may take a chair and put it anywhere in the gardens; the chairs do not complain, nor do they warn, "You'd better rest here. You won't find a place to sit down for quite some distance." (*personification*) In one day, these dull green stars revolve many times around the garden. (*metaphor*)

Write the words *simile, metaphor, hyperbole,* and *personification* on the board. Tell students that the passage contains all the figures of speech listed on the board. Have them read the passage silently. Ask volunteers to underline in the passage the figures of speech. Have other students explain the image and/or comparison that each contains, write the name of the figure of speech next to the line where it is found, and draw a line connecting them. Then follow the suggestions in **Summarize/Reinforce.**

AUDITORY MODEL   Write *simile, metaphor, hyperbole,* and *personification* on the board, pronouncing each as you write it. Then read aloud the passage from the Visual Model. Tell students to listen and to try to identify in the passage the figures of speech listed on the board. Then reread each sentence slowly. Have students raise their hands when they hear a figure of speech, and call on volunteers to identify and name it. Next, have other volunteers describe the images and any comparisons they contain. Then follow the suggestions in **Summarize/Reinforce.**

KINESTHETIC/MOTOR MODEL   Distribute a copy of the passage from the Visual Model to pairs of students. Also write *simile, metaphor, hyperbole,* and *personification* on the board. Explain that the passage contains an example of each of the figures of speech listed. Instruct partners to work together to identify and circle the figures of speech in the passage and then to write the name of each figure of speech next to the line that contains it. Finally, have volunteers explain the image or comparison contained in each figure of speech. Then follow the suggestions in **Summarize/Reinforce.**

3. Summarize/Reinforce

Have students summarize what they learned. (Figures of speech, such as similes, metaphors, hyperbole, and personification, are intended to create vivid images in the reader's mind and make reading more enjoyable.) To reinforce this lesson, have students identify figures of speech in stories or poems they have read recently. Remind them to use the strategies from this lesson to help them appreciate figurative language.

Main Idea and Details

OBJECTIVE: *To understand the relationship between a main idea and its supporting details*

1. Focus

Share the following information with students:

The main idea of a passage expresses what that passage is about. In some passages the main idea is implied rather than stated directly. The details in a passage provide support and evidence for the main idea by citing examples and showing relationships among ideas. Recognizing the main idea and its supporting details helps readers gain a better understanding of what they read.

2. Choose a Teaching Model

VISUAL MODEL Display the following paragraph:

The first great gold rush in the United States began in 1848 when James Marshall discovered gold in the American River at Sutter's Mill in California. The ensuing flood of people to the West Coast resulted in the rapid growth of San Francisco, the nearest ocean port. Ten years later, a gold rush in Colorado led to the establishment of the city of Denver. Later gold rushes brought people to areas throughout the West. Many left when their dreams of sudden wealth died, but some stayed and built new lives for themselves. Together these gold rushes were important to the development of the American West.

Have students read the paragraph silently. Discuss with them the idea on which all the sentences seem to focus. Elicit from students the main idea (These gold rushes were important to the development of the American West.) and the supporting details. Students can write their responses on a web similar to the one shown. Discuss with them how the details support the main idea. Then follow the suggestions in **Summarize/Reinforce.**

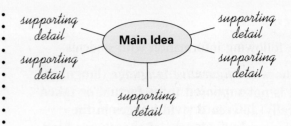

AUDITORY MODEL Read aloud the paragraph from the Visual Model, instructing students to listen for the main idea and supporting details. Reread the paragraph slowly, allowing time for students to take notes. Then draw a blank web on the board, based on the web in the Visual Model. Have students copy the web and fill it in. Ask volunteers to share their webs with classmates and explain how each detail supports the main idea. Then follow the suggestions in **Summarize/Reinforce.**

KINESTHETIC/MOTOR MODEL Duplicate and distribute the paragraph from the Visual Model. Read it aloud, pausing after each sentence to ask whether it states the main idea. When students identify the sentence, have them draw a box around it. Next, ask volunteers to write on the board the sentences from the paragraph under columns headed *Main Idea* or *Supporting Details*. Discuss with students how the details support the main idea. Then follow the suggestions in **Summarize/Reinforce.**

3. Summarize/Reinforce

Have students summarize what they learned. (The main idea is what a passage or story is mostly about. Details help support and explain the main idea.) To reinforce this lesson, have students identify the main idea and supporting details in paragraphs from magazine or newspaper articles. Remind them to use the strategies from this lesson to identify main ideas and details as they read.

Fact and Opinion

OBJECTIVE: *To distinguish between fact and opinion*

1. Focus

Share the following information with students:

A *fact* is a statement that can be proved true or false. An *opinion* is a statement of belief or feeling. Even though an opinion may be supported by facts, it cannot be proved true or false. Readers need to distinguish between facts and opinions in order to understand and evaluate what they read.

2. Choose a Teaching Model

VISUAL MODEL   Display the following passage, explaining that it contains both facts and opinions:

I believe that the automobile presents a great danger to the future of our planet. Automobile exhaust contributes to air pollution. Fossil fuels, which are limited resources, provide gas and oil for cars. In my opinion, human beings are depleting the world's resources at an alarming rate, and automobiles are largely to blame.

Show students these two signs from the American Sign Language alphabet, indicating that the first is the initial letter of *fact* and the second is the initial letter of *opinion*:

F   O

Ask a volunteer to read the excerpt aloud. Then ask other volunteers to read one sentence at a time and sign an *F* or an *O* to indicate whether it states a fact or an opinion. Also have them point out words that gave them clues to their answers. Then follow the suggestions in **Summarize/Reinforce.**

AUDITORY MODEL   Ask students to listen as you read aloud the excerpt from the Visual Model. Have them listen closely in order to identify facts and opinions. Then reread the excerpt, pausing after each sentence, and ask students to identify each as a *fact* or *an opinion*. Have volunteers name words that gave them clues for their answers. Then follow the suggestions in **Summarize/Reinforce.**

KINESTHETIC/MOTOR MODEL   Display the excerpt that appears in the Visual Model. Distribute four index cards to each student. Have students copy one of the sentences from the excerpt on each card. Then ask them to make a border of *F*'s around the card that contains a fact and borders of *O*'s around the cards with opinions. Also have them underline any words in the sentences that gave them clues. Ask them to share their responses. Then follow the suggestions in **Summarize/Reinforce.**

3. Summarize/Reinforce

To check students' understanding of the lesson, have them summarize what they learned. (A fact is a statement that can be proved. An opinion is a statement that expresses a feeling or belief and cannot be proved.) To reinforce the lesson, have students give pairs of facts and opinions about current events that interest them. Remind students to use the strategies from this lesson in evaluating what they read.

Reference Sources

OBJECTIVE: *To understand the uses of important reference sources*

1. Focus

Share the following information with students:

Knowing about various reference sources can help readers find the answers to questions and the solutions to problems. Among reference sources with useful information are a dictionary, an atlas, an encyclopedia, an almanac, a card catalog, and the *Readers' Guide to Periodical Literature*.

2. Choose a Teaching Model

VISUAL MODEL On the board, write these words: *Arctic Circle, oil drilling, Baffin Island, caribou, ice breaker, narwhal, Inuit.* Have students make charts similar to the one below on separate sheets of paper. Then ask them to think of one or more reference sources they could use to find information about each listed topic and to write the names of those sources on their charts next to the topics. When they have finished, ask volunteers to read aloud and explain their responses, describing what information they would expect to find in each source. Then follow the suggestions in **Summarize/Reinforce.**

Topics	Reference Sources
Arctic Circle oil drilling Baffin Island caribou ice breaker narwhal Inuit	

AUDITORY MODEL Write each word listed in the Visual Model on a separate index card. Ask students to take turns choosing an index card, reading the topic aloud, and telling what reference source or sources they would use to find information about that topic. Encourage them to give reasons for their choices and to describe the information they would expect to find in the reference sources they chose. Then follow the suggestions in **Summarize/ Reinforce.**

KINESTHETIC/MOTOR MODEL Ask volunteers to draw across the board a simple pictorial representation of each reference source mentioned in the Focus. Then list below those pictures the topics given in the Visual Model. Ask volunteers to choose a topic and draw lines connecting the topic to the pictures of the reference sources they would use to find information about that topic. Have each volunteer give reasons for choices and erase the lines when he or she is finished. Then follow the suggestions in **Summarize/Reinforce.**

3. Summarize/Reinforce

To check students' understanding of the lesson, ask them to summarize what they learned. (Various reference sources can provide information on many topics.) To reinforce the lesson, arrange a trip to the school library so that students can see what reference sources are available there. Remind students to use reference sources for more information on topics they encounter in their reading.

Author's Purpose and Viewpoint

OBJECTIVE: *To develop inferential meaning by identifying the author's purpose and viewpoint in a selection*

1. Focus

Share the following information with students:

An author may have one or more purposes in writing: to entertain, to inform, to persuade, or to express ideas or feelings. An author may also have strong opinions on a subject and may slant the information presented to support that viewpoint. Readers who recognize an author's purpose and viewpoint are better equipped to judge and accept or reject what they read.

2. Choose a Teaching Model

VISUAL MODEL   Write *entertain, inform, persuade,* and *express ideas and feelings* on the board. Then display the following paragraphs from the selection "Treasure Trove":

Excitement mounted. Next they discovered a low triangular doorway sealed by an enormous stone, and they managed to loosen it enough for Ruz to squeeze behind it and into a vaulted room. He knew instantly that his four seasons of exhausting labor had been rewarded.

Ruz's discovery yielded an enormous amount of information about this civilization. The complicated structure of the temple proves the skill of Maya architects. The carved slab over the stone coffin and the two stucco heads place Maya sculptors among the world's finest. The magnificent jade ornaments demonstrate their talent as craftsmen.

Have a volunteer read the first paragraph aloud, name the author's purpose (entertain), and point to words in the paragraph that support the answer.

Then have a volunteer read the second paragraph aloud, name the main purpose (inform), and point to the word in this paragraph that gives a clue. *(information)* Help students recognize the author's viewpoint (that the Maya were skilled

sculptors and craftsmen) as stated in the last three sentences, and that the purpose here is to persuade. Then follow the suggestions in **Summarize/Reinforce.**

AUDITORY MODEL   Read aloud the first paragraph from the Visual Model. Ask students to listen for words that indicate the author's purpose. (entertain)

As you read aloud the second paragraph, have students listen for a word that tells them that the author's purpose here is mostly to inform. *(information)* Ask volunteers to support this answer. Next, lead students to recognize the author's viewpoint in the final three sentences and the author's purpose (to persuade). Then follow the suggestions in **Summarize/Reinforce.**

KINESTHETIC/MOTOR MODEL   Display the two paragraphs from the Visual Model. Write on the board: *entertain, inform, persuade,* and *express ideas and feelings.* Have students copy each purpose on a separate index card. Read the first paragraph. Ask students to hold up the card that tells the author's main purpose and to explain their choices. With the second paragraph, first ask students to listen for a clue word that is similar to one of the words on their cards. *(information)* Then have them hold up the card that tells the author's purpose and to explain their choices. Also ask them to identify the author's words that reveal a viewpoint and another purpose (to persuade). Then follow the suggestions in **Summarize/Reinforce.**

3. Summarize/Reinforce

Have students summarize what they learned. (Authors write to entertain, to inform, to persuade, or to express ideas and feelings. Authors often express viewpoints or opinions in their writing.) To reinforce the lesson, have students name the purposes of stories or articles they have read, and ask them to name the authors' viewpoints. Remind students to use the strategies from this lesson to identify author's purpose and viewpoint.

Generalizations

OBJECTIVE: *To recognize and to make valid generalizations*

1. Focus

Share the following information with students:

A generalization is a judgment or conclusion reached after gathering information. To be valid, a generalization cannot be too broad, and so it might contain qualifying words such as *most* or *many*. Generalizations are useful because they allow readers to apply what they have learned to new but similar situations.

2. Choose a Teaching Model

VISUAL MODEL Display the following paragraph and diagram:

Hi! Thank you for agreeing to take care of Muttsy while I am away. I hope he won't be too much trouble for you. Here are some suggestions. Like most dogs, Muttsy likes to go for walks. He also likes to play fetch with a stick. He has a typical dog's good appetite, but he prefers cat food to dog food for some reason! His favorite toy is his green rubber bone, and he can chew happily on it for hours. Thanks again.   Your neighbor

Dogs and walks	Dogs at play
Dogs and meals	Dogs' toys

Have a volunteer read the note aloud. Then ask other volunteers to read aloud the boxed headings below the note and use them to form generalizations about dogs as you point to the related sentences in the note. Then follow the suggestions in **Summarize/Reinforce.**

AUDITORY MODEL Read aloud the paragraph from the Visual Model. Ask students to listen for details that can help them make generalizations about dogs. Then duplicate the boxes from the Visual Model on the board. Reread the paragraph slowly. Help students orally state a generalization about dogs to go in each box. Choose students to write those generalizations on the board. Then follow the suggestions in **Summarize/Reinforce.**

KINESTHETIC/MOTOR MODEL Duplicate and distribute the paragraph from the Visual Model to pairs of students. Have students follow along as you read the paragraph aloud. Then draw on the board the boxed headings that follow the paragraph, and have students duplicate them. Ask students to write in each box a generalization about dogs that fits that heading. Have students share their completed diagrams. Then follow the suggestions in **Summarize/Reinforce.**

3. Summarize/Reinforce

Check students' understanding of the lesson by asking them to summarize what they learned. (Valid generalizations are useful in applying information already learned to similar situations.)
the lesson, ask students to give examples of valid generalizations about animals and contrast them with generalizations that are invalid or silly. Remind students to use the strategies from this lesson to help them to be alert for generalizations as they read and to judge their validity.

Comparing/Contrasting

OBJECTIVE: *To use comparison and contrast to better understand facts and concepts*

1. Focus

Share the following information with students:

> *Comparing* **means describing how two facts, objects, or ideas are alike. Words such as** *another, like,* **and** *also* **sometimes signal a comparison.** *Contrasting* **means describing how two facts, objects, or ideas are different. Words such as** *unlike, instead, while,* **and** *although* **sometimes signal a contrast. Comparing and contrasting facts or concepts helps readers better understand and remember what they read.**

2. Choose a Teaching Model

VISUAL MODEL   Refer students to the story "Discovering Gold," and have them read the first two paragraphs on Student Anthology page 222, the first of which begins "Many people were drawn to Dawson . . . " Then write the following chart on the board, omitting the words in parentheses:

	Dawson	Other Cities
wages	*(dust weigher $20/day; teamster $100/day; lawyer $150/day)*	*(less than $2/day)*
currency	*(gold dust or money)*	*(money)*

Have students work in pairs. Ask partners to skim the passage again, taking note of how Dawson compared to other cities of the late 1800s in the way certain professions were compensated and how business transactions were handled. Remind students to look for words signaling similarities and differences. Then have partners duplicate the chart on a separate sheet of paper and fill in the columns. Next, have volunteers complete the chart on the board. Then follow the suggestions in **Summarize/Reinforce.**

AUDITORY MODEL   Refer students to the story "Discovering Gold," and have students follow along in their books as you read aloud the paragraphs indicated in the Visual Model. Ask them to listen for examples of how Dawson compared with other North American cities of the late nineteenth century. Then have students work in small groups. Instruct each group to write the chart headings *Dawson* and *Other Cities* on a sheet of paper. Next, reread the passage slowly, having students compare and contrast under the appropriate headings information about wages and currency, as done in the Visual Model. Remind students to look for certain words that might signal similar or dissimilar ideas. Finally, have volunteers explain the comparisons and contrasts they made. Then follow the suggestions in **Summarize/Reinforce.**

KINESTHETIC/MOTOR MODEL   Refer students to the story "Discovering Gold" and have students silently read the passage indicated in the Visual Model, paying attention to words that signal the similarities and differences between Dawson and other cities. Then ask students to work in groups to create and fill in a chart similar to the one displayed in the Visual Model. Have volunteers show their charts to classmates, using words such as *also, another, while,* and *unlike* to clarify the similarities and differences. Then follow the suggestions in **Summarize/Reinforce.**

3. Summarize/Reinforce

Have students summarize what they learned. (Comparing means telling how facts, concepts, or ideas are alike; contrasting means telling how they are different.) To reinforce this lesson, have students reread other sections of "Discovering Gold" and make comparisons and contrasts. Remind them to use the strategies from this lesson to help them understand facts and concepts as they read.

Making Judgments

OBJECTIVE: *To make critical judgments about literature*

1. Focus

Share the following information with students:

Making judgments often involves evaluating whether or not an action or plan is good, wise, objective, accurate, or valid. Readers can gain experience in making judgments in their own lives by making judgments about the actions and plans of story characters.

2. Choose a Teaching Model

VISUAL MODEL Display the passage that follows. Ask students to read it silently and decide what Zoe's choices of action are.

Zoe had just enough money to buy the bicycle on display in the window of French's bike shop. This was her first thought as she stopped to look at the sleek green 10-speed. The money she owed her brother was the nagging thought that followed. However, with a new bike she could get a paper route and make much more money. She could pay her brother back in no time. Of course, it might look funny when she put her new bike in the garage next to her brother's car, its rear fender scratched because of her carelessness. But she would explain, and he would understand.

Ask students to discuss what Zoe might choose between in order to buy the bicycle. (paying back the money she owes her brother with her savings and spending the savings and paying back her brother at a later time) Have them discuss the decision that Zoe makes and make a judgment about it. Suggest that students fill in a chart similar to the following to organize the information they used to make their judgments. Then follow the suggestions in **Summarize/Reinforce.**

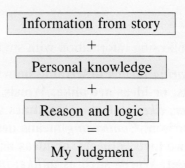

AUDITORY MODEL Tell students that you will read aloud a paragraph that tells about a difficult decision someone has to make. Ask them to listen carefully as you read aloud the passage used in the Visual Model. Encourage students to discuss what might have influenced Zoe to make her decision. Ask them to share their judgment of her decision. Then follow the suggestions in **Summarize/Reinforce.**

KINESTHETIC/MOTOR MODEL Distribute the paragraph used in the Visual Model and ask students to read it silently. Then ask students to make a judgment about Zoe's decision. Have those who agree with Zoe stand on one side of the room, and those who disagree stand on the other side. Ask students to share reasons for their judgments of Zoe's decision and discuss the difficulty of making such a choice. Pairs of students in agreement might fill in a chart similar to the one shown in the Visual Model. Then follow the suggestions in **Summarize/ Reinforce.**

3. Summarize/Reinforce

Have students summarize what they learned. (Making a judgment may mean evaluating which action or plan is wiser, better, or more valid.) To reinforce the lesson, invite volunteers to give examples of situations in which someone might have to make difficult judgments or choices. Remind them to use the strategies from this lesson to help them make judgments about decisions characters make in stories as well as help them make real-life judgments.

Directions

OBJECTIVE: *To follow and give directions accurately*

1. Focus

Share the following information with students:

Paying careful attention to directions, whether giving, reading, or listening to them, helps a person complete a new task correctly and more easily. Sequence and direction words and required materials and supplies are especially important.

2. Choose a Teaching Model

VISUAL MODEL   Remind students that Elena, the main character in "Time: The Missing Element," had to follow certain steps carefully in order to survive in an inhospitable wilderness. Display on the board the steps she followed in rekindling her fire:

1. **First, remove the lean-to of planks that sheltered the fire overnight.**
2. **Next, with a hand held over the ashes, locate the remaining warmth.**
3. **Then blow softly on the warm part of the ashes until the glowing coals appear.**
4. **Tuck a few wisps of dry grass among the coals.**
5. **When flames appear, add a handful of twigs.**
6. **After the twigs are burning, add small sticks.**
7. **When the sticks are burning, add larger pieces of wood.**

After students have read the directions silently, ask volunteers to point to the step on the board that answers each of these questions:

- **What is the first thing to do in rekindling a fire?**
- **How can you find the warm part of the fire?**
- **What do you do to get coals to glow again?**
- **Which size fuel do you add first? Next? Last?**

Have students explain in their own words why it is important to read all of the directions before beginning to follow them. (Possible response: in order to have the necessary materials at hand at the moment when you need them.) Have a volunteer list on the board the materials Elena needed. Then follow the suggestions in **Summarize/Reinforce.**

AUDITORY MODEL   Explain to students that you will read aloud the steps that Elena, the main character in "Time: The Missing Element," had to follow to rekindle her fire when she was stranded in the wilderness. Read aloud the numbered directions that appear in the Visual Model; ask students to listen carefully and then draw a simple picture to go with each step. When they have finished, have them compare their pictures and list orally the materials Elena needed. Then follow the suggestions in **Summarize/Reinforce.**

KINESTHETIC/MOTOR MODEL   Display and read aloud the numbered directions that appear in the Visual Model, explaining that they are the directions that Elena, the main character in "Time: The Missing Element," had to follow to rekindle her fire. Ask pairs of students to illustrate or pantomime each step of the directions. Have the pairs read the directions aloud as they show their art or act out each direction. Have them also draw or list the materials Elena needed. Then follow the suggestions in **Summarize/Reinforce.**

3. Summarize/Reinforce

Check students' understanding of the lesson by having them summarize what they learned. (In following directions, listen carefully for words that indicate order and for needed materials.) To reinforce the lesson, have students give oral and written directions for doing a simple task. Remind students to use the strategies from this lesson when they need to follow or give directions.

Summarizing

OBJECTIVE: *To summarize all or part of a literature selection*

1. Focus

Share the following information with children:

A summary is a statement of the most important information in a passage. To summarize a paragraph or passage, focus on the most important ideas and try to state them in your own words. A summary is much shorter than the original passage and contains only the most important information. Knowing how to summarize helps readers understand and remember what they read, and also helps readers share what they have read with others.

2. Choose a Teaching Model

VISUAL MODEL Duplicate the passage below, and distribute a copy to each student. Read the passage aloud as students follow along silently.

Gorillas are among the most intelligent of primates. Scientists now know why gorillas, who seem to think and communicate, have never developed speech. Their vocal cords and the shape of their tongues do not allow them to form the sounds required for speech.

However, Gorillas regularly use a variety of gestures in their communications with each other. Scientists began to wonder whether gorillas might be taught to communicate with humans through sign language. Dr. Penny Patterson, a scientist at Stanford University, worked with a young female gorilla named Koko and attempted to teach her sign language. The attempt was successful. After four years, Koko had learned the signs for over two hundred words. Communication between humans and gorillas had begun.

Have students work in pairs to summarize the passage. Tell partners to begin by underlining the most important ideas in each paragraph. Then have partners summarize these ideas by restating them briefly in their own words. Have students then combine the paragraph summaries into a single summary statement for the whole passage. Have one student from each pair say the summary aloud. Work with students to write a summary on the board. Then follow suggestions in **Summarize/Reinforce**.

AUDITORY MODEL Read aloud the passage from the Visual Model. Ask students what important ideas they would include in a summary of the passage. Write their responses on the board. Reread the passage as many times as necessary. Then have students form pairs and restate the most important ideas in their own words. Encourage students to try to summarize each paragraph first and then combine those summaries into a single summary for the whole passage. Have several volunteers say their summaries aloud. Then follow suggestions in **Summarize/Reinforce**.

KINESTHETIC/MOTOR MODEL Read aloud the passage from the Visual Model. Have students take notes on the passage. Tell them to write down only the most important ideas. Reread the passage one or more times, as necessary. Have several volunteers share their notes. Then ask each student to circle the ideas that should be included in a summary of the passage. Allow students to compare their notes. Finally, have each student write a summary based on the circled ideas. They should begin by summarizing each paragraph and then go on to combine their paragraph summaries into a summary of the whole passage. Then follow suggestions in **Summarize/Reinforce**.

3. Summarize/Reinforce

Have students summarize what they learned. (A summary is a short way of summing up the most important ideas in a passage. To summarize, restate the most important ideas in your own words.) To reinforce the lesson, have students summarize other selections they have read. Remind students to look for the most important ideas when they read.

Multiculturalism

The literature and activities in *HBJ Treasury of Literature* celebrate cultural similarities and diversity, foster pride in cultural heritage and history, and open a world of possibilities for children. Multiculturalism is most effective when it is infused throughout the curriculum.

Multicultural Literature:

A Celebration of Diversity

The widening scope of multicultural literature

DR. JUNKO YOKOTA LEWIS

Assistant Professor, Department of Curriculum and Instruction at the University of Northern Iowa and Author, HBJ Treasury of Literature

DR. ROLANDO R. HINOJOSA-SMITH

Ellen Clayton Garwood Professor of English and the Mari Sabusawa Michener Chair of Creative Writing at the University of Texas at Austin and Consultant HBJ Treasury of Literature

When one considers the increasing diversity of students in American schools today, the need for literature that reflects the multitude of their backgrounds becomes immediately obvious. All children benefit from having access to a multicultural body of literature. All children develop a sense of pride and increased self-concept by reading about characters with the same heritage as their own and with whom they can identify. And all children are able to develop an understanding of other cultures and see issues from the perspectives of various cultures by having vicarious experiences through multicultural literature. Allowing children to take part in a variety of cultural experiences such as those offered in *HBJ Treasury of Literature* opens the possibilities for future understandings.

The multicultural literature that children read in school must not only be of literary and aesthetic merit, but must portray a culturally-conscious view of the people represented. Without cultural accuracy, it is likely that stereotyped images of people will be perpetuated and that children will develop misinformed images of other cultures.

We are fortunate to be educating children in an age when an ever-increasing number of high-quality multicultural books such as the ones in *HBJ Treasury of Literature* can be found. These books provide a variety of perspectives for children. Some, such as folklore, give insights into the traditions and values of a cultural group. John Steptoe's *Mufaro's Beautiful Daughters* is an example of an African folktale endorsing the belief that greed and selfishness are bad and that kindness and generosity are rewarded.

HBJ Treasury of Literature also contains literature that tells about the experiences of people in other countries. For example, *Bringing the Rain to Kapiti Plain* by Verna Aardema is a cumulative tale that tells the story of a drought in Kenya. In *The Chalk Doll* by Charlotte Pomerantz, a mother shares with her daughter what it was like to grow up in Jamaica.

The multicultural literature found in *HBJ Treasury of Literature* can help children understand the experiences of a cultural group when they are located in the United States.

Books such as *Chin Chiang and the Dragon's Dance* reflect the experiences of Chinese Americans by telling about a dance from the Chinese culture that is popular in America today. *Fiesta!* tells of celebrating the Mexican American holiday Cinco de Mayo. Virginia Hamilton's *The House of Dies Drear* is set in a house where slaves once escaped to freedom through the tunnels. Hamilton shares historical information about slavery and the Underground Railroad. This book reflects experiences unique to African Americans.

Dream Wolf is the story of a Plains Indian boy and a wolf. In it, Paul Goble shares the Native American viewpoint that we must have greater respect for wildlife or it will vanish.

While one role of the multicultural literature in *HBJ Treasury of Literature* is to help children appreciate the uniqueness of various cultures, another is to help children recognize values and experiences common to many cultures.

For example, *My Friends* by Taro Gomi was originally written and illustrated in Japan and intended for a Japanese audience. The book was later translated and distributed in other countries because the concept of learning things from friends has a universal appeal. Likewise, the love between family members is a universal theme found in stories from many cultures.

In Mildred Pitts Walter's "Spending Time with Grandpa," taken from *Justin and the Best Biscuits in the World*, we meet an African American family with strong love for one another. Carmen Lomas Garza's *Family Pictures* also reflects the theme of family bonding.

Including a variety of fine multicultural literature in *HBJ Treasury of Literature* does more than just delight children. It helps prepare them for their roles as global citizens. It allows them to see and appreciate the richness of the increasing diversity within their communities, their nation, and their world. ●

Allowing children to take part in a variety of cultural experiences...opens the possibilities for future understandings.

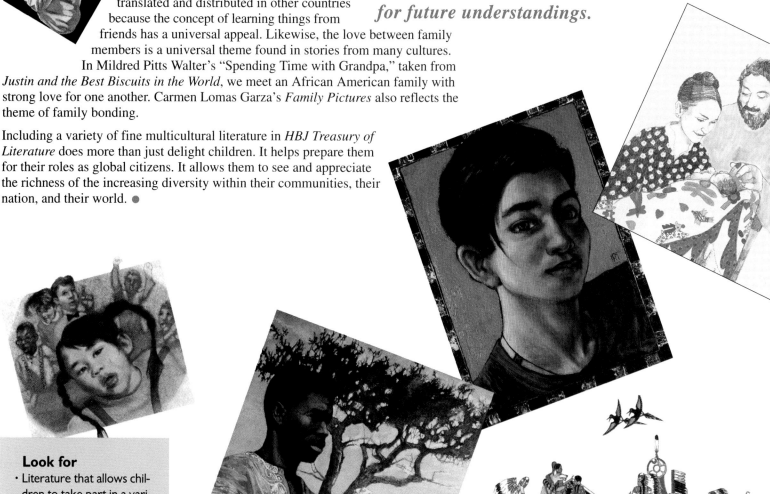

Look for
- Literature that allows children to take part in a variety of cultural experiences
- Literature that portrays a culturally conscious view of the people represented
- Literature that is consistently of the highest literary quality and aesthetic merit

Multicultural Infusion

A curriculum based on the truth of the whole human experience

As with any curriculum movement, the search for truth is the basis for change. It should not be surprising, then, that the search for truth for the whole human experience is at the base of concerns for pluralism in the curriculum.

Multicultural infusion is the vehicle by which pluralism is instilled in the curriculum. The commitment to multicultural infusion is based on the assumption that at one time or another virtually all human groups have played a role in important human events. When diverse cultural groups are not represented in curriculum, that is a relatively sure sign that important truths have been overlooked.

From its conception and throughout its development, the authors and consultants of *HBJ Treasury of Literature* have been committed to truth. The selection of literature for the program was governed by the principle of accurately reflecting diverse cultural groups. The same care went into creating each of the program's components. Multicultural advisors helped shape each phase of the program, acting on a mission to make *HBJ Treasury of Literature* truly represent the people of our nation.

In *HBJ Treasury of Literature*, Cultural Awareness Notes, Multicultural Perspectives, and Multicultural Connections reflect the truth of the human experience. They recognize the contributions of individuals from diverse cultures and the contributions of the cultures themselves. They cultivate in students an appreciation for diversity.

DR. ASA G. HILLIARD III

Fuller E. Callaway Professor of Urban Education, Department of Educational Foundations, Georgia State University and Senior Consultant, HBJ Treasury of Literature

When diverse cultural groups are not represented in curriculum, that is a relatively sure sign that important truths have been overlooked.

We know that learners are more apt to be attracted to materials with which they can identify. However, it is not necessary to contrive situations where this would occur, since the truth of the human experience is that it reflects cultural pluralism. All school subjects should reflect this reality. In fact, pluralism in the curriculum should be seen as an enrichment to the school experience of all students.

HBJ Treasury of Literature offers teachers a socially responsible reading curriculum by helping children in their quest for knowledge and truth. ●

Look for
- Literature that accurately reflects diverse cultural groups
- Cultural Awareness Notes, Multicultural Perspectives, and Multicultural Connections that reflect the truth of the human experience

We believe in assessment that encourages students to share in the responsibility of assessing their learning. Assessment should help teachers and students understand what a student can do successfully rather than emphasize what a student can't do.

Some Old Ideas on Testing Flunk Out

New assessment tools measure what students really know.

DR. ROGER C. FARR

Professor of Education and Director of the Center for Reading and Language Studies at Indiana University and Senior Author, HBJ Treasury of Literature

An assessment program should help teachers and students understand what a student can do successfully rather than emphasize what a student can't do. Assessments should be positive experiences for students — a natural part of the learning process. In *HBJ Treasury of Literature,* assessment tools have been designed to enable every child to experience success.

An effective assessment program provides information not only about *how well* a student reads and writes, but also about *how*. No one improves from merely knowing a score on a test — or from having responses marked as acceptable or unacceptable. There must be an opportunity to review answer choices and drafts of reading and writing.

An effective assessment program encourages students to share in the responsibility of assessment, helping them to become reflective about their developing abilities. In *HBJ Treasury of Literature*, the assessment components include a variety of activities to involve students. These components include a Reading/Writing Portfolio, Portfolio Conferences, Strategy Conferences, and Student Self-Assessment Notes.

No one improves from merely knowing a score on a test....

The assessment activities in *HBJ Treasury of Literature* were developed out of the belief that assessment in a literature-based reading program should not interfere with the enjoyment and development of reading. Rather, it should be a thoughtful guide to help a child increase his or her understanding and appreciation of the power and beauty of literature. Assessment should do these things:

1. **Present Realistic Activities.** Assessments should engage students in activities that resemble ways they actually use reading and writing in everyday life.

2. **Reflect What Is Taught.** Assessment activities should use the skills and strategies that are taught.

3. **Consider Pupil Environment.** Assessment activities should provide opportunities for a student to select the work that he or she thinks is important as well as provide opportunities for the teacher and the student to discuss the student's abilities and interests.

4. **Integrate Language Behaviors.** Assessment should provide opportunities for students to use all of their language skills to accomplish literacy tasks.

5. **Be Ongoing and Congruent with Instruction.** Assessment should provide many opportunities for informal observations, or "kid watching," rather than just formal testing.

Informal Assessment Options

Title	Key Features
Reading/Writing Portfolio	Each student is encouraged to save important examples of his or her writing in the Portfolio. Periodically, student and teacher discuss the Portfolio's contents and note the development of the student's literacy skills.
Informal Assessment Notes	These appear throughout each *HBJ Treasury of Literature* Teacher's Edition lesson plan and give the teacher suggestions for determining when students need help without waiting until the "teachable moment" has passed.
Strategy Conferences	Students are consistently given an opportunity to assess the effectiveness of the strategies they use when they read. The basis for metacognition must be student awareness.
Student Self-Assessment Notes	These appear throughout *HBJ Treasury of Literature* Teacher's Edition lesson plans and help students evaluate their own strategies for working effectively in reader response groups.
Running Records	The teacher keeps an informal account of skills and strategies students use as they read. Running Records provide a window on the reading process and help teachers understand how students are applying reading skills and strategies.

Formal Assessment Options

Title	Key Features
Integrated Performance Assessments	They provide realistic, integrated assessments that give students opportunities to use their reading and writing abilities to engage in authentic, performance activities.
Holistic Assessments	They provide a variety of interesting fiction and non-fiction selections with both multiple-choice and open-ended questions to determine how students are developing as total readers.
Skills Assessments	They provide activities that determine whether students can apply reading skills and strategies. The skills are assessed in the context of words, sentences, and paragraphs rather than in isolation.

An effective assessment program provides information not only about how well a student reads and writes, but also about how.

Look for
- Informal assessment guides
- Student self-assessment opportunities
- Strategy and Portfolio conferences
- Holistic Assessment
- Integrated reading and writing evaluation using authentic literature

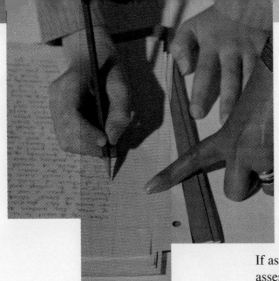

The primary goal is to help the teacher plan an effective instructional program.

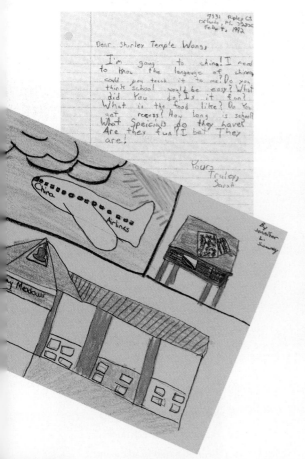

If assessment is to be effective, it must be linked to instructional planning. Each of the assessment components has been developed to serve teacher decision making. The specific interpretation and use of each test for instructional planning are discussed fully in either the *HBJ Treasury of Literature* Teacher's Edition or the manual accompanying the assessment component.

The table below provides an overview of how each of the components serves various teacher decisions. The emphasis is on providing teachers with information that empowers them to make decisions based on the assessment information as well as on their ongoing observations. The columns with two checks ✔✔ indicate a primary use of the assessment for that decision while a single check ✔ indicates a secondary use of the assessment for that decision.

Instructional Decisions

Component	Daily Planning	Unit Planning	Placement
Reading/Writing Portfolios	✔✔	✔	
Informal Assessment Notes	✔✔	✔	
Student Self-Assessment Notes	✔✔	✔	
Running Records	✔✔		
Integrated Performance Assessments		✔✔	
Holistic Assessments		✔✔	
Skills Assessments		✔✔	
Group Placement Test			✔✔
Individual Placement Test			✔✔

Each assessment component provides guidelines for the use and interpretation of that component. However, there are several general guidelines that will help to make the total assessment program more successful.

- Be observant every day. The best assessment tool is a classroom teacher.

- Get students involved in thinking and talking about their reading interests, habits, and development. Self-assessment is the most powerful instrument for bringing about change.

- Rely less often on single assessments and more often on a variety of literacy activities.

- Look for patterns in student responses. Just as a single test provides an incomplete picture, a single response reveals little about whether a student is developing particular reading strategies and skills. ●

Teacher Resources

The resources on these pages will help you customize your literature-based reading program. They include reproducible masters of Response Cards for the discussion of literature, Independent Reading Masters to help with self-selected reading, and Graphic Organizers for applying active reading strategies.

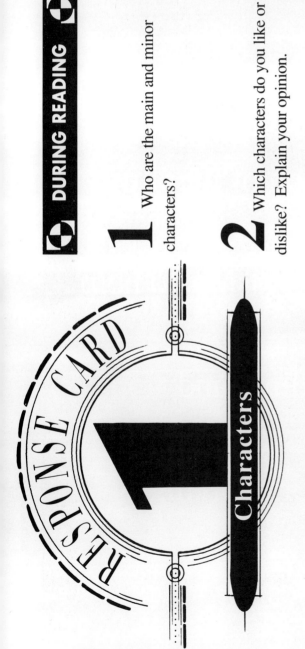

RESPONSE CARD

Characters

1 Who are the main and minor characters?

2 Which characters do you like or dislike? Explain your opinion.

3 Does a character in this story remind you of a character from another story you have read? If so, how are they alike?

4 Choose one character. Why is this character important in the story?

5 Did any of the characters change in the course of the story? If so, how?

6 If you could be any character in this story, who would you be? Why?

7 Suppose you had a chance to interview one of the characters. What would you ask him or her?

RESPONSE CARD

2

Setting

 DURING READING

1 Describe where the story takes place.

2 Have you ever been to a place like this? If you have, how was it like the place in the story?

3 When does the story take place—long ago, in the future, or in the present? Give evidence from the story.

 AFTER READING

4 How did the setting affect what happened in the story?

5 How would the story be different if it were set in a different place?

6 How would the story be different if it were set in a different time?

7 If you could visit the setting for this story, would you go? Why, or why not?

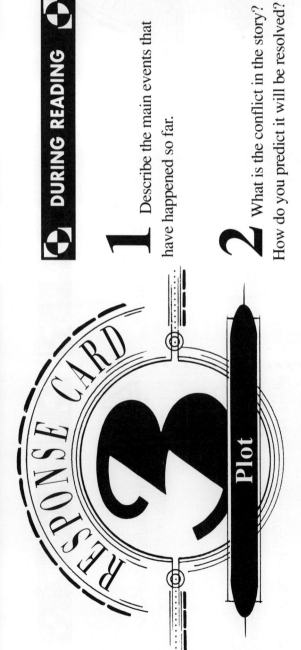

RESPONSE CARD

3

Plot

1 Describe the main events that have happened so far.

2 What is the conflict in the story? How do you predict it will be resolved?

3 What do you think will happen next? What do you think will happen at the end?

4 Describe the main events of the story.

5 What was the resolution to the story? Discuss why your predicted resolution was similar or different.

6 How else might the author have ended the story?

7 What do you think was the best part of the story? Why?

RESPONSE CARDS

RESPONSE CARD

4 Theme/Mood

1 What do you think the theme will be? Explain why.

2 From the title of the story, what did you think this story would be about?

3 What is the mood of the story so far?

4 What do you remember most about the story at this point?

5 What was the theme? Which story events helped you figure it out?

6 Was the theme stated or implied? If stated, tell where. If implied, tell which story events helped you figure out the theme?

7 If you wanted to suggest this story to a friend, what would you say it is mostly about?

8 What was the mood of the story at the end? If it changed, describe where.

 9 What was the funniest, saddest or most exciting part?

RESPONSE CARD

5 Author's Viewpoint

1 What do you know about the author?

2 What is the author trying to tell you? How do you know?

3 Can you tell what kinds of things (people, places, behavior, feelings) the author likes? If so, give evidence from the selection.

4 What tone has the author used? Explain why it matches the author's viewpoint.

5 Do you agree with the author's viewpoint? Why, or why not?

6 What was the author's purpose in writing? How do you know?

7 What else did the author have to know in order to write this article or story?

8 What else could the author have said to support his or her opinion?

RESPONSE CARD

6

Author's Craft

DURING READING

1 Have you noticed foreshadowing in the story? If so, what did you notice?

2 Describe any vivid scene that the author has created up to this point in your reading.

3 What special words has the author used so far to help you see, hear, or feel things in the story?

4 What does the dialogue tell you about the characters? Does it sound the way people really talk? Why, or why not?

5 If the author has used flashbacks, find an example. Why was this technique used here?

AFTER READING

6 What is your favorite word, line, or paragraph in the story? Why is it your favorite?

7 What do you like or dislike about the way the author has written the story?

8 Would you like to read something else by this author? Why, or why not?

9 What was the most important thing you learned from the dialogue in this story?

RESPONSE CARD

7

Responding Freely

1 Work with a partner. Scan the story, and decide whether you will read it silently or aloud.

2 Think about the way the story is organized. Decide with your partner how often you will stop to discuss it.

3 Each time you stop, discuss what you have read. Tell what you think, and listen to what your partner says.

- You might describe things you like or dislike.
- You might discuss things you do not understand.
- You might draw conclusions about what has happened so far or predict outcomes.

4 Read the next section, and discuss it. Continue doing this until you finish the story.

5 Discuss the whole story. Tell what you think, and listen to what your partner says.

- You might describe your favorite part of the story.
- You might discuss the author's writing.
- You might discuss whether what you predicted would happen actually did happen.

RESPONSE CARD

Written Conversation

1 Working with a partner, silently read the pages your teacher suggests.

2 On a sheet of paper, write a comment about what you read. Then write a question about something you didn't understand or something you would like your partner's opinion about.

3 Exchange papers with your partner.

4 Write the answer to your partner's question. Then add a new question to the paper.

5 Exchange papers with your partner again. Answer the new question your partner wrote.

6 Read the rest of the story. Repeat steps 2-5.

7 Discuss the story, using the questions and answers on your paper to help you.

COVER TO COVER

Clues from the outside and the inside can help you choose a book!

Outside

Inside

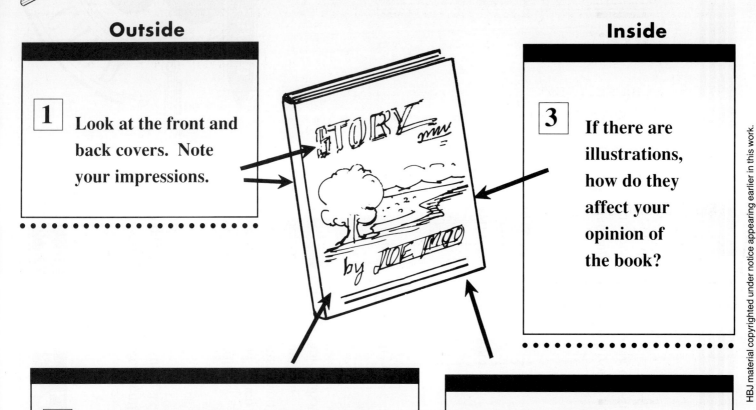

1 Look at the front and back covers. Note your impressions.

3 If there are illustrations, how do they affect your opinion of the book?

2 Have you or people you know read other books by this author? If so, what is your or their opinion?

4 Preview the beginning of the book. What do you think? Is this book for you?

What book did you choose?

Why did you choose it?

READ ALL ABOUT IT!

Complete the newspaper page to tell about your book.

| Weather: a good day for reading | **The Literary Ledger** Date: _____ | " Turning pages into ideas" |

Top Story:

_____
(your name)

Reviews _____
(book title)

Hitting the highlights:

_____
_____
_____
_____
_____
_____

Critic's Corner

I thought this book was
_____

because _____
_____
_____
_____
_____
_____

_____
_____
_____
_____
_____
_____
_____
_____
_____
_____
_____
_____
_____
_____
_____
_____

Special Feature: Cartoon Commentary

Caption _____
_____

Rating:

☐ ★★★ Highly Recommended

☐ ★★ Recommended

☐ ★ Recommended with Reservations

☐ Not Recommended

RESPOND AND BEYOND

Name: _____ **Date:** _____

Title of Book: _____

> Check the box beside the activity you choose to do with your book. Activities with a double arrow (←→) may be done with a partner who has read the same book. Those with a circle (◯) may be done with a group.

Respond

☐ 1. Imagine that you are a publisher's representative trying to persuade a bookstore owner to stock this book. Write what you will say.

←→ ☐ 2. Write a letter to the author, telling what you thought about the book, and asking any questions you may have. Your partner can answer your letter as the author might.

◯ ☐ 3. Choose a dramatic scene from the book to rehearse and present to classmates.

Beyond

☐ 1. Imagine that you are a character from the book. Write a diary entry.

←→ ☐ 2. Read another book on the same topic or by the same author. Discuss similarities and differences between the books.

◯ ☐ 3. Create a mural or collage based on the book. Display it in your classroom.

Make notes about your plans. _____

_____

_____

NOTES AND QUOTES

Name: _____ **Date:** _____

The note pads below may help you keep track of some interesting or amazing things you'd like to remember from your book.

People / Animals / Characters

Places / Setting

Facts or Story Events

New or Interesting Words

ORGANIZING IDEAS

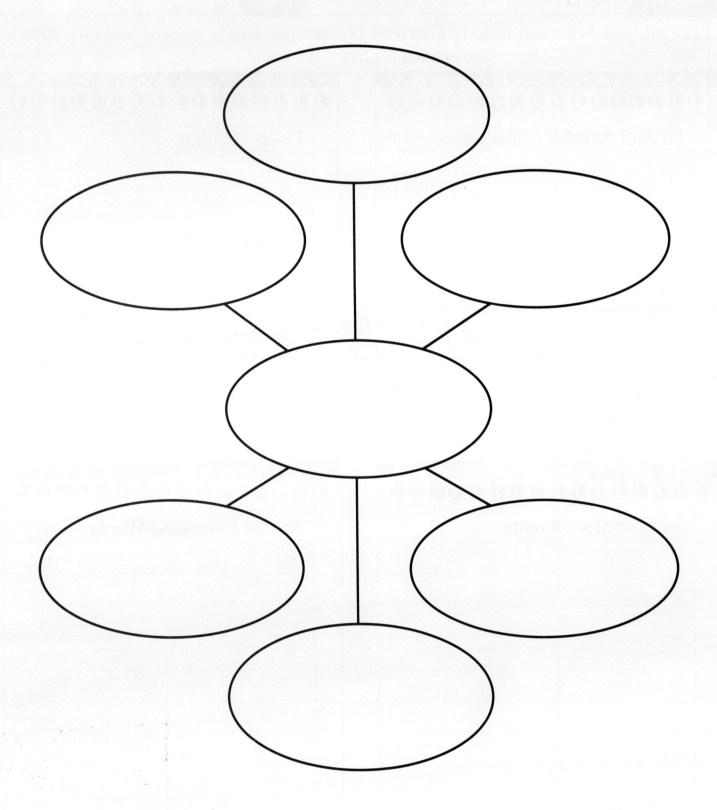

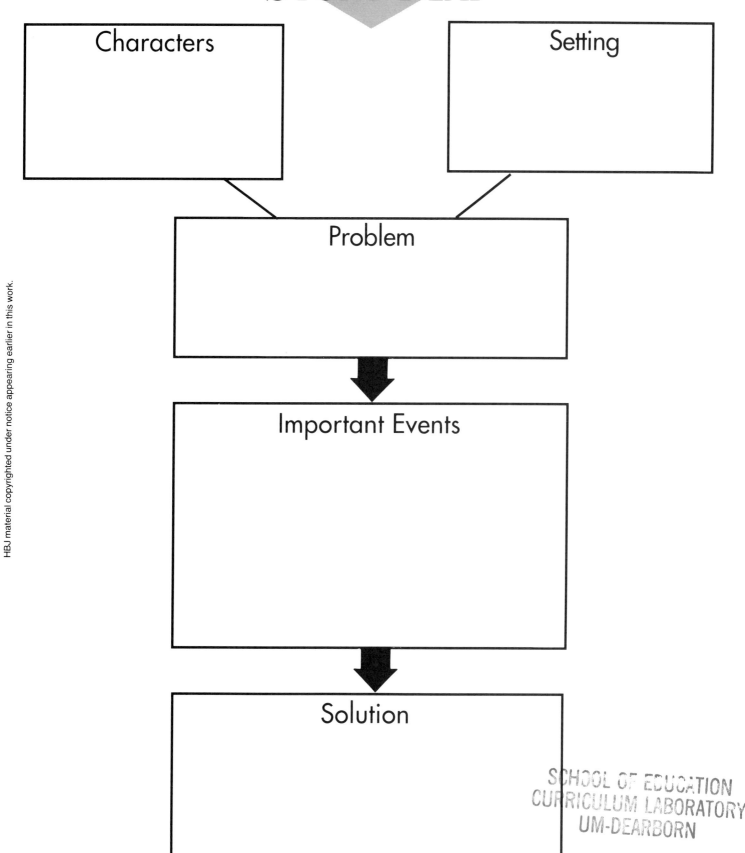

STORY MAP

Characters

Setting

Problem

Important Events

Solution

MAIN IDEA AND DETAILS

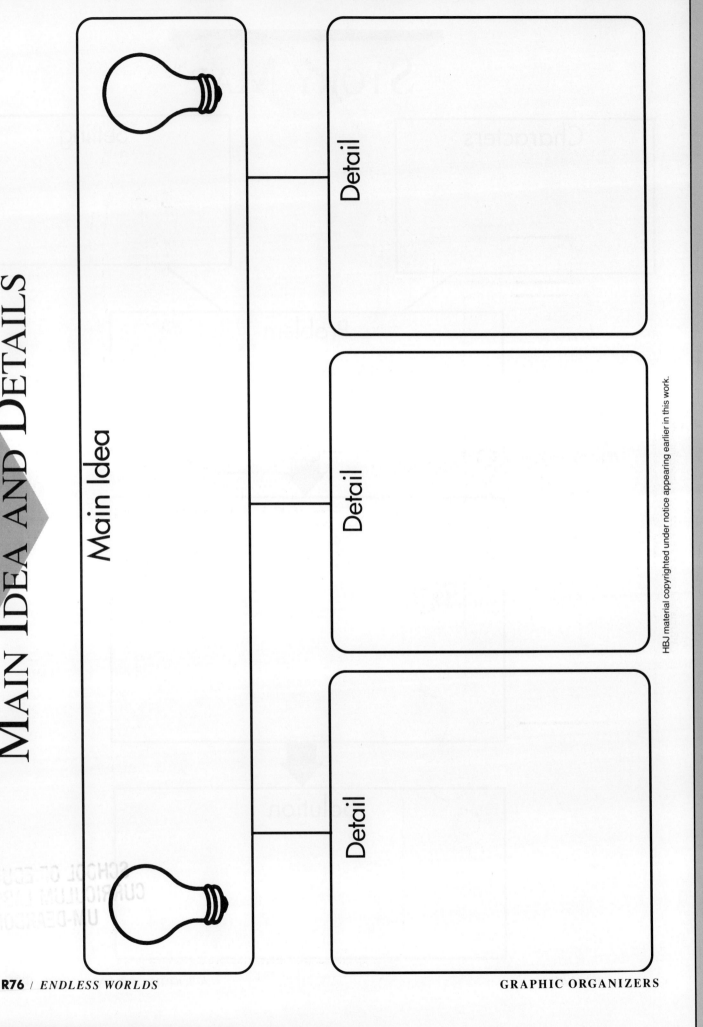

Main Idea

Detail

Detail

Detail

DRAWING CONCLUSIONS

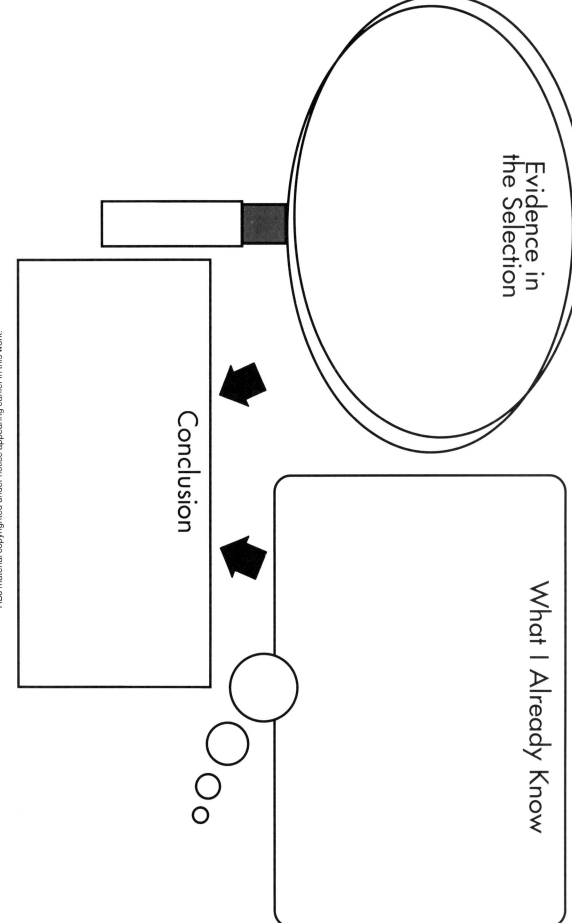

Evidence in
the Selection

Conclusion

What I Already Know

MAKING PREDICTIONS

Information from the Selection	What I Already Know

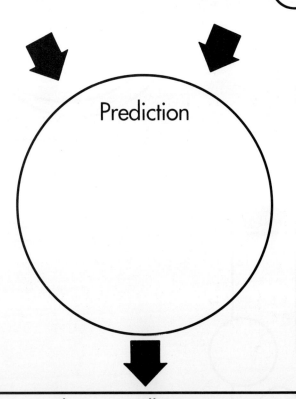

Prediction

What Actually Happens
in the Selection

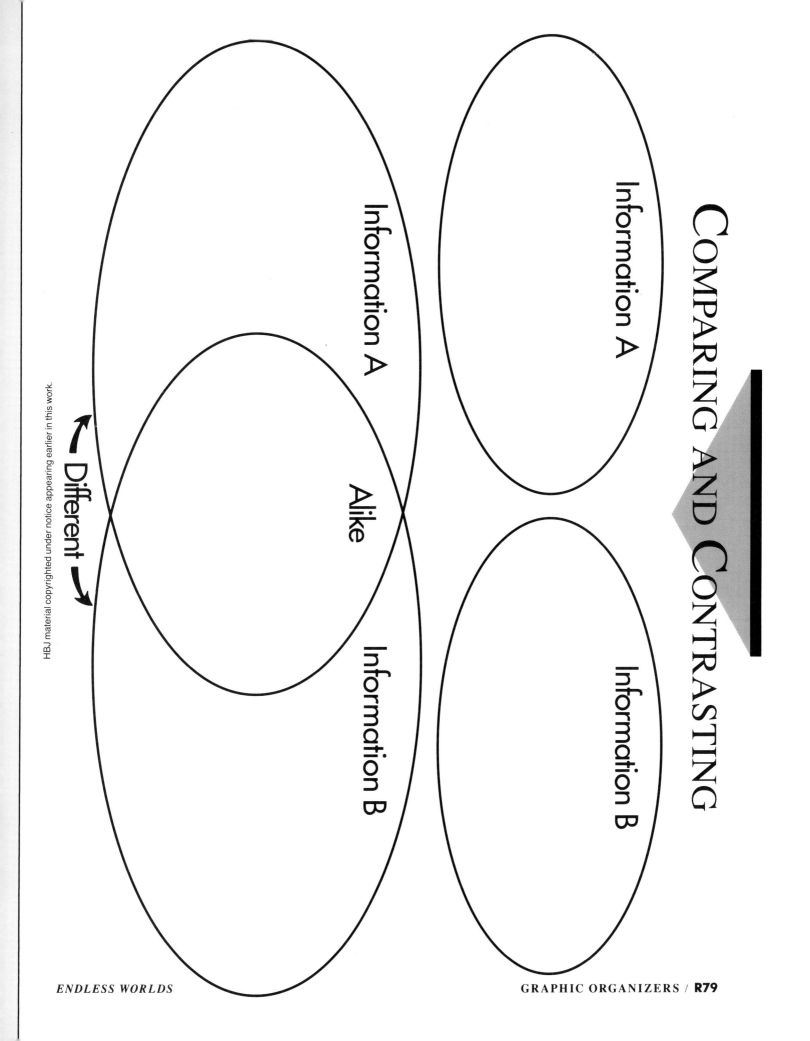

COMPARING AND CONTRASTING

Information A

Information B

Information A

Alike

Information B

Different

MULTIPLE CAUSES AND EFFECTS

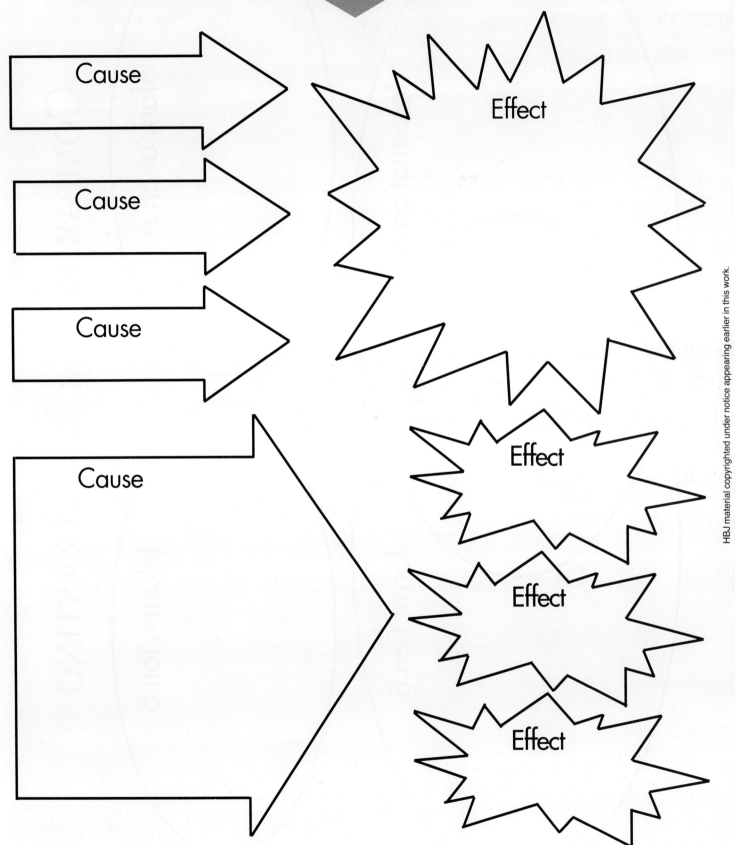

Cause

Cause

Cause

Cause

Effect

Effect

Effect

Effect

HBJ Treasury of Literature
Scope and Sequence

Legend: ▓ = Modeling/Instruction/Application · ◆ = Tested

Grade/Level	1–1	1–2	1–3	1–4	1–5	1–6	2	3	4	5	6	7	8
STRATEGIC READING													
Active Reading Strategies	▓	▓	▓	▓	▓	▓	▓	▓	▓	▓	▓	▓	▓
Read Fiction (Narrative Text)	▓	▓	▓	▓	▓	▓	▓	▓	▓	▓	▓	▓	▓
Read Nonfiction (Expository Text)				▓	▓	▓	▓	▓	▓	▓	▓	▓	▓
Analyze Details	▓	▓	▓	▓	▓	▓	▓	▓	▓	▓	▓	▓	▓
Synthesize Ideas/Information	▓	▓	▓	▓	▓	▓	▓	▓	▓	▓	▓	▓	▓
Make Inferences	▓	▓	▓	▓	▓	▓	▓	▓	▓	▓	▓	▓	▓
Decoding Strategy: Use phonetic/structural analysis plus context to unlock pronunciation	▓	▓	▓	▓	▓	▓	▓	▓	▓	▓	▓	▓	▓
Vocabulary Strategy: Use phonetic/structural/contextual clues to determine meanings	▓	▓	▓	▓	▓	▓	▓	▓	▓	▓	▓	▓	▓
Use Self-Assessment Strategies	▓	▓	▓	▓	▓	▓	▓	▓	▓	▓	▓	▓	▓
COMPREHENSION													
Cause-Effect							◆	◆	◆	◆	◆	◆	◆
Classify/Categorize		◆					◆						
Compare and Contrast							◆	◆	◆	◆	◆	◆	◆
Draw Conclusions							◆	◆	◆	◆	◆	◆	◆
Fact-Fantasy/Nonfact				◆			◆						
Author's Purpose										◆	◆	◆	◆
Author's Viewpoint											◆	◆	◆
Fact-Opinion								◆	◆	◆	◆	◆	◆
Main Idea (Global Meaning)/Details						◆	◆	◆	◆	◆	◆	◆	◆
Make Generalizations											◆	◆	◆
Make Judgments											◆	◆	◆
Paraphrase								◆	◆	◆			
Make Predictions					◆		◆	◆	◆	◆	◆	◆	◆
Referents													
Sequence			◆				◆	◆	◆	◆	◆	◆	◆
Summarize								◆	◆	◆	◆	◆	◆
VOCABULARY													
Key Words/Selection Vocabulary	◆	◆	◆	◆	◆	◆	◆	◆	◆	◆	◆	◆	◆
Synonyms/Antonyms													
Multiple-Meaning Words											◆	◆	◆
Homophones/Homographs													
Context Clues					◆		◆	◆	◆				
Vocabulary Strategy: Use phonetic/structural/contextual clues to determine meanings													
Analogies													
Connotation/Denotation													
Glossary													
Dictionary (for Word Meaning)								◆	◆	◆	◆	◆	◆
DECODING													
Phonics													
Initial/Medial/Final Consonants	◆	◆	◆	◆									
Phonograms													
Short Vowels/Long Vowels		◆	◆	◆	◆	◆							
Consonant Clusters/Digraphs (Initial/Final)		◆	◆	◆	◆	◆							
R-Controlled Vowels							◆						
Vowel Diphthongs/Vowel Digraphs/Variant Vowels							◆						
Schwa													
Decoding Strategy: Use phonetic/structural analysis plus context to unlock pronunciation													
Structural Analysis													
Inflected Forms (With Verbs), With and Without Spelling Changes		◆	◆	◆	◆	◆	◆						
Possessives, Comparatives, Superlatives													
Contractions			◆	◆									
Compound Words													
Syllabication													
Suffixes/Prefixes							◆	◆	◆	◆	◆	◆	◆
Greek and Latin Roots									◆	◆	◆	◆	◆
Spelling Patterns													

▓ **Modeling/Instruction/Application** ◆ **Tested**
Testing options include Unit Skills Assessment, Unit Holistic Assessment, and Unit Integrated Performance Assessment.
For a complete scope and sequence of the kindergarten program, see the Teacher's Edition for that level.

Grade/Level	1–1	1–2	1–3	1–4	1–5	1–6	2	3	4	5	6	7	8
STUDY SKILLS													
Locate Sources of Information													
Use the Library (Parts of, Card Catalog, Computerized Card Catalog, Call Numbers, Database Searching Strategies, *Books in Print, Readers' Guide*)							■	■	■	■	■	■	■
Alphabet/Alphabetical Order	■	■	■	■	◆	■	◆						
Use Sources of Information													
Book Parts	■	■	■	■	■	■	■						
Graphic Aids (Maps, Charts, Graphs, Tables/Schedules, Diagrams, Timelines)						■	■	◆	◆	◆	◆	◆	◆
Compare Information from More Than One Source						■	■	■	■	■	■	■	■
Use Reference Sources (Glossary/Dictionary, Thesaurus, Specialized Dictionary, Atlas/Globe, Encyclopedia, Newspaper, *Books in Print, Readers' Guide*)						■	■	■	◆	◆	◆	◆	◆
Study Strategies (K-W-L, SQ3R, How to Study)						■	■	■	■	■	■	■	■
Content-Area Reading						■	■	■	■	■	■	■	■
Adjust Method/Rate of Reading						■	■	■	■	■	■	■	■
Test-Taking Strategies						■	■	■	■	■	■	■	■
Outlining/Notetaking Strategies						■	■	■	■	■	■	■	■
Follow Directions	■	■	■	■	◆	■	◆	◆	◆	◆	◆	◆	◆
Forms/Applications						■	■	■	■	■	■	■	■
LITERARY APPRECIATION													
Select Books for Individual Needs and Interests	■	■	■	■	■	■	■	■	■	■	■	■	■
Read Full-length Books	■	■	■	■	■	■	■	■	■	■	■	■	■
Literary Elements													
Plot Development													
Storyline	■	■	■	■	■	■	■	◆	◆	◆	◆	◆	◆
Conflict (Internal/External)						■	■	■	■	■	■	■	■
Climax							■	■	■	■	■	■	■
Flashback/Foreshadowing								■	■	■	■	■	■
Theme	■	■	■	■	■	■	■	■	■	■	■	◆	◆
Character (Emotions, Types, Development, Traits)	■	■	■	■	■	■	■	◆	◆	◆	◆	◆	◆
Setting	■	■	■	■	■	■	■	◆	◆	◆	◆	◆	◆
Point of View								■	■	■	■	■	■
Narration						■	■	■	■	■	■	■	■
Dialogue	■	■	■	■	■	■	■	■	■	■	■	■	■
Reader Response Groups/Strategies	■	■	■	■	■	■	■	■	■	■	■	■	■
Author's Craft													
Figurative Language							■	■	■	◆	◆	◆	◆
Characterization		■	■	■	■	■	■	■	■	■	■	■	■
Imagery	■	■	■	■	■	■	■	■	■	■	■	■	■
Mood/Tone	■	■	■	■	■	■	■	■	■	■	■		
Sound Devices (Rhythm/Rhyme/Alliteration/Onomatopoeia)	■	■	■	■	■	■	■	■	■	■	■	■	■
Author's Technique										■	■	■	■
Literary Forms/Genre													
Fiction													
Realistic Fiction		■	■	■	■	■	■	■	■	■	■	■	■
Historical Fiction								■	■	■	■	■	■
Mystery							■	■	■	■	■	■	■
Fantasy	■	■	■	■	■	■	■	■	■	■	■	■	■
Science Fiction	■	■	■	■	■								
Full-length Book	■	■	■	■	■	■	■	■	■	■	■	■	■
Riddle	■	■	■	■	■	■	■	■	■	■	■	■	■
Drama/Play	■	■	■	■	■	■							
Poetry/Song	■	■	■	■	■	■	■	■	■	■	■	■	■
Nonfiction													
Biography/Autobiography	■	■	■	■	■	■	■	■	■	■	■	■	■
Journal/Diary/Letters	■	■	■	■	■	■	■	■	■	■	■	■	■
Essay								■	■	■	■	■	■
Informational Article					■	■	■	■	■	■	■	■	■
How-To Article						■	■	■	■	■	■	■	■
Interview							■	■	■	■	■	■	■
Speech							■	■	■	■	■	■	■
Personal Narrative							■	■	■	■	■	■	■
Folklore (Folktale, Fairy Tale, Fable, Myth, Tall Tale, Legend, Nursery Rhyme)	■	■	■	■	■	■	■	■	■	■	■	■	■

■ Modeling/Instruction/Application   ◆ Tested

Testing options include Unit Skills Assessment, Unit Holistic Assessment, and Unit Integrated Performance Assessment
For a complete scope and sequence of the kindergarten program, see the Teacher's Edition for that level.

Grade/Level	1–1	1–2	1–3	1–4	1–5	1–6	2	3	4	5	6	7	8
MULTICULTURALISM													
Respond to Literature Representing Our Pluralistic Culture	▓	▓	▓	▓	▓	▓	▓	▓	▓	▓	▓	▓	▓
View Concepts/Issues from Diverse Perspectives	▓	▓	▓	▓	▓	▓	▓	▓	▓	▓	▓	▓	▓
Understand the concept that all groups have contributed to society	▓	▓	▓	▓	▓	▓	▓	▓	▓	▓	▓	▓	▓
Acquire attitudes/skills/knowledge to interact successfully with members of diverse groups	▓	▓	▓	▓	▓	▓	▓	▓	▓	▓	▓	▓	▓
LANGUAGE													
Composition													
Writing Process (Prewriting, Drafting, Responding/Revising, Proofreading, Publishing)	▓	▓	▓	▓	▓	▓	▓	▓	▓	▓	▓	▓	▓
Writer's Craft													
Identifying Audience and Purpose	◆	◆	◆	◆	◆	◆	◆	◆	◆	◆	◆	◆	◆
Selecting, Narrowing, Expanding Topics/Gathering Information							◆	◆	◆	◆	◆	◆	◆
Choosing Effective Language							◆	◆	◆	◆	◆	◆	◆
Forms of Writing													
Expository Writing (Comparison/Contrast, Explanation, Letter, News Story, Report, Essay, Directions/Instructions)					▓	▓	◆	◆	◆	◆	◆	◆	◆
Narrative Writing (Stories, Paragraph/s, Personal Narrative, Play, Poetry)	▓	▓	▓	◆	◆	◆	◆	◆	◆	◆	◆	◆	◆
Descriptive Writing/Spatial Order (Titles, Captions, Paragraphs, Stories, Poetry)	◆	◆	◆	◆	◆	◆	◆	◆	◆	◆	◆	◆	◆
Persuasive Writing (Paragraph, Essay, Business Letter)							◆	◆	◆	◆	◆	◆	◆
Cross-Curricular Writing	▓	▓	▓	▓	▓	▓	▓	▓	▓	▓	▓	▓	▓
Skills of Revision													
Correcting Sentence Fragments/Run-Ons								◆	◆	◆	◆	◆	◆
Adding/Deleting/Rearranging Information		▓	▓	▓	▓	▓	◆	◆	◆	◆	◆	◆	◆
Sentence/Word Variety								◆	◆	◆	◆	◆	◆
Unity and Coherence							◆	◆	◆	◆	◆	◆	◆
Using the Conventions of English	▓	▓	▓	◆	◆	◆	◆	◆	◆	◆	◆	◆	◆
Listening													
Participate in Cooperative Groups	▓	▓	▓	▓	▓	▓	▓	▓	▓	▓	▓	▓	▓
Receive Direction/Gain Information/Enhance Appreciation of Language	▓	▓	▓	▓	▓	▓	▓	▓	▓	▓	▓	▓	▓
Respond to a speaker by retelling what was heard, asking questions, and/or contributing information	▓	▓	▓	▓	▓	▓	▓	▓	▓	▓	▓	▓	▓
Analyze/Evaluate Intent and Content of Speaker's Message							▓	▓	▓	▓	▓	▓	▓
Note Details	▓	▓	▓	▓	▓	▓	▓	▓	▓	▓	▓	▓	▓
Visualize	▓	▓	▓	▓	▓	▓	▓	▓	▓	▓	▓	▓	▓
Determine Problem/Solution	▓	▓	▓	▓	▓	▓	▓	▓	▓	▓	▓	▓	▓
Make Justifiable Inferences	▓	▓	▓	▓	▓	▓	▓	▓	▓	▓	▓	▓	▓
Identify Supporting Details	▓	▓	▓	▓	▓	▓	▓	▓	▓	▓	▓	▓	▓
Recognize Persuasion							▓	▓	▓	▓	▓	▓	▓
Identify Mood/Tone							▓	▓	▓	▓	▓	▓	▓
Recognize Bias/Prejudice/Propaganda/Emotional Appeals												▓	▓
Speaking													
Participate in Cooperative Groups	▓	▓	▓	▓	▓	▓	▓	▓	▓	▓	▓	▓	▓
Identify Audience/Purpose		▓	▓	▓	▓	▓	▓	▓	▓	▓	▓	▓	▓
Use a Variety of Words to Convey Meaning	▓	▓	▓	▓	▓	▓	▓	▓	▓	▓	▓	▓	▓
Describe Personal Ideas, Feelings, and Expressions	▓	▓	▓	▓	▓	▓	▓	▓	▓	▓	▓	▓	▓
Orally Retell/Summarize Stories	▓	▓	▓	▓	▓	▓	▓	▓	▓	▓	▓	▓	▓
Entertain Others with Stories, Poems, Dramatic Activities	▓	▓	▓	▓	▓	▓	▓	▓	▓	▓	▓	▓	▓
Give Directions			▓	▓	▓	▓	▓	▓	▓	▓	▓	▓	▓
Share Information	▓	▓	▓	▓	▓	▓	▓	▓	▓	▓	▓	▓	▓
Compare/Contrast							▓	▓	▓	▓	▓	▓	▓
Persuade Others							▓	▓	▓	▓	▓	▓	▓
Develop Skill in Using the Conventions of English	▓	▓	▓	▓	▓	▓	▓	▓	▓	▓	▓	▓	▓
Integrated Spelling													
Apply Spelling Generalizations					◆	◆	◆	◆	◆	◆	◆	◆	◆
Apply Spelling Strategies					▓	▓	▓	▓	▓	▓	▓	▓	▓
Master Frequently Misspelled Words					▓	▓	▓	▓	▓	▓	▓	▓	▓

▓ **Modeling/Instruction/Application** ◆ **Tested**
Testing options include Unit Skills Assessment, Unit Holistic Assessment, and Unit Integrated Performance Assessment.
For a complete scope and sequence of the kindergarten program, see the Teacher's Edition for that level.

ADDITIONAL READING

The following list is a compilation of the additional reading selections taken from the lesson plans.

THE SEA

The Crossing
by Gary Paulsen. Franklin Watts, 1987.

Face to Face
by Marion Dane Bauer. Clarion, 1991.

Hiking and Backpacking
by Gary Paulsen. Simon and Schuster, 1978.

North to the Orient
by Anne Morrow Lindbergh. Harcourt Brace Jovanovich, 1963.

The River
by Gary Paulsen. Delacorte, 1990.

INSIGHTS

The Explorer of Barkham Street
by Mary Stolz. HarperCollins, 1985.

The Miracle Worker
by William Gibson. Bantam, 1962.

Robodad
by Alden R. Carter. G. P. Putnam's, 1990.

Won't Know Until I Get There
by Joan Aiken. Viking. 1982.

The Young Landlords
by Joan Aiken. Puffin, 1989.

GOALS

Aida: A Picture Book for All Ages
as told by Leontyne Price. Harcourt Brace Jovanovich, 1990.

Beezus and Ramona

by Beverly Cleary. William Morrow, 1955.

Discovering the Guitar

by Linda Swears. William Morrow, 1981.

Emily's Runaway Imagination

by Beverly Cleary. William Morrow, 1961.

The Luckiest Girl

by Beverly Cleary. William Morrow, 1958.

Lyddie

by Katherine Paterson. Lodestar, 1991.

Marian Anderson

by Charles Patterson. Franklin Watts, 1988.

The Mouse and the Motorcycle

by Beverly Cleary. William Morrow, 1965.

The Mozart Season

by Virginia Euwer Wolff. Henry Holt, 1991.

Philip Hall Likes Me. I Reckon Maybe.

by Bette Greene. Dell, 1975.

Ribsy

by Beverly Cleary. William Morrow, 1964.

The Science of Music

by Melvin Berger. T.Y. Crowell, 1989.

Trouble's Child

by Mildred Pitts Walter. Lothrop, Lee and Shepard, 1985.

A Very Young Rider

by Jill Krementz. Alfred A. Knopf, 1977.

The Violin Close Up

by Peter Schaaf. Four Winds, 1980.

ADDITIONAL READING

The following list is a compilation of the additional reading selections taken from the lesson plans.

THE STORY

A Day of Pleasure: Stories of a Boy Growing up in Warsaw
by Isaac Bashevis Singer. Farrar, Straus and Giroux, 1963.

The Disappearing Man and Other Mysteries
by Isaac Asimov. Walker, 1985.

Fantastic Voyage
by Isaac Asimov. Houghton Mifflin, 1966.

The Fools of Chelm and Their History
by Isaac Bashevis Singer. Farrar, Straus, and Giroux, 1988.

Homespun: Tales from America's Favorite Storytellers
edited by Jimmy Neil Smith. Crown, 1988.

How Did We Find Out About Computers?
by Isaac Asimov. Walker, 1984.

Isaac Asimov: Scientist and Storyteller
by Ellen Erlanger. Lerner, 1986.

The Night Journey
by Kathryn Lasky. Viking, 1981.

Old Peter's Russian Tales
by Arthur Ransome. Jonathan Cape (London), 1984.

Zlateh the Goat and Other Stories
by Isaac Bashevis Singer. HarperCollins, 1984.

TALES FROM AROUND THE WORLD

The Boy Who Found the Light: Eskimo Folktales
retold and illustrated by Dale DeArmond. Little, Brown, 1990.

The Brocaded Slipper and Other Vietnamese Tales
by Lynette Dyer Vuong. HarperCollins, 1982.

TALES FROM AROUND THE WORLD (cont.)

The Cow-tail Switch and Other West African Stories
by Harold Courlander with George Herzog. Henry Holt, 1974.

Fabulous Beasts
by Alison Lurie. Farrar, Straus, and Giroux, 1981.

Sweet and Sour: Tales from China
retold by Carol Kendall and Li Yao-wen. Houghton Mifflin, 1979.

TALL TALES

Beats Me, Claude
by Joan Lowery Nixon, Viking, 1986.

Davy Crockett, Frontier Hero
by Walter Blair. Lincoln Herndon, 1985.

The Ghosts of Now
by Joan Lowery Nixon. Dell, 1986.

The Gift
by Joan Lowery Nixon. Macmillan, 1983.

Hanna's Hog
by Jim Aylesworth. Atheneum, 1988.

John Henry
retold and illustrated by Gray Gianni. Kipling, 1989.

Mike Fink, King of Mississippi Keelboatmen
by Walter Blair. Greenwood, 1971.

Paul Bunyan
by Esther Shephard. Harcourt Brace Jovanovich, 1985.

The True Story of the Three Little Pigs by A. Wolf
as told to Jon Scieszka. Viking, 1989.

ADDITIONAL READING

The following list is a compilation of the additional reading selections taken from the lesson plans.

THE KLONDIKE

Black Diamonds
by James Houston. Atheneum, 1982.

The Cremation of Sam McGee
by Robert W. Service. Greenwillow, 1987.

Gold! The Klondike Adventure
by Delia Ray. E. P. Dutton, 1989.

Jack London's Stories of the North
by Jack London. Scholastic, 1989.

Racing Sled Dogs: An Original North American Sport
by Michael Cooper. Clarion, 1988.

Snow Dog
by Jim Kjelgaard. Bantam, 1990.

Stone Fox
by John Reynolds Gardiner. T. Y. Crowell, 1980.

White Fang
by Jack London. Scholastic, 1972.

ANCIENT WEALTH

Beyond the Reef
by Todd Strasser. Delacorte, 1989.

The Black Pearl
by Scott O'Dell. Houghton Mifflin, 1967.

ANCIENT WEALTH (cont.)

The Captive
> by Scott O'Dell. Houghton Mifflin, 1979.

Gold and Silver, Silver and Gold: Tales of Hidden Treasure
> by Alvin Schwartz. Farrar, Straus and Giroux, 1988.

The King's Fifth
> by Scott O'Dell. Houghton Mifflin, 1966.

The Lost Wreck of the Isis
> by Robert D. Ballard with Richard Archbold. Scholastic/Madison, 1990.

The Mysterious Maya
> by George E. Stuart and Gene S. Stuart. National Geographic Society, 1977.

Rain Player
> by David Wisniewski. Houghton Mifflin, 1991.

Voices of Japan
> by Carolyn Meyer. Harcourt Brace Jovanovich, 1988.

MEXICO

I, Juan de Pareja
> by Elizabeth Borton de Treviño. Farrar, Straus and Giroux, 1987.

Shark Beneath the Reef
> by Jean Craighead George. HarperCollins, 1989.

Why Corn Is Golden
> by Vivian Blackmore. Little, Brown, 1984.

ADDITIONAL READING

The following list is a compilation of the additional reading selections taken from the lesson plans.

FORTITUDE

Bicycle Rider
by Mary Scioscia. HarperCollins, 1983.

Black Star, Bright Dawn
by Scott O'Dell. Houghton Mifflin, 1988.

Jackie Robinson
by Richard Scott. Chelsea House, 1989.

Moxie
by Phillis Rossiter. Macmillan, 1990.

Sniper
by Theodore Taylor. Harcourt Brace Jovanovich, 1989.

The Wounded Wolf
by Jean Craighead George. HarperCollins, 1978.

Zan Hagen's Marathon
by R. R. Knudson. Farrar, Straus, and Giroux, 1984.

SEARCHING

Going Home
by Nicholasa Mohr. Dial, 1986.

Her Own Song
by Ellen Howard. Atheneum, 1988.

My Name Is Not Angelica
by Scott O'Dell. Houghton Mifflin, 1989.

Poems for Youth
by Emily Dickinson. Little, Brown, 1934.

The Poetry of Robert Frost
edited by Edward Connery Lathem. Holt, Rinehart and Winston, 1970.

The Return
by Sonia Levitin. Atheneum, 1986.

SEARCHING *(cont.)*

Something New Begins: New and Selected Poems
by Lilian Moore. Atheneum, 1982.

The Whispering Wind: Poetry of Young American Indians
edited by Terry Allen. Doubleday, 1972.

COMING OF AGE

After the Rain
by Norma Fox Mazer. William Morrow, 1987.

Big Red
by Jim Kjelgaard. Bantam, 1982.

Danza!
by Lynn Hall. Macmillan, 1981.

Dicey's Song
by Cynthia Voigt. Macmillan, 1982.

Dragonwings
by Laurence Yep. HarperCollins, 1976.

IOU's
by Ouida Sebestyen. Little, Brown, 1986.

The Lost Garden
by Laurence Yep. Silver Burdett, 1991.

The Secret of Gumbo Grove
by Eleanora E. Tate. Franklin Watts, 1987.

The Serpent's Children
by Laurence Yep. HarperCollins, 1984.

Words by Heart
by Ouida Sebestyen. Little, Brown, 1979.

UNIT FIVE OBSERVATIONS

ADDITIONAL READING

The following list is a compilation of the additional reading selections taken from the lesson plans.

EARTH

Barbary
by Vonda N. McIntyre. Houghton Mifflin, 1986.

How Maps Are Made
by John Baynes. Facts on File, 1987.

Journey to the Planets
by Patricia Lauber. Crown, 1982.

Lunar Bases
by Sharon Cosner. Franklin Watts, 1990.

Rainbows to Lasers
by Kathryn Whyman. Franklin Watts, 1989.

This Place Has No Atmosphere
by Paula Danziger. Delacorte, 1986.

Voyagers from Space: Meteors and Meteorites
by Patricia Lauber. T. Y. Crowell, 1989.

SURVIVAL

Catch a Sunbeam: A Book of Solar Study and Experiments
by Florence Adams. Harcourt Brace Jovanovich, 1978.

The Conquest of Everest
by Mike Rosen. Bookwright, 1990.

The Place of Lions
by Erik Campbell. Harcourt Brace Jovanovich, 1991.

A Rumor of Otters
by Deborah Savage. Houghton Mifflin, 1986.

Take a Hike! The Sierra Club Kid's Guide to Hiking and Backpacking
by Lynne Foster. Little, Brown, 1991.

WATCHING NATURE

Bird Watch: A Book of Poetry
by Jane Yolen. Philomel, 1990.

Birds of Prey
by Jill Bailey. Facts on File, 1988.

Drawing from Nature
by Jim Arnosky. Lothrop, Lee & Shepard, 1982.

Henry Reed, Inc.
by Keith Robertson. Viking, 1958.

Henry Reed's Babysitting Service
by Keith Robertson. Viking, 1966.

Henry Reed's Big Show
by Keith Robertson. Viking, 1970.

Henry Reed's Think Tank
by Keith Robertson. Viking, 1986.

An Owl in the House: A Naturalist's Diary
by Bernd Heinrich, adapted by Alice Calaprice. Little, Brown, 1990.

Storm Bird
by Elsie McCutcheon. Farrar, Straus and Giroux, 1987.

ADDITIONAL READING

The following list is a compilation of the additional reading selections taken from the lesson plans.

LOOKING TOWARD OTHERS

Always to Remember: The Story of the Vietnam Veterans Memorial
by Brent Ashabranner. Dodd, Mead, 1988.

Badger on the Barge
by Janni Howker. William Morrow, 1984.

Hank
by James Sauer. Delacorte, 1990.

Into a Strange Land: Unaccompanied Refugee Youth in America
by Brent Ashabranner with Melissa Ashabranner. Dodd, Mead, 1987.

Teacher: Anne Sullivan Macy
by Helen Keller. Greenwood, 1985.

The Times of My Life: A Memoir
by Brent Ashabranner. Cobblehill/Penguin, 1990.

INNOVATIONS

Before the Wright Brothers
by Don Berliner. Lerner, 1990.

Better Mousetraps: Product Improvements That Led to Success
by Nathan Aaseng. Lerner, 1989.

Bouncing and Bending Light
by Barbara Taylor. Franklin Watts, 1990.

Color and Light
by Barbara Taylor. Franklin Watts, 1990.

INNOVATIONS *(cont.)*

Experimenting with Inventions
> by Robert Gardner. Franklin Watts, 1990.

Famous Experiments You Can Do
> by Robert Gardner. Franklin Watts, 1990.

Guess Again: More Weird and Wacky Inventions
> by Jim Murphy. Bradbury, 1986.

Living with Diabetes
> by Barbara Taylor. Franklin Watts, 1989.

SPACE

Astronomy
> by Dennis B. Fradin. Childrens Press, 1987.

The Boy Who Reversed Himself
> by William Sleator. E. P. Dutton, 1986.

Could You Ever Build a Time Machine?
> by David Darling. Macmillan, 1991.

The Day We Walked on the Moon: A Photo History of Space Exploration
> by George Sullivan. Scholastic, 1990.

Radio Astronomy
> by Alan Nourse. Franklin Watts, 1989.

Sweetwater
> by Laurence Yep. HarperCollins, 1973.

CONTENTS BY GENRE

FICTION

DRAMA

NONFICTION

POETRY

AUTHOR FEATURES

INDEX

G ●●●●●●●●●●●●●●●●●●●●●●●

H ●●●●●●●●●●●●●●●●●●●●●●●

Hoff, Darrel, 567A
Hopkins, Lee Bennett, R23B
"How Winter Man's Power Was Broken,"
170–175
Hughes, Langston, 43
Hugo, Victor, 500

I •••••••••••••••••••••••••••

"I May, I Might, I Must," 538
"I Saw a Man," 354
"I Watched an Eagle Soar," 538
"If You Say So, Claude," 197K–205L
"I'm Nobody!," 357
Imagery, 521G–521H
See also Figurative language.
Independent reading
See Additional reading; HBJ Treasury of
Literature Library Books; Options for reading.
Informal assessment
about, R57–60
informal assessment checklist, 109B, 209B,
295B, 399B, 503B, 581B
informal assessment notes, 15B, 30, 41B, 48,
79, 83A, 85, 91B, 95, 106A, 123, 158, 167,
199, 201, 209E, 217, 230, 242, 253, 275,
306, 321A, 323, 340, 350, 355, 369, 385,
418, 446, 477, 519, 530, 547, 569, 576,
577A
portfolio conference, 109B, 209B, 295B, 399B,
503B, 581B
reading/writing portfolio, 15B, 21, 47, 71, 109E,
115, 149, 183, 209E, 215, 239, 267, 295E,
301, 333, 361, 399E, 437, 475, 503E, 509,
541, 561
running records, 15B, 109E, 209E, 295E, 399E,
503E
strategy conference, 41A, 57A, 83A, 91A,
106A, 133A, 146A, 161A, 169A, 197A,
205A, 229A, 236A, 249A, 264A, 283A,
321A, 330A, 347A, 358A, 381A, 396A,
421A, 455A, 481A, 499A, 521A, 535A,
557A, 577A
student self-assessment, 15B, 45B, 57A, 69B,
109E, 146A, 147B, 181B, 207B, 209E,
229A, 237B, 264A, 265B, 293B, 295E,
330A, 331B, 359B, 397B, 399E, 435B,
473B, 501B, 503E, 539B, 557A, 559B, 579B
summarizing the learning, 41F, 41H, 41J, 57F,
57H, 57J, 83G, 83H, 83J, 91F, 91G, 91H,
106G, 106H, 106I, 133F, 133H, 133I, 133J,
146G, 146H, 146I, 161F, 161I, 169F, 169G,
169H, 197F, 197G, 197H, 205F, 205H, 205I,
205J, 229F, 229H, 229J, 236G, 236H, 236I,
249F, 249H, 249I, 249J, 264G, 264H, 264I,
283F, 283G, 238H, 321F, 321H, 330G, 330H,
330L, 347F, 347H, 347I, 347J, 358G, 358I,
358K, 381F, 381H, 396G, 396H, 396J, 421F,
421G, 421H, 455F, 455H, 481E, 481F, 481G,

481H, 499F, 499G, 499H, 521F, 521H, 521I,
521J, 535F, 535G, 535H, 557F, 557G, 557H,
577E, 577F, 577G, 577H
Integrated curriculum
about, R21–28
art, 41K, 57K, 83K, 106K, 109, 146K, 205K,
209, 249K, 264J, 283I, 347K, 358M, 381I,
396K, 421I, 481I, 499I, 502, 503, 557I, 577I
art history, 229K
careers, 169I
computer science, 133K, 421I
drama, 229K
ecology, 481I
economics/math, 229K
foreign languages, 146J
health, 83K, 161I, 236K, 264K, 283I, 321I,
330K, 535I
literature, 577I
math, 41K, 57K, 91I, 106J, 106K, 133K, 146K,
205K, 236J, 283I, 321I, 330J, 347K, 396J,
455I, 521K, 557I, 577I
music, 91I, 106J, 106K, 108, 109, 146K, 161I,
169I, 197I, 208
physical education, 57K, 161I, 249K, 264K,
396J, 521K
science, 41K, 91I, 106J, 133K, 146K, 197I,
205K, 236J, 249K, 264J, 264K, 283I, 321I,
330J, 330K, 347K, 358K, 381I, 421I, 455I,
481I, 499I, 535I, 557I, 577I, 581
social studies, 41K, 57K, 83K, 91I, 106J, 106K,
133K, 146J, 161I, 169I, 197I, 205K, 229K,
236K, 249K, 264J, 283I, 294, 295, 321I,
330J, 330K, 347K, 358L, 358M, 381I, 396J,
396K, 398, 399, 421I, 455I, 499I, 521K,
535I, 557I, 577I, 581
Integrated language arts
about, R26–27B
speaking/listening, 41D, 57D, 83D, 91D, 106D,
106E, 133D, 146D, 161D, 169D, 197D,
205D, 229D, 236D, 236E, 249D, 264D,
264E, 283D, 321D, 330D, 330E, 347D,
358D, 358E, 381D 396D, 396E, 421D, 455D,
481D, 499D, 521D, 535D, 557D, 577D
spelling, 41D, 57D, 83D, 91D, 106E, 109A,
133D, 146E, 161D, 169D, 197D, 205D,
209A, 229D, 236E, 249D, 264E, 283D,
295A, 321D, 330E, 347D, 358E, 381D,
396E, 399A, 421D, 455D, 481D, 499D,
503A, 521D, 535D, 557D, 577D, 581A
See also Spelling, integrated.
writing, 41D, 57D, 83D, 91D, 106D, 106E,
109A, 133D, 146D, 146E, 161D, 169D,
197D, 205D, 229D, 236D, 249D, 264D,
283D, 295A, 321D, 330D, 330E, 347D,
358D, 381D, 396D, 399A, 421D, 455D,
481D, 499D, 503A, 521D, 535D, 557D,
577D, 581A
Integrated spelling
See Integrated langauge arts; Spelling, integrated.
"Integrating the Language Arts," R26
Internal/external conflict, 381E–381F

M

N

O

P

U ....

V ....

W ....

X, Y & Z...............

REVIEWERS

FIELD TEST SITES, MULTICULTURAL ADVISORS, CRITICAL REVIEWERS

Field Test Sites

Vinemont, Alabama
Phoenix, Arizona
Cabot, Arkansas
Conway, Arkansas
Moreno Valley, California
Riverside, California
Sacramento, California
San Diego, California
Bridgeport, Connecticut
Lisbon, Connecticut
New Haven, Connecticut
Land O'Lakes, Florida
Pocatello, Idaho
Donnellson, Iowa
Mohamet, Illinois
Naperville, Illinois
Gosport, Indiana
Spencer, Indiana
Kansas City, Kansas
Mount Sterling, Kentucky
Bossier City, Louisiana
Bridgman, Michigan
Detroit, Michigan
Robbinsdale, Minnesota
Billings, Montana
Nashua, New Hampshire
North Bergen, New Jersey
Chaparral, New Mexico
Brooklyn, New York
Cincinnati, Ohio
New Carlisle, Ohio
Toledo, Ohio
University Heights, Ohio
Beaverton, Oregon
Eugene, Oregon
Portland, Oregon
Fairless Hills, Pennsylvania
N. Huntingdon, Pennsylvania
Philadelphia, Pennsylvania
Estill, South Carolina
Greer, South Carolina
Aberdeen, South Dakota
Nashville, Tennessee
Corsicana, Texas
Dallas, Texas
Grand Prairie, Texas
Harlingen, Texas
Houston, Texas
Katy, Texas
Lewisville, Texas
Lockhart, Texas

McAllen, Texas
Palestine, Texas
Plano, Texas
San Antonio, Texas
Dry Fork, Virginia
Everett, Washington
Vancouver, Washington
Green Bay, Wisconsin

Multicultural Advisors

Dr. James E. Anderson
Associate Professor, Department
of Educational Leadership and
Cultural Studies
College of Education
University of Houston
Houston, Texas

Dr. Mario Benitez
Professor, Department of
Curriculum and Instruction
The University of Texas at Austin
Austin, Texas

Dr. Pat Browne
Director, African-American
History/Multicultural
Education
Indianapolis Public Schools
Indianapolis, Indiana

Dr. Jacob Carruthers
Associate Director and Professor
Northeastern Illinois University
Center for Inner City Studies
Chicago, Illinois

Dr. Nancy Mayeda
Principal
Rooftop Alternative School
San Francisco, California

Dr. Maria E. Morales
Associate Professor and
Director of Undergraduate
Bilingual Education Program
Undergraduate Teacher
Preparation Program
Texas A & I University
Kingsville, Texas

Dr. Cornel Pewewardy
Principal
Mounds Park All-Nations Magnet
School
St. Paul, Minnesota

Dr. Rudy Rodriguez
Professor and Chair, Department
of Reading and Bilingual
Education
College of Education and
Human Ecology
Texas Woman's University
Denton, Texas

Sherry Sellers
Librarian and Multicultural
Specialist
Detroit, Michigan

Dr. Barbara Shin
Principal
Andersen Contemporary School
Minneapolis, Minnesota

Virginia Driving Hawk Sneve
Secondary Counselor
Indian Education and District
Resource for Native-American
Culture
Rapid City, South Dakota

Charlotte Stokes
Teacher Specialist - Social Studies
Alexandria City Public Schools
Alexandria, Virginia

Dr. Bernida Thompson
Principal
Roots Activity Learning Center
Washington, District of Columbia

Marilys Tognetti
Director of Instruction
Dixon Unified School District
Dixon, California

Critical Reviewers

Ginger Abel
Teacher
Peoria Public Schools
Peoria, Illinois

C. Gloria Akers
Principal
James Rhoads School
Philadelphia, Pennsylvania

Claudia Anderson
Teacher
Hawthorne Elementary
Fargo, North Dakota

Margo Angleton
Teacher
Indialantic Elementary
Melbourne, Florida

Karyn Aulwurm
Administrative Specialist
Clark County School District
Las Vegas, Nevada

Hilda Barrett
Teacher
Harper's Choice Middle School
Columbia, Maryland

Diana Bauske
Teacher
Richland Elementary
Richardson, Texas

Florence T. Carter
Teacher
Campbell School
Metuchen, New Jersey

Cicely Cerqui
Coordinator for Elementary
Curriculum
Shoreline Public Schools
Seattle, Washington

Lenore Croudy
Coordinator of Language Arts and
Humanities
Flint Community Schools
Flint, Michigan

Carol DeRita
Teacher
Porter Elementary
Mesquite, Texas

Judee DeStefano-Anen
Assistant Principal/Reading
Specialist
Ella G. Clarke School
Lakewood, New Jersey

Marilyn Dickey
Language Arts Specialist
Shelton View Elementary
Bothell, Washington

Sheila Durante, RSM
Assistant Superintendent for
Elementary Schools
Diocese of Providence
Providence, Rhode Island

Mary Ellen Everitt
Teacher
Antheil Elementary
Trenton, New Jersey

Lisa Fast
Teacher
Escola Americana do Rio de
    Janeiro
Rio de Janeiro, Brazil

Shirley Fields
District Reading Coordinator
Region III
Miami, Florida

Bettie Fitzhenry
Reading Consultant
Killeen Independent School
    District
Killeen, Texas

Ann Carol Franco
Teacher
American School Foundation
Tacubaya, Mexico

Janet Green
Teacher
Whitehouse Primary School
Whitehouse, Ohio

Rilla Hardgrove
Principal
Orchard School
Billings, Montana

Sister Patricia Healey, IHM
Elementary Supervisor
Sisters of the Immaculate Heart of
    Mary
Philadelphia, Pennsylvania

Don Hillyard
Reading Coordinator
Evansville-Vanderburgh Schools
Evansville, Indiana

Sandra Horst
Teacher
Solheim Elementary
Bismarck, North Dakota

Daisy Howard-Douglas
Teacher
Fairfield Court Elementary
Richmond, Virginia

William James
Principal
Durrance Elementary
Orlando, Florida

Karen Jao
Teacher
Taipei American School
Taipei, Taiwan

Mary Jennings
Teacher
Tubman Elementary
Washington, D.C.

Beth Kealy
Teacher
Patterson Elementary
Eugene, Oregon

Jan Keese
District Reading Chair
Ankeny Community Schools
Ankeny, Iowa

Laressa Jane Kschinka
Teacher
American School of The Hague
Wassenaar, The Netherlands

Maya Lagbara, Ed.D.
Assistant Principal
Lida Hooe Elementary
Dallas, Texas

Elizabeth Lolli
Coordinator, Elementary
    Education
Middletown City Schools
Middletown, Ohio

Joyce London
Reading Specialist
Southard School
Howell, New Jersey

Bertha Long-Jackson
Teacher
Jesse Owens School
South Holland, Illinois

Ida Love, Ph.D.
Director of Elementary Schools
Kansas City, Missouri School
    District
Kansas City, Missouri

Constance Major
Reading Specialist
Shawmont School
Philadelphia, Pennsylvania

Jana McCarthy
Language Arts Coordinator
Meridian School District
Meridian, Idaho

Mary K. McCarthy
Reading Specialist
Owyhee Elementary
Boise, Idaho

Bonnie McIntyre
Curriculum Coordinator
Minneapolis Public Schools
Minneapolis, Minnesota

Carlton Mead
Teacher
Whitford Intermediate
Beaverton, Oregon

Hilda Medrano, Ph.D.
Associate Professor
The University of Texas - Pan
    American
Edinburg, Texas

Dr. Jacqueline Mossburg
Coordinator, Staff Development
Fort Wayne Community Schools
Fort Wayne, Indiana

Lawrence Ostopowicz
Reading/Language Arts
    Chairperson
School District of Waukesha
Waukesha, Wisconsin

Charlotte J. Parks
Teacher
Windsor Elementary
Des Moines Public School District
Des Moines, Iowa

Beth Peterson
Teacher
Mount Tabor Elementary
New Albany, Indiana

Evelyn Pittman
Supervisor of Language Arts
Paterson Public Schools
Paterson, New Jersey

Kaye Price-Hawkins
Consultant
Region XIV
Abilene, Texas

Tamara Jo Rhomberg
Reading Specialist
Garlin Kellison Elementary
Fenton, Missouri

David Rubin
Supervisor of Reading
Gateway Center
New Haven, Connecticut

Blanche Ryan
Supervisor of Reading
Indianapolis Public Schools
Indianapolis, Indiana

Janet Sawyer
Teacher
Highland Park Elementary
Austin, Texas

James F. Schindler, Ed.D.
Curriculum Consultant
Jordan School District
Sandy, Utah

Jan Scott
Curriculum Coordinator, K-3
Bossier Parish School System
Bossier City, Louisiana

Sheila Scott
Teacher
Gower Elementary
Nashville, Tennessee

Marsha Shortt
Teacher
Stewart Elementary
Kemah, Texas

Sheldon Shuch, Ph.D.
Director of Curriculum
Community School District Five
New York, New York

Richard Wagner
Language Arts Curriculum
    Coordinator
Paradise Valley School District
Phoenix, Arizona

Mona Warner
ESOL Teacher
Hillsboro Elementary Schools
Hillsboro, Oregon

**Sister Mary Leanne Welch,
    PBVM**
Curriculum Director
Archdiocese of Dubuque
Dubuque, Iowa

Jackie Williams
Instructional Supervisor
Loudon County Schools
Loudon, Tennessee

Lola Williams, Ph.D.
Bilingual Coordinator
Harlingen Consolidated
    Independent School District
Harlingen, Texas

Louverne Williams
Teacher
Holland School
Minneapolis, Minnesota

Sara Jane Wilson
Teacher
Landis Elementary
Alief, Texas

**Sister Marla Ann Yeck, RSM,
    Ph.D.**
Associate Superintendent for
    Curriculum
Archdiocese of Detroit
Detroit, Michigan

Acknowledgments

For permission to reprint copyrighted material, grateful acknowledgment is made to the following sources:

Chelsea House Publishers, a division of Main Line Book Co.: From *Wilma Rudolph* by Tom Biracree. Text copyright © 1988 by Chelsea House Publishers.

Harcourt Brace Jovanovich, Inc.: Pronunciation Key from *HBJ School Dictionary,* Third Edition. Text copyright © 1990 by Harcourt Brace Jovanovich, Inc.

HarperCollins Publishers: From *Julie of the Wolves* by Jean Craighead George. Text copyright © 1972 by Jean Craighead George.

University of Notre Dame Press: From *Barrio Boy* by Ernesto Galarza. Text © 1971 by University of Notre Dame Press.

Illustration Credits

Dave Blanchette, pp. 47B, 93B, 133N, 149B, 197L, 215B, 239B, 301B, 333B, 349B, 405B, 451B, 475B, 483B; Frank Collyer, pp. 146C, 146D, 146E, 146J, 146K; Ric Del Rossi, pp. 15C, 19A, 109F, 169C, 169I, 209F, 283I, 295F, 347K, 399F, 503F; Eldon Doty, pp. 236D, 499C, 499I; John Dyess, pp. 299A, 507A; Richard A. Goldberg, pp. 41C, 41K, 577I; Joni Levy Liberman, pp. 264C, 381C, 381I, 535C; Chris Murphy, pp. 91C, 91I, 205C, 205K, 249C, 321C, 321I; Jack Nebesney, pp. 113A, 229C, 229K, 330C, 358C, 455C, 521C, 521K; Bill Ogden, pp. 21B, 71B, 83C, 83K, 83N, 115B, 161C, 161I, 161L, 183B, 229N, 251B, 264J, 264K, 267B, 321L, 361B, 383B, 396C, 396D, 396J, 396K, 437B, 509B, 521N, 535I, 567B; Stephanie O'Shaughnessy, pp. 106C, 106D, 106J, 106K; Chuck Passarelli, pp. 330D, 358D, 358L, 358M; Tom Powers, pp. 330J, 330K, 421C; John Rice, pp. 213A, 236C, 236J, 236K; Terry Sirrell, pp. 57C, 57K, 197C, 197I, 283C, 347C, 557C, 557I; Ruth Soffer, pp. 249K, 421I, 455I; Joe Veno, pp. 133C, 133K, 264D, 481C, 481I

Photo Credits

(t) top, (c) center, (b) bottom, (r) right, (l) left

T045B, Tony Freeman/PhotoEdit; T057L(tl), Ford Foundation; T057L(bl), Robert Cummins/Black Star; T057L(br), Anthony Neste/Focus on Sports; T069B, Michal Heron; T071A, Courtesy William Morrow & Co.; T083A, Carolyn Soto; T083L(l), Nevada Historical Society; T083L(tr), Rick Friedman/Black Star; T083L(br), Mary McLeod Bethune Foundation; T091J(b), Cameramann; T093A, Christian Steiner; T106L(l), Erich Hartmann/Magnum Photos; T106J(tc), Henry Grossman; T106J(tr), Andanson/Sygma; T106J(b), AP/Wide World Photos; T107B, Jose L. Pelaez/Stock Market; T115A, Wide World Photo; T133A, ISAAC BASHEVIS SINGER; T133L, Granger Collection; T133L(background), Thomas Gilcrease Institute of American History and Art; T146L(l), University of California Riverside Library/Tomas Rivera Archives; T146L(r), Schomberg Center for Research in Black Culture; T147B, Richard Hutchings/PhotoEdit; T161K, Courtesy University of New Mexico Press; T161J(t), David Madison/Duomo; T161J(b), Dave Black/Sportschrome; T169J(l), Jack Spratt/Picture Group; T169R(r), Dennis Stock/Magnum; T181B, Myrleen Ferguson/PhotoEdit; T183A, Courtesy Walter Blair; T197J, Carlos Goldin/D. Donne Bryant; T197K, Courtesy Joan Lawery Nixon; T205L(t), Virginia State Archives; T205L(b), Texas Dept. of Highways; T207B, Bob Daemmrich; T215L(t), Courtesy Stuart J. Sachs/Clarion Books; T229L, Idaho Historical Society Library; T229M, Culver Pictures; T236L(t), Superstock; T236L(c), Bettmann; T236L(b), Wide World Photos, Inc.; T237B, Tom Stewart/Stock Market; T239A, Courtesy Carolyn Meyer; T249L, New York Public Library Picture Collection; T249L(cl, cr, & bl), Granger Collection T251A, Courtesy Houghton Mifflin, Assoc.; T264L(t), Jay W. Sharp/DBI Stock; T264B(b), Marc & Evelyne Bernheim/Woodfin Camp, Assoc.; T265B, Elizabeth Zuckerman/PhotoEdit; T267A, Courtesy Farrar, Straus & Giroux, Inc.; T283J(l), White House Historical Association; T283J(r), U.S. Dept. of Treasury; T293B, David R. Frazier; T321J(t), Suen-O Lindblad/Photo Researchers; T321J(bl), Steve Jackson/Black Star; T321J(bl), Campbell/Sygma; T321K, Courtesy Los Angeles Times; T330L(t), Ken Graham/Allstock; T330L(c), Jeff Schultz/Alaska Stock; T330L(b), Nicholas Devore III/Bruce Coleman, Inc.T331B, Tony Freeman.PhotoEdit; T333A, Michael Mauney; T347L(tl), Robert Foothorap; T347L(tr), Michael D. Freed; T347L(b), Schomberg Center for Research in Black Culture; T359B, Michael Newman/PhotoEdit; T361A, Courtesy Laurence Yep; T381J(r), Courtesy Mote Marien Laboratory; T381J(b), Flip Schulke/Black Star; T383A, Courtesy Ouida Sebestyen; T396L(t), John Running; T397B, David Young-Wolf/PhotoEdit; T405A, HBJ/Rick Friedman/Black Star; T421J(tl), National Sculpture Society; T421J(b), James Sugar/Black Star; T435B, HBJ/Earl Kogler; T455J, Barry L. Runk/Grant Heilman; T473B, Mary Kate Denny/PhotoEdit; T481J(t), The Whaling Museum; T481J(c), Smithsonian Institution; T481J(b), The Granger Collection; T483A, Viking Penguin Children's Books; T499J(tr), Peter Weit/Sygma; T499J(t&l), P. Breese/Gamma Liaison; T501B, HBJ/Maria Paraskevas; T521L(t), Viesti Associates; T521L(l), Springer/Bettmann Film Archive; T521L(r), David R. Frazier; T521M, Paul Conklin; T535J(t), UPI/Bettmann; T535J(c) Jay Freis/Image Bank; T535J(b), Newton K. Wesley; T539B, Tony Freeman/PhotoEdit; T557J(tr), University of Louisiana; T557J(b), The Rochester Museum, New York; T559B, Sandy Roessier/Stock Market; T577J(tr), Adam Woolfitt/Woodfin Camp, Assoc.; T577J(l), Jake Rajs/Image Bank; T1577J(b), Jon Davison/Stockphotos; T579B, Comstock.

Laserdisc

To address the need for integration of technology in curriculum, *HBJ Treasury of Literature Laserdisc* offers videos and images that help build concepts, reinforce strategies, and stimulate critical thinking. Bar codes, linked to lessons in the Teacher's Edition, permit easy access to the visuals.

HBJ LaserVision
Where High Tech Meets High-Quality Literature

With the *HBJ LaserVision* component of *HBJ Treasury of Literature*, a collection of full-motion video and still images, you can reach your students in remarkable ways. The full-motion videos, visual delights of sight and sound, expand the central program themes to help your students focus on important ideas and concepts in a variety of ways. The still images allow you to deliver powerful lessons for your students while they help you access prior knowledge, build background and key vocabulary concepts, stimulate discussion, and inspire writing assignments.

The full-motion videos generate lively discussion with story lines designed to ignite curiosity and encourage a problem-solving approach. Opportunities abound for viewers to use their own knowledge and experiences to predict outcomes, make inferences and judgments, and draw conclusions about characters and their actions. Students come to understand that they can transfer the critical thinking skills they use to analyze situations in the videos to analyze selections in their anthologies, thereby helping them become better readers.

The still images, like the videos, support successful reading of selections and provide inspiration or enhancement for lessons of your own design. Subjects vary from the colors and sights of a variety of cultures to specific topics such as masks, volcanoes, or the baobab trees of Africa.

Today's sophisticated media-viewing youngsters will particularly appreciate the full-motion videos, which vary from animation to music video to comedy. Both the content and visual appeal of the still images are excellent.

Recommendations for placement in the *HBJ Treasury of Literature* Teacher's Editions accompany the bar code stickers for the still images. Suggestions for related critical thinking activities appear in the Teacher's Manual for *HBJ LaserVision*. The Teacher's Manual also includes bar codes for the full-motion videos as well as additional still images.

Throughout the school year, you can instantly access the videos or still images to teach concepts or review and reinforce thinking strategies. *HBJ LaserVision* videos and still images will help you motivate your students to discover the remarkable world of stories and the magic of books.